Handbook of the Economics of Corporate Finance
Volume 1

Private Equity and Entrepreneurial Finance

Handbook of the Economics of Corporate Finance

Volume 1

Private Equity and Entrepreneurial Finance

Edited by

B. Espen Eckbo
*Tuck School of Business, Dartmouth College,
Hanover, NH, United States
Norwegian School of Economics, Bergen, Norway*

Gordon M. Phillips
*Tuck School of Business, Dartmouth College,
Hanover, NH, United States*

Morten Sorensen
*Tuck School of Business, Dartmouth College,
Hanover, NH, United States*

North-Holland

An imprint of Elsevier

ELSEVIER

North-Holland is an imprint of Elsevier
Radarweg 29, PO Box 211, 1000 AE Amsterdam, Netherlands
The Boulevard, Langford Lane, Kidlington, Oxford OX5 1GB, United Kingdom

ISBN: 978-0-12-820149-7
ISSN: 2949-964X

For information on all North-Holland publications
visit our website at https://www.elsevier.com/books-and-journals

Publisher: Zoe Kruze
Acquisitions Editor: Jason Mitchell
Developmental Editor: Naiza Ermin Mendoza
Production Project Manager: Vijayaraj Purushothaman
Cover Designer: Christian J. Bilbow

Typeset by STRAIVE, India

Working together
to grow libraries in
developing countries

www.elsevier.com • www.bookaid.org

Contents

PART II Later stage financing

CHAPTER 4 Private equity financing **139**
Victoria Ivashina

CHAPTER 5 Buyouts: A primer **161**
Tim Jenkinson, Hyeik Kim, and Michael S. Weisbach

PART III   Impact and performance

CHAPTER 7 Stakeholder impact of private equity investments....299
Morten Sorensen and Ayako Yasuda

PART IV Short chapter summaries

Introduction to the handbooks in economics series

The aim of the *Handbooks in Economics* series is to produce Handbooks for various branches of economics, each of which is a definitive source, reference, and teaching supplement for use by professional researchers and advanced graduate students. Each Handbook provides self-contained surveys of the current state of a branch of economics in the form of chapters prepared by leading specialists on various aspects of this branch of economics. These surveys summarize not only received results but also newer developments, from recent journal articles and discussion papers. Some original material is also included, but the main goal is to provide comprehensive and accessible surveys. The Handbooks are intended to provide not only useful reference volumes for professional collections but also possible supplementary readings for advanced courses for graduate students in economics.

Kenneth J. Arrow and Michael D. Intriligator

Introduction to the economics of corporate finance series

Elsevier/North Holland has, in several handbook series, offered comprehensive and accessible research summaries in the field of finance. These volumes began with Volume 9 of *Handbooks in Operations Research and Management Science* in 1995 and continued with two volumes in *Handbook of the Economics of Finance* in 2003 and several volumes in *Handbooks in Finance*, beginning in 2007.

The new series, *Handbook of the Economics of Corporate Finance*, intends to provide comprehensive and accessible updates of central theoretical and empirical issues in corporate finance. The demand for these updates reflects the rapid evolution of corporate finance research, which has become a dominant field in financial economics. The surveys are written by leading empirical researchers who remain active in their respective areas of interest. The dense roadmaps are intended to make the economics of corporate finance and governance accessible not only to doctoral students but also to researchers not intimately familiar with this important field.

B. Espen Eckbo
Volume Series Editor
Tuck School of Business
Dartmouth College
Hanover, NH, United States

Introduction to the first volume

This volume is the first in the new series *Handbook of the Economics of Corporate Finance*. The volume provides eight up-to-date and in-depth chapters covering the rapidly increasing research ranging from early-stage financing of corporate startups to whether the expected return of private equity funds is commensurable with the risk of the underlying portfolio companies. In between, the volume addresses everything from basic contracting, impact of funding sources on corporate innovation, to gender in private equity. The volume also contains convenient short chapter summaries written by the authors themselves. We are grateful for the time and effort the authors, who are all leading experts in this important field of research, have devoted to this volume.

B. Espen Eckbo, Gordon Phillips, and Morten Sorensen
Editors
Tuck School of Business
Dartmouth College
Hanover, NH, United States

Contributors

Michael Ewens
Columbia Business School, New York, NY, United States

Will Gornall
Sauder School of Business, University of British Columbia, Vancouver, BC, Canada

Victoria Ivashina
Harvard Business School, Harvard University, Boston, MA, United States

Tim Jenkinson
Saïd Business School, Oxford University, Oxford, United Kingdom

Hyeik Kim
University of Alberta, Edmonton, AB, Canada

Arthur Korteweg
Marshall School of Business, University of Southern California, Los Angeles, CA, United States

Josh Lerner
Harvard Business School, Harvard University, Boston, MA, United States

Ramana Nanda
Department of Finance, Imperial College London, London, United Kingdom

Gordon Phillips
Tuck School of Business, Dartmouth College, Hanover, NH, United States

Morten Sorensen
Tuck School of Business, Dartmouth College, Hanover, NH, United States

Ilya A. Strebulaev
Graduate School of Business, Stanford University, Stanford, CA, United States

Michael S. Weisbach
Fisher College of Business, Ohio State University, Columbia, OH, United States

Ayako Yasuda
Graduate School of Management, University of California, Davis, CA, United States

Early-stage financing

The contracting and valuation of venture capital-backed companies

1

Will Gornall[a] and Ilya A. Strebulaev[b],*

[a]*Sauder School of Business, University of British Columbia, Vancouver, BC, Canada*
[b]*Graduate School of Business, Stanford University, Stanford, CA, United States*
*Corresponding author: e-mail address: istrebulaev@stanford.edu

Chapter outline

1 Introduction

Venture capital (VC) is a high-touch form of financing used primarily by high-growth, innovative, and risky companies. VC funds invest in these companies on behalf of limited partners, who are mostly large institutional investors. The venture capitalists who manage these funds provide not only financing to companies, but also nonfinancial support such as mentorship, strategic guidance, and network access. While most VC-funded companies fail, some become runaway successes. The seven largest US companies by market capitalization as of the end of December 2021 (Apple, Microsoft, Amazon, Alphabet (Google), Meta (Facebook), Tesla, and Nvidia) received most of their early external financing from venture capitalists. As Gornall and Strebulaev (2021b) show, venture capital-backed companies accounted for 41% of total US market capitalization and 62% of US public companies' R&D spending as of 2020. Among public companies founded within the last 50 years, VC-backed companies account for half in number, three quarters by value, and more than 92% of R&D spending and patent value. Indeed, the US VC industry is in no small way responsible for the rise of hundreds of new large companies over the life of most recent generations.

   Young, innovative companies are unlike most other businesses. Perhaps most importantly, while their investment needs are front-loaded, their cash flows are typically far in the future and uncertain, with success coming from a new product or service that has not yet been rolled out or created. These special circumstances raise numerous economic and business issues and necessitate special forms of financing and particular relationships with financiers. They make it difficult for these companies to access capital through traditional means, such as traditional bank and receivables financing or public equity markets, and cause them to turn to a startup financing ecosystem that includes not just institutional VC funds but also crowdfunding, angel investors, corporate VC, growth equity, and private equity.[a]

---

[a]We use the term "institutional VC" to distinguish traditional VCs that take money from institutional investors from corporate VCs, captive VC funds run by family offices, and other VC-like intermediaries. Institutional VCs are also sometimes called financial VCs in the industry.

Startups often write complicated financial contracts tailored to their specific needs. Indeed, existing empirical and theoretical research emphasizes the centrality of contractual terms in evaluating the relationships between institutional VCs and their portfolio companies (Kaplan and Strömberg, 2003, 2004). The complex nature of contracts and the economic uncertainty these companies face also require the reassessment of the applicability of and modifications to standard financial valuation methods. In this chapter, we analyze the economic foundations of the contractual relationships between innovative companies and their financiers as well as the valuation of such companies and the financial securities that they issue. We aim to detail the economic nature of contracts used in practice in the US and to relate the existing contractual relationships to the mainstream contract theory. While we concentrate on the recent US landscape, our analysis could also be applied to a broader international context, with some necessary modifications.

A note on interpretation before we proceed. For expositional simplicity, we talk in this chapter about "startups." We use this term to refer to the young and innovative companies that use contractual arrangements similar to those of typical companies financed by VC funds or companies whose aim is to raise proper VC financing in the future. For example, we include large but private VC-backed companies under this umbrella.

The chapter proceeds as follows. In Section 2, we provide an overview of key stylized facts about startups and how they lead to contracting frictions. In Section 3, we discuss the various investment contracts used by startups and their associated cash flow rights. In Section 4, we extend that discussion to control rights, and in Section 5, we extend it to multiple rounds of financing. In Section 6, we discuss valuation. Finally, in Section 7, we conclude.

2 Contracting between startups and their investors

By their very nature, startups face many challenges in interacting with investors. In this section, we show that modern economic theories of contracting are ideally suited to understanding both these challenges and how startups and investors respond to them. Principal–agent problems, contractual incompleteness, information asymmetry, insufficient collateral, the inalienability of human capital, and other core contracting frictions bind especially tightly for startups. The startup financing ecosystem, including not just investment managers but also lawyers and limited partners, has evolved to allocate capital to promising innovative ventures despite these many frictions.

Startups operate within the nexus of complex sets of relationships between many interested parties. Fig. 1 shows schematically some of these relationships between company founders and companies, companies and investors, companies and employees, different sets of investors of the same company, and investors and their own investors. All these relationships are interlinked and operate both within the formal contractual relationships as well as informal arrangements based

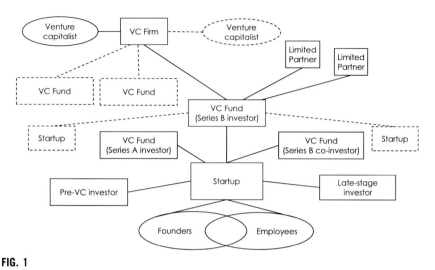

FIG. 1

Relationships between players in the VC ecosystem: This figure schematically illustrates the key relationships between players in the VC ecosystem. *Lines* indicate direct relationships, *dotted lines* indicate relationships tangential to the startup at the bottom-center (e.g., a VC investor's other portfolio companies).

on trust and reputation. Many players in these relationships wear several hats at the same time. For example, a company founder is often both a major common shareholder and a corporate executive, while a VC investor can be a startup board member bound to maximize corporate value, a representative of a VC fund that owns preferred shares in that company on behalf of the fund's investors, and an individual with her own incentives. The player's incentives are never perfectly aligned and the responsibilities of these roles can come into conflict: for example, a potential merger might hurt founders by undervaluing the company while allowing for an early payoff that helps with the venture capitalist's career (Gompers, 1995). Although this chapter's remit is to concentrate on a particular set of contractual relationships, which between companies and their investor, it is important to emphasize that these contracts do not and cannot exist in isolation from a broader set of relationships.

2.1 The life cycle of a VC-backed company

A startup's story starts with one or more passionate entrepreneurs. That individual or team develops an initial idea into a business that may one day become a very large company. Even the best innovative ideas are rarely profitable from day one, which means the startup will need external financing. This financing takes several forms, from an initial investment of the founders' own money and energy, to money raised externally, to perhaps an initial public offering (IPO).

Of course, many, if not most, companies fail on this journey. We use Facebook's financing path to illustrate companies' evolution and the associated financing contracts. There are no hard rules here, with companies raising money in numerous ways, and here we only attempt to lay out the common pattern. We approach classifying startup life cycle stages through the lenses of financing; another useful approach could be to delineate stages based on the company's operational development (Metrick and Yasuda, 2010).

2.1.1 Self-funding

In a company's earliest stage, the founding team develops an idea for a service or a product that they would like to develop and test. This stage may involve product development, market research, building a management team, developing a business plan, and testing the product on a small group of customers.

At this point, the founding team often works for free and usually puts their money into the startup. Family and friends may also contribute. Contracting is generally relatively informal here, with personal relationships helping to deal with the contractual frictions we will later discuss.

In our Facebook example, Mark Zuckerberg, Dustin Moskovitz, Chris Hughes, and Eduardo Saverin all invested time, money, and energy into Facebook's development.[b] They received common equity—the most basic form of ownership. (We discuss the structure of these and the later-mentioned securities in Section 3.)

2.1.2 Pre-VC financing

A fast-growing company will quickly outstrip the financial capacity of its founders. Although the company may still be small in absolute terms and have large gaps in its organizational structure and capabilities, it may still require hundreds of thousands of dollars or even millions of dollars to develop initial prototypes or provide proof of concept.

Companies have a variety of options to fill this financing gap. Angel investors, who are often wealthy individuals investing their own money in arms-length startups, are a common option. Facebook chose this option and raised its first external financing from a consortium of angel investors led by Peter Thiel in the form of a $500,000 convertible note with a $5 million valuation cap.[c] Such notes are a common form of angel financing and combine downside protection with upside potential, with similar Simple Agreement for Future Equity (SAFE) securities often used at this stage in recent years. Financing rounds may also involve common equity issuance or the same securities that VCs receive.

Beyond angel investors, there are several other sources of financing at this stage. Business incubators and startup accelerators often provide a small seed investment

---

[b]See, for example, https://fortune.com/2011/01/11/timeline-where-facebook-got-its-funding/.
[c]https://www.forbes.com/forbes/2011/0214/features-peter-thiel-social-media-life-after-facebook.html?sh=c245616275d1.

along with various types of mentorship and other services. Government grants, such as the Small Business Innovation Research program, are often available and are especially important outside of the United States. Product crowdfunding platforms such as Kickstarter allow startups to presell a product, while equity crowdfunding platforms such as Wefunder or StartEngine allow founders to sell equity to a diverse group of retail investors in a similar manner to an angel round.

Although Facebook raised part of its startup capital from a VC fund, traditional VC funds are less likely to engage at this stage because the scale of investment is too small. However, some VC funds do invest at this early stage, potentially to secure access to the company at a later stage of development. More recently, some VC funds focus on this stage, in the form of the so-called institutional micro-VC funds.

2.1.3 Early-stage venture capital

A company's Series A round is generally its first VC financing (sometimes the first round is also called Series Seed). This money helps companies continue to grow quickly—developing a product and finding an appropriate market fit, expanding their teams, particularly to include marketing and sales executives, testing their business model, and attracting initial customers.

Facebook's Series A came from venture capital firm Accel Partners, which agreed to invest $12.7 million out of its VC fund Accel IX at a reported postmoney valuation of $98 million.[d] This deal came in the form of convertible preferred equity, a type of security that gives investors similar rights to common equity but with additional downside protection and other beneficial provisions.

Many, if not most, innovative companies fail to raise venture capital financing, due to the extreme selectivity of venture capitalists who on average review approximately a hundred investments for every deal they make (Gompers et al., 2020). Still other companies bypass venture capital money altogether, such as Qualcomm that managed to bootstrap its way into being a major public company. However, the overwhelming majority of successful innovative companies need new funding to finance the next growth stage. While recently, some early-stage companies raised funding from angel investors and other entities who are associated more with the seed stage, the traditional route is by raising the first round of institutional VC funding. In a successful scenario, pre-VC financing, such as the one accommodated by angel investors, is typically followed by a VC financing round.

As the company continues to mature, its financing needs continue to grow. A Series A financing round is often followed by other venture capital rounds, such as a Series B round in Facebook's case led by another well-known VC firm, Greylock Partners.

---

[d]See Section 3.1.1 for discussion of this valuation measure. Information on this round and later rounds of Facebook is from Pitchbook.

2.1.4 Late-stage venture capital

As a company's growth continues, it expands its offerings. Revenue may grow strongly at this time, although many companies still do not show a profit. Companies continue raising VC funding that is used toward building a larger management team, marketing, expanding in their original markets, development of new products, or modification of the existing ones.

While venture capitalists continue to invest at this stage, the company's growth and increased professionalism lead to a larger pool of potential investors. Large corporations, often through their corporate venture capital arms, start to become more active, often investing alongside institutional VC firms. For example, Microsoft invested $240 million in Facebook's Series C round.

As the company matures further, other investors come into play. For example, a year and a half before its IPO, Facebook raised a $1.5 billion growth capital round from DST Global, Goldman Sachs, and Goldman Sachs's clients. The expansion in private capital markets has recently led to an explosion of growth equity and private equity funds investing in the asset class (Ewens and Farre-Mensa, 2020). Mutual funds have taken on hundreds of direct investments in late-stage VC-backed companies (Chernenko et al., 2021; Imbierowicz and Rauch, 2020). Direct investments by large institutional investors, such as the Saudi Arabian Public Investment Fund's $5 billion investment in Uber, have also become more regular.

Recently, more innovations are taking place in the late-stage funding market, especially for companies that are perceived as very successful. Under a generic rubric of "pre-IPO" markets, these include companies auctioning their common shares to a wider group of investors and the appearance of secondary markets.

2.1.5 Exit

The VC financing model is built around portfolio company liquidity events, with successful companies going public or being sold. As startup investors, including VC funds, typically sell their stake in the startup at or soon after a liquidity event, they consider such events as exits. Facebook's well-known IPO at a valuation of $81 billion was one of the most successful VC exits ever. Although only a small fraction of VC-backed companies ever become publicly listed, the majority of investor returns and runaway successes in the VC industry come from these companies. In addition to IPOs, companies can go public via direct listings (such as Spotify) or a reverse merger (such as 23andMe's purchase by a blank-check special purpose acquisition company).

Many successful companies are sold, generally to strategic buyers. The sale can take place at any stage of development. At the seed stage, an acquirer may be interested in hiring a management team (the so-called acquihire); at a later stage, an established public company may seek to acquire a successful innovative company. From an investor's perspective, a sale could be successful (the investor generates a profit on its original investment) or unsuccessful. Indeed, a large fraction of sales of VC-backed companies are essentially disguised failures.

Failure followed by liquidation is a common outcome because high-growth innovation is inherently risky and uncertain. These failures occur at each stage of development. While earlier stages are more uncertain and lead to more failed outcomes, there are a fair number of companies that failed to demonstrate their potential at the late stage as well.

2.2 Challenging features of VC startups

Raising money can be challenging even for mature public companies. High growth, innovative startups face additional hurdles. Most of these are well covered by classic models of contract theory. In this section, we discuss several characteristics of VC-backed companies that are worth noting to understand the contractual arrangements.

2.2.1 Nature of the cash flows
2.2.1.1 Uncertain outcomes
As Table 1 shows, startups are, above all, about high uncertainty.[e] A large fraction of VC-backed companies ultimately fail with little or no return to their investors, while a small number are runaway successes. These outliers effectively determine the return of the investor portfolio. All the parties in the VC world thus face extreme uncertainty of outcomes. This uncertainty extends to the cash flows on any single venture and the cash flows of the industry as a whole (Korteweg and Sorensen, 2010; Kisseleva et al., 2020).

Table 1 Startup outcome frequencies.

		IPO	M&A	Failure
Gompers et al. (2020)	Survey	15%	53%	32%
	Venture Source	13%	43%	44%
Puri and Zarutskie (2012)		16%	34%	40%
Ewens and Marx (2018)		6%	41%	28%
Wang et al. (2022)		3%	16%	81%

This table presents some evidence on the frequency of startup outcomes.

---

[e]The composition of Table 1 reflects both the multitude of VC data sources and the challenges of their interpretation. Gompers et al. (2020) report recent evidence on startup outcomes from the survey of over 800 VCs in 2016–2017, as well as historical data provided by VentureSource, one of the main longitudinal VC data sources available. Puri and Zarutskie (2012) use VentureSource, VentureXpert, and Longitudinal Business Database data for firms that receive their first rounds of VC financing between 1981 and 2005. Ewens and Marx (2018) use VentureSource data on firms founded from 1995 to 2008. Wang et al. (2022) report the data on VC-backed companies provided in Crunchbase, a popular open-source database of entrepreneurial companies. Importantly, while some merger and acquisition (M&A) outcomes are successful, many are not and would have been classified as failures using better data.

2.2.1.2 Scarce initial cash flows

Early-stage VC-backed companies, as a rule, are not profitable and many do not even have revenue. Even in the case of success, their profits are typically not sufficient to cover the investment amounts they received as private companies. For example, the year before its IPO and a decade after its founding, the electric car maker Rivian invested almost $1 billion into its business in addition to a $1 billion loss on its core operations. The value of innovative startups does not come from their short-term profitability. Instead, it lies in the expectation of cash flows in the sometimes distant future. Consequently, investors generate returns by selling their stake in the company rather than by getting access to the company's current assets or cash flows. The scarcity of contemporaneous cash flows makes the requirements of traditional debt instruments, such as maintaining an earnings before interest, taxes, depreciation, and amortization (EBITDA) to asset ratio above a minimum threshold, a nonviable option for VC-backed companies.

2.2.1.3 Insufficient collateral

High-growth innovative companies develop new products or services, often in novel industries. Most VC-backed companies are in the technology-related sectors. As a result, VC-backed companies tend to be collateral-poor, which effectively prevents them from using many traditional financing avenues, such as bank debt financing. Some of these companies, especially in the healthcare sector, do own intellectual property, but the values of their patents are often speculative and either difficult to establish and verify or not worth much in case of the company failure.

2.2.2 Nature of the information

2.2.2.1 Double-sided information asymmetry

Entrepreneurs and managers know more about the project than investors. That is particularly salient in our setting because a large share of information about the business and product is soft and nonverifiable (Amit et al., 1998). Although a company's growth and professionalization reduce information asymmetry, it continues to hold to some degree at all stages of the VC-backed company's life cycle, even for the presumably better-informed investors who are also board members. At the same time, investors are more knowledgeable about the market conditions, the funding environment, and the preferences of prospective investors. Given that VC-backed companies continuously raise funding and the company values greatly depend on the market and funding conditions, investors have the upper hand on relevant noncompany-specific information. The resulting double-sided information asymmetry plays a vital role in the dynamics of contractual negotiations.

2.2.2.2 Differences in opinion

The high degree of uncertainty is often complemented by differences in opinion. This can be reflected in disagreements on the startup's potential, with founding teams often being excessively optimistic, or about the direction that the startup should undertake. The most contentious disagreements are often about the suitability of the founders as corporate leaders, with VCs frequently seeking to replace them with professional managers.

2.2.2.3 Difficulty in acquiring information

Risky innovative projects are, by nature, difficult to evaluate. This raises challenges at many layers, from evaluating startups to reporting unrealized investment performance. A particular challenge this creates is that existing investors are more knowledgeable about the company than prospective investors, which can lead to a hold-up scenario, in which existing investors attempt to invest in follow-on rounds at unfair terms to founders or employees.

2.2.2.4 Contractual incompleteness

VC-backed companies present the case of ultimate contractual incompleteness. They face immense uncertainty and a changing environment that necessitates continuous changes to business and financial strategies. Even describing all such eventualities in a contract is inconceivable. As a result, just dividing future cash flow rights is not sufficient: instead, contracts in VC-backed companies prescribe, in greater detail, a corporate governance structure that is often contingent on future outcomes.

2.2.3 Moral hazard

2.2.3.1 Double-sided moral hazard

The incentives of startup founders frequently conflict with those of investors. Founders may enjoy private benefits of control and be subject to the typical host of managerial incentive problems such as shirking or diversion (Kaplan and Stromberg, 2001). Beyond these frictions, founder and investor risk exposures are fundamentally different, with investors enjoying diversified portfolios and founders typically having most of their wealth locked into the startup. The financial and nonfinancial incentives that founders and other employees face play a leading role in contracting and outcomes. Because investor-value add is important, investors, in turn, face their own set of incentive issues regarding effort provision. Different contractual payoffs may further drive a wedge between founder and investor incentives. Differences between investors and managers are often strongest in decisions on raising additional funding and a company exit. For example, some VC investors may face a strong incentive to take a portfolio company public to cement their reputation and raise follow-on VC funds (Gompers, 1995).

2.2.3.2 Inalienable human capital

Founder quality plays a critical role in the success or failure of VC-backed companies, with VC investors reporting that it is the most important factor in their investment decisions as well as in the outcome of their investments (Kaplan et al., 2009; Gompers et al., 2020). Founder departures due to disagreements with investors or other founders lead to the failure of many fledgling startups. Insights from the contracting literature that has been developed on the assumption of the inalienability of human capital (Hart and Moore, 1994; Bolton et al., 2019) are therefore very useful for analyzing the contracting arrangements of VC-backed companies.

2.2.3.3 Multilayer agency problems

In the entrepreneur–investor relationship, investors act as principals. However, investors representing institutional venture capital or private equity funds (general partners of these funds) act on behalf of their investors, known as limited partners. In the general partner-limited partner (GP-LP) relationship, general partners themselves are agents and LPs are their principals. The agency issues in the GP-LP relationship often reverberate into the company–investor relationship. For example, GPs of VC firms that are in the process of raising a new fund are less likely to write their investments off.

2.2.3.4 Many principals and conflicts among them

Mainstream contract theory assumes a principal–agent scenario with either one principal or many principals with aligned preferences. However, the nature of fundraising by VC-backed companies naturally leads to a situation where there are many distinct investors (principals) with occasionally divergent interests. The multitude of investors can lead both to horizontal and vertical problems. At a horizontal level, several investors often form a syndicate at each VC financing round. Members of a syndicate may have divergent interests leading to frictions (Nanda and Rhodes-Kropf, 2019). Vertically, investors in early rounds of funding may have entered at much lower share prices than the later round investors did and may face different incentives on whether the company should be sold or go public. Alternatively, an investor with another very successful company in her portfolio may exhibit different risk attitudes than an investor with a portfolio of mediocre investments. Thus, the entrepreneur–investor conflicts that economic studies of optimal contracts concentrate upon need to be supplemented by the study of investor–investor conflicts. Bartlett (2006) provided the first in-depth analysis of such conflicts within a legal framework.

2.2.4 Ecosystem structure

2.2.4.1 Matching frictions

The importance of VC-value add as well as the diversity of expertise, beliefs, and connections imply that startup-investor fit has significant importance. These inherent features lend both sides bargaining power in negotiating agreements. While early-stage startups generally struggle to raise money, successful startups at a later stage may have much more bargaining power (Gompers et al., 2020). Regions with relatively more VC and related capital supply, such as the California Silicon Valley, have contracts that are more tilted toward founders, while areas with relatively less investor capital, such as many emerging markets, have contracts tilted toward investors.

2.2.4.2 Varying market conditions

The VC capital market is marked by feasts and famines, with VC fundraising often precipitously declining during crises (e.g., in 2001 and 2009) and, conversely, often doubling during booms. The availability of capital shifts bargaining power and leads to significant shifts in both contractual arrangements and total fundraising. Funding downturns are marked by intense competition among startups vying for investors, while booms are marked by "money chasing deals," where investors vie for access to companies perceived to be poised for success.

2.2.4.3 Illiquidity

VC-backed companies are private entities, and investor ownership positions are subject to substantial illiquidity. This illiquidity, present in all closely held companies, is exacerbated in VC-backed companies due to a high degree of asymmetric information. More recently, VC-backed companies have tended to stay private for longer and in response, the secondary market for trading their shares has been steadily growing. Yet, this secondary market is in its relatively nascent form, and fundamental economic factors may prevent it from developing fully. For most VC investors, the only viable option of exit is when the company is sold or goes public.

2.3 Process of contracting in VC-backed companies

While public equity issuance is broadly standardized, startup equity issuances are highly bespoke. Under the Anglo-Saxon legal system, parties to a contract are free to innovate and modify a contract to suit their specific needs within a wide spectrum of possible options. Startups and VCs take full advantage of such flexibility and consequently negotiation over contractual arrangements is an important part of VC fundraising.[f] Although there are several common contract templates,[g] in practice contracts vary widely from one instance to another, not just in terms of superficial structure but also in the underlying economics. These are the fruit of intense negotiations, bargaining power and knowledge of all the parties, and time constraints.

Investors negotiate sophisticated contract terms, including cash flow, control, and voting rights. Kaplan and Strömberg (2003, 2004) describe many of these terms and examine the determinants of the contractual provisions in VC contracts. Gompers et al. (2020, 2021) show that VCs consider investor-friendly contractual features, such as pro-rata rights and liquidation preference, of the utmost importance in the negotiation process.

---

[f]As Kaplan et al. (2007) show, experienced VCs across countries appear to use US-style contracts. Bottazzi et al. (2009) argue legal protections lead to both noncontractible support of startups and contracted downside protections.

[g]See, for example, the National Venture Capital Association model legal documents available at https://nvca.org/model-legal-documents/. Some law firms have their own standardized templates.

Financing rounds commonly involve many investors investing together as part of a syndicate. Generally, one of these syndicate members is a lead investor and is responsible for setting terms and taking an ongoing active governance role. Importantly, there are often investors on both sides of the negotiating table—with any new investment diluting the claims of previous investors. In fact, existing owners frequently increase their stake as part of a financing round, meaning they are simultaneously adding to their stake and diluting it. This helps mitigate some of the information conflicts inherent in fundraising.[h]

It is common for one of the parties to offer a term sheet that summarizes the proposed terms of investment. The term sheet could be offered both by a company and by an investor. For many seed-stage companies, the companies led by founders offer the proposed terms to prospective investors, such as angels. When companies raise institutional VC funding, it is more common for the lead VC investor to propose a term sheet. In either case, the offer of a term sheet is an invitation to the negotiating table rather than a legally binding commitment of financing. Although some term sheet provisions are binding, these provisions cover the process of negotiations (e.g., preventing the company from signing multiple term sheets with different investors) or information nondisclosure of the proposed deal terms. The provisions of the term sheet covering the terms of the investment are usually not legally binding. In seed and early-stage financings, the due diligence process is often largely concluded before the term sheet signing. In late-stage financings, comprehensive due diligence is often initiated after the signing of the term sheet.

Term sheets differ on the completeness of the terms they cover. Negotiations often concentrate on a small number of contractual provisions perceived as important by contractual parties. Negotiating parties also need to take into account that other parties may have a veto over the contract in some circumstances. For example, some existing investors may not participate explicitly in the negotiating process over the new financing round, but their existing contractual rights include the veto power allowing them to prevent a financing from taking place unless specific conditions are met. If negotiations succeed and the deal is implemented, a comprehensive set of legally binding documents is signed. In a typical VC financing, these documents almost always include the stock purchase agreement, the voting rights agreement, the investor rights agreement, etc. It is also common for specific investors to negotiate a side letter, giving them additional protections. Seed stage financings often use a simpler structure with only one signed contractual document, whether a convertible note or a SAFE.

The entire process leads to substantial cross-sectional variation in contracts at all stages of the company life cycle. Financial securities issued by different companies,

---

[h]Investors being simultaneously buyers (of the new securities) and sellers (both as VCs having their existing shares diluted and as company board members issuing shares) can create a new set of conflicts and uncertainties.

whether convertible preferred stocks or convertible notes, vary widely from one company to another across a wide spectrum of contractual provisions, both in cash flow and control rights. Financial securities issued by the same company in different financing rounds may also vary substantially. To provide but just one example, Uber Technologies gave its Series C preferred investors dramatically fewer governance rights than its Series B preferred investors (among other provisions, just one-tenth the voting power of what Series B received), while at the same time increasing their ownership rights by offering them 1.25 times their money back in the event of a sale.

2.4 Economic features of VC contracting

In this section, we briefly discuss several important common economic features of financial securities issued by VC-backed companies.

2.4.1 Separation of cash flow and control rights

As the Uber case illustrates, control rights and cash flow rights are frequently separate. A powerful founder may raise money using securities that give new investors fewer rights relative to their underlying economic interest, such as Uber's dual-class voting structure introduced for their Series C round. Alternatively, and more commonly, investors may have additional control rights and minority protections, such as Uber's Series A investors having a guaranteed board seat and various protective provisions. Divides between cash flow and control rights can be even more extreme. Minority investors commonly have veto rights over specific decisions and outcomes. In some cases, as was the case with Uber's founders, a single group of minority owners might control the board of directors.

2.4.2 Contingent provisions

Many of the contractual terms of the financial securities issued by VC-backed companies are contingent on a specific event occurring in the future. One common yardstick is the share price of the next funding round relative to the share price of the current funding round. Both cash flow rights and control rights of existing claim holders may depend on whether the share price in the new round is below the share price of securities issued in previous rounds. For example, ubiquitous "antidilution" provisions entitle existing owners to more shares if the price of the new round falls below the price at which they invested. Contingent provisions are also widespread in contracts VC-backed companies sign with founders and employees, often in conjunction with a funding round. For example, a common contingent provision is the vesting of the founder and employee shares: if a founder or employee leaves the company within a certain period, she forfeits a portion or the entirety of her shares or stock options.

2.4.3 Multistage financing

VC-backed companies are prolific fundraisers. Multiple financing rounds are common both for successful companies on an upward trajectory and for struggling companies that need to secure funding to avoid failure. Many contractual terms, therefore, consider the impact of future financing. Each round of financing leads to a new round of negotiations between the management team, existing investors, and prospective investors. The flexibility of the contractual environment means that each new round is generally associated with a new financing contract, giving new investors different rights compared to those given in any previous financing. Renegotiations of existing contracts take place often, and therefore investors and other contractual parties expect that provisions they negotiated in the past may be renegotiated in the future. The accretion of these bespoke financing contracts leads to complicated financial structures, especially at a later stage. Understandably, existing investors are interested in protecting their rights ex ante in anticipation of future fundraising rounds as well as ensuring their right to coinvest in the future again. Multistage financing highlights the importance of dynamic contractual thinking as well as real optionality attitudes on behalf of involved parties. Antidilution mentioned above is one such commonly used term. Another one is a protective clause that entitles existing investors to veto any financing that would infringe on some specific rights they are entitled to. For example, an investor class may be able to veto the issuance of any securities that are senior to them in the priority ranking.

2.4.4 Hybrid equity–debt instruments

Common equity and straight debt instruments dominate traditional financial markets, yet are rarely issued to investors in VC-backed companies. Instead, startups issue convertible preferred stock and convertible notes, which are hybrid instruments that combine the elements of both equity and debt securities. In particular, like equity, these securities enable investors to benefit from upside realizations of company value and, like debt, offer investors a degree of downside protection.

2.4.5 Significant minority ownership

VC investors typically aim to be significant minority owners. Unlike private equity funds, they rarely take controlling stakes. Yet unlike the typical mutual fund, they are not content with owning a tiny fraction of any company they invest in. These considerations stem from the double-sided moral hazard problem discussed above: investments are structured to give both founders and investors strong economic incentives. In early financing rounds, investors typically jointly hold minority cash flow rights and voting rights. In response, minority investors tend to negotiate an extensive set of protective provisions that aim to prevent their expropriation. Many of these protective provisions are state-contingent and cover specific decisions. As the company evolves, the accumulated dilution created by repeated minority stakes typically shifts the bulk of both cash flow rights and the majority of control rights to investors. Successive financing rounds dilute the ownership of founders of successful companies from 100% initially to an average of just 12.5% at the time of IPO (Kaplan et al., 2009).

3 Dividing cash flows

In this section, we discuss how financial contracts divide the cash flows of VC-backed companies. We introduce the main types of financial security used by VC-backed companies in their contractual arrangements with investors, founders, and employees. It is important to emphasize that, while we leave the discussion of control rights until the next section for the benefit of exposition, in reality, cash flow provisions and control provisions are closely intertwined and thus any discussion focused solely on cash flow rights without considering control rights is necessarily incomplete.

We start with some notation, which we take from Gornall and Strebulaev (2020). Consider a single VC-backed company. The company has raised money over a series of rounds, with the round i investors being issued security Z_i in exchange for an investment of I_i. The company is currently raising round n by issuing security Z_n in exchange for an investment of I_n. After that issuance, the startup may issue more securities $(Z_{n+1}, ..., Z_N)$ in exchange for additional investment $(I_{n+1}, ..., I_N)$. Each issuance impacts the payoff of all existing securities.

At some future date T, after raising N funding rounds, the company will experience a liquidity event, such as an IPO or M&A exit, and all of the company owners will be paid out. The payoff of a security depends not just on its terms and the company exit value X_T, but also on the terms of the other securities outstanding at the exit time. We write the payoff of security i as $\pi_i(X_T, \mathbb{Z}_T)$, where the set of securities outstanding at time t is denoted by $\mathbb{Z}_t = (Z_0, Z_1, ..., Z_k)$ for the largest k such that $t_k < t$.

While this setup can accommodate any financial contract, Table 2 shows the main financial instruments used in VC-backed companies as well as the qualitative assessment of the frequency with which different types of securities are owned by various

Table 2 Contract usage.

	Founders and employees	Pre-VC investors	VC investors	Late-stage investors
Common equity	**Yes**	Sometimes	Rare	Sometimes
Common stock options	**Yes**	Rare	Rare	Rare
Straight preferred stock	Rare	Rare	Rare	Rare
Convertible preferred stock	Rare	Yes	**Yes**	**Yes**
Straight debt	Rare	Rare	Rare	Rare
Convertible notes	Rare	**Yes**	Sometimes	Sometimes
SAFE	Rare	**Yes**	Rare	Sometimes
Venture debt	Rare	Rare	Sometimes	Sometimes
Warrants	Rare	Rare	Sometimes	Sometimes

This table provides types of securities typically held by different claim holders in startups. Entries in bold are the ones used most often in practice.

claim holders. As the table illustrates, there is a clear separation line: in practice, investors rarely own common equity-like securities, while founders and employees tend to have received common shares and related equity-like ownership claims. We now discuss all of these securities in detail.

3.1 Convertible preferred stock

Most venture capital investors receive convertible preferred shares or a variant of these, thus that is where we start our discussion. While the formal name of these securities in financial contracts is usually "preferred stock," in reality the conversion features they possess are so critical that we will call them convertible preferred stock to emphasize the stylized fact that VC investors rarely receive the traditional preferred stock used by many publicly listed companies.

These convertible preferred stocks follow a basic form and are supplemented with frequent adornments. Table 3 shows the frequency of these terms in various samples.[i] We start by discussing the most important cash flow terms of convertible preferred stock.

3.1.1 Conversion

Investors who own convertible preferred stock have the right to convert their preferred stock into common stock at any time of their choice. This feature is known as optional conversion. As conversion is irreversible (an investor cannot "unconvert"

Table 3 Convertible preferred stock terms.

	KS2003	GS2020	GS2021	NVCA/AUMNI20
Liquidation multiple >1	71	16	4	1–6
Participation	41	20	28	4–11
Cumulative dividend	44	10	n.d.	n.d.
IPO ratchet	n.d.	17	n.d.	n.d.
Redemption	79	n.d.	n.d.	6–12
Seniority	n.d.	48	32	n.d.
Automatic conversion	95	100	n.d.	n.d.
Automatic conversion exemption	n.d.	68	n.d.	n.d.
Antidilution	95	n.d.	n.d.	n.d.

This table shows the frequency of contractual cash flow terms in convertible preferred stocks issued by startups. Values are rounded and given in percentages. n.d. means no data. KS2003 is Kaplan and Strömberg (2003), GS2020 is Gornall and Strebulaev (2020), GS2021 is Gornall and Strebulaev (2021a), NVCA/AUMNI20 is a range across funding rounds from the NVCA/AUMNI "NEW Enhanced Model Term Sheet v2.0."

[i]The data for the NVCA/AUMNI20 entries are taken from version v2.0 of "NEW Enhanced Model Term Sheet" dated July 2020, published by the National Venture Capital Association and Aumni, and available at https://www.aumni.fund/resources/enhanced-model-term-sheet (accessed February 1, 2022).

common shares back into preferred shares), in practice, conversion takes place in conjunction with a liquidity event or, sometimes, for strategic considerations. In addition, preferred stock may be forced to convert into common shares under some conditions, such as the company undertaking an IPO. The forced conversion is known as automatic or mandatory conversion.

To see how conversion (either optional or mandatory) works mechanically, we introduce two further definitions. We define a fully diluted basis as the condition that assumes the conversion into common stock of all outstanding securities at the time that are convertible into common stock. A fully diluted basis assumes that all convertible preferred stock is converted into common stock, and it also assumes that all options and warrants, including the option pool, and which are discussed below, are exercised. We also define postmoney valuation (PMV) as the product of that round's share price (when the security in question is issued) and the company's total number of shares on a fully diluted basis, that is the number of common shares assuming the conversion of all outstanding securities convertible into common stock. PMV is a widely used term in the VC industry, and the PMV of a financing round is often equated to the "value" of a company (more on the valuation in Section 6).

Consider a simple example, in which a company raises a single round of convertible preferred stock from a single investor and subsequently has a liquidity event. The investor paid I_1 for a contract Z_1 at some PMV P_1. At the time of a liquidity event, if the investor converts her preferred stock into common stock, she will get the following payoff:

$$\pi_1(X_T, \mathbb{Z}_T) = \omega_1 X_T, \tag{1}$$

where the fraction of the company that investor owns at time T upon conversion is

$$\omega_1 = \frac{I_1}{P_1} \tag{2}$$

and $\mathbb{Z}_T = \{Z_0, Z_1\}$, where Z_0 are the common shares owned by founders and employees. Conversion allows the investor to gain from high-value exits. Straight debt without a conversion option is standard for most companies but is challenging for startups because of their high failure probabilities. Because these failures often result in an almost total loss for investors, long-term investments without a conversion option would require exorbitant interest or dividend rates. This explains why noncontingent securities, such as straight debt or vanilla preferred stock, are rarely used by such companies, especially in earlier phases of their life cycle.

This explains the essence of the convertibility option inherent in the securities VC investors receive. As we discuss in Sections 3.4 and 3.5, other securities that investors receive, such as convertible notes and SAFEs, also feature a similar conversion provision.

In addition to optional conversion, most share issues include mandatory conversion terms, which can allow a majority of investors to force all investors to convert. These terms arise to prevent a single owner from refusing to convert her shares, which could block or derail a value-creating IPO exit. Such an exit would generally create value but would entail all convertible preferred stock being converted into common stock, which could hurt some of the preferred investors. These investors may have an incentive to block that conversion, which could delay or derail the IPO process. This issue is averted using mandatory conversion terms, which allow a majority of other shareholders to force the conversion of any recalcitrant holdouts, subject to some conditions. The conditions often take the form of the minimum share price, company value, or net IPO proceeds. As can be expected, mandatory conversion reduces the bargaining power and expected payoff of those shareholders who are more likely to be forced to convert against their wishes (most importantly, those who benefit from strong contractual terms or recent investors who may not have met their return targets), and therefore some investors negotiate exceptions to mandatory conversion either based on votes or a class-specific return target. Some mandatory conversion terms are associated with the so-called ratchets that guarantee investors a certain minimum return in IPOs. For example, late-stage investors in a well-known VC-backed company Square negotiated the IPO ratchet, which resulted in a wealth transfer from other shareholders to them when the Square IPO was priced below the original share price they paid. We discuss automatic conversion further in Section 4.1.4.

3.1.2 Liquidation preference

A liquidation preference provides investors with downside protection by allowing them to take a fixed payout in lieu of their conversion option. Because automatic conversion forces investors to convert in an IPO, liquidation preferences are relevant for exits where the company fails or is acquired (together referred to as liquidations). The industry standard is a $1\times$ liquidation multiple, which entitles investors to their money back before common shareholders receive anything, while, more generally, an $L \times$ liquidation multiple entitles investors to receive L times their investment back. In practice, L can be above 1 in times when companies struggle to secure funding or in later funding rounds when the company is not doing well; L is almost never below 1.

By making their claims senior to those of common equity, liquidation preference provides convertible preferred stockholders with downside protection in less favorable outcomes. In exits when the investor can choose either to exercise her conversion right or to stick to her liquidation preference, the investor chooses the strategy that maximizes her payoff. To illustrate, consider again the single round example introduced above. If the investor has a liquidation multiple of L_1, her payoff in an M&A or a liquidation is

$$\pi_1(X_T, \ Z_T) = \max\{ \underbrace{\min\{L_1 I_1, \ X_T\}}_{\text{Liquidation preference}}, \quad \underbrace{\omega_1 X_T}_{\text{Converted payoff}} \}. \tag{3}$$

For sufficiently high exit values, the investor converts. For intermediate exits, the investor waives the conversion option and receives her liquidation preference. For exits below the investor's liquidation preference, the investor receives the entire exit payoff.

There are several economic explanations for the seniority of VC investors over founders. To start with, there are classic stories about why debt-like securities may be preferred to equity-like securities, ranging from asymmetric information (Myers and Majluf, 1984) to agency costs (Jensen and Meckling, 1976). Giving a guarantee to investors makes the ownership retained by founders more sensitive to their effort and inside information and thus reduces these important frictions.

Furthermore, there are several VC-specific phenomena worth discussing. First, there may be a tax benefit to issuing securities other than common shares. As discussed by Gilson and Schizer (2003), the preferential treatment of capital gains over income may give VC employers an incentive to issue in-the-money stock options to their employees in lieu of cash compensation. Tax regulation attempts to prevent the issuance of such in-the-money options; however, the complexity of the capital structure of VC-backed companies gives them substantial leeway in issuing these options (Gornall and Strebulaev, 2021a). Companies may use liquidation multiples and other preferred features that effectively obfuscate their capital structure while enabling this tax-preferred compensation.

Second, the investor may want protection from the different risk preferences and discounting rates of founders. The seniority of investors prevents founders from opting for a quick sale at a price the VC investor may be unhappy with. To illustrate, imagine that the VC invests $10 million at the PMV of $40 million for one-quarter of the company on a fully diluted basis, with the remaining three-quarters belonging to the common shareholders. The next day, the founders (who control the company) receive an offer to sell the company for $8 million. If the investor does not have a liquidation preference, she will get $2 million in such a sale and the founders will get $6 million. Although this is a negative expected value trade, impatient or risk-averse founders might choose the potentially life-changing $6 million and leave the VC with a loss of $8 million. A liquidation preference prevents this trade and leaves the founders with nothing if the company is sold for less than $10 million.

Third, the founders may be (or rather, almost certainly are) irrationally optimistic about the startup's potential.[j] Contracts where founders bear more of the downside risk emerge naturally from such a difference in beliefs, either genuine or signaled. Moreover, these conversion options may help attenuate a founder's desire to window-dress between financing stages (Cornelli and Yosha, 2003).

Finally, liquidation preferences, along with all terms that benefit the current investor, increase the value of preferred shares and along with them the share price and reported PMV (Gornall and Strebulaev, 2021a). This may lead to higher prices paid by investors in these financing rounds, either to play off founder biases, avoid a perception that the company is struggling, or avoid triggering terms contingent on share price declines (see Section 5.1.1).

---

[j]For example, Camerer and Lovallo (1999) found that entrepreneurs choose to enter a market even when the expected value of entering is negative, reflecting the tendency to overestimate their own prospects for success. Studies with related findings include Cooper et al. (1988), Lee et al. (2017), and Arabsheibani et al. (2000).

3.1.3 Participation

Participation rights entitle an investor to both her liquidation preference and her converted payoff. Liquidation preferences are satisfied first, and the residual exit proceeds are then shared among shareholders as if any participating investors had converted. In the VC industry, participation is informally known as "double-dipping," because it entitles the investors to both downside protection and upside participation.

Continuing our single round example but adding participation, the investor's payoff in an M&A exit or liquidation is

$$\pi_1(X_T, \mathbb{Z}_T) = \underbrace{\min\{L_1 I_1, \ X_T\}}_{\text{Liquidation preference}} + \underbrace{\omega_1 \max\{0, \ X_T - L_1 I_1\}}_{\text{Participation}}. \tag{4}$$

Fig. 2 illustrates the hypothetical payoffs of a convertible preferred stock with and without a participation feature. It is clear that participation increases the payoff of investors, and its effect is relatively large at the intermediate exit values. In practice, the management and existing shareholders are averse to participation; many founders consider it unfair. Negotiations around the participation often coalesce at an intermediate solution, participation with a cap. As the name suggests, the cap implies that the participation feature is applied as long as the total payoff to the investor is equal to the product of the original investment and the cap. Adding a cap of C changes the above formula to

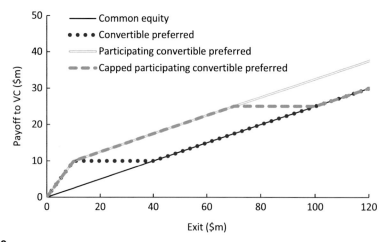

FIG. 2

Impact of conversion, participation, and participation cap on payoffs: This figure shows the payoff of an example investment of $10 million at a PMV of $40 million using common equity, convertible preferred equity, participating convertible preferred equity, and capped participating preferred equity with a cap on total unconverted payout equal to 2.5 times the invested amount.

$$\pi_1(X_T, \mathbb{Z}_T) =$$

$$\max\{\underbrace{\min\ \{L_1 I_1,\ X_T\}}_{\text{Liquidation preference}} + \underbrace{\omega_1 \min\{\max\ \{0,\ X_T - L_1 I_1\}, (C - L_1)I_1\}}_{\text{Capped participation}}, \quad \underbrace{\omega_1 X_T}_{\text{Converted payoff}}\ \}.$$

$$(5)$$

As with liquidation preferences, one economic rationale behind participation is to allow the strategic obfuscation of capital structure and inflation of reported post-money valuations. Additionally, participation could create value by strengthening investor value-creation incentives for intermediate exits, while the standard convertible preferred stock may make investors insensitive to exit value increases in this range (e.g., the flat spot at exits between \$10 million and \$40 million in Fig. 2). However, participation creates a new incentive conflict by reducing payoffs of investors in IPOs where mandatory conversion forces them to convert their shares to common equity and forgo their participating payout.

3.1.4 Seniority

In a liquidation or sale where there is insufficient value to satisfy all liquidation preferences, $X_T < \sum_{j=1}^{N} L_j I_j$, contractual terms that define the relative seniority of investors come into play. While almost limitless complexity is possible, in practice, most seniority structures fall into two categories. First, preferred securities in different funding rounds are "pari passu," that is, they are paid out in proportion to their liquidation preference[k]:

$$\pi_i(X_T, \mathbb{Z}_T) = X_T \frac{L_i I_i}{\sum\limits_{j=1}^{N} (L_j I_j)}. \tag{6}$$

Second, each new round is senior to all prior rounds and has its liquidation preference satisfied before the previously issued securities are paid:

$$\pi_i(X_T, \mathbb{Z}_T) = \min\left\{ L_i I_i, \max\left\{ 0, X_T - \sum_{j=i+1}^{N} (L_j I_j) \right\} \right\}. \tag{7}$$

In practice, companies combine these two structures; for example, a company might initially raise three rounds that are pari passu and later raise two rounds that are each senior to all previous rounds. As shown by Gornall and Strebulaev (2021a), granting seniority to new rounds significantly impairs the value of previous rounds. As such, the terms we see in practice result from a tradeoff between the presumed information asymmetry between investor classes (which seniority alleviates) and the bargaining power of the potentially subordinated existing investors.

---

[k]Note that all preferred securities are still senior to common shares.

3.1.5 Other cash flow provisions

Private VC-backed companies rarely generate cash flows as they use all their cash flow from operations and more, to scale and grow. Thus, they tend not to pay cash dividends and, in most cases, dividends do not play an important role in these contracts. Contractual provisions covering dividends typically state they are paid out when declared by the board and that any dividends paid to common stock are junior to preferred equity. Such "noncumulative" dividends are rarely declared, and so are generally immaterial.

Cumulative dividends can have a large impact; however, they are relatively rare. Such dividends are calculated for each period (typically, 1 year) and the right to receive the dividend is carried forward either until it is paid or until such right is terminated or modified. As startups rarely pay cash dividends, these cumulative dividends accrue and are paid out at the time of exit. While there are many ways these payouts can be structured, one common way is for them to effectively increase liquidation preference over time. Cumulative dividends may be payable only in certain exits, commonly liquidations and sales. In practice, late-stage investors and investors in struggling companies are more likely to negotiate and receive cumulative dividends.

Another typical contractual provision is redemption. Redemption entitles investors to demand the original investment amount back from the company under certain circumstances. As VC-backed companies are usually cash-poor, this provision is unlikely, outside some exceptions, to lead to investors demanding redemption in anticipation of receiving their investment back. Rather, it may provide a bargaining chip to investors in a future round of negotiations. We discuss redemption further in Section 4.4.

Preferred equity typically also contains the so-called antidilution protections, which provide price adjustments in the event of unfavorable future financing rounds. We discuss these terms in Section 5.1.1.

3.2 Common equity

Although investors rarely get common equity at the time of their investment in VC-backed companies, common equity plays a critical role for two reasons. First, as discussed above, investors receive securities that convert into common equity. Second, founders and employees get compensated with instruments derived from common equity, whether common equity itself, restricted stock units (RSUs), or options on common equity.

The cash flow rights of common equity are largely standard and similar to a traditional common equity security. An important exception is vesting, which is ubiquitous to founder and employee securities. Vesting means that the receiver of shares will gain ownership of them over time by satisfying certain conditions. For example, an employee who joins a startup may get an initial option grant that vests over time with their continued employment, which is partially forfeited if that employee quits. Similarly, when founders of the company raise funding from institutional investors for the first time, if not earlier, their ownership is subject to vesting so that they lose shares if they quit or are fired. Economically, these terms align the incentives of employees with those of their employers. If the receiver leaves the company early, she faces a financial penalty by forgoing the unvested portion of her stock compensation. To consider an extreme example, a founder of a startup that raises a first VC round may lose her entire ownership stake in the company if she quits immediately after the round. Founders commonly negotiate for a fraction of their shares to be excluded from such vesting requirements.

This vesting has historically taken place over 4 years and can happen at a time-varying rate. In a cliff vesting, a large fraction of stock ownership is vested on a particular date. In a step vesting, a smaller fraction of shares is vested according to a prespecified plan, usually monthly or quarterly. In practice, many contracts feature both cliff and step vesting. For example, a common 4-year founder vesting plan entitles the founder to a 25% vesting in 1 year (meaning the founder vests 25% of the total package in 1 year), with the rest vesting monthly in equal installments for the remaining 3 years.

Additional "trigger" terms determine what happens to unvested ownership after a sale (when the underlying shares cease to exist). Single-trigger acceleration means that the entire unvested portion of the stock plan is vested upon a prespecified triggering event. Most commonly, such a triggering event is a sale of a company. Another single triggering event could be the involuntary termination of an employee. A double-trigger acceleration means that for the unvested stock to vest, two triggering events must take place. For example, the company is sold and the employee is terminated. These double-trigger clauses are the most common in employment contracts. One reason is that to the extent human capital is expected to be an important asset at the time of the company sale, the acquirer would be wary of acquiring a company where key employees will have no incentives to stay or where there will be additional costs for the acquirer to provide further incentives to retain key employees. Along these lines, acquirers may insist that key employees be subject to "revesting" at the time of an acquisition so that they face a financial penalty if they quit.

3.3 Stock options

Employees joining a VC-backed company often receive an option grant, which allows them to acquire the company's common shares in the future at a certain price by exercising vested options. Stock options are allocated from an option pool, which is an amount of common stock reserved for future employees. The option pool is one of the contractual terms most negotiated between companies and investors because larger option pools at a given PMV mean investors get more shares. It is typical for a company to increase or top-up its option pool at each financing round.

To prevent firms from transmuting an employee's heavily taxed ordinary income into lightly-taxed deferred capital gains, tax regulations require option grants to have a strike price equal to or above the value of the underlying stock. In recent years, this value has been determined based on compliance with Section 409A of the Internal Revenue Service code. Compliance with this regulation can provide option recipients the ability to defer tax and claim it at the lower capital gains rate, in the form of incentive stock options. Other options, such as those given to nonemployees, have less favorable tax treatment and are referred to as nonqualified stock options.[1]

Employees who leave the company or are terminated typically must exercise the vested portion of their options within a short period or let them expire. This posttermination exercise period is usually 90 days and the forced early exercise of options significantly decreases the value of these options to employees.[m]

Employees of VC-backed companies, especially in a later stage of their life cycle, often receive RSUs or restricted stock awards (RSAs) rather than stock options. RSUs are also subject to time-based vesting arrangements similar to the ones stock options have. Moreover, RSUs can be trigger-based, with a trigger like a sale of the company or an IPO. RSAs entitle the employee with the right to purchase the shares at a specified price on the grant date, without vesting. However, the company may have the right to repurchase shares under RSAs at a prespecified price if employees leave or are terminated. Economically, therefore, the vesting process of RSAs and RSUs can be similar. Restricted stock also faces different tax treatment from stock options.

In addition, employee-owned options, RSUs, and common stocks are often subject to various transfer restrictions, such as rights of first refusal (ROFR, see Section 5.2.2) and buyback provisions, which may further lower the value of these assets.

3.3.1 Warrants

VC-backed companies sometimes utilize warrants as a supplementary funding option. A warrant issued by a company is a contract according to which the warrant holder has the right to buy the company's common or preferred shares at a specified price over a specified period. Once a warrant holder exercises her warrant, she receives shares of stock in the company. In this way, warrants are economically similar to stock options. However, they are usually issued to investors rather than employees. They can also be issued to other parties, such as suppliers or customers.

One difference between a stock option and a warrant is that companies issuing warrants are not restricted by the 409A rule; thus, they can set any exercise price. Warrants are often used in combination with other securities or transactions and provide an additional incentive to contracting parties. Examples include a warrant issued in conjunction with a convertible note, a bank loan, or a commercial agreement.

---

[1]The discussion of tax issues related to employee compensation in VC-backed companies is beyond the scope of this chapter. See, for example, https://www.cooleygo.com/isos-v-nsos-whats-the-difference/ for further details.
[m]Carta's 2021Q2 State of Private Markets report shows 90% of the stock options of terminated employees had a less than 95-day posttermination exercise period.

Warrants can be issued both on common stock and preferred stock. Warrants have a specified maturity, up to which they can get exercised. Like preferred stock, warrants may need to get exercised and then converted in a liquidity event, such as a sale or an IPO. Warrants may have vesting arrangements similar to those of stock options.

3.4 Convertible notes

A convertible promissory note is a debt instrument with two primary elements: debt repayment and equity conversion rights. These notes are frequently used to finance preseed, seed, and early-stage companies, which are typically developing and refining their product concepts. Often, convertible notes are the first external financing utilized by these companies. Convertible notes are also sometimes used in later-stage financings, for example, where existing investors are providing temporary financing while the company is raising a new round of funding (also called "bridge" financing).

The debt repayment element of a promissory note defines the principal, interest rate, maturity date, and default provisions with related remedies. The equity conversion element of the note defines the specific event or events that trigger conversion (e.g., a qualifying equity financing round or liquidation), the formula used in converting the debt to equity (i.e., a valuation cap and/or a discount to the per-share price being paid in the next financing round), the type of equity to which the debt would be converted (common stock vs preferred stock, for example), and any additional equity rights attached to the shares converted from the debt such as voting rights and dividend rights. The terms of the convertible note do not establish a specific valuation for the company, rather, they establish a formula (or a choice of formulae) for conversion based on a future event such as a future convertible preferred equity issuance.

A convertible note is typically not secured by the assets of the company, unlike secured bank loans or secured convertible debt instruments. Like convertible preferred stocks, convertible notes are not standardized, uniform financial instruments. Rather the terms discussed below are negotiated by the parties. A common area of negotiation is the conversion terms, meaning the circumstances under which the note will convert into equity securities of the company. Convertible notes can be designed to convert into equity based on a number of potential triggering events, including an equity-financing round (whether a qualified financing or nonqualified), a sale or other change of control of the company, default, or upon maturity. Entrepreneurs and investors will negotiate and agree on conversion terms, including any discount rate (the percentage by which the conversion price per share may be reduced below the price per share of the equity financing) and valuation cap (the maximum company valuation to be used to calculate the conversion price per share).

3.4.1 Principal

The principal of a convertible note is the amount of investment provided by the note-holder to the company through the convertible note. If the note does not convert, it is the amount that the company needs to repay to the investors (plus any accrued interest). If the note is converted, the principal (plus any accrued interest) is the amount used to calculate the number of shares that the note will be converted into. In this latter case, the investor forgoes the principal repayment in exchange for the shares.

3.4.2 Interest rate

Convertible notes, like most debt instruments, feature interest. The early-stage companies that issue convertible notes rarely pay that interest in cash. Rather, the notes accrue the interest, that is, interest is paid via increasing the amount of the note so that, at conversion, the interest also converts into equity securities of the company on the same terms as the principal. At maturity, the total sum of the outstanding principal and accrued interest is due. Upon conversion, the same total sum would typically convert into stock.

3.4.3 Conversion

Convertible notes convert automatically into equity if certain triggers take place. A common trigger that leads to a conversion of principal and accrued interest of the note is an equity financing round. Typically, the equity financing round needs to reach a certain size to be a "qualified financing" to trigger conversion. An additional requirement for qualified financing could be that preferred equity needs to be issued in the financing round. Conversion takes place into the equity issued in a qualified financing round.

A second common conversion trigger is a change in control or a liquidation event. In this case, the note can either be automatically converted into equity or it may simply trigger a repayment event at the greater of principal plus interest or the conversion amount or a multiple of the principal. Conversion can also take place on the maturity date of the note as discussed in Section 3.4.5.

3.4.4 Conversion price, discount, and valuation cap

Conversion associated with a financing round generally occurs at a price lower than that paid by investors in the qualified financing round. For example, with a typical discount of 20%, if investors in the qualified round agreed to pay $1 per share, note-holders will convert at the price of $0.80 per share. This conversion discount is often justified on the grounds of additional time exposure and higher uncertainty facing noteholders compared to investors in the qualified financing round.

Many notes also feature valuation caps. The valuation cap is a term that imposes a ceiling on the price at which a convertible note would convert into the equity security sold at the qualified equity financing. In seed-stage financing, a valuation cap is one of the most important terms of a convertible note. In practice, many variations of a valuation cap are possible and the exact specifics of conversion math are often complicated. Abstracting from those complications, here is a simple example of a valuation cap.

Suppose a convertible note of $1 million specifies a valuation cap of $10 million. If the company raises its next round of financing at a premoney valuation of $8 million[n] —that is, lower than the valuation cap—with a per-share price of $1, the convertible note would be converted at the same per-share price of $1. If, on the other hand, the company's next round of financing has a premoney valuation of $20 million—that is, twice the valuation cap—with a per-share price of $1, the convertible note would be converted into equity as if the premoney valuation is $10 million. The adjusted conversion price is then calculated as $10 million divided by $20 million, which is $0.5 per share. This means that the $1 million convertible note would be converted into 2 million shares, as opposed to 1 million shares without a valuation cap.

The valuation cap mechanism enables the convertible note investor to benefit from the upside of the company after the trigger event occurs. Convertible notes often feature both conversion discount and a valuation cap, which means that the per-share conversion price is the lowest of the discounted per-share price in the next qualified round price per share or the per-share price implied by the valuation cap.

3.4.5 Maturity date and repayment

A note's maturity date is when the principal is due to be repaid along with any accrued but unpaid interest if the note is still outstanding. Some convertible notes have specific terms that call for automatic conversion into equity on the maturity date or entitle the noteholder to an optional conversion into common or preferred equity if the note is still outstanding on maturity. An alternative to repayment or conversion is for the company to negotiate an extension of the maturity date with the noteholders. In practice, such extensions are often granted by investors, because it provides them with the option to convert into the company's stock at a later date if a financing round takes place. However, if the investors refuse to extend the maturity date or the company does not request an extension, the repayment of the note is due at maturity. If the company is unable to repay the note, investors as debt holders can pursue a liquidation process for the company, in which they have seniority relative to any equity outstanding.

3.4.6 Nonpriced round

Convertible note rounds are often referred to as "nonpriced" rounds because they do not explicitly set a share price and, thus, do not have the associated PMV. Instead, their share price is a function of the future financing round that triggers the note conversion. Deferring pricing in this manner allows the notes to be contingent on the

---

[n]Premoney valuation means the agreed valuation of a financing round, excluding the money invested by the new investors. Complications arise as the amount of note may or may not be included in that premoney valuation.

future resolution of uncertainty. However, most of these convertible notes have valuation caps, which anchor the expectations of value for founders and investors. The presence of valuation caps effectively implies the pricing of the round, even though the contractual language around these caps often provides subsequent investors the flexibility to dilute noteholders. Without valuation caps, the conversion deferral can create perverse incentives for investors, as, in many cases, their ownership is a decreasing function of the future round's price, and for managers, who may benefit from deferring a qualified round to dilute the company's noteholders.

3.5 SAFEs

A SAFE is an agreement between an investor and a company that converts into equity at the next financing round if certain conditions are met. SAFEs were developed as an alternative to convertible notes in circa 2012 (Coyle and Green, 2014). They were developed by a team of lawyers working for Y Combinator and intended to be a more straightforward alternative to convertible notes for companies to understand, negotiate, and implement.

As with a convertible note, a SAFE provides for conversion events and can also provide for priority ahead of other equity holders in the event of liquidation. However, unlike a convertible note, a SAFE is not a debt security, and, unlike convertible preferred equity, it is also not an equity instrument. It does not accrue interest or dividends, and it does not generally contain a maturity or repayment date.

A SAFE investment will generally only convert into equity when the company raises a future equity round satisfying certain conditions or in the event of a sale of the company. It is possible that after SAFE financing a company never raises additional equity capital and never sells itself or goes public. In that case, the SAFE holders would continue to hold their securities, earning no interest, receiving no dividends, and never realizing a return of their original investment.

As with other securities we discuss, the specific terms used in SAFEs vary. The investor receives the right to stock in the company at a later date, in connection with specific, agreed-upon triggers. A typical trigger is the sale of equity by the company. The qualified round may include only preferred or both preferred and common equity.

A SAFE, like a convertible note, may feature both a valuation cap and a discount to the conversion price at the time of the triggering event. One of the key benefits of a SAFE is that, in part, because there is a widely available and adopted standard form, it generally requires less negotiation before the investment. A SAFE is a single-document solution that only requires the selection among the several versions of SAFEs the company is going to use as well as the amount of the investment and the valuation cap that applies to the conversion price calculation. Because SAFEs also defer pricing, they give rise to the same incentive issues as convertible notes.

3.6 Venture debt

Venture debt is a type of debt offered by banks, specialized intermediaries, and other creditors to finance VC-backed companies (Davis et al., 2020). In practice, venture debt complements equity financing using convertible preferred stock. It is frequently set up as a bridge loan, to be repaid either in an imminent liquidity event or at the time of the next financing round. Venture debt typically comes with warrants on common equity that enable the creditor to benefit from the upside of the company's value. While venture debt is senior to any common or preferred equity, it typically does not require physical collateral. Venture debt is often issued by companies that have already raised several equity financing rounds.

4 Dividing control

Founders, employees, and investors have diverse interests, beliefs, information, and incentives. These differences make the allocation of decision-making authority critical for startups of all stages. The structure of corporate governance—the allocation of control and voting rights between various stakeholders—is a central topic in startup contracting.

An important distinction between startups and the typical large public company is that startup investors, such as venture capitalists, are active investors who negotiate and exercise substantial corporate governance rights. These investors operate in the context of extreme uncertainty, information asymmetry, institutional constraints, and various underlying agency problems. As a result of negotiations that reflect investor concerns and requirements, the final contractual structure of investment often leads to a separation between cash flow rights and corporate governance rights in an entrepreneurial firm.

For example, early on in the life cycle of a startup, founder–managers are typically majority shareholders and investors are minority shareholders. Keeping much of firm ownership with founders is important given the necessity of raising further funding rounds and the dilution of founder–manager ownership and thus incentives that those rounds entail. However, a minority claim on a company controlled by an often unorthodox founder–manager gives strong impetus for investors to negotiate additional control rights in order to protect their interests. We see the potential for founder–managers to expropriate minority shareholders being checked by an extensive set of negotiated contractual protective provisions. As startups mature and raise further funding rounds, the initially negotiated relationship between investors and founder–managers is further complicated by the addition of new investors eager to negotiate their own control provisions. This means governance disputes arise not just between founder–managers and investors, but also between different classes of investors, for example, between early-stage and late-stage investors who provided funding to the same startup at different prices and with different cash flow rights. In recent years, there have been a lot of calls to improve the corporate governance of large publicly traded companies.[o] This was undoubtedly caused by high-profile

---

[o]There has been a steady rise in corporate governance research in publicly traded firms. For example, Gompers et al. (2003) construct an index of shareholder rights based on governance rules in 1500 public firms and find that firms with stronger shareholder rights had higher firm value, higher profits, higher sales growth, and lower capital expenditures, and made fewer corporate acquisitions. Bebchuk et al. (2009) develop this idea further and construct an "entrenchment" index based on rules that limit shareholders' rights, confirming the previous findings.

scandals that demonstrated to a wider public what defective corporate governance could lead to. A number of high-profile startups also went through tough times recently and were criticized for poor corporate governance. Well-known examples include Uber, Theranos, and WeWork. These and other examples provide powerful anecdotal evidence for the importance of corporate governance.

In this section, we discuss how the entrepreneurial environment shapes corporate governance. We define corporate governance as a set of principles and mechanisms that balances the interests of company stakeholders and affects control over company decision-making. These stakeholders are not only shareholders, whether preferred or common, but also employees, customers, suppliers, regulators, and society at large. Our discussion encompasses both formal mechanisms laid down in laws, precedents, or private contracts, and informal mechanisms such as reputation, entrenchment, and mutual consent.

The structure of cash flow rights (Section 3), namely that investors receive preferred shares, also plays an important corporate governance role. In the incomplete contracts approach, Aghion and Bolton (1992) and their followers forcefully put forward an explanation for debt financing existence and optimality, in which debt provides a "contingent and thus more flexible governance structure for the firm, one which is more responsive to whether good or bad states of the world materialize in the future" (Aghion and Holden, 2011). In the same vein, preferred stock provides contingent financing and, together with many additional corporate governance mechanisms that we discuss here, serves to respond to the challenges the entrepreneurial firm faces.

A traditional perspective on corporate governance is that of a need to resolve multifaceted conflicts of interest between a manager or a founder–manager and an investor. That easily translates to the startup setting, where an entrepreneur, rich with ideas but financially constrained, contracts with an investor, lacking ideas yet with abundant financial resources. While much of the theoretical and empirical work on agency conflicts in an entrepreneurial setting has been along these lines, more recently evidence of conflicts between investors emerged as an important distinctive feature of a VC setting and one that plays an important economic role (Bartlett, 2006). In a public companies context, the conflict is between the managers and dispersed shareholders, acting through the board of directors. In the VC setting, however, there is a small number of minority investors, most of which hold a nontrivial stake in the company and many of which are represented on the board. These investors acquire their stake at different funding rounds, paying different prices and negotiating investor-specific contracts and protections. This leads to interinvestor conflicts that are not part of the traditional agency conflict framework pioneered by Jensen and Meckling (1976) and subsequently applied to the VC setting (Admati and Pfleiderer, 1994; Berglof, 1994; Bergemann and Hege, 1998; Hellmann, 1998; Cornelli and Yosha, 2003; Schmidt, 2003).

It is useful to split formal corporate governance mechanisms into several interconnected categories: shareholder voting, board control, and shareholder protective provisions.

4.1 **Shareholder voting rights**

In startups, especially those that are backed by VC investors, the voting rules could be structured very differently from those in other privately owned corporations or publicly traded companies. One such difference is the identity of shareholders who have the right to vote. We start with a brief description of shareholder voting.

By default, US corporate law makes a number of corporate decisions subject to a shareholder vote, for example, the merger with another entity. Above all, a change of the rules listed in the charter requires shareholder approval. Corporate charters frequently make other decisions subject to shareholder approval as a result of negotiations between founder–managers and various classes of investors. Importantly, most of the cash flow rights discussed in Section 3 are spelled out in the corporate charter. As a result, shareholder voting rules, which determine the process by which shareholders approve these decisions, play an important role. Some examples of provisions that are set out in a corporate charter are as follows:

1. Cash flow rights, such as liquidation preference, conversion rules, and dividend rights;
2. Restrictions on the sale, liquidation, or restructuring of the company;
3. Ownership structure including the classes or series of company shares and the number that can be issued;
4. Board of Directors election procedures; and
5. Protective provisions of specific shareholder classes.

Other decisions do not typically require shareholder approval, including the day-to-day management of company affairs, the allocation of the option pool among the employees within the authorized number of shares set in the corporate charter, and, perhaps most importantly, the firing and hiring of corporate executives, including the CEO.

Corporate votes are undertaken by shareholders. The shares a company issues, and consequently the potential votes, are limited by a company's corporate charter. This document indicates authorized shares (also known as authorized stock or authorized capital stock), which is the maximum number of shares of each class that a company is allowed to issue without further approval by shareholders. The listing of the number of authorized shares in the charter serves as a powerful shareholder protection, as it may prevent the company decision-makers from issuing more shares and thus diluting (some of) the existing shareholders.

Although the number of authorized shares is given in the corporate charter, the number of issued and outstanding shares is not. Issued shares are those that the company has issued to its shareholders. The number of issued shares of each class cannot be above the number of shares that are authorized to be issued for that class. Issued shares could either be outstanding shares or treasury shares. Outstanding shares are owned by shareholders, such as investors or employees. Such ownership may include shares that are in the process of being vested. Outstanding shares that are transferred back to the company are called treasury shares.

The number of authorized common and preferred shares may also contain an additional buffer, which is effectively how many more shares the company can issue without the need to amend the corporate charter. For preferred shares, the buffer usually allows the company to continue fundraising for the same series of preferred stock for some time after the funding round has been agreed upon and, for example, raise money in sequential tranches with the same conditions as already issued preferred shares. For common shares, the authorized number is a bit trickier. First, it takes into account all the conversion options. For example, preferred shareholders should have the ability to convert into common without the need to amend the corporate charter. Second, the authorized number of common shares also includes the agreed-upon employee stock option pool that has not yet been allocated to specific employees, and these shares thus have not yet been issued. Again, the company board would like to be able to issue those shares without amending the charter.

With these preliminary considerations out of the way, we are ready to discuss which shares have the right to vote and, equally important, which shares do not carry such voting rights. This discussion will also help to emphasize the difference between the corporate governance of startups and "traditional" companies, such as public companies or the typical private corporation. Outstanding common shares have the right to vote, as in traditional companies, with the exception of the so-called nonvoting common shares. (Note that these shares would have similar or identical cash flow rights to voting common shares.) In practice, nonvoting common shares are often given to employees who join at a later stage of the company development, with the rationale being not to dilute the voting rights of existing shareholders.

In traditional companies, preferred stockholders do not have the right to vote. In fact, the Securities and Exchange Commission (SEC) chose the distinction in voting rights as the main defining difference between common and preferred stocks.[p] The SEC distinction makes the voting rights of preferred shareholders in startups stand out. Specifically, the convertible preferred shares issued to investors, as a rule, carry voting rights. Preferred shares usually vote on the so-called as converted basis.[q] An as converted basis means that preferred shareholders have the same voting rights that they would have if they were to convert into common shares (without actually having to convert). This implies that only preferred shares that could be converted carry voting rights. Note that preferred shares receive the voting rights of the underlying common shares even without converting, allowing them to retain their other preferred rights.

Restricted stock units—company shares that are issued to employees as a part of compensation—have the same right to vote as the shares that these restricted stock

---

[p]See   https://www.investor.gov/introduction-investing/investing-basics/investment-products/stocks. "Common stock entitles owners to vote at shareholder meetings and receive dividends. Preferred stockholders usually do not have voting rights but they receive dividend payments before common stockholders do, and have priority over common stockholders if the company goes bankrupt and its assets are liquidated."

[q]Some charters give each preferred share a fixed number of votes.

units represent (typically, common shares). Again, not infrequently, these would be nonvoting common shares, which would preclude them from voting. If an employee's shares can vote, that employee can vote them regardless of whether the shares are vested. As discussed in Section 4.3, founders typically agree to have most of their stock subject to vesting, so that they lose many of those shares if they quit within a period after the financing. Unvested shares may be subject to loss; however, they carry the right to vote alongside other shares.

In addition to nonvoting common shares, authorized but not yet issued shares do not carry voting rights until after issuance. Treasury shares, stock options, stock warrants, and debt also do not have voting rights.

4.1.1 Supermajority and supervoting

Startups impose a variety of voting rules. Commonly, a majority of all eligible votes should be in favor for the proposal to be approved, where a majority here means 50% plus one. An alternative structure requires a majority of eligible votes to be cast (a quorum) and a majority of those cast votes being in favor, although these structures are close to equivalent given the highly motivated and concentrated ownership. Supermajority thresholds, requiring votes in excess of a majority, are frequently established in the corporate charter. These typically apply only to certain scenarios and certain investor classes (as discussed below). The existence, frequency, and specificity of these voting thresholds indicate the extent to which shareholders consider supermajority an important protective mechanism. In practice, the selection of a specific threshold often reflects the ownership stake the investor maintains in a specific class of shares upon which such a supermajority voting threshold is imposed. Importantly, as it is common for investors to form syndicates in VC financing rounds, specific thresholds are often set to give a minority investor veto power (see Section 4.1.2).

Standard voting rules imply that one common share has one vote and, similarly, that one preferred share has one vote per common share into which it converts. Alphabet, Meta, and other public companies feature dual-class structures where there are two or more classes of common stock with identical cash flow rights but different voting rights. Such supervoting shares also exist for startups.[r] In recent times, supervoting has generated debates in the VC industry, as a number of companies with supervoting, such as Uber, WeWork, and Theranos, have encountered major scandals.

Supervoting shares entail one class of shares having more votes than another voting class of shares. From the point of view of corporate governance, the critical implication of supervoting is that it leads to further separation between cash flow and voting rights. In practice, supervoting is rarely initiated at the outset of company formation or the first funding round, but rather, as an indication of the bargaining power

---

[r]For the avoidance of confusion, we prefer not to call this a dual-class structure, as startups, of course, have many classes of shares to start with.

of founder–managers, it is introduced later in the startup's lifecycle. Founder–managers who are with the company at that time are the main beneficiaries of super-voting arrangements, which would typically involve a reorganization that creates two classes of common shares. One of these classes has substantially more votes per share than the other, with the founder–managers receiving the class of shares with more votes. Existing investors are often grandfathered in in this arrangement and thus also receive supervoting preferred shares. Other common shareholders (such as employees and founders who left the company) and new investors see sometimes dramatic dilution of their voting power. These arrangements commonly give 10 votes to the high-vote shares, although in some cases, such as that of Theranos, the founder(s) receive 100 votes per share, which all but eliminates the voting power of other shareholders.

How widespread is supervoting? Some of the most prominent startups, such as Alphabet, Meta, and Uber, featured this governance structure. However, the exceptional nature of these companies is part of the reason they had this voting structure—only the "hottest" startups with the most powerful founders are able to negotiate stronger control rights. These companies are exceptional both in governance and (perceived) performance.

4.1.2 Class-level voting

Investors in startups often negotiate specific voting provisions that give them the right to block an action. These are implemented through differential voting scenarios in which separate classes of shares have to approve a proposal. The voting basis is the arrangement of the shareholder classes voting, and such bases may lead to substantial additional voting power for a specific share class.

There are three common voting basis scenarios. In the first scenario, preferred and common shareholders vote "as a single class," meaning that the approval requires the (super)majority of total votes, resulting from adding all common and preferred (on an as converted basis) shares. In the second scenario, preferred shareholders vote as a separate class. In this scenario, without the affirmative vote of the (super)majority of all preferred share votes, voting together but separately from common shares, the proposal cannot be approved.[s] In the third scenario, a subset of preferred investors vote together as a class. This could be a single series of preferred (e.g., Series A) or multiple series (e.g., Series A and B). Such votes exclude not only common shareholders but also other preferred shareholders (e.g., a hypothetical Series C).

In all scenarios, the voting within a basis follows the same majority, supermajority, and supervoting rules discussed in the previous section, with the contract either specifying some fraction of eligible votes being in favor or requiring a quorum and specifying that a (super)majority of the cast votes be in favor of the action. Being part

---

[s]Theoretically common shares also can be entitled to vote as a separate class, but such a provision is exceedingly rare in practice apart from the election of directors, which we discuss separately.

of a narrow voting basis affords substantial control to those investors and, not surprisingly, these provisions are heavily negotiated and precisely delineated in the corporate charter.

To provide a specific example of the protective provisions for which investors negotiate special voting bases, consider the 2015 corporate charter of Blue Apron at the time it was still a startup.[†] In Blue Apron's case, a basis of all preferred shareholders voting together (second scenario) had to approve by vote the following corporate actions:

1. Liquidate the company;
2. Amend the corporate charter;
3. Increase or decrease the authorized number of preferred or common shares;
4. Create new series of stock, unless junior to the preferred with respect to liquidation preference;
5. Declare any dividend;
6. Issue any debt exceeding $10 million;
7. Increase the number of shares reserved under the equity incentive plan;
8. Increase or decrease the size of the board of directors; and
9. Permit any subsidiary to do any of the above.

As can be imputed from this list, the majority of preferred shareholders of Blue Apron effectively controlled many of the most important corporate decisions, particularly financing decisions. Without their approval, the company could not raise a nontrivial amount of financing, pay dividends, or change the size of its board. Such provisions inevitably shift power away from founder–managers to investors. Analysis of these corporate charters indicates that there is substantial heterogeneity among types of protective provisions given to preferred shareholders. Blue Apron's list is by no means atypical, and most startups afford preferred investors similar protections.

The third scenario is the one where a specific series or several series of preferred shareholders must approve an action by voting as a separate class. The frequency of such provisions indicates the perceived potential for a conflict between different classes of investors. Coming back to the example of Blue Apron, Series C Preferred Stock of Blue Apron had to approve the following actions as a separate class (at the time, Blue Apron had four series of preferred stock, Series A, B, C, and D):

1. Create new series of shares of stock that are senior to Series C in liquidation preference or that are convertible into Series C;
2. Increase or decrease the authorized number of shares of Series C preferred stock; and
3. Amend the corporate charter in a way that adversely affects Series C preferred stock.

[†]Fifth Amended and Restated Certificate of Incorporation of Blue Apron, Inc., 05/08/2015.

Given that such provisions give an inordinate degree of influence over corporate decision-making to a specific class of shareholders (and therefore, often, to a specific investor), they are limited to specific actions that act against the interests of the protected class. For example, in Blue Apron's example, the first two provisions prevent the dilution of the ownership stake of the Series C existing shareholders, unless they assent to such a dilution.

Different series of preferred stock may have distinct protective provisions that correspondingly change the voting basis. For example, Series D preferred stock of Blue Apron had the same three provisions that Series C had (in relation to Series D) and additionally had a fourth provision, which in effect made any corporate transaction that constituted a company liquidation (such as a sale) subject to the affirmative vote of Series D preferred shareholders, unless those shareholders' exit proceeds at least equaled their investment amount. Series D therefore had a veto on any company sale in which they would not fully recover their investment—a powerful right.

Academic research has not yet studied the fair value implications of complicated voting structures in the VC setting. Available evidence from public companies suggests that the voting premium effectively bestowed by class voting rules can be very substantial. For example, Rydqvist (1987) and Zingales (1995) have used the Shapley value to measure the value of voting rights in publicly traded firms with more than one class of shares.

4.1.3 Protective provisions

The above examples from Blue Apron's corporate charter are protective provisions. These provisions are contractual clauses that have the goal of preventing the company and its shareholders from taking certain actions without getting the explicit consent of the investors protected by those specific provisions. They thus aim at protecting minority investors against expropriation. Such protective provisions can be very elaborate and diverse (Bengtsson, 2011).

Such protective provisions are in addition to other control rights that VCs negotiate, the most important of which are board seats, as discussed in Section 4.2. One advantage that they offer is a specifically and clearly stated protection in a corporate charter. Such provisions could be verified in court and corporate charters are considered of more import in a court of law than other contracts that firms enter into (Bartlett and Talley, 2017). Another advantage is that the actions of investor directors must be in the company's interest, while the exercise of class rights does not have to be. This means that protective provisions allow investors to capture value in a way that is deleterious to the company, something they may not be able to do as board members (See Section 4.2.2).

A related contractual protection is the information rights negotiated by investors (especially those who are not entitled to designate board seats: see Section 4.2.1). Given the private and often secretive nature of startups, management prefers not to divulge information, including financial status and projections, to all investors. Often, a requirement on the minimum number of shares of company ownership is imposed in order to limit information provisions to a smaller group of larger investors.

Bengtsson (2011) shows that most corporate charters include covenants. Moreover, he identified 12 distinct covenant groups. Tellingly, VC contracts never include financial covenants that force a company to maintain specific levels of interest coverage, working capital, or net worth. The absence of such covenants, the use of which is standard in bank loans and corporate bond contracts, underlies the uncertainties associated with the financial performance of startups and the verifiability of their financial statements. Instead, Bengtsson (2011) shows that all the observed covenants are of negative covenant nature, that is, they are protective provisions and give investors the right to veto a specific corporate action. Some provisions, such as rights to veto changing the size of the board of directors, liquidate a company, or pay dividends to common or preferred stock, are always present. Other provisions, such as veto rights on issuing debt or issuing equity securities junior to preferred shares, are present for the majority of contracts. Other protective provisions, such as changing the current line of business, acquiring other companies, licensing out technology, or changing stock option plans, are included in the minority of contracts. Some protective provisions are rare and company-specific, emphasizing that protective provisions are negotiated as a function of company- and investor-specific determinants.

Research has shown a conflicting relationship between protective provisions and other rights. On the one hand, contracts that provide more preferential cash flow rights to investors have more protective provisions. On the other hand, contracts that give investors more board control lead to fewer protective provisions. Kaplan and Strömberg (2003), Bengtsson (2011), and Bengtsson and Sensoy (2011) also show that the number of protective provisions and cash flow contingencies increases with a startup's age and the stage of its lifecycle.

4.1.4 Automatic conversion

An important protective term concerns automatic conversion. In addition to optional conversion provisions where investors have the right to convert preferred stock into common stock at the time of their choice (see Section 3.1.1), startups typically also have automatic conversion provisions where preferred stock can be forced to convert into common stock under certain conditions. Forced conversion, if implemented, means that investors give up all the rights of preferred stock (both cash flow and control rights) and instead, obtain only rights associated with the ownership of common stock (Black and Gilson, 1998). As the rights of preferred stock are superior to those of common stock, automatic conversion acts as an important check on preferred stock's economic and corporate governance rights. As such, conditions under which automatic conversion is permitted become of crucial importance. Most often, these conditions relate to an IPO and require a minimum common stock price, dollar amount of proceeds, and/or market capitalization for the company. Kaplan and Strömberg (2003) find that IPO-related automatic conversion is present in 95% of the financing rounds in their sample. They also find that often the IPO conditions are set at or above the company's PMV at the financing round, implying that the preferred investors protect themselves from expropriation by other shareholders in less favorable outcomes.

Automatic conversion provisions can be both strengthened and weakened. In some cases, automatic conversion can be initiated outside the IPO if there is a (super)majority of shareholder votes. On the other hand, automatic conversion may be limited to IPOs meeting certain performance milestones, such as a valuation or fundraising target. It may even be separately negotiated for different series of investors, with some investors negotiating automatic conversion only if approved by their class or only if the exit meets a lofty performance target. In a sample of highly valued companies, Gornall and Strebulaev (2020) found that such automatic conversion exemptions were common, especially among later-stage investors.

The importance of automatic conversion provisions stems from the observation that in order to undergo an IPO, it is a standard industry practice for all preferred stock to convert into common in conjunction with the IPO process. Thus, even a small preferred shareholder, by withholding the conversion decision, has the power to control the exit outcome. As such, these provisions point to the resolution of inter-investor conflicts. This especially concerns investors entering at very different price points. While a preferred shareholder with the original issue price of $1 would likely be content with the IPO price of $20, the same cannot be asserted about a preferred shareholder whose price entry point into the company was $30. In addition, investors frequently target cash-on-cash multiples, and an immediate exit at a high internal rate of return (IRR) but a low cash-on-cash multiple may conflict with their goals. This also explains why automatic conversion exemptions are negotiated by later-stage investors as they tend to pay more per share—at least in successful companies.

A related provision is what is known as "drag-along" rights. If certain conditions are met these terms allow a qualified majority of preferred shareholders to force common shareholders to sell their shares as part of a sale of the company. This allows an acquirer to get complete ownership of the company and prevents minority shareholders from obstructing a deal. Once again, the drag-along provision aims at resolving the agency conflicts that could arise between investors and founder–managers. Williams (2017) finds that almost 60% of preferred equity financings feature a drag-along provision.

4.2 Board of directors and control rights

The board of directors is the second major corporate governance mechanism. The board of directors is a group of individuals that represent shareholders in major corporate decisions; indeed, corporate law identifies boards as the main corporate decision-making body. The role of corporate boards in public companies has received substantial attention from corporate governance research (see, for example, Adams, 2017). One of the critical board responsibilities is the oversight of management. In particular, management serves at the pleasure of the board, meaning that the board can relieve any CEO—regardless of whether she is a founder—of their duties at any time, unless such action is specifically allocated away from the board in the corporate charter. In startups, investors play an active part in corporate governance by serving as board members. Investors report that they interact with their portfolio companies and management frequently, often weekly (Gompers et al., 2020). Startup boards, in their oversight of the CEO and the senior management team, frequently remove founder–managers from their executive positions.

Other functions of boards include monitoring and assessing corporate performance, providing strategic guidance, developing corporate policy, approving budgets, and fundraising.[u] While all corporate boards have similar responsibilities, they play a larger role in startups for several reasons. First, the dynamic nature of startups and their innate uncertainty amplify potential conflicts. Second, founder–managers are frequently relatively inexperienced and face the especially challenging task of managing rapid growth. Finally, the numerous active owners and the complex web of financial and governance controls give them a significant intermediation role.[v] For example, Hellmann (1998) shows that board control can be a prerequisite for VC investment, since without that control, the entrepreneur may hold up the value generated by the venture capitalist. As Lerner (1995) and Hellmann (1998) argue, allowing the board to monitor and replace the founder–manager reduces agency costs and is strongly preferred by VC investors.

Much of the existing evidence underlines the distinctions between the structure and the role of the board in public companies and startups. For example, earlier survey evidence by Fried et al. (1998) showed that boards of startups are more involved in both strategy formation and evaluation. Baker and Gompers (2003) show that at the time of the IPO firms backed by VC investors have different board sizes and compositions than other newly public firms. Hochberg (2012) also compares VC-backed and non-VC-backed public firms following their IPOs and finds that VC-backed firms have lower levels of earnings management, more positive reactions to the adoption of shareholder rights agreements, and more independent board structures than similar non-VC-backed firms, which is consistent with better governance.

4.2.1 Election of startup boards
The importance of boards in startups is underlined by the observations that the rules on the election of directors are heavily negotiated and their structure differs markedly from those of traditional companies. In public companies, the candidates for directors are proposed by the nominating committee of the board, approved by the board, and then voted on by all the common shareholders at the annual shareholder meeting (usually by simple majority, even though the multiclass structure may give certain shareholders a blocking power to nominate directors). Contrary to this practice, early-stage companies use often intricate rules that specifically allocate board seats to different groups of owners. Specifically, investors often negotiate for the right to elect one or more directors all by themselves, and the first VC investors typically make financing contingent on receiving a board seat.

---

[u]See Knowles (2009), which lists functions that are central to the board role.
[v]Gao and He (2019) argue that the governance role of boards in private firms is more important because other governance mechanisms are lacking. As we show here, other mechanisms, such as shareholder voting rights and protective provisions, act jointly with board governance for startups.

The board composition of Uber as of May 2016, when it was still a private company, offers an example of board structure.[w] Uber's corporate charter provided for a board of directors comprised of eight voting directors. A separate voting agreement between shareholders detailed who had the right to designate voting directors. These eight were as follows:

(i) One seat was contractually allocated to Series A Preferred stock (and designated by Benchmark, a VC firm that held a majority in Series A);

(ii) One seat was contractually allocated to Series C-2 Preferred stock (and designated by TPG Equity Holdings, a lead investor in Series C-2); and

(iii) Six seats were contractually allocated to Class B Common Stock (out of which one was designated by Expa-1, an accelerator, where the founding partner, Garrett Camp, is also Uber's cofounder; one was held by Ryan Graves, another of Uber's cofounders; one was reserved for Uber's CEO (at the time of the voting agreement it was Travis Kalanick, Uber's leading cofounder); and three seats were unfilled).

Uber had by this time a supervoting share structure, with Kalanick owning about 35% of Uber's supervoting Class B common stock. This gave him substantial influence (but not the outright majority) over whom to appoint as directors on behalf of Class B common stock. According to the lawsuit filed by Benchmark, Kalanick had also approximately 16% of the total voting power, while Benchmark has 20% of the voting power (when voting along with common as a single class) and 36% of the preferred stock voting power. Note also that at the time Uber had four additional classes of stock (Series Seed Preferred Stock, Series B Preferred Stock, Series C-1 Preferred Stock, and Class A Common Stock) that contractually were excluded from voting in an election or removing any of Uber's directors.[x]

Uber illustrates the degree to which various stakeholders can be entrenched on the board. It further illustrates a critical feature of corporate governance arrangements in startups, according to which the number of board seats and the allocation of board seats are contractually determined in the corporate charter and a voting agreement. Board size contractual determination means that any change in the number of directors should be approved by shareholders and, moreover, that various classes of shareholders not infrequently have veto rights over this change. Note that as startups raise successive funding rounds, additional board seats are added ad hoc as new investors negotiate a board position.

---

[w]Some board details are taken from Complaint, Benchmark Capital Partners VII, L.P., v. Travis Kalanick and Uber Technologies, filed in the court of the chancery of the state of Delaware, 08/10/2017.

[x]In fact, to emphasize such exclusion and to avoid any potential lingering uncertainty, Uber's corporate charter had the following provision: "Notwithstanding anything to the contrary contained herein, neither the holders of Series Seed Preferred Stock, Series B Preferred Stock, and Series C-1 Preferred Stock, nor the holders of Class A Common Stock will be entitled to vote in the election or removal of any directors of the Corporation" (Uber Certificate of Incorporation, 07/31/2013, pp. 17).

The contractual allocation of a board seat to a specific class of stock is difficult to rescind. Furthermore, a party with control over the designation of a board member (usually a lead investor of the round in the case of a preferred stock allocation of the board seat) may replace a board member and designate another board member representing its interests at any time without any need for the approval of other shareholders or board members. All this evidence points to the utmost importance of board control and composition.

In addition to the board size and composition, investor contractual agreements often specify the requirements for the composition of various board committees. A frequently encountered requirement is that any board committee (such as the compensation, the investment, and the audit committees) must have either a representative or a majority of directors that represent a specific set of shareholders. Not surprisingly, most often this set of directors is representing the preferred shareholders, that is, investors. This provides further protection to startup investors.

4.2.2 Types of board members

Both academic and industry literature on the corporate governance of publicly traded companies commonly classifies directors into insiders or executive directors, who are the company's senior executives, and outsiders or nonexecutive directors (Adams, 2017). Such a distinction is less informative in the startup setting, given the board membership allocation and active participation of investor board members. Instead, it is more fruitful to classify directors into the following groups.

4.2.2.1 Common directors

Common directors are designated by common shareholders. In startups, especially at an early stage, these directors are typically company founders. An important negotiating issue in the first investor round is often whether all company founders become directors, as adding common directors dilutes the power of investor directors. As a result, the number of common directors is often limited.[y] In the case of multiple founders, there are often agreements between founders that spell out who will become a board member representing common stockholders. Such an agreement could be a formal legal contract or could be more informal. Later in the life of the company, people other than founders are often selected to represent common shareholders. If there is more than one class of common shareholders then, as in the example of Uber, it is often the case that only specific classes have the right to designate a director.

4.2.2.2 Investor directors

Investor directors represent preferred shareholders. Such directors could be designated by all preferred shareholders voting as a single class or, more often, designated by a specific series of preferred shares. In the former case, a separate voting

---

[y]Anecdotally, some solo founders may seek cofounders to ensure they can negotiate two board seats for common directors.

agreement supplements the corporate charter by frequently identifying a specific investor who will have the right to nominate a director.

In practice, lead early-stage investors usually join the boards. For example, when a company raises its first VC round (say, through issuing Series A preferred stock), the lead investor, often a VC fund, will typically have the right to designate at least one director. Often, when a syndicate of investors participates in the round, two or more colead investors have the right to designate one director each. Alternatively, they may need to decide through the voting agreement who will become a director representing this series of preferred stock. Kaplan and Strömberg (2003) found in their sample that VC investors obtain the right to a board seat in over 40% of financing transactions. Evidence given in Ewens and Malenko (2020) suggests that lead early-stage VCs typically obtain a board seat.

4.2.2.3 Joint directors
Joint directors, often called independent directors in the VC literature, are appointed by the mutual agreement of common and preferred shareholders (founder–managers and investors). Often they are outside directors, meaning directors whose sole involvement with the company is in their role as a director. Startups often have joint directors, especially at a later stage of their lifecycle. To what extent joint directors could in practice be designated by a specific class of shareholders or to what extent some shareholders have an unequal power of say in the appointment of joint directors is an unsettled issue.

4.2.2.4 CEO directors
Voting agreements often reserve a separate board seat for the CEO. Note that, at an early stage, it is often one of the founders who becomes the CEO of the company. That founder thus may become a board member by virtue of being the CEO, while another founder may be designated by common shareholders. One difference is that if the CEO is replaced, the previous founder–CEO automatically loses the board seat but not the seat designated by common shareholders. For this reason, in the case of a solo founder, that founder is designated by common shareholders, and the CEO board membership is not needed.

4.2.2.5 Nonvoting directors
In addition to full voting board members, startups also may have nonvoting directors or, as they are often called, board observers. Board observers have the right to participate in (most) board deliberations and receive the same information from the company as full voting board members. However, they have no right to vote as board members. Given the importance of access to information, many investors who do not get to nominate a board member negotiate the right to designate a board observer. In practice, this is especially common in later rounds of funding.

In some cases, there are voting board members who may have "conditional" access to information and "contingent" voting rights. This means that during discussions of some prespecified topics they cannot participate and are excluded from information sharing. These contingencies would be carefully negotiated and specified clearly in contracts. An example is an investment by a corporation either directly or through a corporate venture fund, in which a board member representing their interest "leaves the room" during a discussion of a company sale to a potential competitor.

4.2.3 Board structure

Evidence on board composition suggests that startups have plenty of director representation. In their sample, Kaplan and Strömberg (2003) find that VCs hold approximately 41% of the total board seats, founders (including the CEO as a director) hold 35%, and independent directors hold the remaining 23%.

Despite specific board members being elected by a particular group of shareholders, all board members owe a fiduciary duty of loyalty to the entire company under corporate law. Important corporate actions frequently create a conflict between the economic interests of the firm and one or more classes of shareholders, and the differentially impacted classes may control a board seat. Because board members owe loyalty to the corporation, an investor or other owner could support (oppose) an action as a board member but oppose (support) it as a shareholder during the shareholder voting process or through the other control channels we discuss in this section. However, there is a clear potential for this conflict of interest to bias board member decisions, although this has only recently received particular attention from the courts. Bartlett and Talley (2017) discuss a particular relevant Delaware legal case, which was decided only in 2013. The board of Trados, the startup at the heart of that case, consisted of seven directors, two of whom were company executives, four represented VC investors or had close ties to them, and one was a jointly appointed independent industry expert. Given bleak growth prospects, the board sought to sell a company at a value, in which only preferred shareholders and select executives (through the management incentive plan implemented to incentivize these executives to facilitate the sale of the company) received any proceeds. Common shareholders, who received nothing, sued, alleging that the board violated its fiduciary duties by selling the company rather than continuing to operate it. The court ruling identified a number of problems with the decision-making process of the board and the actions of VC investors on the board. While the court concluded that the fair valuation analysis showed that common stock had no economic value and thus found the board not liable in that specific case, this recent ruling posits an important development in the treatment of frequent conflicts arising in startups.

Another phenomenon underscores the relationship between the board structure in publicly traded companies and startups. In corporate governance discussions of board roles in publicly traded companies, "few features of board structure have generated as much debate in recent years as the staggering of director elections" (Adams, 2017). A board is staggered if only a subset of directors is up for (re-) election every year. Note that by this definition all boards of startups are staggered because seats designated by specific classes of shareholders are not up for reelection at a fixed frequency. Interestingly, evidence from young publicly traded firms, many of which were VC-backed, suggests that one purpose of staggered boards may be to allow founders to continue to influence the firm. For example, Field and Karpoff (2002) document that 36.2% of firms in their sample of 1019 IPOs from 1988 to 1992 have staggered boards. Most of the academic research on the relationship between staggered boards and performance is, however, not applicable to startups.

4.2.4 Board control

With respect to the boards of publicly traded companies, corporate governance research distinguishes between independent and captured boards, the latter being the boards in which a majority of directors are either appointed by management or not truly independent of the management. The nomenclature of captured and independent boards is thus less relevant to early-stage startups because most board members have a substantial financial interest in the company. Instead, in thinking about various board control scenarios, we distinguish between founder-controlled boards, balanced boards, and investor-controlled boards.

A founder-controlled board has the majority of its directors designated by founders (most often through their ownership of the majority of common shares). Evidence suggests that early on in the life of startups, founder-controlled boards are most common. Conversely, an investor-controlled board has the majority of directors appointed by investors. A balanced board is a board in which neither investors (preferred shareholders) nor founders (common shareholders) by themselves constitute a majority of the board, principally due to the presence of joint directors.

The control of the board gives the controlling party an important right to initiate corporate actions. Considered in this light, protective provisions that allow a shareholder to block an action are complementary to the board control. For example, board control may facilitate the ability of investors to sell the firm without internalizing the residual claim of common shareholders (as argued by Broughman and Fried (2010), though see the discussion of recent legal cases above) or make it easier for VC investors to exit their investment over the possible objections of other stakeholders (Fried and Ganor, 2006).

The broad economic mechanisms underlying the control allocation in the firm also apply to board control. For example, as Aghion and Bolton (1992) show, it is beneficial to award control to the founders, if possible, in order to protect founders' private benefits. The opposing factor is the investor participation constraint that may lead to the necessity of investor control. Numerous academic studies have applied economic theories of control to startups, mostly through the prism of an investor holding preferred stock (e.g., Kirilenko (2001) and Schmidt (2003)). However, the issues specific to board control in the startup setting have been scantly discussed in the academic literature to date. A notable exception is the attention paid to these issues by some legal scholars. For example, to explain the existence of joint directors and balanced boards in startups, Broughman (2010) develops an argument, according to which these directors act as an unbiased third party that can prevent opportunistic behavior that would occur in investor-controlled or founder-controlled companies. In this context, jointly appointed directors act as the tie-breaking vote. This limits the opportunism of the founder–manager directors and investor directors and causes them to seek compromises.

Note that disagreements may arise not only between founders and investors, but also between investors and other investors. A common conflict arises between directors representing early rounds and those representing later rounds on the target exit timing, type, and value. Early-stage investors may prefer a faster sale because their earlier (and lower-priced) entry means they have made significant returns but are now winding down their funds. Late-stage investors may prefer to hold out for a potentially higher-value IPO exit because their shares were acquired more recently at a higher price. Indeed, in many cases, the original issue price of early-stage directors is so low relative to that of later rounds that these preferred shareholders may be more attuned to the interest of common shareholders than that of other preferred shareholders. These interinvestor disagreements may play an important role in the board dynamics and resulting control over board decisions. We explore this more fully in Section 5.

Empirical evidence suggests that board control is often exercised by VC investors. Kaplan and Strömberg (2003) found that VC investors controlled the startups' boards in 25% of their sample, while founders controlled the board in 14% of companies. Notably, in the rest of the sample (61%) jointly appointed directors are tie-breaking, resulting in balanced boards. Broughman (2010) found similar distribution in a smaller sample of Silicon Valley startups.

4.3 Founder and employee restrictions

The quality of human capital is key to the outcomes of entrepreneurial companies. VC investors regularly perceive management teams to be the most important factor in their due diligence of investment opportunities (Gompers et al., 2020). Arguably more than in a public company setting, if a startup's management team is disincentivized to provide a high level of effort or leaves the startup altogether, the damage to the company's prospects is substantial if not lethal. As a result, the provision of proper efforts is an important part of negotiations between founder-managers and investors and can be traced to many aspects of contractual arrangements. Of those we already discussed, founder–managers tend to own common shares and thus are junior shareholders relative to the preferred shares owned by investors. In the bad state of the world, seniority of the preferred shares implies that the common ownership of founder–managers may be wiped out. Investors also share in corporate governance and often orchestrate a removal of the CEO (often a company founder) by the board.

In addition to the provisions we discussed, the structure of founder–management compensation (and, to a lesser extent, of the compensation of most employees in startups with perceived important human capital) reflects an attempt to resolve agency conflicts. A large fraction of compensation is tied to the performance of the firm. In the case of founders and senior managers, a share of contingent compensation dominates a noncontingent salary compensation. Foremost among the compensation structure elements is the vesting arrangement, according to which founder–managers receive stock options or shares of restricted stock that vest over time. This vesting arrangement extends to founder equity, implying that if the startup founder opts to leave the company soon after receiving the first round of VC investment, the founder forfeits the entire ownership stake in the company. Shares vest over time according to a prespecified vesting schedule, with a typical duration of 3–4 years. The vesting schedule often includes two components: cliff vesting and incremental vesting. During the initial period of employment (or, for founders, during the initial period after the first VC round, for example, for the first year), no shares vest; instead, a large fraction of shares vest at the same time in a cliff. Subsequently, shares vest incrementally, monthly or quarterly, for the remaining duration of the vesting schedule.

Such a compensation arrangement aligns incentives of the founder–managers and investors and minimizes incentives for managers to shirk or to engage in activities to derive private benefits at the expense of other shareholders. The cliff vesting ensures that if the founder–managers leave firms early on, their entire share ownership is forfeited. Kaplan and Strömberg (2003) find that it is common for startups to include such vesting provisions, especially in first VC financings.

In addition, investors may insist on founder–manager employment contracts including noncompete provisions. These prohibit the founder–manager from working for another firm in the same industry for a specified period of time after they leave the firm. Kaplan and Strömberg (2003) find that noncompete clauses are used in approximately 70% of the financings.[z] Both vesting and noncompete provisions, by making it more expensive for employees to leave the firm, aim to resolve the hold-up problem (Hart and Moore, 1994) that could be particularly severe in an early-stage firm.

4.4 Redemption rights

Redemption rights entitle preferred shareholders to force the company to repurchase their shares under certain conditions, typically at the price they originally paid for those shares or their liquidation preference. From an economic viewpoint, such redemption is similar to demandable debt where creditors can demand the repayment of principal at prespecified times. Although these terms are cash flow rights in form, the fact that startups are generally either wildly successful (making the right irrelevant) or cash-poor (making a cash return impossible) means they function more like control rights in practice and add to investors' arsenal of bargaining tools. Such rights can force the sale of startups that are not on the path to high growth. For example, if an initially promising startup transitions into a so-called lifestyle business that

---

[z]Ewens and Marx (2018) use the changes in state noncompete laws to explore founder replacement and startup performance. They observe that states that are home to many startups, such as California and New York, do not enforce noncompete contracts.

supports employee wages and gives the managers control benefits but affords no possibility of high return, redemption rights allow investors to force a sale or a change in strategy. More broadly, redemption rights mitigate founder–manager moral hazard.

Kaplan and Strömberg (2003) find that almost 80% of financings in their sample featured redemption rights, which is similar to 78% found by Williams (2017) on a larger and more recent sample. At the same time, given the potential potency of these rights, two conditions often must be met before investors can utilize redemption provisions. First, redemption rights can be triggered only after a certain period of time, giving founder–managers some breathing room. Kaplan and Strömberg (2003) find a typical maturity of 5 years. Second, a certain percentage of preferred shareholders are often required to vote in favor in order to trigger redemption rights, indicating the importance of interinvestor conflicts that are associated with redemption.

4.5 Informal control mechanisms

The nature of startups means that control can extend far beyond formal legal rights. Founder–manager power is constrained by the power of the purse. While founder–managers provide key human capital, investors provide financial capital. Founder–managers who defy the will of their investors may find themselves cut off from funding from those investors. The important signaling role of reinvestment and pro-rata rights means this can completely shut a firm out of fundraising (Rajan, 1992).

Investor power is similarly constrained through several mechanisms. First, a founder–manager's human capital can give them outsized bargaining power above and beyond any contract. The departure (or even reduced effort) of a visionary leader could cripple a fast-growing firm, and as such, VCs are unlikely to force the hand of the founders of successful firms. Second, reputation is of paramount importance in the VC world given the fact that VCs rely on deal flow from networks to generate returns (Gompers et al., 2020) and syndication from friendly firms (Hochberg et al., 2007; Nanda and Rhodes-Kropf, 2019). A VC firm that routinely pushes the limits of its control rights in conflicts with founders or other investors can build up a negative reputation in a business where reputation is key to success. Third, the inevitable dilution and renegotiation of future rounds offer multiple opportunities for an unhappy founder–manager (if they remain with the firm) to undermine investor returns.

4.6 Legal system

Beyond specific contractual rights, the legal system provides investors and managers with a variety of standard protections. Investors have some degree of protection against deceit and expropriation by majority owners.[aa] Founders and other common

---

[aa]For example, see the description of the entire fairness doctrine in https://rc.com/documents/PrimeronBusinessJudgmentRule.pdf.

equity holders benefit from some legal precedents that prioritize their claims above those of preferred investors.[ab] Although public legal battles may cause reputational damage and therefore are detrimental to success in the entrepreneurial ecosystem, these rights bound the actions taken by the parties involved. The potential for lawsuits could have a chilling effect on actions taken or give parties bargaining power beyond their contractual rights. For example, some acquirers insist on an overwhelming shareholder vote (say, 90%) in favor of the sale out of fear the dissenting shareholders may initiate the legal action. As another example, the potential for lawsuits from founders over round terms can drive companies to seek arms-length outside investors for new financing rounds. Many of these issues are guided by legal precedents, potentially offering scope for further careful empirical work.

4.7 Across investor variation in control rights

Most of our discussion of control rights has focused on founder–managers and VC investors. This is natural because these parties tend to have the most active corporate governance roles. However, startups have numerous other stakeholders with varying degrees of control.

While early-stage VC investors typically take a major governance role, the angel investors who immediately precede them frequently have little in the way of governance rights. Because debt typically has limited control rights outside of distress and covenant violations, angel investors using the debt-like convertible notes end up with relatively little power. The main lever at their disposal is their right to the return of their principal at the maturity of the notes—which gives rise to a similar power as redemption rights. Investors using SAFEs have even less power because these investments lack even the principal repayment of the convertible notes. Angel rounds using preferred equity can have the same control rights as VCs; however, most convertible notes and SAFE issues offer little in the way of control rights. Angel-led preferred equity investments can come with a board seat; however, this is not typical. Late-stage investors may have different preferences still. For example, Chernenko et al. (2021) show that mutual funds receive redemption rights and IPO-related rights but rarely receive board seats.

4.8 Relationship between cash flow and corporate governance rights

Cash flow rights and corporate governance rights are closely linked. Economic mechanisms may lead to either complementarity or substitutability of these rights in startup financing. For example, an investor may exert a larger degree of control over corporate actions, while providing founder–managers with stronger cash flow

---

[ab]For example, the Trados court argued that "it is the duty of directors to pursue the best interests of the corporation and its common stockholders, if that can be done faithfully with the contractual promises owed to the preferred." (In re Trados Inc. Shareholder Litigation, C.A. No. 1512-VCL, mem. op. (Del. Ch. Aug. 16, 2013)).

rights and relying to a lesser degree on protective covenants. Indeed, Bengtsson (2011) shows evidence that contracts providing preferential cash flow rights to investors or those that do not lead to investor-controlled boards also have more protective provisions. Bengtsson and Sensoy (2011) show that more experienced VC investors, whom they estimate to have superior abilities and who are more frequently joining the boards of their portfolio companies, obtain weaker downside-protecting contractual cash flow rights than less-experienced VC investors. The authors conclude that investors with better governance abilities focus less on obtaining downside cash flow rights, which entail risk-sharing costs, and more on governance aspects of the contract, such as obtaining board representation, during negotiations with entrepreneurs. Similarly, Bottazzi et al. (2008) show, on the sample of European VC firms, that more experienced investors are substantially more likely to be active, including in taking board seats in portfolio companies. Gompers et al. (2010) find that successful serial entrepreneurs do not receive more favorable valuations from VC investors even though their subsequent companies are more likely to be successful. However, Bengtsson and Sensoy (2011) show that serial successful entrepreneurs do, in fact, raise capital at more attractive terms (lower effective valuations) because the VC investors obtain weaker downside protections. This finding underscores the importance of interconnection between cash flow rights and corporate governance.

Empirical evidence by Kaplan and Strömberg (2003) and subsequent researchers shows that both cash flow and control rights can be separated and made contingent on the future states of the world, including observable and verifiable measures of performance. While these provisions are correlated, correlations are far from perfect. For example, Kaplan and Strömberg (2003) show that board control and voting rights are correlated, implying that if investors have the majority of the board, they also tend to have majority share voting rights. They also find that in their sample control rights and cash flow rights are positively correlated as well, even though there is a cluster of companies in which there is a clear separation of the parties' cash flow and control rights. Taken together, these results point out the interconnection between cash flow and corporate governance provisions in startups.

5 Evolution of cash flow rights and control

Successful startups almost invariably raise multiple rounds of funding, with each additional financing round dramatically complicating the company's capital structure. Startups have stayed private longer over the past decade (Ewens and Farre-Mensa, 2020), leading to more financing rounds and increasingly complex capital structures.

Airbnb, shown in Table 4, offers an example of a successful company's fundraising path. It raised multiple rounds from different sources, with round sizes and prices increasing as the company scaled. Each of these rounds in general leads to the dilution of existing ownership claims (Section 5.1), with each new round reducing

Table 4 Airbnb major financing rounds.

Date	Round	Lead investor(s)	Investment ($m)	Valuation ($m)
Nov 2008	Accelerator	Y-Combinator	$0.02	n.d.
Apr 2009	Series Seed	Sequoia	$0.6	n.d.
Nov 2010	Series A	Sequoia and Greylock	$7	$67
Jul 2011	Series B	Andreessen Horowitz	$112	$1,300
Feb 2013	Series C	Founders fund	$200	$2,500
Apr 2014	Series D	TPG	$475	$10,000
Nov 2015	Series E	Hillhouse capital and others	$1,600	$25,500
Jun 2016	Debt	JPMorgan and others	$1,000	N/A
Sep 2017	Series F	CapitalG and TCV	$1,000	$31,000
Apr 2020	Growth equity	Silver Lake and others	$2,000	$18,000
Dec 2020	IPO		$3,490	$41,000

This table presents Airbnb's major financing rounds, as reported by Pitchbook. Valuation is the reported or estimated PMV. n.d. means no data. N/A means data are not available.

all existing shares ownership claims. Shareholders mitigate this through a number of channels, most importantly through reinvestment into successful startups (Section 5.2). Beyond cash flows, each round changes the governance structure of the firm, transferring control from the founders and existing investors toward new investors (Section 5.3).

5.1 Dilution

One of the most important features of multiple financing rounds is that each round dilutes the ownership of all existing shares. Using the notation from Section 3, the fully diluted ownership claim of securities i at the time of exit is equal to their initial ownership claim (I_i/P_i), diluted by all future issuances $(1 - I_j/P_j)$:[ac]

$$\omega_i(\mathbb{Z}_T) = \frac{I_i}{P_i} \prod_{j=i+1}^{N} \left(1 - \frac{I_j}{P_j} \right). \tag{8}$$

Kaplan and Strömberg (2003) find that as the number of rounds progresses, investors, considered as a single class, tend to increase their cash flow and control rights at the expense of common shareholders and thus founder–managers. While this finding has been supported by more recent research, a caveat to keep in mind is that investors do not represent a monolith but rather, as the company raises more financing, their body becomes more dispersed, with often diverging preferences (Bartlett, 2006).

[ac]Option pools and antidilution terms, which we discuss in Sections 3.3 and 5.1.1, respectively, may impact this dilution further.

Investors use multiple avenues to protect themselves from such dilution. First and foremost, they frequently reinvest (Section 5.2), which allows them to counteract dilution by buying more shares. Beyond that, at the time of negotiating their original investment, they often insist on protective provisions and shareholder voting rights that effectively allow them to block a future financial transaction that is substantially adverse to their economic interests. If investors join a syndicate, they may negotiate the pay-to-play provisions, thus increasing incentives for all the investors in the round to provide financing in the future (see Section 5.2.3). Finally, investors routinely negotiate the so-called antidilution rights that offer protection against dilution in unfavorable financing rounds. We discuss this now.

5.1.1 Antidilution

An ideal investment would see the startup posting strong growth, increasing its value, and issuing each subsequent financing round at a higher price in the lead up to a fabulous exit. In practice, this is, of course, not always the case and even successful startups (such as Airbnb) stumble. Poor company performance or changes in the overall market can force a company to raise money at a lower PMV, if it does not fail entirely. As shown in Eq. (8), the lower the PMV of a financing round, the more dilution it creates for existing owners. This impacts both cash flow rights which we discuss here, and control rights which we discuss later. Raising a financing round at a lower price than the preceding round is called a "down round."

Investors routinely negotiate for antidilution rights that offer protection against dilution in unfavorable financing rounds. Antidilution protection is triggered whenever the company issues a new series of preferred shares at a price below that paid by the protected investors. In that event, these provisions increase the number of common shares the protected investor gets upon conversion by adjusting the price at which they convert into common shares.

To show how antidilution protection works, consider the most common form of antidilution, broad-based weighted average antidilution. After each subsequent round $j > i$, the ownership share of existing securities with weighted-average antidilution protection (A^{AD}) increases to

$$\omega_i' = \max\left\{ \omega_i\left(1 - \frac{I_j}{P_j}\right), \omega_i\left(\frac{\frac{\omega_0'}{\omega_0} + \frac{I_j}{P_j}}{1 + \omega_i I_j / I_i}\right) \right\} \quad \text{for } i \in A^{AD}, \tag{9}$$

and the ownership of securities without antidilution protection is correspondingly reduced to

$$\omega_i' = \omega_i \frac{1 - \frac{I_j}{P_j} - \sum_{k \in A^{AD}} (\omega_k')}{1 - \sum_{k \in A^{AD}} (\omega_k)} \quad \text{for } i \notin A^{AD}, \tag{10}$$

where ω_0 is the ownership of common equity.[ad]

Weighted average antidilution protection adjusts the conversion price of the protected securities downward to a value between the price paid by the protected investor and the price paid by the investors in the current round. A stronger form is known as "full ratchet antidilution protection," which adjusts the conversion price downwards all the way to the price of the shares issued in the new round. Kaplan and Strömberg (2003) find that almost 95% of preferred stock financings include some form of antidilution protection. Using a more recent sample, Williams (2017) similarly finds that antidilution protection, mostly broad-based weighted average, is present in approximately 92% of preferred equity financings.

Whether preferred shares feature weighted average antidilution or the more extreme full ratchet antidilution, common equity does not have antidilution protection and therefore typically bears the brunt of these antidilution adjustments to conversion prices. To the extent that common stock is owned by founder–managers or employees who are still instrumental to the startup's success, incoming investors often renegotiate antidilution protection and may threaten to withdraw their investment offer if existing investors exercise their antidilution rights. As a result, antidilution protections are often waived by investors or their impact is attenuated through renegotiation. As an alternative, antidilution exercise could coincide with a stock grant of shares to the continuing senior management, thus providing protection to existing investors and current managers at the expense of other common shareholders, especially the founders who are no longer with the company.

5.1.2 Dilution of downside protections

Beyond dilution of raw ownership, future rounds also dilute the downside protections of existing investors. In a liquidation or sale where there is insufficient value to pay off all investor claims, new investors directly impair the value of existing investors. For example, if all rounds are pari passu, the payoff becomes as follows, with each round diluting downside protection:

$$\pi_i(X_T, \mathbb{Z}_T) = X_T \frac{L_i I_i}{\sum_{j=1}^{N}(L_j I_j)}. \tag{11}$$

New rounds that are senior or have high liquidation multiples lead to even more dilution of downside protection for existing preferred shareholders, as Gornall and Strebulaev (2021a) show. This significantly reduces the ex ante value of investor downside protections.

Beyond just dilution, sometimes the previous series are stripped of their contractual protections. The most extreme form of this is a recapitalization or "cram-down," where preferred shareholders are converted into common equity. These transactions,

---

[ad]In practice, these formulas are expressed in terms of conversion prices rather than ownership fractions.

which typically occur for distressed companies whose investors would otherwise write off the investment, wipe out special contractual provisions of preferred investors.

5.2 Reinvestment

Our Airbnb example shows that investors frequently reinvest in startups. In this section, we discuss the reasons for that investment structure (Section 5.2.1) and how investors protect their right to invest (Section 5.2.2) or even partially commit to reinvesting (Section 5.2.3).

5.2.1 Staging

VCs and many other investors aim to stage their investments in a startup. "Staging" means that at the initial round of investment, the investors inject funding that they know to be insufficient for the company to succeed in the majority of even good states of the world. As a result, investors expect to facilitate further financing in the future, which they make implicitly and explicitly contingent on the interim company performance (Gompers, 1995). Staging serves to protect investors by limiting the exposure to companies that face a high uncertainty and a large probability of failure. From one angle, therefore, staging can be seen as a real option: by investing the small amount necessary to keep the startup exploring its product and business model while uncertainty is partially resolved, investors buy an option to continue investing in the entrepreneurial project in the future.

The VC environment adds two wrinkles beyond a traditional real option setting. First, VC investors tend to form investment syndicates. In the next rounds of funding new investors often enter the fray and lead negotiations. This can dilute existing investors' cash flow and governance rights. Second, VC investors often utilize new financing rounds to renegotiate control rights, especially if the company is not performing as expected. This is consistent with an incomplete contracts framework in which future control rights are contingent on future realizations.

Staging provides strong performance incentives to founder–managers who may have to meet agreed-upon milestones to secure future financing and to ensure they have a higher chance of staying at the helm of the company. These beneficial aspects of staging must counterbalance with a well-known deficiency of dynamic financing, in which the investor does not or cannot commit to providing future funding. Agency conflicts or changing funding market environment may lead to inefficient liquidation in cases in which it would be optimal for the companies to continue operations in the first best case (Holmström and Tirole, 1998).

A related aspect of staging is the information asymmetry between insiders (including existing investors) and outsiders (including new investors). This may lead to a hold-up by existing investors; indeed, if an existing investor refuses to fund the company, it sends a strong negative signal to any potential incoming investor who, as an outsider, is by nature less informed (Rajan, 1992).

An investor needs to ensure that when the time comes for the next fundraising, she has enough funds at her disposal to participate in the financing round if she wishes to do so. Thus, at the time of an initial investment, investors, especially VC funds, allocate a portion of their capital in anticipation of future fundraising. This is known in the industry as "dry powder." For VC funds, which are constrained with respect to both time (because of a limited fund horizon imposed by limited partners) and capital (because of a limited fund size), the dry powder allocation decision is a critical consideration. In addition, anecdotal evidence suggests that VC investors consider their ability to fulfill their implicit commitment to their portfolio companies to be a critical component of their reputation, which allows them to secure access to promising investments in the future.

5.2.2 Pro-rata rights

Pro-rata rights give investors the right, but not the obligation, to invest in future rounds at the same terms as newly incoming investors. They are entitled to invest up to their current ownership share on a fully diluted basis. This allows them to stave off ownership dilution created by future rounds. Investors that utilize pro-rata rights in follow-on rounds thus end up holding preferred shares of different series, even though their fractional ownership of these series varies. For example, a lead investor holding the majority in a specific series of preferred stock may subsequently acquire minority ownership positions in subsequently issued series of preferred stock.

Reinvesting serves several purposes. First, it allows investors to capitalize on their inside information and reinvest in companies they see as undervalued. Second, it allows them to maintain a governance stake. Third, it puts them on both sides of the transaction and partially mediates the effects of mispriced rounds or downside protection dilution.

Existing owners who use their pro-rata rights reduce the amount of the financing round available to the new investor. In many cases, the lead new investors will insist on adjusting special class voting thresholds to ensure they hold the class voting privileges. In others, negotiation can lead to some earlier investors partially waiving their pro-rata rights.

A related contractual term often negotiated with common equity holders (and sometimes with preferred equity holders as well) is the so-called Right of First Refusal (ROFR). ROFR means that if shareholders desire to sell their shares and find a willing buyer, they must provide the company with a notice of proposed sale, and then the company or some of its designated investors may have the right to exercise the ROFR and purchase the shares at the negotiated price.

5.2.3 Pay to play

Pay-to-play terms penalize existing investors who opt not to participate in future financing rounds. The penalty may range from the loss of antidilution protection or other preferred shareholder rights to the automatic conversion of that investor's preferred stock into common stock. These terms are observed only in transactions in which a financing round is organized by a syndicate of investors. In this case, it may be insisted upon by some syndicate members as a protection against other members of the syndicate refusing to finance the company in the future.[ae] The pay-to-play provision helps align incentives by making it costly for investors to shirk from providing financing. As such, this provision signals interinvestor conflicts of interests.

Pay-to-play provisions are less frequent than might have been expected, given the prevalence of investor syndicates in financing rounds of startups. Williams (2017) finds that approximately 9% of preferred equity financings feature a pay-to-play provision. Within that sample, conversion of preferred shares to common is the most frequent punishment for investors refusing to participate in the subsequent financing rounds. Bengtsson and Sensoy (2015) find that pay-to-play provisions are more frequently observed in down rounds and flat rounds compared to up rounds. This suggests that the likelihood of investors abandoning the company in the future in the down round is higher, necessitating contractual intervention to align incentives.

5.3 Control

Startups issue more preferred shares with each successive round of equity funding. New investors gain voting privileges and some may even join the board of directors. As a result, common shareholders, including founder–managers, see their control diluted over time unless they initiate corporate governance changes to retain control rights, such as supervoting. Kaplan and Strömberg (2003) show that founders' voting and board rights decline over financing rounds, while investor rights increase. The board control is more likely to shift from common or founder-controlled to investor-controlled boards (Ewens and Malenko, 2020). Given the contingent nature of many contractual provisions as well as the dependence of bargaining power of new investors on the evolution of company fortunes, we should expect that the evolution of control is contingent on company-specific dynamics. For example, down rounds should lead to a higher likelihood of founder–managers rescinding control of the company (Ewens and Marx, 2018). Bengtsson and Sensoy (2015) show that new lead VCs are weakly more likely to take a board seat if the company performs poorly.

As discussed in Section 4.1, shareholder voting rights typically offer vetoes to specific classes of investors over specific actions. In the early stages of a company's lifecycle, this mostly protects investors against the rent-extracting behavior of founder–managers that is adverse to investors. In later stages, interinvestor conflicts gain importance as investors differ more and more in terms of economic preferences and contractual rights. The fact that each subsequent fundraising results in the issuance of a stand-alone class of shares (typically in the form of a series of preferred stock) underlines the importance of interinvestor differences.

The most consequential decisions are also the situations in which the divergence of interests among investors is at its highest: the choice of the company's exit

---

[ae]See Blaydon (2002) and LeClaire et al. (2005) for practitioner discussion of pay-to-play.

strategy and the timing and conditions of subsequent fundraising. The nature of preferred stock inherently leads to a difference in outcomes for a particular class of investor over a potentially wide range of company exit values depending on whether such exit is a sale (in which case preferred rights, such as liquidation preference, are more protected) or a public listing (in which case automatic conversion ensures the loss of preferred rights). Some investors, especially the late-stage investors investing at higher price points than previous shareholders, demand substantial protective rights against an unfavorable outcome, including a veto in certain cases, or expect a discount to take into account the future value extraction and a value transfer from them to earlier investors and common shareholders.

A prominent example of this is the class-level automatic conversion exception, in which a class of investors can effectively block an IPO unless they receive a certain minimum return on their investment. The veto right over an IPO completion arises because it is the universal practice in the industry that all the convertible preferred stock should convert into common stock in the IPO process. This is contractually accomplished by automatic conversion, which enables the company to force all the preferred shareholders to convert into common stock under certain conditions. Contractual terms can exempt investors from that unless additional, substantially stringent, conditions are met. In the realm of highly valued startups, which are thus closer to the IPO eventuality, these automatic exemption clauses are not infrequent.

6 Valuation of venture capital securities

Valuing assets is central to finance. In the VC context, it facilitates allocating funding to entrepreneurs and investment managers, managing risk, and trading in secondary markets. Unfortunately, startups are fundamentally difficult to value, especially at an early stage of their life cycle. First, given that their profits occur well into the future, their cash flows are inherently difficult to forecast, as discussed in Section 2. Second, as we have discussed at length, startups tend to raise funding numerous times using a variety of complicated contracts. For these reasons, startup investors use various rules of thumb and simplified versions of more traditional financial valuation methods.

We discuss first the valuation of startup cash flows (Section 6.1) before moving on to how valuation is impacted by the contractual terms that we have discussed in the previous sections (Section 6.2).

6.1 Valuing innovative projects

Innovative high-growth startups usually lose money in their early years. These early losses are offset against large future profits that are in the relatively distant future and may not occur at all. In fact, many startups have no real revenue at the time of the first external financings and no profit in the foreseeable future. These properties make it not only difficult to forecast cash flows but also mean that small changes in discount rates have large impacts on valuation. Some of the core parameters of common valuation models in finance (such as β) are nontrivial to estimate for VC as an asset class, let alone at the level of a particular startup (Korteweg, 2019).

Beyond the nature of the cash flows, startup investors struggle to gather information. The founder–managers, who are often the most knowledgeable about the product and customers and thus presumably in the best position to estimate future cash flows, have conflicted incentives in their negotiations with investors. Founders of startups are also well known to be case studies in irrational exuberance. For example, Gompers et al. (2020) show that less than a third of early-stage startups ever meet revenue forecasts. As a result, investors routinely discount founder–manager optimistic expectations. Of equal importance, core determinants of success are perceived to be generally intangible qualities such as managerial ability (Gompers et al., 2020).

These challenges have led VCs and other early-stage investors to eschew the sophistication of traditional valuation approaches and instead to adopt a radically simple, yet powerful, set of valuation techniques. We will discuss three broad families of valuation models used by investors to value startups as stand-alone companies: cash flow-based models, market comparables approaches, and nonquantitative methods. It is important to emphasize that our discussion will be particularly relevant to early-stage startups. As startups mature, traditional valuation methods start playing an increasingly important role in their valuation. The robustness and applicability of these methods depend in large part on the predictability of cash flows, which is naturally greater for more developed companies.

Although these simplified valuation techniques are inherently inaccurate, several channels mitigate the real impact of this inaccuracy. First, staging (Section 5.2.1) attenuates the noise in valuation. For example, an investor who overpaid for Series A may pay a fair price or even a lower than fair price for a subsequent Series B round raised by the same startup (see, e.g., Admati and Pfleiderer, 1994). Second, especially in early funding rounds, the valuation is just one component among the multitude of contractual terms and contractual downside protections (e.g., antidilution) which reduce the cost to investors of pricing errors. Third, startup investors, whether angel investors or VCs, diversify their holdings across multiple startups, leading to pricing errors balancing out further. Note that many of these channels are not available to other claim holders, such as founders and employees.

Beyond these considerations, it is important to note that there is no well-functioning market for startup shares and valuations are outcomes of negotiations between investors and founder–managers (and, more broadly, between investors and a startup's existing claim holders), implying that the bargaining power of the involved parties, as well as the local fundraising environment, are particularly relevant. The notional monetary component of valuation is thus only one ingredient in a complicated contractual outcome, as we show later.

6.1.1 Cash flow-based valuation

The classic method of valuing and discounting cash flows is net present value (NPV) analysis. Early-stage startup investors, such as VCs, adapted the NPV method in several ways to be applicable in their context.

VCs that do use the classic NPV method typically use large discount rates in the range of 25%–30% or higher. These discount rates at face value are much higher than those that one would estimate using methods prescribed in classic finance textbooks and are broadly unrelated to academic assessments of the risks that VCs face.[af] As argued by Gompers et al. (2020), VCs effectively think of IRRs conditional on successful projects. Using excessively high IRRs thus allows VCs to continue using somewhat optimistic cash flow projections and achieve a more realistic aggregate IRR in the face of numerous portfolio company failures. Thus, the discount rates used are designed to partially capture the high level of project-specific idiosyncratic risk by stripping out the individual project characteristics with that of the portfolio of highly uncertain investments. In addition, higher discount rates may also compensate for the fees charged in the VC industry, making the net returns comparable to market alternatives to investors of institutional VC funds (see, e.g., Litvak, 2009; Metrick and Yasuda, 2010).

To appreciate a common adaptation to the NPV method in startup valuation, consider a classic NPV problem, where an investor must pay I in exchange for a security issued by a startup. The startup is high-risk and has q probability of failing in each year, in which case the security becomes worthless. If the startup has not failed, the security generates expected cash flows $X_1, X_2, ..., X_T$ with the terminal payoff X_T corresponding to a time-T liquidity event. Suppose the appropriate risk-adjusted discount rate for the project is r, perhaps coming from a capital asset pricing model. A classic NPV analysis would simply discount these cash flows based on their probability:

$$\text{NPV} = -I + \sum_{t=1}^{T} X_t \left(\frac{1-q}{1+r}\right)^t. \tag{12}$$

Venture capitalists frequently make two key simplifications to this approach. First, they ignore intermediate cash flows and focus only on the security's payoff at the startup's exit. This simplifies the NPV expression to the following:

$$\text{NPV} = -I + X_T \left(\frac{1-q}{1+r}\right)^T. \tag{13}$$

Ignoring intermediate cash flows is justified in the VC context because these cash flows are generally relatively small. Startups rarely pay dividends and instead the major cash flow the investor will receive is simply the exit payoff, whether a sale or IPO.

Second, they bundle failure probabilities into the discount rate. This allows VCs to focus on the upside success in their discounting and offset idiosyncratic risk through an inflated discount rate:

[af]For assessments of the risks and returns that VCs face, see, for example, Cochrane (2005), Harris et al. (2014, 2016), Kaplan and Schoar (2005), Korteweg and Nagel (2016), Korteweg and Sorensen (2010, 2017), Korteweg (2019), and Gupta and Van Nieuwerburgh (2021).

$$\text{NPV}_{\text{VC}} = -I + X_T \left(\frac{1}{1 + r_{\text{VC}}}\right)^T, \tag{14}$$

where r_{VC} is the "VC-specific" discount rate, equal to

$$r_{\text{VC}} = \frac{1 + r}{1 - q} - 1. \tag{15}$$

Several commonly applied VC-specific valuation approaches, such as the so-called Venture Capital Method, utilize these two adaptations.[ag] To summarize, these approaches use two modifications. First, they ignore intermediate cash flows, which is realistic given that most of the startup monetization outcomes that matter for VCs are exit outcomes such as sales or IPOs. Second, the discount rate used by VCs (that they also often call the IRR) includes both the risk-adjusted component r and the risk-unadjusted probabilistic distribution of future cash flows. This explains why, in surveys, VCs report much higher required IRRs (Gompers et al., 2020).

This mechanism also helps explain perhaps the most popular approach to valuation in the VC industry, which seemingly ignores the time value of money completely. Rather than discounting to the initial date, VCs instead set a valuation based on a targeted cash on cash multiple, such as 5 or 10. Cash-on-cash multiples are effectively (expected, required, or realized) multiples of invested capital (MOIC), which is measured as $\text{MOIC} = \frac{X_T}{I}$. Again, note that this measure ignores the intermediate cash flows and the probabilistic distribution of outcomes. However, while it can be perceived that the use of the MOIC valuation completely abstracts from both the time value of money and risk, it is not the case. Using Eq. (13), we can define the break-even required MOIC as

$$\text{MOIC} = \left(\frac{1 + r}{1 - q}\right)^T. \tag{16}$$

Using an investment rule based on such an MOIC, VC investors can expect to break even on average in their portfolio, taking into account both risk and time discounting. In practice, additional considerations, such as the already alluded to economics of VC funds, lead to higher MOIC than break-even ones. Importantly, the fact that VCs require much higher MOIC than could otherwise be expected simply means that, in the "VC financial language," the MOIC measure encapsulates risk and time components. To give a simple quantitative example, if we assume the risk-adjusted cost of capital of $r = 15\%$, exit time of $T = 5$ years, and an ultimate probability of success in the 5%–10% range (all the parameters arguably in the reasonable empirical range), then the break-even MOIC are between 5 and 10, matching those frequently required by early-stage startup VC investors.

[ag]Sahlman (2009) discusses in detail these valuation approaches. In addition, he also considers the impact of dilution, as investors expect that the payoff X_T they receive in the case of success will depend on future funding rounds the startup raises.

6.1.2 Market multiples valuation

The market multiples (also known as market comparables) approach to valuation involves valuing a subject company by comparing it to other similar businesses, often through a so-called value multiple. The idea behind multiples is that similar assets should sell for equivalent prices.[ah] In the case of companies, it is common to measure the market price as a multiple of some form of earnings or revenue variable. Common valuation multiples, in practice, include the ratio of enterprise value (the total market value of all securities of the company including common stock, preferred stock, and debt) to EBITDA, earnings before interest and taxes (EBIT), or revenue. For example, investment bankers use the market multiples method valuing an M&A transaction using public company comparables with often sophisticated adjustments.

As in the case of the NPV method, a typical VC application of the market multiples method is also adapted to fit the context in which startups operate. First, startups typically have negative EBIDTA and negative profit at the time of a VC investment. In their place, VCs use revenue, if there is any, and, if not, monthly active users or other metrics deemed appropriate for the startup in question. The underlying assumption here is that the company will pivot toward profitability at some later point, justifying a valuation based on revenue for a currently money-losing venture or a nonfinancial metric intended to capture the startup's progress and the scale of eventual success.

Second, when performing a market multiples analysis, the key assumption (and a potential source of error) comes from the selection of the similar or comparable businesses (so-called comps) used to value the company of interest. The intent is that these comps should have a comparable form to the subject company. Embedded in each company's valuation multiple are the market's perceptions of the company's future growth prospects, profit margins, and risks. However, no two companies are identical, so identifying appropriate comparable companies requires reasonable judgment about the similarity of the comps to the subject company. In the case of startups, the public company peers traditionally used for market comparables may not be suitable. This applies not only to startups in emerging industries that lack public peers; even public peers in ostensibly similar industries have inherently different growth rates, profitability, and risk. Instead, VCs either look at comparable transactions of other early-stage startups to imply valuation or adjust the public comparables for the differential growth rates.

Third, the unaudited financials of a fast-growing startup are inherently less reliable than those of more mature publicly traded companies. This challenge applies to both the startups themselves and any privately held comparables selected for valuation (that often do not release revenue or valuations). In response, VCs often resort to rules of thumb (e.g., a valuation of $60\times$ monthly recurring revenue), gut feel, and judgment.

[ah]For a practitioner-oriented introduction to the market multiples valuation method see Koller et al. (2010) and Damodaran (2006).

Beyond explicitly using multiples of specific comparable companies, valuation is often based on the perception of the value of a segment of broadly comparable companies. For example, if early-stage prerevenue software-as-a-service startups have secured a PMV of around $10 million in a certain geographical area in the past several months, investors will tend to offer valuations around that number.

6.1.3 Nonquantitative approaches to valuation

The challenges of valuing (especially very) early-stage startups mean that valuation is triangulated from applying judgment-based rules. For example, based on their experience VCs may have a specific target ownership stake on a fully diluted basis. The minimum investor ownership stake may be viewed by investors as necessary to maintain control rights in light of expected future dilution and is often determined by the economic considerations of VC funds rather than a specific startup. The ceiling on the target ownership stake is designed to preserve founder–manager incentives and ensure interest on behalf of future investors. In the very first VC rounds, the ownership stake has historically been within the range between 15% and 30%. In addition, while the expected future cash flows are difficult to estimate, investors can forecast expenses (and thus the amount they need to invest) for the relatively short period of time (typically until the next investment round, that is, over a 12- to 18-month horizon) with much better precision. The PMV then follows from effectively reversing the ownership calculations under contracting (Eq. 2):

$$\text{Postmoney valuation} = \frac{\text{Investment amount}}{\text{Investor fully diluted ownership stake}}. \qquad (17)$$

For example, given a target ownership share of 20% and a company's cash needs of $5 million, VCs triangulate to a PMV of $25 million.

Another approach that might be used in some cases utilizes scoring rules of varying sophistication. They may be entirely qualitative (e.g., the so-called Berkus method[ai]) or a mixture of quantitative and qualitative techniques (e.g., adjusting local valuation norms based on startup quality, as in Bill Payne's scorecard valuation[aj]).

Another approach used frequently by angel investors is to defer valuation using SAFEs or convertible notes. This can be a partial deferral, as with a convertible note with a cap, or a full deferral with an uncapped convertible note. Although superficially appealing, deferring valuation creates its own set of issues and in many instances leads to the implied valuation range, as discussed in Sections 3.4 and 3.5.

6.2 Valuing contractual claims

Much of the academic work on VC valuation has focused on the question of how a startup's financial structure impacts the value of the financial securities it issues. This question lends itself to more formal analysis because we can often start with an

---

[ai]See https://berkonomics.com/?p=131.
[aj]See https://altitudeaccelerator.ca/wp-content/uploads/2012/02/Valuation-Worksheet.pdf.

observed price or prices, such as the price of a security issued in the latest round of funding. Given the price of one security, it is possible in principle to determine the value of the other securities that the company issues, ranging from stock options to common shares to other preferred securities.

Although, in principle, such a value decomposition could be performed at any time, in practice most startups lack a liquid market in *any* of their securities. As such, methodologies that value contractual claims generally price securities using the issuance price of the most recent financing round. For example, at the time SpaceX issued its Series M Preferred Stock, the price that investors paid for that stock was observed, which made it possible to back out the price of SpaceX's Series B Preferred Stock, consistent with the price of Series M shares.

6.2.1 Ignoring contractual terms

In practice, investors not infrequently ignore contractual terms when valuing securities issued by startups. This would mean, for example, assuming that SpaceX's Series A Preferred Stock and its common stock had the same value as SpaceX's Series M Preferred Stock at the time of the Series M issuance. Agarwal et al. (2017) show that mutual funds frequently employ this strategy. Gornall and Strebulaev (2020) report that many finance professionals, both inside and outside of the VC industry, think of the PMV as a fair valuation of the company.

Underlying this strategy is the idea that contractual terms do not matter. Although theoretically incorrect, this may not be an entirely unreasonable assumption in practice. First, the VC investment model is premised on massive successes and abject failures. Given that many contractual terms have value in intermediate and less-than-successful exit outcomes, to the extent investors rely only on extremely successful outcomes, the quantitative implications of some contractual terms may be of lesser importance. Second, the VC investment model is premised on multiple rounds of financing. Indeed, Jenkinson et al. (2019), Bengtsson and Sensoy (2015), and Gornall and Strebulaev (2021a) argue that future round terms may impair the value of securities issued in previous rounds. To the extent that pattern holds more generally, the value of some contractual protections is subject to dilution and is thus less relevant for contemporaneous valuation.

Another consideration, which, in practice, is arguably the most important one, is that the strategy of ignoring future rounds simplifies the task of valuing complicated securities, which could severely tax even knowledgeable experts. Finally, to the extent that market participants are worried about valuation manipulation in illiquid opaque markets, this approach's simplicity seems to tie the hands of fund managers. It is not uncommon for fund managers to mark securities they have in the company to the price established in the most recent round.

However, ignoring contractual terms is not only indefensible on theoretical grounds, but also often leads to substantial mispricing of the company's outstanding securities. To see a clear illustration of this, consider Square Inc.'s October 2014 Series E financing round, in which the company raised $150 million by issuing

9.7 million Series E Preferred Shares for $15.46 per share to a variety of investors.[ak] These shares had the same payoff as common shares if the company did well but additional protections if the company did poorly. The Series E investors were promised at least $15.46 per share in a liquidation or acquisition and at least $18.56 per share in an IPO, with both of those claims senior to all other shareholders. These Series E shares joined Square's existing common shares and Series A, B-1, B-2, C, and D Preferred Shares. Each of these classes of shares had different cash flow, liquidation, control, and voting rights.

After this round, Square was assigned a so-called PMV, as discussed in Section 3.1.1. This PMV is calculated as the product of the most recent round's per-share price and the fully diluted number of common shares (with convertible preferred shares and both issued and unissued stock options counted, based on the number of common shares into which they convert). Square had 253 million common shares and options and 135 million preferred shares following its Series E round financing, for a total of 388 million shares on a fully diluted basis. Multiplying these yields a PMV of $6 billion:

$$\$6 \text{ billion} = \underbrace{\$15.46}_{\text{Series E price}} \times \underbrace{388 \text{ million.}}_{\substack{\text{Total number of} \\ \text{shares in all classes}}} \tag{18}$$

This PMV formula works well for public companies with a single class of shares, as it produces the company's equity market capitalization. Ignoring the contractual terms is equivalent to assuming that this same formula applies to start-ups such as Square and that a PMV equals the equity value of the company. Our previous discussion of cash flow and control rights shows that this is not the case. For example, Square's November 2015 IPO price was $9 per share, over 40% less than the Series E price. Series E investors, on the other hand, were contractually protected and received additional shares until they received $18.56 worth of common stock. Series E shares must have been more valuable than other shares, as they paid out more in downside scenarios and at least as much in upside scenarios. The PMV formula ignores this difference in value. By assigning convertible preferred shares and common shares the same value, the PMV formula ignores the option-like nature of shares and overstates the value of common equity, previously issued preferred shares, and the entire company. The impact on PMV may be enormous. In the case of Square, Gornall and Strebulaev (2020) show that after accounting for contractual terms in a contingent claims framework, the company's fair valuation following its Series E financing round was approximately $2.2 billion, not the $6.2 billion implied by the PMV. Square's reported PMV was 171% higher than the company's implied fair value. In Section 6.2.3, we discuss this framework.

[ak]This example is taken from Gornall and Strebulaev (2020).

6.2.2 Probability weighted expected return method

The probability-weighted expected return method (PWERM) is a way of valuing securities that is similar in spirit to the intuitive cash flow-based valuation approaches discussed in Section 6.1.1. It involves projecting several scenarios out of a startup's possible probability distribution of outcomes, each with the assigned valuation outcome and a probability weight. For each scenario, given the valuation outcome and the financial structure, we can calculate the resulting cash flow "waterfall," determining security-level payoffs. By weighing all these scenarios given the probability weights, the relative value of securities can be inferred.

While intuitive, this method's weakness is that it is almost entirely ad hoc. Deriving scenarios and appropriately weighing them probabilistically requires a large degree of subjective judgment. This makes it difficult to apply PWERM in a consistent and rigorous way and it also may make it open to manipulation.

6.2.3 Contingent claims valuation

The contingent claims methodology takes into account the complicated financial structure of startups and enables the estimation of individual security values using option pricing models. In our context, an important feature of these models is their ability to parsimoniously take into account the entire probabilistic distribution of a startup's future exit scenarios. Beginning with Black and Scholes (1973) and Merton (1974), researchers and practitioners have used share prices to value warrants, options, bonds, and other contracts. Metrick and Yasuda (2010) pioneered this idea in the VC context and developed an option pricing methodology that prices a security and derives an implied firm value under the assumption that the limited partners of the VC fund breakeven, and incorporates many frequently used contractual terms. Gornall and Strebulaev (2020) take this approach further and develop a related option pricing methodology. Such methods are also now widely applied by practitioners, who commonly take the pricing of the most recently issued security and "backsolve" to get the company value; they then use that value to back out the value of each outstanding security.

We now discuss a contingent claim valuation framework for valuing startups, as developed by Gornall and Strebulaev (2020). The basic setup was discussed in Section 3. To discount future cash flows at the time of exit, we need to make assumptions about the company's exit value and exit time. As is common in contingent claims models, we assume that the company's fair value $X(t)$ evolves according to a geometric Brownian motion with volatility σ that grows at the risk-free rate r_f under the pricing measure. This assumption is foundational to many areas of corporate finance and asset pricing. The time to exit is independent of $X(t)$ and exponentially distributed, $T \sim EXP(\lambda)$, where λ is the exit rate (and $1/\lambda$ is the average exit time). As Gornall and Strebulaev (2020) show, these assumptions are reasonable for VC-style investments.[al]

[al]Although we assume an immediate exit, VCs hold shares past the IPO in practice and even generate value by doing so (Gompers and Lerner, 1998).

Consider pricing a round i, in which the company raises I at the PMV of P. We assume that this is the last round before the company's exit and that the round is fairly priced, so that the investment amount I equals the investors' payoff discounted under the pricing measure:

$$I = \mathbb{E}\left[e^{-Tr_f}\pi_i(X_T, \mathbb{Z}_T)\right]. \tag{19}$$

Because $X(t)$ is a geometric Brownian motion, we can rewrite Eq. (19) in terms of a standard normal random variable Z:

$$I = \mathbb{E}\left[e^{-Tr_f}\pi_i\left(X(0)\ e^{\sqrt{\sigma^2 T}Z + (r_f - \sigma^2/2)T}, \mathbb{Z}_T\right)\right], \tag{20}$$

The company's time 0 value is simply the value of $X(0)$ that solves Eq. (20) and fairly prices the round. As an example, consider a standard convertible preferred equity issued in the only financing round. If the round's investors convert, they are entitled to own I/P fraction of the company's common shares. If they do not convert, they retain a claim of I that is senior to common shares. The investors' payoff can be written as

$$\pi_i(X(T), \mathbb{Z}_T) = \max\left\{\frac{I}{P}X(T),\ \min\{I, X(T)\}\right\}. \tag{21}$$

As discussed in Section 4.1.4, most convertible preferred equity shares are also subject to automatic conversion clauses that force these shares to convert into common shares when a trigger event occurs. The trigger event is commonly an IPO that raises a sufficiently large amount of money, referred to as a qualified IPO. In a qualified IPO, preferred shares must convert into common shares, even if doing so reduces their payout (e.g., the IPO share price is below the share price at which the preferred shareholders invested).

To model automatic conversion, we treat the payoffs in the IPO and the M&A separately and write the total payoff of investors in this round as the sum of the payoff in an IPO, $\pi^{\text{IPO}}(X(T), \mathbb{Z}_T)$, and the payoff in M&A or liquidations that cannot trigger automatic conversion, $\pi^{\text{M\&A}}(X(T), \mathbb{Z}_T)$. We then weight these payoffs by the probability of each outcome conditional on the exit value, $p^{\text{IPO}}(X(T))$ and $1 - p^{\text{IPO}}(X(T))$:

$$\pi_i(X(T), \mathbb{Z}_T) = p^{\text{IPO}}(X(T))\pi_i^{\text{IPO}}(X(T), \mathbb{Z}_T) + \left(1 - p^{\text{IPO}}(X(T))\right)\pi_i^{\text{M\&A}}(X(T), \mathbb{Z}_T). \tag{22}$$

The payoff in an M&A exit is just Eq. (21). If an IPO triggers automatic conversion, investors instead get their converted payoff:

$$\pi_i^{\text{IPO}}(X(T), \mathbb{Z}_T) = X(T)\frac{I}{P}. \tag{23}$$

If an IPO does not trigger automatic conversion, investors get the same choice between conversion and the liquidation that they would get in an M&A exit. Common practice dictates that all investors must convert prior to the IPO, so we assume that if an investor is not forced to convert and they do better in an M&A exit, they are able to force an M&A exit.

With this setup in place, the model can accommodate any cash flow contractual terms, including all of those discussed in Section 3, such as liquidation preference, automatic conversion exemptions, IPO ratchets, cumulative dividends, etc.[am] Table 5 (which is reproduced from Table 1 in Gornall and Strebulaev (2020)) shows

Table 5 Impact of contract terms on fair value.

Scenario	Company			Common share		
	PMV ($m)	FV ($m)	Δ_V	PMV ($)	FV ($)	Δ_C
Baseline	1000	771	30%	1	0.78	28%
Liquidation multiple						
1.25×	1000	705	42%	1	0.70	43%
2×	1000	515	94%	1	0.48	109%
Option pool						
0%	1000	810	23%	1	0.78	28%
10%	1000	732	37%	1	0.78	28%
Seniority						
Junior	1000	811	23%	1	0.82	22%
Senior	1000	737	36%	1	0.74	35%
Participation						
With no cap	1000	653	53%	1	0.64	56%
With 2.5× cap	1000	666	50%	1	0.65	53%
IPO Ratchet						
At 1×	1000	640	56%	1	0.62	60%
At 1.25×	1000	573	75%	1	0.55	83%
At 1.5×	1000	508	97%	1	0.47	114%
Automatic conversion veto						
At 1×	1000	646	55%	1	0.63	59%
At 0.5×	1000	680	47%	1	0.67	50%
Investment amount						
$400 million in round B	1000	875	14%	1	0.85	17%
$10 million in round B	1000	698	43%	1	0.72	39%
$400 million in round A	1000	885	13%	1	0.87	14%
$10 million in round A	1000	745	34%	1	0.76	32%

This table shows the fair value that produces a PMV of $1 billion for a startup raising a $100 million round using different contract terms. The "Company" columns report the PMV of the new round (PMV) in millions of dollars, the fair value of the company that makes that round fairly priced (FV) in millions of dollars, and the percentage by which the PMV overstates the fair value (Δ_V). The "Common share" columns report the share price of the round (PMV) in dollars, the fair value of the common shares (FV) in dollars, and the percentage by which the share price overstates the value of common shares (Δ_C).

[am]As this model assumes no future rounds, it accommodates no realistic antidilution protection and ignores the dilution imposed by future rounds. Gornall and Strebulaev (2021a) discuss these assumptions and incorporate future financing rounds in a contingent claims framework.

the impact of contractual terms on valuation in a representative numerical example and calibrated values of parameters: volatility, σ, is 0.9; the exit rate, λ, is 0.25 (implying the average exit value of 4 years); the probability of an IPO exit is an increasing function of X_T (with the specific empirical specification given by Equation (17) in Gornall and Strebulaev (2020)); and the risk-free rate, r_f, is 0.025.

Table 5 considers a startup that is raising $100 million of new VC investment at $1 per share in a Series B round, with a PMV of $1 billion, using standard preferred shares with a conversion option, automatic conversion in IPOs, a guaranteed return of initial investment in M&A exits and liquidation events, and no additional provisions. In the past, this company raised $50 million of VC investment in a Series A round, with a PMV of $450 million, using the preferred shares with the same rights and terms as, and pari passu seniority with, the newly issued shares. Using subscripts to denote the different rounds, $P_A = 450$, $P_B = 1,000$, $I_A = 50$, and $I_B = 100$ (all values in millions). After the current round, if all shares convert, the new investor owns 10% of the total shares, the old investor owns 10%, and the current common shareholders own the remaining 80%.

We define the company's overvaluation, Δ_V, as the ratio of the PMV to the implied fair value. We define the common shares' overvaluation, Δ_C, as the ratio of the most recent round's share price to the fair value of a common share. The results show that a fair value of $771 million correctly prices a VC round with a PMV of $1 billion. The PMV exaggerates the company's value by 30% and the value of common shares by 28%.

The table also shows the impact of specific contractual terms on PMV. A 1.25× liquidation preference increases overvaluation from 30% to 42%, and giving the new investor a 2× liquidation preference increases overvaluation to 94%. A larger option pool increases overvaluation as well. Making the new investor senior increases company (common share) overvaluation to 36% (35%). Giving the new investor participation without a cap leads to a dramatic increase in overvaluation, from 30% to 53%. Caps reduce that overvaluation only slightly in this example.[an] Overvaluation of 55% results if the new investor is exempted from converting in all down-exits. Even exemptions that bind only on low IPOs, such as those below 50%–75% of the PMV, lead to 47%–54% overvaluation. Valuation is also impacted by the size of the investment. A substantial investment of $I_B = $400 million leads to an overvaluation of 14%. At the other extreme, if the new investor only invested $10 million, the overvaluation rises to 43%.

To summarize, the conclusion is that contractual terms can have a quantitatively significant impact on the PMV. Gornall and Strebulaev (2020) apply this framework to the sample of 135 highly valued US startups (the so-called unicorns, that is, private companies with reported PMVs at or above $1 billion). They find that for this sample PMVs average 48% above fair value, with 14 being more than 100% above.

[an]The effect is small in this example because we consider a highly valued company for which successful exits are likely to be high-value IPOs and in which convertible preferred equity is automatically converted. For a smaller company, caps can have a large impact on overvaluation.

One challenge of the valuation framework we presented is that it does not consider the impact of future dilutive rounds. Gornall and Strebulaev (2021a) extend the framework to incorporate the prevalence of multiple rounds of financing. They find that while the pricing of most securities, in practice, is quantitatively relatively unaffected by future rounds, some specific contractual terms (such as liquidation multiples) become dramatically impaired by expectations of future issuance.

The contingent claims methodology is arguably more complicated than other valuation approaches. This complexity means that VC investors, in practice, apply it infrequently. At the same time, the variant of this methodology is now at the center of 409A tax appraisals, used by privately held companies to determine the cost of employee compensation (see Section 3.3).

We have concentrated on studying the influence of cash flow terms on valuation. Although control rights are of extreme importance in startups, the opacity of the VC environment and their qualitative nature has made valuing these terms challenging. While it is clear that control rights can benefit investors and result in nontrivial value transfers, the quantification of that value is, as of yet, not fully known. More research is needed on these, as well as other, issues related to startup valuation.

7 Conclusion

In this chapter, we have discussed the economics of contracting between startups and their investors. We have paid particular attention to the ways contractual terms reflect specific contracting frictions that startups, their founder–managers, and their investors face in practice. The opacity of the startup financing ecosystem has meant that many major theoretical and empirical insights have been developed only recently. Given the importance of startup financing for the broader economy and economic growth, we expect waves of further productive research soon. To that end, we have outlined many issues that warrant further investigation.

Acknowledgments

We would like to thank many researchers and industry practitioners for their valuable input. Gornall thanks the SSHRC for its support. Strebulaev thanks the Venture Capital Initiative at the Stanford Graduate School of Business.

References

Adams, R.B., 2017. Boards, and the directors who sit on them. In: The Handbook of the Economics of Corporate Governance, vol. 1. Elsevier, pp. 291–382.

Admati, A.R., Pfleiderer, P., 1994. Robust financial contracting and the role of venture capitalists. J. Financ. 49 (2), 371–402.

Agarwal, V., Barber, B.M., Cheng, S., Hameed, A., Yasuda, A., 2017. Private Company Valuations by Mutual Funds. Georgia State University (Unpublished working paper).

Aghion, P., Bolton, P., 1992. An incomplete contracts approach to financial contracting. Rev. Econ. Stud. 59 (3), 473–494.

Aghion, P., Holden, R., 2011. Incomplete contracts and the theory of the firm: what have we learned over the past 25 years? J. Econ. Perspect. 25 (2), 181–197.

Amit, R., Brander, J., Zott, C., 1998. Why do venture capital firms exist? Theory and Canadian evidence. J. Bus. Ventur. 13 (6), 441–466.

Arabsheibani, G., De Meza, D., Maloney, J., Pearson, B., 2000. And a vision appeared unto them of a great profit: evidence of self-deception among the self-employed. Econ. Lett. 67 (1), 35–41.

Baker, M., Gompers, P.A., 2003. The determinants of board structure at the initial public offering. J. Law Econ. 46 (2), 569–598.

Bartlett, R.P., 2006. Venture capital, agency costs, and the false dichotomy of the corporation. UCLA Law Rev. 54, 37–116.

Bartlett, R., Talley, E., 2017. Law and corporate governance. In: The Handbook of the Economics of Corporate Governance, vol. 1. Elsevier, pp. 177–234.

Bebchuk, L., Cohen, A., Ferrell, A., 2009. What matters in corporate governance? Rev. Financ. Stud. 22, 783–827.

Bengtsson, O., 2011. Covenants in venture capital contracts. Manag. Sci. 57 (11), 1926–1943.

Bengtsson, O., Sensoy, B.A., 2011. Investor abilities and financial contracting: evidence from venture capital. J. Financ. Intermed. 20 (4), 477–502.

Bengtsson, O., Sensoy, B.A., 2015. Changing the nexus: the evolution and renegotiation of venture capital contracts. J. Financ. Quant. Anal. 50 (3), 349–375.

Bergemann, D., Hege, U., 1998. Venture capital financing, moral hazard, and learning. J. Bank. Financ. 22 (6–8), 703–735.

Berglof, E., 1994. A control theory of venture capital finance. J. Econ. Organ. 10, 247.

Black, B.S., Gilson, R.J., 1998. Venture capital and the structure of capital markets: Banks versus stock markets. J. Financ. Econ. 47 (3), 243–277.

Black, F., Scholes, M., 1973. The pricing of options and corporate liabilities. J. Polit. Econ. 1981, 637–654.

Blaydon, C., 2002. Bury the ratchets. Ventur. Cap. J. 41, 11–12.

Bolton, P., Wang, N., Yang, J., 2019. Optimal contracting, corporate finance, and valuation with inalienable human capital. J. Financ. 74 (3), 1363–1429.

Bottazzi, L., Da Rin, M., Hellmann, T., 2008. Who are the active investors? Evidence from venture capital. J. Financ. Econ. 89 (3), 488–512.

Bottazzi, L., Da Rin, M., Hellmann, T., 2009. What is the role of legal systems in financial intermediation? Theory and evidence. J. Financ. Intermed. 18 (4), 559–598.

Broughman, B.J., 2010. The role of independent directors in startup firms. Utah Law Rev. 2010 (3), 461–510.

Broughman, B., Fried, J., 2010. Renegotiation of cash flow rights in the sale of VC-backed firms. J. Financ. Econ. 95 (3), 384–399.

Camerer, C., Lovallo, D., 1999. Overconfidence and excess entry: an experimental approach. Am. Econ. Rev. 89 (1), 306–318.

Chernenko, S., Lerner, J., Zeng, Y., 2021. Mutual funds as venture capitalists? Evidence from unicorns. Rev. Financ. Stud. 34 (5), 2362–2410.

Cochrane, J.H., 2005. The risk and return of venture capital. J. Financ. Econ. 75 (1), 3–52.

Cooper, A.C., Woo, C.Y., Dunkelberg, W.C., 1988. Entrepreneurs' perceived chances for success. J. Bus. Ventur. 3 (2), 97–108.

Cornelli, F., Yosha, O., 2003. Stage financing and the role of convertible securities. Rev. Econ. Stud. 70 (1), 1–32.

Coyle, J.F., Green, J.M., 2014. Contractual innovation in venture capital. Hastings Law J. 66, 133–182.

Damodaran, A., 2006. Damodaran On Valuation: Security Analysis for Investment and Corporate Finance. Wiley Finance.

Davis, J., Morse, A., Wang, X., 2020. The leveraging of Silicon Valley. University of North Carolina (Unpublished working paper).

Ewens, M., Farre-Mensa, J., 2020. The deregulation of the private equity markets and the decline in IPOs. Rev. Financ. Stud. 33 (12), 5463–5509.

Ewens, M., Malenko, N., 2020. Board Dynamics Over the Startup Life Cycle. (Unpublished working paper).

Ewens, M., Marx, M., 2018. Founder replacement and startup performance. Rev. Financ. Stud. 31 (4), 1532–1565.

Field, L.C., Karpoff, J.M., 2002. Takeover defenses of IPO firms. J. Financ. 57 (5), 1857–1889.

Fried, J.M., Ganor, M., 2006. Agency costs of venture capitalist control in startups. N. Y. Univ. Law Rev. 81, 967.

Fried, V.H., Bruton, G.D., Hisrich, R.D., 1998. Strategy and the board of directors in venture capital-backed firms. J. Bus. Ventur. 13 (6), 493–503.

Gao, H., He, Z., 2019. Board structure and role of outside directors in private firms. Eur. Financ. Manag. 25 (4), 861–907.

Gilson, R.J., Schizer, D.M., 2003. Understanding venture capital structure: a tax explanation for convertible preferred stock. Harv. Law Rev. 116 (3), 874–916.

Gompers, P.A., 1995. Optimal investment, monitoring, and the staging of venture capital. J. Financ. 50 (5), 1461–1489.

Gompers, P.A., Lerner, J., 1998. Venture capital distributions: short-run and long-run reactions. J. Financ. 53 (6), 2161–2183.

Gompers, P.A., Ishii, J., Metrick, A., 2003. Corporate governance and equity prices. Q. J. Econ. 118 (1), 107–156.

Gompers, P.A., Kovner, A., Lerner, J., Scharfstein, D., 2010. Performance persistence in entrepreneurship. J. Financ. Econ. 96 (1), 18–32.

Gompers, P.A., Gornall, W., Kaplan, S.N., Strebulaev, I.A., 2020. How do venture capitalists make decisions? J. Financ. Econ. 135 (1), 169–190.

Gompers, P.A., Gornall, W., Kaplan, S.N., Strebulaev, I.A., 2021. Venture capitalists and COVID-19. J. Financ. Quant. Anal. 56 (7), 2474–2499.

Gornall, W., Strebulaev, I.A., 2020. Squaring venture capital valuations with reality. J. Financ. Econ. 135 (1), 120–143.

Gornall, W., Strebulaev, I.A., 2021a. A Valuation Model of Venture Capital-Backed Companies With Multiple Financing Rounds. Stanford University. (Unpublished working paper). Available at SSRN 3725240.

Gornall, W., Strebulaev, I.A., 2021b. The Economic Impact of Venture Capital: Evidence From Public Companies. Stanford University, Stanford, CA (Unpublished working paper).

Gupta, A., Van Nieuwerburgh, S., 2021. Valuing private equity investments strip by strip. J. Financ. 76 (6), 3255–3307.

Harris, R.S., Jenkinson, T., Kaplan, S.N., 2014. Private equity performance: what do we know? J. Financ. 69 (5), 1851–1882.

Harris, R., Jenkinson, T., Kaplan, S., 2016. How do private equity investments perform compared to public equity? J. Invest. Manag. 14 (3), 1–24.

Hart, O., Moore, J., 1994. A theory of debt based on the inalienability of human capital. Q. J. Econ. 109 (4), 841–879.

Hellmann, T., 1998. The allocation of control rights in venture capital contracts. Rand J. Econ 29, 57–76.

Hochberg, Y.V., 2012. Venture capital and corporate governance in the newly public firm. Rev. Financ. 16 (2), 429–480.

Hochberg, Y.V., Ljungqvist, A., Lu, Y., 2007. Whom you know matters: venture capital networks and investment performance. J. Financ. 62 (1), 251–301.

Holmström, B., Tirole, J., 1998. Private and public supply of liquidity. J. Polit. Econ. 106 (1), 1–40.

Imbierowicz, B., Rauch, C., 2020. The Pricing of Private Assets: Mutual Fund Investments in 'Unicorn' Companies. Deutsche Bundesbank (Unpublished working paper).

Jenkinson, T., Rauch, C., Fu, D., 2019. How Do Financial Contracts Evolve for New Ventures. University of Oxford. (Unpublished working paper). Available at SSRN 3512304.

Jensen, M.C., Meckling, W.H., 1976. Theory of the firm: managerial behavior, agency costs and ownership structure. J. Financ. Econ. 3 (4), 305–360.

Kaplan, S.N., Schoar, A., 2005. Private equity performance: returns, persistence, and capital flows. J. Financ. 60 (4), 1791–1823.

Kaplan, S.N., Stromberg, P., 2001. Venture capitals as principals: contracting, screening, and monitoring. Am. Econ. Rev. 91 (2), 426–430.

Kaplan, S.N., Strömberg, P., 2003. Financial contracting theory meets the real world: an empirical analysis of venture capital contracts. Rev. Econ. Stud. 70 (2), 281–315.

Kaplan, S.N., Strömberg, P., 2004. Characteristics, contracts, and actions: evidence from venture capitalist analyses. J. Financ. 59 (5), 2177–2210.

Kaplan, S.N., Martel, F., Strömberg, P., 2007. How do legal differences and experience affect financial contracts? J. Financ. Intermed. 16 (3), 273–311.

Kaplan, S.N., Sensoy, B.A., Strömberg, P., 2009. Should investors bet on the jockey or the horse? Evidence from the evolution of firms from early business plans to public companies. J. Financ. 64 (1), 75–115.

Kirilenko, A.A., 2001. Valuation and control in venture finance. J. Financ. 56 (2), 565–587.

Kisseleva, K., Mjøs, A., Robinson, D.T., 2020. Firm Dynamics and the Returns to Early-Stage Investment. (Unpublished working paper).

Knowles, M.F., 2009. Report of the task force of the ABA section of business law corporate governance committee on delineation of governance roles and responsibilities. Bus. Lawyer 65 (1), 107–152.

Koller, T., Goedhart, M., Wessels, D., et al., 2010. Valuation: Measuring and Managing the Value of Companies. John Wiley and Sons.

Korteweg, A., 2019. Risk adjustment in private equity returns. Annu. Rev. Financ. Econ. 11, 131–152.

Korteweg, A., Nagel, S., 2016. Risk-adjusting the returns to venture capital. J. Financ. 71 (3), 1437–1470. https://doi.org/10.1111/jofi.12390.

Korteweg, A., Sorensen, M., 2010. Risk and return characteristics of venture capital-backed entrepreneurial companies. Rev. Financ. Stud. 23 (10), 3738–3772.

Korteweg, A., Sorensen, M., 2017. Skill and luck in private equity performance. J. Financ. Econ. 124 (3), 535–562.

LeClaire, J.R., Kendall, M.J., Taft, K.L., 2005. Watchmark ruling clarifies pay-to-play. Ventur. Cap. J. 45, 64. 64.

Lee, J.M., Hwang, B.-H., Chen, H., 2017. Are founder CEOs more overconfident than professional CEOs? Evidence from S&P 1500 companies. Strateg. Manag. J. 38 (3), 751–769.

Lerner, J., 1995. Venture capitalists and the oversight of private firms. J. Financ. 50 (1), 301–318.

Litvak, K., 2009. Venture capital limited partnership agreements: understanding compensation arrangements. Univ. Chic. Law Rev. 76, 161–218.

Merton, R.C., 1974. On the pricing of corporate debt: the risk structure of interest rates. J. Financ. 29 (2), 449–470.

Metrick, A., Yasuda, A., 2010. Venture Capital and the Finance of Innovation, second ed. John Wiley and Sons, Hoboken, NJ.

Myers, S.C., Majluf, N.S., 1984. Corporate financing and investment decisions when firms have information that investors do not have. J. Financ. Econ. 13 (2), 187–221.

Nanda, R., Rhodes-Kropf, M., 2019. Coordination frictions in venture capital syndicates. In: The Oxford Handbook of Entrepreneurship and Collaboration, pp. 351–371.

Puri, M., Zarutskie, R., 2012. On the life cycle dynamics of venture-capital-and non-venture-capital-financed firms. J. Financ. 67 (6), 2247–2293.

Rajan, R.G., 1992. Insiders and outsiders: the choice between informed and arm's-length debt. J. Financ. 47 (4), 1367–1400.

Rydqvist, K., 1987. Empirical Investigation of the Voting Premium. (Unpublished working paper).

Sahlman, W.A., 2009. A Method for Valuing High-Risk, Long-Term Investments: The "Venture Capital Method". Harvard Business School Publishing.

Schmidt, K.M., 2003. Convertible securities and venture capital finance. J. Financ. 58 (3), 1139–1166.

Wang, D., Pahnke, E.C., McDonald, R., 2022. The past is prologue? Venture-capital syndicates' collaborative experience and start-up exits. Acad. Manage. J. 65, 371–402.

Williams, S., 2017. Venture capital contract design: an empirical analysis of the connection between bargaining power and venture financing contract terms. Fordham J. Corp. Financ. Law 23, 105.

Zingales, L., 1995. What determines the value of corporate votes? Q. J. Econ. 110 (4), 1047–1073.

Venture capital and innovation

2

Josh Lerner[a],* and Ramana Nanda[b]

[a]Harvard Business School, Harvard University, Boston, MA, United States
[b]Department of Finance, Imperial College London, London, United Kingdom
*Corresponding author: e-mail addresses: josh@hbs.edu; jlerner@hbs.edu

Chapter outline

Venture capital has done much more, I think, to improve efficiency than anything.
—Kenneth Arrow (1995).

Handbook of the Economics of Corporate Finance, Volume 1, ISSN 2949-964X, https://doi.org/10.1016/bs.hecf.2023.02.002

1 Introduction

One area of consensus among academic economists and policymakers is the need for greater innovation. This concern is rooted in worries about the lagging rate of productivity growth in many Western nations. In the U.S., for instance, the productivity growth rate has reverted in last decade to the anemic levels seen from the late 1970s to the mid-1990s after a short surge in the late 1990s and early 2000s. This pattern is worrisome given the strong connections between innovation, productivity, and economic prosperity.

Moreover, several indications suggest that reigniting productivity growth in future years through innovation will be challenging. Research efficiency is falling sharply across fields (Bloom et al., 2020): ideas appear to be getting harder to find. In addition, large American firms are investing less in R&D, with the decline is concentrated in research (as opposed to development) expenditures (Arora et al., 2021). The roots of this change can be debated: is it a response to the unwillingness of the stock market to reward these activities (as those authors suggest) or to changing corporate incentive schemes (Lerner and Wulf, 2007)? Whatever the causes, the consequences are likely to be substantial, as basic research has long been seen as critical to economic vitality (Griliches, 1986).

Against this sober backdrop, the venture capital (VC) industry appears to be a bright spot in the global innovation landscape. Over the last decade, the amount of capital deployed by VC investors and the number of startups receiving funding has grown substantially (see Fig. 1 for data on U.S. activity[a]). Globally, over $600 billion has been estimated by CrunchBase to be deployed in 2021. This is more than twice the mean level between, 2018 and 2020, and some ten times more than between 2011 and 2013.[b] Entirely new financial intermediaries such as accelerators, crowd funding platforms, and "super angels" have emerged at the early stage of new venture finance, competing with traditional early-stage funds. Meanwhile, mutual funds, hedge funds, and sovereign wealth funds have deployed large sums of capital into more mature, but still private, venture capital backed firms.

In this chapter, we review the research documenting the positive impact that venture capital has on driving innovation. However, despite the optimism articulated by Ken Arrow in the quotation above and by many practitioners before and since, VC also has very real limitations in advancing substantial technological change. As we noted in Lerner and Nanda (2020), there are three issues in particular that seem worthy of further academic research: (i) the very narrow band of technological

---

[a]Creating comparable data series for VC globally over such an extended period is exceedingly challenging. The rate of VC growth globally, however, is certainly greater than that of the U.S. alone. The National Venture Capital Association estimates, for instance, that the U.S. share of world venture capital financing has fallen from 80% in 2006 ti under 50% in, 2018–20 (https://nvca.org/wp-content/uploads/2021/08/NVCA-2021-Yearbook.pdf).
[b]https://news.crunchbase.com/news/global-2020-funding-and-exit/; https://news.crunchbase.com/news/q3-2021-global-venture-capital-report-record-funding-monthly-recap/.

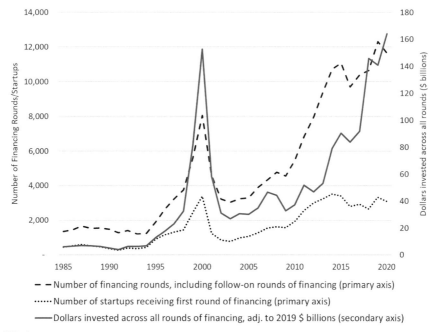

FIG. 1

Evolution of the U.S. VC Industry between 1985 and 2020. Notes: This exhibit reports for the U.S. the number of unique startups receiving an initial round of financing (Primary Axis), the total number of financing rounds, including follow-on rounds of financing (Primary Axis) and the total investment across all rounds of financing in billions of dollars (Secondary Axis) for the institutional VC industry for each year from 1985 to 2020.

Data are compiled from the U.S. National Venture Capital Association's yearbooks and related publications. This is an updated version of a graph in Lerner Josh, Ramana Nanda, 2020. Venture capital's role in financing innovation: what we know and how much we still need to learn. J. Econ. Perspect. 34 (3), 237–261.

innovations that fit the requirements of institutional VC investors; (ii) the relatively small number of VC investors who hold, and shape the direction of, a substantial fraction of capital that is deployed into financing radical technological change, and (iii) the relaxation of the intense emphasis on corporate governance by VCs in recent years. While academics and practitioners have effectively articulated the strengths of the venture model, we believe much less attention has been devoted to these limitations. Yet these features are likely to continue having important real effects on the rate and direction of innovation in the broader economy and are thus too important to ignore.

We begin by tracing the growth of the institutional venture capital industry, and the reasons behind its growth. We highlight how technological and institutional changes in the past two decades have narrowed the focus and concentrated the capital invested by VCs. We highlight recent research examining the potential real effects that these changes can have. We summarizing some recent thoughts of ours about potential adaptations to the venture capital model might enable a broader base of ideas and technologies to receive risk capital.

2 A brief look at the history of institutional venture capital[c]

Entrepreneurs have sought funds to pursue their risky ideas for centuries before the modern VC industry. Indeed, many of its key elements, such as the organization and incentive structures of VC partnerships as well as the use of risk-sharing contracts, can be traced as far as Genoese merchants in the 15th century and American whaling voyages in the 19th century. Other have pointed even further back to the Byzantine cheokoinonia or the Muslim muqarada. The most ambitious have pointed back four millennia to The Code of Hammurabi, which laid out the essential ground rules for these activities (Astuti, 1933; de Roover, 1963; Lopez and Raymond, 1955; Nicholas, 2019).

Whatever the historic antecedents, like many great successes, the modern venture capital has also many putative inventors. J.H. Whitney, established immediately after World War II, has described itself as the first venture firm. So has Bessemer Venture Partners, which began investing the Phipps' family money in 1911.

Most historians, however, trace the origins of the institutional venture capital industry to 1946, when Harvard Business School professor Georges Doriot formed the American Research & Development Corporation.

The genesis of this fund dated to 1945, when a committee of leading Boston citizens came together to consider the challenges of the region and the nation in the post-War era. In their deliberations, the committee was largely motivated by fears about innovation and economic growth. Prior to World War II, the bulk of the financing for entrepreneurial ventures—which were typically too risky for banks to lend to or to go public on a stock exchange—were wealthy individuals. But these individuals were frequently poor investors, being distracted by their far-flung business interests and their wide-ranging other interests. The economy needed new firms, the committee felt, to commercialize the promising new technologies developed during the War. But without some additional avenues to raise financing, they feared, these new entities would not get off the ground. The failure to raise capital would depress the economic health of the region and the nation, and might even lead to a relapse to the debilitating conditions seen in the 1930s. While proposals for aggressive government intervention to fund entrepreneurs had been floated in Washington, the committee objected to these ideas on both practical and philosophical grounds, instead proposing a business to finance new businesses.

---

[c]The reader desiring a more detailed perspective can study the several volumes on the industry's evolution, including Ante (2008), Gompers and Lerner (2001b), and Nicholas (2019).

Within a year, Georges Doriot had assumed the leadership of ARD. Much has been written about Doriot's many accomplishments: an influential Harvard Business School professor, a Brigadier General who played a key role in designing the supply chain for U.S. troops in World War II, a co-founder of INSEAD, the leading European business school, and the like, but surely laying out the template for modern venture capital investing was one of his greatest feats. From its earliest communications, ARD emphasized three aspects of its role:

- Selection. Unlike a bank, which might fund one-half or one-third of the firms that walked in the door, ARD set the bar extremely high. Typically, it funded only 1% to 2% of the business plans it received. Even then, it typically made small investments, with additional funds conditional on the firm making satisfactory progress in advancing its ideas.
- Oversight. Unlike a banker, who would be satisfied with quarterly statements, Doriot emphasized intensive involvement in the companies in which ARD invested. As the firm noted in its promotional material, "The Corporation usually will be represented on the Board of Directors, will assist in the procurement of personnel for key positions, and will endeavor to make available the best possible … assistance." One aspect of this tight governance was that investments were often structured as a preferred debt note, in addition to common stock, which gave the venture capitalists more power—and put more pressure on the entrepreneurs—than had ARD instead just held common stock.
- Value Add. Doriot realized that the path to success for new ventures was not easy. Frequently, these firms lacked the track record or the connections to get attention from potential strategic partners, investment banks, and other actors. By pairing these firms with seasoned mentors who had both credibility and networks, he hoped to give the firms "stamps of approval" that could enhance their probability of success. As he stated, "A team made up of the younger generation, with courage and inventiveness, together with older men of wisdom and experience, should bring success."

The other unquestioned father of the modern industry was General William Draper, a long-serving military officer and occasional industrialist. H founded Draper, Gaither and Anderson (DGA) in 1958 along with Rand Corporation founder Rowan Gaither and Air Force general Frederick Anderson. DGA was notable for its location (it was one of the pioneering firms in Silicon Valley) but particularly for its structure. With a small number of private backers—of its $6 million fund, the venerable investment bank Lazard Frères contributed $1.5 million and the Rockefellers and two other leading families nearly as much—it eschewed the publicly traded structure of earlier funds. Rather it adopted the model that would become standard in the industry, the limited partnership.

In making this choice, the partners were swayed by the difficulties that ARD had faced: for much of its first 15 years, Doriot had struggled to raise capital. After the $500 thousand it had raised from its initial backers, additional funding had been slow to come by. Its profile as a non-dividend-paying entity with losses stretching out for the foreseeable future did not excite many institutions. Moreover, the frequent articles about ARD's social goals of promoting economic development and entrepreneurship raised concerns among investors that financial returns were second order. Early on, a decision was made to raise money by taking ARD public. Even then, no investment bank was willing to underwrite the offering, and it was largely sold off in small blocks to retail investors on a "best efforts" basis. Over the course of the 1950s, the firm frequently dealt with disillusioned investors in the face of portfolio companies that took longer than expected to mature and market turbulence.

While much of this dissatisfaction may have reflected the naiveté of inexperienced investors, even knowledgeable investors criticized ARD's tendency to stick with troubled firms too long. Doriot defended himself spiritedly: "We are really doctors of childhood diseases here. When bankers or brokers tell me I should sell an ailing company I ask them, 'would you sell a child running a temperature of 104?'" But the experience of "zombie" firms like Ionics raised the question of whether the evergreen structure that characterized the ARD fund was appropriate: once the capital was raised, ARD had no obligation to ever return the capital, and could keep on investing until the firm ran out of money or was acquired.

The limited partnership structure that DGA introduced to the venture capital industry addressed several concerns. By raising funds upfront, the venture capitalist received all the money he or she need for the life of the fund. There would be no need to go "back to the well" every year or two for another tranche of capital, as Doriot had been required to. (The one exception related to the fact that investors in venture capital limited partnerships are not typically been required to put in all the capital that they commit to the fund up-front. Rather they promise the funds, and then the general partners draw down the capital as needed. In extraordinary periods, such as after the financial crisis of 2008, there may be real worry that the investors cannot or will not meet their commitments.)

Moreover, the new firm's founders felt that the ARD structure had brought about excessively conservative thinking. As Pete Bancroft, one of the junior investment professionals at DGA noted of their predecessors, "They did not dare as greatly or as well." Much of this could be attributed to the compensation scheme at the Boston firm: everyone, including Doriot, received a salary—there was no explicit link of compensation to performance. Instead, at DGA, not only were the partners major investors (contributing $700,000 of the capital, or more than 10% of the funds), but they also got a significant profit share. In particular, the DGA partners received 40% of the capital gains (well above the 20% to 30% standard in the industry today), in addition to their proportionate share of the amount going to the limited partners.

But at the same time, there were advantages of the new structure for the limited partners. The venture capitalists only raised funds for a set period, typically 7 to 10 years, with the possibility of an extension for a few more. This stipulation provided a distinct time limit for the venture capitalists' activity: there would be no nurturing sick firms indefinitely. Moreover, the investors had the assurance that, ultimately, they would get whatever money remained back. While it would be very hard to dislodge the manager of an "evergreen" fund like ARD without an expensive battle for control of the board, limited partnerships simply wind up. Unless a venture firm can convince investors to ante up for a new fund, they will go out of business.

The partnership structure also addressed investors' concerns by drawing a sharp line between the limited and general partner. The limited partners were limited in the sense that their liability was capped by the amount they invested: if the fund invested in a biotechnology company whose drug unfortunately ended up killing several people during a clinical trial, the general partners running the fund would face many millions of dollars of claims for damages, but the investors would not. This was important to many investors, as an investor putting a few million dollars into a venture fund does not want to have to worry about the risk of losing many, many millions more if something goes wrong with a high-risk investment.

At the same time, the fact that the general partner needed to return to the limited partner for funds meant that the institutional and individual investors who provided capital the funds could have a lot of power. Bill Draper, General Draper's son and the eventual founder of Sutter Hill and a number of other venture groups, related how while working for his father at DGA, they were approached about investing in the first condominium development in Hawaii. The investment appeared to be highly promising, and proved to be highly successful. But mid-way through the due diligence process, Draper was summoned to Rockefeller Center, and dressed down by one of the family office's partners for investing outside of their promised mandate and expertise. He was told in no uncertain terms that the Rockefellers could access such through much more knowledgeable, real estate-focused intermediaries. As a result, they were forced to turn down the investment, which ultimately provided a higher return than any of the deals that ended in DGA's portfolio.

This give-and-take between limited and general partners in venture firms has been part of the territory since the industry's early days. In part, the features in contracts between venture groups and their investors are driven by the need for oversight: less-established groups, where there is more uncertainty about the ability of the investment team, tend to grant the general partner more control, such as terms that limit the kinds of deals the fund can invest in or other activities that the venture capitalists can engage in.

But the numbers of venture capitalists and investors are small, so the structure of these deals is also shaped by supply and demand conditions. A sudden increase in demand for venture capital investing services—if, say, institutional investors suddenly increase their allocation to venture capital funds—should increase bargaining power in favor of the venture investors. Only a small number of venture capitalists may be raising a fund at any particular time, and these firms are likely to be differentiated by size, industry focus, location, and reputation. Meanwhile, managers who allocate alternative investments for institutions often operate under limitations about the types of funds in which they can invest (for instance, rules that prohibit investments into first funds raised by venture organizations) and are pressured to meet allocation targets by end of the fiscal year. As a result, venture groups whose services are in more demand—whether because of a hot market or a successful track record—enter into agreements with more freedom and also with higher levels of fees.

Undoubtedly, the creation of the limited partnership represented an important breakthrough, which addressed many of the drawbacks of evergreen funds such as ARD and paved the way for the modern industry we see today.

Several of the most prominent venture capital firms of today, such as Sequoia Capital, Kleiner Perkins, and New Enterprise Associates were formed in the early-to-mid 1970s to invest in what would become the burgeoning semi-conductor and biotechnology industries. However, the industry began to take off and truly institutionalize in the early 1980s, when pension funds began to allocate some of their capital towards this relatively new asset class.[d] While the allocations of these institutions to private capital in the 1980s were initially very modest, even a small allocation of such a large pool led to very rapid growth of the sector. This transition was followed by the entry of public pensions into this space a decade later, and later by pension and sovereign funds around the globe as these policy changes were replicated elsewhere. Initially, neither private nor public pension funds invested in a dramatically different manner than the institutions and families that preceded them. But their impact was important because of their sheer size, which dwarfed that of the other early investors such as university endowments and insurers.

These funds have financed repeated waves of technological innovation. These include the semi-conductor revolution and diffusion of mainframe computing in the 1960s, the advent of personal computing in the early 1980s, the biotechnology revolution of the 1980s, and introduction of the Internet and e-commerce in the 1990s. VC's role in financing technological revolutions continued in the 2000s, including the widespread diffusion of "smart" mobile communications technologies and the rise of cloud computing. These technologies enabled the rapid growth of products and services catering to both businesses and consumers.

One important aspect enabled by these technologies was the ability to connect and employ widely dispersed sellers of services and goods (frequently dubbed the "sharing economy," and manifested by companies such as Airbnb and Uber). A second enabled substantial improvements in efficiency to existing services and an ability to replicate existing services at much lower price points (e.g., salesforce.com and other companies providing software to businesses and the plethora of "Mobile Apps" available for consumers). Third, several companies replicated business models successful in the U.S. in new markets (with the Chinese companies

---

[d]Much of this change can be traced back to the clarification in of an obscure rule articulated by the Employment Retirement Income Security Act (ERISA) that had originally stated that private pension managers had to invest their funds' resources with the care of a "prudent man"; that is, carefully and conservatively. In early 1979, the Department of Labor ruled that pension-fund managers could take into account portfolio diversification in determining the prudence of an investment. Thus, the ruling implied that the Labor Department would not view allocation of a small fraction of a portfolio to illiquid funds as imprudent, even if a number of companies in the venture capitalist's portfolio failed. That clarification flung the door open for corporate pension funds to invest in venture capital.

Alibaba and Tencent being the most dramatic exemplars). An important consequence of the third approach was the dramatic increase in VC investment in Asia over this period (itself a topic worthy of much closer study).

But the boom in the 2010s was different from earlier cycles in some important respects. The foremost change was the extent to which new types of financial intermediaries entered to fund startup ventures at their earliest and most mature private stages, effectively "squeezing" traditional VC investors and leading the venture capital industry to evolve in important ways.

In examining the evolution of early stage financing of VC-backed ventures, Ewens et al. (2018) document how technological advancements also substantially lowered the cost of starting new businesses in the software and services sectors. The much lower starting capital for new ventures in these sectors implied a fall in the cost of experimentation associated with learning about their potential, leading early stage investors to be more willing to fund less proven (but potentially higher return) ideas and entrepreneurial teams in these sectors. This "spray and pray" investment approach—where financiers provided a small amount of funding and limited governance to a larger number of startups—also created an increasingly important role for business accelerators, which sought to systemize the mentoring and development of inexperienced, first-time entrepreneurs (Hochberg, 2016).

The substantially smaller quantum of capital required to get a business of the ground also led to more opportunities for angel (or individual) investors. These years saw the growth of angel groups (Kerr et al., 2014b) and the institutionalization of angel investors who began to raise small funds (sometimes referred to as "Super Angels"). There was also a rapid growth of online platforms such as AngelList, where groups of individuals could back a lead investor who aimed to replicate some of the systematic diligence and monitoring functions played by traditional venture groups (Agrawal et al., 2016). The contemporaneous rise of crowdfunding and peer-to-peer platforms has had a more mixed legacy, enabling widespread participation in financing startups by the populace, but many of which were also plagued by fraud.

The highly visible successful ventures such as Facebook, LinkedIn, Salesforce and Uber, together with historically low interest rates and frustration with the high fees charged by VCs, also led to sovereign wealth funds, hedge funds, mutual funds, and other public market investors entering venture investing directly (Fang et al., 2015; Lerner et al., 2022). These investors have become major players in the later rounds of companies, participating in the financing of startups after one or more rounds of venture financing. Ewens and Farre-Mensa (2020) estimate that between 2014 and 2016, over three-quarters of the late-stage VC funding came from such non-traditional investors. Indeed, much of the growth in capital that has come from these later stage investors has gone to "unicorns," defied as privately held firms with nominal valuations in excess of one billion dollars. But in the past few years, this pattern has spread as well to the early-stage market, particularly the rise of hedge fund Tiger Global, which has been an aggressive investor in young firms.

Contemporaneous with the increase in direct financings by sovereign funds and others has been the rise of "mega-funds" (VC funds that are substantially larger than historical averages), often financed from the same pools of capital. The most salient of these has been SoftBank's Vision Fund.[e] At the time of its first closing on $93 billion in May 2017 (with an anchor investment of $45 billion from the Saudi Public Investment Fund), it was already 30 times larger than the previous largest VC fund raised (New Enterprise Associates 2015 Fund XV). Softbank would ultimately go onto raise $100 billion for its first fund, and at the end of 2019 was seeking a roughly similar amount for a second fund. This rapid increase in capital deployed by non-traditional investors at 'pre-IPO' stage of venture capital backed firms has also triggered venture firms to raise very large funds, such as the, 2018 $8 billion Sequoia Capital Global Growth Fund III.

3 How the venture capital model boosts innovation

Despite this growth in capital committed to VC over the past four decades, the pool of capital currently under management by US VCs remains small in comparison to the several trillion dollars managed by the broader US private equity asset class, which include buyout and distressed debt funds. Nevertheless, VC is associated with some of the most high-growth and influential firms in the economy. More generally, although comprising less than 0.5% of firms that are born each year (Puri and Zarutskie, 2012), VC-backed firms represent a very significant share of innovative companies that graduate to the public marketplace.

One way illustrate this contention is to examine the impact of venture investing on public firms (Gornall and Strebulaev, 2021). If we look at the subset of firms which were founded after 1968, went public after 1978, and remain traded today (consistent information on venture-backed firms that were acquired or went out of business is hard to find), these firms have had an unmistakable effect on the U.S. economy. In mid-2021, these "newer" firms), venture-backed firms made up one-half of the total number of newer public firms and 77% by value at the end of 2020. But its impact on innovation is truly extraordinary. These firms make up 92% of all R&D spending in 2020, and 93% of all value-weighted patents in 2018.

This success is no accident, as the academic literature has shown. Much work has focused in the tools employed by venture capitalists to monitor and govern, such as the use of staged financing (Gompers, 1995; Neher, 1999), securities that have state-contingent cash flow and control rights (Cornelli and Yosha, 2003; Hellmann, 1998; Kaplan and Strömberg, 2003, 2004), and the active role on VC investors on boards of these firms (Hellmann and Puri, 2000, 2002; Lerner, 1995).

To highlight some of the most important papers in this literature, Kaplan and Strömberg (2004) have examined how venture capitalists think about prospective investments, as well as the dance between investors and entrepreneurs. Drawing from

---

[e]This combination of new entrants deploying small amounts of capital at the early stage with the rise of mega-funds is reflected in fund size statistics: The size of the median fund raised by VC investors has fallen, but there has been an increase in the average size of funds raised by VC firms.

the memoranda that venture funds use to evaluate individual deals, they show that while external factors (such as the evolution of the market) are certainly important, typically the most critical considerations driving whether to invest or note come back to the personal considerations that Doriot highlighted: the depth of the entrepreneur's knowledge, her behavior, willingness to work hard, and ethics.

Meanwhile, the amount of control the VC firm varies. Sometimes VC funding comes with seemingly onerous provisions, regarding the ownership of the equity, control of the board, and division of the proceeds if the firm is liquidated. But these features are not simply complex and onerous for their own stake. Kaplan and Strömberg (2003) show how, consistent with Doriot's vision, that the features of these agreements address the challenges inherent in financing and overseeing young, high-risk entities: Many of the prerogatives the venture capitalists enjoy depend upon the performance of the firm. If the firm does poorly, their venture investors' rights to seats on the board and votes on key decisions will grow to the point where they have full control. (The investors' share of the proceeds in case of the firm being wrapped up will also frequently increase.) As the firm does better, more and more of the control reverts to the entrepreneur. If the firm does very well, and goes public with an attractive valuation, the venture investors will retain their equity stake, but all their other rights will disappear.

The key motivating principle, Kaplan and Stromberg argue, is that venture capitalists only need to take control when things are uncertain or problematic, and will be willing to relinquish it in other circumstances. Swings in control are even more dramatic in cases where uncertainty might be particularly high, such as early-stage firms. Outside directors can play important mediating roles when conflicts do arise (Ewens and Malenko, 2020).

One of the most common control mechanisms used by venture capitalists is the meting out of financing in discrete stages over time, during which the prospects for the firm are periodically reevaluated. As Neher (1999) highlights, staged capital infusion keeps the owner/manager on a tight leash and reduces potential losses from bad decisions. The duration of time between individual rounds of financing varies with the riskiness of the venture and the investors' the need to gather information. Gompers (1995), for instance, shows that early-stage firms receive significantly less money per round. Ventures with more hard assets like factories and equipment— where presumably it is easier to determine what the firm is doing with the funds—receive larger and less frequent financing rounds, while those where the main value is just ideas get small rounds. These results suggest the important monitoring and information generating roles played by venture capitalists, who want to make sure their investment is safe.

The advice and support provided by venture capitalists is often embodied by their role on the firm's board of directors. Lerner (1995) shows that over half the firms in the sample have a venture director with an office within 60 miles of their headquarters, suggesting the hands-on monitoring that these investors provide. Again, there's a clear move towards more control as the entrepreneurial venture gets riskier. In times of crisis—when top manager at an entrepreneurial firm is replaced—venture capitalists are far more likely to be added to the board than when things are going well; a pattern not seen among the other directors.

Another stream of early research has documented the strong persistence in performance of VC funds (Kaplan and Schoar, 2005), which has continued to hold true even as performance persistence in buyout funds has declined (Harris et al., 2020). This might be felt to be consistent with the presence of some innate ability on the part of venture investors. Related work has examined the drivers of this persistence and the degree to which it might be a consequence of differences in skill across investors (Ewens and Rhodes-Kropf, 2015; Hochberg et al., 2007; Korteweg and Sorensen, 2017; Nanda et al., 2020; Sorensen, 2007).

A third stream of work, most relevant for this essay, has documented the rapid growth and economic impact of venture-backed firms (Puri and Zarutskie, 2012). A related literature has sought to distinguish between the value added provided by VCs from their ability to simply select the most promising ventures (Kortum and Lerner, 2000; Hellmann and Puri, 2000. Bernstein et al., 2016; Chemmanur et al., 2011).

Before turning to a discussion of the specific papers, it is worth noting that determining whether financiers help firms is rife with identification challenges. Resolving the "chicken or the egg" dilemma—whether these investors catalyze growth or simply select fast-growing firms to fund—is challenging. For example, venture capital investors claim that the advice and monitoring that they provide to their portfolio companies significantly improve their performance. Many entrepreneurs, however, are skeptical of these claims, and believe that they would have been equally successful without their financiers' assistance. Similarly, it appears that the pace of innovation at many young firms slows after they list on public markets. But does the transition to public equity markets lead firms to stop innovating (as writings on investor short-termism by authors from Michael Porter to Jeremy Stein have suggested), or is it merely that firms go public at their innovative peak?

The impact on innovation of venture capitalists seems particularly substantial. Hellmann and Puri (2000) show this by comparing 170 recently formed firms in Silicon Valley, including both venture-backed and non-venture firms. Using questionnaire responses, they find evidence that venture capital financing is related to product market strategies and outcomes of start-ups. Firms that are pursuing what they term an "innovator strategy" are significantly more likely and faster to obtain venture capital. The presence of a venture capitalist is also associated with a significant reduction in the time taken to bring a product to market, especially for innovators (probably because these firms can focus more on innovating and less on raising money). Furthermore, firms are more likely to list obtaining venture capital as a significant milestone in the lifecycle of the company as compared to other financing events. The results suggest significant interrelations between investor type and product market dimensions, and a role of venture capital in encouraging innovative companies, but identifying a causal effect is challenging with these data.

Kortum and Lerner (2000) visit the same question in a different way, looking at whether the participation of venture capitalists in any given industry over the past few decades led to more or less innovation. Venture funding does have a strong positive impact on innovation. On average, a dollar of venture capital appears to be three to four times more potent in stimulating patenting than a dollar of traditional corporate R&D. The estimates therefore suggest that venture capital, even though it averaged less than 3% of corporate R&D in the United States from 1983 to 1992, is responsible for a much greater share—perhaps 10%—of U.S. industrial innovations in this decade. In short, it seems that venture model does appear to have a substantial economic development impact.

A third example is the work of Bernstein, Giroud, and Townsend. As noted above, while there have been a number of earlier analyses of the relationships between entrepreneurs and their investors, discerning whether venture capitalists simply seek out promising firms or actually accelerate innovative activities poses challenging identification concerns. Most of the earlier studies has shown that the presence of proxies for venture capitalist governance—whether board seats on the firms of their portfolio, the staging of capital, or the use of preferred stock and other contractual tools—increase with proxies for the need for governance (e.g., early-stage firms, cases where CEOs depart the company, etc.). But the extent to which the venture firms take advantage of their greater capacity to provide governance, and the consequences of the decisions to do so, were difficult to discern with the earlier methodologies.

In this paper, the authors exploit the strongly local nature of these investments, which in turn reflects the importance of soft information when monitoring and assessing start-up firms. In order to generate exogenous variation, they use the introduction of new airline routes from central hubs of venture firms (e.g., new routes by United Airlines from San Francisco). This paper shows that the introduction of new routes appears to have a first-order impact on the outcomes of the firms already in their portfolio, this providing convincing evidence that venture governance does matter.

4 Limitations of venture capital model as a spur to innovation

The growth of the venture capital market in the past decade, however, cannot blind us to its limitations as an engine of innovation. We would argue that if the reader anticipates that the growth of venture capital will address the challenge of lagging innovation delineated in the introductory paragraphs, these hopes are excessively rosy. And the changes delineated in the previous section will likely exacerbate, not ameliorate, these challenges.

Much less academic work, however, has focused on the limitations inherent in the venture capital model, many of which may have been exacerbated by the dramatic changes in recent years. We lay out below what we see three distinct areas of concern about venture capital and is ability to successfully spur innovations. While the discussion must be inherently more speculative given the relatively limited work done in this area, we suggest that these questions would well benefit from scholarly attention in the years to come:

4.1 Focus on an extremely narrow slice of technological innovation

Despite the substantial growth of VC in the four decades since the "prudent man" law, in many respects VC still touches a tiny share of firms in the U.S. economy. Even today, only a few thousand new firms each year raise formal VC for the first time, as compared to over annual 500,000 business starts in the U.S. This can be compared to about 16% of new firms in the U.S. that raise external bank financing. Even among high potential firms and those engaged in innovation, Farre-Mensa et al. (2020) found that only 7% of firms that filed for a patent went on to raise institutional venture capital VC. These disparities are likely even more extreme in other nations, where the venture industry is less mature.

Beyond the numbers, VC has been focused on, and has historically only successfully invested in, a very narrow slice of technological innovation, especially information technology and to some extent biotechnology. This focus has narrowed further towards software-oriented businesses in recent years.

Examining the portfolio of a single venture group four decades apart demonstrates the extent of this focus and narrowing.[f] Charles River Ventures was founded by three seasoned executives from the operating and investment worlds in 1970. Within its first 4 years, it had almost completely invested its nearly $6 million first fund into 18 firms. These included classes of technologies that would be comfortably at home in a typical venture capitalist's portfolio today: a start-up designing computer systems for hospitals (Health Data Corporation), a software company developing automated credit scoring systems (American Management Systems), and a firm seeking to develop an electric car (Electromotion, which, alas, proved to be a few decades before its time). Other companies, however, were much more unusual by today's venture standards: for instance, start-ups seeking to provide birth control for dogs (Agrophysics), high-strength fabrics for balloons and other demanding applications (N.F. Doweave), and turnkey systems for pig farming (International Farm Systems). In total, only eight of the initial portfolio companies—or less than half— related to communications, information technology, or human health care.

The fund's portfolio looks very different in December 2021. Of the firms listed as investments, about 90% are classified as being related to information technology comprising social networks, applications for consumers, and software and services related to enhancing business productivity. Approximately 5% of investments are classified as being related to health care, materials and energy.

What has happened to Charles River's portfolio reflects the industry at large.[g] As can be seen from Fig. 2, computer hardware (including semi-conductors, telecommunications and networking equipment, and electronics/instrumentation) dominated

---

[f]This example is drawn from Banks and Liles (1975) and "Charles River Ventures," http://www.crv.com/.

[g]It is difficult to trace accurately fine-grained categories over 35 years because new categories of firms (such as social networks and digital media) have emerged. Moreover, software firms related to industry verticals do not always fit neatly into a single classification. For example, Uber can be classified as transportation, but also as a consumer service. With these caveats in place, our approach is to categorize firms into four broad classifications that are more comparable over time – computer software, computer hardware, business and consumer products/services, and biopharmaceuticals and medical devices.

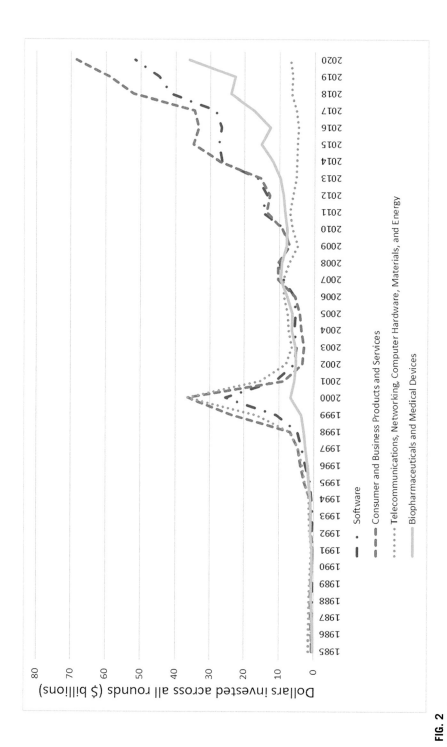

FIG. 2

Venture Capital Investment (in billions of dollars) into U.S. Startups between 1985 and 2020, by Sector. Notes: This exhibit reports investment by VC investors into U.S. startup between 1985 and 2020, broken down by four distinct sectors. Data are drawn from the U.S. National Venture Capital Association's yearbooks and related resources. Consumer and Business Products and Services refer to startups in the following categories: Business Products and Services, Consumer Products and Services, Financial Services, Healthcare Services, IT Services, Media and Entertainment and Retailing/Distribution. Telecommunications, Networking, Computer Hardware and Energy refers to startups in the following categories: Computers and Peripherals, Electronics/Instrumentation, Networking and Equipment, Semiconductors, Telecommunications, Industrial/Energy and Other. Biopharmaceuticals and Medical Devices refers to startups in the following categories: Biopharmaceuticals and Medical Devices and Equipment.

the investments made by VCs in 1985, accounting for over half the dollars invested into startups by VCs. Software and service startups accounted for about 40% of the investments in 1985 while pharmaceuticals and medical devices represented most of the remaining 15%. The exhibit also shows the large shift in focus of VCs away from computer hardware towards software and service businesses over the past 35 years, with a particular acceleration in the past 10–15 years. Biopharmaceuticals and medical devices have maintained approximately the same share of startups receiving funding. However, the chart masks the fact that this investment now comes from fewer VC firms specializing in this sector, as opposed to being part of a broader portfolio of investments for a large number of more generalist VCs.

This industry shift is rational, given the importance of the attractive returns to venture capitalists. VCs are particularly eager to avoid "black holes," which require huge cash inflows before discovering that the technology does not work or the market demand is not there. Thus, funds naturally gravitate to investments in startups where they can learn quickly and cheaply whether the business is likely to be promising, and if they receive good news, reinvest further to finance the scale-up or sell it for an attractive valuation. Software and service businesses, with their lack of technology risk, strong network effects, and increasing returns to scale are amenable to this approach. Clean energy, new drugs, new materials, and many other sectors are less so.

This harsh conclusion is underscored by computations by Sand Hill Econometrics. This firm creates a series of indexes (described in Hall and Woodward, 2004), which seek to capture the gross returns (that is, before management fees and profit sharing) from investments in all active venture transactions in a given category. Their calculation suggest that an investment in the software deals between December 1991 and September 2019 would have yielded an annualized gross return of 24% per annum, far greater than hardware (17%), healthcare (13%), or cleantech (2%). This index further shows that the divergence in these categories has been particularly stark over the prior decade. This in large part explains the number of new firms financed in each sector over the same 35-year period, in particular the dramatic shift towards a focus on software and online service firms.

These considerations highlight that venture capital cannot be seen as a cure-all to the need for more innovation. While venture funding is very efficacious in stimulating a certain kind of innovative business, the scope is highly limited. And to the extent that the enthusiasm for venture capital that would otherwise go to funding innovative expenditures in other settings (e.g., corporate research labs), technological progress in other areas may be "crowded out." One area that has attracted particular concern among U.S. defense officials and others is often called "tough tech"—areas like advanced materials and clean energy that require very long times to develop, yet can yield substantial social returns.

4.2 Concentration of capital in the hands of few non-representative investors

In addition to being focused on a handful of technological areas, venture activity is very concentrated in terms of who invests these dollars. This point might initially appear puzzling, as the National Venture Capital Association estimates that there

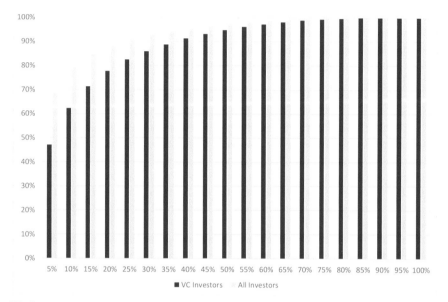

FIG. 3

Concentration of Capital in the U.S. Venture Capital Industry. Notes: This exhibit documents the concentration of capital held by VCs investing in the U.S. Using data from the Pitchbook database, we first created a list of all institutional VC investors that made at least one investment into a US headquartered startup between January 1, 2018 and December 31, 2018. For these investors, we examined the total amount of capital they had raised in the prior 5 years, from 2014 to 2018, amounting to approximately $284 billion raised by 985 investors. As noted above, there has been an increase in the number of non-VC investors putting capital into startups at later stages in recent years, the most notable of which is Softbank's vision fund. Taking such non-traditional investors who also raise funds into account increases the number of investors under consideration to 1074. The x-axis ranks each of these two sets of investors (VC investors and All investors) by the amount of capital they raised between 2014 and 2018. The dark blue bars trace the cumulative capital raised by VC investors and the light blue bars trace the cumulative capital raised by all investors over this period. For example, the top 5% of VC raised just under half of all the capital raised in this period, while the top 5% of all investors raised over two-thirds of the capital raised in this period.

are over 1000 venture capital funds in the U.S. alone at the end of 2020. But as can be seen from Fig. 3 and as we reported in Lerner and Nanda (2020), a few very large VC firms hold the vast majority of capital.

Documenting concentration in the capital invested by VC firms is difficult, because VCs frequently co-invest with each other in the same round of financing, and the databases recording this activity only report the total amount funded rather than breaking this down in terms of the share coming from each investor. To provide a more accurate picture of concentration, therefore, we take an indirect approach: We first created a list of all institutional VC investors that made at least one investment into a US headquartered startup between January 1, 2018 and December 31,

2018. For these investors, we examined the total funds they had raised in the prior 5 years, from 2014 to 2018, amounting to approximately $284 billion raised by 985 investors. Looking at the concentration in the capital raised by these investors provides a good proxy for the concentration in assets under management across institutional VC investors.

Fig. 3 ranks these VC investors by the amount of capital they raised to calculate a concentration curve. As can be seen from the exhibit, the top 50 investors, or about 5% of the VCs, raised half of the total capital over this period. As noted above, there has been an increase in the number of non-VC investors putting capital into startups at later stages in recent years, the most notable of which is Softbank's vision fund. Taking such non-traditional investors who also raise funds into account increases the number of investors under consideration to 1074. Among this larger set of investors, the top 50 investors (still approximately 5%) accounted for 68% of the total capital raised by investors over this period.

These deep-pocketed investors can play a disproportionate role in driving where other investors put their money, beyond the capital that they deploy themselves. This is because investors with smaller sums of capital under management typically focus on investments at the earliest stages of a startup's life, well before the startup is profitable and even has revenue. These early stage venture capital investors often do not have the capital continue financing startups across subsequent rounds to the point where they are generating positive cash flow, a juncture where has traditionally been easier to take firms public or sell them for attractive valuations. Thus, they are dependent on their larger peers continue financing the firms they initially fund and are extremely concerned about financing risk: that the survival of an otherwise healthy startup they back might be threatened by a negative shock to the supply of capital available for such ventures when it is looking for the next round of funding (Nanda and Rhodes-Kropf, 2017). The focus of the large pools of late stage capital can therefore impact the direction of early stage innovation, by shaping where early stage investors are willing to invest.

Undoubtedly, the most dramatic example of this phenomenon is the emergence of the giant Softbank Vision Fund. Venture capitalists have noted that the depth of Softbank's financial firepower has led to shifts in their own investment criteria. If they fund a company, and Softbank chooses to back a competitor, their firm is unlikely to have the financial resources to outlast the SoftBank-backed one. Moreover, it is likely to have trouble raising funding from other VCs. Thus, figuring out what Soft-Bank and other late stage investors want, and investing to cater to their tastes has become a major concern for many early stage investors. Whatever SoftBank's success in raising its next fund, the phenomenon of the deep pockets shaping the industry's investment priorities is unlikely to disappear. This pattern highlights the important role that a relatively small set of financiers can play in shaping the firms that grow and succeed.

Lending particular salience to these concerns of financiers as gatekeepers is the particular nature of these giant capital pools. We highlight three dimensions. First, major venture funds are based in a handful of places. In the U.S., National Venture

Capital Association statistics suggest that three metropolitan areas—the San Francisco Bay Area, Greater New York and Greater Boston account for about two-thirds of the capital deployed by VCs each year.[h] If we look globally, the same phenomenon would surely manifest itself, though good statistics are hard to find. For instance, a tabulation of Pitchbook data between 2015 and 2017 by Florida and Hathaway (2018) concluded that the top the top 25 urban areas accounted for 75% of all disbursements globally. Given this concentration of capital, the start-up community has rearranged itself to "follow the money." Kerr and Robert-Nicoud (2020) provide a fuller discussion of this phenomenon.

Why might this concentration be a cause for concern? On the one hand, economists have long pointed out that there are increasing returns to scale in entrepreneurial and innovative activity. Regions like Silicon Valley have an abundance of resources for entrepreneurs, ranging from excellent engineers used to working long hours for risky stock options, knowledgeable patent attorneys, and of course, lots of financiers. As a result, there are real social benefits from entrepreneurial concentration.

On the other hand, the concentration of venture capital has accelerated the "hollowing out" of innovative activities in many other parts of the world. Venture firms located elsewhere might have chosen very different firms to invest in, given their perspectives on their local economies. More generally, Glaeser and Hausman (2020) have documented in the United States the growing hubs of innovative activity in places far removed from the areas with the greatest economic need, a phenomenon that the growth of venture capital has accelerated.

Moreover, the background of the individual decision-makers at venture firms remains far from representative of the more general population. Fig. 4 (based on data from Lerner and Nanda (2020)), provides a sense of this by focusing on the 417 individuals listed as U.S. based partners of the Top 5% of VC firms documented in Fig. 3.[i] Some firms tend to give partner titles to a larger number of individuals than the true decision makers in the partnership, so we also examine the subset of these individuals who sit on at least one board seat. This further restriction narrows the set of individuals to 265.

Fig. 4 documents the composition of this group, looking at the gender, educational background and location of these individuals. 80% of partners are male, but among the set of partners with at least one board seat, 91% are male. Three quarters of partners with at least one board seat attended either attended an Ivy League school, or one of Caltech, MIT and Stanford. Moreover, nearly 30% of these individuals are

---

[h]https://nvca.org/wp-content/uploads/2019/08/NVCA-2019-Yearbook.pdf and earlier editions archived at https://nvca.org/pressreleases_category/research/.
[i]We used data from the Pitchbook database (https://pitchbook.com/) for this analysis. We screened the investment professionals noted in Pitchbook for each of these firms by restricting them to titles that were one of Managing General Partner, Managing Partner, Founding Partner, General Partner, Senior Partner or Partner and further restricted them to individuals based in the U.S.

	US Based Partners	US Based Partners with at least one board seat
Total Number of Partners	416	265
Share male	82%	92%
Share attended top universities	62%	74%
Share with MBA from Harvard	12%	15%
Share with MBA from Stanford	9%	13%
Share located in Bay area	69%	69%
Share located in Greater Boston	9%	11%
Share located in New York City	14%	11%

FIG. 4

Characteristics of Key U.S. based Investment Professionals in the 50 Largest VC firms. Notes: This exhibit reports characteristics of the key U.S based investment professionals working for the 50 Largest VC firms reported in Fig. 3. Data are drawn from the Pitchbook database. We first restrict investment professionals in these firms to titles that are one of Managing General Partner, Managing Partner, Founding Partner, General Partner, Senior Partner or Partner and further restrict them to individuals based in the US. In column 2, we examine a subset of these individuals who also sit on at least one board seat, as some of the firms in our sample have a larger number of individuals with a "Partner" title than those who make investment decisions or are actively involved in governing startups.

This is compiled from the data presented in table 3 in Lerner Josh, Ramana Nanda, 2020. Venture capital's role in financing innovation: what we know and how much we still need to learn. J. Econ. Perspect. 34 (3), 237–261.

graduates of just Harvard Business School or Stanford Graduate School of Business. In terms of location, 69% are based in the Bay Area alone and over 90% based in either the Bay Area, Greater Boston or New York.

The non-representative nature of the decision makers at these firms is important because of the growing evidence that the lack of diversity among venture capitalists has an impact on what businesses get funded (Calder-Wang et al., 2021; Calder-Wang and Gompers, 2021). Ewens and Townsend (2020) document that male and female investors appear to have gendered preferences (or a differential set of signals about potential cash flows) in terms of the companies they back. Understanding whether such frictions are consequential enough to influence the nature of innovations that are backed and the choice of products faced by consumers is an important question that we believe deserves more research.

A final, more difficult to document concern relates to the criteria that these investors use to make decisions more generally (Gompers et al., 2020). While academics have spent a great deal of time seeking to understand the structure of venture investment agreements and post-deal involvement, the process before the transaction is much less well understood. We know that early stage investors rely heavily on signals of entrepreneur quality (Bernstein et al., 2017), but we know very little as to whether the emphasis on these signals is efficient. Recent work by Cao (2019), for example, shows that information frictions from early stage platforms can lead to systematic downstream effects on firm funding. Given the increasing importance of VC for innovation and growth, understanding the way in which these investors acquire and aggregate signals of a venture's potential and the frictions in this process are a very important and promising area of future research.

4.3 A declining emphasis on governance

The third and final concern that we highlight here has to do with the seeming decline in emphasis on governance in venture capitalist transactions. Venture capital has traditionally been a tough business, with onerous stock purchase agreements (Kaplan and Strömberg, 2003). Moreover, Kaplan et al. (2009) and Ewens and Marx (2018) document, these are not just "paper rights": frequent turnover of management has been the rule.

These patterns have changed dramatically in the past decade. Across the board, "founder friendly" terms appear to have replaced the onerous provisions traditionally demanded by venture capitalists. Several potential explanations can be offered for these patterns.

One may be an increase in competition between venture capitalists associated with the growth documented above. Given the very skewed nature of venture returns, where a few deals generate the bulk of the returns (Hall and Woodward, 2010; Ouyang et al., 2020), the competition to get access to the firms that show potential to generate outsized returns is particularly intense. Reflecting this competition, groups appear to have chosen to outdo each other in the extent of their hospitality towards company founders.

To an economist, however, this explanation is puzzling. If the intensive governance provided by venture capitalists is socially beneficial—as generations of academic analyses would suggest—why would groups choose to abandon it? Should not venture firms compete exclusively by offering entrepreneurs progressively higher valuations (and less dilution of their initial equity stakes) and not be abandoning governance provisions? While more work needs to be done to understand these dynamics, a part of the explanation may be due to the fact that entrepreneurs have a lot of discretion in who they choose to take funding, are strategic in whom they take money from (Hsu, 2004), and may underestimate the need for governance. In an intensely competitive market, some VCs may be tempted to pitch entrepreneur-friendly contracts to founders in an attempt to get access to the most attractive deals.

Another explanation reflects the changing dynamics of both early- and later-stage investing discussed above. First, it has become far cheaper to start a new business, and as a result, the amount of financing entrepreneurs require in the earliest stages has shrunk. It may be that the quantum of capital that firms need at the earliest stage is too small to make it worthwhile for VCs to engage in active governance. Many venture capital firms that have adopted the "spray and pray" investment strategy at the seed stage of financing for ventures are more focused on learning about the potential of a venture before spending time governing them (Ewens et al., 2018). At the same time, the massive inflow of capital from investors who usually focus on the public market may have changed the focus of contractual rights at later stages. A single fund manager in these entities may hold hundreds of separate firms, and have little experience being directly involved with governing the firms in their portfolio. These passive investors are unlikely to have the capabilities to provide effective governance to the entrepreneurial ventures, As Chernenko et al. (2019) document, mutual funds seem far more concerned about ensuring that there is a path to liquidity, reflecting the short-term nature of the capital that they have raised from investors. The changing composition of the capital sources may have also led to a reduced focus on governance.[j]

Whatever the causes, the consequences of this change have been evident in the high-profile ousters of founders of unicorns in recent years. The travails of Theranos, Uber, and We Work illustrate in part the consequences of allowing entrepreneurs with limited prior management experience to raise enormous sums for new ventures with little formal oversight and governance protections. Understanding why traditional VC contractual provisions have faded in importance and their social welfare implications appears to be a promising area of future research for both theorists and empiricists alike.

5 New approaches

As we have argued in this paper, venture capital has been a highly efficacious way to boost innovation, as reflected in the importance of venture-backed companies in economies and stock markets. At the same time, the industry has important limitations. We have highlighted the narrow focus on a few industries in today's venture portfolios, the concentration of decision-making in a handful of key gatekeepers, and the declining emphasis on the corporate governance that has an industry hallmark since its inception.

In the final section, we summarize some elements that may require reconceptualization for the industry to become more effective. These hypotheses, which are designed will provide some ideas to practitioners and academics alike interested in thinking "outside the box," are developed in more length in Lerner and Nanda (2020) and (in regard to the organizational and incentive structure of venture partnerships) in Lerner (2012).

---

[j]Alternatively, VC-backed firms have begun to remain private for longer but the number of partners managing these firms has not grown substantially, implying that each individual VC is spread more thin due to the larger number of commitments on boards of directors of firms. The reasons for the failure of groups to adjust investment team sizes is an important question.

5.1 **Organization of VC partnerships**

Our first set of suggestions relate to the design of venture fund. Since the early days, VC funds have been 8-to-10 years in length, with provisions for one or more 1-to-2 year extensions. Venture capitalists typically have 5 years in which to invest the capital, and then are expected to use the remaining period to harvest their investments.

The uniformity of these rules is puzzling. Funds differ tremendously in their investment foci: from quick-hit social media businesses to long-gestating biotechnology projects. In periods when the public markets are enthusiastic, venture capitalists may be able to exit still-immature firms that have yet to show profits and, in some cases, even revenues. But as discussed above, there has been tremendous variation in the maturation of firms in different industries. Given the reasonable short fund life—and the fact that groups after a few years shift their focus to raising their next fund–it is not surprising that the venture funds have increasingly focused on sectors such as software and social networking, which are characterized by fast innovation "clock speeds." What explains the constancy of the venture fund lives?

One possible explanation is that a reasonably short fund life seems to have been the norm in limited partnerships of all types. The structure of venture capital limited partnerships seem to have been largely borrowed from pools devoted to other endeavors. Many of the other arenas where limited partnerships were employed in the 20th century, such as real estate, oil-and-gas exploration, and maritime shipping, all were reasonably short-lived. In the formative days of venture partnerships, the lawyers drafting the agreements may have gravitated to relatively short fund lives. With the passage of time, such arrangements have been taken as gospel by limited and general partners alike. Another factor behind the persistence of the 10-year agreement has been resistance of limited partners (the investors in the VC funds) to long fund lives. Investors may fear that if they give the funds to a sub-standard venture group for a longer period, they will be stuck paying fees until the end of time for very limited returns. This reluctance may tell us more about the outsized nature of the fees that venture funds receive than about the inherent desirability of a longer-lived fund.

Indeed, the manner in which venture capitalists are compensated has changed little, even as the funds have grown much larger. Venture groups typically receive a share of the capital gains they generate (typically 20%, but sometimes as high as 30%) and then an annual management fee (often between 1.5% and 2.5% of capital under management, though it often scales down in earlier years). Such fees are quite modest for a fund of a few million dollars: it is likely to cover only a very modest salary for the partners once the costs of an office, travel, and support staff are factored in.

But this compensation structure has remained largely unchanged as funds have become substantially larger. And as venture capital groups begin managing hundreds of millions or billions of dollars, substantial "economies of scale" appear: put another way, as a group becomes 10-times larger, expenses increase much less than tenfold. As a result, management fees themselves become a profit center for the firm. And these steady profits may create incentives of their own, not all appealing.

For instance, the temptation to raise a larger fund at the expense of lower returns, the lure doing a sub-par deal so money can be put to work quickly and a new fund can be raised sooner, and a tendency to do excessively safe investments that will not have as much upside, but pose less possibility of a franchise-damaging visible failure.

Just how large a temptation the venture capital compensation scheme can pose is illustrated in the work of Metrick and Yasuda (2010). They show that of every $100 invested by the limited partners, over $23 end up in the pockets of the venture investors. These sums might not be disturbing if they were being driven by incentive compensation: if the very substantial payouts to each partner reflected the large amount of money being made by the limited partners in the fund. But profit sharing is not the most important source of compensation. Instead, almost two-thirds of the income is coming from the management fees, which remain fixed whether the fund does well or poorly. This creates very perverse incentives to raise ever-larger funds and is tied to the greater concentration of capital held by a few investors.

What explains the traditional reluctance of limited partners to push to change these compensations arrangements? Staff members may not really understand the economics of the funds, they may fear that rocking the boat would limit their own ability to get a high-paying position at a fund or an intermediary in the future, or the officers may worry that developing a reputation as an activist would jeopardize their organization's ability to access the best funds. The last concern is a reasonable one. After the giant California Public Employees' Retirement System led a consortium of pension funds who pushed for an overhaul of private equity compensation in the mid-1990s, they were shunned by venture and buyout funds alike. In recent years, we have seen more collective discussion of these issues by limited partners in meetings of Institutional Limited Partners Association. But many of their proposals have modest half-measures to adjust fees without addressing the more fundamental issues.

In our earlier work, we suggest paying greater attention to an alternative model: the way that venture capital groups used to operate. Early venture capital groups, such as Draper, Gaither & Anderson, negotiated budgets annually with their investors. The venture capitalists would lay out the projected expenses and salaries, and reach a mutual agreement with the limited partners about these costs. Such negotiated fees greatly reduce the temptation to grow at the expense of performance and are likely to lead ultimately to more successful and innovative start-ups.

5.2 De-risking ventures

As highlighted above, venture funds invest in stages. This enables them to reinvest in businesses that continue to show promise while abandoning those that do not (Reis, 2011). One of the potential reasons why there has been a dramatic rise in venture capital directed toward software and related ventures is that this industry has seen much more rapid declines in the cost of learning about the ultimate viability of the venture in these sectors. This approach may not be well suited for ventures with substantial regulatory and technology risk, such as clean energy and advanced materials.

The approach to de-risking ventures begins with the process that VCs use to identify promising new ideas. The traditional approach entails entrepreneurs coming to VCs to pitch them new ideas and VCs deciding whether to fund them or not. This approach has the benefit of enabling the investors to maintain an arms-length relationship from the entrepreneurial team, reducing the entrenchment that is sometimes associated with corporate R&D and internal capital markets.

An alternative approach, however, has begun to be used by some VC investors specializing in bio-pharmaceuticals (such as Third Rock Ventures and Flagship Pioneering): to incubate and finance ideas in-house. This process has the benefit of reducing asymmetric information because much of the staff for the team of entrepreneurs comes from within the fund. It also enables the VC firm to fund what it might believe is the most promising idea or approach, as opposed to selecting among a set of ideas that came through the door. In our earlier work, we suggest such new approaches may hold promise for widening the scope of venture capital investment.

It is also natural to wonder whether collaboration of other parties, whether governments, non-profits, and corporations, may also alleviate some of the barriers to financing new ventures in more difficult technologies. Of course, we are not the first to think of this suggestion! Governments have been involved with the promotion of venture capital at least since the creation of the British firm 3i in 1946. Corporations have been collaborating with venture capitalists since the 1960s. And universities and other non-profits have been incubating, mentoring, and directly financing new ventures for much of the last half-century.

But the track record of these collaborative efforts has been quite mixed. There have been numerous successes, such as the Israeli's governments jump-starting of its venture industry through the Yozma program, or many pharmaceutical firms' success in responding to the biotechnology revolution through their venturing initiatives. At the same time, anecdotes abound of naïve officials making poor decisions: for instance, the leadership of Boston University of putting a third of their endowment into a single faculty-founded biotechnology company, an investment that was ultimately sold for pennies on the dollar. Nor does the statistical evidence seem that inspiring: for instance, the Thomson Reuters (now Refinitiv) database suggests that between 1993 and 2013, corporate venture funds lost 4% per annum, at a time when U.S. venture funds has annual returns of nearly 30%.[k]

Elsewhere, though, we argue that these collaborations can be beneficial, but only if they are executed correctly. For instance, the primary mechanism through which U.S. government policy interacts directly with new ventures is through the Small Business Innovation Research program. A striking study by Howell (2017) suggests that the initial Phase I awards have very positive effects on new technology ventures, doubling the probability that a firm receives VC and boosting patenting and revenue. But these Phase I awards made up only 20% of total of $2.8 billion spent on the program fiscal year 2017 (U.S. Small Business Administration, 2018). The bulk of the

---

[k]See Ma (2020) for a more optimistic view.

funding goes to larger Phase II awards, which Howell argues have no positive impacts. Similarly, both Howell (2017) and Lerner (1999) suggest the problematic impact of the companies have managed to capture a disproportionate number of awards. These "SBIR mills" commercialize far fewer projects than those firms that receive just one (or a handful) SBIR grant. But the repeat winners are very effective contestants, as they often have staffs in Washington scouring for award opportunities and lobbying for rules that benefit themselves. In addition to governments, one promising area of recent growth has been the interest among philanthropic organizations to finance more early stage, high risk R&D as a pathway to draw in institutional VC once the technology has been sufficiently de-risked.

6 Conclusion

The growth of venture capital in the past decade, both in the US and worldwide is an important validation of the model. At the same time, the period has brought into sharp relief the structural limitations of the industry. Over the past decades, academics and practitioners alike have highlighted the strengths of venture capital. Understanding and articulating limitations and related financing frictions for high potential ventures, as well as the ability of institutional innovations to address these limitations, is an important challenge to both groups going forward.

Acknowledgments

Josh Lerner is the Jacob H. Schiff Professor at Harvard Business School and a Research Associate at the NBER; Ramana Nanda is a Professor of Entrepreneurial Finance at Imperial College London and a Research Fellow in the Financial Economics Program of the CEPR. Their email addresses are jlerner@hbs.edu and ramana.nanda@imperiral.ac.uk. Harvard Business School's Division of Research provided funding for this work. This essay is based in large part on Lerner (2012) and especially Lerner and Nanda (2020). It draws on the ideas in in Gompers and Lerner (2001a), Kerr, Nanda and Rhodes-Kropf (2014), and Ivashina and Lerner (2019). We owe a debt of gratitude to Paul Gompers, Bill Janeway, Steve Kaplan, Victoria Ivashina, Matthew Rhodes-Kropf, William Sahlman, and especially Felda Hardymon for many helpful conversations over the years. We thank Jeremy Greenwood for pointing out the Arrow interview and to Susan Woodward for the Sand Hill Econometrics data. Lerner has received compensation from advising institutional investors in venture capital funds, venture capital groups, and governments designing policies relevant to venture capital. All errors and omissions are our own.

References

Agrawal, A., Catalini, C., Goldfarb, A., 2016. Are syndicates the killer app of equity crowdfunding? Calif. Manage. Rev. 58, 111–124.

Ante, S., 2008. Creative Capital: Georges Doriot and the Birth of Venture Capital. Harvard Business School Press, Boston.

Arora, A., Belenzon, S., Sheer, L., 2021. Knowledge spillovers and corporate Investment in Scientific Research. Am. Econ. Rev. 111, 871–898.

Arrow, K., 1995. Interview With Kenneth Arrow, Federal Reserve Bank of Minneapolis. https://www.minneapolisfed.org/article/1995/interview-with-kenneth-arrow.

Astuti, G., 1933. Origini e Svolgimento Storico della Commenda Fino al Secolo XIII. S. Lattes & Co., Milan.

Banks, R.L., Liles, P.R., 1975. The Charles River Partnership. Harvard Business School Case no. 375075, p. 1975.

Bernstein, S., Giroud, X., Townsend, R.R., 2016. The impact of venture capital monitoring. J. Financ. 71, 1591–1622.

Bernstein, S., Korteweg, A., Laws, K., 2017. Attracting early stage investors: evidence from a randomized field experiment. J. Financ. 72, 509–538.

Bloom, N., Jones, C., Van Reenen, J., Webb, M., 2020. Are ideas getting harder to find? Am. Econ. Rev. 110, 1104–1144.

Calder-Wang, S.Q., Gompers, P.A., 2021. And the children shall lead: gender diversity and performance in venture capital. J. Financ. Econ. 142, 1–22.

Calder-Wang, S., Gompers, P., Sweeney, P., 2021. Venture Capital's 'Me Too' Moment. Working paper no. 28679, National Bureau of Economic Research.

Cao, R., 2019. Information Frictions in New Venture Finance: Evidence From Product Hunt Rankings. Unpublished working paper.

Chemmanur, T., Krishnan, K., Nandy, D., 2011. How does venture capital financing improve efficiency in private firms? A look beneath the surface. Rev. Financ. Stud. 24, 4037–4090.

Chernenko, S., Lerner, J., Zeng, Y., 2019. Mutual Funds as Venture Capitalists? Evidence From Unicorns. National Bureau of Economic Research Working Paper No. 23981.

Cornelli, F., Yosha, O., 2003. Stage financing and the role of convertible securities. Rev. Econ. Stud. 70, 1–32.

de Roover, R., 1963. The organization of trade. In: Postan, M.M., Rich, E.E., Miller, E. (Eds.), The Cambridge Economic History of Europe: Volume III: Economic Organization and Policies in the Middle Ages. Cambridge University Press, Cambridge (Chapter 2).

Ewens, M., Farre-Mensa, J., 2020. The deregulation of the private equity markets and the decline in IPOs. Rev. Financ. Stud. 33, 5463–5509.

Ewens, M., Malenko, N., 2020. Board dynamics over the startup life cycle. Working paper no. 27769, National Bureau of Economic Research.

Ewens, M., Marx, M., 2018. Founder replacement and startup performance. Rev. Financ. Stud. 31, 1532–1565.

Ewens, M., Rhodes-Kropf, M., 2015. Is a VC partnership greater than the sum of its partners? J. Financ. 70, 1081–1113.

Ewens, M., Townsend, R., 2020. Are early stage investors biased against women? J. Financ. Econ. 135, 653–677.

Ewens, M., Nanda, R., Rhodes-Kropf, M., 2018. Cost of experimentation and the evolution of venture capital. J. Fin. Econ. 128, 422–442.

Fang, L., Ivashina, V., Lerner, J., 2015. The disintermediation of financial markets: direct investing in private equity. J. Financ. Econ. 116, 160–178.

Farre-Mensa, J., Hegde, D., Ljungqvist, A., 2020. What is a patent worth? Evidence from the U.S. patent 'lottery'. J. Financ. 75, 639–682.

Florida, R., Hathaway, I., 2018. The Rise of the Startup City. Center for American Entrepreneurship, Washington.

Glaeser, E., Hausman, N., 2020. The spatial mismatch between innovation and joblessness. Innov. Policy Econ. 20, 233–299.

Gompers, P., 1995. Optimal investment, monitoring, and the staging of venture capital. J. Financ. 50, 1461–1490.

Gompers, P., Lerner, J., 2001a. The Money of Invention. Harvard Business School Press, Boston.

Gompers, P., Lerner, J., 2001b. The venture capital revolution. J. Econ. Perspect. 15 (2), 145–168.

Gompers, P., Gornall, W., Kaplan, S., Strebulaev, I., 2020. How do venture capitalists make decisions? J. Fin. Econ. 135, 169–190.

Gornall, W., Strebulaev, I.A., 2021. The Economic Impact of Venture Capital: Evidence from Public Companies. Stanford University Graduate School of Business Research Paper No, pp. 15–55.

Griliches, Z., 1986. Productivity, R&D, and basic research at the firm level in the 1970s. Am. Econ. Review 76, 141–154.

Hall, R.E., Woodward, S.E., 2004. Benchmarking the Returns to Venture. National Bureau of Economic Research Working Paper No. 10202.

Hall, R.E., Woodward, S.E., 2010. The burden of the nondiversifiable risk of entrepreneurship. Am. Econ. Rev. 100, 1163–1194.

Harris, R.S., Jenkinson, T., Kaplan, S.N., Stucke, R., 2020. Has Persistence Persisted in Private Equity? Evidence From Buyout and Venture Capital Funds. Fama-Miller Working Paper. https://ssrn.com/abstract=2304808.

Hellmann, T., 1998. The allocation of control rights in venture capital contracts. Rand J. Econ. 29, 57–76.

Hellmann, T., Puri, M., 2000. The interaction between product market and financing strategy: the role of venture capital. Rev. Financ. Stud. 13, 959–984.

Hellmann, T., Puri, M., 2002. Venture capital and the professionalization of start-up firms: empirical evidence. J. Financ. 57, 169–197.

Hochberg, Y., 2016. Accelerating entrepreneurs and ecosystems: the seed accelerator model. Innov. Policy Econ. 16, 25–51.

Hochberg, Y.V., Ljungqvist, A., Yang, L., 2007. Whom you know matters: venture capital networks and investment performance. Journal of Finance 52, 251–301.

Howell, S.T., 2017. Financing innovation: evidence from R&D grants. Am. Econ. Rev. 107, 1136–1164.

Hsu, D.H., 2004. What do entrepreneurs pay for venture capital affiliation? J. Finance 59 (4), 1805–1844.

Ivashina, V., Lerner, J., 2019. Patent Capital: The Challenges and Promises of Long-Term Investing. Princeton, Princeton University Press.

Kaplan, S.N., Schoar, A., 2005. Private equity performance: returns, persistence, and capital flows. J. Financ. 60, 1791–1823.

Kaplan, S.N., Strömberg, P., 2003. Financial contracting theory meets the real world: an empirical analysis of venture capital contracts. Rev. Econ. Stud. 70, 281–315.

Kaplan, S.N., Strömberg, P., 2004. Characteristics, contracts, and actions: evidence from venture capitalist analyses. J. Financ. 109, 2173–2206.

Kaplan, S.N., Sensoy, B., Strömberg, P., 2009. Should investors bet on the jockey or the horse: evidence from the evolution of firms from early business plans to public companies. J. Financ. 64, 75–115.

Kerr, W.R., Robert-Nicoud, F., 2020. Tech clusters. J. Econ. Perspect. 34 (3), 50–76.

Kerr, W.R., Nanda, R., Rhodes-Kropf, M., 2014a. Entrepreneurship as experimentation. J. Econ. Perspect. 28 (3), 25–48.

Kerr, W.R., Lerner, J., Schoar, A., 2014b. The consequences of entrepreneurial finance: a regression discontinuity analysis. Rev. Financ. Stud. 27, 20–55.

Korteweg, A., Sorensen, M., 2017. Skill and luck in private equity performance. J. Financ. Econ. 124 (3), 535–562.

Kortum, S., Lerner, J., 2000. Assessing the impact of venture capital on innovation. Rand J. Econ. 31, 674–692.

Lerner, J., 1995. Venture capitalists and the oversight of private firms. J. Fin. 50, 301–318.

Lerner, J., 1999. The government as venture capitalist: the long-run effects of the SBIR program. J. Business 72, 285–318.

Lerner, J., 2012. The Architecture of Innovation. Harvard Business Press and Oxford University Press, Boston and London.

Lerner, J., Nanda, R., 2020. Venture capital's role in financing innovation: what we know and how much we still need to learn. J. Econ. Perspect. 34 (3), 237–261.

Lerner, J., Wulf, J., 2007. Innovation and incentives: evidence from corporate R&D. Rev. Econ. Stat. 89, 634–644.

Lerner, J., Mao, J., Schoar, A., Zhang, N., 2022. Investing outside the box: evidence from alternative vehicles in private capital. J. Financ. Econ. 143, 359–380.

Lopez, R.S., Raymond, I.W., 1955. Medieval Trade in the Mediterranean World: Illustrative Documents Translated with Introductions and Notes. Columbia University Press, New York.

Ma, S., 2020. The life cycle of corporate venture capital. Rev. Financ. Stud. 33, 358–394.

Metrick, A., Yasuda, A., 2010. The economics of private equity funds. Rev. Financ. Stud. 23, 2303–2341.

Nanda, R., Rhodes-Kropf, M., 2017. Financing risk and innovation. Manage. Sci. 63, 901–918.

Nanda, R., Samila, S., Sorenson, O., 2020. The persistent effect of initial success: evidence from venture capital. J. Financ. Econ. 137, 231–248.

Neher, D.V., 1999. Staged financing: an agency perspective. Rev. Econ. Stud. 66, 255–274.

Nicholas, T., 2019. VC: An American History. Harvard University Press, Cambridge.

Ouyang, S., Yu, J., Jagannathan, R., 2020. Return to Venture Capital in the Aggregate. Working paper no. 27690, National Bureau of Economic Research.

Puri, M., Zarutskie, R., 2012. On the lifecycle dynamics of venture-capital- and non-venture-capital-financed firms. J. Financ. 67, 2247–2293.

Reis, E., 2011. The Lean Startup. Crown Business, New York.

Sorensen, M., 2007. How smart is the smart money? A two-sided matching model of venture capital. J. Financ. 62, 2725–2762.

U.S. Small Business Administration, 2018. SBIR/STTR Annual Report. 2017. https://www.sbir.gov/sites/default/files/SBIR%20FY2017%20ANNUAL%20REPORT.pdf.

Small firm financing: Sources, frictions, and policy implications

3

Ramana Nanda[a] and Gordon Phillips[b],*

[a]*Department of Finance, Imperial College London, London, United Kingdom*
[b]*Tuck School of Business, Dartmouth College, Hanover, NH, United States*
Corresponding author: e-mail address: gordon.m.phillips@tuck.dartmouth.edu

Chapter outline

1 Introduction

Small firms form the backbone of the economy. In the United States, they account for over 90% of all firms and over 40% of economic activity. Moreover, startups—the vast majority of which start small—have been shown to play a particularly important role in driving productivity growth and net job creation, making them an important and set of firms to understand for academics and policy makers alike.

Young and small firms also have particular features that make them more susceptible to financing constraints: they may depend more on external finance to support their growth, yet they often have less "hard" data available on which to make funding decisions. This can often lead them to be perceived by financiers as more "opaque" or subject to asymmetric information. In addition, small firms often have a single relationship with financial intermediaries such as banks, making them more subject to informational hold-up by financial intermediaries and hence face worse terms when raising external finance.

But how salient are these financial frictions and to what extent do they have a quantitatively important impact on real outcomes such as employment or productivity growth? In this review, we provide an overview of the large and growing literature on understanding financing constraints facing small businesses with a view to answering these questions.

We start in Section 2 by using representative data from the US Survey of Business Owners (SBO) to describe the main sources of financing for US business owners, broken down by firm size. We also show using data from the SME Finance Monitor that these patterns appear consistent with the financing patterns in the UK. These statistics provide an organizing framework for reviewing the literature on the sources of small firm financing and associated frictions, and also shed light on financing sources that appear under-studied relative to their use by small businesses. For example, credit card financing, both to the owners and the business, stands out as a key area that received comparatively less attention relative to the intensity with which it appears to be used by small firms.

In Section 3, we discuss the aggregate effects of relaxing financing constraints. A key insight from this section is that there appears to be substantial heterogeneity in the findings of different papers in terms of the magnitude of financing frictions facing small firms. These differences seem related to the subsample of entrepreneurs being studied, which highlights the important role of understanding the composition of small businesses when interpreting aggregate effects, both for academics and policy makers looking to enact reforms.

In Section 4, we discuss research on potential technological and policy interventions to reduce financing constraints for small firms. Several elements have contributed to making this an active area of work. First, there is growing availability of microdata on small firm financing with the potential to tie this to longer term firm outcomes. This enables a much deeper understanding of the causes and consequences of financing constraints, as well as an understanding of heterogeneity among different subpopulations of small businesses. Second, there has been a massive rise of financial technology in recent years, both within traditional banks and with new "fintech" startups, several of whom are looking to exploit inefficiencies in small business lending. Studying their impact enhances our understanding of what frictions such fintech might address and what remain. Third, there have been several government interventions aimed at helping small businesses, particularly in the wake of the COVID-19 pandemic, which again enables a deeper understanding of the nature of financing frictions and the policies that might be most effective at alleviating them.

Finally, in Section 5, we provide a brief discussion and conclusion, summarizing what the body of work on small firm financing frictions has taught us and outlining promising areas of further inquiry.

2 Sources of small firm financing

We begin by documenting the sources of finance as reported in the Survey of Business Owners and Self-Employed Persons (SBO). We use data from the 2012 SBO, which is the most recent data available through the Census Bureau's public use API as of the time of writing.[a] The SBO surveys a representative sample of nonemployer (self-employed) and employer businesses in the United States.

We focus on the sources of financing used by employer firms that form the bulk of economic activity. Tables 1 and 2 break down the sources of financing by firm size and separately report the sources of capital used by business owners as part of their startup capital (Table 1) and expansion capital (Table 2). Table 3 provides a similar perspective on financing in the UK using data from the SME Finance Monitor. A number of patterns jump out from these tables: First, although most owners report using some capital to start their businesses, a very large share of business owners did not use *any* capital for expansion in the year prior to the survey. Second, among those using capital for startup or expansion, the most common source of capital appears to be "internal"—personal savings or internal cash flow of the businesses. Only half the business owners report using any form of external finance. Third, consistent with Robb and Robinson (2014), debt is the dominant source of external finance for business owners, both in terms of startup and expansion capital.

We turn next to discussing each of the sources of financing noted in the tables in more detail.

2.1 Personal wealth

As seen in Tables 1 and 2, over 90% of business owners report using personal wealth as part of their startup capital and over a third of business owners report using personal wealth to finance business expansion. The large share of individuals using

---

[a]See https://www.census.gov/data/developers/data-sets.html.

Table 1 SBO startup capital.

	All employer firms	1–9	10–49	50–99	100+
Share using some capital for startup	93%	92%	95%	94%	93%
Among those using startup capital, share that used at least some personal/family savings or assets	83%	85%	75%	76%	94%
Among those using startup capital share that used at least one form of external finance	53%	50%	64%	62%	73%
Business Loan from bank	22.4%	19.7%	31.3%	33.1%	40.4%
Business loan/investment from family/friends	5.1%	4.5%	7.0%	6.0%	8.1%
Personal/family home equity loan	7.3%	7.0%	8.5%	7.6%	7.1%
Business credit card(s) carrying balances	4.5%	4.8%	3.9%	2.3%	2.5%
Personal credit card(s) carrying balances	9.5%	10.1%	7.9%	6.0%	4.8%
Investment by venture capitalist(s)	0.5%	0.4%	0.9%	1.5%	2.4%
Other source(s) of capital	4.0%	3.7%	5.0%	6.0%	7.6%

Note: *This table shows the results on SBO startup capital.*

personal wealth to finance their businesses, combined with a minority of individuals reporting any form of external finance is often seen as a sign that small business owners face credit rationing or related financing constraints (Stiglitz and Weiss, 1981). Moreover, early research on large cash windfalls from bequests measured strong entrepreneurial responses (Holtz-Eakin et al., 1994; Blanchflower and Oswald, 1998), consistent with these bequests unlocking credit constraints.

While such an explanation is intuitive, recent work has also noted the potentially small *demand* for external finance by many small business owners as well as noting identification challenges with using bequests to study financing constraints. Hurst and Lusardi (2004) document that the relationship between household wealth and entry is relatively constant for the bottom 80 percentiles of the wealth distribution and begin rising sharply thereafter, with the relationship between wealth and entrepreneurial entry is strongest in the top 5 percentiles of the wealth distribution. They note that such an exponential relationship between wealth and entry is inconsistent with the presence of credit constraints deterring entry, particularly since the vast majority of entry at the top of the wealth distribution is into industries such as finance, law and real estate that are not at all capital intensive. Instead, they argue that the lifestyle of an entrepreneur is a "luxury good." Those at the top end of the wealth

Table 2 SBO expansion capital.

	All employer firms	1–9 employees	10–49 employees	50–99 employees	100+ employees
Share that used any capital for expansion or making capital improvement(s)	53%	50%	61%	70%	77%
Share that used at least some internal finance for expansion or capital improvements	53%	55%	49%	50%	49%
Personal/family savings or assets	35%	39%	26%	19%	12%
Business Profits or Assets	18%	16%	22%	31%	37%
Share that used at least one form of external finance for expansion or capital improvements	46%	45%	51%	49%	50%
Business Loan from bank	20.0%	16.5%	27.8%	33.7%	37.5%
Business loan/investment from family/friends	1.6%	1.6%	1.9%	1.6%	0.8%
Personal/family home equity loan	4.2%	4.5%	3.9%	2.2%	1.0%
Business credit card(s) carrying balances	10.3%	11.1%	8.8%	5.0%	2.8%
Personal credit card(s) carrying balances	7.8%	9.0%	5.5%	2.8%	0.9%
Investment by venture capitalist(s)	0.4%	0.3%	0.6%	0.9%	1.9%
Other source(s) of capital	1.8%	1.5%	2.1%	2.9%	4.8%

Note: *This table shows the results on SBO expansion capital.*

Table 3 SME Finance Monitor sources of capital.

	All SMEs	0 emp.	1–9 emp.	10–49 emp.	50–99 emp.	100–249 emp.
USE OF EXTERNAL FINANCE[a]	**53%**	**37%**	**49%**	**60%**	**68%**	**68%**
Core products (any)	**45%**	**30%**	**40%**	**50%**	**62%**	**62%**
– Bank overdraft	25%	17%	22%	26%	37%	36%
– Credit cards	24%	14%	19%	29%	36%	39%
– Bank loan	14%	7%	13%	17%	21%	26%
– Commercial mortgage	5%	1%	3%	6%	9%	10%
Other forms of finance (any)	**28%**	**14%**	**24%**	**36%**	**39%**	**41%**
– Leasing or hire purchase	20%	7%	15%	26%	32%	35%
– Loans from directors, family & friends	5%	3%	6%	6%	5%	6%
– Equity from directors, family & friends	2%	1%	2%	3%	3%	3%
– Invoice finance	4%	1%	2%	6%	7%	8%
– Grants	6%	4%	6%	7%	6%	7%
USE OF TRADE CREDIT[b]	**54%**	**31%**	**51%**	**66%**	**64%**	**67%**

Note: Use of Finance among existing SMEs, as reported in 2016 Q3 to 2021 Q2 waves of UK's SME Finance Monitor Survey.
[a]Current use of external finance.
[b]Regularly use of trade credit.

distribution are more likely to want to consume this luxury good. Hurst and Lusardi (2004) also show that bequests in the future are as likely to predict business starts as past bequests, suggesting that they are likely to measure a number of other factors associated with household wealth that are unrelated to alleviating financing constraints. Moreover, more recent evidence that has examined the impact of cash windfalls on the *who* selects into entrepreneurship suggests that rather than alleviating a financing constrain, they may enable those with lower human capital to start firms by relaxing the discipline of external finance (Andersen and Nielsen, 2012; Bellon et al., 2021).

Further evidence of such an argument comes from Hamilton (2000) who shows that nonpecuniary motivations appear to play an important role in explaining the fact that small business owners enter and persist in self-employment even when their predicted earnings in wage employment could be higher. Moskowitz and Vissing-Jørgensen (2002) also suggest the role of nonpecuniary motivations in explaining what they note as a "private equity premium puzzle"—the fact stakes that business owners hold in their (privately held) businesses does not earn the required premium one would expect it to earn given its large and undiversified nature of overall household wealth. Hurst and Pugsley (2011) report direct evidence on the lack of demand for expansion capital among many small business owners. They show that a large share of small business owners do not express any intention or desire to grow larger or to innovate.

Of course, it is important to note that nonpecuniary motivations for becoming and remaining a small business owner are not inconsistent with the presence of financing constraints facing other small business owners who are looking to grow. However, this heterogeneity in the motivations and related capital needs of small business owners is an important issue and a theme that runs through this chapter: it has implications for how we measure the acuteness and the real effects of financing constraints facing entrepreneurs as well as an understanding of what the appropriate policy interventions are likely to be.

2.2 Bank finance

Tables 1–3 show that the majority of external finance used by firms involves debt and that moreover, debt financing from financial intermediaries such as banks is the predominant source of external financing for small firms. A long literature has examined the role of bank financing to small businesses, identifying a number of challenges faced in bank lending to small businesses and the ways in which small businesses and banks try to overcome these.

Perhaps the most salient feature of most small businesses from the perspective of a financier is their *opacity*. Their accounts are not subject to rigorous scrutiny in the same manner as larger and publicly traded firms. In addition, there is often a blurry line between household balance sheets and small business balance sheets. For this reason, small business depend almost exclusively on bank financing as a source of external debt as the informational advantage of banks allows them to more easily overcome challenges such moral hazard and adverse selection relative to arms-length financiers involved in bond financing (Diamond, 1984, 1991).

Early empirical work in this area emphasized the importance of bank–borrower relationships as a way for banks to overcome information challenges, and highlighted how the length of relationships (Berger and Udell, 1995; Berger et al., 2001) and concentration of all banking relationships with one bank were tied to more favorable prices and terms faced by small businesses as was shown early by Petersen and Rajan (1994).

Although banking relationships clearly play an important role in facilitating access to finance for small businesses, subsequent research has also highlighted how bank structure plays an important role in impacting small businesses lending (Berger and Udell, 2002; Berger et al., 2005). Specifically, this work has highlighted how observably similar small businesses appear to get more credit at better terms from smaller community banks when compared to large banks. There is no reason to believe that loan officers in larger banks have less ability to screen and monitor small businesses, but Stein (2002) shows theoretically that this is likely to be driven by the fact that "soft" information is harder to transmit across hierarchies. In smaller banks, information does not have to pass through several layers of hierarchy, providing loan officers an incentive to collect and use "soft" information for their lending decisions. This enables them to provide small businesses with more credit at better terms.

However, banks with decentralized lending structures may not always be best for small business lending. This is because, as noted by Rajan (1992), the informational advantage of banks gives them the ability to extract rents from small businesses—which could be particularly true in markets where there is little banking competition. Consistent with this view, Sapienza (2002) and Erel (2011) find that mergers tend to improve efficiency, but as the local market share of the acquired banks increases, the efficiency effect is offset by market power. When banks become larger, they reduce the supply of loans and increase loan spreads for small borrowers. Similarly, Canales and Nanda (2012) find that decentralized banks give larger loans to small firms and those with soft information. However, decentralized banks are also more responsive to their own competitive environment. They are more likely to expand credit when faced with competition but also restrict credit and charge higher prices when they have market power.

A more recent literature on bank financing for small businesses has documented a substantial decline in Commercial and Industrial (C&I) lending to small businesses, particularly in the wake of 2007 financial crisis and the subsequent Great Recession (Bernanke, 2010; Mills and McCarthy, 2014). This decline seems particularly sharp in markets where the largest banks have more market share (Chen et al., 2017), potentially driven by regulation. Whatever the reasons, the degree to which this is driven by changing demand for bank credit, shifts in the available supply of risk capital or a substitution away from banks to fintech intermediaries all warrant further investigation, as we discuss further in Sections 4 and 5.

2.3 Personal credit

Tables 1 and 2 document the prominent role of home equity loans and lines of credit as a source of financing for business owners, particularly for startup capital. Home equity and credit cards are comparable in size with bank financing in terms of their frequency of use by smaller firms. Indeed, given the blurry line between household and firm balance sheets when it comes to small business financing, a number of papers have discussed the role of secured and unsecured *personal* credit in enabling the entry and growth of small firms.

2.3.1 Home equity financing

When banks' screening technology cannot fully overcome the challenges associated with the opacity of small businesses, they can rely on pledgeable collateral to reduce their loss in the event of default. The ability to repossess collateral in the event of default means that banks may be willing to lend in instances where they are confident about the resale value of the collateral, even if they are unable to assess the firm's ability to repay credit through cash flow from operations.

A number of papers have examined increases in available home equity of the entrepreneurs—either through mortgage reforms (Kerr et al., 2022; Lastrapes et al., 2022; Jensen et al., 2022) or house price increases (Black et al., 1996; Adelino et al., 2015; Corradin and Popov, 2015; Schmalz et al., 2017) and studied how this in turn might enable entrepreneurship. This work finds consistent evidence that increases in the value of housing collateral available to pledge by an entrepreneur increases the likelihood of selection into entrepreneurship, although as we discuss further in Section 3, the magnitude of the effect varies across studies. Interestingly, the role of home equity appears most valuable for relaxing the entry constraint for entrepreneurs. As seen in Table 2, far fewer entrepreneurs report using home equity to finance the expansion of their businesses.

2.3.2 Unsecured personal credit

The willingness of banks to make unsecured loans to small businesses is interesting in itself and likely tied to the massive growth in unsecured consumer credit over the last several decades. The latter has been driven by the increases in data and credit scoring methodology on individuals' ability to borrow and repay credit. Given the greater ability of financiers to gather individual characteristics and model consumer credit behavior compared to credit scoring small businesses themselves, many business owners end up either explicitly or implicitly relying on their personal creditworthiness when raising funding for their businesses. Robb and Robinson (2014) note for example that a large share of startups receive debt financing through the personal balance sheets of the entrepreneur.

The implicit role of personal assets in unsecured lending has been examined most frequently in the context of personal bankruptcy laws, which vary considerably across states. A particular source of variation is the ease with which lenders can access personal assets of individuals in the event that they declare bankruptcy and have unpaid debts. Some states have high exemption limits and prevent lenders from possessing an individual's home, while others have low exemptions, meaning that banks have a higher likelihood of recovering some portion of their principal if a borrower with unsecured credit declares personal bankruptcy. Variation across states terms of the ability of banks to reposes personal assets is likely to have equilibrium effects—higher exemptions are likely to increase demand for unsecured credit, but lower the willingness of financiers to lend. Berkowitz and White (2004) and Berger et al. (2011) document that the supply effect appears to dominate—in that small businesses were less likely to have credit in states with more lenient bankruptcy laws. Robb and Robinson (2014) also note that borrowers in states with higher personal bankruptcy exemptions have lower ratios of debt to personal capital.

One area that has received relatively little attention in literature is the role of credit card financing in supporting small businesses. Anecdotes often suggest that entrepreneurs "max out their credit cards."

Fonseca and Wang (2021) use a dataset that links household and firm liabilities for 1% sample of US individuals with credit scores and document substitution to personal credit when business face constraints in bank financing following the 2007 crisis. Herkenhoff et al. (2021) provide direct evidence of personal credit worthiness and revolving credit on entrepreneurship. They link detailed TransUnion credit records to Census employee and firm data building a panel of over 3 million workers that they follow for close to 10 years. They find that if an individual's unused revolving credit (credit cards and personal lines of credit) increases by 10% in the current year, their potential to start a new firm increases by 0.021% points in the subsequent 2 years. This represents a 7% increase relative to the sample average rate of firm ownership, suggesting a large elasticity of new firm startups to borrowing capacity. They also find that self-employment rates also increase by 0.66% points in the year following a 10% increase in an individual's unused revolving credit. Relative to the sample average self-employment rate of 10.6%, this represents a 6% increase. These elasticities show a large role for consumer credit as part of startup financing.

2.4 Equity financing

A consequence of taking an aggregate perspective on small firm financing is that external equity financing such as venture capital (VC) plays a small role as a share of firms raising external finance. This topic is also covered by other chapters in the Handbook, so we only touch upon a few topics. Da Rin et al. (2013) and Lerner and Nanda (2020) provide more extensive reviews of the literature.

2.4.1 Venture capital

About 0.5% of firms in the SBO report using VC, which is consistent with the other work on the proportion of VC-backed startups in the United States (Puri and Zarutskie, 2012). VC is not appropriate for many firms. From the perspective of entrepreneurs, VC only makes sense when entrepreneurs are willing to forgo substantial dilution in terms of their equity ownership as well cede control to VCs. Nevertheless, VC is a very important source of risk capital for the firms with the highest growth potential in the economy and for those involved in commercializing radical new technologies for whom VC remains one of the only viable sources of external finance.

As evidence of the disproportionate role played by VC-backed firms in the economy, Lerner and Nanda (2020) look at Initial Public Offerings (IPOs) over the 1995–2018 period and report that VC-backed startups account for just under half these IPOs, despite accounting for less than 1% of startups each year receiving a first round of VC financing. These publicly traded VC-backed firms were more likely to have survived as of December 2019, and among the surviving firms accounted for a disproportionate share of R&D expenditure and Enterprise Value—highlighting the importance of the firms backed by VC for aggregate innovation.

A long literature has aimed to document the value added role played by VC investors, and degree to which they play a causal role in impacting firm performance, versus simply selecting firms with the highest growth potential (Kortum and Lerner, 2000; Samila and Sorenson, 2011; Chemmanur et al., 2011; Puri and Zarutskie, 2012;

Bernstein et al., 2016). Much less attention has been paid to frictions associated with receiving VC financing. Lerner and Nanda (2020) point to two such frictions that appear to warrant further inquiry. First, they point to the concentration of funding within networks that tend to be skewed heavily toward male entrepreneurs in a small number of large cities close to where VCs are located. They also point to the narrow band of innovation that VC is focused on financing.

2.4.2 Angel investors, accelerators, and crowd funding

There has also been a substantial rise in the volume of Angel investment since the mid-2000s, in addition to the rise of new financial intermediaries such as Accelerators and Crowd Funding Platforms.

Ewens et al. (2018) trace this rise to the advent of cloud computing starting with Amazon's Elastic Cloud Compute in 2006. They document how this technological shock enabled entrepreneurs to rent space on the cloud instead of making expensive fixed investments in IT-hardware, thereby lowering the cost of experimentation associated with their new product or service by over an order of magnitude. In turn, this lower cost of experimentation unleashed a wave of new entrepreneurs starting firms with much less capital. These shifts changed the investment landscape for early stage VC—creating a "Seed" round of financing—that came before the "Series A" round of VC funding.[b] It also creating the need for new types of intermediaries to address the evolving market for early stage venture finance.

One such intermediary are Accelerators, often referred to as fixed-term, cohort-based "boot camps" for startups that offer educational and mentorship programs for founders, exposing them to a wide variety of mentors, including former entrepreneurs, VCs, angel investors, and corporate executives'. Accelerator programs often culminate in a public pitch event, or "demo day," during which the graduating cohort of startup companies pitch their businesses to a large group of potential investors (Hochberg, 2015).

The rationale for the rise in such intermediaries is provided by Ewens et al. (2018), who note that the fall in the cost of the initial round of financing for startups substantially increases the real option value of the first financing, thereby enabling a greater number high option-value entrepreneurs to be financed—such as younger, less experienced founders with "moonshot" ideas. These entrepreneurs need more intensive support, yet the fact that they are higher option value also means they are more likely to fail which required early investors to find more scaleable forms of providing value added services. The cohort-based nature of Seed Accelerators help overcome this challenge. Additionally, the much larger number of potential investment opportunities made screening substantially more difficult for VCs. The Accelerators provided a way to curate a set of more viable investment opportunities that VCs can learn about during the "demo days."

---

[b]VC funding is made through a process staged investments, with the norm historically being that the first round was referred to as "Series A," the second as "Series B", and so on.

Gonzalez-Uribe and Leatherbee (2018) study the value added role of such Accelerators, as well as trying to distinguish the impact of the mentoring and support from the validation associated with being admitted to the program.

Beyond Accelerators, there has also been a rise in the prominence of Angel investors—individuals investing their own savings into young, private companies (as opposed to institutional investors who deploy capital on behalf of others). In turn, the large rise in the number of investors and investment opportunities has led to intermediaries such as equity compounding platforms.[c] The lack of systematic, high quality data on angel investments makes analysis challenging. Recent research suggests that they may be less sophisticated (Yimfor, 2021) and less sensitive to financial motives of investment (Denes et al., 2020) and may also be more likely to suffer adverse selection. A promising direction of equity compounding appears to be in syndicates of angel investors pooling their funding and expertise, which may enable them to overcome some of the challenges associated with getting the adversely selected investments (Agrawal et al., 2016).

2.5 Trade credit

Although the SBO does not ask business owners about the use of trade credit due to the fact that it is not typically considered as a source of financing from a financial intermediary, data from a comparable survey in the UK called the SME Finance Monitor, highlights how nearly over half of small businesses use trade credit. The use of trade credit is usually seen as an expensive source of borrowing and has therefore been seen as sign that firms may face constraints in financing their working capital with lines of credit from the bank.

More recently, however, a growing literature has also begun to document the degree to which smaller firms in supply chains are effectively financing their customers through trade credit (Barrot, 2016). By being paid weeks after the sale of a good or a service, firms effectively provide short-term corporate financing to their customers. Such interfirm trade credit financing is, in aggregate, three times as large as bank loans and fifteen times as large as commercial paper in the United States (Barrot and Nanda, 2020).

Trade credit claims, recorded as accounts receivable on firms' balance sheets, are typically seen as short-term, liquid, low-risk claims that should be very easy to pledge, and that should not constrain firm growth. Yet over a third of these accounts receivables are believed to sit on the balance sheets of small firms. Media reports seem to suggest that large firms continue to increase their cash flows by extending the time that they pay their small business suppliers, and recent research as found that long payment terms forces financially constrained small firms to cut back investment

---

[c]Rewards-based compounding platform such as Kickstarter help drive certification and raise funding for prototypes through prepayment but do not involve equity finance.

(Murfin and Njoroge, 2015). Understanding the aggregate effects of such delayed payment is an important area of research and discussed in more detail in Section 3.

---

3 Real effects of (relaxed) financing constraints

As we have shown in Section 2, an extensive literature has examined the sources of financing for small businesses, as well as identifying ways in which financiers try to overcome the particular challenges associated with financing young and small firms.

Nevertheless, frictions in the process of screening and monitoring small firms can still lead to credit rationing (Stiglitz and Weiss, 1981). In addition, intermediaries with market power have been shown to restrict credit and charge higher prices, leading to a wedge between the cost of internal and external finance that can lead positive NPV opportunities to go unfunded.

What are the real effects of these frictions? Are they consequential enough to have aggregate effects? Moreover, who benefits most when such constraints are relaxed? Are the effects concentrated among a few firms or impact small firms more broadly? And is the marginal firm that benefits from relaxed constraints of higher quality/productivity than the average unconstrained firm, or just on the margin in terms of productivity? Understanding these questions is not only important for macroeconomic models that are often motivated by financing frictions for entrepreneurs, but also help shed light on the appropriate policy interventions to address financing frictions for small firms (Greenstone et al., 2020; Caglio et al., 2021).

The key empirical challenge that any work needs to address when answering such questions is to isolate exogenous shocks to the supply of small firm credit in a manner that is orthogonal to investment opportunities and firms' demand for credit. Given this empirical challenge, the most credible sources of exogenous variation tend to come from reforms or related "shocks" to the supply of credit to small businesses. We summarize work looking at the real effects of such natural experiments.

3.1 Shocks to the supply of bank credit

Given their importance as a source of financing to small firms, banks and shocks to their ability to lend in a manner that is exogenous to local investment opportunities are an important laboratory for understanding financing constraints for small firms.

3.1.1 US branch-banking deregulation

The US commercial banking sector experienced substantial shifts in their regulatory environment between the 1970s and 1990s, leading to massive shifts in the competitive environment of banks over this period as described in Berger et al. (1995).

Two types of banking restrictions were relaxed over this period. The first related to restrictions on intrastate branching that prevented new bank entry and acquisitions. For example, banks were restricted from opening new branches within states, and multibank holding companies faced restrictions in their ability to convert branches of acquired subsidiary banks into branches of a single bank. The second related to the Douglas amendment to the Bank Holding Act of 1956, which prevented a bank holding company from acquiring banks in another state unless that state explicitly permitted such acquisitions by statute. No state allowed such acquisitions until the late 1970s. States then entered reciprocal regional or national arrangements which allowed their banks to be acquired by banks in any other state in the arrangement. Except for Hawaii, all states had entered such agreements in 1993. These episodes of interstate deregulation culminated with the passage of the 1994 Riegle–Neal Interstate Banking and Branching Efficiency Act, which codified these state-level changes at the national level.

The primary impact of such branch bank deregulations was to enable banks to enter new markets, shifting the competitive environment for banks. Following the deregulations, the number of banks fell by a third between 1977 and 1994. Early work on the impact of the deregulations by Jayaratne and Strahan (1996) and Jayaratne and Strahan (1998) examined bank efficiency and bank entry and growth rates of per capital income and output. Their results suggested that more efficient banks emerged postderegulation and most of the reduction in banks' costs were passed along to bank borrowers in the form of lower loan rates. Consistent with this, Sapienza (2002) and Erel (2011) find that credit supply and loan terms generally improve for small businesses where there is more competition.

Black and Strahan (2002) and Cetorelli and Strahan (2006) were the first papers to examine the real effects of deregulation on entrepreneurship. They measure large increases in entry following the interstate banking deregulations, particularly among smaller entrants with under 10 employees. Kerr and Nanda (2009), Krishnan et al. (2015) and Bai et al. (2018) use comprehensive firm- and establishment-level Census data to study heterogeneity in the types of firms that benefited most from the deregulations.

Consistent with Black and Strahan (2002) and Cetorelli and Strahan (2006), Kerr and Nanda (2009) show that the greatest increase in entry occurred among very small startups. However, they document that the vast majority of this entry comprised new firms that failed within three years of founding. Such churning entry is consistent with the increased access to credit and better loan terms due to the banking deregulations enabling "marginal" entrants who are likely to be weaker. It also helps account for the fact that despite the wide-spread entry documented by Black and Strahan (2002), the aggregate effects in terms of overall firm growth were much more muted.

Nevertheless, Kerr and Nanda (2009) also document that the deregulation did promote larger entrants and a smaller number of entrants that survived more than three years. Consistent with the rise of "stronger" entrants in addition to the more marginal churning entrants, Krishnan et al. (2015) examine the productivity of existing firms following the state banking deregulations and find increases in firm TFP, which is particularly is stronger for firm that were more financially constrained prior to the deregulations.

Bai et al. (2018) begin with similar Census administrative data as the Krishnan et al. (2015) but also combine it with Quarterly Financial Reports data that has comprehensive financing sources for small firms. The Quarterly Financial Reports microdata from the Census allows them to distinguish between debt from commercial banks (bank debt) and debt from other sources (nonbank debt). First, they find that bank deregulation is associated with an economically large increase in the relative growth, and especially labor share growth, of more productive young firms. Second, they show that these small firms make more extensive use of bank credit postderegulation to grow their firms. Moreover, this relative growth increase is important for both labor and capital, and it is not present for older firms.

Importantly, Bai et al. (2018) show that the individual small firm effects they document translate into economically important gains in aggregate industry productivity and that changes in the allocation of labor are important in driving these gains at the firm and industry level. Industry and firm gains are particularly important as they show that while productivity per unit of labor (akin to an IRR) may be relatively flat, if more productive firms expand then overall value (akin to NPV) can increase more.

Not all the margins of banking deregulation have shown to be positive. While most evidence shows increases in commercialization and size, innovation may be less positively impacted. Using patent level and innovator level data, Hombert and Matray (2017) analyzes the effects of intrastate banking deregulation on the number of innovative firms and the movement of inventors across innovative firms. They find support for the hypothesis that in the move toward more banking markets more competitive, more specialized banking relationships that require soft information were adversely affected. They document adverse effects on innovation and inventors moving from small innovative firms, thus find a labor market reallocation of inventors across firms and states. Their results are consistent with small firms without hard assets being hurt by increased competition in banking markets while small firms with fixed assets and hard information benefiting from bank deregulation. Chava et al. (2013) also find mixed effects on innovation when looking at intrastate vs interstate deregulation, while Cornaggia et al. (2015) look at innovation in small and large firms following the interstate deregulation to examine the overall impact on state-level innovation. Note that the shift to commercialization and growth by firms may be viewed as an optimal shift to exploitation from exploration as firms age.

3.1.2 Shocks to bank balance sheets

While the banking deregulations provide one way to examine changes in firm access to capital that are unrelated to specific investment opportunities, a second approach used in the literature has exploited shocks to bank balance sheets as a way to study the resulting transmission to small business lending. The premise behind these papers is that if the shock to bank balance sheets is large enough, banks will face constraints, forcing them to cut back on lending to firms independent of the borrowing firms' investment opportunities.

Schnabl (2012) examines this in an emerging markets context, studying the impact of the 1988 Russian default on the local economy in Peru through the transmission of this external shock to local firm borrowing through these banks' exposure to the Russian crisis. He finds large cuts in lending in Peru by banks that were exposed to the 1998 Russian lending crisis and further documents that local banks do not fully pick up the slack and increase their lending enough to compensate for the lost lending relationships by the international banks.

Chodorow-Reich (2014) examines this in the US context in the aftermath of the 2007 financial crisis by exploiting cross-sectional variation in commercial banks' exposure to Lehman Brothers' bankruptcy. He combines lending data from Dealscan on banking relationships for over 2000 firms from the US Census Longitudinal Business Database (LBD) which has establishment-level employment information for small firms. He examines small firms with less than 50 employees and medium-sized firms with 50–1000 employees. He finds a large negative impact on employment for small and medium-sized firms that had precrisis relationships with lenders that were impacted by the Lehman crisis. He documents a large effect—the withdrawal of credit by lenders accounted for up to one-half of employment declines at these impacted small and medium-sized firms.

Huber (2018) studies a similar decline in small business lending in Germany by Commerzbank in the great financial recession of 2008–10 and shows the effects extend beyond firms with direct banking relationships to include the broader local economy due to aggregate demand and agglomeration spillovers in the most affected counties. These spillover effects are interesting as they document that the real effects of financing frictions facing small firms may not be restricted to the firms themselves, but have broader macroeconomic effects due to the general equilibrium effects.

3.2 Exogenous increases in access to personal credit

A different line of research has examined exogenous increases in access to personal credit, to study the response of entrepreneurship and thereby aim to identify financing frictions facing the founders.

A growing stream of work on the role of housing collateral on entrepreneurship has found a clear role for unlocked collateral enabling entrepreneurship, although the magnitude of the effect varies across studies. In part this is due to the fact that most studies exploit variations in house price increases to study changes in the value of housing collateral, but isolating the causal role of increased collateral on entrepreneurship from other factors that are correlated with increased value of home equity is difficult without individual-level controls. For example, Kerr et al. (2022) find that during the housing market boom of the 2000s, wealthy individuals—who got the largest increases in home equity by virtue of their bigger homes—were also more responsive to entrepreneurial opportunities independent of relaxed constraints. As noted in Section 2, this is consistent with Hurst and Lusardi (2004) who find that wealthy individuals more likely to enter entrepreneurship, often in sectors such as real estate (e.g., as real estate agents), which of course is also a more attractive opportunity during housing booms.

Recent work looking at the sources of small business financing also shows that while prevalent, home equity financing appears to be used by a small minority of businesses. Indeed as noted by Caglio et al. (2021), the majority of bank lending to small firms appears to be based on ongoing business value rather than the value of tangible collateral. Consistent with this, research looking at mortgage reforms (Lastrapes et al., 2022; Jensen et al., 2022; Kerr et al., 2022) documents interesting heterogeneity in the responses, where a small number of individuals have large responses to unlocked housing equity, which also has the potential to shed light on the characteristics of individuals facing financing constraints. Jensen et al. (2022), for example, show that in their context, the response is concentrated among those who were starting businesses in industries where they did not have prior experience, making it harder for financiers to screen them.

Herkenhoff et al. (2021) exploit bankruptcy flags removal from consumer credit reports as a way to exploit an exogenous increase access to personal credit. These removals occur, by law, no more than 10 years after bankruptcy and give rise to large increases in credit ratings while not reflecting large changes in an individual's creditworthiness. They compare bankrupt individuals over time, before and after flag removal. Consistent with prior studies such as Musto (2004) and Han and Li (2011), they show that access to credit increases among the subgroup of individuals who have their bankruptcy flags removed. Their analysis of bankruptcy flag removal is focused on the credit access effect: credit constraints loosen after flag removal, allowing individuals to potentially finance self-employment and entry into new business ownership.

Bos et al. (2018) focus on the way reported delinquencies, that is, skipped payments as opposed to debt discharge, in the Swedish pawn registry affect earnings and self-employment. Bos et al. (2018) show that individuals whose past defaults are publicly available for longer are less likely to have a job, are more likely to be self-employed, and earn lower incomes on average.

With respect to self-employment, Herkenhoff et al. (2021) find that bankruptcy flag removal has a limited effect on the overall stock of self-employed individuals, as some individuals leave self-employment for formal employment and other individuals enter self-employment. Those who transition into self-employment after a bankruptcy flag removal borrow $15k more than those who transition into self-employment prior to flag removal. This finding represents a 12.4% increase in borrowing relative to the sample average. They earn approximately $1000 more Schedule C net income at any time horizon we observe (an increase of about 4% relative to the sample average).

They then use the new Integrated Longitudinal Business Database (ILBD) to measure transitions from self-employment to hiring paid employees in the Longitudinal Business Database (LBD). Focusing on this conditional sample of self-employed individuals examines people who are closer to the active margin of having demand for credit and shows how extra credit affects the tendency to start a new firm that has employees. They find that after flag removal, individuals are more likely to own a business with employees, that is, startup a new firm. Among these new firm startups, these owners borrow, on average, $40,000 more after flag removal, a 33% gain relative to the sample average.

Chatterji and Seamans (2012) study the impact of state-level removal of credit card interest rate ceilings on transitions into self-employment, following the US Supreme Court's 1978 Marquette decision. Prior to this decision, states were allowed to set their own caps on credit card interest rates, but the court ruled that nationally chartered banks could charge the highest allowable rate in their home state, regardless of the interest rate ceiling in the customer's state of residence. This allowed banks to "export" interest rates across state boundaries, subsequently leading many states to remove their credit card interest rate ceilings and significantly increasing credit card companies' efforts to market their cards to individuals. They find that credit card deregulation increased the probability of entrepreneurial entry, and also document heterogeneity in terms of the response, with a particularly strong effect for black entrepreneurs in states with a history of racial discrimination. This finding is consistent with the hypothesis that blacks living in states with a history of discrimination would have been most likely to face credit rationing and hence show the largest response to relaxed constraints on personal credit.

Overall, the entrepreneurial response to relaxed personal credit constraints not only highlights the presence of financing frictions, but helps to isolate the subsample of individuals who had the largest response, and hence shed light on the characteristics of individuals facing financial frictions.

3.3 Accelerated payment of trade credit

As noted in Section 2, trade credit is used by a substantial share of firms in supply chains. Although not based on borrowing from a financial intermediary, it is effectively a source of borrowing from (or lending to) other firms. Since small firms typically have only a few weeks worth of cash on their balance sheets, long payment times can play an important role in preventing expansion and growth.

Barrot (2016) uses a natural experiment that changes trade credit payable terms in France to demonstrate the importance of financial constraints to the entry and survival of small firms. He examines the entry and exit of firms surrounding trade credit regulation reform that went into effect in 2006. This reformed prevented firms from extending to their customers payment terms in excess of 30 days. This reform resulted in a significant 15% reduction in payment terms relative to their prereform level. He examines the entry of exit of firms following this working capital reform. The micro level data set that Barrow uses combines firm-level data with information on business creation and defaults for the universe of French firms, which enables him to carefully analyze how short-term corporate liquidity impacts the entry and survival of financially constrained entrepreneurs. He shows that probability that a trucking firm that receives the benefit of quicker payment causes a decrease in the probability of a bankruptcy filing decreases by 60 bps, a 25% drop with respect to the prerestriction level. Furthermore, this effect is concentrated among small, young, cash poor, highly levered, and low payout firms, which are more likely to be liquidity constrained. His results provide consistent evidence that the previous long payment terms impose substantial liquidity risk on financially weaker firms, forcing them into financial distress to a greater extent than if they were paid earlier.

Using a reform that reduces payment time by the US government, Barrot and Nanda (2020) show that small business contractors to the US government grew faster after the reform. In addition to increased employment growth, firms that benefited from the accelerated payments also begin paying their own suppliers in a more timely manner. Paying suppliers faster led to improvements in their own payment-related credit score within recorded by Dunn and Bradstreet. Barrot and Nanda (2020) also provide an estimate of the cost of financial constraints for small firms. Based on the elasticity of the employment response, They estimate that the implied cost of external finance for treated firms is approximately 40%, which while high, is comparable to the cost of trade credit and of other sources of financing available to small businesses in the wake of the financial crisis.

In looking at the aggregate impact of the accelerated payments, Barrot and Nanda (2020) find that aggregate employment increases, but only in areas where unemployment is high. In tighter labor markets, the positive employment effects of accelerated payments crowd out growth for firms competing in the same labor market, making the overall effect close to zero. This general equilibrium impact of reducing financing frictions is interesting as it highlights the conditions under which reduced credit frictions has a positive aggregate impact vs. simply leading some firms to grow at the expense of others.

3.4 Small business fragility during the COVID-19 pandemic

There are multiple papers that have examined how small firms are impacted through their loss of business and credit during the recent COVID-19 pandemic. We discuss several of these papers here but do not provide a comprehensive survey. The key findings reinforce the conclusion that small businesses are financially fragile and are at risk of failure frequently during downturns and crisis. Also what this recent works shows is that data can be gathered from multiple sources including surveys that are done formally and via online media like Facebook.

Bartik et al. (2020) through an extensive survey shows the impact of the COVID-19 pandemic on small businesses. In addition to its impact on public health, COVID-19 has had a major impact on the economy. They survey more than 5800 small businesses. Several main themes emerge from the results. First, extensive mass layoffs and closures have occurred. They find that 43% of businesses are temporarily closed, and businesses have—on average—reduced their employee counts by 40% relative to the month before the pandemic. Second, consistent with previous literature, they document that small businesses are financially fragile. For example, the median business has more than $10,000 in monthly expenses and less than one month of cash on hand. Third, the majority of businesses planned to seek funding through the CARES act. However, many small business had problems with accessing the aid, such as bureaucratic hassles and difficulties establishing eligibility.

Fairlie (2020) uses data from the current population survey for April 2020 and documents that the number of active business owners in the United States plummeted by 3.3 million or 22% over the crucial two-month window from February to April 2020. The drop in business owners was the largest on record, and losses were felt across nearly all industries and even for incorporated businesses. African–American businesses were hit especially hard experiencing a 41% drop. Latinx business owners fell by 32%, and Asian business owners dropped by 26%. Simulations indicate that industry compositions partly placed these groups at a higher risk of losses. Immigrant business owners experienced substantial losses of 36%. Female-owned businesses were also disproportionately hit by 25%. These findings of early stage losses to small businesses have important policy implications and may portend longer term ramifications for job losses and economic inequality.

Alekseev et al. (2020) survey approximately 1.9 million Facebook users, and 66,297 eligible individuals completed at least part of the survey: 46,669 business owners and managers, 4163 operators of personal enterprises, and 15,435 business employees. They document that firms had seen losses, on average, of over one-half of their business. Not surprisingly small business finances suffered during the pandemic. Many businesses were struggling to pay bills (31.3%), rent (24.9%), wages (24.1%), and debt obligations (23.0%). About 42% of businesses reported having more outflows than inflows in the past month, and 78.2% of businesses were concerned about cash flows over the next 3 months. Importantly, their survey considers sources of financing. They report that only a quarter of the businesses had access to formal sources of financing through a loan or line of credit from a financial institution, and most businesses were reliant on personal savings and informal sources of financing. Finally, they show that these small businesses had deteriorating financial conditions due to the COVID-19 crisis, through lack of access to capital or negative cash flows.

Chodorow-Reich et al. (2022) examine how small and large firms were differentially impacted by their lenders liquidity provision during the recent COVID recession. First, they document that small firms face more onerous terms than do large firms in their credit access to credit lines. Relative to large firms, small firms (i) obtain credit lines more frequently demandable or with much shorter maturity, (ii) post more collateral, (iii) have higher utilization rates, and (iv) pay higher spreads even conditional on other firm characteristics. Second, they examine small firms' borrowing after many small firms obtained Paycheck Protections Program (PPP) loans. Given the more onerous terms they face on their credit lines, small and medium-sized firms did not draw down credit from their banks while larger firms did. Small firms that were able to get PPP loans actually reduced their non-PPP borrowing from banks, while large firms drew down their credit lines.

Autor et al. (2020) indicate that the PPP boosted employment at eligible firms. Following the passage of the CARES Act, employment at eligible firms begins rising relative to employment at ineligible firms. They show that through the first week of June of 2020, the program boosted employment at eligible firms by a median of 3.25%. The upper range of this effect, once scaled by the overall estimated take-up rate in the economy, is 7.5%, which is below a rough upper bound on the likely treatment effect on employment calculated using a subset of about 1500 firms that they identify as having received a loan from the SBA loan-level data. If their results generalize to the full sample of eligible PPP firms, this implies that the PPP increased aggregate US payroll employment by about 2.3 million workers through the first week of June 2020. Balyuk et al. (2021) find that bank relationships matter in small business access to PPP funding. Small firms were more likely to get early access to PPP loans if they had prior bank relationships, especially with small banks

Howell et al. (2021) explores the sources of racial disparities in small business lending. They study the $806 billion Paycheck Protection Program (PPP), which was designed to support small business jobs during the COVID-19 pandemic. PPP loans were administered by private lenders but federally guaranteed, largely eliminating unobservable credit risk as a factor in explaining differential lending by race. Even after controlling for a firm's zip code, industry, loan size, PPP approval date, and other characteristics, they find that Black-owned businesses were 12.1% points (70% of the mean) more likely to obtain their PPP loan from a fintech lender than a traditional bank. Among conventional lenders, smaller banks were much less likely to lend to Black-owned firms, while the Top-4 banks exhibited little to no disparity after including controls. They find that Black-owned businesses' higher rate of borrowing from fintechs compared to smaller banks is particularly large in places with high anti-Black racial animus, pointing to a potential role for discrimination in explaining some of the racial disparities in small business lending. Consistent with this view, they find that when small banks automate their lending processes, and reduce human involvement in the loan origination process, their rate of PPP lending to Black-owned businesses increases.

4 The role of government policy

Having shown the sources of financing and nature real effects of relaxed financing constraints, we turn in this section to discuss potential technological and policy interventions to reduce financing constraints for small firms. We first note that a key insight emerging from the work outlined in Section 3 is that estimated aggregate effects of (relaxed) constraints can vary considerably and that this variation appears to be driven by the underlying heterogeneity in the number and types of firms that benefit the most. This clearly has important policy implications—in particular, the policy response under a view that real effects are small effects for all firms is likely to be quite different compared to a view where there are large effect for smaller subsamples of firms, particularly if it is possible to target such frictions effectively.

4.1 Information about credit worthiness

Beyond understanding heterogeneity, there has also been a massive rise of financial technology in recent years, both within traditional banks and with new "fintech" startups, several of whom are looking to exploit inefficiencies in small business lending (Mills, 2019). Studying their impact enhances our understanding of what frictions such fintech might address and what remain.

As noted in the prior sections, small business rely on banks as a primary source of external finance. The informational advantage of banks comes from their being informed rather than arms-length lenders. Moreover relationship lending and decentralized bank structures contribute to the ability of loan officers to collect and utilize "soft information" to make lending decisions, which has been shown to have substantial predictive power beyond hard information such as credit scores (Iyer et al., 2016). Yet, as noted by Rajan (1992), the informational advantage of banks also gives them market power, that they can use to extract rents from the small businesses. This trade-off, between the ability to collect information and to use it strategically against the small business remains a key trade-off for small businesses. As noted in Section 3, bank competition can play a role in reducing the rent-extraction by banks, but other work has shown this can also come at the expense of relationship lending, which may also reduce the ability to lend in settings where soft information is key.

We discuss two different developments that have the potential to relax this trade-off in a manner different from bank competition. The first entails the role of technology, and the increasing sophistication of machine learning algorithms that can extract great information value from textual and other meta data, and thereby "harden" what has historically been "soft information." Berg et al. (2022) discuss the development of such fintech and note that at present, the advantage of fintech appears to be primarily in terms of the speed with which decisions can be made.

The second entails shifting the control rights associated with the use if the borrowers information to the small business rather than leaving them solely with the incumbent bank—as is the case with regulations related to "Open Banking" (Babina et al., 2022). Shifting the control rights over transaction data (such as, for example, data on receipts and payments coming out of a business' checking account) enable banks with which the small business does not have a relationship to learn about their creditworthiness. There is likely considerable complementarity between technological advantages and regulations such as open banking, as the value of being able to share one's data is greater when competitors are able to study it more effectively.

Overall, however, understanding how such algorithms evolve, and the heterogeneous impact they may have on borrowers is both an important area of research and one that is worth understanding from a regulatory standpoint. For example, Fuster et al. (2022) show how greater flexibility to uncover structural relationships, can lead to disparities in rates received by borrowers. Using data on US mortgages, they find that Black and Hispanic borrowers are disproportionately less likely to gain from the introduction of machine learning algorithms.

4.2 Government as customer

Beyond regulating the way in which information can be used, government can play a role in impacting financing constraints for small businesses through its role as a customer. In the United States, government procurement amounts to 4% of GDP and includes $100 billion in goods and services purchased directly from small firms. As shown by Barrot and Nanda (2020), accelerating payment to small businesses can directly impact cash flows and support firm growth. Chatterji et al. (2014) also provide evidence of how the practice of reserving a proportion of government contracts for minority-owned businesses that was introduced by cities in the 1980s helped reduce the self-employment gap for African American men.

The limitation of this channel is that it can only impact those selling to the government. This can have distributional consequences as well as impact overall efficiency depending on degree to which those selling to the government are either more, or less productive than the typical firm in that industry or region.

4.3 Loan guarantees and direct interventions

In terms of understanding the trade-offs associated with different policy interventions, there have been several government interventions aimed at directly helping small businesses, such as in the wake of the COVID-19 pandemic. Some of these have been undertaken as direct subsidies while others have indirectly subsidized small businesses by working with financial intermediaries. This enables a deeper understanding of the nature of financing frictions and the policies that might be most effective at alleviating them.

The most common approach in which government is typically involved in alleviating financing constraints is through supply side interventions, either by directly financing startups believed to be facing credit constraints as in the case of Small Business Innovation Research (SBIR) programs (Lerner, 2000; Howell, 2017) or through loan guarantee programs such as the Small Business Administration's 7 (a) and 504 programs (Brown and Earle, 2017).

In understanding the potential benefits of direct lending vs. loan guarantees, an intuitive benefit of the latter is that it relies on an existing infrastructure of financial intermediaries who have information about borrowers and are specialized in screening applicants. Nevertheless, the literature has identified several potential downsides associated with loan guarantee programs. First, Lelarge et al. (2010) study the impact of guaranteed loan programs in France and find evidence of risk shifting by banks. Firms receiving guaranteed loans had higher assets, hired more and grew faster. But these firms also had a higher probability of subsequent default suggesting that risker firms received the guarantees.

Second, a number of papers have studied loan guarantees in the context of PPP loans in the wake of the COVID pandemic. The PPP program was structured as a type of guaranteed loan program where firms applied to a participating private lender; once the loan was approved by the Small Business Administration (SBA), the lender would distribute funds to the firm. Loans were forgivable if the firm met certain criteria, including maintaining employment and wages at roughly prepandemic levels. A concern highlighted by this research is the fact that in setting where access to such loans is through financial intermediaries, the relationships of specific firms and their ability to have banks access the loans on their behalf was quite unequal, leading to heterogeneous ability to access the funds in a manner not always tied to the actual needs of the businesses.

Autor et al. (2022) examine the effectiveness of indirect approaches such as PPP and show that the $800 billion dollars preserved 2–3 million job-years of employment at a cost of $170,000 to $275,000 per job. They conclude that only 23%–34% of the funds went directly to workers who would have otherwise lost their jobs. Thus most of the money flowed to business owners and shareholders with about three-quarters of the funds flowing to the upper quintile of households.

Going forward, the growing availability of microdata together with such types of policy interventions have the potential to significantly deepen our understanding of the most effective ways to make supply side interventions and the trade-offs associated with choosing these approaches in emergencies such as the Covid pandemic vs. more normal times.

5 Conclusions

In this chapter, we have examined the sources of small firm financing, evidence of the magnitude of financing frictions and the real effects when they are alleviated, as well as some of the ways in which policy makers continue to help alleviate small firm credit constraints.

Several themes have emerged from this work. First, we document important heterogeneity in the underlying population of small business owners. Much of the entry into business ownership at the top end of the wealth distribution is not in capital intensive industries and appears to be driven by nonpecuniary motivations. Nevertheless, a significant number of small firms that do appear to rely on external finance—both bank finance for their business as well as personal credit of their owners—do appear to face credit constraints, particularly in instances where it seems hard to evaluate their credit worthiness. Understanding whether it is possible to identify firms that are most likely to face such constraints based on ex-ante characteristics is important for an understanding of the actual magnitude of frictions facing these businesses, and more targeted approaches to alleviating these constraints.

In many ways a core challenge in alleviating small firm financing frictions relates to the enduring trade-off between the special ability of banks to utilize soft information and resulting advantage they gain from being able to use this at the expense of the small firms themselves. Regulations that give businesses control rights over their own information, combined with increasing technological advances in machine learning have the potential to learn credit worthiness from attributes that were harder to learn from before. However, as we discussed, such algorithmic approaches appear to have their own downsides in terms of the unequal benefits that accrue to borrowers from such technological advances. Finally although governments across the world provide subsidies as a way to alleviate constraints, there is still a lot to be learned about the relative merits of direct lending vs. loan guarantees and the instances in which one approach might be preferable to the other. These remain some of the many promising avenues of further effort in understanding small firm financing constraints.

Acknowledgments

We thank Tong Yu for research assistance and are grateful to Espen Eckbo and Morten Sorensen for their helpful comments.

References

Adelino, M., Schoar, A., Severino, F., 2015. House prices, collateral, and self-employment. J. Financ. Econ. 117 (2), 288–306.

Agrawal, A., Catalini, C., Goldfarb, A., 2016. Are syndicates the killer app of equity compounding? Calif. Manage. Rev. 58 (2), 111–124.

Alekseev, G., Amer, S., Gopal, M., Kuchler, T., Schneider, J.W., Stroebel, J., Wernerfelt, N.C., 2020. The Effects of COVID-19 on US Small Businesses: Evidence From Owners, Managers, and Employees. National Bureau of Economic Research.

Andersen, S., Nielsen, K.M., 2012. Ability or finances as constraints on entrepreneurship? Evidence from survival rates in a natural experiment. Rev. Financ. Stud. 25 (12), 3684–3710.

Autor, D., Cho, D., Crane, L.D., Goldar, M., Lutz, B., Montes, J., Peterman, W.B., Ratner, D., Villar, D., Yildirmaz, A., 2020. An evaluation of the paycheck protection program using administrative payroll microdata. 22 (Unpublished manuscript).

Autor, D., Cho, D., Crane, L.D., Goldar, M., Lutz, B., Montes, J.K., Peterman, W.B., Ratner, D.D., Vallenas, D.V., Yildirmaz, A., 2022. The $800 Billion Paycheck Protection Program: Where Did the Money Go and Why Did It Go There? National Bureau of Economic Research.

Babina, T., Buchak, G., Gornall, W., 2022. Customer Data Access and Fintech Entry: Early Evidence From Open Banking. SSRN Working Paper 4071214.

Bai, J., Carvalho, D., Phillips, G.M., 2018. The impact of bank credit on labor reallocation and aggregate industry productivity. J. Financ. 73 (6), 2787–2836.

Balyuk, T., Prabhala, N., Puri, M., 2021. Small Bank Financing and Funding Hesitancy in a Crisis: Evidence From the Paycheck Protection Program. Available at SSRN 3717259.

Barrot, J.-N., 2016. Trade credit and industry dynamics: evidence from trucking firms. J. Financ. 71 (5), 1975–2016.

Barrot, J.-N., Nanda, R., 2020. The employment effects of faster payment: evidence from the federal quickpay reform. J. Financ. 75 (6), 3139–3173.

Bartik, A.W., Bertrand, M., Cullen, Z.B., Glaeser, E.L., Luca, M., Stanton, C.T., 2020. How Are Small Businesses Adjusting to COVID-19? Early Evidence From a Survey. National Bureau of Economic Research.

Bellon, A., Cookson, J.A., Gilje, E.P., Heimer, R.Z., Van Nieuwerburgh, S., 2021. Personal wealth, self-employment, and business ownership. Rev. Financ. Stud. 34 (8), 3935–3975.

Berg, T., Fuster, A., Puri, M., 2022. Fintech lending. Annu. Rev. Financ. Econ. 14, 187–207.

Berger, A., Udell, G., 1995. Relationship lending and lines of credit in small firm finance. J. Bus. 68 (3), 351–381.

Berger, A., Udell, G., 2002. Small business credit availability and relationship lending: the importance of bank organisational structure. Econ. J. 112 (477), F32–F53.

Berger, A.N., Kashyap, A.K., Scalise, J.M., 1995. The transformation of the us banking industry: What a long, strange trip it's been. Brook. Pap. Econ. Act. 1995 (2), 55–218.

Berger, A., Klapper, L., Udell, G., 2001. The ability of banks to lend to informationally opaque small businesses. J. Bank. Financ. 25 (12), 2127–2167. https://EconPapers.repec.org/RePEc:eee:jbfina:v:25:y:2001:i:12:p:2127–2167.

Berger, A.N., Miller, N.H., Petersen, M.A., Rajan, R.G., Stein, J.C., 2005. Does function follow organizational form? Evidence from the lending practices of large and small banks. J. Financ. Econ. 76 (2), 237–269.

Berger, A.N., Cerqueiro, G., Penas, M., 2011. Does debtor protection really protect debtors? Evidence from the small business credit market. J. Bank. Financ. 35 (7), 1843–1857.

Berkowitz, J., White, M.J., 2004. Bankruptcy and small firms' access to credit. RAND J. Econ. 35 (1), 69–84.

Bernanke, B.S., 2010. Restoring the Flow of Credit to Small Businesses. Federal Reserve Meeting Series: "Addressing the Financing Needs of Small Businesses", vol. 12. http://www.federalreserve.gov/newsevents/speech/bernanke20100712a.htm.

Bernstein, S., Giroud, X., Townsend, R.R., 2016. The impact of venture capital monitoring. J. Financ. 71 (4), 1591–1622.

Black, S.E., Strahan, P.E., 2002. Entrepreneurship and bank credit availability. J. Financ. 57 (6), 2807–2833.

Black, J., de Meza, D., Jeffreys, D., 1996. House prices, the supply of collateral and the enterprise economy. Econ. J. 106 (434), 60–75.

Blanchflower, D.G., Oswald, A.J., 1998. What makes an entrepreneur? J. Labor Econ. 16 (1), 26–60.

Bos, M., Breza, E., Liberman, A., 2018. The labor market effects of credit market information. Rev. Financ. Stud. 31 (6), 2005–2037.

Brown, J.D., Earle, J.S., 2017. Finance and growth at the firm level: evidence from SBA loans. J. Financ. 72 (3), 1039–1080.

Caglio, C.R., Darst, R.M., Kalemli-Özcan, S., 2021, April. Risk-Taking and Monetary Policy Transmission: Evidence From Loans to SMEs and Large Firms. National Bureau of Economic Research. http://www.nber.org/papers/w28685. Working Paper. Working Paper Series 28685.

Canales, R., Nanda, R., 2012. A darker side to decentralized banks: market power and credit rationing in SME lending. J. Financ. Econ. 105 (2), 353–366.

Cetorelli, N., Strahan, P.E., 2006. Finance as a barrier to entry: bank competition and industry structure in local US markets. J. Financ. 61 (1), 437–461.

Chatterji, A.K., Seamans, R.C., 2012. Entrepreneurial finance, credit cards, and race. J. Financ. Econ. 106 (1), 182–195.

Chatterji, A.K., Chay, K.Y., Fairlie, R.W., 2014. The impact of city contracting set-asides on black self-employment and employment. J. Labor Econ. 32 (3), 507–561. https://ideas.repec.org/a/ucp/jlabec/doi10.1086-675228.html.

Chava, S., Oettl, A., Subramanian, A., Subramanian, K., 2013. Banking deregulation and innovation. J. Financ. Econ. 109 (3), 759–774. https://doi.org/10.2139/ssrn.2174420.

Chemmanur, T., Krishnan, K., Nandy, D., 2011. How does venture capital financing improve efficiency in private firms? A look beneath the surface. Rev. Financ. Stud. 24 (12), 4037–4090.

Chen, B.S., Hanson, S.G., Stein, J.C., 2017. The Decline of Big-Bank Lending to Small Business: Dynamic Impacts on Local Credit and Labor Markets. National Bureau of Economic Research.

Chodorow-Reich, G., 2014. The employment effects of credit market disruptions: firm-level evidence from the 2008–9 financial crisis. Q. J. Econ. 129 (1), 1–59.

Chodorow-Reich, G., Darmouni, O., Luck, S., Plosser, M., 2022. Bank liquidity provision across the firm size distribution. J. Financ. Econ. 144 (3), 908–932.

Cornaggia, J., Mao, Y., Tian, X., Wolfe, B., 2015. Does banking competition affect innovation? J. Financ. Econ. 115 (1), 189–209. https://doi.org/10.1016/j.jfineco.2014.09.

Corradin, S., Popov, A., 2015. House prices, home equity borrowing, and entrepreneurship. Rev. Financ. Stud. 28 (8), 2399–2428.

Da Rin, M., Hellmann, T., Puri, M., 2013. A survey of venture capital research. In: Handbook of the Economics of Finance, vol. 2. Elsevier, pp. 573–648. 2.

Denes, M.R., Howell, S.T., Mezzanotti, F., Wang, X., Xu, T., 2020. Investor Tax Credits and Entrepreneurship: Evidence From U.S. States. National Bureau of Economic Research, Inc. NBER Working Papers 27751.

Diamond, D.W., 1984. Financial intermediation and delegated monitoring. Rev. Econ. Stud. 51 (3), 393–414.

Diamond, D., 1991. Monitoring and reputation: the choice between bank loans and directly placed debt. J. Polit. Econ. 99 (4), 689–721.

Erel, I., 2011. The effect of bank mergers on loan prices: evidence from the United States. Rev. Financ. Stud. 24 (4), 1068–1101.

Ewens, M., Nanda, R., Rhodes-Kropf, M., 2018. Cost of experimentation and the evolution of venture capital. J. Financ. Econ. 128 (03), 422. https://doi.org/10.1016/j.jfineco.2018.03.001.

Fairlie, R.W., 2020. The Impact of Covid-19 on Small Business Owners: Evidence of Early-Stage Losses From the April 2020 Current Population Survey. National Bureau of Economic Research.

Fonseca, J., Wang, J., 2021. How Much Do Small Businesses Rely on Personal Credit? Working Paper.

Fuster, A., Goldsmith-Pinkham, P., Ramadorai, T., Walther, A., 2022. Predictably unequal? The effects of machine learning on credit markets. J. Financ. 77 (1), 5–47. https://doi.org/10.1111/jofi.13090. https://ideas.repec.org/a/bla/jfinan/v77y2022i1p5-47.html.

Gonzalez-Uribe, J., Leatherbee, M., 2018. The effects of business accelerators on venture performance: evidence from start-up Chile. Rev. Financ. Stud. 31 (4), 1566–1603.

Greenstone, M., Mas, A., Nguyen, H.-L., 2020. Do credit market shocks affect the real economy? Quasi-experimental evidence from the great recession and "Normal" economic times. Am. Econ. J. Econ. Pol. 12 (1), 200–225.

Hamilton, B.H., 2000. Does entrepreneurship pay? An empirical analysis of the returns to self-employment. J. Polit. Econ. 108 (3), 604–631.

Han, S., Li, G., 2011. Household borrowing after personal bankruptcy. J. Money Credit Bank. 43 (2–3), 491–517.

Herkenhoff, K., Phillips, G., Cohen-Cole, E., 2021. The impact of consumer credit access on self-employment and entrepreneurship. J. Financ. Econ. 141, 345–371.

Hochberg, Y.V., 2015. Accelerating Entrepreneurs and Ecosystems: The Seed Accelerator Model. Innovation Policy and the Economy. vol. 16 University of Chicago Press, pp. 25–51. http://www.nber.org/chapters/c13584.

Holtz-Eakin, D., Joulfaian, D., Rosen, H.S., 1994. Sticking it out: entrepreneurial survival and liquidity constraints. J. Polit. Econ. 102 (1), 53–75.

Hombert, J., Matray, A., 2017. The real effects of lending relationships on innovative firms and inventor mobility. Rev. Financ. Stud. 30 (7), 2413–2445.

Howell, S.T., 2017. Financing innovation: evidence from R&D grants. Am. Econ. Rev. 107 (4), 1136–1164. https://doi.org/10.1257/aer.20150808.

Howell, S.T., Kuchler, T., Snitkof, D., Stroebel, J., Wong, J., 2021. Racial Disparities in Access to Small Business Credit: Evidence From the Paycheck Protection Program. National Bureau of Economic Research.

Huber, K., 2018. Disentangling the effects of a banking crisis: evidence from German firms and counties. Am. Econ. Rev. 108 (3), 868–898.

Hurst, E., Lusardi, A., 2004. Liquidity constraints, household wealth, and entrepreneurship. J. Polit. Econ. 112 (2), 319–347.

Hurst, E., Pugsley, B.W., 2011. What do small businesses do? Brook. Pap. Econ. Act. 43 (2), 73–142.

Iyer, R., Khwaja, A.I., Luttmer, E., Shue, K., 2016. Screening peers softly: inferring the quality of small borrowers. Manag. Sci. 62 (6), 1554–1577.

Jayaratne, J., Strahan, P.E., 1996. The finance-growth nexus: evidence from bank branch deregulation. Q. J. Econ. 111 (3), 639–670.

Jayaratne, J., Strahan, P.E., 1998. Entry restrictions, industry evolution, and dynamic efficiency: evidence from commercial banking. J. Law Econ. 41 (1), 239–274.

Jensen, T.L., Leth-Petersen, S., Nanda, R., 2022. Housing collateral, credit constraints and entrepreneurship-evidence from a mortgage reform. J. Financ. Econ. 145 (2), 318–337.

Kerr, W.R., Nanda, R., 2009. Democratizing entry: banking deregulations, financing constraints, and entrepreneurship. J. Financ. Econ. 94 (1), 124–149.

Kerr, S., Kerr, W.R., Nanda, R., 2022. House prices, home equity and entrepreneurship: evidence from US census micro data. J. Monet. Econ. 130, 103–119.

Kortum, S., Lerner, J., 2000. Assessing the contribution of venture capital to innovation. RAND J. Econ. 31 (4), 674–692.

Krishnan, K., Nandy, D.K., Puri, M., 2015. Does financing spur small business productivity? Evidence from a natural experiment. Rev. Financ. Stud. 28 (6), 1768–1809.

Lastrapes, W., Schmutte, I., Watson, T., 2022. Home equity lending, credit constraints and small business in the US. Econ. Inq. 60 (1), 43–63. https://doi.org/10.1111/ecin.13026.

Lelarge, C., Sraer, D., Thesmar, D., 2010. Entrepreneurship and credit constraints: evidence from a French loan guarantee program. In: International Differences in Entrepreneurship, University of Chicago Press, pp. 243–273.

Lerner, J., 2000. The government as venture capitalist: the long-run impact of the SBIR program. J. Priv. Equity 3 (2), 55–78.

Lerner, J., Nanda, R., 2020. Venture capital's role in financing innovation: what we know and how much we still need to learn. J. Econ. Perspect. 34 (3), 237–261. https://doi.org/10.1257/jep.34.3.237.

Mills, K.G., 2019. Fintech, Small Business & the American Dream: How Technology Is Transforming Lending and Shaping a New Era of Small Business Opportunity. Palgrave Macmillan.

Mills, K., McCarthy, B., 2014, July. The State of Small Business Lending: Credit Access During the Recovery and How Technology May Change the Game. Harvard Business School. Working Paper 15-004.

Moskowitz, T.J., Vissing-Jørgensen, A., 2002. The returns to entrepreneurial investment: a private equity premium puzzle? Am. Econ. Rev. 92 (4), 745–778.

Murfin, J., Njoroge, K., 2015. The implicit costs of trade credit borrowing by large firms. Rev. Financ. Stud. 28 (1), 112–145.

Musto, D.K., 2004. What happens when information leaves a market? Evidence from post-bankruptcy consumers. J. Bus. 77 (4), 725–748.

Petersen, M.A., Rajan, R.G., 1994. The benefits of lending relationships: evidence from small business data. J. Financ. 49 (1), 3–37.

Puri, M., Zarutskie, R., 2012. On the life cycle dynamics of venture-capital-and non-venture-capital-financed firms. J. Financ. 67 (6), 2247–2293.

Rajan, R., 1992. Insiders and outsiders: the choice between informed and arm's-length debt. J. Financ. 47 (4), 1367–1400.

Robb, A.M., Robinson, D.T., 2014. The capital structure decisions of new firms. Rev. Financ. Stud. 27 (1), 153–179.

Samila, S., Sorenson, O., 2011. Venture capital, entrepreneurship, and economic growth. Rev. Econ. Stat. 93 (1), 338–349.

Sapienza, P., 2002. The effects of banking mergers on loan contracts. J. Financ. 57 (1), 329–367.

Schmalz, M.C., Sraer, D.A., Thesmar, D., 2017. Housing collateral and entrepreneurship. J. Financ. 72 (1), 99–132.

Schnabl, P., 2012. The international transmission of bank liquidity shocks: evidence from an emerging market. J. Financ. 67 (3), 897–932.

Stein, J., 2002. Information production and capital allocation: decentralized versus hierarchical firms. J. Financ. 57, 1891–1921. https://doi.org/10.1111/0022-1082.00483.

Stiglitz, J.E., Weiss, A., 1981. Credit rationing in markets with imperfect information. Am. Econ. Rev. 71 (3), 393–410.

Yimfor, E., 2021. Brokers and Finders in Startup Offerings. SSRN. Working Paper. Working Paper Series 3511164.

Later stage financing

Private equity financing

4

Victoria Ivashina[*]

Harvard Business School, Harvard University, Boston, MA, United States
*Corresponding author: e-mail address: vivashina@hbs.edu

Chapter outline

Throughout this chapter, the term "private equity," or "PE," is used to broadly describe the segment of the alternative industry that uses an illiquid closed-end fund structure to raise capital. This includes a range of private equity investment strategies, such as buyouts, growth equity, and venture capital, but also other alternative asset classes like private debt funds. In other words, much of what is discussed here applies not only to *equity* funds, but also to the private equity industry broadly speaking.

    The goal for this chapter is to impart an understanding of what is unique about the PE funding structure and why it might function differently from other forms of capital. Note that in buyouts and late-stage growth equity investments, the use of debt—not just equity—is central to financing individual investments. So, arguably, the use of leverage is also unique in private equity (see, for example, Fig. 1 in Axelson et al., 2013). This, however, will be addressed in a later chapter devoted

Handbook of the Economics of Corporate Finance, Volume 1, ISSN 2949-964X, https://doi.org/10.1016/bs.hecf.2023.02.004

139

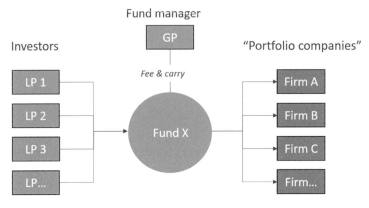

FIG. 1

Traditional fund structure.

Source: Author.

to buyouts. I focus here on how capital for private equity investments is raised and the factors that influence the flow of funds to this industry. I begin with a simple introduction, and the basics of PE funding, but eventually reflect on industry trends and limitations of prevailing forms of private equity investing and what they might look like in the future.

1 The basics

1.1 Traditional fund structures

Although the fund structure in the modern private equity industry looks rather standardized, it did not start this way, and we will return to this fact later. For now, let's just familiarize ourselves with the basics.

Private equity firms are organized as Limited Partnerships in which the private equity firm acts as the General Partner (GP) (also called the "Sponsor") and the investors who provide the majority of the capital as Limited Partners (LPs) (see Fig. 1). Traditionally, PE funds raise capital from external investors through a blind, closed-end fund. Once fundraising is closed, the size of the fund commitments is fixed, the capital "locked," and distributions of the fund are at the discretion of the fund manager. (In contrast, one can invest in or withdraw from a mutual fund at any time.) The blind nature of the fund speaks to the fact that limited partners do not have direct influence over investment decisions, which is not uncommon in the asset management industry. The rights of LPs are defined in the Limited Partnership Agreement (LPA).[a]

---

[a]Individual LPs can receive additional terms through so-called "side letters." It is common, for example, to restrict investments in controversial industries through such side agreements.

There are important differences, not only in the general form of funding in private equity, but also in how capital is drawn from investors. In any other investment vehicle—think mutual or hedge fund—capital is typically transferred to the financial manager at the moment of investment. In private equity, a pension fund would generate a *commitment to fund* capital calls when and if investments or additional capital needs arise. This is what fundraising is. Throughout the fund's life, to receive capital from LPs the GP must send a "drawdown notice" detailing the amount needed from each for an upcoming investment or expense.[b] The GP is typically required to provide ten business days' notice to LPs before the capital is due. LPs are usually allowed to hold uncalled commitments in safe investments, but must have enough liquidity to send the funds requested by the GP. So, unlike other asset classes, investing in private equity requires liquidity management.

If an LP is unable to make payment by the "drawdown date," the GP can send a default warning, and if funding is still not received within a few days the commitment is considered to be in default. The consequences of default for an LP are typically dramatic and may include (i) the GP reducing or withholding distributions from the defaulted LP, (ii) the GP selling the defaulted LP's entire share of the fund to a substitute LP, (iii) the LP ceasing to accrue gains from the fund while continuing to accrue losses, (iv) the LP potentially losing all rights to contribute to the fund in the future, and (v) the LP remaining liable for its share of the commitment plus a default penalty.

"Real Life" Example: LP Capital Commitments

"If any Limited Partners (other than an Excused Partner with respect to a Portfolio Investment) fails to make, in a timely manner, all or any portion of any Capital Contribution, Direct Payment or any other payment required to be made by such Limited Partner hereunder, and such failure continues for five Business Days… then such Limited Partner may be designated by the General Partner as in default under this Agreement (a "Defaulting Partner")…

The General Partner may take any or all of the following actions with respect to a Defaulting Partner (i) reduce amounts otherwise distributable to such Defaulting Partner by 50% as of the date of such Default and withhold the remaining 50% of any future distributions that otherwise would be payable to such Defaulting Partner pursuant to Article VI until the dissolution of the Fund, (ii) cease to allocate any income and gain to such Defaulting Partner with respect to its remaining interest in the Fund, but continue to allocate its pro rata share of losses and deductions, (iii) require such Defaulting Partner to remain fully liable for payment of up to its pro rata share of Organizational Expenses and Fund Expenses as if the Default had not occurred."

Source: *Limited Partnership Agreement, anonymized by the author.*

Fig. 1 depicts the traditional structure of a PE fund. As noted, multiple limited partners contribute money to the fund. In turn, the fund is invested in a range of "portfolio companies" (typically 12–15 investments per fund). The investments

---

[b]For details, see Institutional Limited Partners Association (ILPA), "Capital Call & Distribution Notice Best Practices," https://ilpa.org/wp-content/uploads/2018/03/ILPA-Best-Practices-Capital-Calls-Distribution-Notices_Version-1.1.pdf.

are managed by the GP, which charges a fixed management fee and performance-based fee called carried interest, or "carry." Although the reality is a bit more complex, this is commonly referred to as "2-and-20": 2% fee of assets under management and 20% carry.

Fig. 1 corresponds to the structure of one fund. The life of a fund is limited, a typical fund being expected to return all of its capital in roughly 10 years.[c] But annual extensions are possible. (An illustration of this can be seen in the Oaktree example below.) The continuity of the PE firm depends on the GP's ability to raise the next fund. In short, private equity is funded through a sequence of overlapping closed-end funds (see Fig. 2 for an illustration). The year in which the fund makes its first capital drawdown (typically fees, if not investment) is known as its "vintage year."

Note that repeated fundraising is an important disciplining mechanism in the industry. Funds, even so-called "generalist" funds, tend to have a focus, typically geographic and strategic. For example, a fund that does U.S. large-cap buyouts (the most prominent strategy in terms of fundraising) will avoid venture, "loan-to-own" distress deals or investments in emerging markets. Ex-ante promised or target net return is used as a reference point. Ex-post, to account for macroeconomic fluctuation, returns are compared to those of peers and public benchmarks. A fund that underperforms will struggle to raise the next fund. Of course, this type of response in PE is not as agile and damning as mutual or even hedge fund redemptions. But the idea is roughly the same: the capital is returned over the life of the fund and a limited partner unhappy with the performance or practices of a given fund has the option to not invest in the next fund.

Performance (measured on deployed instead of committed capital) is the most important, but not the only relevant dimension for the GP. Another example where

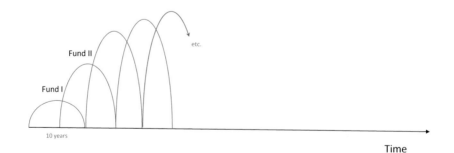

FIG. 2

PE financing over time.

Source: Author.

[c]Eighty-four percent of the sample in a 2019 survey by consultancy MJ Hudson had an initial fund life of ten years. "Private Equity Fund Terms Research," 5th Edition, MJ Hudson, 2019–2020.

pressure is felt is in LPs' expectations that the capital will be put to work relatively quickly. An LP that subscribes to invest with an asset manager charging 2% of committed capital will be eager to see that capital put to work as soon as possible.[d] But it makes little sense to force capital deployment in a fixed amount of time because arrival of the best investment opportunities and time to their closing is not fixed.[e] With this in mind, most investments occur in the first half of the life of a fund, called the "investment period," and most exits in the second half of a fund's life termed the "harvesting period."

So when should a PE manager raise the next fund? The simple idea is that as an investment manager you do not want to run out of money to invest. The industry is too competitive, and delays in closing might lead you to lose a coveted target. (Think of the analogy of bidding on a house when you have to formalize a mortgage application while another bidder is offering cash.) Raising a fund within the same strategy too soon (or raising too big a fund for that matter) can be problematic for several reasons.[f] Ideally, the next funds are raised towards the end of existing funds' investment period.[g] The length of the fundraising (also called subscription) period naturally varies greatly depending on a number of factors including fund size, firm reputation, performance track record, and current market environment, but is generally about one year.

"Real Life" Example: Structure of Closed-end Funds

"Oaktree's closed-end funds are typically structured as limited partnerships that have a 10- or 11-year term and have a specified period during which clients can subscribe for limited partnership interests in the fund. Once a client is admitted as a limited partner, that client is required to contribute capital when called by us as the general partner, and generally cannot withdraw its investment. These closed-end funds have an investment period that generally ranges from three to five years, during which Oaktree is permitted to call the committed capital of those funds to make investments. As closed-end funds liquidate their investments, Oaktree typically distributes the proceeds to the clients, although during the investment period Oaktree has the ability to retain or recall such proceeds to make additional investments. Once a fund has committed to invest approximately 80% of its capital, Oaktree typically raises a new fund in the same strategy, generally ensuring that it always has capital to invest in new opportunities."

Source: *Oaktree Capital Group, Form 10-K, December 31 2020, p. 9.*

---

[d]Performance measurement in private equity is from the moment the capital is "at work" and not from the fund closing date. Although this means that there are no strong direct incentives to make investments sooner rather than later, the GP will be on the hook to clear an 8% preferred return on all capital drawn from the LP, which includes annual fees, before it can access carry.

[e]In addition to the pressure of expectations, the annual fee structure typically declines in the second half of a fund's life. For example, if a 10-year fund charges a 2% annual fee of committed capital, after five years (i) the base of the fee shifts from committed to invested capital, and (ii) it typically gradually declines on an annual basis until reaching 1%.

[f]For example, see "The Private Equity Firm That Grew Too Fast," *The New York Times*, April 24, 2015. Issues of overlapping funds are discussed in Victoria Ivashina and Jeffrey Boyar, "Berkshire Partners: Party City," Harvard Business School Case 218-028.

[g]In the first years of a fund's life, it is not uncommon to include "recycling provisions" that make a provision for the PE fund to reinvest proceeds from early exits.

Fixed percentage fees are controversial in the industry. Limited partners are sharply aware of PE being an expensive asset class. As the PE industry became increasingly competitive over the industry's roughly forty-year history, returns became compressed and more uncertain, whereas compression of fees has not been nearly as dramatic. Say a fund is $10 million; 2% translates to $200,000 per year in fees. With this budget, an investment team is expected to close two or three deals per year, each of which requires exhaustive due diligence on the market, financials, legal, management, etc. Let's also hope that the GP is not closing on the first two deals that came to the fund. So actually the GP needs to do due diligence on a much bigger set of deals and in some strategies (like VC or early-stage growth equity) source these deals. And the investment team needs something to live on as well. With a fund this size it is easy to see that fees are a necessity. The story is different if the fund is $10 billion, charging 2% and closing two or three deals per year. It is difficult to build a case for the costs of deal origination and closing scaling proportionately for large deals. In this case, the leftover for the GP is substantial, as is the certainty of the fees. A $10 billion fund represents $1 billion in almost guaranteed fees over the first 5 years alone, regardless of the quality of investments. This creates a critical tension in the industry, especially as the mega PE firms handling much of the capital in the industry have consolidated.

1.2 The J-curve

We earlier introduced the idea that PE deploys funds gradually during the first half of a fund's life and, by construction, exits these investments in the second half of the fund's life. (The average holding period moves around 5 years, and historically has been slightly higher. When valuations are high, however, as they were at the end of 2021, the investment holding period is slightly less than five years.) This leads to the concept of the "*J*-curve," which captures the unique distribution of LPs' cash flows over the life of a fund (see Fig. 3).

Put yourself in the shoes of an LP. The *J*-curve tells you that after committing your capital you will be facing "capital calls" for several years with only the book

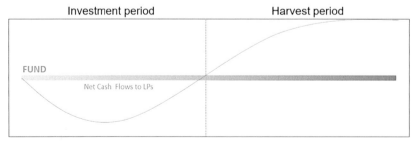

FIG. 3

The *J*-curve.

Source: Author.

value of your investments to show.[h] As noted earlier, after it is committed and before it is called capital is in the hands of LPs, but it has to be held in liquid and relatively safe investments to be able to meet capital calls. This intrinsic part of investing in private equity is reflected neither in the *J*-curve nor in the measurement of the returns to private equity. But it is important for an LP to understand that constraints on how committed capital is invested before it is called will affect the overall return on capital allocated to alternatives.

Capital is drawn from LPs for two reasons: asset management fees and investments. Investment opportunities arrive over time and are exited, on average, after five years. Distributions from full or partial exits as well as intermediate dividends lead to an eventual reversal of returns into net positive cash flows to LPs. Gradual deployment of capital (and certainty of fees) and long holding periods result in a deepening of the *J*-curve. The trajectory of the negative cash flows in PE investments is quite different from investing in the public market, in which a single investment is deployed in one day.

Although LPs might have little control over the distribution of cash flows from a PE fund, there are tactics available to mitigate some of the effects of the *J*-curve across their private investment portfolios. A reduction in fees or change in calculation basis can help LPs, however, standardized industry practices can make such adjustments difficult.[i] Recently active growth of a secondary market, and specifically funds specialized in secondary investments, has been gaining significant traction among LPs in part due to *J*-curve mitigation. In simple terms, a secondary fund purchases LP stakes in the primary fund. Typically, this occurs after an existing LP has been invested in a fund for a number of years such that the secondary fund is largely invested and close to distribution early in its life.[j] The portfolio effects outlined in the *J*-curve are generally important considerations for LPs. Relatedly, the J-curve effect is not a secondary consideration when an LP decides to pursue exposure to private assets or the PE asset class by investing in secondary funds, funds of funds more broadly, or pursuing co-investments and direct investments. We return to this later.

As we look at the *J*-curve and relate it to the earlier observation that the next fund is typically raised before the existing fund runs out of money, it should become clear that by the time an existing LP is invited to invest in the next fund few realizations have taken place. This means that there is little "hard" proof of existing PE performance before capital is committed to the next fund. As an LP, you will still be relying

---

[h]The capital call for an individual LP in a fund is proportional to the value of its committed capital within the fund.

[i]For indirect evidence of variations in terms across limited partners, see Begenau and Siriwardane (2023). Although favorable terms for anchor investors are more typical, anchor investors are more valuable for early funds or funds in new strategies.

[j]For a deep dive into secondaries, see Victoria Ivashina, Luis Viceira, John Dionne, and Alys Ferragamo, 2021, "PE Secondaries: Blackstone Strategic Partners," Harvard Business School Case 9-222-027.

heavily on the information that originally led you to invest with the first fund. Earlier, we mentioned that funds' flow response is not as sharp in PE as in, say, mutual funds, but it still acts as a disciplining mechanism. Now we can further clarify that the outflow is likely to react on about a 10-year frequency, a piece of the dynamic that is essential to understanding why despite being highly competitive, the PE industry is slow to correct some of its most criticized practices.[k]

1.3 Subscription lines

Given that the topic of this chapter is private equity financing, we should address the use of "subscription lines," or "lines of credit." These are generally low interest credit facilities used by PE funds to finance all or part of an acquisition.[l] These credit facilities do not exist in the absence of LPs' capital subscriptions, but are in fact secured by the LPs' commitments (hence, the term "subscription lines"). This explains the low interest rate on such credit lines; the likelihood of CalPERS or the Yale endowment defaulting on their commitments to private equity are, after all, clearly negligible.[m] Naturally, not every fund is able to raise capital from such prominent institutions, so underlying the broader phenomenon of subscription lines is some variation in LTV (loan-to-value) and/or cost of the line.

Using credit lines enables GPs to delay the capital call from LPs. A fund that needs to close on an acquisition calls the capital from the bank (*in addition* to the debt package at the deal level) to temporarily fund *equity* capital in the deal. Fig. 4 illustrates the mechanics.

Why do this? Let's begin with benign reasons for which the use of credit lines was originally conceived. First, the lines provide liquidity management flexibility. As illustrated in the previous section, for an LP liquidity management is not a trivial part of investing in private equity, and on the GP side the timing of investment opportunities and closure are not precise. In a large buyout, for example, there are many things that PE investors do not control. There is a competitive sales process and the need for board and regulatory approval. Yet the GP needs financing lined up to fund the acquisition when the deal is closed. The debt leg of the financing is typically secured ahead if the acquisition occurs through a bridge loan.[n] It is not surprising that, on the debt side, this (contingent) short-term liquidity provision is outsourced to banks (e.g., see Kashyap et al., 2002). For different reasons, a similar

---

[k]See Victoria Ivashina and Josh Lerner, *Patient Capital*, an entire book devoted to a discussion of frictions in the PE industry grounded in many years of research by the authors and colleagues in the profession.

[l]During the credit boom that followed the Great Financial Crisis, some of the largest private equity firms also received credit lines at the firm (vs. fund) level. This is a different, additional form of leverage.

[m]Let's also not forget about the earlier described consequences of defaulting on a commitment.

[n]Also, "staple financing," the debt financing for a transaction arranged by the seller, is typical in large cap transactions. This is another common practice for ensuring a smooth closing process once all conditions are met.

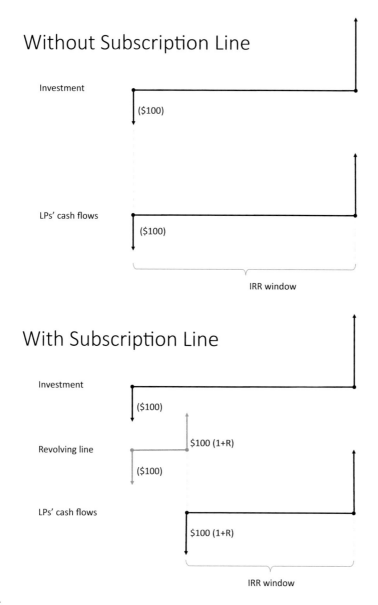

FIG. 4

Cash flows on an individual investment.

Source: Author.

risk of short-term funding delays arises on the equity side. Again, it is intuitive to use banks to ensure the temporary funding provision. This, in turn, enables LPs to handle liquidity in a more sophisticated way than just having their committed capital in quasi-cash, and to better manage the *J*-curve.

The use of subscription lines was pervasive at the end of 2021, and attracted a lot of criticism and awareness by LPs due to some additional consequences. We noted earlier that performance calculation for PE investments is computed from the moment capital is deployed. As can be seen in Fig. 4, because (direct) deployment of LP capital is delayed as a consequence of the use of a subscription line, the window over which performance is calculated shrinks. This, in turn, increases the Internal Rate of Return ("IRR"), a primary performance measure for many LPs. Although small subscription lines carry an interest rate (more so when they are used, but there is some minimal cost just for having a line outstanding), any interest charged over the period during which the line is drawn is an expense borne by the deal (not surprisingly, as there is no free money). The overall profit available to LPs is thus reduced, as captured in the Multiple of Money measure (the other common performance metric of PE performance that captures the ratio between money invested and money returned).[o] In IRR calculations, the boost from the shrinking horizon over which the return is computed outweighs the negative impact of the cost of the credit line. This opportunity to artificially enhance the IRR, and in the world of uncertain PE performance and capital chasing top quartile funds, might make a significant difference in fundraising. Research by Preqin related to funds of 1990 to 2007 vintage showed subscription line use to contribute to a median change of about 1% in IRRs.[p]

There are some additional critiques surrounding the use of subscription lines. For example, carry (the performance-based component of GP compensation) is conditional on a hurdle return on drawn capital (typically set at 8% of IRR). So the ability to inflate the IRR allows earlier GP performance-related fees. Depending on the performance of the fund, this can reduce the net profits received by LPs.[q]

In response to the increased use of subscription lines in the industry, the Institutional Limited Partner Association (ILPA) issued updated guidance in June 2020 related to "Enhancing Transparency around Subscription Lines of Credit." Among other things, the guidance advocates for increased transparency in performance metric reporting. It is a concise and worthwhile read for those interested in the subject. It is fair to say that standardization of the most sensible practices on the LP side is impeded by (i) divergent practices and objectives of different limited partners, and (ii) restricted access to funds, specifically, to the top performing funds. This make it easy for a majority of LPs to do things "differently" from its pears, and expect that they can deliver above average performance.

---

[o]Multiple of Money (MoM), Multiple of Invested Capital (MOIC), and Total Value to Paid In (TVPI) are different names for the same concept: if you invest $100 and receive $250 5 years later, your multiple is 2.5x.

[p]For details, see "How Big Is the Impact of Credit Lines on Fund Performance Really," *Private Equity International*, September 2019.

[q]For a broader discussion of subscription lines, see Victoria Ivashina and Terrence Shu, "Subscription Lines Dilemma," 2019, Harvard Business School Case 220-025. Also, Howard Marks' letter to the shareholders from April 18, 2017 "Lines in the Sand," https://www.oaktreecapital.com/docs/default-source/memos/lines-in-the-sand.pdf.

1.4 Who are the limited partners?

A private equity fund is a specialized financial intermediary (an asset manager) that manages money primarily for large institutional investors. In academic research focused on the behavior of financial intermediaries, a great amount of attention is devoted to understanding intermediaries' incentives and constraints. What is fascinating in the context of PE is that we have financial intermediaries on both the LP and GP side. Each side brings its own set of complex issues that influence the state and evolution of the PE industry. Above, we elaborated on the mechanics of the PE manager's job. Let's shift attention to the LPs.

As Fig. 1 illustrates, a single (well-established) private equity fund consists of a range of different LPs. According to Preqin, of the top-100 LPs by size of commitment to private equity, nearly 50% are pension funds (about 5% being private, and the rest public). For example, California Public Employees' Retirement System (CalPERS), California State Teachers' Retirement System (CalSTRS), New York State Common Retirement Fund, Florida State Board of Administration, Teacher Retirement System of Texas, and Washington State Investment Board are among the largest LPs. Fund of funds, insurance companies, and other asset managers each represent about 10% of the largest LPs. These are followed by sovereign wealth funds and endowment plans.[r] The general pattern is that all are investors with a long-term liability structure (which is why investing in an illiquid long-term asset class is suitable for their portfolio).

Fundraising is an intense process (on both ends). A GP would want a reasonably diversified base of LPs to avoid any hiccups on capital calls and minimize the time and resources devoted to fundraising for the next funds. Ideally, the LP base will include institutions with which a GP has an ongoing relationship to facilitate the fundraising process. All of which is to say that, for funds in the $1–$5 billion range, the general composition of the LP base is not going to be representative of the overall distribution of the LPs, whereas for larger PE firms the composition of LPs essentially represents the market, as can be seen in the KKR example below.

Coordination among investors is important to understanding the relationship dynamic between LPs and GPs. Once a fund is closed, it is typical to establish a Limited Partner Advisory Committee (LPAC) to advise the GP on issues that might arise. Imagine, for example, that an attractive merger opportunity presents itself for a company in a PE portfolio. But it requires additional capital, which can only come from a different fund. These types of decisions or waivers of some of the conditions in the LPA agreement would need to be approved by the LPAC. Broadly, the three main roles of an LPAC relate to (i) waiver under the original LP agreement, (ii) conflicts of

---

[r]Preqin, "The Private Equity Top 100," Special Report, February 2017. Of course, these general statistics for investor type hide the importance of individual investors. For example, the top-5 LPs include not only Canadian Pension Plan Investment Board (CPP IB) and California Public Employees' Retirement System (CalPERS), but also Abu Dhabi Investment Authority (ADIA) and Government of Singapore Investment Corporation (GIC).

interest facing the GP in investment or operating decisions (such as the example of the follow-up acquisition above), and (iii) general oversight. This will become relevant when discussing the trend of lengthening the fund horizon.

"Real Life" Example: 2020 KKR & Co Investor's Breakdown

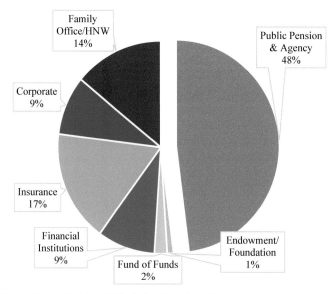

Note: This chart is compiled from KKR & Co., Form 10-K, 31 December 2020, p. 25. According to this filing, the numbers are based on the AUM of Private Markets investment funds, Private Markets co-investment vehicles, Public Markets separately managed accounts, and Public Markets investment funds. The numbers exclude general partner commitments, assets managed through CLOs, and strategic partnerships in which KKR has a minority ownership interest.

2 Beyond the fund structure: Co-investments and direct investments

The most prevalent option for accessing private equity is to invest via a fund and take a traditional LP role (Fig. 1). LPs that invest through a traditional fund have no decision-making power over the selection and timing of investments.

At the other end of the spectrum are LPs that choose to invest directly in private companies and execute deals alone. This is typically referred to as "direct investment" (vs "fund investment"). Although in the absence of an intermediary there are no associated fees and carry payments, direct investing requires significant internal resources to source, perform due diligence, structure, monitor, and potentially exit private investments. Typically, the kind of direct deals that enable LPs to keep costs under control are debt as opposed to equity deals and specialized infrastructure deals. For multiple reasons, LPs tend to lack the capacity for operational or other active management, value-add common in the buyout, growth equity, and venture capital space (i.e., traditional private equity strategies). So, although direct investing by LPs has become commonplace, it rarely competes for deals with traditional funds.[s]

The most prominent way to save on fees and carry while investing in private equity is to co-invest alongside a private equity fund. As of 2020, co-investing was estimated at $55–$60 billion of deal flow per year.[t] A co-investment opportunity enables an LP to invest in a deal through a fund *and, in parallel*, through a co-investment vehicle that has a reduced fee and carry structure (see Fig. 5). There is significant variation in fee and carry (the same is true for fund investment), but compared to fund investment, co-investment vehicles charge roughly half the fee and carry. So in a "2-and-20" compensation scheme (2% fee and 20% carry), the co-investment vehicle would, on average, charge 1% and 10%. With co-investing, fees and carry are negotiated separately, and GPs could offer zero fees and carry to large LPs.[u]

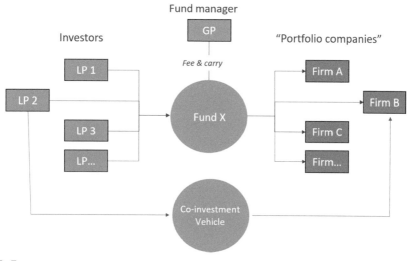

FIG. 5

Co-investment structure.

Source: Author.

---

[s]For details of direct and co-investments, see Victoria Ivashina, Federica Gabrieli, and Jérôme Lenhardt, 2017, "PFA Pension: Expansion of Alternatives Portfolio," Harvard Business School Case 218-025.
[t]See Private Funds CFO, 2020, "Conflict over co-investment terms," https://www.privatefundscfo.com/conflict-over-co-investment-terms/.
[u]The fee structure on co-investments can also be complicated by how the broken-deal costs are allocated in transactions. For example, fee and carry could be zero, but co-investments associated with additional cost charges for broken-deals.

The typical co-investment process starts with the GP identifying a deal open for co-investment. Not surprisingly, these often tend to be large deals that require additional capital. This is consistent with evidence in Fang et al. (2015) and Braun et al. (2020). From this perspective, the GP benefits from the process as co-investing enables the fund to do larger deals without increasing concentration risk and can strengthen relationships with LPs. Whereas in the past, large investments would be co-led by multiple GPs, now additional capital is frequently raised through co-investment.

Key to co-investment is the availability of deals on both the GP and LP side, co-investment arrangements affording LPs a right, but not an obligation, to invest. This is important to keep in mind when analyzing heterogeneity in costs and performance from investing in private equity across LPs. Differential access to co-investments yields different costs, even for LPs within the same fund, and because LPs have discretion with regard to dialing up or down or rejecting specific co-investments, outcomes even for LPs with co-investment rights become difficult to compare.

Importantly, deal selection highlights a potential risk of co-investment for LPs. Naïve thinking would suggest that, as illustrated in Fig. 5, every co-investment is also in the fund and, presumably, incentives are well aligned. So shouldn't something that is good for an LP at a 2-and-20 cost structure be good at a discount structure? In fact, it depends on whether the GP is equally good at sourcing, managing, and exiting deals of traditional size as well as deals multiples of that size, which is often what become available for co-investment. Scaling of GPs' skills and capabilities should not be taken for granted. Additionally, to the degree that co-investments are crowding out deals previously co-led by multiple GPs, should we assume that such partnerships were not particularly beneficial for value creation (despite the high cost structure)? After all, we are replacing what would be a partnership of, say, two GPs, both of which claimed to be active, with a GP plus passive co-investors. If there is no crowding out, and deals available for co-investment are deals that otherwise would not be done, then they are riskier deals and we have a different problem on our hands.[v]

GPs typically have far more information about specific deals and the complete universe of deals than LPs, which have only a short amount of time in which to perform due diligence. This could lead to a possible adverse selection problem in which the GP sends only below-average quality deals (compared to the fund). The naïve intuition isn't completely off, however; the adverse selection problem cannot be too large because, as fund performance is ultimately affected, it is in GPs' interest to pursue only reasonably high-quality deals in order to maintain good relationships with their LPs.

---

[v] I am only emphasizing deal size differences here because that is a prominent feature of co-investments. That said, there are other reasons deals become available for co-investment that speak even more directly to the potentially riskier profile of co-investment deals, which is the point I am trying to make here.

Nowadays, any LP with significant access to co-investments would necessarily have in-house capabilities for dealing with adverse selection by performing due diligence on and evaluating deals GPs make available for co-investment. This is especially important given that due diligence must typically be done within a limited timeframe. Larger LPs that put a lot of value on the selection process claim to invest in as few as 5% of co-investments made available to them. Given these additional expenses, co-investing programs may not be suited to smaller LPs. Preqin reported that in 2020 approximately 75% of LPs with more than $50 billion in AUM, compared to fewer than half of investors with less than $1 billion in AUM, were already, or considering, co-investing.[w]

This is the conceptual background of co-investment. An empirical study published in 2015 compared the performance of early co-investment programs (Fang et al., 2015). The study used data on 390 direct investments (103 of which were co-investments) made between 1991 and 2011 by seven global institutional investors. The advantage of this sample was that it enabled the researchers to see the complete investment programs of seven large limited partners. The co-investment deals, on net, were found to underperform the investments of the corresponding fund as measured by IRR or multiple, but still outperformed the public market. In that sense, it might have been a reasonable allocation by LPs (and might also make sense from a *J*-curve management perspective). But these findings did contrast sharply with the general perception that co-investments would deliver fund-level returns at a cheaper cost and therefore beat fund performance.

Although Braun et al. (2020) also examined the relative performance of co-investments using a large sample of investments, it is difficult to compare the two studies due to differences in the sample and performance metrics. I would expect that for deals within a given fund, market-adjusted performance (which is what the latter study used) should not generate significantly different results. But there are other dimensions on which the study differs from the above-referenced study. Braun et al. conclude that the *large* sample of co-investments (they look at 1,106 co-investment deals) performs about the same in gross terms as the fund investments from 1981 to 2010. Putting aside measurement differences, this is an intriguing finding.

Co-investments have grown significantly over the past decade, during which time there has been active discussion in the industry largely converging to the view that co-investments are attractive if done right.[x] It is surprising to see that in the early years of co-investments, when awareness of the challenges of the space were less pronounced, an LP might have been fine pursuing co-investments. Although tying these results to individual LPs' holdings and their performance might be harder, the discrepant results of the two studies might hint at mistakes in selection by LPs filtering the co-investments to pursue from the universe available to them.

---

[w]See Preqin, 2020, "2020 Preqin Global Private Equity and Venture Capital Report," p. 48.
[x]For example, in a 2019 Cambridge Associates report entitled, "Ready, Steady, Co-Invest," the risk of adverse selection, significant resources and expertise needed to evaluate investments, and tight response times are highlighted as the top-3 challenges for LPs pursuing co-investments.

3 Trends in private equity financing

3.1 Fund flow into private equity

Investor demand for private capital investment continued at a strong pace at the end of 2021, with total funds raised growing year-to-year (excluding a minor drop in 2020 reflecting COVID-19 market uncertainty). Between 2010 and 2019, global fundraising grew at an annual average rate of about 13.4%, clearly above the growth rate of the underlying economies. Most funds are located in the United States and Europe, as is most LP capital.[y]

This is a global trend driven to a large degree by the near-zero interest rate environment precipitated by the Great Financial Crisis. On average, in the ten years following the financial crisis, allocations to private equity and real estate nearly doubled, representing about 20% of assets under management in 2017 for pensions in many of the largest economies (Ivashina and Lerner, 2019b). In the study sample alone, the authors found a $1.8 trillion shift by pension funds to alternatives between 2008 and 2017, leading them to argue that the global nature of the sharp rise in and timing of PE commitments by pension funds points to interest rates being trapped at near zero.

One might ask why, given that interest rates have been low for more than a decade now, we see such robust growth in allocations to PE. First, as pointed out earlier, fundraising is slow to react in private equity. Only one exit might be secured before an LP is asked to commit capital to the next fund (the rest being held in an illiquid position and marketed at book value). Perhaps not surprisingly, fund early exit decisions are not made at random.[z] This means that the information an LP might have to date is likely to have a positive bias, as fundraising success is heavily dependent on early exits, especially for younger PE firms or firms that might have recently faced adversity. Second, again as noted earlier, access to individual private equity funds is often relationship based. Third, you cannot scale up allocation to private equity in a significant way over a short period of time. Say that a pension fund decides in 2010 that it is ready to deploy a significant fraction of its capital to private equity, but many of the private equity firms are not currently taking capital commitments (recall that fundraising has a roughly 5-year frequency). Although public assets can be purchased (or sold) at any time, private equity opportunities are discrete and occur with low frequency. Lastly, an LP might want to smooth its exposure to the *J*-curve, which means that it would not want to commit capital to funds with the same vintages.[aa]

---

[y]According to Private Equity International, as of mid-2021, 206 of the 300 largest PE firms were operating in North America, 50 in Europe, and 43 in Asia-Pacific. "PEI 300," *Private Equity International*, June 10, 2021.

[z]See, for example, Barber and Yasuda (2017), Brown et al. (2019), and Chakraborty and Ewens (2018).

[aa]For example, in a 2019 interview, the chief investment officer at Washington State Investment Board (a $128 billion pension) pointed out that "PE portfolio construction is best done gradually and organically over time and must come at the same pace allowed by the governance structure, investment policies and the LP's diligence capabilities on hiring the talent pool. [...] Every time we increased our PE allocation it has taken us years to fulfill that. In the last two decades, we went from 15 percent to 23 percent, but each time we managed that increase very carefully." Source: *Private Equity International*, July 9, 2019.

As a result, fundraising that we see today is largely a function of decisions taken after the Great Financial Crisis. The natural prediction based on this observation is that (in the longer run) the fund flow to private equity will stabilize, as rates (and therefore the relative appeal of the fixed income asset class) cannot fall any further.

Of course, additional trends might be at least partially offset by other developments in the industry. One factor might be retail's entry into private equity driven in part by the entry of U.S. defined contribution pension plans to the asset class. Another trend that characterized the past few years and is likely to continue forward is the rise in "non-flagship" funds, or funds in adjoined strategies, such as private credit, opportunity funds, and secondaries, among others.[ab] Expansion is particularly pronounced in larger GPs, the average number of "fund families" now reaching seven different products offered by the same PE firm from just a single offering in 2000.[ac] These additional products provide further avenues for capturing higher capital allocations from existing LPs.

I now discuss two additional trends that will continue to be in the spotlight in the years to come.

3.2 Lengthening of the fund horizon[ad]

Although we tend to associate private equity with long-term capital, the reality is that the bulk of the industry is focused on a 5-year holding horizon for individual investments. Five years to exit, in turn, leads to a prioritization of goals and operational strategies that show credible results in 4 years, at which point the GP can initiate the sale process, which takes about a year.[ae] It should be easy to see that the need and opportunities for sophisticated active management surpass initiatives that can show results in 4 years.

Beyond investment opportunities, fundraising, which, due to overlapping fund structures, occurs at roughly 5-year intervals, is a hassle. Given the opaqueness of private investments, limited partners want to meet senior investment professionals and know their record and involvement with the deals, which all takes time. Moreover, fundraising is an "over-the counter" process: the LP-GP engagements and negotiations are bilateral. Consequently, the fundraising period typically extends over a year or more and is a costly process for the private equity firm.

Taking a step back, the modern PE industry developed after World War II. Two American venture capital firms, American Research and Development Corporation (ARD) and J.H. Whitney & Co, founded in 1946, are believed to have shaped the

---

[ab]The term "non-flagship" might be outdated, as many PE firms' expansion into adjoined strategies has been the engine of growth.

[ac]"A year of disruption in the private markets," *McKinsey Global Private Markets Review 2021*, April 2021.

[ad]A related discussion appears in Ivashina (2022).

[ae]I should acknowledge that I implicitly argue that the Modigliani and Miller theorem is violated and liability structure matters for firm operations. The underlying reason for this is the level of uncertainty associated with the type of investments pursued by private equity firms including start-ups, turnaround, execution of growth through acquisitions, and distress, among other strategies.

modern private equity firm. As is common today, ARD was originally formed as a blind closed-end fund. Georges Doriot is credited with emphasizing the importance of the fund structure (as opposed to deal-by-deal financing) to facilitate a speedy flow of capital to attractive opportunities. ARD, however, was funded through a public market, arguably because the institutional investor base (as well as modern portfolio theory) was not yet developed, and not because of the vision of the superiority of an unlimited holding horizon. Nevertheless, it is interesting that private equity funding structures of the future might more closely resemble those of these early precursors than the funding structures that predominate today.

In recent years, private equity has become increasingly focused on raising funds for "permanent" or "perpetual" capital vehicles.[af] There are a few funds that have a true perpetual structure.[ag] For the most part, however, the trend refers to stretching fund life beyond the traditional 10 years, and there are a couple of common ways to achieve this. Return targets (and average fees) for longer hold funds are typically lower due to a focus on steady cash-flow investments. The end return is justifiable due to accrued returns on investments held over a longer horizon, whereas traditional fund investments involve significant taxes, closing costs, and reinvestment leakage, despite higher per investment return.

"Real Life" Example: What is Perpetual Capital?

In 2020, Blackstone raised more than $8 billion for a second Perpetual Fund offering. As of December 2020, Blackstone reported Perpetual Capital Asset Under Management at $134.9 million.

Blackstone definition of Perpetual Capital within its 2020 10K filing:

"Perpetual Capital" refers to the component of assets under management with an indefinite term, that is not in liquidation, and for which there is no requirement to return capital to investors through redemption requests in the ordinary course of business, except where funded by new capital inflows. Perpetual Capital includes co-investment capital with an investor right to convert into Perpetual Capital."

Note: This information is compiled from The Blackstone Group Inc., Form 10-K, 2020. The quote is taken from p. 6.

It might be that over the next few years raising funds with longer than a 10-year life for mainstream strategies, such as large-cap buyouts, will become the norm. But already we have seen the acceptance of multiple practices that facilitate stretching the holding period. I discuss several of these.

Cross-fund investments—Imagine that a firm has a highly successful investment in Fund IV. Seven years down the road the investment is still in the portfolio and continues to have a lot of growth potential, which requires addition funding. Fund

---

[af]For example, see "Private-Equity Firms Create Funds that Are Built To Last," *Wall Street Journal*, January 1, 2019.
[ag]See, for example, Victoria Ivashina and Jeffrey Boyar, 2018, "Granite Equity Partners," Harvard Business School Case 219-040.

IV, approaching its life end, could easily exit its investment by selling it to a strategic or financial buyer. But should Fund IV sell (fully or partially) this deal to its Fund V? This is a fascinating question that is at the core of many business school cases. A decade or so ago, the prevalent answer would have been "no": it is a matter of discipline, and the nature of the PE industry is such that investments need to be exited in a duly prescribed manner. In the current environment, this is no longer so clear, and more and more firms have held the same investment across multiple funds.

A key risk to be managed in the transfer of ownership interests between funds is the fair valuation of the stake being disposed of, it being an illiquid asset. The conflict here is evident—most certainly the fair value will not be the same as the actual value, and, in our example, this will create winners and losers among LP investors in Fund IV and Fund V. The problem is messy, but the goal is to introduce as much objectivity into the valuation as possible, and there are several not-mutually exclusive techniques for doing so. These include (i) obtaining a third-party fairness opinion to address valuation concerns, (ii) partnering with other reputable PE funds, and (iii) getting approval from the LPAC.

Secondary transaction—This is not a direct way for a GP to stretch a fund's life, but it is a significant PE market development that facilitates other fund ever-greening practices. "Secondary" or "LP-led secondary" transactions are sales (complete or partial) of one LP's fund investments to another LP. There is no GP involvement in this transaction other than that such sales typically require a GP's agreement. So just as with a publicly traded stock, an investor can acquire a position in the primary market (during the IPO) or in the secondary market. Between 2001 and 2019, global secondary deals in the PE market grew from $2 billion to $88 billion, accelerating in the last decade.[ah] It is still small compared to the size of the industry, but growing very fast. Normalization of secondary transactions in the PE space provides a source of liquidity for LPs and lifts pressure from GPs to deliver liquidity and verified valuation though a traditional exit.

GP-led secondary transaction—This type of transaction differs from the one described above in being initiated, structured, and overseen by the GP. Activity in the GP-led secondaries market has been increasing in recent years, the value of such deals being estimated to have reached $30bn in 2020.[ai] There are a couple types of transactions that fall under the "GP-led secondary" umbrella. The simpler one involves a Special Purpose Vehicle (SPV) structure termed a "Continuation Vehicle." The idea is to move an existing asset or assets from an older fund to the continuation vehicle. LPs can either "cash out" and sell their

---

[ah]For a deep dive into secondaries, see Victoria Ivashina, Luis M. Viceira, John D. Dionne, and Alys Ferragamo, 2021, "PE Secondaries: Blackstone Strategic Partners," Harvard Business School Case 222-027.
[ai]See "Continuation funds: How GPs are holding on for longer," PitchBook, February 3, 2021.

interests in the original fund or roll over their investment into the new SPV. The SPV typically has updated fund terms and economics alongside an extended life cycle for the assets. A concrete example of such transactions is the sale of Gatwick, Britain's second-busiest airport. The arrangement allowed investors to continue owning the asset after the original fund's lifecycle end.[aj]

A more complex example of this type of transaction, also known as a "stapled" deal, is a transaction in which the GP simultaneously extends the holding period for existing assets by transferring them into a new fund *and* fundraising additional capital from new LPs into that fund.[ak]

Can the trend of horizon lengthening take off at significant scale (not vis-à-vis historical levels, but with respect to the size of the industry)? It is not clear. Most of the structures currently used are highly complex at their core, and the fundamental problem of visibility into value and management of private assets remains. Exits are still the clearest window into fund performance.

3.3 Investing for good

One industry innovation trend of a particular interest for the next decade is the focus on ESG (environmental, social, and governance)-related strategies. Recent years have witnessed unparalleled growth in capital directed to ESG-related strategies, one quarter of all ESG funds raised since 2015 having been raised in 2020:Q1 alone.[al] European LPs lead their U.S. and Asian counterparts in their commitment to supporting ESG-related strategies including climate change, energy transition, and diversity and inclusion (D&I).[am]

The first key barrier to overcome is to understand the true effect of ESG actions on investor returns. Data are currently lacking confirming a correlation between top quartile ESG performance within a company and higher returns to shareholders.[an]

A second challenge is that ESG metric development is in its infancy. "ESG is broad and amorphous, notoriously hard to define. We lack time-tested standards for measuring either results or impact," read the Bain & Company 2021 Global Private Equity Report. According to the same report, only half of the 431 PE firms that have signed the UN Principles for Responsible Investing (PRI) monitor ESG principles for more than 90% of their portfolio companies. On the LP side, a preview of the 2022 ILPA and Bain & Company ESG Measurement Report indicates that fewer than 20% of LPs request ESG KPI reporting from GPs. In sum, as of early 2022, superior performance of ESG strategies is yet to be demonstrated on a large

---

[aj]"Gatwick Investors Transfers Stake to Fellow Shareholders," *The Daily Telegraph*, January 13, 2020.

[ak]An example of this kind of transaction can be found in Victoria Ivashina and Jeffrey Boyar, 2018, "Enfoca: Private Equity in Peru," Harvard Business School Case 219-030.

[al]Ibid.

[am]"Global Private Equity Report," Bain & Company, 2021, p. 29.

[an]"A year of disruption in the private markets," *McKinsey Global Private Markets Review 2021*, April 2021, p. 53.

scale, even without any apparent constraints on how to measure ESG or which aspects to emphasize.

That said, there is clearly a lot of attention to the ESG field, so another important and interesting question to ask is, "Does private equity (as opposed to public markets) play a different role in propelling the ESG agenda, and why?"

One argument is that for public and B2C firms, retail investors and consumer pressure might be the most effective ESG governance mechanism. A good example is diversity on corporate boards. Whereas an overwhelming majority of newly appointed independent directors of S&P500 companies have been women and minority men, private equity firms have been lagging on this front for the simple reason that they are private.

However, there are other reasons to believe that private equity might be better positioned to be on the forefront of the ESG agenda. Many believe that it is easier to build a sustainable business with a diverse and inclusive culture than to change a mature business to comply with these principals, and those who put weight on this intuitive idea would argue that VC-activity will be central to ESG adoption. We can take this idea further: buyout firms excel at turnarounds, and to the degree that we believe that ESG adoption is comparable to a turnaround buyout firms might play a role.[ao] Of course, in both of these examples, given the mixed evidence on large sample performance, ESG as a central focus of VC or buyout is unlikely to justify the costs of the asset class.

Shifting attention to LPs' needs from a portfolio perspective, a promising trend coming from some large European limited partners is a focus on achieving net-zero CO_2 emissions at the portfolio level.[ap] This is where private capital—and perhaps direct investments by pension funds more so than traditional fund investments—can push the private asset class by pursuing timberland and infrastructure projects in renewable energy, among other projects.

Overall, ESG will continue to be a relevant topic, and things will continue to evolve actively on this front, likely led by regulators and compliance, at least in the U.S. market. For the private equity industry, the focus on ESG is likely to accelerate the growth of infrastructure asset classes and do so through non-traditional private equity structures like LP-GP partnerships and direct LP investments. Within traditional VC and buyouts strategies, the ESG focus is likely to lead to compositional shifts at the GP portfolio level. However, in the absence of clarity on performance advantages, and given the cost of this asset class, it is unlikely that a focus on ESG will lead to a significant capital inflow for the private equity fund industry.

[ao]See the academics discussion at the IPC Oxford Private Equity Research Symposium on May 27, 2021 entitled, "The Future of Private Equity." The proceedings of this symposium can be found in the *Journal of Applied Corporate Finance*, 2021, 33(3).

[ap]See, for example, recent PFA strategic announcement https://english.pfa.dk/news-archive/2020/05/10/14/48/pfa-is-committed-to-zero-co2-emissions/.

Acknowledgments

Victoria Ivashina is a Lovett-Learned Professor of Finance at the Harvard Business School (HBS) and co-founder and co-head of HBS's Private Capital Project. Professor Ivashina is the author of many HBS case studies and notes in the field of private equity, and co-author of two books, *Patient Capital: The Challenges and Promises of Long-Term Investing* and *Private Equity: A Case Book*. She directed the development of the HBS Online course on Alternative Investments, and since 2010 has been teaching Private Equity Finance, an elective course in the Harvard Business School MBA program. She also teaches and co-heads the Private Equity and Venture Capital executive education program.

I am grateful to Cathy Basquel (HBS MBA'2021) and Alys Ferragamo for exceptional assistance in developing this chapter.

References

Axelson, U., Jenkinson, T., Strömberg, P., Weisbach, M.S., 2013. Borrow cheap, buy high? The determinants of leverage and pricing in buyouts. J. Fin. 68 (6), 2223–2267.

Barber, B.M., Yasuda, A., 2017. Interim fund performance and fundraising in private equity. J. Fin. Econ. 124, 172–194.

Begenau, J., Siriwardane, E., 2023. How do private equity fees vary across public pensions? J. Fin. forthcoming.

Braun, R., Jenkinson, T., Schemmerl, C., 2020. Adverse selection and the performance of private equity co-investments. J. Fin. Econ. 136, 44–62.

Brown, G.W., Gredil, O.R., Kaplan, S.N., 2019. Do private equity funds manipulate reported returns? J. Fin. Econ. 132, 267–297.

Chakraborty, I., Ewens, M., 2018. Managing performance signals through delay: evidence from venture capital. Manage. Sci. 64, 2875–2900.

Fang, L., Ivashina, V., Lerner, J., 2015. The disintermediation of financial markets: direct investing in private equity. J. Fin. Econ. 116 (1), 160–178.

Ivashina, V., Lerner, J., 2019b. Looking for Alternatives: Pension Investments around the World, 2008 to 2017. Working Paper.

Kashyap, A., Rajan, R., Stein, J., 2002. Banks as liquidity providers: an explanation for the co-existence of lending and deposit-taking. J. Fin. 57, 33–73.

Further reading

Ivashina, V., Lerner, J., 2019a. Patient Capital: The Challenges and Promises of Long-Term Investing and Private Equity: A Case Book. Princeton University Press.

Ivashina, V., 2022. When the Tailwind Stops: The Private Equity Industry in the New Interest Rates Environment. Long Term Investor (LTI@UniTO) Inaugural Report, CEPR.

Buyouts: A primer

Tim Jenkinson[a], Hyeik Kim[b], and Michael S. Weisbach[c],*

[a]*Saïd Business School, Oxford University, Oxford, United Kingdom*
[b]*University of Alberta, Edmonton, AB, Canada*
[c]*Fisher College of Business, Ohio State University, Columbia, OH, United States*
Corresponding author: e-mail address: weisbach.2@osu.edu

Chapter outline

1 Introduction

Thirty-two years ago, Jensen (1989) predicted that the public corporation would be "eclipsed" and largely replaced by other forms of organization. While that prediction looked a bit foolish when its publication was immediately followed by the 1990s IPO boom, after 2000 it proved to be remarkably prescient. Consistent with Jensen's prediction that the public corporation would decline in importance, there has been a more than 50% decrease in the number of public US firms since its peak of 7509 in 1997: at the end of 2020, there were only 3530 investible stocks available for the Wilshire 5000.[a] At the same time, the size and importance of private capital markets have increased dramatically. Private capital markets now raise more than $1 trillion every year and invest not just in private firms, but also in publicly traded firms, real estate, and privatization of publicly owned institutions.

A new set of financial institutions has developed that has enabled private capital markets to thrive. In this paper, we will explain how these institutions function, present up-to-date evidence on them, and discuss the relevant academic literature. Our discussion focuses on the buyout component of private capital markets, which is sometimes referred to as the leveraged buyout (LBO) market because of the extensive use of debt in these transactions.

Most investing in the private capital markets occurs through funds, which, as we discuss in Section 2, are structured as limited partnerships. In a buyout fund, the limited partners (LPs) make capital commitments that can be drawn down at the discretion of the fund managers, known as the general partners (GPs). These "draw-downs" are used to acquire portfolio companies, which are managed and ultimately sold by the fund. The returns that the LPs receive come from the difference between the cost and the sale price, plus any dividends received.

To raise a fund, the GPs must offer potential LPs a sufficiently attractive return distribution to induce them to invest in the private market rather than in alternatives. Investments in buyout funds tend to be riskier, due to the extensive use of leverage, and less liquid than those in public markets. In addition, their fees and profit shares are substantially higher than vehicles that invest in public securities such as mutual funds. Private market returns, net of these high fees and profit shares, must deliver a premium over comparable public market returns to induce suppliers of capital to invest. Yet, despite this high hurdle, investors have chosen to make extremely large capital commitments to buyout funds because their expectations of returns are high enough to justify taking on the additional risk and illiquidity.

How do buyout funds manage to earn sufficiently high net returns to induce LPs to invest? Part of the answer is the real changes that the GP can make in its portfolio firms. Sometimes the GP does as Jensen (1989) argues and creates value by reducing wasteful expenditures of free cash flow. But not always—often the value increases come from other sources such as strategic expansions or consolidations, professionalization of management combined with pecuniary incentives for them, providing the firm with capital at times when it does not have other sources of finance, or privatization of an inefficient government operation. In addition, GPs can produce returns for their investors by transferring value from other parties, in particular tax authorities, via the greater use of debt, which is normally tax deductible (within limits).

---

[a]As reported by https://www.investors.com/news/publicly-traded-companies-fewer-winners-huge-despite-stock-market-trend/. See Doidge et al. (2018) for data and discussion about the decrease in public listings over recent years. We present numerous statistics on private capital markets in Section 4.

Recent literature has documented that it is not just the government which is targeted for wealth transfers; it appears that there are, in some circumstances, systematic wealth transfers from customers, workers and suppliers to buyout fund investors.

Intellectually, the buyout sector provides a plethora of questions to study. There are theoretical questions: How should funds be set up and managers compensated? To what extent does private contracting allow for more efficient resource allocations than a reliance on public markets? There are questions related to portfolio theory and capital markets: How much capital should be allocated to this asset class? How should capital be split between various subsectors (buyouts, VC, real estate, etc.)? How does one go about measuring the risk and return of a fund that makes only around 10 investments, many of which have only one cash outflow and one cash inflow over a 12–15 year period? To what extent do LPs and/or GPs have measurable skills? Corporate finance questions abound: How much value is created by the highly leveraged financial structure of most buyouts? What do GPs do to their portfolio firms to increase their values? Do they transfer wealth from other parties (workers, governments), or do they improve the efficiencies of operations? And perhaps the most important questions concern management and leadership, since at the end of the day, most of the increases in the value of the portfolio firms are likely to come from better managerial decisions: How do private equity funds decide on the managerial teams of their portfolio firms? What do they do to motivate and monitor these teams?[b]

The academic literature has just scratched the surface in its understanding of these and related questions. To make things more complicated (and more fun to study), buyout funds constantly innovate and come up with new types of investments and organizational structures. The private capital market has matured to the point that most major firms today have relied on said markets at some point, and this trend is likely to continue. A useful mantra for those of us who study the private equity industry is that: *Private capital markets are at least as important and far more interesting than public capital markets in the 21st Century economy.*

We begin our discussion of buyouts by explaining in Section 2 how buyout funds are structured and exactly how they work. We discuss the relationship between three broad questions in this section: (1) how is capital intermediated from investors to buyout funds, (2) how do buyout funds structure investments into portfolio companies, and (3) how are the management of portfolio companies incentivized by the buyout fund owners?

Starting with the first question, funds that manage assets for investors are an important form of organization that is not as well understood by most economists as it should be. Most buyout funds are set up as closed-end limited partnerships.

---

[b]It probably is not a coincidence that one of the most successful buyout general partners, David Rubenstein of Carlyle, has his own youtube series on successful leadership. See: https://www.youtube.com/channel/UCqsN9MYiu1mKSAsYoF6ppTg.

The "ultimate management company" is often a partnership itself, although some have become public companies. Under the ultimate management companies are the fund advisors, who are contracted by the fund to source, diligence, and negotiate deals, and manage them after they are acquired. We discuss a number of issues related to the structure of the fund and its relationship with its LPs, including fees, co-investment opportunities, and the use of lines of credit and other techniques that enable funds to leverage their entire funds. We particularly focus on the manner in which the interests of GPs and LPs in buyout funds are aligned.

The second question relates to the financing of buyouts. As their name suggests, a key feature of LBOs is an extensive use of leverage. Most buyouts secure the leverage against the assets of the portfolio companies. The structure of the debt has some distinct features. We present statistics on the use of leverage, and provide a detailed example illustrating the way in which the debt of a typical buyout is structured.

The third question relates to the relationship between buyout funds and the management teams of their portfolio companies. GPs seek alignment of interests with management, and achieve this by, in most cases, requiring management to acquire significant equity stakes in the portfolio companies. In addition, they structure the equity portion of the capital structure so that such management returns are amplified in the case of success. The details of such remuneration structures are closely guarded, although much progress has been made in liberating data on the private equity sector for academic scrutiny. However, some general trends are clear, and we finish Section 2 with a discussion of the way in which management incentives are structured.

While Section 2 discusses the nuts and bolts of the way in which buyouts are structured, Section 3 focuses on why they occur in the first place. Buyouts deliver returns to investors by improving the performance of the companies that they buy. It is the expectation of these performance improvements that drive the growth of the industry. The ability of a buyout fund to secure capital commitments depends on investors' expectations of its return relative to their relatively high hurdle because of the buyout sector's risk, fees, profit shares, and illiquidity.

How do buyout funds go about improving the performance of portfolio firms? Our discussion follows Kaplan and Strömberg (2009), who classify the changes brought on by buyout funds as *financial engineering*, *operational engineering*, and *governance engineering*. The most important element of financial engineering in a buyout is the dramatic increase in portfolio firms' leverage. This leverage induces the firms' managers to focus their energies on activities that generate the cash necessary to service the higher interest payments. In doing so, managers will decrease the capital available for wasteful investments, which will increase their firms' values. Operational engineering consists of the way in which buyout funds immerse themselves in the operations of their portfolio companies. Funds often will have operating partners who specialize in helping companies in the particular industries that the fund targets. Finally, governance engineering refers to the improvements in corporate governance brought on by the funds. These improvements typically include smaller but more active boards (compared with similar public companies), and much stronger financial incentives for top management.

Buyout funds almost always link their provisions of financing with control rights. Normally these involve a majority of ownership, but sometimes funds will take minority positions with other rights, such as board seats or the ability to increase their ownership to a majority if pre-specified financial targets are not met. Theoretically, associating financing with control allows funds to make investments that more passive investors cannot. If an investment is positive NPV and a particular strategy not favored by current management is followed, a buyout fund can make the investment and force the management to adopt its favored strategy or change the management team if they will not. In addition, buyout funds are flexible in the types of investments they make. They operate without the mandates that limit other types of investors so that they have more potentially valuable investments available to them. For example, a fund whose stated strategy is to provide equity will often be able, if they think it likely to be profitable, to provide debt to a distressed firm with the hope of negotiating a swap into a controlling equity position.

Section 3 also details some of the particular strategies that buyout firms adopt. These strategies vary from "bust up" LBOs designed to sell off assets and reduce cash flow, to expansions in which the fund provides capital for "bolt on" acquisitions to a firm, to transition-oriented deals where the fund provides an exit for some of the firm's owners while allowing others to remain in control. By being flexible in their investing strategy, buyout funds are able to come up with many ways in which they can earn returns for their investors.

Section 4 provides facts about buyouts which starts with a brief history describing the evolution of the sector. Buyout markets tend to be correlated with the credit cycle. Purchase price multiples and debt contributions tend to go up (down) during economic booms (busts) but returns show a counter-cyclical pattern: years when relatively little capital is raised tend, ultimately, to produce the best returns. While in the past, trade sales to corporate acquirers were the dominant way of exiting, secondary transactions whereby one buyout fund sells to another have become increasingly common. Fund fees have deviated surprising little from the 2 and 20 model—a 2% annual management fee and 20% profit share, or "carried interest"—even as buyout funds have increased dramatically in size.

Section 5 surveys academic research on buyouts. Such research on buyouts and on private capital markets more generally faces two major hurdles. First, the firms that are acquired in buyouts are private after they are acquired, and the majority are private prior to being acquired as well. Consequently, the quantity of data that is available to researchers is far lower than for research on public firms. Furthermore, data on private equity funds themselves—in particular fund cash-flows, fees, details of limited partnership agreements, etc.—are difficult to obtain. Data availability is, in general, improving and there have been some important initiatives that have made research-quality data more readily available for researchers.[c] Second, even if all private data were available publicly, much data that is commonly used for public firms and markets simply do not exist for private firms and markets. In particular, there are no market prices for firms or funds that are not publicly traded (a few are). And funds receive cash flows from their portfolio companies only at the time of acquisitions portfolio firms, exists, as well as the occasional dividend.

The limited availability of cash flow data combined with the lack of market data for firms and funds makes measuring funds' risk and return much more complicated than the comparable exercise for public firms. For this reason, much research addresses the issue of measuring the funds' returns and the extent to which these returns justify their risk and illiquidity. The most common metric for measuring private equity returns has become the Public Market Equivalent (PME) return. However, this measure has issues of concern to which answers are not obvious, such as how to adjust it for risk, and the appropriate public market benchmark against which to measure a fund's return. For example, should a European fund be benchmarked against European stock market indices, which have underperformed American stock market indices in recent years (making European funds look good relative to American funds that are measured relative to a higher benchmark)? Nonetheless, while studies vary depending on methodology, most find a PME for buyout funds >1, implying that these funds do beat the public markets against which they are compared.

Another topic of research concerns the investors in buyout funds. Investors must decide how much capital to allocate to the sector, and the particular funds to which to commit capital. Portfolio theory does not provide much guidance for these decisions since historical risk and return are so difficult to measure. In addition, given the changes in the industry, past performance is not likely to be a good predictor of future performance anyway. In addition, the choice of funds in which an institution allocates capital can dramatically influence its returns. There have been studies suggesting that these choices are not random. General Partners do appear to differ in their skill to earn returns, and Limited Partners differ in their skill at evaluating General Partners' skills.

An important strand of the literature on buyouts concerns the underlying source of their returns. A number of studies have documented that portfolio firms' cash flows usually increase. But the reason why they increase can vary substantially. Sometimes, funds create value through the approaches discussed in Section 3. However, funds can also transfer wealth from other parties, including workers, the government, suppliers, and customers. Clearly, the source of portfolio firms' increased

---

[c]In particular, we would highlight the role played by the Private Equity Research Consortium (PERC), which provides access to Burgiss data and programming support to analyze the data. PERC also runs conferences encouraging interaction between academics and practitioners working, or investing, in private equity. More information on PERC is available at https://uncipc.org/index.php/initiativecat/private-equity/

cash flows is an important issue for many reasons, especially public policy toward buyouts, and is likely to be a continuing area of research in the future.

Finally, there is interesting work studying contracting issues in buyouts. As discussed in Section 2, buyouts have a complicated contractual structure, which is likely to be an important driver of their performance. Important research has studied the nature of this contractual arrangement, the extent to which it is consistent with contracting theory, and whether it leads to agency problems between LPs and GPs, and between GPs and portfolio firms.

2 What are buyouts and how do they work?

In this section, we discuss three questions. First, how is equity finance intermediated between investors and the fund? In other words, what is the LP–GP arrangement? We characterize the way in which buyout funds are structured, finance is provided by investors, and fund managers are compensated and regulated. Second, how does a buyout fund finance the purchase of, and design the financial structure of, portfolio companies? Leveraged Buyouts, as their name implies, use significant amounts of debt in their capital structures. We discuss the way in which this debt is structured alongside the equity from the fund. Third, we complete the circle by discussing the financial arrangements that are negotiated between the portfolio companies and their management teams. In particular, we discuss the structure of the equity incentives that management face. One mantra of the private equity industry is to align the interest of all parties, and the extent to which such alignment is achieved is an overarching focus of this section.

2.1 Investors and funds

There are many possible structures that could conceivably be used to make investments in private companies. In the early days of private equity, publicly listed structures were used, such as business development corporations in the United States or investment trusts (such as Investors in Industry, which became 3i) in the United Kingdom. These are typically structured as closed-end funds, which raise capital on public markets via an IPO, and secondary offerings, and then invest in private companies. They can recycle realizations back into new portfolio companies (and are therefore referred to as "ever-green" funds), and must adhere to various rules relating to the distribution of profits to investors in order to retain favorable tax status.[d] Such structures are still used, and are one of the easiest ways in which individual investors can gain exposure to buyouts, but they are not the most common way in

---

[d]For instance, in the United States a requirement for Business Development Corporations to retain their status as regulated investment companies, they must distribute over 90% of their profits to shareholders. With Regulated Investment Company status, no corporate income tax on profits is paid by the Business Development Corporation.

which buyout funds are organized. However, there has been work studying these structures—which are typically traded on stock markets since they do not have a fixed life—as a way of measuring the returns associated with private equity.[e]

2.1.1 Funds as limited partnerships

The dominant form of LBO fund structure has become the Limited Partnership, which is also used for many other forms of what used to be called "alternative assets" but are by now mainstream—assets such as hedge funds, private credit funds, energy funds, etc. There are two main reasons why Limited Partnerships have become the standard fund structure: (1) tax efficiency for investors, (2) incentive structures and tax efficiency for fund managers.

First, we explain the structure of such funds. In most countries, and certainly those in which private equity is active, it is possible to form limited partnerships, which are a form of partnership in which some of the partners (typically institutional investors) contribute only finance and are not involved in investment decision-making. These investors are referred to as Limited Partners (confusingly, they are Limited Partners of the Limited Partnership). We will use the abbreviation LP to refer to the investors (as limited partners) rather than the partnership itself. The liability of such investors is limited to their invested capital. This limitation is critical for a large institutional investor, with the sort of deep pockets that could attract litigious claimants (for example, if an operating company acted in an anti-competitive way or was negligent). Such investors would not be as protected if they purchased a stake directly in a company and exercised some element of control, for instance, by having board representation. The Limited Partnership structure allows investors to hold significant stakes in private companies without exposing themselves to the risk of litigation.

A Limited Partnership requires a General Partner (GP) to manage the fund and make the investment decisions. In principle, the GP has unlimited liability for the debts and any claims against the partnership. Again, the language is confusing in this respect: often individuals are referred to as General Partners, but the formal General Partner of the fund is typically a separate legal entity, so that individuals do not bear the risks associated with unlimited liability.

Fig. 1 provides an overview of the various entities and the important financial flows. There can be differences in these structures across countries, but the diagram illustrates some key features. First, in any structure, there will be an ultimate management company that is established by the initial founders. This company is sometimes referred to as the "GP"; however, the terminology can be confusing because as each individual fund has a General Partner and the ultimate management company (UMC) does not have to be a partnership (it is common in the United States for this entity to be an LLC). This ultimate management company essentially controls the brand of the fund manager, decides on strategy, and can finance the launching of

---

[e]See Jegadeesh et al. (2015).

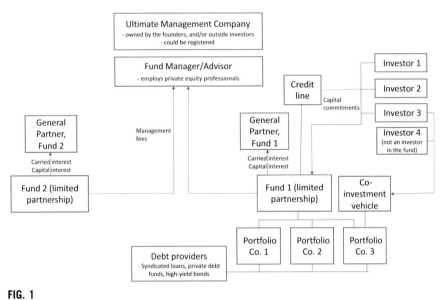

FIG. 1

The typical GP-LP structure.

new funds (for legal work, marketing, investor meetings, etc.). Outside investors can own a stake in the UMC, and a number of the most well-known UMC's have gone public in recent years. Such outside capital can be used to launch new fund strategies (such as private debt, or funds focused on new geographies) so that the founders do not have to provide all the required funds. It can also enable founders to take some money off the table, by selling part of their stake in the UMC. This strategy of investing in UMCs has become very popular, with large funds being managed by Blackstone, Goldman Sachs, and Neuberger Berman (through their Dyal Capital Partners subsidiary) that are dedicated to investing in such stakes. Some of these funds that invest in GP stakes have gone public in recent years.

The second important entity in a buyout structure is the Fund Manager, which is sometimes referred to as a Fund Advisor. This entity employs private equity professionals and provides services across the various funds that are raised. Certain individuals can be focused on particular funds, but often they will provide input into investment decisions across funds.

The third important entity is the Fund. The Fund will engage the Fund Manager to source, diligence, and select deals, in return for a management fee. The UMC will typically raise a number of funds (as they are of limited life and so naturally self-liquidate), and each fund will be established as a separate limited partnership. As noted above, the partnership consists of investors (LPs) who provide capital but do not participate in the investment decisions, and whose liability is limited to their invested capital, and a General Partner, who takes investment decisions and has unlimited liability. To address this potentially unlimited liability, GPs are typically set up to be "thin" organizations with few assets or employees, and which (somewhat ironically) are usually themselves a limited liability entity (such as an LLC). Consequently, the investment decisions are made at the level of the Fund Manager/Advisor, where the investment professionals are employed.

The distinction between the three entities—the UMC, the Fund Manager/Advisor, and the General Partner—is often not made, and the short-hand of "GP" is used to cover the combination of roles. We will also generally adopt this shorthand, except where there are important distinctions that affect incentives or economics.

The fourth type of entity is the portfolio companies that are acquired by the Fund. LBO funds usually take controlling stakes in the portfolio companies in which they invest. In many cases, this control will involve purchasing all the equity and repaying its existing debts. The "Enterprise Value" of these portfolio companies (i.e., the debt and equity) is paid for partly by the Fund, and partly with external debt arranged by the GP. This debt is raised on the basis that it will be a liability of the portfolio company, rather than the Fund. For this reason, debt providers often refer to LBO GPs as "financial sponsors," because they sponsor the raising of debt on behalf of the portfolio companies. We examine the financing and structuring of portfolio company investments in detail in Section 2.2.

The final, increasingly important entity is co-investment vehicles. In LBOs, it is common for some part of the equity in portfolio firms to be made available to investors outside the fund structure. These investors are often also investors in the Fund—as depicted by investor 3 in Fig. 1—but they need not be (as in the case of investor 4). There has been limited academic research so far on the issues relating to co-investment. Braun et al. (2020) identify several potential motivations for GPs to offer co-investment opportunities. For deals that require a large amount of equity relative to the fund size, the simple motivation may be portfolio diversification. Funds put limits on the proportion of equity that can be invested in any single deal and arranging for some equity to be invested via a separate vehicle can provide the equity above the maximum that the fund can contribute. An alternative approach is to team up with a fund run by another GP in a "club deal," but these have become less common since SEC investigations into possible anti-competitive behavior relating to such deals.[f]

A key feature of co-investments is that they typically involve no, or much reduced, management fees and carried interest payments to the GP that organizes the deal.[g] For LPs in the fund, therefore, they are able to invest additional capital at a lower cost, although this practice will lead to more concentration in their portfolios. Consequently, co-investment opportunities are prized by LPs, who often seek information on the likely extent of such opportunities at the time they are making fund commitments.

The fact that some co-investment is offered to investors (as represented by investor 4 in Fig. 1) who are not LPs in the Fund is more controversial, since they will

---

[f]See Keyte and Schwartz (2016). Private Equity and Antitrust: A New Landscape. *Antitrust, 31*, p.21. for details about private equity and antitrust.
[g]Co-investors will sometimes be charged a one-off transaction fee, and will also share in the costs of due diligence, debt arrangement, etc., since these will generally be passed onto the portfolio company.

avoid paying fees to the GP through the fund structure. When GPs do offer such opportunities to outside investors, it is often in the hope that they will become LPs in future funds. Also, some large investors are increasingly able to act quickly and at scale to participate in deals from the start (sometimes referred to as "primary co-invest") and so play a similar role to that of a GP in a club deal. This is particularly true of sovereign wealth funds, some public pension funds (Canadian public pension funds were pioneers as co-investors), and large fund of fund managers, who have large amounts of capital to deploy and use co-investments to boost the net return of their vehicles.

The academic literature on co-investments has tended to focus on whether there is adverse selection in the choice of deals, meaning that the GP is more likely to offer the LPs co-investment opportunities on their worse deals. The first paper to study this issue was Fang et al. (2015), who found evidence of adverse selection based on data from seven large LPs. However, this finding has been challenged by Braun et al. (2020), who built a large dataset of co-investments and found no evidence that the returns earned, gross of fees, on deals offered for co-investment are significantly different from the remaining deals in a given fund. The growth in the significance of co-investment in LBO deals suggests this is an area that will attract more analysis in the future.

2.1.2 Fund governance

The key document that governs the operation of the Fund is the Limited Partnership Agreement (LPA). This document proscribes the sorts of investments the Fund Manager may enter into, the specific individuals (known as "key persons") who will devote their time to managing the fund, the obligations of the LPs, how much capital will be invested by the GP, and the fees and profits shares to be paid to the GP, etc. We discuss fund economics separately in the next section, but there are several other significant features of LPAs.

First, funds usually have a defined life of 10 years (although some funds with longer and shorter lives have been raised). GPs normally have the option to extend the fund's life for 3 more years, and even further extensions (with the agreement of the LPs) are common. The average life of a buyout fund is, in practice, around 13 years from the initial closing until the sale of the last portfolio firm. LBO funds are self-liquidating vehicles in that when they realize investments in portfolio companies, the proceeds are returned to the investors rather than re-invested in other companies.[h] In addition to defining the fund life, the LPA will also specify the investment period—typically the first 5–6 years of the fund life—during which capital can be drawn down at the discretion of the GP without consulting the LP. After that point, investments are typically limited to those in process, those pursuant to existing commitments, and follow-on investments.

---

[h]Some recycling of capital into new investments may be possible, depending on the terms of the LPA.

Second, investors commit capital to the fund, but this capital is only "called" when it is required by the GP to complete a transaction or to pay fund expenses. In other words, investors who want to invest a certain amount of money into private equity funds have to "over-commit" more capital to funds than they actually would like to be invested, since <100% of their commitments will be drawn down at any particular point in time. Knowing how much to over-commit is complicated, as the GP controls both when they draw down capital contributions and when the portfolio companies are sold. For this reason, LPs typically use cash-flow modeling to estimate when capital will be drawn down and returned based on historical data from previous funds. Given that funds only call capital when it is required for a particular deal, the way performance is measured takes account of the timing of the actual cash flows. IRRs remain, despite the strong academic health warnings that have been issued (see, e.g., Phalippou (2009)), one of the main performance metrics used by LPs, and, as we explain in the next section, an important component of fund economics.

One recent development, which has a significant impact on the relevance of IRRs, is that GPs of LBO funds are increasingly asking LPs for permission to establish subscription lines of credit. These are short-term loans from financial institutions to the fund. Fig. 1 illustrates the way in which they enable the GPs to pay for transactions without initially calling capital from the LPs. These lines of credit are essentially short-term leverage at the fund level, in that the fund borrows the money to invest in portfolio companies. The commitment of the LPs to send money to the fund whenever it is demanded is the collateral for these loans. Given that most investors in LBO funds are large, reputable investors, and it is very rare for an LP to default on a capital call, such debt is low risk and cheap.

However, there are limits on the length of time that such debt can be used in respect of any investment, which is typically no more than 6–24 months. At one level, the use of subscription credit lines can be convenient for the LP: they should enable the GP to call capital less regularly and more predictably—for example, once a quarter, or annually. On the other hand, the impact of initially borrowing the money to invest in portfolio companies typically will increase IRRs—since the time that LP funds are invested will be shorter. This impacts the economics of the funds, as we shall explain later.

The alternative motivations for the growth of such credit facilities have been analyzed by two recent papers. Schillinger et al. (2020) find that subscription credit lines are mainly a cash-flow management tool and have only moderate effects on final fund performance. In contrast, Albertus and Denes (2020) find substantial distortions in reported IRRs and suggest that subscription credit lines are more common among poorly performing funds. This latter result is, on the face of it, surprising in that such facilities are established at the inception of the fund, and so a GP will not know how well the fund will subsequently perform.

The debate regarding subscription credit lines is yet to be concluded. However, we view this as part of a more general trend toward the increased use of debt in all parts of LBO structures. For example, GPs are often able to borrow the funds they commit to the fund, using future management fees as collateral. Whether this reduces their effective "skin in the game"—as they do not necessarily need to dip in their own savings to pay for their capital contribution—is debatable, but the practice is not universally welcomed by LPs.

Furthermore, although subscription credit lines are, by construction, short-term in nature, there is a developing trend toward "NAV lines" of credit. These allow funds to potentially borrow money against the asset values of existing portfolio companies, for example, to accelerate distributions or to support portfolio companies late in a fund's life. Essentially, these NAV lines layer leverage at the fund level on top of the leverage that is used to buy the companies in the first place, as we discuss in Section 2.2. There is also an increasing use of "preferred equity" in fund structures, whereby the fund sells a preferred equity stake in the fund, which again can be used to facilitate distributions. These will also have the effect of leveraging the remaining investments, as the first call on returns is the preferred equity. Therefore, while until recently the leverage in LBOs was at the level of the portfolio company, the situation has become significantly more complicated in recent years, and leverage can now be seen at many different points in LBO structures, although the use of such credit facilities and borrowing is by no means universal. We see this as a potentially interesting topic for future research if the relevant data becomes available.

The third important feature of LBO funds is that they are "blind pools" of capital, meaning that once the LPs have made their capital commitments, they have no say on the choice of companies that are acquired. Therefore, during the 5–6 year investment period, the GP essentially controls the LP's checkbook, and also determines when the committed capital is drawn down, the investments are exited, and the proceeds are returned to investors. This structure gives little control to investors once they have made a commitment to the fund. This lack of control can be particularly important in periods of financial crisis or when asset values change dramatically. For example, during the global financial crisis in 2008, the value of most assets fell considerably, which resulted in a "denominator effect" whereby the undrawn commitments (which were fixed in dollar terms) increased the projected share of private equity beyond levels anticipated by some investors. In other words, the nature of private equity investing creates a "commitment risk" that could result in suboptimal asset allocations for investors. Furthermore, in periods of financial crisis, when the premium on liquidity can be high, private equity funds are still able to call capital from investors. This puts them in an unusual and privileged position, but at the expense of their investors who may be required to fund investments at a time when cash flow is scarce.

One response to the lack of control over commitments and distributions has been the development of secondary markets for investor stakes in funds. In such a secondary market, an LP will sell both their investments in the fund and the liability for future draw downs. Typically, the LPA will require LPs to ask for permission to sell their stakes (and future commitments) to the fund, but such permission is usually granted unless something is unattractive about a potential buyer, such as being required to reveal information about the fund (e.g., the returns) and its portfolio companies to the public. This applies particularly to investors (such as public pension schemes) that are often subject to the various Freedom of Information Acts that apply in the United States, United Kingdom and other countries. Such trading of LP stakes has grown significantly in recent years (see Nadauld et al. (2019)).

Various other secondary markets have emerged, which have significantly increased the choices available to investors. In particular, there is now an active market for purchasing portfolios of companies from the fund. The latter type of transaction is often performed toward the end of the life of a fund, to facilitate a final distribution and winding-up of the fund. The purchaser is often a fund that is raised specifically to invest in secondary stakes. The returns on such secondary funds have been impressive, which has led to a dramatic increase in their capital under management; as of the summer of 2022, Blackstone alone has invested $66 billion in secondary funds.[i]

Another common secondary market transaction is known as a "continuation fund." These funds acquire one or more of the remaining portfolio companies from the existing fund and give LPs the choice of rolling over all, or a part of, their investment into the continuation vehicle. Clearly, such transactions are sensitive for at least three reasons. First, the GP is managing both the fund that is selling the asset, and the vehicle that is buying the asset. Being on both sides of a transaction is a recipe for conflicts of interest. Too low a price benefits the shareholders of the continuation fund at the expense of the shareholders of the original fund. And too high a price will lead to a higher IRR for the original fund, which can be advantageous to the GP since it will allow him to raise larger funds in the future (see Chung et al. (2012)). In addition, the fees on continuation fund vehicles are subject to considerable debate with LPs, as GPs are able to "write up" the value of the companies as the basis for charging management fees, and enable the GP to expand the assets they manage, since these vehicles are additional to their normal sequence of funds.

However, there is also a logic behind these deals: for some companies, where the GP anticipates that significant incremental growth can be achieved, the use of continuation vehicles can make sense for LPs, as they can share in the portfolio companies' upside for a longer period. In a sense, the popularity of continuation funds points out a weakness of existing 10-year fund structures. It seems likely that the alternative approach of lengthening the fund life and holding the assets within the fund for longer will also become more prevalent in the future.

Such innovations have significantly increased the liquidity of private equity investments in recent years, although many of the investors in such funds (such as pension funds and sovereign wealth funds) have little need for liquidity.[j]

---

[i]This value was taken from the Blackstone website in July 2022: https://www.blackstone.com/our-businesses/strategic-partners/
[j]See Nadauld et al. (2019) and Boyer et al. (2021) for more information about these secondary markets.

2.1.3 Fund economics

Buyout funds receive three potential sources of revenue: management fees, carried interest payments and, in some cases, fees from portfolio companies. As we explain, management fees and portfolio company fees are related, and so we discuss these first, before turning to carried interest.

Management fees for LBO funds have traditionally been around 2% per annum (initially of commitments, and eventually of invested capital)—and form part of the characterization of private equity as having a "2 and 20" cost to investors. A recent analysis by Lim (2022) of around 6000 LBO funds finds remarkably little variation in such fees: the median fee remains 2% with the mean only slightly lower at 1.9%, and a standard deviation of 0.2. Given the huge growth in the size of LBOs, and the economies of scale that exist, it is remarkable how little fees have fallen. For instance, Lim finds that the median fee for funds that are in the top quartile by size in each vintage year is still 1.8%. The sheer scale of such fees for multi-billion dollar funds has meant that the original mantra of private equity (management fees keep the lights on, but we only get rich on carried interest) simply does not hold anymore for large buyout managers. In Fig. 1, the management fee is illustrated as flowing directly from each Fund to the Fund Manager, but in practice this would often flow into the GP and then out to the Fund Manager, and, if profits remain, to the UMC.

It should be noted that this headline fee is normally charged for the investment period on committed capital, rather than invested capital. Therefore, for the first few years of the fund the management fees can be a considerable drag on returns—which almost inevitably go negative initially—and a very large proportion of the net asset value of the fund in the early years. Initial investments take time to be re-valued and management fees, charged based on the entire committed capital, have an immediate negative effect on returns. Indeed, this phenomenon has been given a name—the J-curve—and has been the subject of books written on the details of private equity investing (see, for example, *J-Curve Exposure* by Mathonet and Meyer (2007)).

However, it is important to realize that the management fee is typically reduced after the investment period. According to a recent survey (Hudson (2020)), such "management fee step-downs" after the investment period are observed in 95% of funds. Management fees can decrease after the investment period in a variety of ways. First, the management fee rate could be reduced, but still calculated based on the entire committed capital, including money that has already been drawn down, invested, exited and returned to investors by this point. Second, the management fee could remain the same in percentage terms, but the fee basis can be reduced to the capital that is still invested, usually calculated as the book value of the initial investment net of the cost of any realized investments. Finally, some LPAs specify both that percentage management fees are reduced and that the fee basis is changed to invested capital. However, such a dual approach is less commonly observed in practice, other than in some large buyout funds.

In the first study of the economics of private equity funds, Metrick and Yasuda (2010) found that, on an *ex-ante* basis, management fees comprised around two-thirds of GPs' expected revenues. Lim (2022) focuses on realized returns and finds a somewhat lower proportion—just over 50%—of actual revenues for buyout GPs comes from management fees. However, this is still a high proportion, and for large funds, such revenues will amount to much more than the costs of running the fund. The existence of significant, predictable profits from multiple funds is one of the driving forces of the sale of stakes in the ultimate management companies.

In addition to the management fees that are charged directly to the LPs, in some LBO funds, fees can also be charged by the GP to portfolio companies. Such fees are associated with services such as on-going monitoring, arranging transactions, etc. Some of these fees are questionable: surely on-going monitoring of investment is a service that should be covered by the management fee? However, other services provided by the GP substitute for those that might otherwise need to be provided by a third party. For example, a GP might provide corporate finance advice related to debt restructurings or acquisitions, for which the portfolio company would otherwise pay fees to an investment banker. An interesting discussion of such arrangements and the questions they raise about governance is provided by Phalippou et al. (2018).

However, where such fees are charged, they are often partially or fully offset against the management fees charged to LPs. In recent years, 100% offsets have become common, meaning that any revenues associated with a set of services, as specified in the LPA, are offset in a given year against management fees. The devil is in the detail, since some services are carved out from the 100% offset and can result in additional revenues flowing to the GP. One might ask why such portfolio company fees are charged at all, if they are subsequently netted off against management fees. Aside from the potential additional revenues for the GP from services not covered by the offset, the main reason for the arrangement is often tax related. For example, in the United Kingdom, GPs have to charge value-added taxes on management fees, which cannot normally be reclaimed by the LP. In contrast, the taxes on any services charged to the portfolio company can normally be offset. While it is clear from an economic perspective that management fees are no lower whether they are paid by the LP or the portfolio company, this can add complexity to tracking the cost of private equity investments. Furthermore, in the case of co-investment vehicles, there are often no fees to waive, and therefore investors in such vehicles will not be indifferent to the level of portfolio company fees charged.

The final component of GP remuneration is a "carried interest" in the fund, usually equal to 20% of a fund's net profits. In contrast to management fees, either charged to the LP or the portfolio company, which do not depend on the performance of the investments, carried interest is a direct function of a fund's performance. Unlike venture capital funds, carried interest for most LBO funds is only paid after a "preferred return" has been earned by the LPs. This is defined in terms of an IRR, which is referred to as the *hurdle rate*. The most commonly observed hurdle is 8%.

In the sample of LBO funds studied by Lim (2022) 85% had precisely an 8% hurdle, 2.4% had a hurdle between 8% and 10%, and 5% between 6% and 8%. The remainder had no hurdle rate. Once the preferred return has been achieved, GPs share the profits through their carried interest. This carried interest proportion is almost always 20%: in Lim's sample, 95.8% of GPs had precisely a 20% carried interest, with 1.5% having a lower share and only 2.8% having a higher share.

From an economic perspective, this clustering of carried interest, and preferred returns, is surprising: one would expect the successful GPs to appropriate a higher share of the profits over time. However, the gains to success seem to accrue largely through growing the fund size while keeping the management fee constant. A notable feature is that the hurdle must be cleared before carried interest is earned, but it is a "disappearing" rather than a "hard" hurdle. A hard hurdle would stipulate that the GP would only share in profits *in excess of* the preferred return. However, in the case of LBO funds, once the LPs have received their preferred return, the LPA will stipulate a catch-up rate whereby the GPs receive more, or often all, of the next available cash until the overall profits are shared 80/20. For this reason, the hurdle rate is only of significance for funds that perform relatively poorly, or in adverse market conditions: if a fund returns, say, a 15% IRR, the extent of carried interest payments will be the same whether or not the fund had a hurdle rate (as long as the hurdle rate was sufficiently below 15%, of course). Therefore, when some successful GPs have managed to negotiate away the preferred return in subsequent funds, this results in the strange outcome that future payments will only be higher if future fund performance is low. Removing hurdles hardly contributes to an alignment of interest, as GPs continue to earn performance fees even when profits are low.

There are some important details about the way carried interest is calculated, in particular relating to the cashflow "waterfall." While the overall size of carried interest payments is based upon the performance of the fund as a whole, there can be important differences in the timing of such payments. There are two main approaches, which are known as "American waterfalls" and "European waterfalls." An American waterfall tracks capital contributions (and an allocable portion of funded expenses) and distributions from realized investments. Furthermore, carried interest begins to be distributed as soon as the IRR on such investments exceeds the hurdle. For instance, if a $500 m fund has called $100 m, and quickly returns $300 m (and so comfortably exceeds any normal hurdle rate), the GP would receive 20% of the profit to date, i.e., $40 m (20% of the $200 m profit). Of course, the remaining $400 of capital has yet to be invested, and the fate of these remaining investments will determine the ultimate carried interest payment. For instance, if that $400 m was invested for a loss, and resulted in distributions of only $300 m, the overall fund would only yield a profit of $100 m. Providing the IRR still exceeded the hurdle rate—which is likely given the way IRRs are calculated given the impact of early distributions—a provision in almost all LPAs known as a "clawback" would require $20 m of the carried interest assigned to the GP to be returned to the LPs. However, if these sums had already been paid out to the GPs they would have paid taxes on the sums received, and LPAs normally stipulate that any clawback is capped at the net after-tax carried interest received.

Given the obvious issues relating to paying out profits on early investments before all the capital has been invested, many funds now use an approach commonly referred to as a European waterfall. Under a European waterfall, carried interest is not paid until the fund has returned all the capital contributions, including those for management fees paid by investors, and the preferred return. Therefore, carried interest payments under a European waterfall typically occur much later in the fund life. The LPs will receive cash earlier under a European waterfall than in an American waterfall, so this should result in higher IRRs to LPs, holding cash flows constant and ignoring tax considerations. One of the few academic papers to focus on these differences in the timing of cashflows is Hüther et al. (2020), using evidence from venture capital contracts, which use similar waterfalls. Intriguingly, they find that funds that use the more "GP-friendly" American waterfall tend to have higher returns. This result could occur because of selection—higher quality funds are able to negotiate with their LPs to use an American waterfall, which enable GPs to receive their carry sooner.

One important question remains about carried interest: which individuals in the GP receive it? From the investors' perspective, carried interest is an important way in which their interests are aligned with those of the fund managers, but this assumes that the people putting in the effort to find attractive targets for acquisition and making the decisions are personally receiving a reasonable share of any profit sharing. This issue has two important considerations.

First, the increasing tendency for the UMC to be listed publicly (for instance, KKR, Blackstone, Apollo, etc.) means that a proportion of the economics of each fund will flow to the shareholders of the listed entity, rather than to the current LBO fund managers. Furthermore, even if the UMC is not itself listed, it has become increasingly common, as noted earlier, for stakes to be sold to specialist funds or even to large LPs (such as US public pension schemes or sovereign wealth funds). In both cases, some incentive effects of the carried interest on those doing the deals will be reduced. Some investors have used this dilution of the alignment of interest as a screen to determine which funds to consider.

Second, even if none of the carried interest has been "sold" to outside investors, the distribution of the carry between those working for the fund and the UMC can vary widely. For instance, the founders of the UMC may no longer be involved on a day-to-day basis with the running of the latest funds but may still take a significant share of the carried interest. In many respects, this practice is reasonable: the founders took risks and invested capital and labor in establishing the initial funds, and later funds "stand on the shoulders" of the earlier funds' reputations. However, founders continuing to take a share of the carry after their active involvement in investments has ended has the same dilutive effect on incentives as selling a stake in the UMC.

In both cases, the underlying issue is the way in which funds manage succession. How founders cash out, if at all, is a common issue across professional service firm partnerships. This issue is likely to become an important topic of research as more LBO (and other) partnerships face such succession issues. However, information on the distribution of carried interest is particularly difficult to obtain, at least for academic researchers. Since LPs increasingly ask questions about this as part of their fund due diligence, it will hopefully only be a matter of time before data on the distribution of fund economics becomes widely available. To date, the only paper that has looked in detail at this issue is Ivashina and Lerner (2019). These authors examine 717 private equity partnerships and find that the allocation of carried interest is divorced from past success as an investor. However, the allocation is heavily influenced by whether an individual is a founder, and that a lack of carried interest to the currently active partners results in departures and the spawning of new partnerships.

The overall effect of carried interest and management fees is to drive a considerable wedge between gross returns earned by the fund and net returns received by the LPs. Clearly, the magnitude of this wedge will depend on the performance of the fund, but, on average, the difference between gross and net LBO fund IRRs tends to be around six percentage points.

2.1.4 Taxation

As noted at the start of this section, one of the over-arching reasons why partnership structures are employed for LBO funds is taxation: both for the GP and LP. From the perspective of the LP, aside from ensuring limited liability for LPs, such fund structures are "tax transparent," meaning that no taxation is levied at the fund level. This is important, since many investors in private equity funds are tax exempt, and so will pay no taxes on the capital gains or income they receive. The limited partnership structure enables investors to benefit from the same tax treatment they would receive if they owned private companies directly, but with the additional advantage of limited liability.

From the perspective of the GP, there is in most countries a substantial benefit from the partnership structure: carried interest is typically taxed at capital gains tax rates rather than income tax rates. In most countries, the effective rate of taxation of capital gains is (often considerably) lower than that applying to income. This difference can occur simply from lower rates of taxation since any profits earned by the portfolio company will have been subject to corporate taxation. However, in the case of LBOs, the extensive use of debt can significantly reduce, or eliminate entirely, corporate taxes. The lower effective rate can also derive from any "tapering" of capital gains tax rates depending on how long assets are held for. In many countries, policymakers have attempted to reduce taxes on entrepreneurs and long-term investors by having a reducing rate of capital gains tax depending on the length of time an asset is held. Given that portfolio companies are often held for several years, those in receipt of carried interest payments may also be able to benefit from such "taper relief."

Maximizing capital gains tax treatment can take other forms as well, including various ways in which management fees can be turned into carried interest payments. The carried interest itself can be vested into offshore vehicles (or, in the United States, tax-sheltered accounts such as Roth IRAs) that can delay the payment of capital gains taxes, in some cases indefinitely. These arrangements are complex and the extent to which they are available to GPs varies across jurisdictions, but the tax advantages are perhaps the main reason why partnership structures have emerged as the dominant way of organizing buyout, and other private capital, funds.

It is not surprising, therefore, that taxation of carried interest has been one of the most contentious issues facing the private equity industry, with newly elected political leaders around the world pledging to change the tax treatment. However, changing the tax treatment of carried interest is easier said than done, as witnessed by the inability of recent US presidents, like Obama or Trump, to follow through on their desired reforms. The difficulty of changing the tax treatment of private equity occurs because the individuals who benefit from carried interest do invest capital to receive their share of the proceeds of any investment. Therefore, in this fundamental sense, what investors receive as carried interest really is a capital gain. While, in economic terms, this gain comes from the partners' labor in their nurturing of the investments—and so is more akin to a bonus for good performance—most countries have found it difficult to write rules to tax carried interest as labor income.

2.1.5 Regulation

In this section, we have been discussing the relationship between the LP and GP, and the extent to which alignment of interest is achieved. Given that most LBO funds are only accessible (at least directly, rather than through fund-of-fund structures) by institutional investors, much of the regulation of the fund itself tends to be through private contracts, that is, the limited partnership agreement. However, fund managers are, in general, regulated by national regulators. This has not always been the case. For example, US fund managers were often able to avoid regulation under the Investment Advisors Act of 1940, on the basis that they had few, large clients. However, the Dodd-Frank (Wall Street Reform and Consumer Protection) Act that became law in 2010 swept away these exemptions, and any fund advisor managing more than $150m in assets became regulated by the Securities and Exchange Commission (SEC). The SEC started regular examinations of LBO fund managers, including whether the GP stuck to the terms of the limited partnership agreement, and concluded that around one-third of such agreements were being violated in practice, though the materiality of such violations seems to have varied greatly. This led to some high-profile settlements by the GPs, although often without admitting that violations had, in fact, occurred.

Regulation has also become more extensive in Europe. The most significant piece of recent legislation has been the adoption within the European Union of the Alternative Investment Fund Manager Directive (AIFMD), which became effective in July 2013. Under the AIFMD, any manager of an "alternative investment fund" (as opposed to entities such as mutual funds, which are subject to the separate Undertakings for Collective Investments in Transferable Securities, UCITS) must be registered with, and are subject to regulation by, their national regulators. As with the Dodd-Frank Act, the AIFMD was passed in the wake of the financial crisis of

2008, amid fears that alternative assets might lead to systemic risks. It covered not only LBO funds, where it is hard to see any potential for systemic risks, as well as hedge funds, where such risks clearly exist.

The trend toward increased regulation of LBO funds is inevitable as the proportion of assets—many of them in high-profile and, in some cases, politically sensitive companies—increases. This has, in general, resulted in even more complexity in the structure outlined in Fig. 1. For example, in order to obtain a European passport for marketing funds throughout the EU, it is necessary to have a regulated fund manager within the EU.

2.2 Funds and portfolio companies

Having discussed the relationship between funds and their investors, we now turn to the way in which LBO funds structure their acquisitions of portfolio companies. A key distinguishing feature of LBOs, in contrast to venture capital or expansion capital deals, is that they normally acquire relatively mature companies that have regular cash flows. This cash flow is critical to support the leverage that is a defining feature of LBOs. In this section, we first describe LBOs' capital structures and how the sources of debt have changed significantly over time.

2.2.1 LBO deal structures

In an LBO, the fund contributes the equity (alongside any co-investment vehicles) that is used to purchase portfolio companies, and this equity is supplemented with significant amounts of debt. Since most LBOs are "control deals" in which a majority of, if not all, the equity is purchased, the fund normally borrows against the assets it intends to acquire. This is clearly not possible in the case of minority investments—for instance in venture capital deals—since the majority owners (e.g., the entrepreneurs) would not accept debt, secured against their own venture, as a means of payment! The fund itself does not take on debt, although in the short-term the equity contributions from LPs may be debt-financed using subscription credit lines, as discussed in the previous section.

Since many transactions are competitive, with investment banks running an auction involving interested potential acquirers, it is necessary for all bidding buyout funds to obtain commitment letters from debt providers (who typically charge a fee for this service). The most relevant metric for the debt providers is the stability and predictability of the future cash-flows that will be generated by the portfolio company, which will be used to pay the interest on the debt. In particular, in LBO transactions, there is a focus on earnings before interest, tax, depreciation, and amortization (EBITDA), which gives a measure of the available cash that could (at least in the short-term) be used to pay interest. Since EBITDA makes no allowance for capital expenditures, an alternative variant that is frequently used is EBITDA minus "normalized" CapEx.

The capital structure used in U.S. LBO transactions can be seen in the chart below. There has been a noticeable upward trend in LBO valuations, in terms of

EBITDA multiples, although valuations fell in 2009 following the global financial crisis. The near-zero interest rates on government debt through the 2010s have reduced the cost of debt and are likely to have been a major cause of the increase in valuations in this period. The most recent data, for 2019 and 2020, suggests that valuation multiples have continued to increase slightly, reaching an average of 11.4 × for 2020.[k] European LBOs have followed a similar trend.

Total debt as a proportion of purchase prices (i.e., enterprise values) hit a peak before the financial crisis at around 60%. The majority of debt in LBOs is in the form of senior secured, or "first lien" debt—as shown in Fig. 2. Such debt was traditionally supplied by banks, and, given the unusually leveraged structure of the portfolio companies, is often referred to by the somewhat unusual term "leveraged loan." These loans are arranged by a lead bank and are then usually syndicated to other banks and lenders. Many of these "syndicated loans" ended up in collateralized loan obligation (CLO) funds and were one example of banks becoming focused on generating fees (commitment fees, arranging fees, etc.) using their balance sheet capacity, but not holding onto the loans themselves. This approach is known as the "originate and distribute" business model. Were such debt to be rated by credit rating agencies, which in general it is not, it would often be classified as sub-investment grade. However, by bundling together loans from many different companies and then slicing them into tranches of varying seniority, CLOs can create securities that have high investment grade ratings (along with junior tranches that are much riskier).

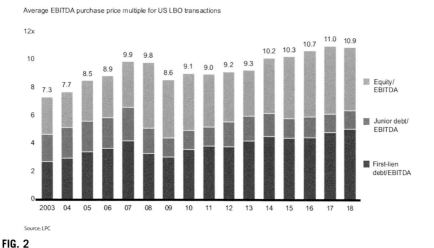

Average EBITDA purchase price multiple for US LBO transactions

Source: LPC

FIG. 2

Valuations and capital structure of LBOs.

[k]See fig. 8 in the 2021 Global Private Equity Report published by Bain, available at https://www.bain.com/globalassets/noindex/2021/bain_report_2021-global-private-equity-report.pdf

In addition to the senior secured debt, it is common for LBOs to raise additional, subordinated debt, sometimes referred to as "junior" or "second lien" debt. Traditionally, such debt was often provided by specialist investors, including hedge funds. As the name implies, such subordinated debt often has a longer maturity than the senior debt—so the latter is paid off first—and has lower priority than the senior debt in the event of bankruptcy or liquidation. There can be multiple tranches of subordinated debt, including mezzanine debt, which will often be the riskiest. Mezzanine debt sometimes includes equity-like features such as warrants—and hence is considered to be at the mezzanine level between debt and equity.

2.2.2 An example of an LBO deal structure

To give an example of the structure of lending used in a typical LBO, in Fig. 3, we illustrate the capital structure of the 2006 LBO of Kwik-Fit, which is a tire and exhaust system repairer based in the United Kingdom, by PAI Europe IV fund.[1] This deal had a typical pre-financial crisis structure. The purchase price of £773.5 m equals a multiple of 8.1× EBITDA. This enterprise value includes any existing debt, which would have to be repaid on such a change of control. The financing of the acquisition comprised 25% equity (from the fund, with some contributions from management) and 75% debt (from banks and other providers).

The debt was structured into five tranches, along with two credit facilities. Starting with the latter, such credit facilities are established to minimize cash

	Amount (£m)	Terms	Pricing (spread over LIBOR)	Multiple of EBITDA
Enterprise Value	773.5			8.1 x
Equity	191.0 (25%)			2.0 x
Debt				
Term Loan A	140	7 year amortizing	2.25%	
Term Loan B	135	8 year bullet	2.50%	
Term Loan C	135	9 year bullet	3.00%	
2nd Lien	75	9.5 year	5.00%	
Total senior secured debt	485.0			5.1 x
Mezzanine	97.5	10 year	4.5% + 5% PIK	
Total Debt	582.5 (75%)			6.1 x
Revolving credit facility	40	7 year	2.25%	
Capex facility	50	7 year	2.25%	

FIG. 3

A typical pre-GFC capital structure: Kwik Fit, 2006.

[1]This example is taken from Axelson et al. (2013).

holdings necessary for covering normal operational needs, and thereby maximizing net debt. In general, facilities are not normally included in the calculation of debt, as they are undrawn at the time of the transaction, and the banks that provide such facilities normally require that they are reduced to zero at regular intervals (to distinguish such facilities from term loans). The loans themselves were structured with three tranches of 1st lien debt, that is, the Term Loans A, B and C. These rank pari passu in seniority, but the A loan is less risky because it is repaid earlier, being amortizing, and has a shorter (7 year) maturity than the B and C loans. An important feature of LBOs is the length of such term loans: 7–9 years is quite typical, which is much longer than the maturity of most public company debt. Having long maturity debt reduces refinancing risk, which, in the case of Kwik Fit, would have been a major benefit when the financial crisis hit 2 years after the LBO.

Another important feature of LBO debt is that much of it is non-amortizing, with the principal being repaid at the end of the term in a "bullet" payment. This is the case in this example, with the B and C tranches being bullet loans and the C having a 1 year longer term than the B loan. Such bullet loans reduce the ongoing cash flows to the lender, which are limited to interest payments, and can thereby increase the quantity of debt that is used for the LBO. Given the higher risks—both associated with the structural (if not legal) subordination of the tranches, and the differing amortization schedules—the B and C loans have slightly higher margins than the A loans.

When no regular repayments of the principal are required, lenders may negotiate a "cash sweep" whereby some proportion of available cash flow each year is used to repay the principal amount. In effect, this makes the amortization schedule contingent on firm performance, and so reduces the risk of default, at least in the short-term.

In the Kwik Fit deal an additional tranche of 2nd Lien debt was raised. This 2nd Lien debt ranks below the A, B and C Term Loans in terms of seniority, but is still classified as part of "senior secured debt." Relative to the C term loan, the 2nd lien debt has a slightly longer maturity, and pays an interest margin that is noticeably higher at 5%. This reflects the market's perception of how the debt is becoming significantly riskier as leverage is being stacked up. However, the private equity sponsors chose to increase leverage even further using a mezzanine loan. This again had a slightly longer maturity than the 2nd lien debt and required the firm to pay a margin of 4.5% (over LIBOR) interest in cash, with additional interest—known as pay-in-kind, or PIK—being rolled up and added to the principal amount outstanding. The total cost of this riskiest tranche of debt is clearly significant—with a total margin over LIBOR of 9.5%—and such rates reflect risks that are arguably closer to equity. In a sense, the private equity sponsor is therefore deciding on the size of its exposure to the deal (as it could have contributed more equity in place of the mezzanine loan) and the riskiness of its investment.

2.2.3 The growth of private debt
Traditionally, the main providers of leverage for LBOs were banks and some specialist lenders such as mezzanine funds. However, in recent years the provision of debt to fund LBOs has changed significantly with the emergence of private debt funds.

Private debt funds are structured in a similar way to private equity funds, raising money from institutional investors as an LP–GP structure, with a finite life and charging a management fee (often around 1%, but charged on invested rather than committed capital) and a carried interest on the profits. Such funds grew quickly after the 2008 financial crisis as some of the banks that were major players in the leveraged loan market reduced the extent of such lending (for instance, RBS, which was the dominant lender to LBOs in Europe, effectively withdrew completely from the market). As banks faced increasing capital requirements, including for leveraged lending, private debt funds moved into the vacuum and grew rapidly. Institutional investors, facing near-zero yields on their fixed income investments, were attracted to these funds, which provided a diversified portfolio of loans that were actively managed over the life of the fund (unlike many of the bank-originated loans that were sold into CLOs).

Private debt funds lend to most types of companies, including publicly listed and private companies. However, a significant proportion of private debt has been used to fund LBOs. As private debt funds have moved into the space left by banks, there have been some innovations. In particular, private debt funds are often prepared to provide both the senior and junior debt—which has become known as uni-tranche lending—which can make it easier and quicker for buyout funds when arranging the debt for an LBO transaction, as they only have to deal with one potential lender. This is increasingly the case since private debt funds have grown significantly in scale, with market leaders such as Oaktree, Ares and GSO raising multi-billion dollar funds. Research on the lending practices and the risk and returns of private debt funds is currently limited, in part because the number of funds that have matured and where outcome returns for investors can be observed are still relatively few. One of the few studies to date is Munday et al. (2018) which provides early evidence of the performance of the various types of private credit strategies, with the best returns being associated with direct lending. Private debt funds are likely to be an important topic for research in future years.

2.3 Portfolio companies and management

Having explained the relationship and alignment of interest between investors and funds, and the financial structure used by funds to finance their acquisition of portfolio companies, we now turn to the way that LBO funds provide incentives to the management team of the portfolio companies. As with information about the distribution of carried interest within a fund, there is relatively little information in the public domain regarding the incentives given to management teams of portfolio companies. However, some general observations are possible.

First, the existing management team, prior to the LBO, often does not survive the acquisition. One of the ways in which private equity owners can add value is by improving management, and in many cases, this means replacing the existing CEO and/or other senior officers. However, the arrival of an LBO owner does not always lead to a management change. In many cases, the fast pace of decision-making (driven by the buy-to-sell model and focus on metrics such as IRRs), an increased focus on data, driving out inefficiencies, and the other improvements brought by the LBO can be empowering and motivating for management. But for others who are used to less active owners and not excited by the strategic plans of the buyout fund, the arrival of private equity owners can lead to their exit.

Second, many LBO funds now retain a roster of industry experts with operational experience who are closely involved in the due diligence stage of a potential transaction and are involved in the on-going leadership and/or improvement projects of the portfolio company. Such executives are often called "operating partners" of the LBO fund, and they will tend to focus on particular sectors (such as retail, hospitality, or industrial) where experience can be particularly valuable. If the LBO fund wins the deal, such operating partners can be installed as Chair of the portfolio company to provide a direct link with the fund on a day-to-day basis. Such operating partners will usually be paid by the portfolio companies during their period of involvement, or fees for their services may be charged by the fund to the company. Equity incentives can be provided at the portfolio company level, which can reduce the share of the carried interest on the fund required for such operating partners. In a sense, their incentives become more "deal-by-deal."

Third, whether or not the management team remains the same, a defining feature of LBOs is the increased use of leverage, which reduces free cash flow and acts as a disciplining effect on management, as originally noted by Jensen (1986). Many LBO targets operate with very low leverage and enjoy the stability of owning assets (specifically property) rather than having to make contractual payments (such as rents). As noted in the previous section, LBOs are conducted by the fund arranging significant amounts of debt financing to acquire the company, and the debt is then pushed down into the portfolio company. Having gained control of the company, there will often be subsequent balance sheet transactions, such as selling off property. The proceeds of such sales can be used to reduce leverage or to make special dividend payments to the fund, which can have a substantial effect on IRRs. In virtually all LBO transactions, however, the management must operate with far less financial flexibility because of much higher leverage.

The final aspect of the management contract that is critical to the LBO model is equity incentives. The typical transaction involves significant equity stakes being bought by the executive team, so that the alignment of interest flows from the investors to the fund (via carried interest) to the portfolio company (via equity stakes). These equity stakes are leveraged by the debt taken on by the portfolio company. However, they are leveraged further by the structuring of the equity. An example of a typical structure is presented in Fig. 4.

In this example, a portfolio company is bought for $1000 m, with $300 m of equity and $700 m of debt. The debt is structured as $400 m of senior debt, which we assume amortizes over time, and $300 m of junior debt (with a bullet payment at maturity). To align interests, LBO funds almost always insist that management owns a significant stake in the firm's equity. However, since the equity in the deal comprises $300 m, a 10–20% stake in the deal would cost $30–60 m, which could be

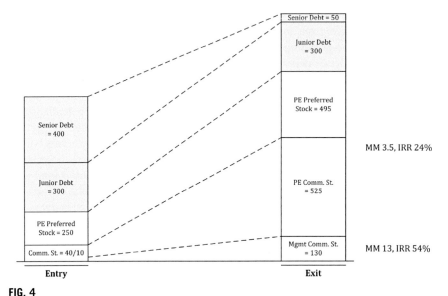

FIG. 4

The structuring of debt and equity in LBOs.

beyond the net worth of a typical management team. Consequently, at the time of the transaction, the equity may itself be split into tranches, with the majority being preferred stock, which earns a fixed rate of return, and the remaining being the common stock. In the example, we assume that $250m of the equity is provided by the fund in the form of preferred stock, along with a $40m investment in the common stock. The remaining $10m is invested by the management team, who, in this example own 20% of the common stock (but none of the preferred stock). Given that the preferred stock has a fixed rate of return, in this example 12%, from the perspective of the management team the preferred stock adds additional leverage and risk to their equity in addition to the debt.

Evidence on the structuring of the equity in LBOs is sparse, particularly for US deals where private companies are not required to publish their accounts. The way in which deals are structured can differ, depending in part on the tax treatment of preferred shares, with a common alternative being the use of a shareholder loan (at a fixed rate of interest) being provided by the fund in place of the preferred shares. Either way, the intention is to give the management team significant "skin in the game" via very highly leveraged equity stakes.

The example in Fig. 4 demonstrates how significant the gains for management can be. We assume that exit occurs after 6 years, and that the total enterprise value has increased by 50% to $1500m. Given the typical duration of amortizing senior debt, most of that would have been repaid after 6 years—we assume a balance of 50 remains. The junior bullet payment debt is still outstanding. The preferred stock, with a 12% interest rate, will have increased to $495m, providing the LBO fund close to a 2× return on that part of the original investment. The remaining value—in this case $655 m—accrues to the common stockholders. Assuming the fund invested $40 m in the common stock, this turns into $525 m. Combining their holdings of preferred stock and common stock, the LBO fund makes a 3.5× return on its investment. Recall that the increase in the enterprise value is only 50%, demonstrating the impact of debt on amplifying equity returns (and, of course, risk).

From the perspective of the management team the returns are spectacular: their original $10 m investment turns into $130 m over the 6-year period. Such "life-changing" potential returns are precisely what LBO funds seek to offer management teams, who have by far the sharpest incentives. This can be seen not only on the upside, their 13× return on investment, but also on the downside. Had the company not performed as planned, and the enterprise value had fallen, relative to the entry price, by 10% or more, then the management team's equity stake would be worthless, with all remaining value accruing to the PE fund via their preferred stock.

Therefore, the management team in a typical LBO structure is highly incentivized to produce financial returns and to exit the investments relatively quickly, since they will not realize the value of their equity until a purchaser is found. For those with the appropriate risk appetite, working as an executive in an LBO can be one of the most attractive roles in the corporate world. Extraordinary potential rewards are combined with highly engaged owners who are focused on rapid value creation, with much less of the scrutiny—from the press or analysts—that executives of public companies attract. If a large payout occurs, it is seldom a matter of public record, as the details of the capital structure are usually hidden from public scrutiny. There are no shareholder votes on remuneration, and no reporting of bonuses—these are all matters decided privately with the fund. Indeed, over time a cadre of serial LBO executives has emerged who move from one transaction to the next, often with a gap to draw breath between deals, and who develop close relationships with particular (or even multiple) LBO funds. Such trusted executives are an important, and richly rewarded, part of the LBO ecosystem.

It seems likely that a significant part of the success of LBO funds in creating value derives from being able to attract very talented management, who are highly incentivized to produce financial returns in collaboration with the fund. It is, of course, difficult to isolate the impact of management when the counterfactual is difficult to observe. This is another area that is ripe for future research, for instance, analyzing whether investment plans and execution were successfully achieved, or whether good (or bad) outcomes were more attributable to luck (or lack thereof). As individual executives undertake serial engagements over time, it may be possible to test for the existence of individual skill (e.g., by testing for individual fixed effects) in the same way as has been done for CEOs of public companies. However, as with many issues involving private equity, data is often the issue. At present, while deal-level returns data are becoming available (see, e.g., Braun et al. (2017)), details of management compensation contracts remain largely hidden.

In conclusion, this section has described the manner in which capital is provided to funds, how funds acquire companies, and how those companies attract and incentivize management. The mantra of private equity has always been alignment of interest, and the arrangements we have documented explain how this is achieved. However, in the case of LBO funds, competition for capital and deals have resulted in significant increases in fund size and, as we shall show, a noticeable reduction in returns, certainly relative to public markets. For large LBO funds, alignment of interest has, in our view, declined over time. This is chiefly because management fees have not reduced as fund sizes have increased, despite the obvious economies of scale. The fund managers and owners of the management company "brand" can earn handsome returns even if investors are disappointed. Some LBO funds have responded to excess demand from investors by removing hurdle rates, the only impact of which is to pay carried interest to the fund even when returns are low. From an economic perspective, one might expect successful GPs to increase the carry percentage and for management fees to be more cost-based, but in practice carry percentages only rarely deviate from the standard 20%.

In this respect, LBO funds differ noticeably from VC funds. There are many VC GPs where they choose to limit fund size growth, charge fees that are broadly in line with costs, and, if successful, charge higher carried interest. Whether LPs eventually drive some change in their negotiations with LBO GPs remains to be seen; there were signs of change after the global financial crisis in 2008, such as the development of best practice limited partnership agreements by the Institutional Limited Partners Association (which have been revised regularly and are, at the time of this writing, in version 3.0). However, since then, investor allocations have been increasing significantly to private equity—both LBOs and VC—and consequently GPs have been able to defend the status quo. However, ultimately this status quo will only be sustainable if net returns to investors, on a risk-adjusted basis, remain attractive to investors.

3 How do buyouts create returns for their investors?

Understanding the way buyouts are structured, however, does not address the more fundamental issues of why they occur at all and why they have become so prevalent in recent years. Buyout sponsors earn returns for their investors by making profits on the purchase and sale of their portfolio companies, sometimes receiving dividends during the period in which they own the companies. A buyout fund will seek to acquire a company if the expected return its GPs anticipate from their period of ownership exceeds their cost of capital.

This cost of capital, however, is a relatively high target. To invest in a buyout fund, a potential investor must anticipate that the fund will earn high enough returns to compensate for the fund's fees, its risk, and its illiquidity. As noted in the previous section, the "2 and 20" fee structure drives a significant wedge between gross and net returns. Furthermore, the leverage of their portfolio firms results in buyout funds having relatively high equity betas, even though buyout funds often target relatively non-cyclical businesses with lower asset betas. Consequently, the systematic risk of buyout funds and hence the required rate of return they demand for their investments is likely to be higher than that for publicly traded companies. We discuss the issues involved in estimating fund betas and returns in detail in Section 5.

The impact of illiquidity on required returns is harder to quantify but undoubtedly meaningful. Buyout funds require investors to make capital commitments for very long periods of time. Most funds have a 10-year life, and, with extensions, it is typically at least 12 years before a fund exits all its investments. Although opportunities to sell stakes in a fund before its investments are exited have increased over time, these remain limited and may incur significant costs.[m] Investors in a buyout fund have no say in the decisions about the timing of the fund's return of capital. Rational investors should only become limited partners in a buyout fund when they feel that the fund's returns, *net of the fees the fund charges*, are likely to exceed those of the public market by enough to offset the fund's risk and illiquidity.

For these reasons, the most natural investors into buyout funds are those for whom illiquidity is less important. Examples of such investors are those investing for the very long-term, such as sovereign wealth funds, endowments, pension funds (especially those which are growing, with contributions exceeding withdrawals), etc. that have relatively low liquidity demands. In such cases, the required liquidity premium may be very modest. However, for other investors, the unpredictable nature of capital calls and distributions means that access to adequate, as Swensen (2009) calls "non-disruptive sources of liquidity," such as credit lines, are critical to minimize liquidity risks.

3.1 Improving portfolio firms' values

How does a buyout fund go about earning these high returns? Part of the game is buying companies for less than their underlying value. Sometimes buyout funds can find proprietary deals and can purchase a target company without competition from other funds. These deals tend to be purchased at lower prices than comparable firms that are sold at auctions run by investment banks, so the purchase prices could be less than warranted by the firms' underlying value. However, despite what GPs often say, most relatively mature firms—that are the main target of buyout funds—are in fact bought at an auction, and the prices paid are likely to reflect the market's perception of the firms' fundamentals.[n]

Consequently, to earn returns sufficiently high to entice limited partners to invest, a buyout fund must have a strategy to improve the value of the firms that they purchase. A useful way of characterizing the alternative ways in which GPs can improve the value of their portfolio firms was proposed by Kaplan and Strömberg (2009): *financial engineering*, *governance engineering*, and *operational engineering*.

---

[m]See Nadauld et al. (2019) for estimates of the costs of trading in this market.
[n]Gompers et al. (2016) survey private equity GPs, and the median percentage of deals that are proprietary they report is 50%, which seems to be biased upwards given today's market (see table 20 of their paper).

Financial engineering refers to the way in which buyout firms optimize capital structures. As discussed in the previous section, LBOs are financed with substantial debt—far higher than observed in comparable publicly traded companies. Axelson et al. (2013) document that in their sample of over 1000 buyouts, the median deal has a 70% debt to total capital ratio, which is roughly the proportion of equity in a typical public company. Therefore, buyouts tend to invert the capital structure, with debt becoming the main source of finance in place of equity. Jensen (1986, 1989) proposes that in addition to creating tax shields, this leverage adds value by reducing the agency costs of free cash flow. Leverage creates pressure on managers to generate cash and inhibits growth that is counter to the interests of shareholders. By adding leverage to portfolio companies, their value increases because the need to use cash for interest payments reduces wasteful investments.

Buyout funds also substantially change the governance of their portfolio firms. Such governance engineering has at least two main components. First, the executives running the portfolio companies will, in general, have equity stakes that are much higher than prior to the buyout, especially when the firm was previously publicly traded. It is common for management (collectively) to hold stakes of around 10% or more in private equity-backed companies. Second, boards of directors in portfolio companies tend to be relatively small and more active, meeting fairly frequently. In public corporations, there is a natural tendency for boards to become less effective over time (see Hermalin and Weisbach (1998) and Acharya et al. (2008)). By substantially increasing pecuniary incentives and creating a more active board, GPs can increase the value of their portfolio firms through improved corporate governance.

Buyout funds are deeply involved with the operations of their portfolio companies. Such operational engineering is an important element of buyout funds' investment process. When a buyout fund acquires a firm, they normally have a plan for improving the firms' operations. There is no magic formula that characterizes the way that buyout funds change the operations of their portfolio firms. Sometimes they cut back on wasteful investments, sometimes they take advantage of scale economies or synergies by providing financing for "add on" acquisitions, and sometimes they professionalize a firm's management team. There has been an increasing trend toward funds having a roster of "operating partners" who come with deep industry expertise and take on the role of Chair of the company after it is acquired. Because competition makes funds pay full price and investments have a high required rate of return, private equity partnerships must be able to substantially increase the profitability of any firm they acquire if they are to be successful.

3.2 Flexibility and the importance of control rights

An advantage that private equity funds have over other investors is that they have the ability to base their choice of investments on the financial, governance and operational changes that they hope to make post-investment. Most investors purchase existing securities such as stocks or bonds whose returns are beyond their control, as they play little, or no, role in governance. While some investors, in particular activist hedge funds, exert influence through "voice"—engaging with the board of directors—most investors are passive. If they are dissatisfied with the current management their only option is to "exit"—selling their stakes. In contrast, buyout funds are *active and controlling investors* and will, in general, not make investments unless they have the power to influence the firms in which they invest. In most buyouts, the fund acquires a majority voting stake in the portfolio company and consequently has voting control. However, even if a buyout fund takes a minority investment, it almost always obtains substantial control rights, often a board seat and always a significant shareholding that enables the fund to approve important firm-level decisions. Whenever the GPs feel they can increase the value of their investments, buyout funds will utilize these control rights to influence their portfolio firms' policies and, if necessary, to change the management team.

The returns of private equity funds come about in large part because the funds are able to undertake investment strategies that are simply unavailable to passive investors. For example, a fund might make an equity investment in a company that is contingent on the management cooperating with specific operational changes such as selling one business and expanding another. Or it might purchase a firm that has high-quality but underutilized assets, which is a positive NPV investment only if the acquirer has the ability to change the management team and improve the way that the assets are used. What makes each of these investments sufficiently profitable to meet the high cost of capital for buyout funds (as a result of their high fees, high risk, and low liquidity) is a fund's ability to combine the purchase of a portfolio firm's equity with the changes necessary to increase the value of the portfolio firm.

Many buyout funds have become more specialized over time. Buyouts in their modern form began in the 1980s. At that time, most funds were generalist and invested in many different industries. Since then, funds have become more specialized. Today it is common for funds to focus on a few industries. By doing so, funds' GPs become experts in these industries. They can hire full-time specialists who help them evaluate firms in these industries and manage the firms once they are acquired.

But while private equity funds do focus on particular sectors, they are not contractually limited to investing only in these sectors. They can and do take advantage of opportunities in other sectors when opportunities present themselves. Sometimes GPs raise funds explicitly to take advantage of short-term market opportunities as quickly as possible. For example, Blackstone has raised funds called "Tactical Opportunities" that are designed to invest in whatever sectors are attractive at the time, which as of 2022 had $35 billion in capital commitments.[o] Between December 2015 to March 2016, there was a sharp decline in oil prices, so the "Tac Ops" fund invested heavily in the energy sector. It did not have to approach investors when the opportunity occurred, because it had the capital already committed and was able to invest immediately. Starting in June 2016 the fund shifted its focus to the cybersecurity and cloud computing sectors which were taking off at that time.

---

[o]See https://www.blackstone.com/our-businesses/tactical-opportunities/.

Presumably, this fund will be able to shift into new sectors in future years as they become attractive to investors, and ultimately realize high returns for their investors.

Private equity funds have the flexibility not only to make financial, governance and operational changes to their portfolio firms, but some also can invest in whatever kinds of securities that it thinks will be most profitable. In a typical buyout, a fund purchases a controlling stake in the firm's equity while adding substantial leverage. But sometimes the fund can buy a minority stake of the equity that leaves the current management in control, perhaps with the right to take control if the management does not meet objectives. Or it can provide equity to a publicly traded corporation (known as private investment in public equity, or PIPE). Or it can invest in risky debt with the hope of exchanging it for equity (and control) in a restructuring. All these strategies, and others, are used by buyout funds as ways of earning returns for the limited partners in their funds. Since partners at private equity funds have strong pecuniary incentives and no restrictions on the type of investments they can make, GPs are always coming up with new ways to increase returns to their limited partners through creative investing strategies.

3.3 Alternative strategies to increase portfolio firms' values

Buyout funds have several common investment strategies. These strategies are the key to making buyouts profitable and generating the sorts of gross returns that will attract capital and pay for the significant management fees and carried interests to the GP. In Table 1, we provide a taxonomy of some of the most frequently observed strategies employed by GPs. Some of these relate to the pre-existing nature of the target company (e.g., family-owned or part of a conglomerate) whereas others relate to the general ways in which buyout funds transform businesses. Strategies are in no way mutually exclusive, and in practice the investment thesis of the GP will include elements of many different ways to create value.

3.3.1 Free cash flow

The early 1980s LBOs were mostly of large public firms. In many of these deals, the underlying source of value was that the firm had been wasting the firm's resources on value-decreasing investments. Jensen (1986), after observing a number of such deals, came up with one of the most important ideas in the finance literature, the "free cash flow" problem. He posited that when firms have assets that generate substantial cash flows and do not have any positive NPV projects available, they will tend to invest anyway, even if the projects that are available happen to be negative NPV. Jensen viewed leveraged buyouts as a market solution to the free cash flow problem. LBOs can increase the value of firms with assets that produce more cash than can be deployed in valuable investments by forcing the firms to use cash flow to pay interest on the debt and rather than invest it in wasteful projects. The value increase for such a buyout would come from the reduction in the quantity of value-destroying projects in which the firm invests.

Table 1 Common strategies used in buyouts to create value.

Strategy	Main features	Comments
Reduce free cash flow	Increasing leverage significantly, interest payments reduce free cash flow to focus management on generating profits and reduce wasteful expenditure	The "classic" strategy, as articulated by Jensen (1986), and still adopted in most buyouts. But since all GPs can raise leverage, such "financial engineering" is only now a competitive advantage relative to corporate acquirers. Working capital is managed by increased use of revolving credit facilities
Refocus operations	Identify and sell non-core assets, allowing increased focus on, and investment in, the highest margin/growth parts of the business	Many companies become complex portfolios of different businesses providing few synergies, but reducing idiosyncratic risk for management. Buyout funds can reassess the importance of each asset—free from any legacy decisions or arguments—and sell or close down those that are not core, thereby simplifying operations and allowing management to focus on value creation in the core business
Enhancing executive management	Replacement of Chair, CEO or other senior executives	Not all buyouts involve widespread departures of executives, but it is common for the buyout fund to bring in one of its roster of "operating partners" to chair the board. The suitability of the C-suite will be a key focus of due diligence, and succession plans will be produced where required, with a focus on bringing in proven industry experts especially those familiar with the demands of working with buyout fund owners
Operational efficiencies	Common strategies involve improving IT systems to enhance management information, increased out-sourcing, re-negotiating supplier contracts, closing less efficient plants	Such "operational engineering" has become more important as financial engineering has become a more generic competency. Reductions in employment are often focused on less productive establishments, with more productive parts of the business growing

Continued

Table 1 Common strategies used in buyouts to create value.—cont'd

Strategy	Main features	Comments
Scale economies	Roll-ups of fragmented sectors and accelerated expansion	The roll-up strategy often involves a series of add-on acquisitions in fragmented sectors, which can often be achieved at low valuation multiples relative to the multiples associated with the market leaders. Scale can also be achieved by taking a business that has been focused domestically to other international markets, and by accelerating expansion within existing markets
Corporate orphans	Divesting business units from large conglomerates that have become focused on their core business	Many companies have become conglomerates over the years, with a range of different businesses that have only a loose economic logic tying them together. The more peripheral business units—the corporate orphans—can suffer from a lack of attention at the overall board level and may be starved of funds to invest in the business. Acquiring such business units from their parent company and giving them full attention and access to capital and expertise has been an important strategy for buyout funds
Privatization	Taking state-owned enterprises into the private sector	State-owned enterprises frequently lack autonomy, strong management and access to finance. Buyout funds can be an alternative to public listing of such businesses, and can add particular value in cases where the management needs to be improved and for assets that have not traditionally been owned privately
Transition in ownership	Enabling transition for companies which are owned by individuals or families	Businesses that grow and flourish without ever becoming public companies can often have ownership concentrated in a few individuals or a family and can face challenges in terms of succession and realization of wealth. Buyout funds can help on both fronts, bringing in management expertise and enabling the founders to exit over a period of time

Table 1 Common strategies used in buyouts to create value.—cont'd

Strategy	Main features	Comments
Distressed investments	Buying companies that are facing financial distress	This is a specialist strategy, as it requires a different set of skills related to, inter alia, acquiring and re-negotiating particular tranches of debt, restructuring existing fixed commitments, such as property leases or supplier contracts, dealing with legacy pension liabilities etc. Funds focusing on such situations are often referred to as distressed debt funds, but they often become the dominant equity owner in the same way as a buyout fund

A classic example of the free cash flow leading to a buyout was the 1988 purchase of RJR-Nabisco by KKR in 1988, which was vividly described in Burrough and Helyar's *Barbarians at the Gate*. This book colorfully describes the wasteful investments that RJR-Nabisco undertook before the buyout that RJR-Nabisco financed with cash from cigarette sales. KKR was willing to pay more than double the pre-buyout price for RJR-Nabisco largely because of the value created by cutting back on wasteful investments.

3.3.2 Refocus operations

Another characteristic of many of the 1980s LBOs is that much of the inefficient investments the firms made before they were bought out diversified the firms away from their main line of business. Consequently, many of these firms were split up after they were taken private. It often turned out that the sum of the parts were worth more separately than when combined in a single company. The presumption underlying these "de-conglomerate" buyouts is that such ill-fitting parts should not have been combined in the first place.

Both the funds' GPs and the portfolio firms' managers are strongly motivated to increase the value of their portfolio firms. Sometimes the way to increase value is to expand one particular product line while cutting back on another. A buyout fund will examine the operations of a firm it acquires, divest the portions that do not contribute to the core mission and invest in those that do. Often prior management has an emotional attachment to its historical investments or suffers from the sunk cost fallacy. A buyout fund can take a fresh look at the firm's operations without such biases, which can lead them to make value-improving changes.

3.3.3 Enhancing executive management

Sometimes a firm's problems stem not from its assets but its management. A potential source of value that can motivate a buyout is a potential management change. In a significant proportion of buyouts, the CEO, CFO or other senior executives are replaced, either immediately or after a few months (as the existing executives can be helpful in knowing where the "bodies are buried!"). Many buyout funds have "operating partners" who specialize in improving the performance of underperforming companies, either as the chair of the board, or the CEO. In addition, funds have connections with other top executives, some of whom they have worked with on prior deals, who can replace the managers of a portfolio firm if they are not performing sufficiently well.[p]

3.3.4 Operational efficiencies

Buyout funds often can increase production efficiency through several methods. Sometimes they lay off workers and sometimes they hire more. They modernize production methods, closing inefficient plants and investing in newer ones (Davis et al., 2014). Production can be moved to different locations that have lower labor costs, and contracts with suppliers can be renegotiated or new suppliers found. There are many ways in which buyout funds can make the operations of portfolio firms more efficient.

3.3.5 Scale economies: Roll ups and expansions

A common strategy of buyout firms is to take advantage of the scale economies inherent in businesses with fixed costs. For example, a doctor's or dentist's office usually has a manager for scheduling, negotiations with insurance companies, etc. Combining such offices can lead to more efficient utilization of such managers. A classic strategy of private equity firms is to "roll up" multiple such businesses in a region and combine them. These deals create efficiencies in part by better utilizing fixed assets, and by achieving other economies of scale (such as in purchasing). Ideally, when the newly formed company is sold, its cash flows are larger than the sum of the cash flows of the smaller companies would be. In addition, the sale is likely to be at a higher multiple since potential buyers prefer to acquire larger, more efficient firms. A recent example of a roll-up strategy has been seen in the cinema sector, where large numbers of smaller cinema operators have been rolled up into a few dominant chains.

Related to a roll-up is an expansion strategy. In an expansion, a buyout fund acquires a portfolio of firms, and at the time of the purchase, commits to financing "add on" acquisitions for the portfolio firms. These deals are usually in sectors where there are unexploited scale economies. The commitment to financing add-on acquisitions makes the original deal more attractive to the firm's managers, who can ultimately run a larger entity, assuming they are retained in their jobs.

---

[p]For discussion and evidence on the way in which CEO changes are an important element buyout of buyout firms' strategies, see Gompers et al. (2022).

Consequently, expansion strategies are a way of both facilitating the original purchase of portfolio firms and increasing their value after they are acquired.

3.3.6 Corporate orphans

Sometimes divisions in a firm get out of favor with top management and do not get sufficient resources to maximize their value.[q] These divisions are sometimes referred to as "corporate orphans," since they suffer from inattention from the parent firm. Corporate orphans can prove to be excellent targets for buyout funds. Given an incentivized management team and resources, buyout funds can often increase these firms' values substantially and earn high returns from these deals.

3.3.7 Privatization of state-owned enterprises

State-owned enterprises are often notoriously badly managed. Consequently, when they are privatized, there is much scope for improvement. Private equity funds can acquire these companies, help foster efficiencies, and increase returns through this process. The way in which state-owned enterprises are privatized varies by country. Much of the privatization in recent years has been in China, which is because it has many inefficient former state-owned enterprises. In many Chinese deals, the fund usually does not take a controlling position, since having the government with a meaningful equity stake is very helpful in doing business in that country (see Lerner and Jin (2012)).

3.3.8 Transitions in ownership

Often in privately held companies, transitions can be problematic. Founders can retire with no clear successors. And family firms can have some family members (or other investors) who wish to liquidate their stake while others want to continue managing the company. In such a situation, an investment by a buyout fund can add value by easing the transition. The fund can purchase the equity from the investors who want to exit but not the equity of those who want to remain. In such deals, control can be negotiable; a common solution is for the buyout fund to start off with a minority stake that becomes a controlling stake if objectives negotiated at the time of the deal are not met. Such an approach not only provides incentives to meet the objectives after the deal is consummated, but also motivates the management team not to overstate their forecasts to ensure that the objectives are set realistically (see Hardymon et al. (2007) for an example of such a deal).

3.3.9 Mitigating distress

When firms enter financial distress, they usually try to arrange a restructuring in which firms deliver by swapping some of their debt for equity. However, most holders of debt are passive and do not actively engage with corporate governance.

---

[q]See Scharfstein and Stein (2000) for a formal model of such behavior.

In addition, when debt is diffusely held, coordination problems can inhibit distressed firms from being able to complete value-increasing restructurings (see Gertner and Scharfstein (1991)). These inefficiencies present an opportunity for private equity firms to create value by facilitating restructurings in distressed firms. Typically, they purchase a large stake in the "fulcrum" debt, which is the most senior debt that would not get paid in full in a liquidation. By doing so, the fund hopes to negotiate a restructuring in which they can convert the debt to equity, gain control of the company, and enact changes to the firm's operations.

3.3.10 Other private equity strategies

This list of strategies covers the main ways in which buyouts add value to portfolio firms. However, there are many other related private equity strategies that are not technically buyouts but share some characteristics. Two in particular are worthy of mention. First, a recent trend has been for private equity funds, instead of buying firms, to take long-term leases to operate infrastructure, such as airports, toll roads, or electric utilities instead of acquiring ownership of those assets. Funds designed for these investments have raised enormous amounts of capital in recent years. Between 2015 and 2019, these funds invested $388 billion and have $217 billion of dry powder available as of 2019.[r] Infrastructure assets offer relatively safe cash flows and can earn much higher returns than those available from the fixed income market. The reason why private equity funds can offer these higher yields is that they typically can improve the operating performance of the assets.[s]

Second, although not a buyout, but an interesting type of private equity deal worth mentioning is the Private Investment in Public Equity. In a PIPE, a private equity or hedge fund negotiates a private placement with a public company. Since private equity funds charge higher fees and have higher net-of-fee required returns than other intermediaries investing in public equities such as mutual funds, they cannot satisfy their investors by simply purchasing public equities on the exchange. Usually, the firms raising capital from a PIPE do not have access to other sources of finance and for this reason, are willing to structure the transaction to provide the private equity fund a high enough expected return to induce them to invest. Specifically, funds almost always purchase the equity at a discount to the public market price, and often receive warrants in addition to the equity at this discounted price (see Lim et al. (2021) for details and statistics on PIPE transactions).

3.4 Wealth transfers

While buyout funds purport to increase the value of their portfolio firms by creating efficiencies using the strategies just described, they also can increase value by transferring wealth from other parties to themselves. This idea was originated by

---

[r]See https://www.ey.com/en_us/private-equity/how-pe-infrastructure-funds-are-getting-new-options.
[s]See Andonov et al. (2021) and Howell et al. (2022) for recent research about infrastructure funds.

Shleifer and Summers (1988), and the extent to which possible wealth transfers motivate buyouts, as well as mergers and acquisitions more broadly, has been an important topic of research.

Perhaps the most important source of wealth transfers is from the government from reduced corporate taxes (see Kaplan, 1989b). The evidence that buyout funds pay lower corporate taxes is indisputable, since they employ much higher leverage. However, there is uncertainty about the amount of value that is transferred through tax reductions, and whether the benefits of such financial engineering accrue to the investors in the fund rather than the vendors of the companies that are acquired.

In addition, there are studies that evaluate whether buyout funds achieve their returns in part by cutting corners on quality, safety, working conditions, investment, R&D, etc. In general, the evidence is mixed and varies across sectors. However, it should be emphasized that the main constraint facing any buyout fund is the need to sell their portfolio companies to willing buyers. Cutting corners, reducing costs in an unsustainable way, reducing product quality and similar actions that transfer wealth from a firm's customers or employees are tempting to boost short-run financial results, but are unlikely to maximize the price an acquirer will pay for a portfolio firm.

4 Facts about buyouts
4.1 A brief history of the industry

Since the first leveraged buyout in the 1960s, the buyout sector has grown tremendously. Total buyout assets under management have grown to about $2.5 trillion as of 2020. The sector has experienced several booms and busts that have been highly correlated to the business cycle. This section discusses facts related to the buyout market, across time and geography, to help understand the dynamics of the market as a whole and to provide intuition as to how the market will develop in the future.

The leveraged buyout market began in the 1960s when public companies made acquisitions funded mainly by debt, which were then called "bootstrap transactions."[t] A well-known early deal was the acquisition of Pan-Atlantic Steamship Company in 1955 by a financier named Malcom McLean. To finance the deal, McLean borrowed $42 million and raised $7 million through preferred stock. After the acquisition, McLean invested in containerized shipping, which increased efficiency in the shipping business.[u]

The idea of using a highly leveraged transaction to take companies private was adopted by investors such as Victor Posner, who created the term "leveraged buyout."[v] Leveraged buyouts gained popularity when investment companies were

---

[t]See Vadapalli, 2007. *Mergers, Acquisitions and Business Valuation.* Excel Books India for a detailed history of the LBO market.
[u]See https://www.pbs.org/wgbh/theymadeamerica/whomade/mclean_hi.html.
[v]See Trehan (2006). The History of Leveraged Buyouts. *4Hoteliers.*

established with relatively small amounts of equity, with the intention of buying much larger companies by raising debt secured on the assets of the target. Early investors were Jerome Kohlberg, Henry Kravis, and George Roberts who established KKR and raised $30 million in 1978, and companies like Thomas H. Lee Partners, Cinven, Forstmann Little & Company, Welsh, Carson, Anderson & Stowe, Candover, and GTCR. Most of these firms remain large private equity investors today. Among these, Cinven and Candover, both based in London, were among the earliest European buyout firms when private equity spread outside the US market in the 1980s.

The 1980s saw a proliferation of LBOs, a number of which were "hostile." As the market developed there were some iconic deals that shaped the future of the industry. One of the first was Wesray Capital's investments in Gibson Greetings in 1984, which was exited in a $290 million IPO 16 months after acquisition and generated a profit of $66 million for Wesray. The rising stock market in the 1980s helped enable profitable exits for many buyouts, and investment bankers were increasingly prepared to provide significant leverage to finance LBOs. Michael Milken at Drexel Burnham Lambert become famous for developing the market for high-yield debt financing for buyouts, which were commonly referred to as "junk bonds." Supported by the ready availability of high-yield debt, the size of buyout deals quickly snowballed with the most famous deal ever executed occurring in 1989: the acquisition of RJR Nabisco by KKR for around $25 billion.[w]

However, by the end of the 1980s, the market started to overheat and several large buyouts like Federated Department Stores, Revco, Walter Industries, FEB Trucking, and Eaton Leonard went into bankruptcy under the burden of their high-yield debt, and rising interest rates. RJR Nabisco itself was financially constrained under the huge interest burden, despite significant asset sales that were used to repay debt. It eventually had to be recapitalized, with KKR putting in additional $1.7 billion in 1990. Not only did high-yield debt begin to default but large buyouts in the late 1980s had to cut expenses aggressively, often through layoffs, as free cash flow became constrained. The boom cycle came to an end in the early 1990s, which also witnessed public companies adopting anti-takeover defenses like poison pills, which protected themselves from hostile bids.

After the recession of the early 1990s, and in response to the failures and criticisms of the earlier deals, buyouts returned in the mid-1990s with an increased focus on generating long-term value for their portfolio companies. Transactions had much lower leverage, with debt to value ratios of 20–40% compared with the 85–95% in the 1980s. Thomas H. Lee Partners' success with Snapple Beverages in 1992 was a watershed deal that led to entry into the sector. Only 2 years after the takeover, Lee took Snapple Beverage public and sold it to Quaker Oats for $1.7 billion, resulting in a $900 million profit. The credit market started to open up again with investors willing to lend capital to finance LBOs, and the mid-1990s saw a second bloom in the

---

[w]See Burrough and Helyar, 1990. Barbarians at the Gate. *Harper and Row.*

industry with a number of important deals like Duane Reade, Sealy, KinderCare Learning, J. Crew, Domino's, Regal Entertainment, Oxford Health Plans, and Petco.

The sharp stock market decline in 2000 hit the buyout market hard, especially deals in the telecommunication sector. The credit market started to tighten up again and the number of deals decreased sharply. Two partnerships that were hit particularly hard were Hicks Muse Tate & Furst and Forstmann Little & Company, both of which had invested in technology companies right before the internet bubble burst.[x]

Valuation multiples were much lower in the early 2000s, which was commonly attributed to tighter lending conditions. In addition, most of the deals that were done were relatively small. However, those deals that were made during this time turned out, on average, to be very profitable.

The mid-2000s saw a third boom in the buyout market. Decreased interest rates and loose credit conditions led to a number of very large deals. At the same time, regulation changes relating to public equity markets, such as the Sarbanes-Oxley Act, made private ownership more attractive. Fundraising and deal volume increased substantially, with buyout funds investing a record $280 billion in 2006 and $290 billion in 2007. The largest buyout deals that were made in this period included the acquisition of Georgia-Pacific Corp (2005), Albertson's (2005), EQ Office (2007), Freescale Semiconductor (2006), Ally Financial GMAC (2006), Chrysler (2007), First Data (2007) and TXU (2007).

The buyout boom came to an abrupt halt with the Financial Crisis in 2008. The credit market dried up completely when investment banks were struck by defaults in the mortgage market. Debt financing became highly constrained, the market for collateralized loan obligation (CLO) funds (into which much LBO debt was sold) froze, and the number of buyout transactions dropped significantly.

However, both the equity market and the buyout market rebounded relatively quickly, and deal volume has steadily been increasing since 2009. The continued economic recovery over the next decade resulted in a huge growth in the buyout sector, which today manages around $2.5 trillion in assets. The growth and entry of GPs has resulted in significantly more competition for deals in both the US and Europe, both of which are now relatively mature markets. One implication of this increased maturity of the buyout market is that there is increased competition for deals, which could potentially lower returns for buyout investors.

As we are writing this chapter, we are in the middle of the Covid-19 pandemic. What was remarkable in this crisis was the fast rebound of buyout deals—and, indeed, valuations—after the initial impact of the pandemic at the start of 2020. The window of opportunity for investing at depressed values was only open for a few months before markets recovered and prices increased. Furthermore, at the start of the pandemic buyout funds were sitting on record amounts of undrawn capital commitments (dry powder) and this resulted in a very active buyout market from mid-2020 onwards.

---

[x]See Forbes. (2001). Forbes Faces: Thomas O. Hicks. *Forbes*.

Having given this brief historical overview of the development of the buyout sector, the sections below will present detailed evidence on how buyouts have evolved over time and across different regions.

4.2 The evolution of the buyout market

Fig. 5 illustrates the evolution of the buyout market. Fig. 5A presents the amount of capital and the number of funds raised in the buyout market each year, across different geographic regions since the mid-1990s. Fig. 5B presents the number and the total value of buyout deals across time and region and the total value of deals made each year. Fig. 5C presents buyout deals in comparison to the total M&A market in the United States. Fig. 5A and B are generated from data provided by Preqin and Fig. 5C is generated by data from Thomson via OneBanker.

From Fig. 5A and B, we see that the number of funds, deals, the total value of deals as well as the amount of capital raised strongly co-move with the credit cycle. Prior to the 2000 stock market decline, the amount of capital raised had more than tripled over the prior 5-year period. The number of deals increased substantially in 2000 as well but fell dramatically the following year. During the 2001–2003 recession, there were not many deals. The market heated up when the credit market boomed—with loosened credit conditions—in the mid-2000s. Capital raised during 2007 was around $250 billion, about 2.5 times the amount raised in 2004. The number of deals also hit a peak at about 4600 deals in a single year in 2007 and buyout deals comprised about a quarter of total M&A activity.

After the 2008 Financial Crisis, US capital-raising was cut in half in 2009. Given its dependence on the availability of debt financing, the buyout market was hit harder than the overall M&A market. Buyout deals comprised only 7% of the total M&A deal value in 2009, in comparison to 24% in 2007. The buyout market recovered relatively quickly after the Financial Crisis and has stayed buoyant, even through the 2020–21 pandemic.

Recent years have seen a large increase in the number of funds and capital raised. The number of deals remains below the level of 2007, but the deal value exceeds the 2007 level, which suggests that there is more capital being raised relative to the number of deals, and that funds are paying higher price per deal. Not surprisingly, there have been concerns from the media that there is now too much money chasing too few deals.[y] And the US market seems to be at the core of the problem compared to other regions; the increase in the amount of capital raised is mainly driven by the US market, while the number of deals made in the United States has not changed much since 2007.

Table 2 presents the distribution of the number of deals within a fund for each year and across different geographical regions. The table was generated from deal-level data provided by Preqin.

---

[y]As reported by https://www.wsj.com/articles/buyout-funds-have-money-to-burn-and-thats-a-problem-1503680385.

Panel A

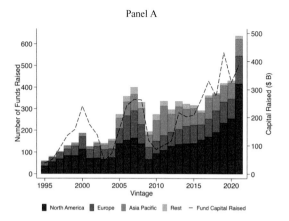

Panel B

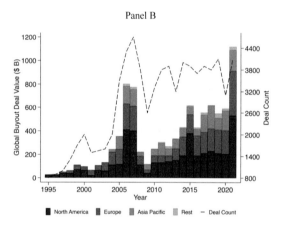

Panel C

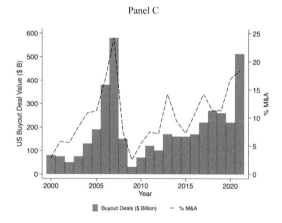

FIG. 5

The overall evolution of the buyout market. This figure shows the overall evolution of the buyout market. (A) The number of funds (bar, left Y-axis) and the capital raised by these funds (dashed line, right Y-axis). The sample includes periods from 1995 to 2021 in regions such as North America, Europe, Asia Pacific, and the Rest of the World. The data is provided by *Preqin*. (B) The total value of buyout deals (bar, left Y-axis) and the total deal count (dashed line, right Y-axis). The samples include periods from 1995 to 2021 in regions such as North America, Europe, Asia Pacific, and the Rest of the World. The data is provided by *Preqin*. (C) The capital invested in buyout deals (bar, left Y-axis) and the percentage of buyout deals out of the total M&A activities (dashed line, right Y-axis). The sample includes periods from 2000 to 2021 in the US market only and the data is provided by *Refinitiv*.

Table 2 The number of deals in a fund.

Number of deals in a fund

	Obs.	Mean	Std	Min	p25	p50	p75	Max
North America								
1995–2000	297	9.36	9.06	1	3	7	12	51
2001–2007	653	15.85	18.76	1	4	10	19	174
2008–2009	169	18.14	18.98	1	5	13	23	107
2010–2016	715	12.89	15.32	1	4	8	16	147
Mean	458.5	14.06	15.53	1	4	9.5	17.5	119.75
Europe								
1995–2000	146	9.04	9.81	1	3	6	12	85
2001–2007	425	13.13	14.32	1	5	9	16	117
2008–2009	120	12.07	11.36	1	5	9	15	59
2010–2016	416	10.33	10.66	1	3	7	13	74
Mean	276.75	11.1425	11.5375	1	4	7.75	14	83.75
Asia Pacific								
1995–2000	32	3.69	2.55	1	1.5	3	5.5	9
2001–2007	161	6.87	5.9	1	2	5	10	31
2008–2009	74	5.57	5.24	1	2	4	8	33
2010–2016	304	5.27	5.31	1	1.5	3	7	29
Mean	142.75	5.35	4.75	1	1.75	3.75	7.625	25.5
Rest								
1995–2000	8	4.25	3.28	1	1.5	3.5	6.5	10
2001–2007	66	7.11	5.82	1	3	6	8	27
2008–2009	31	4.87	4.93	1	1	4	6	24
2010–2016	98	4.16	3.85	1	2	3	5	27
Mean	50.75	5.0975	4.47	1	1.875	4.125	6.375	22

This table shows the number of deals in a fund broken down by time and region. The sample includes funds with vintage years from 1995 to 2016 in regions such as North America, Europe, Asia Pacific, and the Rest of the World. The first column presents the vintage year groups. We report the number of funds, mean, standard deviation, the minimum, the bottom 25%, 50%, and 75%. The data was provided by Preqin.

The average number of deals per fund varies by region. On average, North American funds have 13 deals in a fund, with European funds having slightly fewer at 11. However, Asian funds and funds from the rest of world are smaller and more concentrated, having only on 5 deals per fund on average. The distribution is highly right skewed for all years and geographical regions. While the median number of deals are around 9 and 8 for North American and European funds, some funds have well over a hundred investments, many of which are small investments in deals that are syndicated by other GPs.

In the non-US market, European funds follow a similar pattern as the North American funds. The largest number of deals in a fund appeared during the 2000s before the Financial Crisis and dropped significantly during the crisis, due to the decline in the number of mega funds raised during the period. Meanwhile, the number of deals made in funds from Asia-Pacific grew substantially during the 2000s and is currently between 5 and 6.

4.3 Assets under management and dry powder

Fig. 6A presents statistics on assets under management over time and across regions. The data are provided by Burgiss. We observe two buyout booms in Fig. 6A, during the 2005–2007 and 2016–2021 periods. The North American and Asian markets grew particularly rapidly during these two periods. Other than during the Financial Crisis, the buyout market grew continuously over the past 20 years, setting a record-level of asset under management in recent years. As of 2021, the assets under management by the buyout funds have reached almost $2.7 trillion combining the three regions: $1.7 trillion in North America, $700 billion in Europe, and $270 billion in Asia.

Fig. 6B presents the amount of uncalled committed capital (dry powder) across time and location. Despite the strong pace of investments being made since the mid-2010s, fundraising has been sufficiently high so that the quantity of dry powder available for future investments has increased as well. The total quantity of worldwide dry powder reached a peak of about $800 billion in 2020. Because there is so much dry powder available, there has been increased competition for deals which is likely a reason for the high valuation multiples for deals occurring in recent years.

Although the amount of assets under management has reached the peak in 2021, we observe a decline in the amount of dry powder in 2021, mostly coming from North America. Analyst reports have attributed the decline to the sharp increase in the public-to-private (P2P) transactions in North America and in Asia. Especially, during 2021, there has been a surge of software P2P deals that are large in value which naturally absorbed a lot of dry powder from the buyout funds that were waiting to be spent.[z]

---

[z]See https://www.bain.com/globalassets/noindex/2022/bain_report_global-private-equity-report-2022.pdf

Panel A

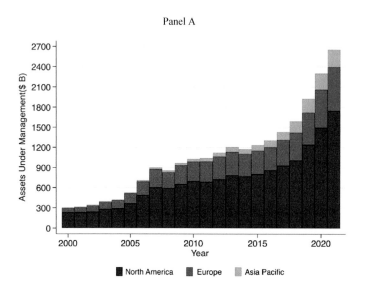

Panel B

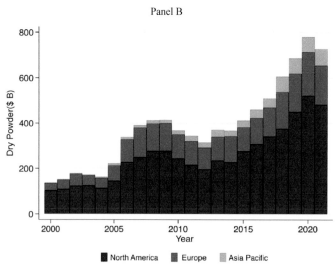

FIG. 6

AUM and Dry powder. This figure shows the asset under management (A) and the amount of dry powder (B) in the buyout market across time and region. The sample includes periods from 2000 to 2021 in North America, Europe, and Asia Pacific. The data is provided by *Preqin*.

4.4 Fund performance over time by location

Table 3 presents the distribution in fund performance by vintage year and geographical region. Panel A presents performance measured using the TVPI (Total Value to Paid In Capital) and Panel B presents PME (Public Market Equivalent) returns.

Table 3 Buyout fund performance by vintage year and region.

Vintage	North America				Europe				Asia Pacific			
	Mean	95th	50th	5th	Mean	95th	50th	5th	Mean	95th	50th	5th
Panel A. TVPI												
1995	1.59	2.71	1.53	0.61	0.59	0.60	0.60	0.60	0.88	0.90	0.84	0.78
1996	1.71	2.68	1.39	0.36	1.93	2.42	1.80	1.47	1.08	1.08	1.08	1.08
1997	1.51	2.17	1.21	0.58	1.96	2.23	1.83	0.91	1.46	1.51	1.50	1.48
1998	1.31	2.44	1.44	0.35	2.09	2.85	1.53	1.15	1.14	1.62	1.38	0.73
1999	1.46	2.63	1.57	0.29	1.85	2.11	1.65	0.30	1.08	1.12	1.04	0.96
2000	1.85	2.92	1.74	0.49	2.17	2.61	1.72	0.95	1.87	1.97	1.58	1.49
2001	1.97	3.01	1.93	0.91	2.15	2.91	1.94	1.12	3.59	3.57	3.11	2.65
2002	1.93	2.54	1.81	1.06	2.15	3.29	1.91	1.36	2.84	2.36	2.36	2.36
2003	2.06	3.31	1.77	1.08	2.09	2.92	1.78	0.58				
2004	1.79	3.00	1.61	0.94	1.68	2.71	1.80	0.85	1.73	2.17	1.67	0.86
2005	1.61	3.03	1.54	0.73	1.57	2.09	1.45	0.81	1.51	2.32	1.48	0.79
2006	1.56	2.77	1.63	0.71	1.29	2.47	1.58	0.53	1.35	1.94	1.31	0.37
2007	1.71	2.88	1.73	0.77	1.41	2.35	1.50	0.69	1.73	2.84	1.54	0.62
2008	1.70	2.98	1.68	0.62	1.62	2.31	1.56	0.58	1.37	3.07	1.50	0.64
2009	2.09	4.27	2.04	0.72	1.53	2.31	1.74	1.09	1.20	1.77	1.47	1.10
2010	1.84	3.05	1.84	0.88	1.47	2.75	1.73	0.50	1.52	3.40	1.48	1.07
2011	2.06	3.28	1.90	0.94	1.67	2.91	1.78	0.94	1.38	2.35	1.81	0.91
2012	1.87	2.90	1.81	0.84	1.73	2.34	1.63	1.15	1.77	2.44	1.62	1.35
2013	1.85	2.83	1.76	1.17	1.61	2.82	1.58	1.29	1.53	3.30	1.48	1.13
2014	1.92	3.21	1.67	0.84	1.85	2.97	1.53	1.11	1.48	1.76	1.50	1.29
2015	1.76	2.80	1.50	1.11	1.60	2.03	1.52	1.13	1.38	1.62	1.40	0.90

Continued

Table 3 Buyout fund performance by vintage year and region.—cont'd

Vintage	North America				Europe				Asia Pacific			
	Mean	95th	50th	5th	Mean	95th	50th	5th	Mean	95th	50th	5th
2016	1.62	2.61	1.53	1.01	1.51	1.81	1.39	1.06	1.49	2.00	1.43	1.00
2017	1.64	2.31	1.54	1.12	1.48	1.83	1.21	0.74	1.58	1.84	1.59	1.39
2018	1.35	1.77	1.26	1.01	1.31	1.76	1.15	0.75	1.24	1.49	1.00	0.84
2019	1.28	2.02	1.13	0.74	1.13	1.40	0.94	0.52	1.26	1.74	1.13	0.94
2020	1.09	1.43	1.00	0.16	1.28	3.00	0.87	0.20	1.01	1.36	0.99	0.29
2021	1.19	1.24	1.00	0.63	0.98	0.83	0.58	0.33	0.97	0.99	0.93	0.86
(All)	1.69	3.05	1.56	0.71	1.60	2.68	1.51	0.65	1.48	2.50	1.43	0.74
Panel B. PME												
1995	1.11	1.7	1.03	0.4	0.43	0.43	0.43	0.43	0.71	0.72	0.68	0.64
1996	1.27	1.87	1.11	0.29	1.27	1.58	1.47	0.95	0.94	0.94	0.94	0.94
1997	1.24	1.85	1.03	0.59	1.69	2.10	1.52	0.80	1.28	1.32	1.26	1.19
1998	1.2	2.27	1.44	0.35	1.91	2.90	1.47	1.10	1.02	1.47	1.14	0.74
1999	1.27	2.09	1.39	0.28	1.51	1.64	1.37	0.32	1.08	1.09	1.06	1.02
2000	1.4	2.6	1.34	0.47	1.77	1.97	1.39	0.88	1.63	1.69	1.34	1.31
2001	1.47	2.38	1.52	0.66	1.53	2.01	1.44	0.75	2.97	2.92	2.68	2.43
2002	1.42	1.85	1.32	0.8	1.48	2.43	1.43	1.10	2.39	1.99	1.99	1.99
2003	1.55	3.01	1.33	0.73	1.60	2.06	1.43	0.41	1.52	1.78	1.51	0.75
2004	1.35	2.31	1.25	0.66	1.36	2.10	1.39	0.73	1.32	2.25	1.30	0.71
2005	1.15	2.09	1.05	0.45	1.32	2.01	1.21	0.64	1.04	1.40	0.93	0.32
2006	1.01	1.69	1.08	0.51	1.03	1.83	1.21	0.43	1.12	1.78	1.04	0.42
2007	1.02	1.71	1.08	0.47	1.05	1.64	1.19	0.46	0.92	1.91	0.93	0.42
2008	1.02	1.6	0.93	0.37	1.12	1.58	1.07	0.37	0.74	1.04	0.88	0.73
2009	1.17	1.84	1.19	0.51	1.06	1.62	1.19	0.82	0.88	2.24	0.80	0.65

2010	1.01	1.7	1.01	0.52	0.98	1.87	1.24	0.34	0.88	1.43	1.07	0.47
2011	1.13	1.82	1.14	0.53	1.17	2.15	1.29	0.61	1.15	1.58	1.04	0.82
2012	1.13	1.8	1.12	0.57	1.26	1.63	1.30	0.79	1.03	1.82	1.09	0.73
2013	1.13	1.81	1.1	0.68	1.24	1.92	1.28	0.99	1.06	1.37	1.11	0.86
2014	1.2	2.01	1.05	0.5	1.47	2.32	1.32	0.87	0.96	1.19	1.01	0.64
2015	1.13	1.6	1.03	0.71	1.32	1.71	1.26	0.95	1.05	1.31	1.02	0.72
2016	1.05	1.68	1.06	0.7	1.25	1.49	1.23	0.91	1.21	1.41	1.25	1.00
2017	1.16	1.68	1.12	0.8	1.27	1.54	1.06	0.70	0.97	1.18	0.83	0.65
2018	1.02	1.32	0.98	0.76	1.13	1.52	1.04	0.70	1.03	1.45	0.93	0.80
2019	1.02	1.59	0.92	0.59	0.97	1.29	0.87	0.55	0.89	1.24	0.77	0.26
2020	0.93	1.25	0.87	0.14	1.08	1.88	0.76	0.24	0.97	0.99	0.91	0.83
2021	1.12	1.16	0.95	0.63	0.94	0.81	0.56	0.31	0.71	0.72	0.68	0.64
(All)	1.17	1.97	1.06	0.49	1.26	2.00	1.20	0.56	1.07	1.79	1.01	0.53

The table shows the performance distribution of buyout funds. The sample includes funds with vintage years from 1995 to 2021 in North America, Europe, and the Asia Pacific. Panel A presents the total value paid-in (TVPI) as the performance measure, and panel B presents the public market equivalent (PME) as the performance measure. The benchmark public equity index for North America is S&P 500, MSCI Europe for Europe, and MSCI World for Asia. Both tables present the mean, the bottom 95%, 50%, and 5% performance across vintage years and regions. The data is from Burgiss.

All these returns are net of management fees and carried interest; in other words, they are the returns that the LPs actually receive. However, for funds that have not yet distributed all their capital, reported returns value not yet exited deals at NAV, which likely understates the performance they will ultimately achieve.

Overall, it is evident that the buyout market has almost always outperformed public markets in each region. An exception are funds investing in the Asia-Pacific region, where we see many vintage years in which buyouts have underperformed public markets.

There is a counter-cyclical pattern to returns, with higher returns for funds with vintage years during recessions. However, calls and distributions tend to be higher when economic conditions are strong. If we compare 1995–1999 to 2000–2002 and 2005–2007 to 2008–2009, we observe that funds raised during the 2000–2002 recession and the 2008–2009 Financial Crisis had higher returns than before these crises when the market was at near a peak. Interestingly, PMEs are also higher during the down cycles indicating that buyout funds can take advantage of depressed markets, when competition from corporate acquirers is likely to be lower.

4.5 Purchase prices and leverage multiples

Fig. 7 presents the average EBITDA-to-purchase-price (enterprise value) multiples by year for US and European markets. The data come from the LCD global.

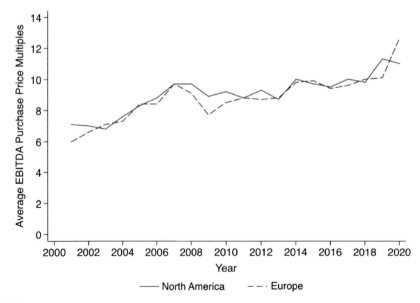

FIG. 7

The average EBITDA purchase price multiples. The figure presents the average EBITDA purchase price multiples. The sample includes deals invested from 1999 to 2020 in the United States and in Europe. The data is from the *LCD global*.

Purchase price multiples have increased over time, with the average multiple being around 11–12 times EBITDA in 2020. To some extent, these high multiples reflect movements in interest rates: as interest rates fell after the Financial Crisis, the cost of capital was reduced and asset values rose. In addition, the increased competition for deals resulting from the high quantities of dry powder also probably explains some of the increase.

Multiples appear to be pro-cyclical. During the downturns in the early 2000s and during 2007–2008, we see a clear downward movement in price multiples. On the other hand, during the boom cycles, such as 2005–2007 and 2014–2020, we see a noticeable increase in multiples. Yet, the median PME and TVPI during 2005–2007 and 2014–2020 in Table 3 suggest the buyout market being over-heated during the periods, as the buyout fund performance is lower.

Fig. 8 presents the average contributions of equity and debt over time for US and European deals. On average, 55% and 60% of the contribution comes from debt financing for the US and European markets, respectively. To examine the numbers by splitting the samples based on time, pre-crisis, the debt contribution used to be around 68% for both markets while the debt multiples remained around 4.7 and 5.4 for the US and European markets, respectively. During the Financial Crisis, the debt contribution went down to about 50% of the total with debt multiples around 2.4 and 3.9 for the US and European markets, respectively. Post-crisis, the debt contribution remained to be about a half, but the debt multiples recovered to the points where they used to be in the pre-crisis period. This pattern occurs because the deals have become more expensive, and the purchase price multiples have increased post-crisis. The recent 5–6 years have especially seen a huge increase in the purchase price multiples with tech buyouts being particularly expensive ($\approx$16–22$\times$ EBITDA).

In the United States, credit conditions started to slowly recover from the financial crisis in 2009, while in Europe, tight credit supply remained until 2012. In recent years, there have been more generous equity financings in the United States and the debt contribution to buyouts has been decreasing trend.

4.6 Exits

Table 4 presents information on the different routes by which the LBO fund exits their deals, broken down by time and region. The table is generated from the deal-level data provided by Preqin from 1990 to 2019. Most buyout deals in the 1990s were in North America and Europe. The largest number of deals in both North America and Europe at the time were exited through trade sales, which are sales to corporate acquirers, followed by IPO which was the second most popular exit type. The two types combined were responsible for 66% and 60% of all exits for North America and Europe, respectively. Buyout markets in Asia and the rest of the world were not very popular during the 1990s, with only a few exit deals, mostly by trade sales and IPO. In particular, the most popular exit route in Asia during the time was through an IPO.

Panel A

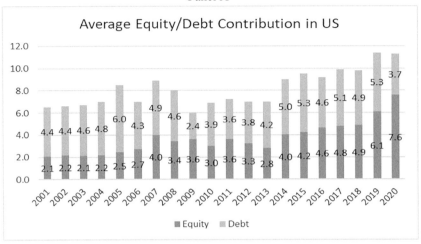

Panel B

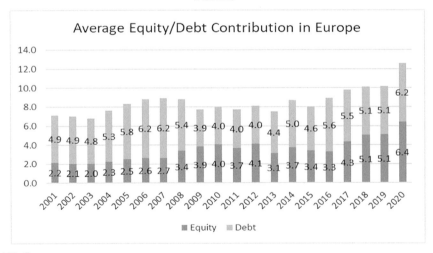

FIG. 8

Average equity and debt contribution. The figures show the average equity to debt contribution of buyout deals in the United States and Europe. The sample includes deals invested from 2001 to the first quarter of 2020. The data is from *LCD global*.

In the 2000s, trade sales were the most popular form of exit for all regions. About 37% of all exits were through trade sales during this period. The IPO market cooled for North America and Europe, and the share of IPO exits shrank to below 10% for both regions. Instead, as the number of buyout funds increased, buyout funds became active buyers of deals, and sales to other GPs, which is known as a secondary buyout,

Table 4 Exit types.

Exit Type	Geography	1990s	2000s	2010s
IPO	North America	199	389	472
Merger		44	302	1339
Private Placement		25	207	805
Recapitalization		9	165	526
Restructuring		5	208	342
Sale to GP		73	885	3083
Sale to Management		8	60	118
Trade Sale		302	1571	4765
Unspecified Exit		92	349	550
Write Off		4	227	358
IPO	Europe	125	241	401
Merger		6	148	706
Private Placement		9	90	556
Recapitalization		2	54	176
Restructuring		1	76	259
Sale to GP		28	966	2828
Sale to Management		7	159	347
Trade Sale		145	1409	3724
Unspecified Exit		143	519	576
Write Off		0	60	224
IPO	Asia	12	184	649
Merger		2	22	126
Private Placement		1	92	783
Recapitalization		0	2	39
Restructuring		0	10	48
Sale to GP		1	68	458
Sale to Management		0	12	95
Trade Sale		7	210	1054
Unspecified Exit		5	66	312
Write Off		0	9	43
IPO	Rest	2	43	117
Merger		0	10	68
Private Placement		0	17	93
Recapitalization		0	0	7
Restructuring		0	1	8
Sale to GP		1	27	159
Sale to Management		0	6	29
Trade Sale		3	104	396
Unspecified Exit		0	38	143
Write Off		0	2	13

The table presents the buyout deal distribution by exit types, geography, and time horizons (decades). The sample includes deals that are from 1990 to 2019 in North America, Europe, Asia Pacific, and the rest of the World. The data is from Preqin.

became the second most popular form of exit. Asia and the rest of the world followed similar trend—the share of IPO exits went down, and the share of sales to other GPs increased, but IPO exits were still the second most popular exit route.

In the 2010s, there was an increasing trend in the share of sales to other GPs exits, and a decreasing trend in the share of IPO exits persist in both North America and Europe. More than a quarter of deals in North America and Europe was exited through sale to other GPs, while trade sales were still the most popular exit route. Asia and the rest of the world followed a similar pattern, but these two regions have experienced an immense increase in the share of exits through private placements. For Asia, private placements are now the second most popular exit type.

Across all regions and time, sales to manager exits are rare; on average, 2% of all exits are by selling to the portfolio company managers. The write-off is also very rare, comprising only 1% of all exits. However, in North America, the fraction was as high as 5% during the Financial Crisis.

4.7 Fund fee distribution

Table 5 presents the fund fee structure distribution over time and geographical region. The table is generated from Stepstone fund fee data.[aa] Table 5 confirms the fact that 2–20 (i.e., 2% of annual management fee and 20% of carried interest) is the most widely used fee structure in private equity. There is a remarkable consistency in carried interest, with about 95% of GPs charging exactly 20%. Management fees do vary more widely. The median management fee has remained around 2%, except in Europe where it has gone down slightly to 1.8 in recent years (2016–2020). The median GP stake in the fund is around 4.5% in North America but slightly lower in Europe or Asia.

One thing to note is that the data is from 1970 to 2020 and since 2020, the management fee for most buyout funds have gone down to 1.5%.

5 The academic literature on buyouts

Given the large increase in the volume of buyouts in recent years, it is not surprising that there has been a corresponding increase in academic research on buyouts. This research has yielded several insights about buyouts' performance, their investors, and the role that governance plays, both in terms of the buyout funds themselves and also about the portfolio firms in which they invest.[ab]

An important consideration in all empirical research about buyouts is the availability of data. Data on almost all aspects of private equity is of far worse quality than

---

[aa]We thank Wayne Lim for providing this Table. A more in-depth analysis of private equity fund economics can be found in Lim et al. (2021).
[ab]An earlier survey that discusses a number of studies we are not able to cover here is Eckbo and Thorburn (2013).

Table 5 Fund fee structure

Vintage	Fund Size ($M)				Management Fee (%)					Carry (%)					GP Share of Fund (%)			
	N	Mean	Median	SD	N	Mean	Median	SD	Fraction =2%	N	Mean	Median	SD	Fraction =20%	N	Mean	Median	SD
Panel A: North America																		
1970–2000	906	307	150	528	112	1.9	2	0.4	75.00%	109	20.1	20	1.6	95.40%	107	4.5	3	5.25
2001–2005	609	472	252	685	119	2	2	0.2	85.70%	122	20.1	20	0.9	96.70%	121	4.6	2.7	4.54
2006–2010	411	753	364	1307	119	2	2	0.2	75.60%	118	20	20	0.8	96.60%	116	4.2	3	3.51
2011–2015	266	1048	550	1409	102	2	2	0.2	78.40%	102	20	20	1.2	97.10%	100	4.6	2.7	4.94
2016–2020	173	1643	750	2832	63	2	2	0.2	74.60%	64	19.9	20	0.6	98.40%	63	4.3	2.5	6.62
Panel B: Europe																		
1970–2000	478	290	150	490	18	1.9	2	0.3	72.20%	19	19.4	20	2	89.50%	16	3.9	2.5	4.66
2001–2005	351	433	223	664	30	1.9	2	0.3	63.30%	31	20.1	20	1	90.30%	30	3.8	2	4.32
2006–2010	229	683	314	1080	33	2	2	0.2	66.70%	35	20.1	20	0.9	97.10%	30	3.3	2	3.12
2011–2015	137	973	380	1602	30	1.9	2	0.2	63.30%	31	19.8	20	1.4	96.80%	30	2.8	2	2.32
2016–2020	86	1483	515	1957	25	1.8	1.8	0.2	40.00%	25	20.2	20	1	96.00%	23	5	3	8.12
Panel C: Asia																		
1970–2000	178	342	126	603	13	2	2	0.3	69.20%	12	20.8	20	2.9	91.70%	11	4.9	2	5.78
2001–2005	115	407	200	736	14	2	2	0.4	64.30%	13	20.8	20	2.8	92.30%	10	3	2	2.84
2006–2010	77	692	332	1102	20	1.9	2	0.1	75.00%	20	20	20	–	100.00%	18	5	2.3	6.41
2011–2015	51	1114	500	1600	21	1.9	2	0.2	76.20%	21	20	20	–	100.00%	21	2.8	2	2.61
2016–2020	20	1845	920	1937	13	1.9	2	0.2	76.90%	13	20	20	–	100.00%	13	2	2	0.74

This table presents statistics of the fee contract between GPs and LPs in buyout funds. The buyout fund sample includes vintage years from 1970 to 2020 in North America, Europe, and Asia. Panels A, B, and C presents buyout fund fee contracts in North America, Europe, and Asia, respectively. The sample includes only GP's main buyout funds (side vehicles, non-main strategies, etc. excluded) that are bigger than 5m in 1990 dollar terms. The 4 columns after vintage represent the number of funds, mean, median, and standard deviation of fund size (in $ million), columns 6–10 present the number of funds with management fee data available, mean, median, standard deviation of management fee, and the fraction of funds with 2% management fee, columns 11–15 present the number of funds with carried interest data available, mean, median, standard deviation of carry, and the fraction of funds with 20% of carry, and columns 16–19 present the number of funds that disclose GP's share of fund, mean median, and standard deviation of GP's share of fund.

comparable data on public firms. Since buyout funds and their portfolio firms are private, there does not exist price data from trades at regular frequencies for either funds or their portfolio companies. In addition, much of whatever data that does exist is usually private and not accessible to researchers. Finally, the data that is available publicly, especially relating to performance, can be selectively revealed, which can give scholars a misleading picture of the private equity industry. Addressing these issues is a major consideration in many of the papers discussed below.

5.1 Fund performance

Much research about private equity funds, and buyout funds in particular, concerns their performance. Measuring funds' risk and return, and the extent to which it is "abnormal," is much more challenging than for other types of securities. To understand why, recall that any fund makes a relatively small number of investments (averaging around 10 per fund). If a fund makes 10 investments, then the fund's cash flows for its entire existence, usually lasting between 12 and 15 years, will consist of only 10 draw-downs from the LPs (as well as regular demands for management fees) and various distributions of cash flows back to the LPs when the portfolio firms are exited (depending on whether the exit is via a sale to another purchaser, or via a series of share sales following an IPO). In addition, there will sometimes be intermediate cash flows if portfolio firms pay dividends, which could be substantial if the portfolio firm is recapitalized. The key point, however, is that a private equity fund has a relatively small number of cash flows, which are spread over a long period of time. These cash flows tend to be skewed, with some deals losing capital but others being "home runs" and returning high multiples of invested capital.

These infrequent cash flows make an understanding of buyout fund returns much more difficult than the returns of more frequently traded assets. Several research questions follow from this issue. How does one assess whether the return of one fund, which consists of a small number of cash flows over a long time period, is sufficiently high to justify its risk? Moreover, can we tell whether the performance of the industry as a whole has been high enough to justify the enormous amount of capital that it has been committed to it? Finally, to what extent is past performance, either at the level of the GP or across GPs, relevant for predicting future performance, given that the environment is very different today than it has been historically, with many of the obvious buyout targets no longer available?

5.1.1 Measuring fund performance

Despite the drawbacks that are emphasized in introductory finance classes, the two most common measures of private equity performance are the internal rate of return (IRR), and the cash multiple of invested capital (multiple). Gompers et al. (2016) survey general partners, and find that over 90% rely primarily on these two measures. In addition, this survey suggests that GPs focus on absolute performance rather than risk-adjusted performance measures.

Although these measures are what practitioners most frequently use, they have several weaknesses. The multiples approach ignores many factors that investors should care about, such as the time an asset is held, interest rates, and the opportunity cost during the holding period—for instance reflected in the returns earned in public markets. IRR is a noisy measure of performance and its use can lead GPs to act against the best interest of their LPs. The IRR measure is usually distorted in a way where high IRRs are usually higher than the effective rate of returns and low IRRs are usually lower than the effective rate of returns (Phalippou, 2008). Focusing on IRR can lead to an exaggeration in measured performance and volatility, which could lead the managers to act in a way that conflicts with the LPs. Specifically, to boost the IRR, managers may terminate good investments too early when it is more favorable for the LPs to hold the investment longer at a lower rate. Or managers may engage in regular dividend recapitalizations, which result in short-term cash flows to investors—thereby boosting IRRs—but which have little impact on investment multiples (since debt is simply substituted for equity, leaving enterprise values unchanged).

A natural way to improve over IRR would be to adjust for market-wide movements and measure abnormal performance relative to a benchmark. Recently, the Direct Alpha approach developed by Gredil et al. (2014), which produces an annualized excess return, has gradually been adopted by some GPs and LPs, although conventions change very slowly in private equity. While IRR data is publicly available for most (but not all) funds, data on the magnitude and timing of cash flow distributions have historically been only available to the fund's investors. In recent years, however, cash flow data has become available through some data sources, in particular Burgiss (who also provide Direct Alpha measures of performance).

Using early cash flow data from Thomson VentureXpert (TVE), Kaplan and Schoar (2005) argued that investors should rely on a performance measure that values a fund's cash flow distributions relative to the returns on the public equity market (called the "Public Market Equivalent" or PME).[ac] A fund's PME is calculated as the discounted sum of cash flow distributions, where the discount factor is the return that an investor would have received over the same period in the public market, most commonly measured by the return on the S&P 500 over the same period. A PME equal to 1 represents the breakeven point where the fund's performance is equivalent to the performance of the public market, and PME higher or lower than 1 indicates the fund's outperformance or underperformance relative to the public equity market. This calculation implicitly assumes that the funds have betas equal to 1, which, as we discuss below, is probably lower than the funds' true betas.

Relying on this PME measure, studies have shown that there is a variation in performance of PE across different times and data sources. Kaplan and Schoar (2005) themselves, using TVE fund cash flow data from 1980 to 2001, found that

---

[ac]This measure was originally developed by Long and Nickels (1996).

the average PME for buyout is 0.97, which suggests a slight underperformance of PE relative to the public equity market. Using the same TVE data but a different approach to dealing with valuations of funds that had not been updated for several quarters, Phalippou and Gottschalg (2009) concluded that the performance of buyout funds was, net of estimated costs, around 3% lower than that of public markets. However, it was subsequently found by Stucke (2011) that the TVE data was biased downwards. The lack of updating of fund valuations in that dataset reflected the fact that the LPs and GPs had stopped responding to requests for data, rather than (as assumed by Phalippou and Gottschalg) that the valuations of the remaining companies were zero if they had not been updated for some while. As time went on, the IRRs on this stale data went down whereas on average the valuations employed by buyout funds of their remaining portfolio companies are, on average, conservative. Therefore, in reality, valuations tend to rise over the later years of a fund.

Academic research on private equity returns took a significant step forward with the formation of the Private Equity Research Consortium, which reached an agreement with Burgiss, a private markets data analytics firm, to make their data available, free of charge, to academics. The first authors to take advantage of this data are Harris et al. (2014) who analyzed the merits of the Burgiss data, which is derived entirely from LPs, relative to the other main data sources. Consistent with the finding of Stucke (2011), Harris et al. found the TVE data to be an outlier compared with the other data sources, and to be downward biased. Using the high-quality cash flow data from Burgiss et al. found that U.S. buyout funds had actually consistently outperformed public markets. The average PME of 1.22 implied that U.S. buyouts significantly outperformed the S&P500 over their sample period.

A number of other studies, using different samples, have come to similar conclusions. Higson and Stucke (2012) use a sample of 1169 buyout funds from Cambridge Associates between 1980 and 2008 and find that the median PME for these funds is 1.13. Axelson et al. (2013) estimate PME from publicly available databases and find a relatively high estimate (1.36). With a proprietary database from a single large LP for buyouts from 1984 to 2010, Robinson and Sensoy (2016) find a PME of 1.18. More recently, Harris et al. (2018) using the Burgiss fund-of-funds database from 1987 to 2007 report a PME of 1.14, reflecting the additional layer of fees associated with fund-of-funds. Although there are some variations in estimates, the above mentioned papers all conclude that the buyout funds outperform the public market during the 1990s and early 2000s. One exception is Phalippou (2014) who finds contrary evidence using small-cap indices as a public market benchmark, arguing that this benchmark is the appropriate one to use since the average buyout fund mainly invests in small and value companies. However, in recent years, small cap indices have significantly underperformed large cap ones, suggesting that this finding would no longer hold.

5.1.2 Adjusting for risk

While most studies found a PME for buyout funds >1, it is nonetheless unclear whether their returns can be considered abnormally high. Investing in a buyout fund involves taking on the additional risk coming from the high leverage that general partners use to finance purchases of the portfolio companies, as well as the illiquidity associated with a long-term commitment of capital. It is difficult to know how much this risk and illiquidity should add to the required cost of capital. The methods for measuring risk commonly used for securities that trade continuously are not usable for private equity funds that have such few cash flow realizations, and which trade themselves infrequently—if at all—on the secondary market.

How does one adjust buyout returns for risk? How valid is the implicit assumption underlying the PME analysis that the buyout funds' betas equal 1? What about liquidity—do investors demand an illiquidity premium? How should one even think of estimating the risk of a fund for which the only data are the prices at which it buys and sells 10 companies over a 12- to 15-year period?

One possibility is to start with the notion, emphasized by Axelson et al. (2014), that the return on a buyout fund is simply the return on the portfolio firms, adjusted for the change in leverage brought on by the LBO. To use this approach to estimate a fund's risk, one would start with an estimate of the beta of the portfolio firm before it is acquired and apply the standard formula from Modigliani-Miller Proposition 2 to adjust for leverage.[ad]

Unfortunately, this calculation ignores several important considerations. First, the firms that tend to be targeted by buyout firms tend to be less risky than average, so their pre-buyout equity betas are probably lower than 1. Second, while 50% is lower than the typical buyout leverage ratio at the time of the deal, portfolio firms usually pay down some of their debt and increase their value while owned by the buyout funds. Therefore, the average leverage ratio over the entire period the portfolio firm is owned by the fund can be substantially less than the leverage at the time of purchase. Finally, the standard MM calculation assumes that the beta of the firm's debt equals zero. However, buyout debt is sufficiently risky that the beta of buyout debt is likely to be positive (see Kaplan and Stein (1990)). All of these factors will lead buyout betas to be less than the MM calculation would suggest.

There have been a number of studies that have used a variety of methods to estimate fund betas, as well as the alphas that are implied from these betas and the fund returns. Driessen et al. (2012) use the generalized method of moments to measure the alphas and betas by allowing dynamic discount rates. They find that buyout funds have betas of about 1.3 but no evidence of outperformance. In contrast, Ewens et al. (2013) use fund cash flow and NAV data from *Venture Expert* (VE), LP sources, and *Preqin* covering years from 1980 to 2007, and report the beta loadings to be 0.7 with a positive alpha of 1.2%. Using the three factor model, they report the alpha to be 0.9% which is still positive. Ang et al. (2018) construct a quarterly time series return indices using fund-level cash flow data from 1996 to 2015 and find that the market beta of buyouts is around 1.2 and the alpha is 4%. However, they report

---

[ad]According to the standard formula from Modigliani-Miller Proposition 2, beta of a levered firm is the weighted average of security betas (i.e., $\beta_L = \beta_E \frac{E}{E+D} + \beta_D \frac{D}{E+D}$). If the firm has a beta of 1 (as is definitionally true for an average firm) and one applies a 50% leverage ratio, then the implied beta should be about 2 under the assumption that the debt beta is 0.

that the alpha drops to 1% when they control for the Fama and French 3 factor model and -3% when they control for the Pástor and Stambaugh four factor model.

These studies estimate betas and alphas for the net of fee fund-level returns, which is what is relevant for LPs who invest in buyout funds. An alternative approach is to use deal level information to estimate the betas of each portfolio firm. Using the deal-level, gross-of-fee cash flow information for 2075 buyout deals that are managed by 250 funds from 1994 to 2007, Axelson et al. (2014) report a market beta of 2.4 and an alpha of 8.6%. The authors argue that using deal level rather than fund level data is a superior way to estimate funds' risk. They provide a simulation suggesting the source of discrepancy in beta loadings between previous studies and their study comes from the types of data being used. Moreover, Axelson et al. argue that using fund-level IRRs brings downward bias in beta estimation, whereas estimates using deal-level data are unbiased. Buchner and Stucke (2014) also report buyout performance gross of fees and show that the beta lies between 2.7 and 3.15 and alphas are around 5%. Similarly, Franzoni et al. (2012) use deal-level monthly cash flow data provided by the Center for Private Equity Research (CEPRES) and report positive alphas gross of fees after only controlling for the market risk.

Theoretically, gross of fee estimates of beta should be higher than net of fee estimates. Since carried interest tends to be higher when times are good, the fees themselves will have positive betas. Therefore, netting the fees from a fund's return will lower its beta. Axelson et al. (2014) argue that the difference between gross of fee betas and net of fee ones could be as high as 0.5, which could explain some of the difference between studies.

There have been other approaches to estimate alphas and betas for buyout funds. Jegadeesh et al. (2015) gather a sample of publicly traded private equity funds and estimate alphas and betas for these funds using methods that have become standard for the estimation of risk and return of public securities. These authors report betas of 0.7 and alphas close to zero. Boyer et al. (2021) use data on private equity secondary market transactions, and estimate alpha and beta based on this index. They find that the widely used NAV-based indices tend to significantly understate the volatility of PE and show that the transaction-based buyout index has a beta of around 1.75. Moreover, the transaction based hedonic indices show that buyouts do not outperform the public equity market on a risk-adjusted basis.

Another approach to evaluating risk in private equity funds has been proposed by Korteweg and Nagel (2016), who propose a generalized PME (GPME) that adjusts for firm risk. This approach is promising as it has the advantages of the PME approach while accounting for firm-level risk at the same time. Boyer et al. (2021) extend the Korteweg and Nagel method and show that, in the context of their index, it can be used to estimate time-varying risk-premia as well.

Overall, there is no consensus on the risk of private equity investments, and the extent to which they earn an excess return after adjusting for risk. As Axelson et al. (2014) point out, the disparity in the magnitude of beta and alpha across the literature can be affected by the types of data used in the analysis. For example, studies that use

NAV-based fund-level returns tend to report betas that are closer to the market and studies that use transaction-based or a deal-level cash flow data tend to report relatively high betas.

If transaction-based or deal-level data is more reflective of market values than NAV-based data and the PE performance does not outperform the public equity market when adjusting their risk, an interesting question concerns why PE investment is so popular even though their performance has not been great. Investors certainly need to consider the illiquid nature of the asset class, which even amplifies the question of why PE is becoming so popular. One of the possible explanations could be that leverage in buyouts is not as risky as in public firms so that the Modigliani and Miller calculation when estimating beta may not apply to buyouts. Moskowitz and Vissing-Jørgensen (2002) briefly discuss possible reasons why investors would invest in private equity despite high risk and low return characteristics. They argue that there could potentially be more tolerance in entrepreneurial risk, large non-pecuniary benefits, skewed preferences, and misperceptions of risk. It seems clear that more research needs to be done to resolve this puzzle.

5.1.3 Performance persistence

A fundamental issue in our understanding of delegated portfolio management is the extent to which good performance comes from luck, or if the managers of the portfolios have skill that enables them to perform persistently well. Investors' views about this issue guide their portfolio decisions, since it does not make sense to spend effort finding the best managers if fund performance does not vary with managers' abilities.

One way to address this issue is to measure the extent to which any measured performance persists over time. For mutual funds, the approach dates back to classic work by Jensen (1968), and after many papers, the answer is still somewhat inconclusive. Since there is no strong evidence that selecting mutual funds based on the perceived skill of fund managers leads to abnormal returns, many finance professionals advise their clients to invest in index funds and avoid trying to pay to select the best managers. However, the answer is much different for buyout funds—there does appear to be some evidence of performance persistence in private equity funds. The evidence suggests that GPs' skill varies, and consequently LPs are correct to spend effort selecting those they believe to be the best.

The first study to measure performance persistence in private equity is Kaplan and Schoar (2005), who find that high (and low) returns tend to persist over the subsequent funds raised by a particular PE family. Robinson and Sensoy (2016) confirm the Kaplan and Schoar (2005) finding, providing evidence for performance persistence using a larger sample of buyout funds. These papers suggest that GPs' skills do differ, so choosing GPs based on their past track record is likely to increase an LP's performance.

Recently, there have been several papers revisiting the issue of performance persistence in more detail using better data. These papers have been able to replicate the earlier findings; however, they find that the evidence became weaker after 2000.

Braun et al. (2017) employ deal-level cash flow data and find that although persistence still exists, it has become substantially weaker in recent years (2001–2012). The interesting innovation in this paper is the use of deal-level data. Clearly, as we have discussed, the performance of buyout funds takes a long time to realize, and so comparing the performance of two funds can span a period of two decades or more. Braun, Jenkinson and Stoff strip off the fund wrapper and look at persistence at the GP level across deals.

More recently, Harris et al. (2020) use cash flow data from Burgiss and look at fund-level persistence using traditional performance metrics and also the performance at the time that GPs were raising their next fund. This is an interesting lens through which to analyze persistence, as it represents the information that is available to LPs at the time at which they have to make commitments to future funds. While they find some persistence in buyout performance—when measured by the final, or most recent, fund valuations—the paper finds little evidence of investable persistence in buyouts. The relationship between the return at the time of fundraising, which is what investors observe, and the final performance of the next fund, is essentially random. Therefore, using this more accurate representation of the information available to investors, these authors find little evidence of return persistence for buyouts. They do find, however, much stronger evidence of persistence for VC funds, across all measures and time periods.

Particularly, when measuring performance persistence, separating skill from luck is a fundamental issue. For example, even though estimates from regressions tell us that top quartile funds tend to perform well in the next fund on average, this does not necessarily mean that an investor can choose any fund in the top quartile and can earn high returns. Past performance can be a noisy measure as it contains the luck element. Such noisy measures have less investable persistence as it is hard for LPs to identify whose past performance is due to luck or skill.

Several papers have examined performance persistence by focusing on the source of its variance. Using a variance decomposition model, Korteweg and Sorensen (2017) isolate fund variance into three components: long-term persistence, overlapping economic conditions, and idiosyncratic variance (i.e., luck). They find that luck explains a lower portion of buyout fund returns than venture capital returns, and that buyouts have higher long-term persistence. Rossi (2019) confirms the results of Korteweg and Sorensen (2017) and finds that persistence explains 5–15% of the performance variation. However, Rossi also finds evidence that PE fund returns are expected to mean revert in the future and that high-growth PE firms were on average lucky in the past. By this logic, high-growth follow-on funds should underperform their preceding funds even absent decreasing returns to scale.

Overall, the academic evidence suggests that the extent to which buyout funds have a persistent component in their performance is rather limited. Therefore, it is likely to be difficult for investors to identify the best funds using just statistical measures of performance. An LP's skill in determining the quality of GPs using other sources of information than just prior performance is a potentially important factor affecting the returns they achieve from their portfolio.

5.2 **Limited partners**

Investors in private equity funds (i.e., LPs) are usually institutional investors such as public or corporate pension funds, endowments, advisors (including fund-of-funds), insurance companies, banks, and finance companies. Consequently, LPs are also delegated managers for their own investors. In addition, LPs sometimes play a significant role in PE investments when they participate in co-investments or make direct investments themselves. There have been several recent papers that have studied the role of LPs, which we discuss in this section.

5.2.1 *LP performance*

LPs vary in terms of their organizational structure, investment objectives, and sophistication. Practitioners claim that there is substantial heterogeneity in LPs. Much of this heterogeneity occurs across different types of LPs, but there are also substantial differences in the resources and experience within LPs serving similar constituencies. For example, Swensen (2009) argues that endowments' higher flexibility enabled them to invest heavily into alternative assets like private equity well before most institutional investors. And within a class of investors such as endowments, the largest and most active investors tend to have the most resources available to identify and evaluate alternative funds.

One of the first papers that studied heterogeneity in performance across different types of LPs is Lerner et al. (2007). This paper examines 838 funds with vintage years between 1991 and 1998, in which 352 LPs invested. It finds that endowments earn an annual return of 21%, which is substantially larger than the returns earned by all other types of LPs. Sensoy et al. (2014) reexamine this idea using a larger sample covering more funds over a longer time period, with 14,830 investments by 1852 LPs during 1991–2006. They replicate Lerner et al. (2007)'s finding that for funds raised between 1991and 1998 endowments did indeed outperform other investors. However, as the industry matured and became more well understood and "commoditized," the difference across classes of LPs went away. In the early years of the industry, knowledge of how it worked was valuable and led to higher returns, but over time as this knowledge became common to all investors, these differences disappeared.

Cavagnaro et al. (2019) extend the analysis from classes of LPs to individual LPs and evaluate the extent to which individual LPs have skill in making investment decisions. These authors use data covering 30,915 investments made by 2314 LPs into private equity funds between 1991 and 2011. They use a bootstrap approach that simulates LPs' return distribution under the assumption that they are identically skilled and compare with the actual LP return distribution. Cavagnaro et al. (2019) find that compared to the bootstrapped distribution, the return distribution shows consistency in LPs' performance. Further, they extend the Bayesian approach of Korteweg and Sorensen (2017) and find that a standard deviation increase in skill leads to 1–2% increase in annual returns. The implication of these results is that LPs' skill does appear to affect returns to a meaningful degree.

While previous papers find evidence that difference in LPs' skill affects performance, the nature of LPs' objectives can also have an effect on their returns. Hochberg and Rauh (2013) explore investment patterns and investment performance of LPs over the period 1980–2009 and find that public pension funds tend to overweight their investment in in-state firms compared to other LP classes. However, these in-state investments earn lower returns than similar out-of-state investments. The paper further relates the overweight in in-state investments to political pressures facing public pension funds. Overall, their evidence suggests that political pressure can be costly, as it leads state pension funds to invest in local funds that earn lower returns than they could achieve absent political pressure.

Barber et al. (2021) find evidence that some investors do care about the nonfinancial role of private equity funds. The paper examines whether some investors are willing to accept lower returns for nonpecuniary benefits by investing in "impact funds," that supposedly invest in socially desirable companies. It considers a sample of 4659 funds, including 159 impact funds with vintage years from 1995 to 2014 and estimates the willingness to pay for impact across LP types. The paper finds that the IRR of impact funds is 4.7% lower than traditional funds. Using a hedonic pricing framework, the authors estimate that investors are willing to give away 2.5–3.7% of expected excess IRR for nonpecuniary objectives. In terms of heterogeneity of willingness to pay across LPs, they find that development organizations, financial institutions, and public pensions exhibit a positive willingness to pay.

One of the important aspects of LPs that could affect their performance, but has been underexplored in the literature, is their demand for liquidity. LPs' liquidity demand could affect the weight they place on liquidity, which could affect the LPs' returns (see Lerner and Schoar (2004)). We do not know much about the way in which LPs' preferences regarding liquidity affect their investments, especially the amount of capital they commit to private equity and their choices of funds.

Overall, the evidence suggests that some LPs consistently outperform others and that their skill accounts for a significant portion of their performance. Likely reasons for this disparity in performance are differences in skill, as well as political pressures to invest locally and in impact funds.

5.2.2 Direct investments and co-investments

Recently, there has been an increase in direct investments by institutional investors. These direct investments are sometimes initiated by the LPs themselves and sometimes take the form of co-investments in which the institution invests alongside a GP. Direct investing potentially allows institutions access to the private equity market without having to pay the substantial fees associated with investing through a fund. However, it is not obvious that the returns earned by direct investing are larger than the net of fee returns they would receive by investing through a fund. GPs have skills in negotiating investments and adding value to portfolio companies that are likely to be better than the abilities of most institutional investors. And co-investment opportunities potentially suffer from adverse selection in which GPs do not offer such opportunities on their best deals, only their more marginal ones. Evaluating the extent to which these and related issues are empirically relevant has been the subject of some recent research.

Fang et al. (2015) consider these issues using proprietary data from seven large LPs involving 390 direct private equity investments made between 1991 and 2011. They find that most of the direct investments outperform the public market but that the outperformance is concentrated in buyouts rather than venture capital. However, compared to the corresponding funds with which they invest, buyout co-investments underperform while solo direct investments do well. The paper attributes the underperformance of co-investments to adverse selection of investments in which GPs only invite LPs to their more marginal deals.

Using a larger sample of 1016 co-investments made by 458 LPs between 1981 and 2010, Braun et al. (2020), in contrast to Fang et al. (2015), find no evidence of adverse selection in LP co-investments. They find that gross PMEs for co-investments are similar to the returns on deals from the corresponding fund that are intermediated by GPs. Moreover, they observe no differences in co-investment performance across LP classes and document that, because of lower fees and carried interest payments to GPs, co-investments outperform the corresponding fund, net of fees. As institutions' direct investing and co-investing increases in the future, this area is likely to see much more useful research.

5.3 Sources of returns

While the existence of return persistence and other tests suggest that GPs who are successful on average are more skillful than other GPs, the nature of these skills is not obvious. How exactly do GPs increase the value of their investments? There are many potential sources discussed above in detail in Section 3. Understanding the extent to which each potential source of value is empirically important has become an important area of research.

Jensen (1986, 1989) argues that a major source of the value created by buyouts is the substantial pecuniary incentives that GPs and top management teams have following buyouts. In addition, he argues that the high leverage of portfolio firms leads these firms not to waste the free cash flows that are generated by their operations. Jensen is an early proponent of the view that buyouts create their returns by increasing firms' efficiency. The alternative viewpoint, originally espoused by Shleifer and Summers (1988), is that much of the return buyouts generate occurs not from efficiency increases but from transfers from other stakeholders. This view argues that many of the gains from buyouts (and other takeovers) come from wealth transfers from workers, bondholders, and the government. Such two contrasting, but not necessarily mutually exclusive, views have led to much research about whether private equity funds do increase the values of portfolio companies. And if they do in fact increase value, how do they do it?

5.3.1 Value creation to portfolio companies

The earliest papers on buyouts focus on their value creation and find support for the view that the early buyouts in their sample do increase the value of the portfolio firms. Kaplan (1989a) documents that there are substantial increases in portfolio companies' cash flow. These increases appear to come from improved incentives and not from reductions in employment. Smith (1990) finds positive operational returns that are not a result of a reduction in advertisement, R&D or increased layoffs. Lichtenberg and Siegel (1990) examine a large sample of manufacturing establishments of management buyouts in United States and conclude that there tends to be an increase in total factor productivity. Baker and Wruck (1989) conduct a case study of the O.M. Scott & Sons Company and show that the company's operational improvement was not due to a reduction in costs. They find an increase in R&D and Marketing & Advertisement investments after the acquisition.

These early studies have used samples that are relatively small, as they mostly focused on U.S. public-to-private deals. Subsequent research has extended the analysis to larger samples that exploit plant-level data or patent data to effectively capture the productivity or innovation of target firms. Davis et al. (2014) utilizes the Longitudinal Business Database that covers a large sample of buyout firm establishments. Their findings suggest that buyouts bring an increase in total factor productivity through efficiency improvements. GPs accelerate exits in less productive establishments and increase entries in more productive ones. Lerner et al. (2011) explore US patent data and find that patents are more likely to be cited post-buyout. Their result implies that there is no evidence of myopic management in buyouts. Using US deal-level proprietary data, Acharya et al. (2013) show that high abnormal returns of buyouts are attributed to improvement in sales and operating margins while target firms are private.

Outside the United States, Harris et al. (2005) find similar patterns using a manufacturing establishment database from the United Kingdom. Boucly et al. (2011) employ over 800 French LBO deals and show that target firms become more profitable relative to a control group. They find that buyouts help relax credit constraints and allow to take growth opportunities. Firms that are in industries that rely more on external financing experience larger growth.

Bernstein and Sheen (2016) focus on restaurant buyouts and identify the particular operational changes brought on by the buyouts. They find that restaurants become cleaner, safer, and better maintained after the buyout. The paper exploits the franchise structure of the restaurants as a clever way to identify the causality between PE buyout and improved maintenance. The authors compare the chain-owned restaurants to the franchisee-owned ones, where the groups of restaurants are similar to one another except for their ownership structure.

Several papers examine the way in which portfolio companies bought by buyouts perform during bad times. Johnston-Ross et al. (2021) examine the role of private equity during the 2008 Financial Crisis. They compare banks that were acquired by private equity and banks that were acquired by banks to measure the effect of PE intervention on these banks during the Crisis. Johnston-Ross et al. find that PE backed banks are less likely to go bankrupt and perform better during the Crisis period. The relatively good performance of these firms leads to faster recovery of the local economies in which they operate. Similar to Johnston-Ross et al. (2021), Bernstein et al. (2019) find that PE backed companies decreased investments less than their peers and had increased financings, higher asset growth, and increased market share during the 2008 Crisis. These papers all provide evidence suggesting that private equity plays a positive role in helping firms survive economy-wide crises.

5.3.2 Wealth transfers

Critics of private equity often argue that rather than adding positive value to portfolio companies, GPs earn their returns by transferring wealth from stakeholders. There are a number of studies that suggest that such transfers are responsible for some of the returns earned by private equity funds. Guo et al. (2011) studies a sample of 192 buyouts completed between 1990 and 2006. The paper first shows that the risk adjusted returns to pre- (post-) buyouts are substantially high. They further explore the relative contributions to these returns. In contrast to the findings using 1980s samples, the median operating performance of buyouts is comparable to the performance of benchmark firms. Since operational improvements appear to be minimal, the inference from Guo et al. (2011) is that GPs earn returns by taking advantage of mispricing in the market, the tax advantages of debt, and by transferring wealth from employees.

Since many of the ways in which private equity funds can transfer wealth vary across industries, a number of studies have focused on samples of buyouts in individual industries. Gupta et al. (2021) examine the effects of PE ownership on patient welfare at nursing homes using administrative patient-level data. They find that a nursing home that is purchased by a private equity fund has an increase in the probability of death by 10%, and a decline in nursing availability and overall staffing. Furthermore, they find evidence of a systematic shift in operating costs away from patient care to non-patient care items like monitoring fees, lease payments, and interest payments. In contrast, Gandhi et al. (2020) evaluate the performance of private equity backed nursing homes during the COVID-19 pandemic and find that private equity ownership was associated with a decrease in the probability of confirmed cases and a lower probability of personal protective equipment shortages.

Eaton et al. (2020) studies the effect of PE ownership on for-profit higher education, using 88 private equity deals involving 994 schools. Similar to the findings of Gupta et al. (2021), this paper finds that the new ownership transfers wealth from students by increasing tuition but not the quality of education. After buyouts there are lower graduation rates, as well as lower loan repayment rates and earnings for the students who do graduate.

Overall, the literature has found evidence of both wealth creation and wealth transfers from buyouts. Buyouts appear to create substantial efficiencies on average. However, there is also evidence that some of these gains come at the expense of other stakeholders, in several different ways. The combination of the two effects is what generates the returns that limited partners receive from their investments in buyout funds.

5.4 Agency problems between GPs and LPs

There are two main governance relationships in private equity. First, funds invest in portfolio companies and must govern those companies. Second, the funds themselves are managed by general partners, who govern the fund on behalf of the limited partners and have a fiduciary duty to make decisions in their interests.

An important issue in delegated portfolio management literature is whether the contracts between managers and investors are optimally set so to align the interests of both parties. Since private equity investments require LPs' capital to be tied up for more than 10 years without any discretion on investment decisions, it is especially important that the contract is well designed to protect LPs' interests. Several studies have examined the nature of agency problems between GPs and LPs.

5.4.1 Agency conflicts from contracts

Axelson et al. (2009) provide a theoretical explanation of the PE fund structure, which they argue arises because of agency problems between GPs and LPs. In this model, the most efficient way to finance buyouts is through a structure that pools deals within funds and also requires funds to raise additional capital for each deal. Such a structure, together with strong incentives for managers, leads to a structure similar to what is observed in practice. It is second-best efficient, meaning that it is the best that can be achieved but still contains some inefficiencies. In certain circumstances, it will lead to value-increasing investments to be ignored while in others, value-decreasing investments will be undertaken.

Robinson and Sensoy (2013), Degeorge et al. (2016), Arcot et al. (2015), and Kim (2021) report findings consistent with the notion that contracts between GPs and LPs are designed to minimize agency costs. However, these contracts do not induce the first-best outcome. Robinson and Sensoy (2013) find that GPs distort the timing of distributions around the waterfall date so that they can receive carry and avoid the risk of investment declining in value. They also show that to earn management fees, GPs delay the liquidation of poorly performing deals. Similarly, Arcot et al. (2015) and Degeorge et al. (2016) find that funds that are under pressure to invest prior to the end of the investment period tend to engage more in secondary buyouts that end up underperforming. Kim (2021) studies how the 2 and 20 fee structure that has been widely adopted by buyout funds can in fact lead GPs to make investments that appear to be negative NPV and against the interest of LPs, presumably to maximize their GPs' fees. The pattern is more prominent among more experienced GPs who do not need to establish a reputation and funds that have earned high returns earlier that are likely to have already met LPs' return expectations.

5.4.2 Return manipulation

Another agency-related issue concerns the manipulation of valuations during fundraising. Since a fund's fees are a function of its size, GPs have incentives to increase the funds' size. Given that prior returns strongly affect LPs' commitments (see Chung et al. (2012)), increasing NAV prior to fund-raising could potentially increase reported performance and hence lead to larger capital commitments. The extent to which this practice occurs has been the topic of some interesting research.

Jenkinson et al. (2013) analyze 761 funds in which *Calpers* invested to evaluate whether funds tend to be aggressive or conservative in valuation and change their reporting behavior around the time of fund-raising. In addition, they measure the extent to which investors could rely on interim returns to predict final fund returns. Jenkinson et al. (2013) find that overall fund valuations are conservative and are likely to be smoothed, except when GPs are raising their next fund. During the fundraising period there is an inflation in fund valuation and reported returns. Moreover, they show that interim returns are a poor predictor of funds' final performance.

Barber and Yasuda (2017) look at fund-level cash flows and quarterly NAV data for more than 800 US-focused funds raised between 1993 and 2009 to study whether PE firms tend to time their fundraising during valuation peaks of their current funds. They find that GPs do time the market and fundraise during the valuation peaks. While peaks during the fundraising period are clearer for funds that have high realizations, they also find evidence of peaks due to upward NAV reporting among low reputation GPs with few realizations. Moreover, markdowns of reported NAV are observed after fundraising among GPs with a low reputation. Brown et al. (2019) revisit the issue using a much larger and granular sample from *Burgiss* that includes daily cash flows and quarterly NAV reports of 2071 funds. These authors find that underperforming managers tend to inflate the reported returns, while outperforming one's report returns in a more conservative manner. However, they also find that those underperforming managers that inflate returns are less likely to raise a subsequent fund.

Several papers have documented the existence of agency conflict between GPs and LPs in buyouts. Given the long-term nature of the commitment and the number of decisions that are delegated to the GPs, some agency problems are inevitable. Contracts between GPs and LPs align their interests well as possible, but some residual conflict remains.

5.4.3 Emerging conflicts

The buyout model has evolved considerably over the years, and some issues we have identified are sufficiently new that they have yet to attract academic interest, or at least publications. One area that we highlight in this section on agency conflicts is the increasing prevalence of continuation vehicles, which we briefly discussed in Section 2.

To some extent, the emergence of continuation funds can be traced back to the limited life structure of buyout funds. Some assets may offer the prospect of generating attractive returns for many years under the private equity governance model, and yet GPs are expected to liquidate their funds after 10 years or so. Until recently, such companies often ended up being traded in a secondary transaction, in which the original fund sells the firm to a second fund. These transactions sometimes created issues for those LPs who were in funds run by both the selling and buying GPs: essentially, these LPs continued to hold the asset but had paid significant transactions fees and crystalized carried interest for the selling GP. However, the buyer and seller were distinct, so the negotiated price presumably was "fair."

However, conflicts of interest are much more likely in the case of continuation vehicles where the GP sells the company from the main fund into a continuation vehicle that it also manages, and in which not all of the original fund investors participate. Since being both a buyer and a seller on a transaction is a recipe for potential conflict (not to mention lawsuits) such transactions typically involve an outside investor—often a secondary fund, or new investors who are not in the original fund—which helps to establish the price for the asset.

While the incentives to participate in a continuation vehicle, rather than exit and take the proceeds of the intermediate sale at that point, are often finely balanced, the incentives for the GP are much clearer. First, they will crystalize carry on the sale from the fund. However, investors will typically expect GPs to reinvest a significant proportion of their gains into the continuation vehicle. Second, the basis for the management fee will change. Recall that management fees are often based on invested capital in the second half of a fund's life. If an asset has grown significantly in value, then the fee basis will be written up in the continuation vehicle. For this reason, even though the management fee rates negotiated on continuation vehicles are often lower—say 1% rather than 2%—the increase in the fee basis will often more than compensate for this. Third, as noted earlier, increasingly the panacea for buyout funds is to grow management fees by expanding assets under management. Continuation vehicles play into this strategy very effectively, as the exit from the original fund can help to facilitate the raising of the GPs next fund while they continue to manage some of the original assets for much longer via continuation vehicles. Therefore, the move away from selling well-performing assets to other GPs can be seen as a natural way to expand fee income, albeit one beset with potential conflicts. This development is very recent, but future research will undoubtedly evaluate these funds' performance, as well as the way in which the conflicts of interest are managed.

6 Conclusion

The 20th century witnessed the growth of public capital markets, which allowed investors to participate in the growth of companies and resulted in the separation of ownership from control. Arguably, one of the remarkable developments in finance in the 21st century has been the growth of private capital markets, and the re-emergence of a close link between ownership and control. The value of a strong relation between ownership and control is an important reason for the enormous growth of the buyout industry in recent years.

Private capital markets typically operate through funds, which raise capital commitments and invest this capital in companies. The growth in private funds has been fueled by the huge growth in the size of key institutional investors, in particular those associated with public pension schemes, sovereign wealth funds and, increasingly, rich individuals. In recent years, private funds have raised commitments of about $1 trillion annually from such institutional investors, and currently have more than $2 trillion in "dry powder" that could be invested at the discretion of the funds' General Partners. While these funds use the capital for different types of investments, the largest amount is raised for buyouts of existing companies, approximately $400 billion annually. This paper attempts to understand the buyout market and the reasons why it has grown to become such an important part of the economy.

Investors provide capital to buyout funds when their expectations are that the funds' returns will be sufficiently high to offset their risk, illiquidity and the significant fees and profit shares charged by the fund managers. To earn these returns, buyout funds acquire portfolio companies, manage them for a period of time, then exit their position and return investors' capital. Almost all deals involve substantial increases in leverage that sharpen incentives and amplify—in both directions—the returns to the funds' equity investments. The change in the value of the portfolio companies comes mostly from improvements in the performance of the portfolio firms that are acquired and then sold by the buyout funds. However, part of any value increase can come from transfers from others, in particular tax authorities who may receive lower corporate tax payments as a result of the increased use of interest tax shields on debt. The ability of buyout funds to improve the value of their portfolio firms is the primary factor affecting their returns, and consequently the flow of capital into the buyout sector.

Underlying buyout funds are a complex set of contracts that have evolved over time and have become fairly standardized across funds. The two most important of these are the contract between the investors and the funds and the contract between the funds and the portfolio companies. As the companies that manage private funds have grown and raised multiple funds that often spread into different geographies or asset classes, contracts linking these management companies and the individual funds they manage have been developed. These contracts are designed to ensure that all parties have strong pecuniary incentives to increase the value of the portfolio companies and consequently, the returns of the funds themselves. However, as funds become very large, the alignment of interest between investors and fund managers can weaken, as management fees—which have been surprisingly sticky as funds have increased in size—have become a significant source of profit for fund managers. Furthermore, as the sector has matured, the ultimate owners of the fund management company have sold off stakes to outside investors, and some private equity managers have even gone public. All these developments reduce the alignment of interests between fund managers and their investors. Section 2 describes these contracts and the institutional environment of buyout funds in detail.

There are many strategies that funds have developed for increasing the values of their portfolio companies. The iconic deals of the 1980s were predominately acquisitions of firms with cash-generating assets for which additional leverage would reduce wasteful spending of their free cash flows. Over time, however, several other approaches have become common. Expansions, industry consolidations, ownership transitions, privatizations of public enterprises, and acquisitions of distressed assets are among the growing number of strategies that have become popular with buyout funds.

Private equity funds have proved to be a remarkably efficient vehicle for enacting many types of changes in portfolio firms. Their general partners are highly motivated to think of new ways to increase firms' values and have been extremely creative in coming up with new ways to do so. As a result, there is no one magic formula that characterizes what buyout funds do to generate returns. There is every reason to suspect that funds will continue to develop new approaches to increasing the values of their portfolio companies, so that the list of strategies presented in Table 1 will look very incomplete in the future.

Academic research on buyouts has been active over recent years. Yet, there is much more research to be done. The study of buyouts is interdisciplinary, covering both of the main fields within financial economics (asset pricing and corporate finance), but also relating to labor economics, industrial organization, management, and accounting. The buyout sector has become an important asset class to institutional investors. However, it is not obvious what the appropriate weight buyouts should take in well-diversified portfolios, nor is it clear what are the risk, expected returns or liquidity premia associated with buyout funds. Understanding the source of these returns, and the way they are the consequence of changes in the corporate policies of the portfolio firms has been an important area of research.

Some of the important policy changes buyout funds enact in their portfolio firms relate to corporate financial decisions, choice of top management and their compensation, and corporate strategy, their competitive strategies, and their methods of production. An underlying issue in much of this research is whether the gains come from wealth creation or wealth transfers. The answer to this question will impact perceptions on the role of buyouts in the economy.

There has been much work devoted to understanding the financial structure of public corporations. Portfolio companies of buyout funds can be understood using many of the principles that have been developed for public corporations. However, the frictions that make public corporations and markets interesting to study—asymmetric information, agency problems, illiquidity, etc.—are all much more problematic in private markets than in public ones. Therefore, there is much to be learned about private firms and markets using tools that have been developed in the literature. Given the current size and growth rates of private capital markets, research along these lines is likely to be fruitful. Private capital markets have become at least as important, and far more interesting to study, than public capital markets.

Acknowledgments

We would like to thank Peter Cornelius, Harry DeAngelo, Rui Gong, Eduard Inozemtsev, Chris Kallos, Minsu Ko, Josh Lerner, Daisy Wang, Cynthia Yin, and Grace Zhang for valuable comments on earlier drafts.

References

Acharya, V., Kehoe, C., Reyner, M., 2008. The voice of experience: public versus private equity. McKinsey Q. 28, 1–7.

Acharya, V.V., Gottschalg, O.F., Hahn, M., Kehoe, C., 2013. Corporate governance and value creation: evidence from private equity. Rev. Financ. Stud. 26 (2), 368–402.

Albertus, J.F., Denes, M., 2020. Private equity fund debt: capital flows, performance, and agency costs. In: Performance, and Agency Costs (May 26, 2020).

Andonov, A., Kräussl, R., Rauh, J., 2021. Institutional investors and infrastructure investing. Rev. Financ. Stud. 34 (8), 3880–3934.

Ang, A., Chen, B., Goetzmann, W.N., Phalippou, L., 2018. Estimating private equity returns from limited partner cash flows. J. Financ. 73 (4), 1751–1783.

Arcot, S., Fluck, Z., Gaspar, J.M., Hege, U., 2015. Fund managers under pressure: rationale and determinants of secondary buyouts. J. Financ. Econ. 115 (1), 102–135.

Axelson, U., Strömberg, P., Weisbach, M.S., 2009. Why are buyouts levered? The financial structure of private equity funds. J. Financ. 64 (4), 1549–1582.

Axelson, U., Jenkinson, T., Strömberg, P., Weisbach, M.S., 2013. Borrow cheap, buy high? The determinants of leverage and pricing in buyouts. J. Financ. 68 (6), 2223–2267.

Axelson, U., Sorensen, M., Strömberg, P., 2014. Alpha and Beta of Buyout Deals: A Jump CAPM for Long-Term Illiquid Investments. London School of Economics (LSE). Unpublished working paper.

Baker, G.P., Wruck, K.H., 1989. Organizational changes and value creation in leveraged buyouts: the case of the OM Scott & Sons Company. J. Financ. Econ. 25 (2), 163–190.

Barber, B.M., Yasuda, A., 2017. Interim fund performance and fundraising in private equity. J. Financ. Econ. 124 (1), 172–194.

Barber, B.M., Morse, A., Yasuda, A., 2021. Impact investing. J. Financ. Econ. 139 (1), 162–185.

Bernstein, S., Sheen, A., 2016. The operational consequences of private equity buyouts: evidence from the restaurant industry. Rev. Financ. Stud. 29 (9), 2387–2418.

Bernstein, S., Lerner, J., Mezzanotti, F., 2019. Private equity and financial fragility during the crisis. Rev. Financ. Stud. 32 (4), 1309–1373.

Boucly, Q., Sraer, D., Thesmar, D., 2011. Growth lbos. J. Financ. Econ. 102 (2), 432–453.

Boyer, B., Nadauld, T.D., Vorkink, K.P., Weisbach, M.S., 2021. Discount rate risk in private equity. In: Evidence From Secondary Market Transactions. National Bureau of Economic Research (No. w28691).

Braun, R., Jenkinson, T., Stoff, I., 2017. How persistent is private equity performance? Evidence from deal-level data. J. Financ. Econ. 123 (2), 273–291.

Braun, R., Jenkinson, T., Schemmerl, C., 2020. Adverse selection and the performance of private equity co-investments. J. Financ. Econ. 136 (1), 44–62.

Brown, G.W., Gredil, O.R., Kaplan, S.N., 2019. Do private equity funds manipulate reported returns? J. Financ. Econ. 132 (2), 267–297.

Buchner, A., Stucke, R., 2014. The Systematic Risk of Private Equity. (Working paper).

Burrough, B., Helyar, J., 1990. Barbarians at the Gate. Harper & Row, New York, USA.

Cavagnaro, D.R., Sensoy, B.A., Wang, Y., Weisbach, M.S., 2019. Measuring institutional investors' skill at making private equity investments. J. Financ. 74 (6), 3089–3134.

Chung, J., Sensoy, B.A., Stern, L., Weisbach, M.S., 2012. Pay for performance from future flows: the case of private equity. Rev. Financ. Stud. 25 (4), 3259–3304.

Davis, S.J., Haltiwanger, J., Handley, K., Jarmin, R., Lerner, J., Miranda, J., 2014. Private equity, jobs, and productivity. Am. Econ. Rev. 104 (12), 3956–3990.

Degeorge, F., Martin, J., Phalippou, L., 2016. On secondary buyouts. J. Financ. Econ. 120 (1), 124–145.

Doidge, C., Kahle, K.M., Karolyi, G.A., Stulz, R.M., 2018. Eclipse of the public corporation or eclipse of the public markets? J. Appl. Corp. Financ. 30 (1), 8–16.

Driessen, J., Lin, T.C., Phalippou, L., 2012. A new method to estimate risk and return of nontraded assets from cash flows: the case of private equity funds. J. Financial Quant. Anal. 47 (3), 511–535.

Eaton, C., Howell, S.T., Yannelis, C., 2020. When investor incentives and consumer interests diverge: private equity in higher education. Rev. Financ. Stud. 33 (9), 4024–4060.

Eckbo, B.E., Thorburn, K.S., 2013. Corporate restructuring. Found. Trends Financ. 7 (3), 159–288.

Ewens, M., Jones, C.M., Rhodes-Kropf, M., 2013. The price of diversifiable risk in venture capital and private equity. Rev. Financ. Stud. 26 (8), 1854–1889.

Fang, L., Ivashina, V., Lerner, J., 2015. The disintermediation of financial markets: direct investing in private equity. J. Financ. Econ. 116 (1), 160–178.

Forbes, 2001. Forbes Faces: Thomas O. Hicks. *Forbes*.

Franzoni, F., Nowak, E., Phalippou, L., 2012. Private equity performance and liquidity risk. J. Financ. 67 (6), 2341–2373.

Gandhi, A., Song, Y., & Upadrashta, P. (2020). Have Private Equity Owned Nursing Homes Fared Worse Under COVID-19? Working paper.

Gertner, R., Scharfstein, D., 1991. A theory of workouts and the effects of reorganization law. J. Financ. 46 (4), 1189–1222.

Gompers, P., Kaplan, S.N., Mukharlyamov, V., 2016. What do private equity firms say they do? J. Financ. Econ. 121 (3), 449–476.

Gompers, P., Kaplan, S. N., & Mukharlyamov, V. (2022). The Market for CEOs: Evidence from Private Equity. Working paper.

Gredil, O., Griffiths, B. E., & Stucke, R. (2014). Benchmarking Private Equity: The Direct Alpha Method. Working paper.

Guo, S., Hotchkiss, E.S., Song, W., 2011. Do buyouts (still) create value? J. Financ. 66 (2), 479–517.

Gupta, A., Howell, S.T., Yannelis, C., Gupta, A., 2021. Does Private Equity Investment in Healthcare Benefit Patients? Evidence from Nursing Homes. National Bureau of Economic Research. No. w28474.

Hardymon, F., Lerner, J., Leamon, A., 2007. Brazos Partners and Cheddars' Inc. Harvard Business School Case 9-806-069.

Harris, R., Siegel, D.S., Wright, M., 2005. Assessing the impact of management buyouts on economic efficiency: plant-level evidence from the United Kingdom. Rev. Econ. Stat. 87 (1), 148–153.

Harris, R.S., Jenkinson, T., Kaplan, S.N., 2014. Private equity performance: what do we know? J. Financ. 69 (5), 1851–1882.

Harris, R.S., Jenkinson, T., Kaplan, S.N., Stucke, R., 2018. Financial intermediation in private equity: how well do funds of funds perform? J. Financ. Econ. 129 (2), 287–305.

Harris, R.S., Jenkinson, T., Kaplan, S.N., Stucke, R., 2020. Has Persistence Persisted in Private Equity? Evidence from Buyout and Venture Capital Funds. National Bureau of Economic Research. No. w28109.

Hermalin, B.E., Weisbach, M.S., 1998. Endogenously chosen boards of directors and their monitoring of the CEO. Am. Econ. Rev., 96–118.

Higson, C., & Stucke, R. (2012). The Performance of Private Equity. Working paper.

Hochberg, Y.V., Rauh, J.D., 2013. Local overweighting and underperformance: evidence from limited partner private equity investments. Rev. Financ. Stud. 26 (2), 403–451.

Howell, S. T., Jang, Y., Kim, H., & Weisbach, M. S. (2022). All Clear for Takeoff: Evidence from Airports on the Effects of Infrastructure Privatization. Working Paper.

Hudson, M.J., 2020. Private Equity Fund Terms Research, fifth ed. MJ Hudson.

Hüther, N., Robinson, D.T., Sievers, S., Hartmann-Wendels, T., 2020. Paying for performance in private equity: evidence from venture capital partnerships. Manag. Sci. 66 (4), 1756–1782.

Ivashina, V., Lerner, J., 2019. Pay now or pay later? The economics within the private equity partnership. J. Financ. Econ. 131 (1), 61–87.

Jegadeesh, N., Kräussl, R., Pollet, J.M., 2015. Risk and expected returns of private equity investments: evidence based on market prices. Rev. Financ. Stud. 28 (12), 3269–3302.

Jenkinson, T., Sousa, M., & Stucke, R. (2013). How Fair Are the Valuations of Private Equity Funds? Working paper.

Jensen, M.C., 1968. The performance of mutual funds in the period 1945-1964. J. Financ. 23 (2), 389–416.

Jensen, M.C., 1986. Agency costs of free cash flow, corporate finance, and takeovers. Am. Econ. Rev. 76 (2), 323–329.

Jensen, M.C., 1989. Eclipse of the public corporation. Harv. Bus. Rev.

Johnston-Ross, E., Ma, S., Puri, M., 2021. Private Equity and Financial Stability: Evidence from Failed Bank Resolution in the Crisis. National Bureau of Economic Research. No. w28751.

Kaplan, S.N., 1989a. The effects of management buyouts on operating performance and value. J. Financ. Econ. 24 (2), 217–254.

Kaplan, S.N., 1989b. Management buyouts: evidence of taxes as a source of value. J. Financ. 44 (3), 611–632.

Kaplan, S.N., Schoar, A., 2005. Private equity performance: returns, persistence, and capital flows. J. Financ. 60 (4), 1791–1823.

Kaplan, S.N., Stein, J.C., 1990. How risky is the debt in highly leveraged transactions? J. Financ. Econ. 27 (1), 215–245.

Kaplan, S.N., Strömberg, P., 2009. Leveraged buyouts and private equity. J. Econ. Perspect. 23 (1), 121–146.

Keyte, J.A., Schwartz, K.B., 2016. Private equity and antitrust: a new landscape. Antitrust 31, 21.

Kim, H., 2021. Opening the Black Box in Private Equity: When Interests Conflict between GPs and LPs. Unpublished Dissertation, Ohio State University.

Korteweg, A., Nagel, S., 2016. Risk-adjusting the returns to venture capital. J. Financ. 71 (3), 1437–1470.

Korteweg, A., Sorensen, M., 2017. Skill and luck in private equity performance. J. Financ. Econ. 124 (3), 535–562.

Lerner, J., Jin, Y., 2012. Hony, CIFA, and Zoomlion: Creating Value and Strategic Choices in a Dynamic Market. Harvard Business School Finance case, (811-032).

Lerner, J., Schoar, A., 2004. The illiquidity puzzle: theory and evidence from private equity. J. Financ. Econ. 72 (1), 3–40.

Lerner, J., Schoar, A., Wongsunwai, W., 2007. Smart institutions, foolish choices: the limited partner performance puzzle. J. Financ. 62 (2), 731–764.

Lerner, J., Sorensen, M., Strömberg, P., 2011. Private equity and long-run investment: the case of innovation. J. Financ. 66 (2), 445–477.

Lichtenberg, F.R., Siegel, D., 1990. The effects of leveraged buyouts on productivity and related aspects of firm behavior. J. Financ. Econ. 27 (1), 165–194.

Lim, W. (2022). Private Equity Economics: Compensation and Growth Dynamics. Working paper.

Lim, J., Schwert, M., Weisbach, M.S., 2021. The economics of PIPEs. J. Financial Intermediation 45 (1), 1–14.

Long, A. M., & Nickels, C. J. (1996). A Private Investment Benchmark. Working paper.

Mathonet, P.-Y., Meyer, T., 2007. J-Curve Exposure. Wiley.

Metrick, A., Yasuda, A., 2010. The economics of private equity funds. Rev. Financ. Stud. 23 (6), 2303–2341.

Moskowitz, T.J., Vissing-Jørgensen, A., 2002. The returns to entrepreneurial investment: a private equity premium puzzle? Am. Econ. Rev. 92 (4), 745–778.

Munday, S., Hu, W., True, T., Zhang, J., 2018. Performance of private credit funds: a first look. J. Altern. Invest. 21 (2), 31–51.

Nadauld, T.D., Sensoy, B.A., Vorkink, K., Weisbach, M.S., 2019. The liquidity cost of private equity investments: evidence from secondary market transactions. J. Financ. Econ. 132 (3), 158–181.

Phalippou, L. (2008). The Hazards of Using IRR to Measure Performance: The Case of Private Equity. Working paper.

Phalippou, L., 2009. Beware of venturing into private equity. J. Econ. Perspect. 23 (1), 147–166.

Phalippou, L., 2014. Performance of buyout funds revisited? Rev. Financ. 18 (1), 189–218.

Phalippou, L., Gottschalg, O., 2009. The performance of private equity funds. Rev. Financ. Stud. 22 (4), 1747–1776.

Phalippou, L., Rauch, C., Umber, M., 2018. Private equity portfolio company fees. J. Financ. Econ. 129 (3), 559–585.

Robinson, D.T., Sensoy, B.A., 2013. Do private equity fund managers earn their fees? Compensation, ownership, and cash flow performance. Rev. Financ. Stud. 26 (11), 2760–2797.

Robinson, D.T., Sensoy, B.A., 2016. Cyclicality, performance measurement, and cash flow liquidity in private equity. J. Financ. Econ. 122 (3), 521–543.

Rossi, A., 2019. Decreasing Returns or Reversion to the Mean? The Case of Private Equity Fund Growth. Working Paper, University of Arizona.

Scharfstein, D.S., Stein, J.C., 2000. The dark side of internal capital markets: divisional rent-seeking and inefficient investment. J. Financ. 55 (6), 2537–2564.

Schillinger, P., Braun, R., & Cornel, J. (2020). Distortion or Cash Flow Management? Understanding Credit Facilities in Private Equity Funds. *Working paper*.

Sensoy, B.A., Wang, Y., Weisbach, M.S., 2014. Limited partner performance and the maturing of the private equity industry. J. Financ. Econ. 112 (3), 320–343.

Shleifer, A., Summers, L., 1988. Breach of Trust in Hostile Takeovers. vol. Corporate University of Chicago Press. https://doi.org/10.2307/2234106.

Smith, A.J., 1990. Corporate ownership structure and performance: the case of management buyouts. J. Financ. Econ. 27 (1), 143–164.

Stucke, R. (2011). Updating History. Working paper.

Swensen, D.F., 2009. Pioneering Portfolio Management: An Unconventional Approach to Institutional Investment, Fully Revised and Updated. Simon and Schuster.

Trehan, R., 2006. The History of Leveraged Buyouts. *4Hoteliers*.

Vadapalli, R., 2007. Mergers. Excel Books India, Acquisitions and Business Valuation.

Gender and race in entrepreneurial finance

Michael Ewens*

Columbia Business School, New York, NY, United States
*Corresponding author: e-mail address: michael.ewens@columbia.edu

Chapter outline

1 Introduction

This chapter reviews the intersection of race, gender, and entrepreneurial finance with the broad goals of providing the background and citations for those interested in contributing to the field. Few academics or PhD students decide to read a chapter like this one without some previous interest in the topic signaled in the title and abstract. I will thus spare the reader a lengthy introduction that tries to generate excitement about a research topic while convincing them that no one has answered the important questions. Instead, let me briefly motivate the topic and then clarify the chapter's setting, objectives, and target audience.

Why do we need a chapter such as this? To start is Table 1, which shows the representation of women and minorities of all genders in the entrepreneurial finance market. I start with a normative statement that these numbers are too low. One need only compare the proportion of high-growth startups that are women-run (12%–28%) to their population representation or labor force participation Calder-Wang and Gompers (45%, 2021) to see why this is called the "entrepreneurship gender gap." Similar comparisons for Black entrepreneurs (1%–10%) reveal similar gaps. The sources of these disparities are many and not necessarily an indictment on investor's preferences or bias. In fact, that is the whole point of many academic articles on the topic: what explains the disparities? Is it a skills gap, wealth inequality, educational differences, culture, norms, or investor bias? Or perhaps some historical institution led to differences in human capital that persist today. That said, an unspoken motivation throughout the remaining sections is equality of participation across all stages of the startup life cycle. Why? Beyond how they correlate with characteristics like wealth, education and pre-entry economic characteristics, race, gender, ethnicity, and other innate characteristics should not predict participation or success in entrepreneurship ex-ante.

Recent events and controversies in the venture capital and private equity industry show that this topic is likely to be top-of-mind for practitioners and policy makers for years. Several investors and limited partners have reacted to these developments with resignations and firings. Others have taken a proactive approach to address concerns about underrepresentation (Section 7.2). Understanding if and how demographic characteristics matter from startup founding to exit is critical to assessing the industry's progress.

Our setting is the financing of high-growth entrepreneurial firms in the United States. Many of the topics covered in the chapter apply to all small businesses, but several will be specific to venture capital, angel investors, and private equity. Berger and Udell (1998) show that the external financing of small businesses demands researchers' attention. They highlight the unique setting of entrepreneurial finance where insiders contribute a substantial amount of capital and tap the private equity markets as the firm develops. The high level of informational opacity distinguishes it from the public firm setting and plays an important part in understanding the financing life cycle. This life cycle involves multiple players—banks, angels, VCs, private equity firms—and thus presents situations where bias, stereotypes, and discrimination could affect underrepresented founders. The informational opacity found at nearly every stage only exacerbates the frictions underlying most models of discrimination.

1.1 Chapter objectives

Here is what you should expect out of this chapter.

- It will present a framework for understanding how gender and race matter for startups raising capital from banks, angel investors, venture capitalists, or private equity firms. I present a simplified version of the entrepreneurial firm life cycle and describe the major players.
- Summary of the motivating "facts" about participation of women and minorities in startups. After reviewing dozens of papers using disparate datasets, all the facts about firm formation, capital raising, growth, and outcomes needed to be collected one place.
- One faces a daunting and ever-expanding list of economic theory and review articles to read before testing theories or even building databases. Section 5 is thus a financial economist's summary of the economics of discrimination. It provides the citations, terminology, and models for researchers interested in testing the myriad alternative explanations when exploring differential treatment by race or gender. When appropriate, the section attempts to tie the models' predictions to the entrepreneurial finance setting.
- Present a review of the contemporary literature in entrepreneurial finance—with an economics and finance bias—related to race and gender. This is the section you might skip to if you are seeking cites to add to your own project (though I cannot promise I did not miss some). Rather than put a list of citations and one sentence summaries of papers into paragraphs of text, the literature review attempts to connect the work and summarize its lessons for future work.
- The remaining sections of the chapter look forward and provide a guide for researchers interested in exploring topics in the area. It presents recent and ongoing changes to the financing and entrepreneurship landscape. These changes could change the race and gender "facts," while providing useful variation for testing theories. The main section of the chapter ends with a list of unanswered questions and unexplored subareas that demand more attention.
- Appendix provides references for data sources, methods for assignment of race and gender, and a review of methods used to detect discrimination.

As will be clear as you proceed through the chapter, I devote more time to gender issues than to race. This focus is not a statement about relative importance. Instead, it is a by-product of several factors. The literature across fields has spent considerable time on gender relative to race. Part of this attention stems from data constraints because gender is more often recorded and measured with minor error. Similarly, minority participation rates (whatever their causes) are often so low that standard regression estimation has weak statistical power. Next, several of the models of entrepreneurial entry, preferences, risk, and stereotypes better map to gender than race. Simply, it is more difficult to connect historical or social events to clear—though perhaps unintended—to differences between genders, but there are clear connections for race and ethnicity. As we discuss in Section 6, there is a lot of room in the literature for studies on race and ethnicity.

Beyond its overview of the economics of entrepreneurship, Parker (2018) provides an extensive survey of topics around female and minority entrepreneurship. His review extends beyond this chapter's focus on the US private equity and startup markets, so I encourage interested readers to look there for international evidence.

1.2 Intended audience

I write this chapter for two audiences. First, I aim to provide a literature review and "facts assessment" for practitioners and policymakers who do not have the will or time to review dozens of academic papers. Sections 1 and 2 achieve this, while Table 1 summarizes the baseline facts. The second audience—research faculty, PhD, and masters students—will find these sections only part of the story. Here, I aim to provide a resource for those who seek to conduct research at the intersection of private equity and discrimination broadly speaking. Numerous members of this audience will have financial and economic theory mastered, yet lack knowledge of the unique institutional setting of private equity and high-growth entrepreneurship. These readers may also have less experience with the rich and extensive discrimination literature in labor economics. Section 6 summarizes research on economics and econometrics of discrimination and bias, which forms the foundation of the main literature review. The review of the economics of discrimination literature in Section 6 can guide observational studies or experiments but should not be viewed as a comprehensive literature review of that field (see comprehensive reviews cited).

1.3 Entrepreneurs and firms

The set of entrepreneurial firms raising external finance is large and varied. This chapter focuses on a small, but influential subset: high-growth startups and their investors. The literature review will focus on young, small business that have some intention to grow or hire employees. A standard defense of focusing on these firms—despite their rarity—argues that young, innovative firms are drivers of innovation, employment, and economic growth (Akcigit et al., 2022).

Table 1 Representation statistics in entrepreneurial finance.

	% Women	% Black	Notes/Source
Panel A: New firms (before capital)			
Incorporated firms (NLSY)	28%	10% (Nonwhite)	Share of self-employed individuals in incorporated firms from NLSY79 1982–2012 (Levine and Rubinstein, 2017, Table 1 Panel B)
CA/MA newly incorporated firms	22%		Newly incorporated firms in California and Massachusetts, 1995–2005 (Guzman and Kacperczyk, 2019)
Entrepreneurial entry rate (relative)	64% (lower rate)	78% (lower rate)	The relative rate of the adult, nonbusiness owner population that starts a business (both incorporated and unincorporated, employers or nonemployers) each month, averaged 1996–2020 (Fairlie and Desai, 2021, Table 2 and Table 3)
Small business owners	29.9%		Women-owned firms as a percentage of all in 2012. Surveys of Business Owners (Robb et al., 2014, Appendix 3)
Team size/employment at start (relative to men)	7% smaller/20% fewer employees		Ewens and Townsend (2020, Table 2 "Team size") [7%]. Hebert (2020, Table 2, Panel E) [20%]
High-growth startups (subset of new firms)			
Incorporated firms CA/MA	17%		Share of female-led startups in top 10% high-growth startups in California and Massachusetts, 1995–2005 (Guzman and Kacperczyk, 2019, Table 2)
Equity crowdfunding startups	16%		The percentage of startups with female founders. Startups based in the United Kingdom, 2012–2017 (Hellmann et al., 2021, Table 2, Panel A)
Angel-backed startups	16%–28%	19.4%	For gender: firms with female CEO/founders as a percentage of the entrepreneurs that are seeking angel capital (Ewens and Townsend, 2020, Table 1, Sohl, 2020). For race: the share of minority-owned firms in the entrepreneurs that presented their business concept to angels (Sohl, 2020).
Innovation goals (relative to men)	19%–40% lower		Hebert (2020, Table 2) "High-growth oriented" [19%]. Global Entrepreneurship Monitor 2021 Table A7 (Bosma and Levie, 2010), US-based startups: relative rate of starting innovative product or service-based firm [40%].
"High impact" startups	12.4%		Percentage of firms with female founder whose sales have at least doubled over a 4-year period and which have an employment growth quantifier of two or more over the same period with employee-size 1–19 from 2004 to 2008, SBA data (Tracy, 2011, Table 15)

Panel B: Capital raising by founder (at least one women or minority)

Bank finance: relative rate of business loans	50% less likely	The relative rate of black vs nonblack small businesses acquiring small business bank finance. 2004–2011 KFS (Fairlie et al., 2022, Table A.4)
All VC fundraising (deals)	14.5%	2.4% (+Latino)	Women: US deal value for female-founded companies as a share of all VC deal in 2020. PitchBook Venture Monitor Q4 2021 (p23). Black: Share of dollars invested in startups founded by black or Latino entrepreneurs. Crunchbase "Funding to Black & Latinx Founders" report, 2020.
Incorporated firms with VC	10%		Share of female-led startups across firms that get venture capital in California and Massachusetts, 1995–2005 (Guzman and Kacperczyk, 2019, Table 2)
Form D filers (private capital raising)	10%	4% (Black & Hispanic)	Percentage of nonfinancial firms that raise capital in reliance on Regulation D, 2010–2019 (Yimfor, 2021)
Early-stage capital/angel	21%–24%	11.5%	The percentage of women entrepreneurs received angel investment (the yield rate) in Q1,2 2019 (Sohl, 2020). The percentage of female/nonwhite startup CEOs in 2018. 2019 ACA Angel Funders Report (p. 13).
Small business fundraising	34.6%		Percentage of financial capital invested in women-owned businesses, Kauffman Firm Survey 2016 (Coleman and Robb, 2009, Table 3)
Equity crowdfunding success	Same		Using equity crowdfunding data in the UK, Hellmann et al. (2021, Table 4) find gender does not have a significant effect on campaign success.
Crowdfunding success (Kickstarter) (relative)	6% higher		[HTML]FFFFFWomen entrepreneurs have a higher rate of success (82%) than men (76%). Kickstarter, 2009–2012. Gafni et al. (2021) also see Greenberg and Mollick (2017).

Panel C: Investors and funds

Angel investors	26.5%–30%		For 2020 (26.5%), the number is US VC deal count in female-founded companies with female angel participation as proportion of all deals with angel participation. All In Female Founders in the US VC Ecosystem 2021 (p. 19). For 2021 (30%): "The Angel Investor Market in Q1Q2 2021: A Market Stabilizing During the Vaccine Rollout", Center for Venture Research, December 15, 2021.
VC Investors (GPs)	16%	22% (nonwhite)	Female GPs as a share of all US GPs. All In Female Founders in the US VC Ecosystem 2021 (pp. 8–9). Percentage of female/nonwhite employees among investment partners in 2020. Deloitte VC HumanCapital survey March 2021 (Figs. 1 and 2)
VC funds controlled	5.6%		"Women in VC" report October 2020, "The Untapped Potential of Women-led Funds." "Women-led funds." Funds I–III using Preqin as benchmark for all funds.
PE funds controlled	7.2%		Share of women/minority-owned firms in all funds (Lerner et al., 2021).

Continued

Table 1 Representation statistics in entrepreneurial finance—cont'd

	% Women	% Black	Notes/Source
Panel D: Outcomes			
Newly public firm (IPO) CEOs	<1%–3%		Shontell, 2021 (BusinessInsider), Nasdaq data, 2020 (1%).
			Percent Women by Function in All EGF IPOs from 1996–2010 [3%] (Kenney and Patton, 2015, Table 4)
Successful VC exits founders	19.4%		Share of female-founded companies in venture-backed exits in 2019. All in Female Founders and CEOs in the US VC Ecosystem 2020 (pp. 18).
Share of total exit valuations in VC	8.7%		Share total exit valuation associated with female-founded companies in all VC exits (2019). All in Female Founders and CEOs in the US VC Ecosystem 2020 (p. 18).
Incorporated firm acquired or IPO	7%		Share of female-led startups across firms that got IPO or acquisition in California and Massachusetts, 1995–2005 (Guzman and Kacperczyk, 2019, Table 2)
Angel-backed startups success	42% (lower rate)		The relative rate of startups that got IPO or acquisition. First-time fundraising events for US startups founded between 2010 and November 2015 (Ewens and Townsend, 2020, Table 2 Panel B)

The table reports statistics on the participation of women and minorities across multiple stages of the startup life cycle. "% women" is the percentage of firms with at least one female founder (unless otherwise showed). "% Black" is the percentage of firms with at least one black founder. Sometimes, this column is the percentage of nonwhite or minority founders. The "Notes/Source" column provides a short summary of the variable and references.

2 Why race and gender?

A chapter that provides an in-depth review of the theory and empirical results of race and gender in entrepreneurial finance is useful for several reasons. The facts about gender and race are the most common motivation in the papers reviewed (see Table 1). Here, the representation of women and minorities in entrepreneurial firms looks much like the 1970s labor and education markets that formed the basis for a large economics literature. For example, women run less than a quarter of VC-backed start-ups, while since 1996 whites start new firms at a 23% higher rate than blacks (documented in Section 4). Historical issues surrounding discrimination—wealth disparities, education gaps, and cultural norms—also exacerbated the sizeable gaps in participation and funding. All these frictions showing up in the entrepreneurial finance setting result in complicated policy solutions, but given the importance of entrepreneurial firms to economies, the marginal returns to solving the problems are high.

Next, unlike the small one-establishment business with a single founder-employee, most of these firms of interest face financing constraints and must raise outside capital. Such constraints give rise to business relationships with investors such as angels, venture capitalists, and private equity firms. Even within a well-functioning entrepreneurial finance market where all players are attempting to maximize firm value, there are inevitably conflicting incentives. For example, the entrepreneur may want to remain in control to benefit from nonpecuniary benefits (Moskowitz and Vissing-Jørgensen, 2002; Ewens and Farre-Mensa, 2020), while venture capitalists want to pursue high-growth for the goal of a large exit. How race and gender interact with this complex environment is still an open question and can provide insight into financial intermediation more broadly. Finally, founding, financing, and growing high-growth startups are each an environment where players have different information sets and beliefs. It is unfortunately an ideal setting for topics around discrimination, stereotypes, and other issues of discrimination.

Next, there are many reasons to think that the classic model of discrimination in Becker (1957) where markets can temper prejudice, particularly applies to venture capital and private equity. On the one hand, intermediaries receive high-powered incentives to maximize fund returns and, for venture capital, have so few "shots on goal" that bias or discriminatory behavior is costly. In a world without discrimination, race and gender are likely to have no impact on entrepreneurial success. The chapter's focus on high-growth startups suggests that this prediction is even stronger. The success and failure of these companies hinges on a complex assortment of resource collection, luck, and technical skill. All these facts could lead one to form a strong null hypothesis that prejudice-based discrimination (i.e., taste-based) will be absent in the chapter's setting.

Despite the aforementioned factors, there are many reasons that discrimination by race or gender may persist. Information asymmetries are quite extreme, particularly when compared to lending settings (banks) or companies with clear, physical assets that can act as collateral for loans and are possibly easier to value. Information asymmetries about types or quality are the starting point for numerous theories of discrimination (see Section 5). Next, various investors—angels, individuals, and VCs—decide on "gut feelings" or after personal meetings with entrepreneurs (Gompers et al., 2020; Hu and Ma, 2021). These subjective decisions are ripe for the emergence of bias or stereotypes.

So, beyond discrimination as a topic being important to understand, diagnose and hopefully solve in any setting, I believe that this is particularly important in entrepreneurship and venture capital. Even if a reader is not interested in venture capital or entrepreneurial finance per se, the unique features of the setting may provide insights into the broader fields of discrimination.

3 From founding to financing to exit

I next describe a simplified version of the typical startup path founding decision to eventual exit of an investment by an investor (and return realization for a founder). The goal is to show that the process' complexity and length can translate into many gender or race disparities that can compound over time: founding choices, financing likelihood, startup growth, and eventual startup exits (e.g., IPOs). The setting applies to most US-based startups intending to grow, hire employees, for those that are relatively less intensive regarding physical capital, and pursue innovation. As highlighted by Kerr and Nanda (2011), founders who aim to form these types of firms are much more likely to suffer from financing constraints because they cannot access the traditional debt markets such as banks. Such firms thus need to raise outside equity financing. The complexity of the environment reveals that there are various opportunities for bias or differential treatment to emerge, disadvantaging women, and minorities.

3.1 Founding decision

Start first with the founding decision by an individual entrepreneur with a positive net present value project given the required inputs (capital, time, labor, and advice). I simplify this founding decision into two parts. The first is the actions taken prior to the decision that makes the individual confident that—conditional on all the other components falling into place—she can achieve the goal of founding and realizing a return that justifies the risk. Here, we have a situation where a founder may require significant education or work experience. For example, starting a biotech firm requires scientific expertise, while starting an enterprise software venture requires sales expertise. Note that this first stage of analysis relates to topics at the heart of labor economics: occupational choice, human capital investment, compensation, etc. The second step is the choice of firm type, scale, industry, location, and long-term goals. Among many other things, the founder's choices here affect the type and amount of capital required and the team characteristics demanded by the business.

3.2 Postfounding: Gathering resources and growing the firm

Now suppose that we have a founder who believes that she has the requisite skills and experience to attempt firm formation. She must now gather resources. This includes finding cofounders (Wasserman, 2012), hiring early employees (Sorenson et al., 2021), retaining lawyers and accountants, and identifying intellectual property. Much of this requires capital. Absent a pile of personal or family wealth, she must seek outside capital. Enter the financiers.

In our simple setting, this founder's idea is not well-suited for bank debt because the firm lacks assets that can act as collateral and has no expectations of revenues in the near term. Section 4 details the typical sources of early-stage nonbank finance, but for this exercise, we will assume she must approach individual investors, such as angels, or institutional investors (e.g., VCs). Angel investors typically invest their own money (Kerr et al., 2014), while the latter are sophisticated financial intermediaries with the goal of maximizing returns for their own investors (here, limited partners). Approaching these investors, the founder may encounter a problem: they may have a threshold for firm progress, such as a working prototype or customers (i.e., "Come back when you have some traction.").[a] Thus, the founder will require her own equity, sweat equity or an asset such as a home equity that she can borrow against (Kerr et al., 2022).[b] Suppose the founder gathers her own resources to achieve the first required milestone for these investors and successfully raises equity financing. Now she must run a startup.

Among many steps, growing a startup involves hiring, investing in physical or intangible assets, acquiring customers, and continuing to raise capital to finance it all (every 12–18 months for VC-backed startups).[c] Since 2002, the typical startup that raises venture capital raises 2.7 rounds of financing,[d] while conditional on at least one financing, raises $29 m. Thus, the founder must repeat a similar financing step detailed above. Taking outside capital from sophisticated investors also introduces potential conflicts between the founder/firms and the capital provider. Even if available, bank debt demands regular interest payments and loan payback. Outside equity investors have their own return expectations and investment horizons. For the latter, a venture capital investor invests out of a fund that has a finite investment window (4–5 years) and limited life that generates a demand to liquidate their position (Metrick and Yasuda, 2010). These investors will often demand some control rights (Kaplan and Strömberg, 2003) beyond their equity position. Thus, beyond using her newly raised capital for hiring and investment, the founder must work with her investor's demands in mind.

---

[a]See Gompers et al. (2020) for survey evidence on the VC deal and investment process.
[b]The Goldsmith-Pinkham and Shue (2020) finding that women earning lower returns on housing will likely only exacerbate the relationship between home equity and entrepreneurship for women.
[c]Author's calculation using VentureSource. All follow-on financing events (i.e., not first financing events) of startups with at least one venture capital investor and first financed between 2002 and 2017.
[d]Author's calculation using VentureSource. All startups backed by venture capitalists first financed between 2002 and 2019.

3.3 **Realizing value**

In the last step, the firm and its investors will seek to realize a return by liquidating their position in the fund. This typically occurs through an initial public offering (sell shares to the public) or acquisition (sell shares to another firm).[e] A startup's final valuation and terms depend on the growth achieved, which depends (in part) on how much money it has raised. How could gender or race matter at this stage (all else equal)? The exit decision is a joint decision of the board of directors, which is commonly controlled by the investors in the later stages of the startup's life (Ewens and Malenko, 2022). Negotiation is thus between the founder and board members, on the one hand, and between the firm and the acquirer or institutional investors and underwriters (in an IPO offering), on the other hand.

3.4 **Guiding our analysis**

This simplified story of the high-growth startup reveals the steps where discrimination, bias, nepotism, stereotypes, and differential treatment can affect observed choices or outcomes:

1. Founding decision, precapital raising
2. Resource gathering (e.g., financial and human capital)
3. Growing the firm with active investors
4. Exiting the firm

The theories of these behaviors and preferences will play a different role in each step. The setting clarifies that any analysis of one stage—e.g., the differences in racial representation in CEO founders at IPO—is a function of a potentially extensive set of decisions. Researchers must account for these facts when planning their analyses, while policymakers with limited resources should target solutions that address the sources of underlying differences.

4 **Facts about founders, startups, and investors**

This section sets the stage for the economic framework and literature review by presenting some fundamental facts about entrepreneurs, capital providers and outcomes related to race and gender. It is a preview of the deeper literature review of recent research that explicitly tests for discrimination or bias. Table 1 summarizes the major facts about gender and race representation.

Of course, any numbers presented here that show differential outcomes by race and gender do not address whether discriminatory actions or biased preferences exist. Nonetheless, univariate statistics can be informative on their own. This is not the first survey to document the participation of women and minorities in startups. The Diana

---

[e]For benchmark exit rates, see Ewens and Farre-Mensa (2020).

Project's[f] researchers provided the first comprehensive analysis of female-founded firms raising venture capital.[g] In a series of reports (Brush et al., 2001, 2004; Brush, 2008), the researchers documented a persistent 30-year underrepresentation by female-founded firms in terms of angel and venture capital.

The table presents five settings: the founding decision, the firm formation choice (e.g., industry and size), raising capital, investor characteristics, and outcomes. It aims to report statistics as of 2020–21, but many are older. The main statistics of interest will include participation or basic firm characteristics by gender and race, where the unit of observation is typically the startup. Here, female- or Black-founded means that the startup had at least one woman or black founder. Note that many cells are blank because I could not find reliable data sources for the statistics. These gaps provide directions for future data collection and research. The focus here on Black entrepreneurs rather than other minorities such as Latinos (a larger proportion of the US population) is worth mention. As with the overall focus on gender, this is because the data is limited on other ethnicities and unfortunately there are too few papers with these samples.

Table 1 focuses on the across-gender or across-race comparison for benchmarking. This approach works well in the context of US population shares: 50% women, 13.4% Black and 18.5% Latino (Census, 2019 Population Estimates Program).[h] Another useful benchmark is the labor force participation rates in 2020: 56.2% for women (similar across races), 67.7% for white men, 62.6% for Black men and 75% for Hispanic men. Gompers and Wang (2017b) provide other useful benchmarks that condition on education and career choices Gompers and Wang (2017b, figs. 1 and 3). For example, women earn over 57% of bachelor's degrees since 2010 and half of all lawyers are women. Thus, we can compare the low rates of Black entrepreneurship in Table 1 to Black representation in awarded bachelor's degrees (9%) and doctors or lawyers (approximately 5%) since 2010.

4.1 Founding decision: When, how, and with whom

Panel A of Table 1 provides statistics about the differences in entrepreneurial entry by gender and race. Across multiple time periods and geographies, the pattern is apparent: women and Blacks are significantly less likely than men and whites to form new firms. For example, Fairlie and Desai (2021) use the monthly Current Population Survey to show that men started new business at a 64% higher rate than women from 2019 to 2020 Fairlie and Desai (2021, table 2), while from 1996 to 2020 blacks started new businesses at a 22% lower rate than whites. The new business formation data encompasses an enormous set of companies that are not the focus of this chapter (e.g., nonemployers or nonincorporated); however, the gender and racial gap is large and persistent. The share of female founders from the NSLY (28%), Survey of Small

---

[f]See https://www.dianaproject.org.
[g]For an earlier review of female-founded firms, see Brush (1992).
[h]See https://www.census.gov/quickfacts/fact/table/US/RHI725219.

Business Owners (29.9%) and newly incorporated CA/MA firms (22%) are each significantly below any population, education, or occupation benchmarks. This gap motivates both this chapter, and the literature summarized in Section 6. Next, the row "Team size/employment at start" asks whether female-founded firms look different from their male-founded counterparts at founding. Data from AngelList and French incorporation databases show that founding team size and number of employees at startup are significantly smaller in startups founded by at least one woman.

The next part of Panel A in Table 1 considers the subset of high-growth startups. There are multiple ways to define such firms, such as sales growth and incorporation type. The participation rate of women is almost uniformly lower than the baseline entrepreneurial entry. For example, Guzman and Kacperczyk (2019) find only 17% of high-growth startups are founded by women, while Sohl (2020) survey and Ewens and Townsend (2020) data from AngelList show 16%–28% participation among angel-backed startups. Other than the Sohl (2020)survey showing 19.4% of angel-backed startups were founded by minorities, there is little data on Black or minority founder participation for these types of firms. According to the 2021 Census population estimate, this 19.4% is below the 25% non-White share of the population.[i]

4.2 Raising capital: Sources and amounts

The facts above show that even before institutional capital is raised, the representation of women and most minorities falls significantly below their population and labor force participation. In this section, we consider the set of founders that have entered entrepreneurship and have raised some capital.

Started in 2004 and run through 2011, the Kauffman Firm Survey (KFS) is a longitudinal survey of new US businesses. As detailed by Coleman and Robb (2009), the survey collects information about the owners and business related to physical location, industry, employment, profits, intellectual property, and financing at founding and beyond. A major advantage of such data is the ability to avoid survivorship bias inherent in any database that conditions on firm financing. The data allow Coleman and Robb to look within-industry at-founding financing choice, limiting concerns about industry sorting by founders. The authors document that women-owned new businesses start with relatively less capital, raise less debt and equity postfounding and are more likely to rely on personal sources of finance than male-owned firms (studies with similar patterns include Fairlie and Robb (2009a) and Constantinidis et al. (2006)). Fairlie et al. (2022) use later waves of the KFS to explore capital access issues at firm formation and follow firms as they grow. Black-founded firms raise less initial capital of all types, but primarily external debt. Panel B of Table 1 reports that black-owned business in the KFS are 50% less likely to use small business bank finance than other startups.

---

[i]See https://www.census.gov/quickfacts/fact/table/US/PST045221.

The next two rows of Panel B show that women and minorities are underrepresented among VC-backed startups in 2020: 14.5% for women, and 2.4% for Hispanics and Black. Gompers and Wang (2017b) present a study of the time series of VC-backed startups. The headline numbers are clear: women run 10% of VC-backed startups since 1990 (as of 2015), while black founders run only 2% of firms.[j] They find that although these groups have increased their participation in education or career paths historically found in founder or VC investor resumes, their participation in startups lags. For example, the female participation rate in the financial industry is three to four times higher than that found in VC-backed startups (e.g., since 2010, 34% of investment bankers were women, compared to 9% of venture capitalists). This ability to benchmark racial and gender participation among financed firms using bachelor's degree rates, professional jobs and postgraduate degrees is a powerful means of assessing the sources of disparities. Ideally, researchers can continue to build individual-level data that can control for these factors at the founder-level.

The rest of Panel B in Table 1 paints the same picture as these initial statistics. Women represent 10% of high-growth startups that raise VC in CA or MA, 10% of Form D filers raising multiple types of private equity, 21%–24% of angel capital and 34.6% of small business capital in the KFS survey. These disparities only disappear in the relatively newer financing environment of crowdfunding. Both reward-based and equity-based crowdfunding (details in Section 7) show negligible differences in capital raising by gender. This equality suggests increased investor participation can help shrink the entrepreneurship gender gap.

4.3 Investors

Often labeled as "gate-keepers," venture capitalists—and to a lesser extent angel investors—have the power to determine the small set of startups that receive external equity financing (Puri and Zarutskie, 2012). Where preferences or bias for entrepreneurs among investors persist (i.e., each gender prefers to invest in its own gender), one solution to the founding and financing gaps is increased participation by women and minorities on the supply side of the market. Panel C of Table 1 suggests that there is still a long way to go on this front. Some 26%–30% of angel investors and 16% of general partners at VC firms are women.[k] Blacks make up 4% of the latter. The main decision-makers in private equity are the individuals that control the funds that invest in startups (e.g., managing directors). Here, the gap widens. A little over 5% of VC funds in 2020 are women-managed, while 3.8% of PE funds (VC, growth equity, etc.) from 2011 to 2016 were run by minorities. Section 7.3 discusses market and government programs aimed at closing the supply side gender and racial gaps.

---

[j]Using a sample of VC-backed startups from 2011 to 2013 provided by Pitchbook, Brush et al. (2018) find that the percentage of firms with a female executive increased from 9% to 18%. The authors found that these management teams raise less capital (even within the same industry).
[k]There are other decision-makers at VC firms such as managing directors who could also impact the gender or racial composition of the portfolio.

4.4 Outcomes

Consider now the set of financed or founded startups and take as given the distribution of gender or race in these firms. We next ask how outcomes differ by these characteristics. Such an analysis is, of course, limited by the facts described above: firms founded by women or minorities are different at founding (e.g., smaller, lower growth industries, less startup capital). We thus will present simple summary statistics that do not account for these differences and then highlight work that attempts to control for such factors.

One of the most comprehensive studies of differences in entrepreneurial success by race is Fairlie and Robb (2009b)'s study of small businesses in the Census data. For the set of businesses founded between 1992, they find that compared to white-owned firms, black-owned firms are 54% less likely to have at least $10,000 in profits and fail at a 20% higher rate. Panel D of Table 1 presents additional statistics on outcome differences by gender. Some 1%–3% of new IPOs have a female CEO since 1996, while female-founded VC-backed startups successfully exit at rates above their participation rates (19.4% exit rate vs 14.5%). The latter fact suggests that any discriminatory behavior resulting in lower founding or funding rates for women cannot be easily justified by differences in expected outcomes. This news is mixed when we consider the set of CA or MA-incorporated firms, where the 7% exit rate is below participation. Similarly, female-founded VC-backed startups' exits account for only 8.7% of total value and angel-backed startups have a 42% lower success rate than male-founded firms (Ewens and Townsend, 2020).

4.5 Putting it all together

Table 1 paints a clear picture of the entrepreneurship gap in terms of both race and gender. Women and Blacks are underrepresented at all stages of the entrepreneurial process regardless of the benchmark used (i.e., population, labor force participation, etc.). It presents a snapshot in time that when compared to statistics from early versions of the same sources, has weakly improved over the last decade. However, the rates of convergence suggest that it will take at least another three decades to reach equality (e.g., 3.45% per year growth in VC dollars to female-founded startups). Finally, there are also major data gaps in Table 1 for participation and outcomes by race. While these data gaps are slowly being addressed by investors and data providers (Section 7.3), a more systematic approach by academics or policy makers is warranted.

5 Economics of discrimination

This section presents a short primer on the economics of discrimination. The aim here is to provide the minimum background on the area for researchers in entrepreneurial finance or private equity who want to explore topics of race or gender. It also provides guidance for data collection steps and the host of alternative explanations that emerge in discrimination analysis.

This section does not provide the full review of the literature, which can be found in Cain (1986) (labor market; wages and income), Altonji and Blank (1999) (labor market; theory and empirical), Ross and Yinger (2002) (consumer lending), Blank et al. (2004) (measurement and detection), Fryer Jr (2011) (race and education), Charles and Guryan (2011) (literature review), Bertrand and Duflo (2017) (field experiments), Neumark (2018) (experiments in labor market) and Small and Pager (2020) (sociology). For a complete listing of economic research published in the top ten economics journals, see the appendix file of Bohren et al. (2019b).

5.1 Definitions and terms

Before summarizing the major economic theories of discrimination, it is useful to set terms and definitions.

5.2 Prejudice

Becker (1957) treats prejudice as a distaste for or aversion to cross-racial contact or interactions. The Latin *praejudicium* is "a preliminary hearing or presumption" and related to *praejudicio* "to prejudge" (Schneider, 2005). In the context of the discrimination and bias literature, this always has a negative connotation, but of course, prejudice can be positive. Schneider (2005) defines prejudice as "the set of affective reactions we have toward people as a function of their category memberships." (p. 27)

5.3 Discrimination

"Discrimination" is used in a variety of ways, depending on the speaker (economist vs sociologist) and setting (legal or academic). The definition used in the chapter is sometimes labeled "canonical" discrimination or taste-based discrimination. As Becker (1957) highlights, psychology has the first word on its definition, defining discrimination as when an individual's behavior toward another is not tied to "objective" fact.[1] However, such a definition is limiting because such actions can be both positive or negative. Instead, Becker proposes to let an individual's actions in the market provide the definition:

> *If an individual has a "taste for discrimination", he must act as if he will pay for something either directly or as reduced income, to be associated with some persons instead of others.*

Becker (1957, p. 12)

---

[1]A similar definition for discrimination is found in Schneider (2005): "Unjustified use of category information to make judgements about other people" (p. 29).

This definition clarifies that discrimination is an act. Within economics, this act involves a market transaction.[m] As we will see, there is a role for beliefs in the study of discrimination and differential outcomes by category, but the primary discrimination definition stems primarily from preference.

The bulk of research on discrimination sits broadly in labor economics. The extensive review of this literature in Altonji and Blank (1999) defines labor market discrimination as "a situation in which persons who provide labor market services and who are equally productive in a physical or material sense are treated unequally in a way that is related to an observable characteristic such as race, ethnicity or gender." (p. 3168). Here, "unequal" is different wages or demand for labor. Finally, the Heckman (1998) definition provides some guidance for empirical tests:

> At the level of a potential worker or credit applicant dealing with a firm, racial discrimination is said to arise if an otherwise identical person is treated differently by virtue of that person's race or gender, and race and gender by themselves have no direct effect on productivity. Discrimination is a causal effect defined by a hypothetical ceteris paribus conceptual experiment–varying race but keeping all else constant.
>
> **Heckman (1998, p. 102)**

We will discuss types of discrimination below.

5.3.1 Stereotypes

As the review of the entrepreneurial finance literature below demonstrate, the concept of stereotypes emerges in many settings where an outside capital provider evaluates an entrepreneurial investment opportunity. The earlier theoretical literature on discrimination (Phelps, 1972; Aigner and Cain, 1977; Beck et al., 2010; Arrow, 1973) assumed employers, landlords, etc. held and acted upon rational beliefs. Incorporating incorrect beliefs or stereotypes can impact how one tests for discrimination and constructs research designs.

As shown by Schneider (2005), pinning down a definition of stereotypes is difficult.[n] He offers a simple starting point: "stereotypes are qualities perceived to be associated with particular groups or categories of people" (p. 24). The economics literature has settled on defining stereotypes as "biased beliefs" (Hull, 2021) and "miscalibrated beliefs" (Egan et al., 2022). Bordalo et al. (2016) present a model where stereotypes emerge when:

> A decision maker assesses a target group by over- weighting its representative types, defined as the types that occur more frequently in that group than in a baseline reference group. Stereotypes formed this way contain a 'kernel of truth': they are rooted in true differences between groups.
>
> **Bordalo et al. (2016, p. 1753)**

---

[m]Nepotism is a close cousin to discrimination.
[n]Simply see the documented history of definitions (pp. 16–17).

A key feature of their model is that stereotypes are "context dependent" where an agent's assessment of an individual's target group depends on the chosen reference group.

5.4 Homophily

In its simplest form, homophily is strong "relationship between association and similarity." (McPherson et al., 2001). A common primary source for the concept of homophily is Lazarsfeld et al. (1954), who present two types. Status homophily is connected to formal or informal status, such as race and gender and value homophily, which is based on beliefs and values. Nearly all the tests or discussions of homophily in the literature reviewed below focus on status homophily.[o]

5.5 Framework

Detecting discrimination often reduces to an evaluation of an estimated regression coefficient. Therefore, consider a simple linear model connecting outcomes of interest in this chapter—e.g., firm founding, capital raising, revenues, or success—to firm and founder characteristics. The model provides a way to define discrimination.[p] Let the outcome of interest be financing amount Y:

$$Y = \gamma X + \beta Z + \epsilon \tag{1}$$

The vector X contains the characteristics that predict financing amount (e.g., investment opportunities, industry, profitability) and Z is a zero-one variable for gender, race, or ethnicity. If X contains all the variables that the researcher believes matter for financing outcomes and it is exogenous and Z is uncorrelated with ϵ, then $\hat{\beta} < 0$ reveals discrimination. Of course, any observational data from interesting economic environments used to estimate (1) rarely satisfy these conditions. The standard arguments about confounding omitted variables and sample selection when discussion estimates of (1) can be tied to the theories of discrimination below. For example, real-world data rarely includes all observables that correlation with outcome Y and those omitted could correlate with gender Z (e.g., risk preferences). It is possible that Z matters for financing or firm success (e.g., a firm performs better when a woman is in charge) but it simple captures the omitted variables. Finally, elements of X are endogenous: minorities face discrimination before raising capital and thus have different levels of X.

This final explanation is highlighted by Altonji and Blank (1999). They stress the distinction between the typical focus of empirical research—"current [...] market discrimination"—takes as given observed characteristics of entrepreneurs, often ignoring the effects of those characteristics on market outcomes ("premarket [...]

---

[o]One interesting area of study related to value homophily relates to the matching of investors and founders by risk tolerance or partisanship.
[p]Some of this structure is inspired by David Autor's lecture notes (https://economics.mit.edu/faculty/dautor/courses) and the framework in Ewens et al. (2014).

discrimination", p. 3169). For example, discriminatory behavior affects human capital investment in an entrepreneur's early life and results in different observables when researchers study the market outcomes.

The omitted variable concern notwithstanding, a literature has used (1) regressed by group to direct tests of discrimination. The major example of this is the Oaxaca-Blinder decomposition (Blinder, 1973; Oaxaca, 1973; Oaxaca and Ransom, 1994).[q] The basic intuition is that the in-group (e.g., whites or men) observed outcomes, such as wages can provide a benchmark relationship between observables and outcomes. Assuming the regression model is not missing relevant unobserved predictors (rarely), then one can estimate the role of observable differences (e.g., education, location, experience) separately from the discrimination component in the cross section of outcomes. Importantly, these methods provide bounds given the limited control variables available in many settings.

The next sections discuss the various models of differential treatment. Each section also summarizes how the typical research question in entrepreneurial finance could approach empirical tests of discrimination.

5.6 Taste-based discrimination

The traditional definition of discrimination presented in Section 5.1 is a close approximation to our first model of discrimination. Taste-based discrimination assumes that the decision-maker has a taste or disutility from hiring or investing in a certain group. This distaste for the out-group leads to a conscious decision to either not hire, pay lower wages, invest less capital, or demand more equity. This last feature of the model leads to common empirical tests. Agents acting in ways consistent with taste discrimination should sacrifice profits or returns (in partial equilibrium). The model predicts that for workers with the same observable characteristics, black or female workers will receive lower wages and be hired less often. A challenge (Arrow, 1973) with these two predictions is market equilibrium (though there is debate, see Charles and Guryan, 2008).

5.6.1 Tests and data for entrepreneurial finance

As we will see with the alternative models of discrimination and clear from (1), a simple difference in financing success (hiring) or outcomes (wages) is not enough to prove the existence of taste-based discrimination. One indirect way to rule it out is to study outcomes tied to financial performance. Suppose that investors prefer founders of the same gender because of a distaste for the opposite sex. Their willingness to pay for this disutility should manifest itself in worse outcomes (e.g., exit rates) when they invest in the same gender. Some examples of these tests include Fisman et al. (2017) study of lending in India and Ewens and Townsend (2020) analysis startup exit rates by investor gender. An important requirement here is identifying the gender of both sides of a relationship (e.g., investor–founder or employer–worker).

---

[q]See Jann (2008) for a Stata package of these decompositions that is careful about statistical inference.

5.7 **Statistical discrimination with correct beliefs**

Statistical discrimination (Phelps, 1972; Arrow, 1973; Aigner and Cain, 1977) posits that differential treatment by race or gender can emerge without a distaste by an individual.[r] One need only incorporate a combination of imperfect information and a (correct) correlation between characteristics (race, gender) and outcomes. One can view agents acting in ways consistent with this form of discrimination as a type of signal extraction problem. Indeed, Aigner and Cain (1977) present a model where a group characteristic not only signals productivity, but the variance of the signal difference by group status (this matters because of employer risk aversion). The Phelps (1972) and Arrow (1973) approaches work off the assumption that group status predicts quality and groups (in-truth) differ in average qualities.

Many researchers attempt to separate taste vs statistical discrimination explanations for their results.[s] This separation is challenging because models of statistical discrimination concern unobservable expectations and information sets. Not only that, but tests of statistical discrimination also need to account for the issues in discussed in Heckman and Siegelman (1993): when groups (gender or race) have the same expected quality, differences in the variance of those qualities can lead to spurious conclusions about the existence of discrimination.[t] Some examples of papers that have some success separating the two theories include Marx (2022), Mobius and Rosenblat (2006), Oreopoulos (2011), and Ewens and Townsend (2020) and the papers highlights in the Guryan and Charles (2013) review. In sum, researchers must approach any "tests for statistical discrimination" carefully because the model incorporates several critical assumptions.

5.7.1 *Tests and data for entrepreneurial finance*

Viewing statistical discrimination as signal extraction problem suggests it will be a major source of differential treatment in entrepreneurial finance settings. Investors face extreme levels of information asymmetry at the financing decision and after. Thus, many researchers explore heterogeneity in information or experience to separate taste vs statistical explanations. At the heart of most tests is some variation on information levels, information quality, or experience. For example, investors with more experience investing in women should have better assessments of their relative quality (absent taste-based explanations). Similarly, financial settings where entrepreneurs provide rich information or have repeated interactions of investors should exhibit different (smaller) gaps in outcomes by gender or race. Each of these cases have variation in the cross section or over time in the amount of information asymmetry and thus a predicted difference in value of the race or gender signal on their own.

---

[r] See Fang and Moro (2011) for a thorough review of the theoretical literature on statistical discrimination

[s] For a skeptical view of the possibility of such separation, see Neumark and Rich (2019).

[t] Neumark (2012) provides a test and method to extract discrimination in this setting following the framework.

5.8 Statistical discrimination with incorrect beliefs

If testing for taste vs statistical discrimination was not difficult enough, suppose that the expectations or beliefs about group quality were incorrect or biased. Inaccurate beliefs throw a wrench into standard approaches to detecting discrimination. Bohren et al. (2019a) describe two sources of such inaccurate beliefs and document the resulting identification challenge. One framework generates such beliefs in dynamic learning settings (Bohren et al., 2019b), from heuristics (Fiske, 1998), or the representativeness heuristic (Bordalo et al., 2016). Incomplete information, particularly about the data-generating process that produces information available to an employer or evaluator, can also generate inaccurate beliefs. This collection of research appears to have moved the expanded the default specification for tests of discrimination to at least allow for the possibility of incorrect or biased beliefs.

5.8.1 Tests and data for entrepreneurial finance

As shown by Bohren et al. (2019a), incorporating inaccurate beliefs results in a major identification problem, limiting one's ability to test for taste vs statistical discrimination separately. Statistical discrimination with inaccurate beliefs can often confound results. All hope is not lost, but the bar is much higher if one wants to rule out this type of statistical discrimination. Bohren et al. (2019b) show that along with collecting the standard decisions made by investors (e.g., finance or not) and information available to investors (e.g., industry, capital demand) one must first "collect data on the subjective beliefs of evaluators" (p. 5).[u] For example, a survey (Stanley, 2022) of investors commonly found in private equity funds shows that while they aim to invest in underrepresented money managers, the investors believe this comes at a financial performance cost. The more difficult step requires the researcher collect "data on the true outcome distributions […] required to determine whether beliefs are accurate" (p. 5). Ideally, this outcome data would be sourced from outside the researcher's own sample.

Hu and Ma (2021) are one of the first to take this path in entrepreneurial finance. Researchers interested in separating the three types of discrimination in this area may have to incorporate surveys into their research design and find a representative sample of entrepreneurial outcomes. Perhaps the literature should coalesce around a set of outcome distributions for researchers to use in discrimination studies. If these challenges are not overcome, the researcher must at least be careful to interpret results with the likely inaccurate beliefs confound as an explanation.

5.9 Other models of differential treatment

These three types of discrimination exhaust the explanations addressed in the literature reviewed in the next section. These models each represent a form of direct discrimination. Three alternative, nondirect perspectives are worthy of discussion as the

---

[u]Hull (2021) presents a set of tests that allow for inaccurate and accurate statistical discrimination, while having the ability to rule out canonical taste-based discrimination.

literature develops. The first is implicit discrimination, summarized in Bertrand et al. (2005). This type of discrimination is subconscious and supported by evidence from the social psychology literature. The authors propose the use of the Implicit Association Test (IAT) (Greenwald et al., 1998) either before a research design is implemented or on a subset of subjects in one's observational data study.

Most economists and their discrimination models assume deliberate actions. Small and Pager (2020) highlight the role institutional racism: "something other than individuals may discriminate by race" or "differential treatment by race that is either perpetuated by organizations or codified into law." (p. 52) Organizations—firms, governments, etc.—can discriminate even if individual agents have no such preference. For example, layoff rules based on seniority in firms or organizations where discrimination historically limited upward mobility of women and minorities can generate differential treatment without taste or statistical motivations. Similarly, hiring based on referrals in a world with homophily in network formation may weaken diversity.[v]

The third framework—systemic discrimination—considers the cumulative impact of direct and indirect discrimination. Bohren et al. (2022) summarize the fundamental feature of this approach: any analysis of direct discrimination that simply conditions on characteristics like wealth, education, or income fails to incorporate discrimination's role in any disparities in these nonrace or nongender characteristics. For example, many settings involve unbiased decision-makers who use these observable characteristics in their decisions while being unaware that the characteristics' correlate with group characteristics. This information gap can lead researchers to incorrectly conclude there is direct discrimination, when systemic is at play. Bohren et al. (2022) presents a measurement solution for systemic discrimination that uses a combination of observables and random variation of race or gender to separate the direct from the systemic.

Last, the framework of Eq. (1) and the empirical tests reviewed below each assume a clean, unambiguous signal of race or gender. Race is, however, not a simple binary variable because it is not a biological fact. The "constructivist" perspective from the sociological literature complicates traditional empirical tests of discrimination. Rose (2022) summarizes this:

> *The constructivist argues that race exists not as a natural, but as a social category forged over hundreds of years of political and historical processes. As a result, while individuals may observe others' physical traits, they interpret race; race in data and economic models therefore reflects both physical facts about people and the potentially non-neutral mental models people use to digest those facts.*
>
> **Rose (2022, p. 2)**

---

[v]Less relevant for our setting are Legal frameworks that often result in disparities by race or gender and have long-lasting impacts (e.g., redlining in real estate markets).

Rose (2022) reviews tests for discrimination—both taste and statistical—with this alternative perspective of race and presents modifications to methods (instruments) or assumptions (i.e., which observable factors matter for decisions) that can incorporate a constructivist view. This sociology-motivated approach is likely to grow in importance along with the others detailed above.

5.9.1 Tests and data for entrepreneurial finance

These alternative explanations for differential treatment by race and gender pose challenges for entrepreneurial finance researchers. The explanations tied to organizational issues such as referral networks or firing rules as most likely to apply to how venture capital firms are managed (less so for startups given their age). Research discussed in Section 6 shows that diversity is an issue for modern private equity investors and gender (and likely racial) composition matters for investment strategy. Some work has been done on how VC firms are organized or (Gompers and Lerner, 1999; Ivashina and Lerner, 2019; Malenko et al., 2021), but it is not known what role they play in the gender or racial gaps. Last, data on private startups rarely has clean variables for race, while investors have limited interactions with founders during fundraising. The constructivist perspective of racial identity suggests that incorporating racial perceptions into discrimination analyses will be fruitful in entrepreneurship research.

6 Race and gender patterns: Review of the literature

I now summarize the literature on the role of gender and race in entrepreneurial finance, covering topics from economics, labor, finance, and entrepreneurship. This section follows the frameworks presented in Section 3: founding the firm, gathering resources (what and from whom) and outcomes. Each section will look back on the theories discussed above. There are settings or choices where individuals must bring their own resources—both financial and human—and others where they must interact with outsiders (e.g., investors or the public). In the latter situation, we can consider the information and beliefs frameworks. Finally, each subsection summarizes the major lessons from the literature and important next steps in terms of unanswered questions or missing data.

6.1 Resources

Several steps must be completed before an entrepreneur founds a firm and raises capital. Starting a firm often requires personal capital before founding (Robb and Robinson, 2014). An extensive literature explores the connection between an individual's wealth and entrepreneurial entry. Indeed, the facts about startup capital discussed in Section 4 suggest that personal, prefounding resources of the founder matter for the decision. Evans and Jovanovic (1989) conclude that liquidity or financing constraints bind, and an individual's wealth has predictive power for entrepreneurship. Bradford (2003) documents wealth accumulation differences between black and white entrepreneurs, finding that the former hold a lower fraction of family wealth. Derenoncourt et al. (2022)'s 160-year panel shows this wealth disparity has been a persistent feature of the economy with unclear paths for convergence in the medium term. On top of these wealth disparities, Levine and Rubinstein (2017) show that income and household structure matters as well: entrepreneurs (self-employed in incorporated firms) tend to come from high-income, two-parent households.

Hurst and Lusardi (2004) push back against claims that wealth is a major predictor of entrepreneurship. Rather, they find that the relationship between the two is flat, except in the right tail of the wealth distribution. Kerr and Nanda (2011) address the mixed evidence on the role of wealth and entrepreneurship by highlighting the heterogeneity of startups—high-growth and innovative vs small business—and how this interacts with capital demand. One stream of research supporting a role for studies home equity valuation (i.e., collateral) and entrepreneurship (see Fairlie and Krashinsky, 2012; Corradin and Popov, 2015; Harding and Rosenthal, 2017; Schmalz et al., 2017).[w] Indeed, the 2007 Survey of Business Owners (SBO) shows that home equity supported the initial funding of 12% of employer–businesses in the United States (Kerr et al., 2022) bring rich Census data to the question to discover that many of the users of home equity for startup capital are confined to less productive, lower educated founders. Although they conclude that changes in home equity cannot explain increases in entrepreneurship, their results and others illustrate that personal savings and collateral are key resources for entrepreneurs.

Some parts of a founder's human capital depend on unequal distribution of wealth and information in the economy. We find one example in the Fairlie and Robb (2007a) analysis of small business performance. They find striking differences in sales, profits, employment, and closures between white and black-owned business. The missing pieces that help explain these differences are lower work experience in family businesses and business in their startup industries. This result shows that disparities beyond wealth or collateral could generate differences in race or gender in high-growth firms.

Lessons and next steps. The racial and gender disparities in resources necessary to become a high-growth entrepreneur are unlikely to dissipate in the short-run. Thus, researchers using observational data to understand the role of race and gender should continue to incorporate these facts into their modeling and interpretation of results. In its simplest form, coefficient estimates are affected by a host of economically important omitted variables. As with any other empirical analysis, the solution is not inclusion of imperfect proxies for antecedents to entrepreneurship. These proxies could be related to discrimination, "caus[ing] the unexplained differences to understate the role that discrimination" in the gap in outcomes.[x] Instead, the proxies related

---

[w]Also see Bellon et al. (2021) who study the effect of wealth shocks and business formation.
[x]Guryan and Charles (2013, p. F419).

to founder backgrounds and resources should be improved with a renewed focus on building deep rather than broad samples of entrepreneurs.

6.2 Entry and founding

This section of the chapter is extensive. There are several reasons for this attention to the supply-side of entrepreneurial outcomes. First, recall the facts documented in Section 4: the set of new firms—before raising capital—have low participation rates by women and most minorities. Any analysis of differences in financings, growth and outcomes by gender or race must benchmark using the entry rates. Similarly, these antecedents should inform empirical or theoretical analysis in terms of control variables or economic mechanisms. For example, because childhood social networks play an important role in labor market decisions, any analysis will have a likely unobserved confound. We may be unable to control for these founder or investor characteristics, however, understanding its scope will help us assess coefficient bias through standard omitted variable arguments. Third, some theories of discrimination incorporate beliefs about type and its correlation with race or gender. The academic literature provides us a starting point for correct beliefs about these objects. Finally, although much of the surveyed literature focuses on entrepreneurial choice, the frictions and predictors are generally about labor market choices. They thus also affect the entry and characteristics of bank loan officers, angel investors, venture capitalists and crowdfunding participants.

6.2.1 Career goals and flexibility

Workers evaluate the choice of becoming an entrepreneur much like they evaluate becoming a doctor, botanist, or surf instructor. One important factor is compensation and its relationship to hours worked. Running an entrepreneurial firm is appealing to many because of the nonpecuniary benefits (e.g., Moskowitz and Vissing-Jørgensen, 2002), which includes the ability to set one's hours, schedule, and task list. High-growth entrepreneurial firms in innovative sectors are likely at the extreme of hours required and flexibility demands on their founding team.[y] Where running these firms affords more flexibility, compensation or hours required than alternative career options, there is scope for different choices by gender (less so for race). Goldin (2014) analysis of the changing gender wage gap provides critical insights for female entrepreneurs.

Goldin (2014) first documents that the while the gender wage and income gap has shrunk over the last 40 years, sizeable gaps remain. Those gaps are prominent in high-paying occupations, which are the industries and professions where women have made some of the largest gains in experience and education. Next, she finds that those industries with persistently large gaps in "business" (examples include

---

[y]The chapter's focus on high-growth entrepreneurial firms that intend to hire employees implies that we do not discuss the forms of entrepreneurship (e.g., self-employment) that may be more valuable for individuals requiring flexibility. See Parker (2018, Section 8.2.2) for a discussion of this topic.

"Chief executive and legislator," "Financial manager," "Economist" and "Accountant and auditor")[z] Goldin argues the variation in the gender gap can partially be explained by occupations' differences in "job flexibility." For example, occupations that require not just many hours worked, but the specific block of hours worked: some jobs require 70 hours a week, but only some that do must pay twice the pay of the 35-hour position. These nonlinear earnings profiles could cause differential pay by gender if demands for flexibility are different. The model presented in the paper has direct implications for entrepreneurs, as it rests on imperfect substitutability between workers. As Goldin writes, the entrepreneur "cannot fully delegate responsibility." (p. 1104). The facts and theory presented in Goldin (2014) are central to our understanding of the initial gender gap in entrepreneurship.[aa]

Entrepreneurial ventures require significant time, and those pursuing high-growth strategies have high failure rates. The decision to become a full-time entrepreneur requires leaving wage employment. Researchers have shown (Mincer and Ofek, 1982; Light and Ureta, 1995; Albrecht et al., 1999) that interruptions to waged careers result in lower earning when workers return. Gottlieb et al. (2022) study whether improvements in job protections around parental leave encouraged more entrepreneurship. The results show that the risk of lower pay to experiment with entrepreneurship could inhibit entry. The paper's setting of mother parental leave highlights one channel through which this career risk could disproportionately affect aspiring female entrepreneurs. Other legal institutions can inhibit entry by underrepresented groups or increase the risk of failing after founding. For example, Marx (2022) finds that legal risks around noncompete rules disproportionately discourage entry by female entrepreneurs and results lower use of their professional networks when seeking talent.

6.2.2 Family concerns

Issues surrounding family and motherhood could be connected to preferences for hours' flexibility. I discuss two recent papers in this literature, which are part of a larger literature extensively summarized in Parker (2018). Researchers have explored correlations between job protections, childcare, and healthcare provision (e.g., Thébaud, 2015) and entrepreneurship, however, few have found causal links. Zandberg (2021) asks whether access to reproductive care and control over the time of having a child affects women's choice to become an entrepreneur. He finds that access to abortion correlates with female entrepreneurship and isolates a causal channel using law changes that impacted access. The results demonstrate that part of the gender participation gap could be explained by family considerations that

---

[z]See the online appendix with the full breakdown here: https://www.aeaweb.org/articles?id=10.1257/aer.104.4.1091.
[aa]Also see Lombard (2001) for an estimation of the tradeoff between flexible work hours and self-employment.

disproportionately impact women. Core (2020) investigates similar questions using Italian data and finds similar results. The effects of lower maternity risk are largest for innovative entrepreneurs.

6.2.3 Early-life experiences

What role do early-life experiences play in explaining the gap in entrepreneurial entry between men and women and whites and blacks? Consider first the choice to patent or innovate, a feature of many high-growth startups. Many entrepreneurial firms pursue innovative business ideas and patent. Thus, the pool of innovators and inventors provides a useful benchmark for an important subset of entrepreneurs. Bell et al. (2019) use linked tax records and patented inventions to separate the role of ability and environment in the choices to become an inventor. Several important facts emerge that inform the entrepreneurship and private equity literature. Race, gender, and wealth all strongly predict a child's probability of inventing. The gap by race and gender does not disappear after controlling for early childhood math test scores, demonstrating that environment drives innovative choices. Girls' eventual choice of specific patent industry depends on whether they grew up in an area where women inventing in the same innovative area. This shows that role-model and social networks can explain much of the differences in patenting choices.

Most researchers are not fortunate enough to have data on the full history of entrepreneurs or investors. Instead, they often have databases of existing (rather than potential) startups or those that have raised outside capital. When combined with work on intergenerational predictors of entrepreneurship (e.g., Lindquist et al., 2015), Bell et al. (2019) show that researchers in entrepreneurship and PE must incorporate the complex—and often unobserved—supply-side and prefounding decisions in any analysis of race or gender.

A large labor literature (surveyed in Ioannides and Loury (2004)) documents a connection between early-life social networks and information sharing to job market outcomes. Several studies explore these questions for the decision to become an entrepreneur. Mishkin (2021) documents that a woman's propensity to become an entrepreneur depends on whether her father was an entrepreneur. However, this channel is dampened when she has brothers. The paper argues that roughly 15% of the gender gap in entrepreneurship could be explained by this crowding out effect in early childhood. Additional evidence of experiences and network effects in found in Einiö et al. (2019). They find entrepreneurs create products that match their own demographics or experiences with certain groups. As most entrepreneurial firms are small and have few products, we can draw a connection between these results and industry of founding. Angel investors and venture capitalists are also susceptible to early-life experiences on their investment decisions. Duchin et al. (2021) show that CEO's backgrounds, such as where they grew up and what type of high-school they attended, can predict how much they prefer to invest in projects managed by men.

Where one grows up also predicts entrepreneurship. Guiso et al. (2021) show that whether an individual grows up in an area with many firms predicts entrepreneurial entry. The results suggest that early-life social networks and contacts are likely unobservable factors in any analysis of gender or race in entrepreneurship.[ab]

6.2.4 Stereotypes

Another explanation for the gender gap in entrepreneurship is stereotypes (Schneider, 2005; Bordalo et al., 2016), where both entrepreneurs and their potential investors hold beliefs that genders have productivity advantages in some industries or activities. These beliefs can impact the extensive margin (entry), startup industry, capital demand and investor reaction to gender. This section briefly summarizes some important results that could help us understand the founding decision differences by gender. Reuben et al. (2014) conducts an experiment that reveals subjects hold stereotypes that men perform better at math than women. The differences in subject behavior changed little when provided full information about the potential hire.[ac] Although their analysis applied to science career outcomes, expectations about this treatment could lead women to self-select into different industries, while investors that hold such stereotypes may prefer male founders.

Culture and self-stereotypes can also explain some of the sorting of women (less so by race) into certain industries. Laboratory evidence suggests that stereotypes of self and others could impact founding team formation choice and investors' assessment of such teams. Coffman (2014) shows that individuals contribute less to team production when individuals match with gender-incongruent tasks (Coffman, 2014). Several papers document female founders sort into "gender-congruent" industries (e.g., Hebert, 2020; Gompers and Wang, 2017b; Goldin, 2014). The tendency for occupational sorting will emerge in the discussion of financing outcomes, but there are possible positive effects. In their work on innovators in patents, Koning et al. (2020) document that the increased representation of female inventors coincides toward with a shift toward inventions that are better matched to the needs of women ("female-focused patents"). The innovative choices of lead inventors do not appear to be a simple substitution of inventor gender, but a shift in the composition of inventions. This result has implications for the continued increase in female and, to a lesser extent, minority participation in entrepreneurial firms and private equity.

6.2.5 Preferences and beliefs

The final set of topics around the entrepreneurial founding decision concerns beliefs and preferences. To start, consider the financial calculation faced by a potential entrepreneur. An entrepreneur's founding decision depends on her assessment of the expected utility, weighed against the risk and outside options. Moskowitz and

---

[ab] Also see Markussen and Røed (2017) show that entrepreneurial peers predict entrepreneurship in Norway. For a theoretical treatment of networks and employment choice see Calvó-Armengol and Jackson (2004).

[ac] Del Carpio and Guadalupe (2022) conduct a similar analysis using a field experiment and conclude that the differential treatment for women could result in lower job applications to male-dominated sectors.

Vissing-Jørgensen (2002) document the returns to private equity or entrepreneurial investment do not exceed that of public firms. In contrast, Levine and Rubinstein (2020) argue that self-employed workers who choose to incorporate their firm earn more than their salary-earning counterparts do.[ad] Given the higher risk and low diversification associated with running a small business, if the expected return is indeed lower, then one must rationalize the entrepreneurial choice. The authors show that large nonpecuniary benefits or over-estimates of success could help explain these choices. These conclusions inform the results documented below because unequal capital access or discrimination by investors are impediments after the evaluation of the risk-return tradeoff. If the returns to entrepreneurship are worse for women or minorities (e.g., because of worse capital access or human capital), then the role of nonpecuniary benefits or expectations of success must be larger to justify entry.

Next, an individual's beliefs about their own ability and the abilities of their team can affect their decision to become an entrepreneur. Bordalo et al. (2019) and earlier work in Coffman (2014) find that individuals of all genders have lower self-confidence about their expected performance and are less willing to contribute idea in areas where their gender is stereotypically underrepresented. Their results speak directly to the investor–founder interaction at the deal formation stage because they show that stereotypes also impact beliefs about others. The experimental setting provides direct evidence for one source of incorrect beliefs and likely plays a role in some patterns observed in early-stage financing described below. Stereotypes about oneself and beliefs about the ability likely play a role in the occupational sorting observed in the economy, and startup industry choice specifically (Scott and Shu, 2017; Gompers and Wang, 2017b; Ewens and Townsend, 2020; Hebert, 2020). Last, women may hold themselves to higher standards when making choices about seeking capital or gathering resources (Chari and Goldsmith-Pinkham, 2017; Kolev et al., 2020) or have lower reported self-evaluations than men when interacting with investors (Exley and Kessler, 2022). Evidence for this characteristic's impact on entrepreneurs is found in Howell and Nanda (2019) who show that random exposure to venture capitalists investors improves the chance of raising VC only for men. The gender difference stems from female entrepreneurs' reluctance to reach out to potential investors for capital.

An extensive literature explores differences in risk tolerance, preferences for competition and willingness to negotiate by gender.[ae]Biasi and Sarsons (2020) results on differences in bargaining outside the lab are informative for startup formation. They find that after a law change that allowed for flexible pay, a pay gap

---

[ad]Add to this debate about the return to entrepreneurship any "founder penalty" related to the cost of leaving wage employment. The argument is that employers may be concerned about fit with former entrepreneurs. Kacperczyk and Younkin (2021) conduct audit and experimental studies that show a penalty for male, but not female exfounders.

[ae]This discussion ignores personality traits of entrepreneurs. An extensive review of the literature and unanswered questions is in Kerr et al. (2017).

between male and female teachers emerged (it did not exist prior) and is driven by male teachers' higher propensity to negotiate. Importantly, this difference is entirely driven by men's increased likelihood of bargaining with a male superior (there are no differences between the genders when the superior is female). Combined with experimental results (Babcock and Laschever, 2009; Dittrich and Leipold, 2014; Exley and Kessler, 2022), these differences in negotiation preferences could have effects on the interaction between founders and investors. On one hand, the bulk of VCs are white males (Gompers and Wang, 2017b). On the other hand, negotiating over sales of equity securities, board seats and other control rights is complex. Thus, preferences and skills in negotiation could impact entry choice and outcomes (e.g., through valuation or control rights).[af] Moreover, whether gender differences in risk tolerance are innate or driven by social stereotypes (e.g., see Booth and Nolen (2012) who use of variation in same-sex schooling) may not impact observational data on investor choices.

Next, differences in risk tolerance and preferences for competition emerge in nearly all studies of gender in entrepreneurship. Results that show entrepreneurs are more risk tolerant (e.g., Hvide and Panos, 2014). Croson and Gneezy (2009)'s review article provides a complete overview of the theory and empirical literature, which can be succinctly summarized as follows: women are more risk averse and more averse to competition than men.[ag] These differences have clear implications for entry decisions and assessments of founders by investors and have been tested in different ways in Ewens and Townsend (2020) and Hebert (2020). To date, there is only sparse evidence for the role of these preference differences in the founding decisions or funding outcomes.

The last set of beliefs concern the individual's expectations about treatment by capital providers. If the founder knows little about the entrepreneurial ecosystem or gender gap in founding, they need only look at the facts about the wage gap (Blau and Kahn, 2017). Their own experiences with the standard labor market may mimic what researchers have found in audit studies with large employers (Bertrand and Mullainathan, 2004; Kline et al., 2021, 2021). One challenge faced by women and minorities raising capital is investors' perceptions about differences in participation rates or outcomes. Indeed, as presented in the discussion of economic theories of discrimination, beliefs are central to how researchers separate explanations for differential treatment. If an investor believes that the lower participation rate of blacks follows from human capital or risk preference differences, then any differential treatment observed in the data could be explained by statistical discrimination. Alternatively, if the differences are believed to stem from past discrimination or opportunities, then differential outcomes at the investor stage could have little to do with bias or discrimination by investors. Rich survey and experimental

---

[af]Wiswall and Zafar (2018) find that undergraduates differ in preferences for job flexibility (women prefer) and these differences translate into college major and eventual job choice.
[ag]Examples of laboratory work on these topics is Niederle and Vesterlund (2007) and Buser et al. (2014).

evidence in Alesina et al. (2021) show that beliefs about inequities depend on political affiliation and for teenagers, their parents' political affiliation. Such work extended to investors in private equity and venture capital would be an important step in the literature.

Finally, potential founders may simply assume the worst when they gather resources for their new firm. Fairlie et al. (2022) show just a possibility in their study of credit access differences by race (discussed more below). The most striking result from the work concerns the business owners' attempts to close the gap by seeking more finance. Here, they find that fear of rejection matters:

> *Black entrepreneurs apply for bank loans less frequently than white entrepreneurs. This stems largely from differences in the fear of rejection. Overall, Black entrepreneurs are about three times more likely to state that they did not apply for credit when needed for fear of having their loan application denied. [...] even black founders in the top quartile of the credit score distribution are more than twice as likely to report a fear of denial than white founders with below median credit scores.*

Fairlie et al. (2022), p. 5)

This result is a reminder that equilibrium-thinking should guide interpretations of empirical results. Researchers should assume that underrepresented founders have read chapters like this and formed correct assessments of their success likelihoods, which impacts observed entry rates that researchers use.

Lessons and next steps. This section summarized a literature that helps us understand the gender and racial gap in participation of both founders and private equity investors. Any analysis of differential outcomes in funding or success must incorporate these explanations. In most datasets, the explanations are complex omitted variables that confound the estimation of objects like the coefficient estimate on "Female." The topics above are nonexhaustive but should capture the bulk of the mechanisms that could generate differential entry. More research and improved data will help researchers continue to disentangle the relative roles of these channels. Researchers in entrepreneurial finance may benefit from moving into the lab to explore preference and beliefs in entrepreneurial settings.

6.3 Raising capital

This section summarizes the literature on the differences in financing outcomes for women and minorities. Absent significant personal wealth or collateralizable assets, founders of high-growth startups need to raise outside capital. Frictions in this step— i.e., financing or liquidity constraints—are the focus of large literature in economics and finance (e.g., Beck et al., 2000; Black and Strahan, 2002; Kerr and Nanda, 2011). Finance academics spend much of their research energy on financial characteristics of firms, ignoring all the other critical parts of running a new business. For example, Bhandari and McGrattan (2021) find that "sweat equity"—the business owners' time and expenses to manage and build a business in the United States—is the same magnitude as the value of the fixed assets in those businesses. This section's analysis of capital raising applies to this setting, where those expenses (and fixed assets) demand that the firm raise external financing.

6.3.1 Debt

I now summarize the recent literature on borrowing by entrepreneurs and small business. This is an ideal place to start, as Robb and Robinson (2014) find that newly founded firm's early top financing sources are personal balance sheets and external debt. The bank finance setting is relatively simple: startup seeks loan, meets bank loan officer(s), loan officer decides whether to extend loan and, if extended, on what terms. One natural place to look for impacts of gender and race is at the loan officer step. Such data is difficult to acquire in the United States and, to my knowledge, has been explored rarely in small business lending.[ah] However, research on bank lending in India (Fisman et al., 2017) finds that loan officer and lenders personal characteristics predict lending. Lenders are more likely to lend to individuals with the same ethnicity, and those loans outperform others in the lender's portfolio.

Blanchflower et al. (2003) is one of the first studies investigating discrimination in small business lending.[ai] Using the 1993 and 1997 National Surveys of Small Business Finances, they explore borrower expectations and lending success rates by race. As shown in Fairle et al. (2022), black borrowers in these surveys expect to be rejected for credit and often do not even attempt to apply for loans. They document a higher loan denial rate for black applicants after controlling for a host of creditworthiness variables, education, wealth, and industry. Conditional on successfully borrowing, black business owners are charged higher interest rates (again, even after a large set of controls are included). When combined with the lower rate of application due to fear of rejection, these results point to significant barriers to credit for black small business owners.

One positive view of the lending market for underrepresented minorities and women is the credit score system. Indeed, the Federal Reserve concluded that credit score models can predict credit outcomes and exhibit no bias against a particular race or gender (see Braunstein, 2010). Robb and Robinson (2018) find that forward-looking credit scores have similar predictive power with borrower characteristics across race.

Several studies investigate small business lending and entrepreneurship. Robust differences between cost of credit also appear in a study of female borrowers in Italy (Alesina et al., 2013). A common concern with such differences in the cost of debt is unobserved differences in risk. The authors find no evidence that female borrowers are riskier than their male counterparts. Another study of Italian small business borrowers (Bellucci et al., 2010) shows that female borrowers have more difficulty

---

[ah]There is some evidence that loan officer gender is predictive of loan portfolio performance (Beck et al., 2013).

[ai]A related Blanchard et al. (2008) study exploits similar data to explore the types of discrimination that could explain differential treatment of black, Hispanic, and female small business borrowers.

acquiring credit, though the cost of acquired credit is like that of male borrowers. This is also a rare study that connects borrower and loan officer gender, finding that female loan officers demand less collateral from female borrowers. Consistent with discrimination in lending markets, Chatterji and Seamans (2012) show that exogenous increases in access to credit card debt leads to more entrepreneurial entry for Black entrepreneurs.

Finally, Fairlie et al. (2022) revisit the question of small business credit access for Black entrepreneurs. The long time series of survey waves in the KFS allow them to track firms' ability to make us for any early-stage financing constraints. As found in other work, Black entrepreneurs struggle to raise external debt at founding. This disadvantage remains up to 8 years after firm founding, suggesting that information and firm experience do not close the gap.

The collection of results on debt finance for startups founded by disadvantaged minorities and women paints of picture of fundraising deficiencies. Few studies have at their disposal clean exogenous variation to tease out discrimination from incorrect beliefs or stereotypes. That said, the rich data on loan applications used in many of the research goes a long way toward ruling out standard rational explanations for gaps in debt finance.

6.3.2 Equity financing

After external debt, a common source of capital for the high-growth startups is equity provided by angel investors, venture capitalists, or private equity investors. Before detailing the literature on the role of gender and race in financing outcomes, consider some of the startup characteristics investors use in their investment decisions. In their survey of 885 investors, Gompers et al. (2020) seek to understand the venture capitalist's decision-making. Most important for this chapter are their results on the role of the founding or management team.[aj] The survey results show that VCs rank management team as the most important characteristic both for evaluating investment opportunities and assessing investment success. Thus, there is a clear path for gender or race to (implicitly or explicitly) to enter the financing outcomes reviewed below.

Gompers et al. (2020) also details the deal evaluation process (i.e., preinvestment screening). The interactions between investors and founders seeking capital involve direct inquiries from the former, pitches/presentations to investors in organized events or direct contact by entrepreneurs (Gornall and Strebulaev, 2020). These interactions often require that the investor make quick decisions with limited information, again providing an opportunity for stereotype formation, statistical discrimination, and inference of race in the constructivist view. Several studies of the deal evaluation stage show gender and race can emerge in decision-making.

[aj]Also see Bernstein et al. (2017) for an experiment on angel investors' investment preferences. They similarly find that management team is the main feature of the startup for evaluation.

First, evidence from founder video investment proposals (i.e., pitches) shows that investors respond to intangible characteristics, such as positivity, and treat genders differently in funding decisions based on delivery characteristics (Huang et al., 2021; Hu and Ma, 2021). Brooks et al. (2014) show in multiple settings that investors prefer the same pitches when presented by men, while attractiveness of the entrepreneur has additional predictive power. At the prefunding stage, Kanze et al. (2018) document that investors ask male and female founders different questions. Questions posed to women are more likely to address issues around not losing capital or maintaining gains. The authors argue that investors' gendered focus translates into different funding levels by gender.[ak] Combined with the possibility that investors have costly, limited attention, the prefinancing information-gatherings setting may only amplify issues of incorrect beliefs and prejudice (e.g., Bartoš et al., 2016).

Absent a clear experimental strategy or clean exogenous variation that impacts the composition of founders, researchers have instead focused on creating comprehensive samples of firms that are plausibly seeking capital. With a sample of startups that demand outside capital, it is relatively easy to document any gaps in participation by gender or race. Challenges emerge when one aims to explain the gaps. As we will see, researchers focus on empirical predictions of the economic theories of discrimination detailed in Section 5. Ewens and Townsend (2020) build a risk set of capital-raising startups from data provided by AngelList.[al] The website platform allowed entrepreneurs to postinvestment opportunities and investors to signal interest in multiple ways. Some 16% of the entrepreneurs on the platform are women, again demonstrating stark differences in entry rates by gender. Male investors—over 90% of all active investors on the platform—express less interest in female-founded startups that are otherwise observationally like their male peers. This pattern reverses among the set of female investors.[am] Simply, investor gender predicts differential treatment by gender.[an] Using rich data on the entrepreneurial firms and founders, they rule out risk preference or monitoring advantage explanations. A test of outcome differences within the male investors' portfolios shows that the preference for male founders is best explained by bias.

[ak]The differences in questions at the early stage may also translate into how the VCs interact with their portfolio companies. For example, Egan et al. (2022) find that male bosses are more likely to fire or punish female employees after misconduct.

[al]Becker-Blease and Sohl (2007) surveyed angel investor platforms, gathering data on the founder proposals. They can thus ask what fraction of financing proposals are from female founders and what fraction successfully raise capital. They find that while only 9% of proposals originate from female founders, they experience similar funding success rates than male founders.

[am]Similar patterns are found in Einiö et al. (2019) who document homophily patterns among female-founded startups. Female-founded firms are more likely to raise capital from female investors and hire female inventors.

[an]In the long-run, increased participation by female investors could thus dampen gender gaps. Evidence for changing composition of investors is found in Calder-Wang and Gompers (2021). They show that male venture capitalists are more likely to hire female partners in their firm when they have daughters.

Two recent studies use near-population-level datasets of startups to study an ideal risk set of potential capital raising firms. Hebert (2020) studies the populations of incorporated startups in France to explore differences in founding and financing rates. Some 26% of firms have female founders and those firms are 18% less likely to raise external finance than male-founded firms. This capital raising disadvantage reverses when the analysis focuses on gender-dominated industries: women in women-dominated sectors are more successful in raising capital. Outcomes tests show that founders in sectors not dominated by their own gender outperform, which suggests investors use a higher threshold. The evidence is consistent with investors using context-dependent stereotypes when evaluating startups. Guzman and Kacperczyk (2019) build a similar sample of US incorporated firms to study questions about the entrepreneurship gender gap. They first document that 17% of all such firms or those with a clear growth orientation are female-founded. These firms are 63% less likely to raise external finance. The authors decompose these differences in funding success and conclude that the majority is explained by initial firm characteristics. Differences in signals about firm growth prospects and investor sophistication suggest that much of the remaining funding gap could be explained by statistical discrimination.[ao] These two papers demonstrate that rich observational data and a clean set of capital-seeking startups can provide insight on gender or racial funding gaps. The main challenges for teasing out explanations stem from incomplete information about the demographics of available investors and what information is available in their investment decision.

Some research suggests that women are not always at a disadvantage when seeking to or raising early-stage equity. First, Gornall and Strebulaev (2020) conduct a large field experiment that sent cold emails from fictional founders to real investors.[ap] The experimental variation allows them to ask what is the effect of race (Asian) and gender on the response rates? They find a positive effect of female names, which is broadly consistent with some of the summary of other experiments summarized in Bertrand (2020).[aq] Combined with the results summarized above, the evidence suggests that bias in the later stages (e.g., Ewens and Townsend, 2020; Hebert, 2020) must reverse this early-stage preference for women. Next, Scott and Shu (2017) find that highly qualified women from MIT are less likely to become an entrepreneur if their idea lacks intellectual protection. However, women who decide to pursue their idea-full time experience no disadvantage at raising VC than their male counterparts. This result has limited generalization to broader gender gap and discrimination topics. Conditioning on entry generates a sample of founders who may be higher

---

[ao]These results do not incorporate the subsequent literature on incorrect or biased beliefs, so conclusions about the presence of standard statistical discrimination are limited.

[ap]Also see Zhang (2020) for a set of field experiments on this issue. Bias for or against female and minority entrepreneurs depends on expectations of investor interaction with the startup.

[aq]Data from surveys of angel investors platforms in Becker-Blease and Sohl (2007) shows that financing proposals sent by women to angel platforms experienced no difference in funding success than male founders.

quality or difference risk preferences than the overall population of interest (the same critique applies to all studies that condition of fundraising).

6.3.3 Other capital sources

Venture capital, angel financing, and external debt are just part of the capital options available to entrepreneurs. Recent changes in the debt and equity landscape allow the "crowd" to evaluate and invest in startups. Some argue increasing participation of retail investors and other nontraditional investors in entrepreneurial firms will increase competition and ensure that discrimination is more costly. As a preview, the evidence is mixed whether the crowd behaves differently than institutional investors. One area studies peer-to-peer lending platforms. Duarte et al. (2012) find that lenders on Prosper.com incorporate the appearance of the borrower in their decision. Borrowers whose pictures appear more trustworthy are more likely to raise funds and pay less for credit. They also find that those that appear more trustworthy have better credit scores and lower default rates. Pope and Sydnor (2011) find that black borrowers on the same platform raise debt at lower rates and, when successful, pay higher interest rates. There is no evidence that women experience lower rates of funding.

Younkin and Kuppuswamy (2018) and Gafni et al. (2021) study reward-based crowdfunding sites. The former finds that offerings managed by Black entrepreneurs are less successful at raising capital. Gafni et al. (2021) find that, on average, female entrepreneurs are more successful, while backers (i.e., investors) prefer to contribute to same gender projects. The most recent change in the crowdfunding market is the introduction of equity sales (since 2016). We need more time and data for definitive answers on questions related to race and gender in this area.[ar]

Lessons and next steps. The evidence on capital raising by women and minorities paints a picture of disparities across multiple platforms and sources. The three major types of discrimination detailed in Section 5 play some role in these patterns. For those studies that can identify the characteristics of investors, there is clear evidence of matching by own gender and some evidence in favor of taste-based explanations. The literature's next steps involve collecting better data about the supply and demand-side of the market, possibly adding surveys to assess expectations, stereotypes, and true outcome distributions (Bohren et al., 2019a,b; Hu and Ma, 2021).

6.4 Outcomes

This last section asks whether gender or race of financed entrepreneurs predicts their startups' success. Parker (2018) provides a thorough review of female and minority entrepreneurial firms' performance across a range of small firm types. We first consider venture capital-backed firms.

[ar]Bapna and Ganco (2021) conduct a field experiment using a company raising $846,000. Email solicitations to the 8050 subjects (i.e., the crowd) show that female investors prefer female founders, but male investors exhibit no differential treatment.

Raina (2019) shows that the among VC-backed startups, female-founded firms underperform. He exploits variation in the characteristics of the startup's investors, finding that female underperformance is confined to those backed by male venture capitalists. The results suggest that even overcoming the gender or racial gaps at founding or financing may not translate to outcome equality. The differences could be explained by resource allocation choices of male investors or mismatch of skills between founder and investor. One countervailing force to this issue is the changing diversity of VC firms (e.g., Capital, 2021; Funds, 2019). Here, Calder-Wang and Gompers (2021) find that more VC funds with a more diverse team of general partners (in gender) perform better at the deal and fund-level.[as] Gompers et al. (2022) provide additional evidence that gender and racial composition of investing firms matters for the partner's performance, and, by extension, the investments made by investors. They find female VCs underperform their male colleagues by 10%–15%. This difference stems from female VCs' lower benefit from their colleague's skills and experience. Given the active role that VCs play in startups and the known matching within-gender, the incomplete resource sharing among VC partners poses significant costs to female and minority entrepreneurs.

The underrepresentation of Black and Latino founders in VC-backed startups results in insufficient information to make definite statements about outcomes. We can learn much about relative performance by race from the Fairlie and Robb (2008) work using Census data on small business. The story that emerges is best summarized by the authors:

> *[A] substantial proportion of black firms are less successful, leading to average outcomes that are worse than for white firms. In contrast to these patterns, Asian American-owned firms have average outcomes more similar to–and sometimes better than–those of white-owned firms. Overall, these racial patterns in business outcomes have remained roughly unchanged over the past two decades.*
>
> **Fairlie and Robb (2008, p. 2)**

These differences manifest as lower profits, higher closure rates and a striking difference in annual sales ($439,579 and $74,018 for white and black-owned business, respectively). Fairlie and Robb (2007b) connect these outcome differences to detailed histories of entrepreneurs beyond the usual education and experience controls. They show that although business inheritance differs by race, it cannot explain success outcome variation. Instead, Black entrepreneurs' lower experience working in both a previous family business and in their startup's industry helps explain much of the residual gap in startup performance. These human capital differences venture capitalists and private equity investors significant opportunities to add value to these black-owned startups. **Lessons and next steps**. This section documents actual differences in outcomes for startups run by women and black founders. Given the other features of early-stage financing, it is challenging to disentangle the sources of these disparities.

[as]Gompers et al. (2016) find that investing firms also exhibit within-group matching (e.g., by ethnicity).

It does not take much to argue that, at the least, lower rates of financing success, lower financing amounts and higher costs of capital put these firms at a disadvantage. We need more research to separate out the role of preexit differences driven by discrimination and any role gender or race by at the exit itself (e.g., discrimination, risk tolerance)

7 Changes to the financing landscape

The disparities documented across the startup life cycle and studied in the literature reviewed here could change for many reasons. In this section, we discuss three areas where change is most likely to impact gender and race in startups. The first is the regulatory environment that has changed the early-stage financing environment. Next, the changing supply of capital and technology connecting investor to investment impacts bargaining power. The last area represents directed efforts by governments and private entities to address the disparities head-on. Beyond a summary of the financing landscape, this section provides directions for future researchers' data collection efforts or searches for natural experiments.

7.1 Regulatory changes

Since 2010, new federal legislation and the changes implemented by the Securities and Exchange Commission have resulted in several major deregulations of the private capital markets. Congress, the White House, and regulators were motivated by (perceived) low capital access for some startups and an inability for retail investors to gain exposure to the private capital markets. Perhaps most relevant for our discussion here is the "democratization of capital access" for entrepreneurs and private firms. Each change attempted to lower barriers for entrepreneurs seeking to raise private capital, connect retail investors to startups, or lower the chances that traditional early-stage investors triggered costly regulatory triggers (see Ewens and Farre-Mensa, 2022, for a thorough review). If successful at lowering barriers, then the literature surveyed above provides some predictions about affects for women and minorities.

- *Equity crowdfunding*: part of the 2012 JOBS Act and implemented in 2016, companies can sell equity securities on registered platforms up to $1.07 million per year. In 2021, this upper limit was increased to $5 million.
- *Solicitation*[at] : The JOBS Act also allowed startups to publicly solicit capital under Rule 506 if all purchasers of the securities are accredited investors and the issuer takes reasonable steps to verify that the purchasers are accredited investors.
- *AngelList no action letter*: In March 2013, the SEC effectively approved the creation of the AngelList platform that helped to connect startups seeking capital

---

[at]See https://www.sec.gov/info/smallbus/secg/general-solicitation-small-entity-compliance-guide.htm.

with accredited investors and institutional investors.[au] The SEC's response spawned several product offerings that facilitated early-stage capital raising on AngelList's website (previously interpreted as a solicitation)

- *Reg A+*: Often called the "mini-IPO", the JOBS Act increased the amount of capital that could be raised in this type of public offering.
- *Regulation D changes*: The JOBS Act changed part of the most used registration exemption Regulation D. For example, Rule 504 allows firms to raise up to $5 million from an unlimited number of investors of any type (up from $1 million).

How if at all should these changes impact the facts documented in Section 6? Insofar as the barriers to high-growth entrepreneurship are driven by capital providers bias or information asymmetries, then these regulatory changes should increase investor competition and lower the cost of capital (e.g., Arrow, 1973). Such a view seems to be the common defense for such changes and was clear in the naming of the JOBS Act titles (e.g., "Access to Capital for Job Creators" and "Private Company Flexibility and Growth"). Work showing that banking deregulation improves capital access to small business points to such a channel (Black and Strahan, 2002; Kerr and Nanda, 2011). Increased competition between capital providers may not always lead to smaller gaps in race and gender. As Charles and Guryan (2008) summarize, if the market has imperfect information, imperfect competition, or adjustment costs (Lang et al., 2005), racial or gender gaps can persist if there are biased preferences.[av] Altonji and Blank (1999) summarize a theoretical literature where search costs are added to labor models and argue that increased competition does not always solve the issue (see Borjas and Bronars, 1989 and subsequent papers by Black, 1995 and Bowlus and Eckstein, 2002).[aw]

Several of the changes include increases in information about available investments and investors. The crowdfunding and A+ rules require disclosures by firms and platforms. Related, the AngelList and similar platforms (e.g., FundersClub) that allow for limited solicitation have effectively provided standardized information for potential investors. Rather than deal sharing through personal networks over email or coffee, these platforms create some uniformity for offering documents and even facilitate communication on-platform. Thus, parts of the regulatory changes may lower information barriers for investors.

Gender and racial gaps in entrepreneurial firms raising capital could also decline after the changes because they encourage entry on not just more investors, but more capital providers from underrepresented groups. Indeed, Lerner (2019) finds that VC and PE funds managed by minorities have increased 3.5% to over 5% from 2002 to 2017, while Pitchbook (2022) shows the percentage of female venture capitalists

---

[au]See https://www.sec.gov/divisions/marketreg/mr-noaction/2013/angellist-15a1.pdf

[av]These models are best thought of as racial or other-gender "distaste" where workers do not want to work with out-groups (nor employers hire).

[aw]The idea in most of these models is that the whole distribution of prejudicial taste of firms drives results rather than just the standard marginal firm as argued in Becker (2010).

(GPs) in VC funds increased from 12% in 2019 to 15.4% in 2021. The barriers discussed in Section 6 could equally apply to an entrepreneurial investor from underrepresented groups seeking to build investment portfolios for others. Some products introduced by AngelList aim to help investors build their portfolios and find deals. For this channel to work at shrinking the financing gap, we need not assume that homophilistic preferences, industry sorting and even prejudice disappear. Instead, such preferences and actions can continue so long as the new entrant inventors continue to have own-type preferences in investing.

There are other reasons to predict that these changes that increased regulatory thresholds and advertising rules would have little impact on female and minority entrepreneurs. Both groups tend to cluster in industries with lower capital needs and, in some cases, ask for less capital within the industry. Higher thresholds for capital raising regulation avoidance will not help here. The increased ability to solicit capital publicly requires both an audience and, more importantly for inequality, an audience screened by income or wealth. If disadvantaged groups have worse networks or lower wealth levels, then these deregulations may not improve capital access.

Several research questions emerge from this discussion. First, is there any direct evidence that disadvantaged groups have used these rule changes to raise capital? It would be interesting to see a full aggregation of capital raised by race and gender that incorporates VC, angel, crowdfunding, etc. Second, what model of the investor landscape—substitutability, mobility, value-add and competition—could help us understand the complex interactions between the startup financing frictions documented here and entry by new investors?

7.2 Market changes

Connected to some of these recent regulatory changes are macro-level changes to private equity markets and financing technology. Each could have similar predicted impacts on access to capital for startups and deal flow for investors. In each case, the changes to the financing ecosystem may weaken of the power of the gatekeepers and thus attenuate the role of bias or discrimination.

7.2.1 Changes to capital supply

The private equity financing landscape has changed significantly over the last 25 years (Ewens and Farre-Mensa, 2022). The changes can in part be explained by regulatory changes, but otherwise appear to be driven by participation of new investors and financial innovations. At the same time, academic and anecdotal evidence shows that the balance of power between capital supply and demand has shifted to the latter. The growth of private capital markets can be partially tied to a major deregulation in 1996 which lowered the barriers to private equity across state, while allowing private equity investors to raise larger funds (Ewens and Farre-Mensa, 2020). The authors find that since 1996, valuations paid by early-stage investors have increased significantly. Valuations of VC-backed startups have only continued to climb in the last decade.[ax] Researchers have also documented higher levels of participation by nontraditional investors: mutual funds (Kwon et al., 2020; Agarwal et al., 2021; Chernenko et al., 2021), hedge funds (Aragon et al., 2018), growth equity investors and limited partners (Lerner, 2019). This shift in investor composition translates to an increased supply of capital and presumably more competition between investors. Any lowering of the cost of capital for entrepreneurs or higher probability of raising follow-on financing (Nanda and Rhodes-Kropf, 2016) could disproportionately benefit disadvantaged entrepreneurs.

Other changes are worth mentioning as they likely have similar effects but have not been explored in depth in the context of race and gender. Researchers have documented an increase in venture debt, a relatively new form of nondilutive finance used by VC-backed startups (Davis et al., 2020). Data from Pitchbook[ay] shows significant growth in secondary liquidity for VC-backed startups in the last 10 years: $500 million per year from 2012 to 2015 to roughly $2 billion since 2015. Such liquidity offered to startup founders lowers their risk and could have long-term impacts on entry choice. Finally, new proposed rule changes could have consequences for the supply of capital provided to venture capitalists and private equity funds. In 2020, the Department of Labor issued a letter[az] detailing a potential change to 401(k) rules that would allow private equity fund investments. Not only would this change increase the supply of capital to the PE industry, but it would also increase the diversity of the limited partner (i.e., investors in PE) pool. The myriad of supply level and composition changes detailed here demands new investigations from the perspective of race and gender.

7.2.2 Fintech and data availability

The high-growth financing landscape has also experienced several technological changes that could impact gender and racial disparities. First, Ewens et al. (2018) show that introducing Amazon Web Services changed the capital needs of startups. This change affected the characteristics of funded startups, the types of investors and investor governance choices. Most of these changes coincided with relatively cheaper capital and thus lowering barriers for disadvantaged entrepreneurs and investors. New entrepreneurial firms themselves are introducing novel financing for startups that could change the bargaining power between investor and founder (e.g., Stripe's capital offering, Pipe's nondilutive financing from recurring revenue). Investors are also the beneficiaries of innovation in this space with new technologies that should lower the barriers to entry for women and minorities, angel investors and GPs (e.g., AngelList, Carta, Stripe and Aumni among others). Finally, startups are

---

[ax]See the Pitchbook 2021 Q2 Valuations Report (https://pitchbook.com/news/reports/q2-2021-us-vc-valuations-report. For example, the median early-stage valuation increased approximately $9 million in 2011 to $22 million in 2020.

[ay]Author's calculation searching for VC-backed startups with secondary transactions (September 2021). https://my.pitchbook.com/?pcc=522996-49.

[az]See https://www.dol.gov/newsroom/releases/ebsa/ebsa20200603-0.

often at a disadvantage when raising capital from sophisticated investors demanding complex securities in return for capital (e.g., Kaplan and Strömberg, 2003; Ewens et al., 2022. Since 2007, new data providers covering VC and private equity have emerged.[ba] Possibly in response to competition, these data providers produce regular, informative reports on valuation (Pitchbook valuation report, 2020), deal terms (Silicon Valley Venture Capital Survey from Fenwick and West), exits and investors (2021 Preqin Global Private Equity & Venture Capital Report). To the extent that these data providers can lower information asymmetry, this could improve the prospects of entrepreneurs, particularly those outside the networks or experience where such knowledge is common.

7.3 Targeted programs and funds

One reason we might predict that government interventions in entrepreneurial finance might help mitigate differential outcomes by race or gender in entrepreneurship is the government's nonfinancial motives. The nonprofit sector is thus a natural place for alternative solutions to the entrepreneurship gaps documented in the chapter. Indeed, a host of such groups have emerged in the last decade. These include Venture Forward by the NVCA (underrepresented groups), All Raise (women entrepreneurs), VCFamilia (Latino investors) and BLCK VC (black investors).

That said, it is still unclear what the optimal mechanism is for addressing the gaps in funding and outcomes. If one accepts that bias or discriminatory preferences are slow to disappear and existing investors have market power, then nonmarket solutions, such as the government and nonprofits, are a reasonable strategy. It is also not clear what part of the startup life cycle (Section 3) is best to target. Table 1 shows that even sizeable gaps exist at the earliest founding decision, pointing to programs targeting education and early resource gathering. Addressing frictions for firms founded by women and minorities that successfully raise capital is more difficult, as one must work with existing investors.

8 Ideas for future research

The constant evolution and adaptation of entrepreneurial firms and their ecosystems provide ample opportunities for researchers to fill some gaps in the literature summarized above. Technological change can affect the economic frictions faced by both the supply and demand sides. Regulatory changes can shift the balance of power. This section details some unaddressed topics at the intersection of entrepreneurial finance, gender, and race.

[ba]Three of the major data providers on private equity and venture capital were formally launched after 2007: Pitchbook (in 2007), CB Insights (in 2008) and Crunchbase (in 2015).

- Many cells in Table 1 are empty because of incomplete data or a lack of studies focused on race. Additional data is required before we can understand the gap in high-growth entrepreneurship by race. Several organizations have attempted to fill these gaps with surveys or proprietary data (e.g., Capital, 2021; Lerner, 2019), opening the door to academic to expand and provide continuity.
- Deeper analysis of the Altonji and Blank (1999) distinction between "current market discrimination" and "premarket discrimination" for entrepreneurs. The role of wealth, networks, education, and information differs by race or gender before any founding decisions are made. Understanding these disparities (e.g., Derenoncourt et al., 2022) and their own sources is critical to any policy implications.
- Similarly, there is an entrepreneurship policy implication of the Boerma and Karabarbounis (2021) model of wealth accumulation. They argue that "centuries-long exclusions lead Black [households] to hold pessimistic beliefs about risky returns and to forgo investment opportunities after the wealth transfer" (p. 1). This friction makes investment/entrepreneurship subsidies relatively more effective that direct transfers. It would be interesting to explore the relative effectiveness of past race-based entrepreneurship policies on the wealth gap. The paper also suggests that there are racial differences in beliefs about risk returns that could help explain differences in entrepreneurial entry.
- We know little about how expected rejection or poor deal terms explain the low rate of participation by women or minorities in entrepreneurship. Survey evidence on this question would be an important first step, particularly among would-be entrepreneurs.
- A stark pattern of changing bargaining power between entrepreneurs and investors has emerged in several areas. Valuations for startups are increasing (Ewens and Farre-Mensa, 2022), contract terms are becoming more entrepreneur-friendly, founders are more likely to have dual-class shares (Aggarwal et al., 2022) and corporate governance power has shifted to entrepreneurs (Ewens and Malenko, 2022). How do these bargaining power shifts impact the gender or racial gap at entry and financing?
- The literature reviewed above finds that cost of credit differs by race and gender. Many entrepreneurial firms sell complex securities that are a combination of cash flow and control rights (e.g., Kaplan and Strömberg, 2003; Ewens et al., 2022). If one incorporates these terms into the prices paid to entrepreneurs, do the gaps between races and gender change?
- Addressing the host of explanations for differential treatment stemming from the models in Section 5 is significantly easier when the data at the researcher's disposal has information about both supply and demand. Demographics about investors, loan officers and, most important, information about the set of investments considers by these players are critical to understanding the channels at play.
- The role of geography in capital availability is a common topic for policymakers who are trying to improve capital access for local entrepreneurs. Researchers have shown that entrepreneurs often move in response to this agglomeration of

resources (Conti and Guzman, 2021; Chen and Ewens, 2023). These issues likely only exacerbate the resource constraints, particularly for minorities.

- Sarsons et al. (2021) demonstrate bias in credit attribution by gender in the academic setting, while Exley and Kessler (2022) show that women are less optimistic in self-evaluations. Investors and coexecutives as startups may exhibit similar biases in startups, leading to suboptimal resource allocation or refinancing decisions.

- The patterns of own gender matching found in several papers often motivate predictions about increased participation of female and minority investors. On one hand, this response to gaps in financing and outcomes does not address any deeper issues of stereotypes or bias. On the other hand, the entrepreneurial finance ecosystem has only recently experienced an increase in underrepresented group participation on the supply-side. These new investors are more likely to be inexperienced, which could affect the impacts of their entry. Exploring the real impacts of investor entry would be fruitful.

- This review and existing research have focused primarily on two groups: women and blacks. More research is needed on other disadvantaged groups, with the caveat that many of the differential treatment explanations such as stereotypes or risk preferences do not connect as cleanly to race or ethnicity.

- Major questions about access to capital and outcomes could be revisited using the "constructivist" perspective (Rose, 2022) discussed in Section 5.9. The suggestion in Rose (2022) for instruments that shift perceptions of race point to new experiments, while the normative choices around decision-relevant observables could be guided by expanded surveys following Gompers et al. (2020).

- This handbook's private equity topic is only partially covered in this chapter. It has no discussion of the larger parts of the private equity landscape: buyouts, growth equity, mezzanine, and distressed debt. I am unaware of any published work in this area. One explanation is that gender or race is difficult to map to the typical transaction. For example, when a buyout fund takes a public company private, there are often several general partners (GP) running the deal. This fact makes assigning gender or race to a deal difficult. However, after the private equity firm acquires a target or takes a controlling stake, the setting begins to mimic that explored in the chapter. Topics of interest here could include the role of GP team gender or racial composition on PE deal performance or deal structure. GPs in buyout funds often reorganize top managers, inviting analysis of manager selection and possibly compensation.

9 Conclusion

This chapter reviews the literature on the intersection of entrepreneurial finance, race, and gender. While significant progress has been made studying the gaps in participation and funding by gender and race (see Table 1), the entrepreneurial finance literature has numerous databases to build and unanswered questions to answer. This chapter aims to provide the tools and knowledge to guide this process with a thorough review of the economics of discrimination and empirical literature on discrimination in entrepreneurial finance. The benefit of answering these questions is not simply improving academia's knowledge of an important economic phenomenon. Discovering the sources of differential treatment and outcomes in startups will guide policy solutions for agents in the marketplace (e.g., investors and entrepreneurs) and regulators.

Acknowledgments

The chapter's companion website can be found at https://foundinggaps.com. I thank Kexin Feng for excellent research assistance, Minmo Gahng for help with IPO data and Joan Farre-Mensa, Sean Wang, and Emmanuel Yimfor for their early feedback.

Appendix A Data sources

This section lists the major data sources used by researchers in the papers referenced above. This list is nonexhaustive but should nonetheless provide an excellent starting point for interested researchers.

- **Current Population Survey:** used for the Kauffman Foundation "Early-stage Entrepreneurship" reports. From Fairlie and Desai's summary of the index: The CPS is a monthly survey of approximately 60,000 households and is the official source used to calculate the household-based measure of the unemployment rate by the US Bureau of Labor Statistics. These surveys, conducted monthly by the US Census Bureau and the US Bureau of Labor Statistics, represent the entire US population, and contain observations for over 130,000 people each month. The survey primarily asks questions focused on the employment status of household members, including whether they are unemployed, out of labor force, wage/salary worker, or a business owner (p. 3).
- **Venture capital databases:** coverage of startups, financings, investors, and outcomes
  - These include Pitchbook, CB Insights (VentureSource), Crunchbase, Preqin and Thompson VentureXpert.
- **Form D data:**[bb] regulatory filings with the SEC for securities registration exemption requests. Includes startups that raise outside equity and convertible debt and has information about directors, executives, startup location, capital raised, and security type.

[bb]https://www.sec.gov/dera/data/form-d. See Ewens and Malenko (2022) Internet Appendix for details on Regulation D compliance and issues with Form D availability.

- **Small Business Credit Survey:** survey of small business credit conditions run by the 12 regional Federal Reserve banks.[bc] The survey has been run since 2014, with additions for race and gender variables in the last few years.
- **Kauffman Firm Survey** [bd]
  - panel data covering 4928 startups from 2004 to 2011 that have information on financing choices, financing outcomes, creditworthiness, and credit expectations.
- **OpenCorporates**[be] (related Startup Cartography Project[bf]): incorporation data for most of the United States. It provides information on new firms and some information on outcomes.
- **Survey of Business Owners** (last run in 2012)[bg]: survey of all firms with less than 500 employees that included information on firm size, use of financial services, and the income and balance sheet.
- **5-Percent Public Use Microdata Sample** (PUMS) Files (2000)[bh]: 5% sample of US Census individual data. See Fairlie et al. (2022) for their data on marriage rates by race.
- **Job Patterns for Minorities and Women in Private Industry** (EEOC)[bi]: "periodic reports from public and private employers, and unions and labor organizations which show the composition of their workforces by sex and by race/ethnic category" (see Gompers and Wang, 2017a).
- **Global Entrepreneurship Monitor**[bj]: "carries out survey-based research on entrepreneurship and entrepreneurship ecosystems around the world. GEM is a networked consortium of national country teams primarily associated with top academic institutions." Data are available on entrepreneur behavior, attitudes, and institutional setting for most countries in the world.
- **General Social Survey**[bk]: survey on "what Americans think and feel about such issues as national spending priorities, crime and punishment, intergroup relations, and confidence in institutions."

Appendix B   Identifying race and gender

This section discusses several of the methods used by researchers to identify race and gender in data that may lack such identifiers. The potential bias in any algorithm (Obermeyer and Mullainathan, 2019) should inform any use of the suggestions below.

[bc]See https://www.fedsmallbusiness.org/about.
[bd]See https://www.kauffman.org/entrepreneurship/research/kauffman-firm-survey/.
[be]See https://opencorporates.com.
[bf]See https://www.startupcartography.com/data.
[bg]https://www.federalreserve.gov/pubs/oss/oss3/nssbftoc.htm.
[bh]https://www2.census.gov/census_2000/census2000/PUMS5.html.
[bi]See https://www.eeoc.gov/statistics/job-patterns-minorities-and-women-private-industry-eeo-1.
[bj]See https://www.gemconsortium.org/data.
[bk]See https://gss.norc.org.

B.1 Gender

Several public and commercial datasets provide mappings of probabilities or race and gender using first names. A popular source of name-gender mapping is the Social Security Administration's database.[bl] An open-source R package "gender" allows users to connect to other government databases.[bm] Commercial providers with API access include Genderize.io and Gender API.[bn] They built these name databases for American and Northern European datasets. Pictures can also assign gender; however, privacy issues appear to result in brief lives for many of the services.[bo]

B.2 Race

Race assignment can use pictures as with gender. Surname databases such as the Decennial Census Surname Files[bp]. and related APIs[bq] are the most popular way to assign a probability of race to an individual.

References

Agarwal, V., Barber, B.M., Cheng, S., Hameed, A., Yasuda, A., 2021. Private Company Valuations by Mutual Funds. Working paper.

Aggarwal, D., Eldar, O., Hochberg, Y.V., Litov, L.P., 2022. The rise of dual-class stock ipos. J. Financ. Econ. 144 (1), 122–153.

Aigner, D.J., Cain, G.G., 1977. Statistical theories of discrimination in labor markets. ILR Review 30 (2), 175–187. https://doi.org/10.1177/001979397703000204.

Akcigit, U., Dinlersoz, E., Greenwood, J., Penciakova, V., 2022. Synergizing ventures. J. Econ. Dyn. Control., 104427.

Albrecht, J.W., Edin, P.-A., Sundström, M., Vroman, S.B., 1999. Career interruptions and subsequent earnings: a reexamination using Swedish data. J. Hum. Resour., 294–311.

Alesina, A.F., Lotti, F., Mistrulli, P.E., 2013. Do women pay more for credit? Evidence from Italy. J. Eur. Econ. Assoc. 11 (suppl 1), 45–66.

Alesina, A., Ferroni, M.F., Stantcheva, S., 2021. Perceptions of Racial Gaps, their Causes, and Ways to Reduce Them. Working Paper 29245.

Altonji, J.G., Blank, R.M., 1999. Chapter 48 Race and gender in the labor market. In: Handbook of Labor Economics, vol. 3. Elsevier, pp. 3143–3259. http://www.sciencedirect.com/science/article/pii/S1573446399300390.

Aragon, G.O., Li, E., Lindsey, L.A., 2018. Exploration or Exploitation? Hedge Funds in Venture Capital. Social Science Research Network, Rochester, NY, https://doi.org/10.2139/ssrn.3251086. https://papers.ssrn.com/abstract=3251086. Working Paper ID 3251086.

[bl]See https://www.ssa.gov/oact/babynames/limits.html.
[bm]See https://rdrr.io/cran/gender/man/gender.html.
[bn]See https://genderize.io/ and https://gender-api.com/.
[bo]As of chapter submission, this service was available: https://www.kairos.com.
[bp]See https://www.census.gov/data/developers/data-sets/surnames.html.
[bq]See https://www.census.gov/programs-surveys/decennial-census/data/api.html.

Arrow, K.J., 1973. The theory of discrimination. In: Discrimination in Labor Markets, Princeton University Press, pp. 1–33.

Babcock, L., Laschever, S., 2009. Women don't ask. In: Women Don't Ask, Princeton University Press.

Bapna, S., Ganco, M., 2021. Gender gaps in equity crowdfunding: evidence from a randomized field experiment. Manag. Sci. 67 (5), 2679–2710. https://doi.org/10.1287/mnsc.2020.3644.

Bartoš, V., Bauer, M., Chytilová, J., Matvejka, F., 2016. Attention discrimination: theory and field experiments with monitoring information acquisition. Am. Econ. Rev. 106 (6), 1437–1475. https://doi.org/10.1257/aer.20140571.

Beck, T., Levine, R., Loayza, N., 2000. Finance and the sources of growth. J. Financ. Econ. 58 (1–2), 261–300.

Beck, T., Behr, P., Guettler, A., 2013. Gender and banking: are women better loan officers? Rev. Financ. 17 (4), 1279–1321.

Beck, T., Behr, P., Guettler, A., 2010. Gender and Banking: Are Women Better Loan Officers? Social Science Research Network, Rochester, NY, https://doi.org/10.2139/ssrn.1443107. https://papers.ssrn.com/abstract=1443107. Working Paper ID 1443107.

Becker, G.S., 1957. The Economics of Discrimination. University of Chicago Press.

Becker, G.S., 2010. The Economics of Discrimination. University of Chicago Press, ISBN: 978-0-226-04104-9.

Becker-Blease, J.R., Sohl, J.E., 2007. Do women-owned businesses have equal access to angel capital? J. Bus. Ventur. 22 (4), 503–521. https://doi.org/10.1016/j.jbusvent.2006.06.003.

Bell, A., Chetty, R., Jaravel, X., Petkova, N., Van Reenen, J., 2019. Who Becomes an Inventor in America? The Importance of Exposure to Innovation. Q. J. Econ. 134 (2), 647–713. https://doi.org/10.1093/qje/qjy028.

Bellon, A., Cookson, J.A., Gilje, E.P., Heimer, R.Z., 2021. Personal wealth, self-employment, and business ownership. Rev. Financ. Stud. 34 (8), 3935–3975. https://doi.org/10.1093/rfs/hhab044.

Bellucci, A., Borisov, A., Zazzaro, A., 2010. Does gender matter in bank-firm relationships? Evidence from small business lending. J. Bank. Financ. 34 (12), 2968–2984. https://doi.org/10.1016/j.jbankfin.2010.07.008.

Berger, A., Udell, G., 1998. The economics of small business finance: the roles of private equity and debt markets in the financial growth cycle. J. Bank. Financ. 22 (6), 613–673. https://doi.org/10.1016/S0378-4266(98)00038-7.

Bernstein, S., Korteweg, A., Laws, K., 2017. Attracting early-stage investors: evidence from a randomized field experiment. J. Financ. 72 (2), 509–538. https://doi.org/10.1111/jofi.12470.

Bertrand, M., 2020. Gender in the twenty-first century. AEA Papers Proc. 110, 1–24. https://doi.org/10.1257/pandp.20201126.

Bertrand, M., Duflo, E., 2017. Field Experiments on Discrimination. In: Banerjee, A.V., Duflo, E. (Eds.), Handbook of Economic Field Experiments (January). Handbook of Field Experiments, vol. 1. North-Holland, pp. 309–393 (Chapter 8).

Bertrand, M., Mullainathan, S., 2004. Are Emily and Greg more employable than Lakisha and Jamal? A field experiment on labor market discrimination. Am. Econ. Rev. 94 (4), 104.

Bertrand, M., Chugh, D., Mullainathan, S., 2005. Implicit discrimination. Am. Econ. Rev. 95 (2), 94–98. https://doi.org/10.1257/000282805774670365.

Bhandari, A., McGrattan, E.R., 2021. Sweat Equity in U.S. Private Business. Q. J. Econ. 136 (2), 727–781. https://doi.org/10.1093/qje/qjaa041.

Biasi, B., Sarsons, H., 2020. Flexible Wages, Bargaining, and the Gender Gap. National Bureau of Economic Research, https://doi.org/10.3386/w27894. https://www.nber.org/papers/w27894. Working Paper 27894.

Black, D.A., 1995. Discrimination in an equilibrium search model. J. Labor Econ. 13 (2), 309–334.

Black, S.E., Strahan, P.E., 2002. Entrepreneurship and bank credit availability. J. Financ. 57 (6), 2807–2833. https://doi.org/10.1111/1540-6261.00513.

Blanchard, L., Zhao, B., Yinger, J., 2008. Do lenders discriminate against minority and woman entrepreneurs? J. Urban Econ. 63 (2), 467–497. https://doi.org/10.1016/j.jue.2007.03.001.

Blanchflower, D.G., Levine, P.B., Zimmerman, D.J., 2003. Discrimination in the small-business credit market. Rev. Econ. Stat. 85 (4), 930–943. https://doi.org/10.1162/003465303772815835.

Blank, R.M., Dabady, M., Citro, C.F., Blank, R.M., 2004. Measuring Racial Discrimination. National Academies Press, Washington, DC.

Blau, F.D., Kahn, L.M., 2017. The gender wage gap: extent, trends, and explanations. J. Econ. Lit. 55 (3), 789–865. https://doi.org/10.1257/jel.20160995.

Blinder, A.S., 1973. Wage discrimination: reduced form and structural estimates. J. Hum. Resour. 8 (4), 436–455. https://doi.org/10.2307/144855.

Boerma, J., Karabarbounis, L., 2021. Reparations and Persistent Racial Wealth Gaps. National Bureau of Economic Research, https://doi.org/10.3386/w28468. https://www.nber.org/papers/w28468. Working Paper 28468. Working Paper Series.

Bohren, J.A., Haggag, K., Imas, A., Pope, D.G., 2019a. Inaccurate Statistical Discrimination: An Identification Problem. National Bureau of Economic Research, https://doi.org/10.3386/w25935. http://www.nber.org/papers/w25935. Working Paper 25935.

Bohren, J.A., Imas, A., Rosenberg, M., 2019b. The dynamics of discrimination: theory and evidence. Am. Econ. Rev. 109 (10), 3395–3436. https://doi.org/10.1257/aer.20171829.

Bohren, J.A., Hull, P., Imas, A., 2022. Systemic Discrimination: Theory and Measurement., https://doi.org/10.3386/w29820. https://www.nber.org/papers/w29820. Working Paper 29820. Working Paper Series.

Booth, A.L., Nolen, P., 2012. Gender differences in risk behaviour: does nurture matter? Econ. J. 122 (558), F56–F78. https://doi.org/10.1111/j.1468-0297.2011.02480.x.

Bordalo, P., Coffman, K., Gennaioli, N., Shleifer, A., 2016. Stereotypes. Q. J. Econ. 131 (4), 1753–1794. https://doi.org/10.1093/qje/qjw029. https://academic.oup.com/qje/article/131/4/1753/2468882.

Bordalo, P., Coffman, K., Gennaioli, N., Shleifer, A., 2019. Beliefs about gender. Am. Econ. Rev. 109 (3), 739–773. https://doi.org/10.1257/aer.20170007.

Borjas, G.J., Bronars, S.G., 1989. Consumer discrimination and self-employment. J. Polit. Econ. 97 (3), 581–605.

Bosma, N., Levie, J., 2010. Global Entrepreneurship Monitor: 2009 Global Report. Global Entrepreneurship Research Association, London. https://strathprints.strath.ac.uk/28208/.

Bowlus, A.J., Eckstein, Z., 2002. Discrimination and skill differences in an equilibrium search model. Int. Econ. Rev. 43 (4), 1309–1345.

Bradford, W.D., 2003. The Wealth Dynamics of Entrepreneurship for Black and White Families in the U.S. Rev. Income Wealth 49 (1), 89–116.

Braunstein, S.F., 2010. Credit Scoring: Testimony Before the Subcommittee on Financial Institutions and Consumer Credit, the Committee on Financial Services. US House of Representatives.

Brooks, A.W., Huang, L., Kearney, S.W., Murray, F.E., 2014. Investors prefer entrepreneurial ventures pitched by attractive men. Proc. Natl. Acad. Sci. U.S.A. 111 (12), 4427–4431. https://doi.org/10.1073/pnas.1321202111.

Brush, C.G., 1992. Research on women business owners: past trends, a new perspective and future directions. Enterp. Theory Pract. 16 (4), 5–30. https://doi.org/10.1177/104225879201600401.

Brush, C.G., 2008. Women entrepreneurs: a research overview. In: Basu, A., others (Eds.), The Oxford Handbook of Entrepreneurship, online edn, Oxford Academic, 2 Sept. 2009. https://doi.org/10.1093/oxfordhb/9780199546992.003.0023. (Accessed 26 April 2023). https://www.oxfordhandbooks.com/view/10.1093/oxfordhb/9780199546992.001.0001/oxfordhb-9780199546992-e-23.

Brush, C., Carter, N.M., Gatewood, E.J., Greene, P.G., Hart, M., 2001. The Diana Project: Women Business Owners and Equity Capital: The Myths Dispelled. Babson College Center for Entrepreneurship Research Paper 2009-11.

Brush, C.G., Carter, N.M., Gatewood, E.J., Greene, P.G., Hart, M., 2004. Gatekeepers of Venture Growth: A Diana Project Report on the Role and Participation of Women in the Venture Capital Industry. Working Paper.

Brush, C., Greene, P., Balachandra, L., Davis, A., 2018. The gender gap in venture capital-progress, problems, and perspectives. Ventur. Cap. 20 (2), 115–136. https://doi.org/10.1080/13691066.2017.1349266.

Buser, T., Niederle, M., Oosterbeek, H., 2014. Gender, competitiveness, and career choices. Q. J. Econ. 129 (3), 1409–1447. https://doi.org/10.1093/qje/qju009.

Cain, G.G., 1986. The economic analysis of labor market discrimination: a survey. In: Handbook of labor economics, vol. 1. Elsevier, pp. 693–785.

Calder-Wang, S., Gompers, P.A., 2021. And the children shall lead: gender diversity and performance in venture capital. J. Financ. Econ. 142 (1), 1–22.

Calvó-Armengol, A., Jackson, M.O., 2004. The effects of social networks on employment and inequality. Am. Econ. Rev. 94 (3), 426–454. https://doi.org/10.1257/0002828041464542.

Capital, H., 2021. Black & Latina Women Investors in VC. https://harlem.capital/how-are-black-latina-women-investors-breaking-into-vc/.

Chari, A., Goldsmith-Pinkham, P., 2017. Gender Representation in Economics Across Topics and Time: Evidence From the NBER. Social Science Research Network, Rochester, NY. https://papers.ssrn.com/abstract=3066692. Working Paper ID 3066692.

Charles, K.K., Guryan, J., 2008. Prejudice and wages: an empirical assessment of Becker's The Economics of Discrimination. J. Polit. Econ. 116 (5), 773–809.

Charles, K.K., Guryan, J., 2011. Studying Discrimination: Fundamental Challenges and Recent Progress. National Bureau of Economic Research.

Chatterji, A.K., Seamans, R.C., 2012. Entrepreneurial finance, credit cards, and race. J. Financ. Econ. 106 (1), 182–195. https://doi.org/10.1016/j.jfineco.2012.04.007.

Chen, J., Ewens, M., 2023. Venture Capital and Startup Agglomeration. Working Paper.

Chernenko, S., Lerner, J., Zeng, Y., 2021. Mutual funds as venture capitalists? Evidence from unicorns. Rev. Financ. Stud. 34 (5), 2362–2410.

Coffman, K.B., 2014. Evidence on self-stereotyping and the contribution of ideas. Q. J. Econ. 129 (4), 1625–1660. https://doi.org/10.1093/qje/qju023.

Coleman, S., Robb, A., 2009. A comparison of new firm financing by gender: evidence from the Kauffman firm survey data. Small Bus. Econ. 33 (4), 397–411. https://doi.org/10.1007/s11187-009-9205-7.

Constantinidis, C., Cornet, A., Asandei, S., 2006. Financing of women-owned ventures: the impact of gender and other owner -and firm-related variables. Ventur. Cap. 8 (2), 133–157. https://doi.org/10.1080/13691060600572557.

Conti, A., Guzman, J.A., 2021. What is the US comparative advantage in entrepreneurship? Evidence from Israeli migration to the United States. Rev. Econ. Stat., 1–45.

Core, F., 2020. Female innovative entrepreneurship and maternity risk., https://doi.org/10.2139/ssrn.3539508. https://papers.ssrn.com/abstract=3539508.

Corradin, S., Popov, A., 2015. House prices, home equity borrowing, and entrepreneurship. Rev. Financ. Stud. 28 (8), 2399–2428.

Croson, R., Gneezy, U., 2009. Gender differences in preferences. J. Econ. Lit. 47 (2), 448–474. https://doi.org/10.1257/jel.47.2.448. https://www.aeaweb.org/articles?id=10.1257/jel.47.2.448.

Davis, J., Morse, A., Wang, X., 2020. The Leveraging of Silicon Valley. National Bureau of Economic Research, https://doi.org/10.3386/w27591. https://www.nber.org/papers/w27591. 27591.

Del Carpio, L., Guadalupe, M., 2022. More women in tech? Evidence from a field experiment addressing social identity. Manag. Sci. 68 (5), 3196–3218. https://doi.org/10.1287/mnsc.2021.4035.

Derenoncourt, E., Kim, C.H., Kuhn, M., Schularick, M., 2022. Wealth of Two Nations: The U.S. Racial Wealth Gap, 1860–2020., https://doi.org/10.3386/w30101. https://www.nber.org/papers/w30101. Working Paper 30101. Working Paper Series.

Dittrich, M., Leipold, K., 2014. Gender Differences in Strategic Reasoning. Working Paper.

Duarte, J., Siegel, S., Young, L., 2012. Trust and credit: the role of appearance in peer-to-peer lending. Rev. Financ. Stud. 25 (8), 2455–2484. https://doi.org/10.1093/rfs/hhs071.

Duchin, R., Simutin, M., Sosyura, D., 2021. The origins and real effects of the gender gap: evidence from CEOs' formative years. Rev. Financ. Stud. 34 (2), 700–762. https://doi.org/10.1093/rfs/hhaa068.

Egan, M., Matvos, G., Seru, A., 2022. When Harry fired Sally: the double standard in punishing misconduct. J. Polit. Econ. 130 (5), 1184–1248.

Einiö, E., Feng, J., Jaravel, X., 2019. Social Push and the Direction of Innovation. Social Science Research Network, Rochester, NY, https://doi.org/10.2139/ssrn.3383703. https://papers.ssrn.com/abstract=3383703. ID 3383703. SSRN Scholarly Paper.

Evans, D.S., Jovanovic, B., 1989. An estimated model of entrepreneurial choice under liquidity constraints. J. Polit. Econ. 97 (4), 808–827. https://doi.org/10.1086/261629.

Ewens, M., Farre-Mensa, J., 2020. The deregulation of the private equity markets and the decline in IPOs. Rev. Financ. Stud. 33 (12), 5463–5509.

Ewens, M., Farre-Mensa, J., 2022. Private or public equity? The evolving entrepreneurial finance landscape. Annu. Rev. Financ. Econ. 14, 271–293.

Ewens, M., Malenko, N., 2022. Board Dynamics Over the Startup Life Cycle. Working Paper.

Ewens, M., Townsend, R.R., 2020. Are early stage investors biased against women? J. Financ. Econ. 135 (3), 653–677. https://doi.org/10.1016/j.jfineco.2019.07.002.

Ewens, M., Tomlin, B., Wang, L.C., 2014. Statistical discrimination or prejudice? A large sample field experiment. Rev. Econ. Stat. 96 (1), 119–134.

Ewens, M., Nanda, R., Rhodes-Kropf, M., 2018. Cost of experimentation and the evolution of venture capital. J. Financ. Econ. 128 (3), 422–442. https://doi.org/10.1016/j.jfineco.2018.03.001.

Ewens, M., Gorbenko, A., Korteweg, A., 2022. Venture capital contracts. J. Financ. Econ. 143 (1), 131–158.

Exley, C.L., Kessler, J.B., 2022. The gender gap in self-promotion. Q. J. Econ. 137 (3), 1345–1381.

Fairlie, R.W., Desai, S., 2021. National report on early-stage entrepreneurship in the United States: 2020. SSRN Electron. J. https://doi.org/10.2139/ssrn.3810193. https://www.ssrn.com/abstract=3810193.

Fairlie, R.W., Krashinsky, H.A., 2012. Liquidity constraints, household wealth, and entrepreneurship revisited. Rev. Income Wealth 58 (2), 279–306.

Fairlie, R.W., Robb, A.M., 2007a. Why are black-owned businesses less successful than white-owned businesses? The role of families, inheritances, and business human capital. J. Labor Econ. 25 (2), 289–323.

Fairlie, R.W., Robb, A.M., 2007b. Why are black-owned businesses less successful than white-owned businesses? The role of families, inheritances, and business human capital. J. Labor Econ. 25 (2), 289–323. https://doi.org/10.1086/510763. https://www.journals.uchicago.edu/doi/abs/10.1086/510763.

Fairlie, R.W., Robb, A.M., 2008. Race and Entrepreneurial Success. The MIT Press, Cambridge, MA.

Fairlie, R.W., Robb, A.M., 2009a. Gender differences in business performance: evidence from the characteristics of business owners survey. Small Bus. Econ. 33 (4), 375–395.

Fairlie, R.W., Robb, A.M., 2009b. Gender differences in business performance: evidence from the characteristics of business owners survey. Small Bus. Econ. 33 (4), 375. https://doi.org/10.1007/s11187-009-9207-5.

Fairlie, R.W., Robb, A., Robinson, D.T., 2022. Black and white: access to capital among minority-owned startups. Manag. Sci. 68 (4), 2377–3174. https://www.nber.org/papers/w28154.

Fang, H., Moro, A., 2011. Theories of statistical discrimination and affirmative action: a survey. In: Benhabib, J., Bisin, A., Jackson, M.O. (Eds.), Handbook of Social Economics (January). vol. 1. North-Holland, pp. 133–200 (Chapter 5).

Fiske, S.T., 1998. Stereotyping, Prejudice, and Discrimination. McGraw-Hill.

Fisman, R., Paravisini, D., Vig, V., 2017. Cultural proximity and loan outcomes. Am. Econ. Rev. 107 (2), 457–492. https://doi.org/10.1257/aer.20120942. https://www.aeaweb.org/articles?id=10.1257/aer.20120942.

Fryer Jr, R.G., 2011. Financial incentives and student achievement: evidence from randomized trials. Q. J. Econ. 126 (4), 1755–1798.

Funds, D., 2019. Women Leading Venture Report. https://differentfunds.com/women-leading-venture-2019/.

Gafni, H., Marom, D., Robb, A., Sade, O., 2021. Gender dynamics in crowdfunding (Kickstarter): evidence on entrepreneurs, backers, and taste-based discrimination. Rev Financ. 25 (2), 235–274, https://doi.org/10.1093/rof/rfaa041.

Goldin, C., 2014. A grand gender convergence: its last chapter. Am. Econ. Rev. 104 (4), 1091–1119. https://doi.org/10.1257/aer.104.4.1091.

Goldsmith-Pinkham, P., Shue, K., 2020. The Gender Gap in Housing Returns. National Bureau of Economic Research, https://doi.org/10.3386/w26914. https://www.nber.org/papers/w26914. Working Paper 26914.

Gompers, P., Lerner, J., 1999. An analysis of compensation in the US venture capital partnership. J. Financ. Econ. 51 (1), 3–44.

Gompers, P.A., Wang, S.Q., 2017a. And the Children Shall Lead: Gender Diversity and Performance in Venture Capital., https://doi.org/10.3386/w23454. http://www.nber.org/papers/w23454. Working Paper 23454. Working Paper Series.

Gompers, P.A., Wang, S.Q., 2017b. Diversity in Innovation. National Bureau of Economic Research, https://doi.org/10.3386/w23082. http://www.nber.org/papers/w23082. Working Paper 23082. Working Paper Series.

Gompers, P.A., Mukharlyamov, V., Xuan, Y., 2016. The cost of friendship. J. Financ. Econ. 119 (3), 626–644.

Gompers, P.A., Gornall, W., Kaplan, S.N., Strebulaev, I.A., 2020. How do venture capitalists make decisions? J. Financ. Econ. 135 (1), 169–190. https://doi.org/10.1016/j.jfineco.2019.06.011.

Gompers, P.A., Mukharlyamov, V., Weisburst, E., Xuan, Y., 2022. Gender gaps in venture capital performance. J. Financ. Quant. Anal. 57 (2), 485–513.

Gornall, W., Strebulaev, I.A., 2020. Gender, Race, and Entrepreneurship: A Randomized Field Experiment on Venture Capitalists and Angels. Social Science Research Network, Rochester, NY, https://doi.org/10.2139/ssrn.3301982. https://papers.ssrn.com/abstract=3301982. Working Paper ID 3301982.

Gottlieb, J.D., Townsend, R.R., Xu, T., 2022. Does career risk deter potential entrepreneurs? Rev. Financ. Stud. 35 (9), 3973–4015.

Greenwald, A.G., McGhee, D.E., Schwartz, J.L.K., 1998. Measuring individual differences in implicit cognition: the implicit association test. J. Pers. Soc. Psychol. 74 (6), 1464.

Greenberg, J., Mollick, E., 2017. Activist choice homophily and the crowdfunding of female founders. Adm. Sci. Q. 62 (2), 341–374.

Guiso, L., Pistaferri, L., Schivardi, F., 2021. Learning entrepreneurship from other entrepreneurs? J. Labor Econ. 39 (1), 135–191. https://doi.org/10.1086/708445.

Guryan, J., Charles, K.K., 2013. Taste-based or statistical discrimination: the economics of discrimination returns to its roots. Econ. J. 123 (572), F417–F432. https://doi.org/10.1111/ecoj.12080.

Guzman, J., Kacperczyk, A.O., 2019. Gender gap in entrepreneurship. Research Policy 48 (7), 1666–1680. https://ideas.repec.org/a/eee/respol/v48y2019i7p1666-1680.html.

Harding, J.P., Rosenthal, S.S., 2017. Homeownership, housing capital gains and self-employment. J. Urban Econ. 99, 120–135.

Hebert, C., 2020. Gender stereotypes and entrepreneur financing., https://doi.org/10.2139/ssrn.3318245.

Heckman, J.J., 1998. Detecting discrimination. J. Econ. Perspect. 12 (2), 101–116. https://doi.org/10.1257/jep.12.2.101. https://www.aeaweb.org/articles?id=10.1257/jep.12.2.101.

Heckman, J.J., Siegelman, P., 1993. The urban institute audit studies: their methods and findings. In: Clear and Convincing Evidence: Measurement of Discrimination in America, Urban Institute Press, Washington, DC, pp. 187–258.

Hellmann, T.F., Mostipan, I., Vulkan, N., 2021. Gender in start-up financing: evidence from equity crowdfunding. Available at SSRN 3768361.

Howell, S.T., Nanda, R., 2019. Networking Frictions in Venture Capital, and the Gender Gap in Entrepreneurship. Harvard Business School. https://ideas.repec.org/p/hbs/wpaper/19-105.html.

Hu, A., Ma, S., 2021. Persuading Investors: A Video-Based Study. Social Science Research Network, Rochester, NY, https://doi.org/10.2139/ssrn.3583898. https://papers.ssrn.com/abstract=3583898. ID 3583898. SSRN Scholarly Paper.

Huang, X., Ivković, Z., Jiang, J., Wang, I., 2021. Swimming With the Sharks: Entrepreneurial Investing Decisions and First Impression. Working Paper.

Hull, P., 2021. What Marginal Outcome Tests Can Tell Us About Racially Biased Decision-Making. National Bureau of Economic Research.

Hurst, E., Lusardi, A., 2004. Liquidity constraints, household wealth, and entrepreneurship. J. Polit. Econ. 112 (2), 319–347. https://doi.org/10.1086/381478.

Hvide, H.K., Panos, G.A., 2014. Risk tolerance and entrepreneurship. J. Financ. Econ. 111 (1), 200–223. https://doi.org/10.1016/j.jfineco.2013.06.001.

Ioannides, Y.M., Loury, L.D., 2004. Job information networks, neighborhood effects, and inequality. J. Econ. Lit. 42 (4), 1056–1093. https://doi.org/10.1257/0022051043004595.

Ivashina, V., Lerner, J., 2019. Pay now or pay later? The economics within the private equity partnership. J. Financ. Econ. 131 (1), 61–87. https://doi.org/10.1016/j.jfineco.2018.07.017.

Jann, B., 2008. The Blinder-Oaxaca decomposition for linear regression models. Stata J. 8 (4), 453–479.

Kacperczyk, O., Younkin, P., 2021. A founding penalty: evidence from an audit study on gender, entrepreneurship, and future employment. Organ. Sci. 33 (2), 716–745. https://doi.org/10.1287/orsc.2021.1456.

Kanze, D., Huang, L., Conley, M.A., Higgins, E.T., 2018. We ask men to win and women not to lose: closing the gender gap in startup funding. Acad. Manage. J. 61 (2), 586–614. https://doi.org/10.5465/amj.2016.1215.

Kaplan, S.N., Strömberg, P., 2003. Financial contracting theory meets the real world: an empirical analysis of venture capital contracts. Rev. Econ. Stud. 70 (2), 281–315. https://doi.org/10.1111/1467-937X.00245. https://academic.oup.com/restud/article/70/2/281/1586768.

Kenney, M., Patton, D., 2015. Gender, ethnicity and entrepreneurship in initial public offerings: illustrations from an open database, Res. Policy 44 (9), 1773–1784.

Kerr, W.R., Nanda, R., 2011. Financing constraints and entrepreneurship. In: Handbook of Research on Innovation and Entrepreneurship, Elgar, Cheltenham, pp. 88–103.

Kerr, W.R., Lerner, J., Schoar, A., 2014. The consequences of entrepreneurial finance: evidence from angel financings. Rev. Financ. Stud. 27 (1), 20–55.

Kerr, S.P., Kerr, W.R., Xu, T., 2017. Personality Traits of Entrepreneurs: A Review of Recent Literature. National Bureau of Economic Research, https://doi.org/10.3386/w24097. https://www.nber.org/papers/w24097. Working Paper 24097. Working Paper Series.

Kerr, S.P., Kerr, W.R., Nanda, R., 2022. House prices, home equity and entrepreneurship: evidence from US Census micro data. J. Monet. Econ. 130, 103–119.

Kline, P., Rose, E., Walters, C., 2021. Systemic Discrimination Among Large U.S. Employers. National Bureau of Economic Research, Cambridge, MA, https://doi.org/10.3386/w29053. http://www.nber.org/papers/w29053.pdf. w29053.

Kolev, J., Fuentes-Medel, Y., Murray, F., 2020. Gender differences in scientific communication and their impact on grant funding decisions. AEA Papers Proc. 110, 245–249. https://doi.org/10.1257/pandp.20201043.

Koning, R., Samila, S., Ferguson, J.-P., 2020. Inventor gender and the direction of invention. AEA Papers Proc. 110, 250–254. https://doi.org/10.1257/pandp.20201045.

Kwon, S., Lowry, M., Qian, Y., 2020. Mutual fund investments in private firms. J. Financ. Econ. 136 (2), 407–443.

Lang, K., Manove, M., Dickens, W.T., 2005. Racial discrimination in labor markets with posted wage offers. Am. Econ. Rev. 95 (4), 1327–1340.

Lazarsfeld, P.F., Merton, R.K., et al., 1954. Friendship as a social process: a substantive and methodological analysis. Freedom Control Mod. Soc. 18 (1), 18–66.

Lerner, J., 2019. Diversifying Investments: A Study of Ownership Diversity and Performance in the Asset Management Industry. Knight Foundation.

Lerner, J., Dewan, R., Ledbetter, J., Billias, A., 2021. Knight diversity of asset managers research series: Industry. In: John, S., James, L. (Eds.), Knight Foundation, and Bella Private Markets.

Levine, R., Rubinstein, Y., 2017. Smart and illicit: who becomes an entrepreneur and do they earn more? Q. J. Econ. 132 (2), 963–1018. https://doi.org/10.1093/qje/qjw044. https://academic.oup.com/qje/article/132/2/963/2724553.

Levine, R., Rubinstein, Y., 2020. Selection into entrepreneurship and self-employment. National Bureau of Economic Research.

Light, A., Ureta, M., 1995. Early-career work experience and gender wage differentials. J. Labor Econ. 13 (1), 121–154.

Lindquist, M.J., Sol, J., Van Praag, M., 2015. Why do entrepreneurial parents have entrepreneurial children? J. Labor Econ. 33 (2), 269–296. https://doi.org/10.1086/678493.

Lombard, K., 2001. Female self-employment and demand for flexible, nonstandard work schedules. Econ. Inq. 39 (2), 214–237. https://doi.org/10.1111/j.1465-7295.2001.tb00062.x.

Malenko, A., Nanda, R., Rhodes-Kropf, M., Sundaresan, S., 2021. Investment Committee Voting and the Financing of Innovation. Social Science Research Network, https://doi.org/10.2139/ssrn.3866854. https://papers.ssrn.com/abstract=3866854. Working Paper ID 3866854.

Markussen, S., Røed, K., 2017. The gender gap in entrepreneurship - the role of peer effects. J. Econ. Behav. Organ. 134, 356–373. https://doi.org/10.1016/j.jebo.2016.12.013.

Marx, M., 2022. Employee non-compete agreements, gender, and entrepreneurship. Organ. Sci. 33 (5), 1701–2083.

Marx, P., 2022. An absolute test of racial prejudice. J. Law Econ. Org. 38 (1), 42–91.

McPherson, M., Smith-Lovin, L., Cook, J.M., 2001. Birds of a feather: homophily in social networks. Annu. Rev. Sociol. 27 (1), 415–444. https://doi.org/10.1146/annurev.soc.27.1.415.

Metrick, A., Yasuda, A., 2010. The economics of private equity funds. Rev. Financ. Stud. 23 (6), 2303–2341.

Mincer, J., Ofek, H., 1982. Interrupted work careers: depreciation and restoration of human capital. J. Hum. Resour. 17 (1), 3–24. https://doi.org/10.2307/145520.

Mishkin, E., 2021. Gender and sibling dynamics in the intergenerational transmission of entrepreneurship. Manag. Sci. 67 (10), 5969–6627. https://doi.org/10.1287/mnsc.2020.3790.

Mobius, M.M., Rosenblat, T.S., 2006. Why beauty matters. Am. Econ. Rev. 96 (1), 222–235. https://doi.org/10.1257/000282806776157515.

Moskowitz, T.J., Vissing-Jørgensen, A., 2002. The returns to entrepreneurial investment: a private equity premium puzzle? Am. Econ. Rev. 92 (4), 745–778. https://doi.org/10.1257/00028280260344452.

Nanda, R., Rhodes-Kropf, M., 2016. Financing risk and innovation. Management Science 63 (4), 901–918. https://doi.org/10.1287/mnsc.2015.2350.

Neumark, D., 2012. Detecting discrimination in audit and correspondence studies. J. Hum. Resour. 47 (4), 1128–1157. https://doi.org/10.3368/jhr.47.4.1128. http://jhr.uwpress.org/content/47/4/1128.

Neumark, D., 2018. Experimental research on labor market discrimination. J. Econ. Lit. 56 (3), 799–866.

Neumark, D., Rich, J., 2019. Do field experiments on labor and housing markets overstate discrimination? A re-examination of the evidence. ILR Rev. 72 (1), 223–252. https://doi.org/10.1177/0019793918759665.

Niederle, M., Vesterlund, L., 2007. Do women shy away from competition? Do men compete too much? Q. J. Econ. 122 (3), 1067–1101. https://doi.org/10.1162/qjec.122.3.1067.

Oaxaca, R., 1973. Male-female wage differentials in urban labor markets. Int. Econ. Rev. 14 (3), 693–709. https://doi.org/10.2307/2525981. https://www.jstor.org/stable/2525981.

Oaxaca, R.L., Ransom, M.R., 1994. On discrimination and the decomposition of wage differentials. J. Econ. 61 (1), 5–21. https://doi.org/10.1016/0304-4076(94)90074-4.

Obermeyer, Z., Mullainathan, S., 2019. Dissecting racial bias in an algorithm that guides health decisions for 70 million people. In: FAT* '19. Proceedings of the Conference on Fairness, Accountability, and Transparency, January, Association for Computing Machinery, New York, NY, USA, p. 89.

Oreopoulos, P., 2011. Why do skilled immigrants struggle in the labor market? A field experiment with thirteen thousand resumes. Am. Econ. J. Econ. Pol. 3 (4), 148–171.

Parker, S.C., 2018. The Economics of Entrepreneurship, second ed. Cambridge University Press, Cambridge, ISBN: 978-1-107-17066-7, https://doi.org/10.1017/9781316756706. https://www.cambridge.org/core/books/economics-of-entrepreneurship/0E162493BAC1F3FCD0123518B0AF29FE.

Phelps, E.S., 1972. The statistical theory of racism and sexism. Am. Econ. Rev. 62 (4), 659–661. https://www.jstor.org/stable/1806107.

Pitchbook, 2022. 2022 Half-Year Update: Female Founders Remain Resilient | PitchBook. https://pitchbook.com/news/articles/2022-female-founders-venture-capital.

Pope, D.G., Sydnor, J.R., 2011. What's in a picture? Evidence of discrimination from Prosper. com. J. Hum. Resour. 46 (1), 53–92. https://doi.org/10.3368/jhr.46.1.53.

Puri, M., Zarutskie, R., 2012. On the life cycle dynamics of venture-capital- and non-venture-capital-financed firms. J. Financ. 67 (6), 2247–2293. https://doi.org/10.1111/j.1540-6261.2012.01786.x.

Raina, S., 2019. VCs, Founders, and the Performance Gender Gap. Social Science Research Network, Rochester, NY, https://doi.org/10.2139/ssrn.2846047. https://papers.ssrn.com/abstract=2846047. Working Paper ID 2846047.

Reuben, E., Sapienza, P., Zingales, L., 2014. How stereotypes impair women's careers in science. Proc. Natl. Acad. Sci. U.S.A. 111 (12), 4403–4408.

Robb, A.M., Robinson, D.T., 2014. The capital structure decisions of new firms. Rev. Financ. Stud. 27 (1), 153–179. https://doi.org/10.1093/rfs/hhs072.

Robb, A., Robinson, D.T., 2018. Testing for racial bias in business credit scores. Small Bus. Econ. 50 (3), 429–443. https://doi.org/10.1007/s11187-017-9878-2.

Robb, A., Coleman, S., Stangler, D., 2014. Sources of economic hope: women's entrepreneurship. Available at SSRN 2529094.

Rose, E.K., 2022. A constructivist perspective on empirical discrimination research. J. Econ. Lit., 30.

Ross, S.L., Yinger, J., 2002. The Color of Credit: Mortgage Discrimination, Research Methodology, and Fair-Lending Enforcement. MIT Press.

Sarsons, H., Gërxhani, K., Reuben, E., Schram, A., 2021. Gender Differences in Recognition for Group Work. J. Polit. Econ. 129 (1), 101–147. https://doi.org/10.1086/711401.

Schmalz, M.C., Sraer, D.A., Thesmar, D., 2017. Housing collateral and entrepreneurship. J. Financ. 72 (1), 99–132.

Schneider, D.J., 2005. The Psychology of Stereotyping. Guilford Press, ISBN: 978-1-59385-193-4.

Scott, E.L., Shu, P., 2017. Gender gap in high-growth ventures: evidence from a university venture mentoring program. Am. Econ. Rev. 107 (5), 308–311. https://doi.org/10.1257/aer.p20171009.

Shontell, A., 2021. Hundreds of startups go public every year. In: Only 20 are founded and led by women. Business Insider. https://www.businessinsider.com/female-entrepreneurs-face-obstacles-taking-companies-public-2020-12.

Small, M.L., Pager, D., 2020. Sociological perspectives on racial discrimination. J. Econ. Perspect. 34 (2), 49–67. https://doi.org/10.1257/jep.34.2.49.

Sohl, J., 2020. The Angel Market in 2019: Commitments by Angels Increase With a Significant Rise in Deal Valuations. (White Paper).

Sorenson, O., Dahl, M.S., Canales, R., Burton, M.D., 2021. Do startup employees earn more in the long run? Organ. Sci. 32 (3), 587–604.

Stanley, M., 2022. Asset Owners and Investing in Diversity: Intention Versus Action. https://www.morganstanley.com/articles/pension-fund-investment-prioritize-diversity.

Thébaud, S., 2015. Business as plan B: institutional foundations of gender inequality in entrepreneurship across 24 industrialized countries. Adm. Sci. Q. 60 (4), 671–711. https://doi.org/10.1177/0001839215591627.

Tracy, S.L., 2011. Accelerating Job Creation in America: The Promise of High-Impact Companies. US Small Business Administration, Office of Advocacy.

Wasserman, N., 2012. The Founder's Dilemmas: Anticipating and Avoiding the Pitfalls That Can Sink a Startup. Princeton University Press.

Wiswall, M., Zafar, B., 2018. Preference for the workplace, investment in human capital, and gender. Q. J. Econ. 133 (1), 457–507. https://doi.org/10.1093/qje/qjx035.

Yimfor, E., 2021. Brokers and Finders in Startup Offerings. Working Paper.

Younkin, P., Kuppuswamy, V., 2018. The colorblind crowd? Founder race and performance in crowdfunding. Manag. Sci. 64 (7), 3269–3287. https://doi.org/10.1287/mnsc.2017.2774.

Zandberg, J., 2021. Family comes first: reproductive health and the gender gap in entrepreneurship. J. Financ. Econ. 140 (3), 838–864. https://doi.org/10.2139/ssrn.3362347.

Zhang, Y., 2020. Discrimination in the Venture Capital Industry: Evidence From Two Randomized Controlled Trials. Working Paper.

Impact and performance

III

Stakeholder impact of private equity investments

Morten Sorensen[a],* and Ayako Yasuda[b]

[a]*Tuck School of Business, Dartmouth College, Hanover, NH, United States*
[b]*Graduate School of Management, University of California, Davis, CA, United States*
*Corresponding author: e-mail address: morten.sorensen@tuck.dartmouth.edu

Chapter outline

1 Introduction

Private equity investments are growing, as documented extensively elsewhere in this volume. A major form of private equity is buyouts, also known as leveraged buyouts (LBOs), where private equity funds, also known as buyout funds, acquire majority equity stakes in portfolio companies using large amounts of debt financing. Buyout funds are active investors, and they are intimately involved with and exert substantial control over the portfolio companies they acquire. In fact, it is reasonable to consider private equity ownership as a separate corporate governance form—distinct from, for example, being a publicly-traded or a family-owned business. There is now a substantial body of academic literature that investigates the implications of this governance form for (i) the portfolio company itself (including its management), (ii) employees and other stakeholders, and (iii) the broader society, including consumers, governments, the environment, and the industry. This chapter summarizes this literature and its main findings. We further review the nascent literature on impact funds—a type of dual-objective private equity fund—and frame its findings within the rapidly-growing literature on the environmental, social and governance (ESG) and sustainable investing.

1.1 Existing surveys

In addition to the other chapters in this volume, there are other academic surveys of private equity. Brown et al. (2020) provide a historical perspective of the development of the private equity industry and its performance. Kaplan and Strömberg (2009) describe the organization of private equity firms and their effects on the operations of portfolio companies. Metrick and Yasuda (2011) highlight the importance of private ownership, and the information asymmetry and illiquidity associated with private ownership, as a key explanatory factor of what makes private equity different from other asset classes. Eckbo and Thorburn (2013) reviews the literature on leveraged buyouts in a broader survey on corporate restructuring. Renneboog and Vansteenkiste (2017) reviews the literature on public-to-private LBOs, including the impact of the LBOs on stakeholders.

In contrast to these other surveys, this survey focuses on the impact of private equity ownership on the broader society and aims to shed light on critical market, industry, and regulatory factors that determine when the impact of private equity ownership is positive or negative, and for whom. A key insight is that there is an inherent ambiguity in the sign of the relationship between private equity ownership and the societal impact of the firm's activities when the private equity fund managers do not internalize those societal impacts in their objective functions.

1.2 Early studies

The modern version of buyouts dates back to the 1980s. The seminal acquisition of RJR Nabisco by Kohlberg, Kravis, and Roberts & Co, vividly described in the book "Barbarians at the Gate" (Burrough and Helyar, 1990) took place in 1988. Earlier studies of buyouts focused on the impact of private equity ownership on shareholders. Kaplan (1989a) analyzes data for 76 buyouts (LBOs and management buyouts) and documents that these transactions were followed by significant increases in operating margins and cash flows for the involved portfolio companies, both measured in absolute terms and relative to similar public companies. In another early study, Lichtenberg and Siegel (1990) find that the total factor productivity (TFP) increases for U.S. manufacturing companies that were acquired in buyouts. While recent studies add nuance and depth to our understanding of private equity transactions, the general conclusion that private equity transactions on average create value for, or at least do not harm, shareholders of portfolio companies emerged during this period and remains unchallenged.

1.3 Traditional dichotomy: Jensen (1989) vs Shleifer and Summers (1988)

Discussions of the impact of buyout transactions are often framed as a horse race between the views of Shleifer and Summers (1988) and Jensen (1989). Jensen (1989) emphasizes efficiency gains from private equity transactions. In particular, he argues that public companies suffer from agency problems due to free cash flows, and that private equity ownership with increased leverage can mitigate this problem and both improve social welfare and create gains for shareholders. While he recognizes the possibility of shareholder gains being offset by losses to other financial constituencies (e.g., bondholders) and stakeholders (e.g., employees), he argues that these losses are smaller and short-term compared to the efficiency gains that are long-term, such that takeovers are socially desirable.

In contrast, Shleifer and Summers (1988) emphasize that returns from private equity can often result from transfers from stakeholders, such as employees and suppliers, and not from efficiency gains. Thus, private equity gains need not equate social welfare gains. By the same token, worker layoffs need not equate social welfare loss, though the authors point out that "the redistribution is probably antiegalitarian." (p. 35).

In addition, Shleifer and Summers (1988) note that there are potential negative spillover effects from buyouts, such as the decline of the local economy after factory closures. They propose a particular mechanism of efficiency loss due to breach of implicit contracts. These negative spillover effects could result in overall social welfare loss and make private equity socially undesirable.

While Shleifer and Summers (1988) conjecture that the negative impact of private equity dominates and propose a particular theory of breach of implicit contracts, they do not conduct systematic empirical studies to measure the actual impact. Likewise, although Jensen (1986, 1989) conjectures that the positive impact of private equity dominates and posits that private equity solves a particular agency problem due to free cash flows, he does not conduct systematic empirical analysis to isolate this channel relative to other mechanisms.

In practice, both the positive and negative impacts of private equity can be present in a given transaction. Magnitudes of either effect can vary; as a result, the observed shareholder gains can be consistent with (i) efficiency gains alone, (ii) wealth transfers alone, or (iii) both efficiency gains and wealth transfers. Furthermore, each of these cases may or may not be accompanied by negative externality effects on the broader economy. Empirical findings of efficiency gains—often perceived to be in support of Jensen's arguments—do not necessarily reject Shleifer and Summers' concerns about shareholder gains due to transfers, and likewise, findings of employment loss—often perceived to be in support of Shleifer and Summers' arguments—do not necessarily reject Jensen's theory about efficiency gains. Therefore, instead of testing these hypotheses against each other in a horserace as if they are mutually exclusive, it is more informative to investigate the magnitudes and prevalence of the two effects, while allowing them to be simultaneously present.

One insight that has collectively emerged in the literature in the last three decades is that the pre-deal ownership type matters. Formerly-publicly-traded companies that get acquired by private equity firms (public-to-private deals) undergo systematically different transformations than formerly-privately-owned companies (private-to-private deals), with differential impact on the stakeholders and the broader society. Wealth transfers appear more predominant in public-to-private deals, whereas productivity gains and growth are associated more with private-to-private deals. Interestingly, private-to-private deals are typically less leveraged and more growth-oriented, and thus neither fit the inefficiently-run, cash-cow target architype that Jensen identified, nor are explained by the breach of implicit contracts à la Shleifer and Summers. This heterogeneity in value-generating mechanisms and outcomes underscores the limitation of any sweeping generalization about the social impact of private equity ownership/governance.

2 Incentives in private equity

There are several excellent descriptions of the organization and structure of private equity firms, including in the other chapters of this volume. To establish the terminology and economic relations for our discussion, we review a few central features below, but this is not meant as a comprehensive overview.

A private equity firm manages one or more funds. Each fund raises capital from a group of limited partners (LPs), typically pension funds and other institutional investors. The firm serves as the general partner (GP) of the fund, which is typically organized as a 10-year limited partnership. The fund uses the capital to acquire private assets, and the fund's type is determined by the nature of these assets. Two common types of private equity funds are venture capital funds that acquire equity stakes in young start-ups and buyout funds that acquire equity stakes in more mature companies.

Note that the term "private equity" is sometimes used to refer to either (i) the entire private equity asset class encompassing venture capital, growth, buyout, and distress investing, and (ii) buyout investing alone, which is the largest category of private equity in terms of assets under management. In this chapter, we focus mostly on the literature that studies buyout funds and their portfolio companies, except when we discuss impact funds, where most funds raised early in this category (and thus studied in the academic literature) were venture capital funds and buyout impact funds came into existence only in the last few years as of the writing of the chapter.

The day-to-day operations of a fund are managed by its general partner (sometimes this is structured as a separate management company, but for our purposes we simply refer to this as the general partner). The general partner decides which companies to acquire, how to manage these acquired portfolio companies, and when and how to sell them again. The general partner also decides when to raise follow-on funds and manages this fundraising process. In return, the general partner receives management fees and carried interest. Management fees are charged by the general partner for managing the limited partners' capital and they are around 2% annually of the fund's total committed capital. Carried interest is the general partner's profit share, which is typically 20% of the fund's overall profits.

2.1 Incentives for maximizing deal profits

Consider, in isolation, a single deal where a buyout fund acquires a portfolio company. The private equity structure provides the general partner with strong incentives for maximizing the profits from this deal. The general partner typically receives carried interest of 20% of the fund's profits, although this does not necessarily mean that the general partner's marginal benefit of increasing the profit from the deal by one dollar is exactly 20 cents, due to complications such as the fund being underwater due to losses in other deals, hurdle rates, and catch-up provisions.

These complications are typically second-order, though, and in most situations the general partner has strong incentives to maximize the profits generated in each deal.

An analytical framework, known as the buyout model, is useful for illustrating the implications of these incentives. In this framework, a buyout fund purchases a portfolio company with enterprise value EV_0 and excess cash EC_0. The enterprise value, EV_0, is the economic value of the company's ongoing business, which is typically the present value of its future free cash flows. Excess cash, EC_0, is the cash available to the company that exceeds the cash needed to sustain its ongoing operations. The zero subscripts indicate that these amounts are dated at the time just after the private equity fund acquires the company. The sum of the enterprise value and the excess cash is the company's total value, and it equals the combined value of the company's equity and debt.

The buyout fund finances the acquisition with debt, D_0, and equity, E_0:

$$EV_0 + EC_0 = D_0 + E_0 \qquad (1)$$

The debt, D_0, is the portfolio company's debt just after the closing of the private equity transaction, which is often substantially larger than the company's debt before the transaction, meaning that the private equity fund pays some of the acquisition price by taking on new debt in the portfolio company. Economically, this is analogous to a home buyer financing part of the purchase of a house by taking out a mortgage. The equity, E_0, is the remaining part of the purchase price, which is paid by the private equity fund, and this is also the initial value of the private equity fund's equity stake in the portfolio company.

A similar relationship holds at the time of the exit when the portfolio company is sold by the private equity fund. Using subscript one to denote the values at the time of this sale, the price of the equity, E_1, reflects the company's updated enterprise value, excess cash, and debt at the time of the exit. Again, it holds that:

$$EV_1 + EC_1 = D_1 + E_1 \qquad (2)$$

The fund's profit (or loss) from the deal, denoted P, derives from the change in the value of the fund's equity. This change is:

$$P = E_1 - E_0 = (EV_1 - EV_0) + (EC_1 - EC_0) - (D_1 - D_0) \qquad (3)$$

This expression shows that the profit from a private equity deal consists of three components. It arises from an increase in the enterprise value of the portfolio company, $EV_1 - EV_0$, corresponding to an increase in its economic value. It arises from the excess cash accumulated by the portfolio company during the holding period, $EC_1 - EC_0$. And it arises from the reduction in the portfolio company's debt during the holding period, $D_1 - D_0$.

One implication of this framework is that an immediate way for a private equity fund to increase the profits from a deal is to increase the portfolio company's enterprise value, i.e., increase its economic value as perceived by the acquirer in the future exit. Indeed, a survey of private equity firms by Gompers et al. (2016) reports that these firms place a heavy emphasis on adding value to their portfolio companies. The sources of added value, in order of importance, are increasing revenue, improving incentives and governance, facilitating a high-value exit or sale, making additional acquisitions, replacing management, and reducing costs. All of these sources directly serve to increase the portfolio company's enterprise value at the time of the exit.

The framework also shows the limits to how private equity funds can create profits in a deal. For example, an increase in the amount of leverage used to finance a deal does not mechanically increase the dollar amount of profits from the deal. An increase in leverage typically increases both D_0 and D_1, by largely similar amounts, so the effect mostly cancels out in the last term of the framework (the increases in the amounts may not exactly offset since, for example, an increase in initial leverage increases interest payments during the holding period, which may reduce either excess cash or limit the portfolio company's debt repayment over the holding period; these effects, however, are largely second order).

However, by making the cost basis of equity investment E_0 smaller for a given dollar amount of profit, an increase in the initial leverage does tend to increase the *return* on the equity investment, while also making it riskier.[a] Interest tax shields generated from higher leverage also contribute to increasing the enterprise value of the firm, ceteris paribus. Gompers et al. (2016) find that two-thirds of private equity investor survey respondents say they raise as much debt as the market will bear and that limited partners in private equity funds focus more on absolute performance as opposed to risk-adjusted returns.

As another example of the economics of a deal, a portfolio company can pay a special dividend to the fund. Such a dividend would be paid out of the portfolio company's excess cash, and it would thus reduce the price at which the portfolio company is sold in a future exit. In the framework, a special divided is offset by a corresponding reduction in the excess cash, leaving the fund's profits from the deal largely unchanged (again, the changes may not be exactly similar, and the profits may not be exactly unchanged, due to changes in interest payments and other similar effects).

Other considerations may influence the fund's decision to pay a dividend. For example, a special divided could allow the private equity fund to return capital to its limited partners earlier, which can increase the fund's internal rate of return (IRR) even if the dollar amount of profits remains largely unchanged. This effect would encourage funds to pay special dividends.

Alternatively, the reduction in the portfolio company's excess cash following a special dividend may affect the portfolio company's operations. If the portfolio company suffers from being liquidity constrained it would reduce its enterprise value.

---

[a]Suppose $EV_0 = 100$, $EC_0 = 10$, $EV_1 = 120$, and $EC_1 = 10$. In a low-leverage case, suppose $D_{L0} = D_{L1} = 50$; it implies that $E_{L0} = 100 + 10 - 50 = 60$ and $E_{L1} = 120 + 10 - 50 = 80$, so the return on equity investment is $(E_{L1}/E_{L0}) - 1 =$ is $(80/60) - 1 = 33\%$. In contrast, in a high leverage case, suppose $D_{H0} = D_{H1} = 100$; it implies that $E_{H0} = 100 + 10 - 5 = 100 = 10$ and $E_{H1} = 120 + 10 - 100 = 30$, so the return on equity investment is $(E_{H1}/E_{H0}) - 1 =$ is $(30/10) - 1 = 200\%$.

The fund only benefits from the dividend, but it suffers both from the reduction in excess cash, which is as large as the dividend, plus the loss arising from the decrease in the portfolio company's enterprise value, and a dividend that negatively affects the portfolio company's operations would therefore normally reduce the fund's overall profits from the deal. Hence, this effect would discourage funds from paying special dividends. In their investigation of corporate tax filings from leveraged buyouts during 2005 to 2009, Cohn et al. (2014) find that portfolio companies only make limited dividend payments, and they find no evidence that private equity firms "strip" value from otherwise healthy portfolio companies.

2.2 Incentives of a fund, deal flow

The above discussion considered the profits from a single deal. However, a fund typically invests in several deals, with 10–15 deals being normal numbers. The general partner's carried interest typically depends on the fund's aggregate profit across all deals net of management fees, where management fees are the total amount paid to the general partner during the lifetime of the fund:

$$Fund\ Profits = \Sigma_d\, P_d - Management\ Fees \qquad (4)$$

Deals are indexed by d, and P_d is the profits from deal d, as defined above. Management fees are specified contractually at the inception of a fund and are independent of the fund's performance. However, since management fees come out of the fund's committed capital, larger management fees will reduce the amount of capital available for investing in portfolio companies. Existing research finds that as much as two-thirds of the present value of the general partner's compensation comes from management fees (Metrick and Yasuda, 2010).

To maximize carried interest, holding the set of deals constant, the general partner would simply maximize the profits in each deal. However, holding the set of deals constant is not a trivial assumption. Private equity firms are concerned about their ability to identify and invest in attractive deals, but that may require maintaining a certain reputation to be able to access this "deal flow." Hence, even pure profit maximization at the fund level means that the private equity firm must be mindful about how its actions in a given deal affect the firm's reputation and ability to invest in other attractive deals. It is not inconsistent with profit maximization that a private equity firm leaves money on the table in a specific deal to maintain a reputation as a reasonable investor that other potential portfolio companies would want to work with in future deals. This reputational concern, for example, may induce a private equity owner to incur costs to maintain more stringent regulatory compliance standards in sectors where the framework is transparent and well-enforced than non-private equity owners. On the other hand, the same private equity owner may reverse its policy once the regulation is rolled back.

2.3 **Incentives of private equity firms, raising future funds**

Private equity firms typically manage a series of funds. The general partner's ultimate incentives arise from its concern about its aggregate management fees and carried interest across all its funds. Holding the set of funds constant, a general partner maximizes its aggregate compensation by considering both management fees and fund profits, as defined in Eq. (4) for each fund. The aggregate compensation is:

$$Firm\ Revenue = \Sigma_f \left[h_f \left(Fund\ Profits_f \right) + \text{Management fees}_f \right] \tag{5}$$

The function h_f captures the private equity firm's profit share for each fund, indexed by f. This function is weakly increasing in the fund profits, and a simple version of this function is $h_f(p) = \max(0, 20\%\ p)$, although this function can be more complex due to hurdle rates, catch-up provisions, and other features of the fund's "waterfall."

However, holding the set of funds constant is again not a trivial assumption. The sum is over both current and future funds, and Chung et al. (2012) argue that about half of a private equity firms' incentive pay arises from the effects of its current fund performance on its ability to raise future, typically larger, funds, which generate management fees and carried interest. The other half comes from carried interest earned on the current fund. Metrick and Yasuda (2010) and Chung et al. (2012) find that successful buyout fund managers increase their pay by scaling up the size of future funds rather than by increasing their compensation per dollar managed. The capital for these funds is provided by limited partners, which are typically institutional investors, such as pension funds, university endowments, and sovereign wealth funds. Hence, another concern for a private equity firm is whether the firm's investments and actions are consistent with the preferences and priorities of the limited partners and whether these investments and actions promote the private equity firm's future fundraising.

To summarize the above discussion, the incentives facing private equity firms and the general partners managing their funds are more complex than they may immediately appear. It may be natural to think that the large profit share—in the form of a 20% carried interest—simply means that private equity investors only maximize short-term profits in each deal above all else. However, the private equity organizational form creates more complex incentives for the private equity investors. First, a private equity fund only profits when a portfolio company is sold in an exit, and the sales price depends on the portfolio company's future economic viability. Hence, it is unlikely that extracting short-term profits at the expense of long-term viability is a significant source of profits for private equity funds. Second, a substantial part of a private equity firm's business hinges on its ability to make future investments in companies. Therefore, private equity firms may be concerned about maintaining a reputation for being reasonable investors even if this means leaving money on the table in a specific deal. Third, the private equity firm's ability to raise future and larger funds and earn both management fees and carried interest from those funds, hinges on the firm acting according to the preferences and priorities of limited partners. How these various trade-offs are resolved in practice is an empirical question.

2.4 Growth of environmental, social, and governance (ESG) investing and private equity

In recent years, an increasing share of limited partners who invest in private equity funds have integrated environmental, social, and governance (ESG) issues into their investment analysis. As a sign of increasing demand for ESG-conscious investment practices, as of March 2020, 3038 organizations representing $103.4 trillion in asset under management have become signatories to the United Nations Principles of Responsible Investment (UNPRI). These principles state that the signatories commit to "[i]ncorporate ESG issues into investment analysis," "[i]ncorporate ESG issues into our ownership policies and practices," and "[s]eek appropriate disclosure on ESG issues by the entities in which we invest."

There are two distinct motivations behind investors' push to incorporate ESG issues into their investment analysis. One is based on materiality, or the idea that the ESG practice of business has material impacts on their future financial performance, and therefore it is within the realm of asset managers' fiduciary duty to the beneficiary of its financial assets to incorporate ESG-related information into its investment analysis. Under this branch of responsible investment, the goal is still wealth maximization, but ESG issues are value-relevant and therefore should be disclosed and monitored just like other material information. This materiality-based motivation is consistent with U.S. fiduciary investors' recent push to incorporate ESG into their investment practice.

The other motivation is based on impact investing, or the idea that limited partners enjoy non-pecuniary benefits from generating positive externalities via their investments. This type of responsible investment is called dual-objective or double-bottom line because investors explicitly seek to generate both financial returns and positive societal impact at the same time. Indeed, 88% of UNPRI signatories are either investment managers or asset owners, and the UNPRI states that incorporation of ESG issues both fulfills the signatory's fiduciary duty as institutional investors, and also "may align investors with broader objectives of society." Notably, European fiduciary investors are permitted (and even required) to take into consideration broader social and public interests when screening their investments, while U.S. fiduciary investors are under strict regulatory guidelines to consider only the financial impact of investment decisions (or consider non-financial impact only when it is guaranteed not to lower financial return). This explains to a large degree the difference in expressed preferences and priorities of American vs European investors toward ESG and sustainable investments.

While European institutional investors have been quicker to integrate ESG issues into their investment process, in the last several years the pace of adoption has accelerated even among the American institutional investors. For example, in his influential annual letter to the CEOs of the largest corporations, the BlackRock CEO Larry Fink wrote: "[A] company cannot achieve long-term profits without embracing purpose and considering the needs of a broad range of stakeholders" (Fink, 2020) and "with the world undergoing the largest transfer of wealth in history: $24 trillion from baby boomers to millennials. As wealth shifts and investing preferences change, environmental, social, and governance issues will be increasingly material to corporate valuations." (Fink, 2019) Also, climate risk is increasingly seen as an investment risk, endangering sustainability of investment portfolios. In response, major asset managers and asset owners around the world have started planning for transitions to net-zero portfolios, or portfolios with net-zero greenhouse gas emissions.

Pedersen et al. (2021) build an ESG-adjusted capital asset pricing model in which three types of investors differ in their preferences and information sets with respect to assets' ESG characteristics, and their respective portfolio decisions affect equilibrium asset prices and returns. ESG-motivated investors derive utility from holding high-ESG score assets. ESG-aware investors use firms' ESG scores to update their views on risk and expected returns. ESG-unaware investors are unaware and therefore ignore ESG scores. In the model, ESG-aware investors may get superior outcomes when ESG scores convey value-relevant information. This insight suggests that materiality of ESG information may drive limited partner demand for ESG disclosures by private equity funds, even if they are not ESG-motivated investors.

Given this accelerating shift in investors' preferences for ESG incorporation, general partners in private equity firms are responding by committing to greater ESG disclosures and in some cases raising impact funds that explicitly target generation of positive externalities. Indeed, Preqin reports that "[s]ince 2011, more than 4,400 ESG-committed private capital funds have closed, totaling $3.06tn in combined assets" (Preqin, 2020). This is consistent with the incentives of general partners to maximize their ability to raise future funds by catering to the preferences of their limited partners.

3 Private equity management model

As described in Section 2, private equity funds use a contractual format of finite-life, closed-end limited partnerships that provide general partners with a particular set of incentives and access to their portfolio companies. What does this imply about the effect of private equity ownership on the shareholders, other companies' stakeholders, and society at large? The literature has mostly focused on analyzing the principal-agent problem between portfolio company shareholders and their managers, and how the private equity model purports to solve this agency problem better than public companies can solve it (Jensen, 1989). In contrast, the effect of the private equity management model on portfolio company stakeholders and other parties in the society at large is underexplored. In this section, we (i) review the proposed private equity solution to the principal-agent problem, (ii) posit the private equity model as a potential solution to the ESG monitoring problem of responsible investors, and (iii) point out the ambiguity of the relationship between private equity ownership and the impact on stakeholders.

3.1 Principal-agent problems in public corporations

The literature has identified three ways in which managers of public corporations may behave in value-destroying manners from shareholders' point of view. First, Jensen (1986, 1989) argues that when managers have too much discretion over how to spend any free cash flows of the company they manage, they tend to engage in empire building by investing in projects with negative net present value (NPV) to increase the managers' spheres of influence, and/or to consume private benefits. Second, Bertrand and Mullainathan (2003) find that, when public company managers are shielded from takeovers by state laws, they invest less, pay higher wages to themselves and their peers, and enjoy the quiet life, to the detriment of profitability and productivity of the companies. Finally, while public investors scrutinize hard information such as quarterly earnings and stock returns, they face free-riding problems and lack incentives to produce soft information about a manager's efforts, ability and quality. Subsequently, this narrow focus on quarterly earnings and share prices by public market investors leads to short-termism by company managers, which in turn destroys shareholder values by distracting the managers from long-term strategic thinking and investment horizons (see Bebchuk and Weisbach, 2010 for a survey). Moreover, all three of the agency problems are exacerbated when boards are captured by insiders. Both regulators and firms themselves propose using independent directors as a remedy for these agency problems, and the literature documents some benefits associated with independence of directors (e.g., Chhaochharia and Grinstein, 2006). However, independent directors' effectiveness as monitors depends on their own incentives, and thus can be diminished due to lack of information access, busy-ness, or both (see Bebchuk et al., 2010; Fich and Shivdasani, 2012).

3.2 Posited solutions with private equity management Model 1.0: Traditional view

Kaplan and Strömberg (2009) identify three value-creating activities associated with the private equity management model: Financial engineering, governance engineering, and operational engineering. Each of these activities is characterized as a potential solution to the aforementioned principal-agent problem in public corporations. First, under financial engineering, buyouts typically result in the elevated leverage ratios for portfolio companies for a sustained period of time. Jensen (1986, 1989) argues that pledging future cash flows to repay the debtholders reduces the agency problems and leads managers to engage in less empire building. Moreover, the higher interest payments increase the present value of the interest tax shields, thus enhancing the value of the company, as long as the cost of financial distress does not increase significantly as a result. These are described as the financial engineering aspect of the private equity management model.

Second, under governance engineering, private equity sponsors typically obtain majority ownership of the portfolio companies they acquire, which eliminates the free-rider problem of monitoring public companies and enables the private equity sponsors to closely monitor their portfolio company executives using both hard and soft information about the executives' managerial performance. Combined with the lack of public stock prices and extended holding period, the monitoring focus shifts from short-term earnings management to long-term value realization. Additionally, portfolio company executives are typically given greater equity incentives under private equity ownership than when they are publicly held. Meanwhile, they enjoy less generous perks (e.g., less frequent use of private jets) than their public company counterparts. Since the equity shares are privately held and lack liquidity, executives are incentivized to realize long-term capital gains for the company, which they can unlock only after the investments are exited, rather than short-term upswings in the stock prices.

Finally, private equity firms accumulate in-house industry and operating expertise by hiring operating partners with operating backgrounds and an industry focus who then apply this expertise to add value to their portfolio companies. Kaplan and Strömberg (2009) note that, while financial and governance engineering were common by the late 1980s, operating engineering was added in more recent years to private equity firms' repertoire of value-creating tools. Private equity firms use this industry-specific know-how to identify attractive targets, to develop value creation plans, and to implement the plans.

3.3 Posited solutions with private equity management Model 2.0: Growth, competency, and non-financial outcomes

While the early literature analyzed the private equity management model through the lens of fixing what is broken in the public company governance mechanism, more recently the literature has expanded its focus to the rationale behind private-to-private private equity transactions. After all, most private equity transactions are private-to-private deals, so how can the private equity funds unlock value for companies that already have concentrated ownership and illiquidity? The literature offers two possibilities. First, many private companies face limited access to capital, and this constrains their ability to grow. By unlocking the access to both debt and equity capital, the private equity sponsors may spur growth in the private companies they acquire. Second, private companies may lack the scale, name recognition, and prestige of public companies to attract professionalized managers (e.g., MBA graduates), and thus be less effective at executing their corporate strategy. By becoming associated with prominent private equity firms, which routinely recruit professional executives for their portfolio companies and often have in-house operating partners with senior industry expertise, private companies may improve the managerial skill level of their personnel.

The recent push by institutional investors to incorporate ESG factors into their investment process creates yet another possibility that the private equity management model offers a differential outcome for investors with pro-social or pro-environmental preferences. For example, Hart and Zingales (2017) argue that when (i) shareholders have pro-social preferences, (ii) profit-making and damage-generating activities of companies are non-separable, and (iii) government cannot perfectly internalize negative externalities through laws and regulations, then companies should seek to maximize shareholder welfare rather than market value. Prosocial investors in the model are ethical in plausibly limited ways: If put to a vote, they put positive weight on externalities generated by their decisions, but without such votes they are "willing to hold shares in tobacco or gun or oil companies, and indeed will pay full price for these shares" (p. 267). This and the atomistic weight of individual shareholders creates an "amoral drift," a tendency for public companies to "underweight social surplus much more than privately held companies" (p. 258). Focusing on public companies, the authors propose allowing broader shareholder proxy voting on corporate policy as a mechanism to implement the welfare-maximizing objective that aggregates the preferences of the shareholders. This proposal is interesting because the private equity fund structure allows limited partners and general partners to write contracts that fix the identities of the limited partners and aggregate their preferences at the time of the inception of the fund. Moreover, the weight of individual investors in the partnership and in the ownership structure of each portfolio company is substantial, and thus prevents the amoral drift. Though Fama (2021) raises concerns about the difficulty of coordinating heterogenous and multidimensional ESG preferences of investors in public companies, the 10-year commitment requirement of private equity funds prevents limited partner turnover and temporal shift in aggregate investor preferences. Thus, the debate on ESG incorporation raises a possibility that private equity-owned companies make choices that are more consistent with social preferences of their ultimate owners than either public companies or non-private equity private companies.[b]

3.4 Ambiguity of the effect of private equity management model on stakeholders and society at large

While research suggests that the private equity management model has a positive effect on shareholder value, its effect on the company's other stakeholders or society at large is less clear. For example, suppose a private equity fund takes over a portfolio company and provides its executives with high-powered incentives of significant long-term equity stakes. The company executives, in response, implement heavy investments in high-growth divisions, upgrade the company's IT system, and upskill its high-skilled labor through IT training, while automating and offshoring low-skill jobs and divesting non-performing divisions. On the one hand, this might result in

---

[b]Also see Broccardo et al. (2021), Pedersen et al. (2021), and Pástor et al. (2021).

rent extraction from the company's manufacturing plant employees, who face either job losses, or wage and benefit reductions, as posited in Shleifer and Summers (1988). On the other hand, the same strategy implementation may also result in enhanced rent sharing with the so-called knowledge workers of the company, who experience upskilling, productivity increases, and thus wage and benefit increases.

Likewise, the effects of high-powered incentives of private equity portfolio company executives on the company's customers, the government/taxpayers (via tax revenues or subsidy payments), industry-level innovation, or the environment are a priori ambiguous and remain open empirical questions. This is natural in the sense that the logic/rationale of the private equity management model is traditionally shareholder-centric, and the effects on other related parties are side products of the pursuit of a single-objective maximization. One exception is the newly emerging realm of impact investing, which is an explicitly dual-objective investment model where investors intentionally wish to pursue financial as well as non-financial goals simultaneously.

4 Impact on management, productivity, and efficiency

4.1 Executives, management, board of directors

It is common for private equity investors to replace a portfolio company's management in connection with a private equity transaction. In a survey of (mostly U.S.-based) private equity investors, Gompers et al. (2016) find that CEOs and CFOs are replaced in 30.6–42.9% of private equity transactions and that 57.8% of the surveyed private equity firms routinely recruit their own senior management teams. Biesinger et al. (2020) study value creation plans for the individual deals of (mostly emerging market) private equity funds; 20% of the plans explicitly mention replacing the CEO, 20% mention replacing the CFO, and 26% of the plans mention replacing other managers.

Replacing managers matters. Looking at buyout transactions, Guo et al. (2011) find that operating cash flows improve more when the private equity firm replaces the CEO at or soon after the buyout. Focusing on the individual CEOs of the portfolio companies and their personalities and traits, Kaplan et al. (2012) report that a CEO's execution ability is particularly important for a successful outcome. Interestingly, Biesinger et al. (2020) reach a similar conclusion from the value creation plans. They find that the action items that are actually implemented are more important than the specific choice of strategy, with diminishing returns to making plans ever more detailed, leading them to conclude that "execution is the key."

Given this focus on the management, it is perhaps unsurprising that portfolio companies tend to have better management practices. In an extensive study of management practices, Bloom et al. (2015) conduct about 15,000 interviews with managers in about 10,000 manufacturing plants in 34 countries and score their management practices. They find that private equity-owned companies have better management practices than most other company types such as family-run, founder owned, or government owned firms. The only exception is dispersed shareholder firms (e.g., publicly-listed firms), which have similar levels of the management score as private equity-owned firms. They find a significant gap in the quality of management practices between private equity-owned portfolio companies and the practices of family-owned and other private companies. This gap is robust not only in developed countries but also in developing countries—where private ownership of companies is more prevalent and where capital markets are less developed than in developed economies–suggesting that in those countries private equity acquisition is an important mechanism through which better management practices are introduced to private companies. This finding is noteworthy because most companies are private companies, especially in developing countries with less developed public markets, and these private companies are the typical targets of private equity acquisitions.

An important aspect of management practice is management compensation. Gompers et al. (2016) report that private equity investors use more aggressive compensation packages to incentivize the senior management of portfolio companies. In 61.1–65.1% of the transactions in their study, the private equity investors specifically mention improved managerial incentives as a source of increased value. Cronqvist and Fahlenbrach (2013) find that private equity investors increase the CEO's base salary and bonus by 25%, with the salary increases concentrated among newly appointed CEOs. About half of the equity grants to portfolio company CEOs only vest at the time of an exit event, such as a sale or IPO of the portfolio company, which aligns the CEOs' incentives with the investors' need for a timely exit. Severance contracts for portfolio company CEOs are also stricter with respect to unvested equity, which is often forfeited. Cronqvist and Fahlenbrach (2013) further report that private equity investors are less likely to tie CEO compensation and bonuses to qualitative, nonfinancial, and earnings-based performance measures. Instead, CEO compensation and bonuses depend on more quantitative targets, such as cash flow-based measures (e.g., EBITDA) with less accounting discretion. Bloom et al. (2015) find a slightly weaker relation in their global survey of management practices. They report that private equity-owned companies provide significantly stronger managerial incentives with more direct links to the managers' effort and ability. However, only the unconditional difference is statistically significant, and it becomes insignificant when they include country, company, industry, and other controls. Nevertheless, the broader evidence suggests that private equity ownership provides CEOs with steep financial incentives to align the managers' interests with the interests of the private equity investor.

Another related aspect of management practice is managerial turnover. Interestingly, while private equity investors are initially more likely to replace management at the time of the buyout transaction, Cornelli and Karakas (2015) document that once the deal is completed, private equity investors are less likely to replace management going forward. They attribute this lower turnover rate to private equity investors having more inside information and being more effective at monitoring the managers, which in turn allows the private equity investors to evaluate the managers' performance over a longer time horizon relative to their publicly-traded counterparts. Consistent with this interpretation, Bloom et al. (2015) find that portfolio companies have particularly strong monitoring practices (described as "practices around continuous performance measurement, improvement, and feedback") as compared to other types of companies.

Cornelli et al. (2013) use monitoring reports from the European Bank for Reconstruction and Development (ERBD) to study determinants of individual turnover decisions. The reports allow them to distinguish between the role of "soft" and "hard" information when the boards of portfolio companies replace the CEO. Interestingly, soft information seems to play a larger role than hard information. One interpretation is that private equity investors have closer and more direct connections to the managers and boards of their portfolio companies, and that these investors are therefore less likely to replace a CEO for bad performance that is due to external factors, e.g., bad luck. Instead, they argue, private equity investors are more deliberate when replacing CEOs. In contrast, boards of publicly-traded companies appear to place less weight on the reasons for poor performance. To identify the causal effect, the authors exploit staggered governance reforms that increase boards' personnel authority to dismiss CEOs and find that forced CEO turnover causes improved firm performance.

Acharya et al. (2009) explore the board dynamics of UK-based portfolio companies in more detail. They confirm that CEOs are replaced in connection with private equity transactions, as mentioned above, and they also interview 20 chairpersons and CEOs that have experience with both public and private boards. Contrasting the board structures of private equity-owned portfolio companies with the structures in UK public companies (PLCs) in the FTSE 100, they report that private equity boards are more efficient and have a more concentrated focus on value creation. PLC boards suffer from being larger, being more focused on quarterly profits and market expectations, and having greater concerns about the reactions of external stakeholders than the impact of their decisions on business performance. They identify three main characteristics of private equity boards: they are well-aligned with a focus on value creation, clearly articulate and insist on strategic and performance priorities, and have a greater engagement by the board members. In their sample, three-quarter of the interviewees report that private equity boards add more value than PLC boards. None reported that the public counterparts were better.

4.2 Productivity and efficiency

In his classical analysis of the agency problems facing different types of companies, especially conglomerates, and the value of the private equity governance model, Jensen (1989) focuses on the "free cash flow problem" in poorly governed companies. This agency problem arises when mature companies with stable cash flows and few profitable investment opportunities make wasteful investments to promote managerial empire building (see also Jensen 1986). According to Jensen (1989), the ability to mitigate this problem is a main benefit of private equity ownership. In support of the free cash flow hypothesis, Opler and Titman (1993) find that high cash flow firms with low Tobin's q are more likely to be acquired in a buyout. A more direct test of this hypothesis is the study by Edgerton (2012) of corporate fleets of private jets. Larger jet fleets typically reflect wasteful managerial perks, and consistent with Jensen's hypothesis Edgerton (2012) finds that private equity-owned portfolio companies have significantly smaller fleets than other publicly-traded or private companies, on average, and he finds clear reductions in fleet size after public companies are taken private in buyouts. Many public companies have fleets that appear large by the standards of private equity-owned companies, which he argues is consistent with agency problems in these public companies, although with the caveat that excessive fleets are far from ubiquitous in public companies.

Early Studies: Although Jensen (1989) originally focused specifically on the "free cash flow problem," a number of other contemporaneous studies found more general improvements in the productivity of portfolio companies, and they generally reported that the increases in productivity were not primarily due to reductions in employment.

In their study of a single prominent transaction, Baker and Wruck (1989) explore the highly levered 1986 acquisition of the O.M. Scott & Sons Company as a divisional buyout from the ITT conglomerate. Baker and Wruck report that "operating performance improved dramatically following the buyout" with sales increasing by 25% and earnings before interest and taxes increasing by 56%. The improvements are attributed to three factors: the constraints imposed by high leverage, changes in managerial compensation, and improvements in monitoring and advising of Scott's top management. Moreover, they find no evidence that the improvements came at the expense of employees, although annual employment declined by 9% through natural attrition over the first 2 years following the buyout. Additionally, the improvements were not caused by a reduction in spending on R&D, marketing, or capital expenditures, which actually increased by 23% after this buyout.

Other early studies, using larger samples of private equity transactions, largely confirm these findings. Kaplan (1989a) find substantial increases in operating income, net cash flows, and market value in a sample of 76 portfolio companies, and he argues that these increases are due to improved managerial incentives and reduced agency problems, not transfers from employees.

Smith (1990) reports similar increases in operating cash flows in a sample of 58 portfolio companies, and she highlights the role of improved working capital management and managerial incentives. She also confirms that the increase in operating returns is not due to layoffs or reductions in advertising, maintenance, or research and development, although she does find a decline in capital expenditures.

Muscarella and Vetsuypens (1990) consider 72 reverse LBOs, i.e., transactions where a portfolio company that was previously public and is taken private in a private equity transaction is later listed again in an IPO. As part of the IPO process, the company must disclose several years of financial statements, and these reverse LBOs therefore offer a view into the financials and operations of portfolio companies before and after the private equity transaction, although the subsample of portfolio companies that undergo this specific sequence of transactions may not be representative. Consistent with the previous studies, Muscarella and Vetsuypens (1990) find that portfolio companies in their sample show significant improvements in profitability, mainly due to cost reductions. They do not find evidence of reductions in employment.

Finally, Lichtenberg and Siegel (1990) use Census data for 72 portfolio companies to study changes in total factor productivity (TFP). In the 3 years following a buyout the average TFP increases by 8.3% relative to the industry average. Consistent with the above studies, they do not find any change in the employment of production workers (blue-collar), and they report cumulative increases in the compensation of these production workers of 2.3–3.6%. The employment of non-production workers (white-collar), however, declines by 8.5%.

Later Studies: Later studies of private equity transactions that took place during the 1990s and 2000s find more mixed results and generally do not find statistically significant effects on productivity and profitability. In an unpublished working paper, Leslie and Oyer (2008) contrast portfolio companies with publicly-traded comparable companies. Like Muscarella and Vetsuypens (1990), Leslie and Oyer study reverse LBOs—i.e., portfolio companies that were publicly traded before being acquired by a private equity fund and which became publicly traded again when the fund listed them in an IPO. Their sample contains 144 such transactions taking place from 1996 to 2005. They report that top managers of portfolio companies have substantially higher-powered compensation contracts. These managers own more equity, have lower base salaries, and have a larger fraction of variable compensation. In terms of operational improvements, they find that portfolio companies improve the measure Sales per Employee. However, they find no statistically significant changes in their other performance measures: Return on Assets (ROA), EBITDA/Total Assets, and Employees/Total Assets.

As a brief aside, when interpreting such accounting measures of operating performance, a concern is whether portfolio companies engage in more aggressive earnings management. Katz (2009) finds that private equity-backed companies have higher earnings quality than those that do not have private equity sponsorship, engage less in earnings management, and report more conservatively both before and after the IPO. These findings are consistent with tighter monitoring and reputational considerations exhibited by buyout investors.

Following Leslie and Oyer (2008), Guo et al. (2011) revisit the productivity impact of private equity in a sample of 194 public-to-private U.S. buyout transactions from 1990 to 2006, with deal values exceeding $100 million. They find an 11% increase in EBITDA and net cash flows. They also find some improvements in operating performance, although these are not statistically significant.

Cohn et al. (2014) study 317 buyouts of previously public companies, taking place from 1995 to 2007, using earnings and revenue information from corporate tax filings. Consistent with the above studies, in this sample of public-to-private transactions, they find no significant effects on Return on Sales, Return on Assets, and their measure of economic value added (EVA).

Following up on the previous study, however, Cohn et al. (2022) use similar tax filings to study 288 buyouts, taking place from 1995 to 2009, but now focusing on buyouts of private companies. Interestingly, their findings are different in this sample of private-to-private transactions. They find a moderate but significant increase in profitability, both in absolute terms and relative to the industry. Moreover, they find large and rapid increases in revenue after a buyout, which they argue reflects both organic and acquisition-driven growth. Their interpretation is that for private targets, unlike for public targets, a main source of value creation is unlocking growth opportunities by relaxing financing constraints. The relatively active market for acquisitions of U.S. private companies enables private equity acquirers to use portfolio companies as platforms for acquiring other small companies. While buyouts of public companies may alleviate overinvestment problems, their results suggest that buyouts of private companies solve underinvestment problems. They find no evidence that financial engineering is a significant source of value creation for buyouts of private companies, since these companies already have relatively high levels of leverage and therefore only see a smaller increase in leverage following the transaction.

Davis et al. (2014) use Census data to investigate, among others, the effects of U.S. buyouts on the total factor productivity (TFP) of manufacturing plants. For this analysis, they have TFP data for 286 multiunit manufacturing companies acquired by private equity firms between 1980 and 2003. The risk of a plant exiting in the 2 years after the acquisition depends critically on the productivity of the plant. In the bottom tercile of the TFP distribution, the exit probability is significantly higher for plants operated by private equity-owned portfolio companies than for plants operated by companies in the control group. In contrast, there are no significant differences in the exit probabilities in the middle and top terciles. They report a similar pattern for the opening of new plants. Plants opened by private equity-owned companies are substantially more likely to be in the top tercile and significantly less likely to be in the bottom tercile of the TFP distribution than plants opened by companies in the control group. For continuing plants, they do not find evidence of changes in productivity relative to plants in the control group. Overall, they summarize their findings as evidence that private equity firms reallocate activity to raise TFP, that the large TFP advantage of portfolio companies reflects a concentration of new plants in the upper part of the TFP distribution and exits of plants in the lower end of the TFP distribution, and that their results refute the view that the returns to private equity rest entirely on private gains to financial engineering and wealth transfers from other stakeholders.

In a recent working paper, Davis et al. (2021) revisit the analysis using an extended sample and refined empirical methods. Their results, while preliminary, show even larger average productivity gains when both manufacturing and non-manufacturing industries are included in the sample. Moreover, this analysis also suggests that there are significant differences between public-to-private and private-to-private buyouts, consistent with the different findings in Cohn et al. (2014), focusing on public-to-private transactions, and Cohn et al. (2022), focusing on private-to-private transactions.

Studies of Non-U.S. Transactions: The studies mentioned above have primarily studied U.S.-based portfolio companies. It is interesting to supplement these studies with studies of buyouts in other countries. Other countries have different regulatory and governance systems. They typically have relatively more privately held companies, and they may have capital markets that make it more difficult for these companies to raise external capital, leaving them more capital constrained. Other countries also often have better data for portfolio companies than what is available for U.S. private companies. Interestingly, studies of non-U.S. buyouts find more consistent evidence of operational improvements than studies of U.S. buyouts during the same periods. This difference may be due to differences in the nature of buyouts in these counties or to the composition of buyouts in these other countries having relatively more private than public targets.

In an early study of non-U.S. buyouts, Bergström et al. (2007) consider the entire universe of 73 Swedish buyout exits, exceeding $5 m, during the period 1998 to 2006. They find substantial and significant improvements in EBITDA margins and ROIC, and smaller increases in revenue, which are less statistically significant. Moreover, employment and wage levels in their portfolio companies have not declined relative to the levels in comparable Swedish companies. A natural concern about this study is selection bias, since the sample is a sample of realized exits. Portfolio companies that have gone bankrupt or are being held for extended time periods may be underrepresented in this sample, although Bergström, Grubb, and Jonsson argue that this is rare in Sweden and therefore unlikely to affect their results.

Bouchly et al. (2011) find even stronger effects in a sample of 839 French buyouts from 1994 to 2004. They use financial statements from tax filings to track the portfolio companies before and after the buyout, and they find large and statistically significant growth in profitability, employment, sales, and capital expenditures. From 4 years before to 4 years after the transaction, employment grows by 18%, assets grow by 12%, and sales grow by 12%, on average, relative to comparable companies. Interestingly, this growth is concentrated in portfolio companies that are privately-held before the buyout, i.e., private-to-private transactions, as opposed to divisional buyouts or buyouts of publicly-traded companies. In France, these privately-held companies are often owned by an individual or a family that is cashing out of its business. Moreover, the improvements are concentrated in portfolio companies in industries that rely more on external capital. Overall, the evidence suggests that private equity investments relax credit constraints for portfolio companies and that this benefit may be particularly important in France due to its relatively underdeveloped capital markets, at least during this sample period. The findings and interpretation appear consistent with Cohn et al. (2022) and Davis et al. (2021), discussed above, who study recent buyouts of U.S.-based private companies, and who also find strong growth and evidence of private equity investments alleviating capital constraints for private portfolio companies.

Focusing on innovation and patenting, Amess et al. (2016) study 407 U.K. buyouts between 1998 and 2005. They find a 6% increase in quality-adjusted patent stock 3 years after the buyout, but the improvement in innovation is even stronger for private-to-private transactions and for portfolio companies in financially dependent industries, which is also consistent with private equity investments relaxing financial constraints in portfolio companies and facilitating their investments in innovation activity. Nikoskelainen and Wright (2007) and Renneboog et al. (2007) provide further UK evidence, and Cumming et al. (2007) provide a literature review of global evidence related to governance and financial and real returns to private equity.

However, studying European acquisitions more generally, and excluding private equity transactions, Erel et al. (2015) find significant increases in investments, reduced cash holdings, and lower investment cash flow sensitivities after these acquisitions, which they interpret as evidence that financial constraints are reduced for target companies in general acquisitions, and not just for private equity-driven ones.

Role of General Partners: Acharya et al. (2013) study the role of general partners in a sample of 395 buyout acquisitions of European portfolio companies from 1991 to 2007. They find that the EBITDA to Sales ratio increases by 0.4% annually, on average relative to the sector mean, and that the deal multiple, EBITDA to Enterprise Value, increases by around 1, on average relative to the sector mean. They interpret these improvements as the causal impact of private equity ownership, which creates economic value through operational improvements. Interestingly, they go further and explore the identities and backgrounds on the individual general partners that are responsible for managing each transaction. Deal partners with an operational background, typically ex-consultants or ex-industry managers, are associated with greater outperformance in "organic" deals where the portfolio company mainly improves internally. In contrast, partners with a background in finance, e.g., ex-bankers or ex-accountants, are associated with "inorganic" and M&A driven strategies.

Echoing the heterogeneity of value-creation strategies employed by private equity firms, Davis et al. (2021) find that employment effects of private equity ownership is highly persistent over time at the private equity firm level. Spaenjers and Steiner (2021) study specialist vs generalist private equity firms investing in the U.S. hotel industry and find that specialist private equity investors are associated with value creation through operational performance improvement. In contrast, generalist private equity investors are more associated with value creation through cheaper source of debt financing. Biesinger et al. (2020) find systematic differences across funds in their ability to achieve the objectives set out in the value creation plans for their deals. Funds with focused, homogeneous portfolios of predominantly minority positions are better at implementing these plans than other funds. Focusing on a single industry, Bernstein and Sheen (2016) find that private equity firms with specific experience in the restaurant industry do significantly better than firm with more general operational experience.

4.3 Financial distress and bankruptcy

A natural concern is whether the high leverage imposed on portfolio companies in connection with a private equity deal makes the company more financially fragile. In a study of U.S. private equity deals, Hotchkiss et al. (2021) find that private equity-backed companies have higher leverage and default at higher rates than other companies borrowing in leveraged loan markets. However, conditional on being in default, private equity-backed companies restructure more quickly and more frequently out of court, and private equity owners are less likely to be wiped out in this process.

Wilson and Wright (2013) consider a sample of UK companies, focusing on UK private equity deals during 1995 to 2010. Controlling for size, age, sector and other conditions, they report that portfolio companies in private equity-backed buyouts are no more likely to become insolvent than other similar companies.

Neither study considers the externality cost of distress and bankruptcy on other stakeholders or the broader economy. Thus, while private equity investors may avoid some of the negative impact of distress and bankruptcy despite the high leverage of portfolio companies, the impact on other stakeholders and the broader economy remains under-studied.

5 Impact on employees and other stakeholders

A common concern about private equity is that it does not actually create value but instead expropriates value from a broader set of the portfolio company's stakeholders. As mentioned earlier, in their seminal work, Shleifer and Summers (1988) study this question in the context of hostile takeovers and conclude that "transfers from stakeholders to shareholders could make for a large part of the takeover premium" (p. 53), including transfers from workers, suppliers, and the government (in the form of tax savings from high leverage). They note, however, that private equity encompasses both hostile takeovers and friendly M&As, and they are "targeted at very different companies" and represent difference "economic processes." This observation echoes the heterogenous outcomes on growth and productivity documented in Section 4 for public-to-private vs private-to-private transactions.

5.1 Employment and wages at portfolio companies

The two most comprehensive studies of the effects of U.S. buyouts on employment and wages are Davis et al. (2014) and the follow-on study Davis et al. (2021).[c]

---

[c]Kaplan (1989a) finds that raw median employment growth (excluding divestitures) of large public-to-private buyouts is 4.9% and negative but insignificant when industry-adjusted. Faccio and Hsu (2017) find evidence of higher job creation by targets of politically connected private equity firms than non-connected private equity firms. Consistent with an exchange of favors story, politically connected private equity firms increase employment more during election years and in states with high levels of corruption.

Davis et al. (2014) use U.S. census data to track employment at 3200 portfolio companies and their 150,000 establishments that were acquired by private equity funds from 1980 to 2005. They match portfolio companies and establishments to similar controls and follow the targets and matched controls over several years after the private equity transaction. They find that portfolio companies reduce employment by <1% relative to control firms in the first 2 years, but this small net effect masks larger differences at the establishment level. Specifically, private equity owners actively re-allocate employment across existing establishments by reducing employment or exiting establishments altogether at some locations, while expanding employment at other locations. Further, portfolio companies create more greenfield jobs at new establishments than control firms. Portfolio companies also acquire and divest more than controls. Finally, earnings per worker in portfolio companies declines by 2.4% relative to controls.

Expanding on this original study, Davis et al. (2021) examine U.S. private equity buyouts from 1980 to 2013, increasing the sample to about 3600 targets and 6.4 million total company-level observations. The main insight of this follow-on study as it relates to employment impact of private equity buyouts is the sharp contrast in outcomes between public-to-private vs private-to-private deals: Employment shrinks 13% over 2 years after buyouts of publicly-listed firms relative to control firms, but expands 13% after buyouts of privately-held firms. The authors argue that "[f] or targets that trade publicly before the buyout, private equity groups may focus on tackling the agency problems … whether manifested as excess headcounts, wasteful perquisites, or value-destroying 'pet projects.'" They also point out that the results are consistent with the workforce re-contracting hypothesis (through the breach of implicit long-term contracts) of Shleifer and Summers (1988). In contrast, at targets that were privately held before buyouts, the main constraints that private equity ownership addresses are the access to capital markets and managerial competence, not agency costs.

Antoni et al. (2019) study 511 German private equity buyouts and match establishment-level data with individual data. They find that buyout establishments reduce employment by 8.96% relative to controls, due to an increase in the separation rate by 18.75% and an increase in the hiring rate of 9.79%. The active job creation and destruction results resemble those of Davis et al. (2014, 2021). While the large average job losses at the establishment level appears to be at odds with Davis et al. (2014, 2021), note that Antoni et al. (2019) do not include new establishments that are opened after the buyouts, which Davis et al. (2014, 2021) do include. Employment at existing establishments in Davis et al. (2014), for example, declined by 3% relative to controls for U.S. buyouts.

Evidence on the effect of private equity ownership on wages is mixed. Part of the empirical challenge is that it is difficult to isolate wage changes for a given job from compositional changes in the overall mix of jobs in the total employment pool. Researchers typically observe the total compensation and the headcount, rather than wages for specific workers. Thus, the average compensation per worker could change after buyouts due to compositional changes, even if the wage for each position remains unchanged. In the U.S., Davis et al. (2021) find that compensation per worker rises in divisional targets while it falls for private-to-private deals. The changes are not statistically significant for public-to-private and secondary deals. The authors suggest that increases at divisional buyouts may reflect "job title upgrading"—i.e., pay increase that comes with new titles (e.g., CEO as opposed to divisional manager) and increased responsibilities, mostly concentrated at top managerial positions. In another earlier U.S. study, Lichtenberg and Siegel (1990) find that wages for white-collar workers decline after buyouts, whereas those for blue-collar workers remain unchanged.

In a study of 1350 UK buyouts, Amess and Wright (2007) find that LBOs have significantly lower wage growth than non-LBOs. Similarly, Antoni et al. (2019) find that the average German buyout target employee loses €980 in annual earnings relatives to employees at control group firms, or 2.8% of median earnings. Note that Antoni et al. (2019) overcome the data issues described above by using individual worker-level data.

Fang et al. (2022) study private equity buyouts matched to French administrative data and find that employee pay gaps between young and old, men and women, and mangers and non-managers decrease after the buyout. Compositional effect drives these results: the companies replace expensive employees with cheaper ones and the remaining employees receive small pay increases. The results suggest that wage inequality declines as a side effect of private equity pursuing profit maximization. The compositional change is consistent with the overall active re-allocation and shuffling of jobs by private equity reported in Davis et al. (2021).

5.2 Impact on workers' welfare

Most existing studies on employment and private equity are focused on jobs (positions) rather than workers (individuals). Several papers shed light on the impact of private equity ownership on career outcomes of workers who were employed at portfolio companies at the time of buyouts, and determinants of variation in their outcomes. Focusing on individual workers as the unit of analysis and tracing them over time after departures from portfolio companies is useful for understanding the distributional impact of private equity ownership on stakeholders and the broader society. It also helps evaluate evidence of wealth transfers as opposed to value creation, as suggested by Shleifer and Summers (1988): "[t]o see whether the parties that lose association with the acquired firm suffer wealth losses, one must trace their subsequent employment."

Reporting from Sweden, using employer-employee linked register data, Olsson and Tåg (2017) study the differential incidence of unemployment among workers performing different job tasks and at different positions within the wage distribution at portfolio companies. They find that workers performing automatable routine tasks at targets that lagged behind peers in productivity pre-deal were 10.2 percentage points more likely to experience unemployment spells, and workers performing off-shorable job tasks were similarly 8.6 percentage points more likely to experience unemployment spells. This is despite the fact that there is little evidence of average changes in unemployment after the buyouts; in other words, the unemployment increases are unevenly distributed and is concentrated in workers whose job tasks were replaceable by either internal IT investment in automation or by offshoring. Routine task workers experience 12.7% decrease in labor income after separation from the portfolio company, suggesting that they receive lower wages at a new job. Both findings of unemployment and lower labor income are consistent with wealth transfers from separated workers to acquired companies. At the same time, productivity gain at low-productivity companies from automation and offshoring is consistent with value creation. Finally, layoffs are concentrated among workers in the middle of the wage distribution at portfolio companies, thus supporting the notion that private equity ownership accelerates job polarization within portfolio companies.

The polarization result appears somewhat at odds with the French results in Fang et al. (2022), who report that expensive (older, male) workers were more likely to separate and are replaced by cheaper (e.g., younger) workers, resulting in lower wage inequality within firms. However, Olsson and Tåg (2017) note that the elevated unemployment results in their study are concentrated in low-productivity Swedish firms, which may be more similar to the U.S. public-to-private targets studied in Davis et al. (2014), whereas high-productivity Swedish firms may resemble growth-oriented French portfolio companies studied in Bouchly et al. (2011). Thus, it is possible that public-to-private and private-to-private deals also have opposite wage distributional effects. In a similar vein, Lambert et al. (2021) find that reduction in job satisfaction is stronger after public-to-private buyouts than private-to-private ones.

Antoni et al. (2019) study German buyouts and find that managers and older workers are not more likely to be fired than other types of workers, but conditional on leaving the portfolio companies they appear to have a more difficult time finding new jobs with equivalent pay. In contrast, low-wage workers are more likely to be fired but will quickly start at another low-wage job. Consequently, managers and older workers are worse off than other workers as a result of buyouts.[d] On the other hand, the authors also find that jobs that require stronger IT skills increase in 2 years after buyouts, consistent with private equity implementing investments in IT upgrading that increases productivity of skilled workers while replacing less-skilled workers with automation.

Focusing more on the spillover effects of IT upgrading investments on the welfare of skilled workers at portfolio companies, Agrawal and Tambe (2016) study long-term career paths of employees at portfolio companies relative to matched non-private equity employees. First, they find that portfolio companies hire more IT workers relative to controls in years after 2000, suggesting that private equity

---

[d]Also see Gornall et al. (2021) which find that declines in job satisfaction levels after LBOs are associated with decreased job security and are worse for employees with worse outside options and longer tenure.

firms regard IT upgrading as part of their operational improvement strategies, especially after the Internet/e-commerce boom of the late 1990s. Second, they find that employees at portfolio companies experience 6–9 percentage points longer employment spells relative to control groups, both while working at the target firms and after separating from them and moving to other employers. The effect is driven by workers whose jobs are transformed by IT diffusion (including production), consistent with the interpretation that these workers are now expected to acquire IT-complementary skills on the jobs, which then become transferrable skills that help the workers advance their careers both within and outside of the original employers. Further, workers who perform IT-complementary tasks experience shorter unemployment spells after leaving the portfolio company and earn higher long-run wages.

Beyond long-run employability and wage growth at the worker level, Cohn et al. (2021) present evidence of a large, persistent decline in establishment-level workplace injury rates after buyouts of publicly-traded U.S. companies. Annual injuries per employee fall by 0.74 to 1.00 percentage points relative to control groups, or 11.1–15.0% of the pre-buyout mean. The injury rates decline more sharply at firms that were under more short-term performance pressure before buyouts (e.g., more analyst coverage, transitory institutional ownership, and discretionary accruals). The authors argue that the results dovetail with the view that "the private nature of private equity ownership promotes long-term investment by removing a firm from the scrutiny of public markets."

The studies reviewed in this section illustrate the bifurcated outcomes for worker welfare depending on (1) pre-private equity ownership status (public or private) and (2) whether IT complements or substitutes your job. For either workers at private-to-private targets or workers who perform IT-complementary tasks in their jobs, private equity ownership is associated with increased employment and improved long-run wage growth in general. In contrast, for either workers at public-to-private targets or workers who perform automatable or offshorable tasks, private equity ownership is associated heightened risk and longer spells of unemployment, and slower long-run wage growth.

5.3 Other stakeholders

Brown et al. (2009) find that suppliers to LBO companies experience significantly negative abnormal returns at the announcements of downstream LBOs. They also find that suppliers who have likely made substantial relationship-specific investments are more negatively affected, both in terms of abnormal stock returns and reduced profit margins, than suppliers of commodity products or transitory suppliers. Interestingly, the results are not present for recapitalizations, suggesting that "increases in leverage *combined* with changes in organizational form result in supplier price concessions." The results are consistent with wealth transfers from suppliers to portfolio companies under the new management who may use the elevated leverage as a commitment device to drive harder bargains with suppliers.

6 Impact on broader society

In this section, we review the literature that examines the impact of private equity on broader society. As discussed in Section 3, the effect of high-powered incentives of private equity portfolio company executives on the broader society is ambiguous and remains an open empirical question. As shown below, one emerging insight from the extant literature is that the welfare outcomes for the broader environment and society depend on the regulatory and competitive structures within which the private equity portfolio companies operate. In competitive industries and industries that rely little on governments as payers, private equity ownership tends to result in enhanced consumer welfare, whereas in more concentrated industries and industries heavily dependent on governments as payers, private equity ownership can lead to the pursuit of profit maximization at the expense of consumers. Similarly, the impact of private equity ownership on the environment is sensitive to the regulatory regimes under which the private equity portfolio companies operate, and the incentives the regulations give to the company executives.

6.1 Impact on consumers through portfolio company products and services

As private equity funds transform their portfolio companies' operations, what impact will they have on consumers who either purchase products and services from the portfolio companies themselves or their competitors? For private equity ownership to have any impact on consumers, the private equity management model needs to include some operational engineering elements, and not just financial engineering elements. Moreover, even when operational engineering is at work, its impact on consumers can be positive or negative. Indeed, the literature finds divergent results depending on the competitive structure of the sectors that companies operate in. In lightly regulated, competitive industries with price-elastic demand, private equity ownership of private targets tends to be associated with enhanced consumer welfare via improved service, flat prices, and greater product variety. In contrast, in more heavily regulated, or government-subsidized industries, especially when operating in low-competition markets, private equity ownership can lead to diminished consumer welfare via higher prices, lower service quality, or both.

6.1.1 Competitive industries

Bernstein and Sheen (2016) study the impact of private equity ownership on the operations of fast-food chains by studying comprehensive health inspection records at franchise locations in Florida. The authors find that restaurants become cleaner, safer, and better maintained after private equity buyouts, suggesting that private equity owners use their industry expertise to improve the business operations of their portfolio companies in the chain restaurant industry. Importantly, causal inference is made possible by comparing franchise-owned and private equity-owned restaurants. Improved health inspection performance is associated with greater customer satisfaction and restaurant profitability, so these operational changes enable private equity to achieve financial gains while also generating benefits for restaurant customers.

Fracassi et al. (2021) use micro-level retail scanner data to compare product varieties and prices of consumer products sold by private equity-owned and non-private equity-owned companies in retail stores. The authors find that private equity-acquired companies increase sales by 50% compared to matched control companies, not by increasing prices but by launching new products and expanding geographically to new store locations. Their sale growth squeezes their competitors' products out of shelf space. Interestingly, these results are driven entirely by private-to-private deals. The findings are consistent with growth-oriented buyouts of capital-constrained, privately-owned companies. In contrast, public targets raise prices and reduce sales for existing products, echoing earlier results in Chevalier (1995a,b) who find that private equity-acquired supermarket chains (most of which were public targets) tend to increase prices in local markets with other, highly leveraged rivals. Ewens et al. (2022) study private equity investments in local newspapers and find that production of local news content declines, digital circulation increases, and the risk of the newspaper going out of business decreases following private equity acquisitions, which is consistent with cost reductions.

In summary, private equity acquisition tends to have benign impact on consumers when targets are private and/or operate in competitive markets with low barriers to entry. When the targets are public or operate in less competitive local markets, private equity acquisition can result in higher prices and reduced sales or product availability to consumers.

6.1.2 Regulated or subsidized industries

The private equity management model manifests itself differently when it acquires targets in regulated or subsidized industries. In this section, we review evidence from the healthcare and education sectors.[e]

Healthcare Sector Evidence: The healthcare sector is highly regulated, where revenues of healthcare providers are highly dependent on the reimbursement rates accepted by either the government payers (e.g., Medicare) or private insurers. Since consumers (recipients of healthcare services) typically do not fully pay out of pocket, incentives for providers to compete on price are considerably weaker. The opaqueness of the reimbursement process also makes it difficult for consumers to shop on prices ex ante. Finally, it is difficult to assess ex ante the product or service quality, though pro-competitive policies can mitigate this. These features appear to significantly shape the way in which private equity ownership impacts the healthcare service quality and price that consumers receive.

---

[e]Also see Howell et al. (2022) which study PE ownership effect on privatized airports and find that both local competition and alignment of incentives among regulators and stakeholders help generate positive effects on firm performance even in a highly regulated setting.

Gupta et al. (2020) study the impact of private equity ownership on the quality of care for short-stay Medicare patients at for-profit nursing homes. They find that nursing staffing declines, while bed utilization increases, resulting in improved operational efficiency. However, the efficiency comes at the expense of declining quality, i.e., higher short-term mortality and lower incidence of Five Star ratings at private equity-owned facilities. The authors emphasize that because nursing homes largely rely on Medicare and Medicaid programs (that pay fixed rates per patient 3per day) for revenue, main levers for increasing profitability are staffing cost reduction, admitting more lucrative Medicare patients, and making them stay longer. In a complementary study, Huang and Bowblis (2019) study the impact of private equity ownership on patient outcomes for long-stay Medicaid residents by comparing private equity-owned and non-private equity-owned for-profit nursing homes. In contrast to Gupta et al. (2020) that find declining health outcomes for short-stay post-acute elderly patients for private equity-acquired facilities, Huang and Bowblis (2019) find no significant difference between private equity -owned and non-private equity-owned for-profit nursing homes for long-stay Medicaid (non-elderly disabled) patients. Braun et al. (2020) similarly find no difference in health outcomes at PE- vs non-PE-owned nursing homes.

It is interesting that even in the highly regulated nursing home industry, the impact of private equity ownership on consumers is not uniform. What can explain the divergent findings? Gandhi et al. (2021) suggest (i) heterogenous local market competitiveness and (ii) private equity managers' heightened responsiveness to competitive incentives may be key. They find that private equity acquirers compete on quality in locally competitive markets by increasing high-skilled registered nurse staffing more aggressively, while doing so only modestly in less competitive markets. They also document that, after the introduction of the Five Star System that improves transparency of staffing quality to consumers, private equity-owned facilities in competitive local markets increased staffing expenditure significantly whereas in low-competition markets they decreased staffing expenditure. Thus, even within the same industry, the impact of private equity ownership can differ depending on the competitive incentives the companies receive in the marketplace.

Beyond quality, other researchers have looked at private equity ownership's effect on consumer healthcare spending. Liu (2021) uses insurance claims data of privately insured individuals to study the impact of private equity entry to local hospital markets on healthcare spending by consumers. Counterfactual analyses of structural model estimations suggest that if private equity ownership of hospitals were banned, healthcare spending in local markets where private equity is present would drop by 11%. Higher healthcare spending in private equity-affected markets is driven mostly by higher negotiated prices with insurers, rather than with higher hospital service utilization. Rival hospitals in local markets also raise prices but only if they share a common insurer with private equity-backed hospitals. In addition to superior negotiation expertise of private equity owners, the bargaining model estimation implies that credible bankruptcy threat of highly-leveraged private equity-backed hospitals weakens the bargaining position of insurers, leading to higher prices. Furthermore, consistent with non-pecuniary benefit enjoyed by non-profit hospitals, price increases are larger when non-profit hospitals are acquired by private equity. In sharp contrast to the nursing home industry where the government payout rate is fixed, operational efficiency is barely changed under private equity ownership; instead, the prices charged to insurers for the same quality service is sharply increased. To the extent that insurers pass on their increased spending to consumers via increased premiums, the study implies that private equity ownership of hospitals is detrimental to patient-consumer surplus via increased prices, while quantity and quality of services rendered are insignificantly changed.

Education Sector Evidence: Higher education is another sector where, similar to the healthcare sector, government subsidies (federal student aid for low-income students) are crucial sources of revenues and many customers (students) pay subsidized tuition, thus weakening the providers' incentives to compete on price. The net tuition that students will pay (after grants and loans) is opaque, making it difficult for students to shop on price. There is a reputational incentive not to compete on price by providers, as high price is used as a signal for high quality. Finally, it is difficult to measure the quality of education both ex ante and ex post.

Eaton et al. (2020) study the impact of private equity acquisition on for-profit colleges' actions. The authors find that private equity acquisition leads to higher tuition and per-student debt, while education inputs, graduation rates, and earnings among graduates decline. Government aid is exploited more aggressively, and while loan repayment rates are lower, schools are not hurt because of government loan guarantees. The findings suggest that profit maximization through exploitation of government subsidies and loan guarantees may result in worse outcomes for customers (students) both through poorer education quality and higher prices.

For-profit schools, private equity-owned or not, appear to exploit federal aid programs and charge higher tuitions while capturing federal subsidies (Cellini and Goldin, 2014). Eaton et al. (2020) argue that high-powered incentives of private equity ownership induce private equity-owned schools to more aggressively pursue profit maximization at the expense of students and the federal government.

6.2 Impact on governments and taxpayers

The private equity management model can affect government revenues and expenditures through several channels. First, financial engineering reduces tax liabilities of portfolio companies via increased interest tax shields (Kaplan, 1989b). While this reduces tax collection from the private equity portfolio companies, governments may collect more taxes from banks who collect the increased interest payments from the portfolio companies, so the net effect is likely moderated. Second, private equity-backed companies may engage in other tax- and cost-avoidance activities as part of a shareholder value-creation strategy, including regulatory arbitrage. Note that with non-leverage-related tax reductions, government tax revenues are effectively reduced (not recovered from banks). Third, private equity-backed companies may engage in aggressive subsidy capture or risk-taking behavior that potentially costs taxpayers in events of distress or defaults by either the companies themselves or their stakeholders.

Interest Tax Shields: Cohn et al. (2014) study U.S. federal corporate tax return data and find that private equity-acquired companies' leverage remain elevated even several years after the buyout, suggesting that private equity takeovers represent a one-time permanent change in the capital structure of the companies. Elevated leverage creates value via increased present values of interest tax shields and implies reduced corporate tax revenues from private equity portfolio companies. This suggests that as a greater portion of companies in the economy are acquired by private equity, permanently higher leverage of these companies leads to significantly lower corporate tax revenues for the governments, all else equal.

Non-Leveraged-Based Tax Avoidance: Badertscher et al. (2013) study private U.S. companies with public debt and find that private equity-owned companies engage in greater tax avoidance than management-owned companies. Extending this study, Olbert and Severin (2020) study European buyouts and find that target companies' effective tax rates decrease by 15% after the private equity buyout. Targets engaging in post-buyout tax avoidance invest less in physical assets and employment and fit the category of buyouts that create value via cost cutting rather than growth. The authors examine industry-wide real effects and find that private equity ownership reduces overall corporate tax revenues and industry-wide effective tax rates without creating positive spillovers for other tax bases (e.g., consumption tax). Together, these findings suggest that some private equity investors impose a negative externality on local domestic governments through increased tax avoidance.

In a study of private equity investments in life insurance companies, Kirti and Sarin (2020) also report that private equity-owned insurers aggressively engage in tax arbitrage by reinsuring their contracts with subsidiaries domiciled in tax havens with 0% corporate tax rates.

Collectively, these papers suggest that minimizing tax payments is one of the value-creation strategies pursued by private equity owners, especially for companies with moderate growth prospects, and this has a potential negative effect on domestic government tax revenues.

Indirect Effects on Governments and Taxpayers: Before the Financial Crisis of 2008–09, poorly-rated private-label asset-backed security (ABS) holdings required a higher capital charge. But in the aftermath of the Crisis, insurance regulators exempted insurers from this capital charge requirements to prevent massive fire sales of downgrade private-label ABS by insurers. Becker et al. (forthcoming) and Koijen and Yogo (2016) document that U.S. insurance companies, under pressure for reaching-for-yield in a low-interest environment, exploit this regulatory forbearance by holding high-yielding ABS while avoiding capital charge.

With these industry dynamics as a backdrop, Kirti and Sarin (2020) study private equity ownership of life insurance companies and find evidence that private equity ownership exacerbates this regulatory arbitrage incentive. The authors document that acquired insurers aggressively engage in regulatory arbitrage by selling high-rated but low-yielding corporate bonds and buying poorly-rated and high-yielding ABS within days of the buyouts. The compositional changes of their portfolios increase profitability of the private equity-owned insurers but elevates the riskiness of their portfolios and may exacerbate a hidden cost on taxpayers in the event of distress or failures of these insurers.

This finding echoes the findings of Eaton et al. (2020), which show that private equity ownership exacerbates the distortions in the regulatory framework exploited by for-profit schools targeting students who receive federal aid. Since student defaults are guaranteed by the federal government, for-profit schools lack incentives to enable students to acquire enough earning power to repay the loans or to keep the loan amount down at a sustainable level. Similarly, since insurance companies are not punished via higher capital requirements to hold risky ABS after the removal of regulatory capital requirements for ABS in 2009, their incentives are distorted to hold high-yield ABS without regard to their credit risk. While all for-profit schools and insurers are given distorted incentives, private equity ownership is shown to induce more aggressive exploitation of the regulatory arbitrage opportunities.

As a counterpoint, Johnston-Ross et al. (2020) study private equity participation in the failed bank resolution process during the 2008–2009 Financial Crisis and find that private equity acquirers helped stabilize the financial system by providing capital to failed bank resolutions and saving taxpayers resolution costs in the process. The authors find that private equity investors acquire banks in poorer health and in need of greater capital injection ex ante, and yet these banks recover better (i.e., keep branches open and re-grow deposits). The private equity owners are repeat bank acquirers and introduce highly experienced and skilled management teams to failed banks, often with turnaround expertise. The authors estimate that private equity acquisitions allowed the FDIC to reduce the resolution costs by $3.63 billion.

It is interesting that even in the highly regulated and subsidized industry of banking, private equity incentives and the government incentives seem to be better aligned in the case of failed bank resolution during the crisis, whereas they appear to be more misaligned in for-profit healthcare and education. What determines the degree of (mis)alignments between private equity and public interests, and what policy interventions, if any, can mitigate them, is an important avenue for future research.

6.3 Impact on the environment

As discussed in Sections 2.4 and 3.3, a growing share of limited partners in private equity funds require that ESG be incorporated into the funds' investment processes. Whether their motivations are materiality-driven or impact-driven, limited partners who invest across public and private assets increasingly demand to know whether private portfolio companies that private equity funds invest in promote good environmental practice. The empirical evidence on this question is currently quite limited, and there is an acute need for more research. The question on private equity's role on the environment relates to a broader and growing literature on green banking and investor responsibility for monitoring the environmental impact of projects or companies that they fund.

Shive and Forster (2020) study mandated disclosures of greenhouse gas emissions of U.S. companies and find that, while private independent companies pollute less and are less likely to incur EPA violations than their public counterparts, private equity-owned companies do not differ from public companies in their emissions and violation rates. For a subset of utility companies for which reduction in emissions is shown to be costly and for which electricity output is measurable, the results hold after scaling, suggesting that public and private equity-owned companies eschew the costly pro-environmental actions and choose instead to narrowly maximize profits, going close to the legal limits and thus incurring more actions and violations from the EPA. In contrast, independent owners appear to take more costly pro-environmental actions relative to their counterparts. In light of the argument by Hart and Zingales (2017), see Section 3.3, the findings are consistent with the view that both the public company management and private equity-backed company management do not internalize pro-environmental shareholders' welfare, at least in the sample period of 2006–2017. It is possible that the environmental impact of portfolio companies' real activities was not a salient concern for limited partners in most of the sample period, and it would be interesting to see if private equity responds differentially (relative to public companies) to the heightened concerns for ESG performance among institutional investors in the post-Paris Accord era.

Bellon (2020) studies satellite imaging and administrative datasets for fracking wells to study the impact of private equity ownership on pollution decisions at individual well locations. On average, private equity ownership leads to a significant reduction in use of toxic chemicals for extraction and CO_2 emissions from flaring. However, this average effect hides significant heterogeneities. Portfolio companies increase pollution in locations and periods where environmental liability risk is low, such as when the environmental regulation on federal land was rolled back. Overall, high-powered incentives to maximize shareholder value may benefit environmental outcomes when the risk of environmental regulation is high.

These studies confirm the insights from other studies of private equity firm behavior in regulated industries: high-powered incentives of private equity owners is a double-edged sword, and can either powerfully aid the policy goals when incentives are well aligned with the policymakers' intended goals (e.g., failed bank resolutions), or significantly exacerbate the distortion in the framework when incentives are misaligned (e.g., federal aid capture, oligopolistic price bargaining between hospitals and insurers, capital regulation forbearance in insurance, and roll-backs of environmental regulation on federal land). Collectively, the emerging evidence suggests that regulators need to consider the impact of the high-powered incentives of private equity when assessing the market impact of a given regulatory policy or decision.

6.4 Impact on innovation and industry spillovers

As discussed in Section 5, the impact of private equity ownership on the company's real outcomes diverges between public-to-private and private-to-private deals. The shareholder value-creation proposition for public-to-private deals tends to be centered around efficiency gains and cost cutting. This is in contrast to the relaxation of capital constraints and top-line growth for private-to-private deals. This raises a question on the aggregate impact of private equity penetration on industry-wide innovation level, and whether the sign of the impact depends on the composition of public and private companies in an industry. A related second questions is whether public targets' pre-deal level of innovation is optimal, either from shareholders' or societal perspective.

6.4.1 Public-to-private deals

Lerner et al. (2011) study U.S. public-to-private buyouts and find that, while the level of patenting is unchanged post-buyouts, the patents in the post-buyout programs are better cited, and more narrowly focused. Ayash and Egan (2019) study U.S. public-to-private buyouts using a difference-in-difference approach and find that, compared to the matched control companies, private equity-owned companies reduce patent flows by one-third, driven by both a decline in new patents (23%) and fewer purchases (7%). The difference in inferences between the two studies stems in part from the fact that patenting level generally increased over time in the sample period. In a contemporaneous study, Cumming et al. (2020) study international public-to-private buyouts and find that private equity-backed buyouts are associated with a significant reduction in patents, patent citations, and innovator employment.

6.4.2 Private-to-private deals

Amess et al. (2016) study UK private equity buyouts and find that for private-to-private deals, quality-adjusted patent stocks increase by 14%, accompanied by relaxation of financial constraints. In contrast, quality-adjusted patent stocks weakly decline in the case of public-to-private deals. The findings are consistent with the view that private-to-private deals tend to provide growth equity, employ less leverage, and target smaller companies that hold growth options but are capital constrained. Driver et al. (2020) find that private equity-held firms, though equally innovative as other private firms, skew their strategies toward development and away from research; however, their study does not differentiate between public-to-private and private-to-private deals.

6.4.3 Aggregate impact

The divergent findings for public-to-private and private-to-private deals on innovation suggest that the aggregate impact of private equity penetration on a given industry depends on the composition of public and private companies in an industry that become private equity targets. An industry where private equity targets are primarily public (private), all else equal, is expected to experience an aggregate decline (increase) in innovation activities after an increase in private equity ownership. Since this composition varies from sector to sector and country to country, the average impact across industries or countries is a priori ambiguous. The impact can also change over time, as the composition changes.

There is a related older literature that documents a negative relationship between indebtedness and innovation for publicly-traded companies and for public-to-private transactions (Baysinger and Hoskisson, 1989; Hall, 1990; Long and Ravenscraft, 1993). According to these studies, it is the elevated leverage rather than the private equity ownership that negatively impacts the company's propensity to invest in long-term and hard-to-assess investments in innovation. It is important to note that the debate on this question during the 1990s was tempered by the fact that private equity targets were mostly old-economy sector companies whose level of innovation was low even before the buyout. Since most innovative companies in the economy, e.g., Silicon Valley tech companies, were not suitable LBO targets, the impact of private equity acquisition on the aggregate economy was thought to be limited. For example, Hall (1989) argued that "[e]ven if all of this R&D spending went away after going private, this would make a very small dent in overall industrial R&D."

In contrast, today's private equity invests in every sector of the economy, including IT and healthcare, and many of the buyout deals in these high R&D-intensity sectors employ leverage. For example, in 2021 about 40% of U.S. private equity deal values were in IT and healthcare sectors (PitchBook, 2022). Enterprise software companies, for example, have become prime buyout targets as the SaaS, or Software-as-a-Service business model has become the industry norm and given management more tools to smooth out cash flows across periods. This is a recent phenomenon, and the literature has not closely examined the effect of either private equity ownership or higher leverage on innovation in high-tech industries. As the share of these high R&D-intensity companies and sectors in the economy grows rapidly, the aggregate effect of private equity penetration in these sectors on the innovation of the portfolio companies themselves and spillover effects on competitors remains an open question.

6.5 Impact investing and private equity

One of the recurring findings on the impact of private equity on the broader society and the environment is the importance of aligning shareholder preferences with the broader public interest. Any misalignment due to distortion in the regulatory framework tends to be magnified under private equity ownership because of the high-powered incentives of the private equity management model to maximize shareholder value.

What if investors in private equity funds have explicitly prosocial incentives and impose their preferences on the private equity management model? Impact funds are private equity and VC funds that explicitly pursue dual objectives of both financial return and generation of positive (either social or environmental) externality. In essence, much like how nonprofit hospitals may internalize the positive externality of provision of quality healthcare in the local community as nonpecuniary benefit, impact funds aim to internalize the positive externality that the fund's portfolio companies generate as nonpecuniary benefit to fund investors. As investors pressure for-profit companies to adopt prosocial practice, e.g., net-zero pledges to fight climate change, a debate arises as to how for-profit companies can credibly commit to such pledges that are costly and impact profits negatively. Will the private equity fund mechanism work more or less effectively than the public company governance mechanism to induce prosocial behavior in the portfolio companies? What will be the return implications of imposing such preferences on fund activities?

Broccardo et al. (2021) study voting and exiting as two strategies employed by prosocial investors and consumers to pressure companies to choose clean (vs dirty) technology.[f] The authors build a model that is meant for public companies and advocate for proxy voting as a more effective mechanism to induce clean technology adoption than divestment. However, in practice it may be hard to implement a proxy voting solution to gather the collective preference of public company investors who are free to trade the stocks at a moment's notice. In contrast, the closed-end fund structure, a small and fixed set of limited partners, and illiquidity of fund interests create a more stable structure in which to articulate the prosocial goal of the fund and execute a long-term strategy to adhere to the goal. Limited partners will then vote with their feet when it is time to decide whether to re-up for the next fund the general partners raise, based on the combined financial and non-financial (environmental and/or social) performance of the first fund.

Geczy et al. (2021) study limited partnership contracts of impact funds and find that impact funds give limited partners advisory roles that enable them to perform substantial oversight over deal selection, due diligence, conflict of interest, and other material fund activity. At the same time, the study finds that impact funds typically do not tie manager compensation explicitly to impact outcomes. The use of informal governance rather than explicit contracting to monitor impact performance raises several questions: Is this contracting form optimal or a reflection of a still nascent and rapidly evolving industry? Does it indicate the inherent difficulty of impact measurement, or uncertainty about the relationship between impact and financial performance and investors' ambiguity toward the trade-off? Clearly, more research is needed to answer these questions.

Pástor et al. (2021) analyze financial and real effects of sustainable investing in an equilibrium where (i) companies can either create positive (green) or negative (brown) externality and (ii) investors derive utility (disutility) for holding green (brown) assets, care about companies' aggregate social impact, and care about climate risk. In the model, pro-social investors' willingness to forgo return in exchange for investing in green-tilted portfolio lowers green companies' cost of

---

[f]Also see Pursiainen and Tykvova (2021) for a study of how customers "vote with their feet" in response to announcements of buyouts of retail brands.

capital. Climate risk also increases brown companies' expected return. Pro-social investors enjoy "investor surplus" despite earning negative alpha. This equilibrium framework is useful in understanding expected financial returns of impact funds. Impact fund investors derive utility from holding impact funds that generate positive impact, and thus are rationally willing to invest in them even though their expected financial return alone may be lower than that from investing in non-impact private equity funds.

Taking this insight to the fund-level financial performance data, Barber et al. (2021) estimate random-utility/willing-to-pay models and find that limited partners accept 2.5–3.7 ppts lower IRRs ex ante for impact funds, compared to comparable non-impact funds. The result is consistent with the view that investors derive non-pecuniary utility from investing in impact funds, thus sacrificing financial return. Development organizations, foundations, financial institutions, public pensions, Europeans, and United Nations Principles of Responsible Investment signatories have high willingness-to-pay for impact. Unpacking the channels behind this heterogeneity across investor types, the authors find that, on one hand, investors with mission objectives and/or facing political pressure have high willingness-to-pay; on the other hand, those subject to fiduciary duty-related restrictions against dual-objective investments are reluctant to invest in impact funds, likely for fear of running afoul of the regulation. These results are consistent with the predictions for pro-social investors in Pástor et al. (2021): pro-social investors earn negative alpha in expectation but are rationally willing to do so because of nonpecuniary utility they derive from holding impact funds in their portfolios.

Do impact funds actually generate positive externalities? Does the externality they generate correlate positively or negatively with the fund's financial returns? And within a given fund, does the externality each portfolio company investment generates correlate positively or negatively with the fund's financial returns from the investment? How does a fund measure the externality generated at each portfolio company, and how does the company attribute the externality generated to the investment by the impact fund vs other investments it receives? These are just examples of a myriad of questions that remain open and are fruitful areas of future research.

7 Open questions and suggestions for further research

As discussed throughout the chapter, many questions remain open for future research and are summarized below.

Why do private equity-backed companies tend to exploit regulatory arbitrage and tax avoidance more aggressively than non-private equity-backed peers? Faccio and Hsu (2017) suggest that some private equity firms may benefit from political connections. Do such connections also enable them to pursue either regulatory capture or tax avoidance more successfully or at lower cost?

In regulated or subsidized industries, distortion in incentives given by the regulatory framework tends to get magnified when combined with high-powered incentives of private equity. What policy interventions, if any, can mitigate the misalignment of incentives between private equity and public interests?

While in the past private equity deals are concentrated in low-tech, consumer or industrial sectors, today more than a third of private equity investments are in IT and healthcare, the most innovation-driven segments of the economy. What is the aggregate impact of private equity's greater presence in the tech industry on innovation? Does it depend on the composition of public-to-private vs private-to-private deals? What else matters?

How should impact funds govern and provide incentives for impact generation at the portfolio companies? If implicit rather than explicit contracting is optimal, what is the underlying mechanism? This is a broader question for governing ESG practice at public and non-private equity-backed private companies, too, and there is a potential for innovating on contracting that may have broader applicability for aligning shareholder preferences with the broader public interest.

Acknowledgments

We thank Gordon Phillips (editor) for helpful comments and suggestions. All errors and omissions are our own. Morten Sorensen, Dartmouth College, Tuck School of Business, 100 Tuck Hall, Hanover, NH 03755, email: morten.sorensen@tuck.dartmouth.edu; and Ayako Yasuda, University of California Davis, Graduate School of Management, 3206 Gallagher Hall, Davis CA, 95616-8609, email: asyasuda@ucdavis.edu.

References

Acharya, V., Kehoe, C., Reyner, M., 2009. Private equity vs. PLC boards in the U.K.: a comparison of practices and effectiveness. J. Appl. Corp. Financ. 21 (1), 45–56.

Acharya, V., Gottschalg, O., Hahn, M., Kehoe, C., 2013. Corporate governance and value creation: evidence from private equity. Rev. Financ. Stud. 26 (2), 368–402.

Agrawal, A., Tambe, P., 2016. Private equity and workers' career paths: the role of technological change. Rev. Financ. Stud. 29 (9), 2455–2489.

Amess, K., Wright, M., 2007. The wage and employment effects of leveraged buyouts in the UK. Int. J. Econ. Bus. 14 (2), 179–195.

Amess, K., Stiebale, J., Wright, M., 2016. The impact of private equity on firms' innovation activity. Eur. Econ. Rev. 86, 147–160.

Antoni, M., Maug, E., Obernberger, S., 2019. Private equity and human capital risk. J. Financ. Econ. 133, 634–657.

Ayash, B., Egan, E.J., 2019. The Effect of U.S. Public-to-Private Leveraged Buyouts on Innovation. Working Paper.

Badertscher, B., Katz, S., Rego, S., 2013. The separation of ownership and control and corporate tax avoidance. J. Account. Econ. 56, 228–250.

Baker, G.P., Wruck, K.H, 1989. Organizational changes and value creation in leveraged buyouts: the case of the OM Scott & Sons Company. J. Financ. Econ. 25 (2), 163–190.

Barber, B., Morse, A., Yasuda, A., 2021. Impact investing. J. Financ. Econ. 139, 162–185.

Baysinger, B., Hoskisson, R.E., 1989. Diversification strategy and R&D intensity in multiproduct firms. Acad. Manage. J. 32 (2), 310–332.

Bebchuk, L.A., Weisbach, M.S., 2010. The state of corporate governance research. Rev. Financ. Stud. 23 (3), 939–961.

Bebchuk, L.A., Grinstein, Y., Peyer, U., 2010. Lucky CEOs and lucky directors. J. Financ. 65 (6), 2363–2401.

Bellon, A., 2020. Does Private Equity Ownership Make Firms Cleaner? The Role of Environmental Liability Risks. Working Paper.

Bergström, C., Grubb, M., Jonsson, S., 2007. The operating impact of buyouts in Sweden: a study of value creation. J. Priv. Equity 11, 22–39.

Bernstein, S., Sheen, A., 2016. The operational consequences of private equity buyouts: evidence from the restaurant industry. Rev. Financ. Stud. 29 (9), 2387–2418.

Bertrand, M., Mullainathan, S., 2003. Enjoying the quiet life? Corporate governance and managerial preferences. J. Political Econ. 111 (5), 1043–1075.

Biesinger, M., Bircan, C., Ljungqvist, A., 2020. Value Creation in Private Equity. Working Paper.

Bloom, N., Sadun, R., Van Reenen, J., 2015. Do private equity owned firms have better management practices? Am. Econ. Rev. 105 (5), 442–446.

Bouchly, Q., Sraer, D., Thesmar, D., 2011. Growth LBOs. J. Financ. Econ. 102, 432–453.

Braun, R.T., Yun, H., Casalino, L.P., Myslinski, Z., Kuwonza, F., Jung, H.-Y., Unruh, M.A., 2020. Comparative performance of private equity-owned US nursing homes during the COVID-19 pandemic. JAMA Netw. Open 3 (10).

Broccardo, E., Hart, O.D., Zingales, L., 2021. Exit vs. Voice. Working Paper.

Brown, D.T., Edward Fee, C., Thomas, S.E., 2009. Financial leverage and bargaining power with suppliers: evidence from leveraged buyouts. Finance 12, 196–211.

Brown, G., Harris, B., Jenkinson, T., Kaplan, S., Robinson, D., 2020. Private equity: accomplishments and challenges. J. Appl. Corp. Finance 32 (3), 8–20.

Burrough, B., Helyar, J., 1990. Barbarians at the Gate. HarperBusiness.

Cellini, S.R., Goldin, C., 2014. Does federal student aid raise tuition? New evidence on for-profit colleges. Am. Econ. J. Econ. Policy 6 (4), 174–206.

Chevalier, J., 1995a. Do LBO supermarkets charge more? An empirical analysis of the effects of LBOs on supermarket pricing. J. Financ. 50 (4), 1095–1112.

Chevalier, J., 1995b. Capital structure and product-market competition: empirical evidence from the supermarket industry. Am. Econ. Rev. 85 (3), 415–435.

Chhaochharia, V., Grinstein, Y., 2006. Corporate governance and firm value: the impact of the 2002 governance rules. J. Financ. 62, 1789–1825.

Chung, J.-W., Sensoy, B., Stern, L., Weisbach, M., 2012. Pay for performance from future fund flows: the case of private equity. Rev. Financ. Stud. 25 (11), 3259–3304.

Cohn, J., Mills, L., Towery, E., 2014. The evolution of capital structure and operating performance after leveraged buyouts: evidence from U.S. corporate tax returns. J. Financ. Econ. 111 (2), 469–494.

Cohn, J., Nestoriak, N., Wardlaw, M., 2021. Private equity buyouts and workplace safety. Rev. Financ. Stud. 34 (10), 4832–4875.

Cohn, J., Hotchkiss, E., Towery, E., 2022. Sources of value creation in private equity buyouts of private firms. Rev. Financ. 26 (2), 257–285.

Cornelli, F., Karakas, O., 2015. CEO Turnover in LBOs: The Role of Boards. Working Paper.

Cornelli, F., Kominek, Z., Ljungqvist, A., 2013. Monitoring managers: does it matter? J. Financ. 68 (2), 431–481.

Cronqvist, H., Fahlenbrach, R., 2013. CEO contract design: how do strong principals do it? J. Financ. Econ. 108, 659–674.

Cumming, D., Siegel, D.S., Wright, M., 2007. Private equity, leveraged buyouts and governance. J. Corp. Finance 13 (4), 439–460.

Davis, S., Haltiwanger, J.C., Handley, K., Jarmin, R., Lerner, J., Miranda, J., 2014. Private equity, jobs, and productivity. Am. Econ. Rev. 104 (12), 3956–3990.

Davis, S., Haltiwanger, J.C., Handley, K., Lipsius, B., Lerner, J., Miranda, J., 2021. The (Heterogenous) Economic Effects of Private Equity Buyouts. Working Paper.

Driver, J., Kolasinski, A.C., Stanfield, J.R., 2020. R&D or R vs. D? Firm Innovation Strategy and Equity Ownership. Working Paper.

Eaton, C., Howell, S.T., Yannelis, C., 2020. When investor incentives and consumer interests diverge: private equity in higher education. Rev. Financ. Stud. 33, 4024–4060.

Eckbo, B.E., Thorburn, K.S., 2013. Corporate restructuring. Foundations and Trends® in Finance. 7 (3), 159–288.

Edgerton, J., 2012. Agency problems in public firms: evidence from corporate jets in leveraged buyouts. J. Financ. 67 (6), 2187–2213.

Erel, I., Jang, Y., Weisbach, M.S., 2015. Do acquisitions relieve target firms' financial constraints? J. Financ. 70 (1), 289–328.

Ewens, M., Gupta, A., Howell, S., 2022. Local Journalism Under Private Equity Ownership. Working Paper.

Faccio, M., Hsu, H.-C., 2017. Politically connected private equity and employment. J. Financ. 72 (2), 539–573.

Fama, E., 2021. Contract costs, stakeholder capitalism, and ESG. Eur. Financ. Manag. 27, 189–195.

Fang, L.H., Goldman, J., Roulet, A., 2022. Private Equity and Pay Gaps Inside the Firm. Working Paper.

Fich, E.M., Shivdasani, A., 2012. Are busy boards effective monitors? In: Corporate Governance. Springer, Berlin, Heidelberg, pp. 221–258.

Fink, L., 2019. Profit & Purpose. BlackRock Website (https://www.blackrock.com/corporate/investor-relations/2019-larry-fink-ceo-letter).

Fink, L., 2020. A Fundamental Reshaping of Finance. BlackRock Website (https://www.blackrock.com/corporate/investor-relations/2020-larry-fink-ceo-letter).

Fracassi, C., Previtoro, A., Sheen, A., 2021. Barbarians at the store? Private equity, products, and consumers. J. Financ.

Gandhi, A., Song, Y., Upadrashta, P., 2021. Have Private Equity Owned Nursing Homes Fare Worse Under COVID-19? Working Paper.

Geczy, C., Jeffers, J., Musto, D., Tucker, A., 2021. Contracts with (social) benefits: the implementation of impact investing. J. Financ. Econ. 142 (2), 697–718.

Gompers, P., Kaplan, S.N., Mukharlyamov, V., 2016. What do private equity firms say they do? J. Financ. Econ. 121, 449–476.

Guo, S., Hotchkiss, E.S., Song, W., 2011. Do buyouts (still) create value? J. Financ. 66 (2), 479–517.

Gupta, A., Howell, S.T., Yannelis, C., Gupta, A., 2020. Does Private Equity Investment in Healthcare Benefit Patients? Evidence from Nursing Homes. Working Paper.

Hall, B. (1989). Corporate Restructuring and R&D: Hearing before the Subcommittee on Science, Research and Technology of the Committee on Science, Space and Technology, U.S. House of Representatives, 101st Cong. 43 (testimony of Bronwyn Hall).

Hall, B., 1990. The impact of corporate restructuring on industrial research and development. Brookings Pap Econ. Act. Microecon. 1990, 85–135. The Brookings Institution.

Hart, O., Zingales, L., 2017. Companies should maximize shareholder welfare not market value. J. Law Finance Account. 2, 247–274.

Hotchkiss, E., Smith, D., Strömberg, P., 2021. Private equity and the resolution of financial distress. Rev. Corp. Finance Stud. 10 (4), 694–747.

Huang, S.S., Bowblis, J.R., 2019. Private equity ownership and nursing home quality: an instrumental variables approach. Int. J. Health Econ. Manag. 19, 273–299.

Gornall, W., Gredil, O., Howell, S., Liu, X., Sockin, J., 2021. Do Employees Cheer for Private Equity? The Heterogenous Effects of Buyouts on Job Quality. Working Paper.

Jensen, M.C., 1986. Agency costs of free cash flow, corporate finance, and takeovers. Am. Econ. Rev. 76, 323–329.

Jensen, M., 1989. The eclipse of the public corporation. Harv. Bus. Rev. 67 (5), 61–74.

Johnston-Ross, E., Ma, S., Puri, M., 2020. Private Equity and Financial Stability: Evidence from Failed Bank Resolution in the Crisis. Working Paper.

Kaplan, S., 1989a. The effects of management buyouts on operating performance and value. J. Financ. Econ. 24 (2), 217–254.

Kaplan, S., 1989b. Management buyouts: evidence of taxes as a source of value. J. Financ. 44 (3), 611–632.

Kaplan, S., Strömberg, P., 2009. Leveraged buyouts and private equity. J. Econ. Perspect. 23 (1), 121–146.

Kaplan, S., Klebanov, M.M., Sorensen, M., 2012. Which CEO characteristics and abilities matter? J. Financ. 67 (3), 973–1007.

Katz, S., 2009. Earnings quality and ownership structure: the role of private equity sponsors. Account. Rev. 84 (3), 623–658.

Kim, H., Howell, S.T., Jang, Y., Weisbach, M.S., 2022. All Clear for Takeoff: Evidence from Airports on the Effects of Infrastructure Privatization. Working Paper.

Kirti, D., Sarin, N., 2020. What Private Equity Does Differently: Evidence from Life Insurers. Working Paper.

Koijen, R. S. J., and Motohiro Yogo (2016) Risks of life insurers: recent trends and transmission mechanisms. In Felix Hufeld, R. S. J. Koijen, and Thimann C. (eds.), The Economics, Regulation, and Systemic Risk of Insurance Markets, Chapter 4. Oxford: Oxford University Press.

Lambert, M., Moreno, N., Phalippou, L., Scivoletto, A., 2021. Employee Views of Leveraged Buy-Out Transactions. Working Paper.

Lerner, J., Sorensen, M., Strömberg, P., 2011. Private equity and Long-run investment: the case of innovation. J. Financ. 66 (2), 445–477.

Leslie, P., Oyer, P., 2008. Managerial Incentives and Value Creation: Evidence from Private Equity. Working Paper.

Lichtenberg, F., Siegel, D., 1990. The effects of leveraged buyouts on productivity and relate aspects of firm behavior. J. Financ. Econ. 27, 165–194.

Liu, T., 2021. Bargaining With Private Equity: Implications for Hospital Prices and Patient Welfare. Working Paper.

Long, W.F., Ravenscraft, D.J., 1993. LBOs, debt and R&D intensity. Strateg. Manag. J. 14, 119–135.

Metrick, A., Yasuda, A., 2010. The economics of private equity funds. Rev. Financ. Stud. 23 (6), 2303–2341.

Metrick, A., Yasuda, A., 2011. Venture capital and other private equity: a survey. Eur. Financ. Manag. 17, 619–654.

Muscarella, C., Vetsuypens, M., 1990. Efficiency and organizational structure: a study of reverse LBOs. J. Financ. 45 (5), 1389–1413.

Nikoskelainen, E., Wright, M., 2007. The impact of corporate governance mechanisms on value increase in leveraged buyouts. J. Corp. Finance 13 (4), 511–537.

Olbert, M., Severin, P.H., 2020. Private equity and taxes, Proceedings. Annual Conference on Taxation and Minutes of the Annual Meeting of the National Tax Association 113, 1–63.

Olsson, M., Tåg, J., 2017. Private equity, layoffs, and job polarization. J. Labor Econ. 35 (3), 697–754.

Opler, T., Titman, S., 1993. The determinants of leveraged buyout activity: free cash flow vs. financial distress costs. J. Financ. 48, 1985–1999.

Pástor, L., Stambaugh, R., Taylor, L., 2021. Sustainable investing in equilibrium. J. Financ. Econ. 142 (2), 550–571.

Pedersen, L.H., Fitzgibbons, S., Pomorski, L., 2021. Responsible investing: the ESG-efficient frontier. J. Financ. Econ. 142 (2), 572–597.

PitchBook, 2022. 2021 Annual US Private Equity Breakdown. PitchBook Website (https://pitchbook.com/news/reports/2021-annual-us-pe-breakdown).

Preqin, 2020. Preqin Impact Report: The Rise of ESG in Alternative Assets. Preqin Website (https://www.preqin.com/insights/research/reports/preqin-impact-report-the-rise-of-esg-in-alternative-assets).

Pursiainen, V., Tykvova, T., 2021. Retail Customer Reactions to Private Equity Acquisitions. Working Paper.

Renneboog, L., Vansteenkiste, C., 2017. Leveraged buyouts: motives and sources of value. Ann. Corp. Gov. 2 (4), 291–389.

Renneboog, L., Simons, T., Wright, M., 2007. Why do public firms go private in the UK? The impact of private equity investors, incentive realignment and undervaluation. J. Corp. Finance 13 (4), 591–628.

Shive, S.A., Forster, M.M., 2020. Corporate governance and pollution externalities of public and private firms. Rev. Financ. Stud. 33 (3), 1296–1330.

Shleifer, A., Summers, L., 1988. Breach of trust in hostile takeovers. In: Corporate Takeovers: Causes and Consequences. University of Chicago Press.

Smith, A.J., 1990. Corporate ownership structure and performance: the case of management buyouts. J. Financ. Econ. 27 (1), 143–164.

Spaenjers, C., Steiner, E., 2021. The Value of Specialization in Private Equity: Evidence from the Hotel Industry. Working Paper.

Wilson, N., Wright, M., 2013. Private equity, buy-outs and insolvency risk. J. Bus. Financ. Acc. 40 (7–8), 949–990.

Risk and return in private equity

Arthur Korteweg*

Marshall School of Business, University of Southern California, Los Angeles, CA, United States
*Corresponding author: e-mail address: korteweg@marshall.usc.edu

I am grateful to Douglas Cumming, Nicola Giommetti, and the handbook editors
for helpful comments and suggestions.

Chapter outline

Handbook of the Economics of Corporate Finance, Volume 1, ISSN 2949-964X, https://doi.org/10.1016/bs.hecf.2023.02.008

1 Introduction

Investments in private equity (PE) have increased dramatically over the last 25 years.[a] The 2020 NACUBO-TIAA Study of Endowments reports that U.S. college and university endowments allocate 22.8% of their assets to leveraged buyout and venture capital strategies, and another 6.9% to private debt and private real estate. Similarly, U.S. pension plans invest nearly 20% in alternative asset classes, which includes private equity, and pension funds in many other developed countries also have double-digit allocations to alternatives (Ivashina and Lerner, 2018).[b]

With the growing role of PE in investors' portfolios, assessing its risk and return has taken on increased importance. This chapter surveys the literature, covering both methodology and empirical results.

Several methodological issues prevent the direct application of standard asset pricing techniques to the private equity setting. Most importantly, returns are generally not observed at a regular frequency, reported fund valuations are often stale or biased in other ways, and portfolio company outcomes are frequently missing for failed investments. Moreover, payoff distributions are highly skewed. The chapter describes methods developed specifically to deal with these problems, distinguishing between approaches for fund-level and investment-level data, since they solve distinct econometric problems.

The empirical literature focuses on venture capital (VC) and leveraged buyout, historically the two dominant strategies within the PE space. Estimates of risk and return vary substantially, depending on the data source, sample period, and methodology used. For example, Fig. 1 shows the distribution of capital asset pricing model (CAPM) beta estimates, a measure of systematic risk, for VC and buyout from

---

[a]I define private equity to include all forms of PE investments, including leveraged buyout, venture capital, private real estate, private debt, infrastructure, and others.

[b]Whereas private markets have grown in importance, publicly traded firms now represent a smaller proportion of the economy than they did in the 1970s (Schlingemann and Stulz, 2022). However, most of the decrease in the prominence of public markets occurred prior to the rapid acceleration in private equity investments that started in the 1990s (see also Espen Eckbo and Lithell, 2021).

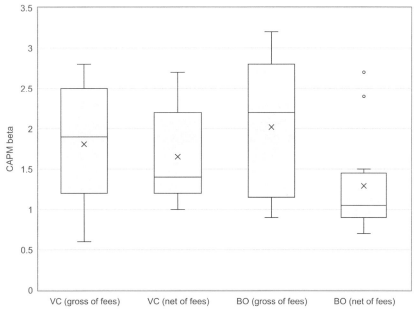

FIG. 1

Distribution of Capital Asset Pricing Model (CAPM) beta point estimates from the literature on venture capital (VC) and leveraged buyouts (BO). The figure shows separate box plots for gross-of-fee and net-of-fee estimates (typically from individual investment-level and fund-level data, respectively) for each strategy. The bottom and top of each box are the first and third quartiles of the distribution. The center line is the median. The mean is marked with an "x." The distributions of VC gross and net of fees betas is based on 10 and 11 estimates, respectively. The buyout gross and net of fees distributions are based on 5 and 12 estimates. The box plots include estimates from the following papers (each paper contributes at most one beta to each distribution, but some papers contribute estimates to multiple plots): Gompers and Lerner (1997), Peng (2001), Woodward and Hall (2004), Bilo et al. (2005), Cochrane (2005a), Hwang et al. (2005), Anson (2007), Ewens (2009), Woodward (2009), Korteweg and Sørensen (2010), Phalippou (2010), Groh and Gottschalg (2011), Driessen et al. (2012), Franzoni et al. (2012), Ewens et al. (2013, 2016), Axelson et al. (2014), Buchner and Stucke (2014), Jegadeesh et al. (2015), Ang et al. (2018), Peters (2018), Buchner (2020), Agarwal et al. (2022), Brown et al. (2021a), Boyer et al. (2022b), Stafford (2022).

the literature. For each strategy, the figure shows the estimates based on pre-fee investment-level data and after-fee fund-level data. Most papers find that VC and buyout are riskier than investing in the public stock market index, which has a beta of one by construction. But the point estimates vary widely, with some papers estimating betas less than one and others reporting estimates over 2.5.

Data quality and coverage have improved significantly in recent years, and researchers have started to adopt similar methodologies, most notably approaches that use stochastic discount factors, such as the public market equivalent metric. This has led to some convergence in estimates. Put differently, the variation in Fig. 1 over-states the uncertainty about estimates to some extent, as the papers included in the figure were not cherry-picked based on any judgment regarding the quality of the data or methodology used to arrive at the results, or even whether they estimate the risk of a reasonably similar set of firms or funds. Still, Fig. 1 underscores an important result regarding the uncertainty about estimates in PE that permeates the literature.

Despite the uncertainty, the weight of evidence from the PE literature suggests the following main takeaways (in addition to the insights on the level of market risk from Fig. 1):

- Relative to a market beta-matched investment in public stocks, the average VC fund earned positive risk-adjusted returns net of fees before the turn of the millennium. Since then, most studies have found average net-of-fee fund returns that are either statistically insignificant or negative.
- The average leveraged buyout fund earned positive net-of-fee returns relative to a market beta-matched public stock portfolio for the entire period since its early growth in the 1980s.
- Beyond market risk, VC looks like an investment in small growth stocks, whereas buyout tends to load on value but does not have a consistently meaningful size loading.
- Liquidity risk is important, but the size of the liquidity premium is still an open question.
- Other risks matter: idiosyncratic risk appears to be priced in VC, both in the time-series and the cross-section. Term structure and credit market risk factors also play a role. However, more work is needed to explore these, and other factors. When additional risk factors are accounted for, the net-of-fee risk-adjusted performance of both VC and buyout is lower, in many cases insignificant and in some cases negative.
- Gross-of-fee risk-adjusted return estimates appear high relative to net-of-fee estimates. The literature has not yet determined whether this difference is explained by fees alone, or whether it stems mainly from differences in data or methodology. Similarly, differences in beta estimates, which appear to be higher in gross-of-fee data, have not been satisfactorily explained.
- Investors' experience in alternative PE vehicles such as co-investments, which have grown dramatically in recent years, depends on the qualities and match between the investor and manager. Private funds of funds in VC have performed on par with direct VC funds, but weaker in buyout.
- Publicly traded PE vehicles do not generate statistically significant risk-adjusted returns (either positive or negative) by most estimates.

Several topics are not covered in this chapter, such as the evidence on return persistence, the large heterogeneity in performance across types of investors (i.e., limited partner or LP) and managers (i.e., general partner or GP), the debate regarding GP skill vs luck, and the LP's portfolio allocation decision. Korteweg and Westerfield (2022) provide an in-depth survey of these questions. The source of any value creation, that is, whether PE creates value at portfolio companies, is also not considered (this is the subject of the chapter by Sørensen and Yasuda in this same handbook volume). Finally, the performance of buyout debt, venture debt, private investments in public equity (PIPEs), angel investments, and entrepreneurs are not covered, although the tools and techniques described in the chapter are applicable to these investments as well.

The chapter is structured as follows. Section 2 describes the institutional setting of the PE industry. Section 3 discusses methods for fund-level data and presents results for main funds. Section 4 turns to the empirical evidence on alternative PE vehicles and funds-of-funds, and Section 5 covers publicly traded PE vehicles. Section 6 considers investment-level data and methods, and Section 7 concludes and lists open questions for future research.

2 Institutional setting

This section provides a brief overview of the PE industry for readers who are unfamiliar with its institutional setting. It may be safely skipped by those versed in the ins and outs of private equity. I present a level of detail that will suffice for the purpose of this chapter without intending to be comprehensive. There are many excellent books and articles with more complete descriptions of the inner workings of private equity, such as Lerner et al. (2012).

2.1 Funds

Traditionally, investors gain exposure to private equity by investing in funds. Funds are pools of capital that are raised and managed by a private equity firm. They are legally structured as limited partnerships with a finite lifetime, typically 10 years, after which they are liquidated.[c] The PE firm professionals serve as General Partners (GPs) and the investors are the Limited Partners (LPs). This structure is common across the different PE subclasses. The key difference between these strategies is the types of assets or securities they invest in. For example, venture capital (VC) funds invest in startup companies, buyout funds buy more seasoned, often struggling, firms (using leverage to help finance the purchase), real estate funds invest in office buildings, warehouses, shopping centers, and other (typically commercial)

---

[c]The (limited) partnership fund structure for highly risky investments has a long history. See, for example, Korteweg and Sensoy (2023), and references therein.

properties, and private debt funds invest in fixed income products (for example, corporate loans and bonds, or structured credit products. These are also known as private credit funds). There are also funds that invest in other PE funds (secondary funds and fund-of-funds). Sacrificing accuracy for ease of exposition, I will henceforth refer to the fund's investments as portfolio companies.

Table 1 presents descriptive statistics of PE funds raised since 1980, when private equity funds started to gain rapid popularity due to the passage of the 1979 ERISA

Table 1 Descriptive statistics for private equity funds.

	VC	Buyout	Real estate	Private debt	Natural resources	Infra-structure
Number of funds	1470	1300	1435	723	291	144
Fund size ($m)	248	1333	574	868	914	2067
	(150)	(500)	(269)	(438)	(410)	(999)
Liquidated (%)	46	38	38	29	33	13
Number of firms	569	431	380	244	92	65
Fund performance						
TVPI						
Mean	1.89	1.80	1.42	1.41	1.55	1.28
Median	1.38	1.61	1.38	1.30	1.30	1.22
St. Dev.	2.43	1.23	0.51	0.50	1.05	0.51
Skewness	7.81	8.46	0.81	2.78	4.18	1.29
Exc. Kurtosis	92.51	134.78	3.12	14.88	25.38	4.64
IRR (%)						
Mean	14.79	16.19	11.79	11.19	14.94	9.59
Median	9.22	14.00	11.58	10.02	9.54	8.78
St. Dev.	37.64	21.04	14.90	13.15	42.73	16.87
Skewness	5.91	4.85	0.89	1.55	9.77	−0.68
Exc. Kurtosis	58.68	63.72	33.11	39.71	126.56	16.15
PME (KS)						
Mean	0.96	1.11	0.96	1.01	0.94	0.86
Median	0.98	1.10	0.97	0.98	0.86	0.90
St. Dev.	0.42	0.32	0.26	0.19	0.30	0.24
Skewness	1.25	0.30	0.83	1.09	1.72	−1.27
Exc. Kurtosis	6.38	0.33	8.62	2.30	5.05	2.01

This table shows descriptive statistics for a sample of closed private equity funds with a North American geographic focus for vintage years ranging from 1980 to 2019. Funds of funds, secondary funds, co-investments, and venture debt funds are excluded. Each column represents a different private equity strategy. Fund size is in millions of U.S. dollars. Number of firms is the count of the number of unique PE firms in the sample. The same firm may raise multiple funds. TVPI is the total value to paid-in capital multiple, IRR is the internal rate of return, and PME (KS) is the Kaplan and Schoar (2005) public market equivalent using the S&P 500 as the benchmark. Reported fund sizes are averages, with medians in parentheses. Fund performance statistics are computed across all funds and vintages for each strategy, based on cash flow and Net Asset Value data reported as of year-end 2019. Exc. Kurtosis is the kurtosis of the distribution in excess of the Normal distribution (which has kurtosis of 3).
Source: Preqin.

"prudent man" rule (which made it feasible for pension funds to invest in PE) and a substantial reduction in the capital gains tax rate that was implemented around the same time. The number of funds, as well as their typical size, varies by strategy. There have been well over 1000 funds raised in venture capital, buyout, and real estate until the 2019 vintage year, the end of the sample period, in part due to these strategies having been around the longest.[d] Natural resources and especially infrastructure funds are more recent additions to the private equity scene, so naturally there have been fewer funds raised in these spaces over the sample period. The largest funds are raised in buyout and infrastructure, with average (median) fund sizes of $1.3 billion ($500 million) and $2.1 billion ($999 million). Private debt and natural resource funds are also quite large at $868 million ($438 million) and $914 million ($410 million). In contrast, the average fund in venture capital is only $248 million, with a median fund size of $150 million. The heterogeneity in fund sizes across PE classes depends on factors such as the typical size of an individual investment and the targeted number of investments per fund, among others.

The fund's GPs are responsible for putting in all the hard work, from sourcing new investments to negotiating and executing deals, managing the portfolio, and ultimately harvesting the gains. Unlike mutual funds and ETFs, they are active investors. For example, in venture capital and buyout, GPs serve on the board of their portfolio companies and provide a variety of value-added services, including monitoring and corporate governance (Lerner, 1995; Hellmann and Puri, 2002; Baker and Gompers, 2003; Edgerton, 2012; Bernstein et al., 2016; Ewens and Marx, 2018), operational experience and strategic advice (Bharath et al., 2014; Davis et al., 2014; Bernstein and Sheen, 2016; Bisinger et al., 2020; Cohn et al., 2020; Fracassi et al., 2022), human resources (Amornsiripanitch et al., 2019; Hellmann and Puri, 2002), innovation (Lerner et al., 2011), and relieving financial constraints (Boucly et al., 2011; Cohn et al., 2020; Fracassi et al., 2022).

The LPs are investors such as pension funds, endowments, insurance companies, sovereign wealth funds, and wealthy individuals. They are pure capital providers and are not actively involved with running the fund: they do not have any control over individual investment and sale decisions, or how the portfolio assets are managed. Instead, they negotiate a contract with the GPs at the time of fundraising, called the LP Agreement (or simply LPA), which describes each party's rights and responsibilities.

2.2 Fund cash flows

An important feature of PE funds is that the money committed by LPs is not immediately transferred to the fund. The LPA allows for an "investment period" (also known as the commitment period), usually 4–6 years (3 years for real estate and private debt funds), in which the fund is allowed to make investments in new portfolio

---

[d]Vintage year can be defined in various ways. A common definition used by researchers is the year of the fund's first capital call to LPs (capital calls are explained below). Even though fundraising typically takes 6 months to a year from first raise to final close, funds often have multiple closings so that GPs can start calling capital and invest before the final close.

companies. LPs hold on to their capital until the GPs identify a desired investment (or when management fees need to be paid; more on fees in the next section). At this point the GPs issue a capital call to the LPs. Capital calls (also referred to as "contributions") are pro rata to fund commitments, for example, an LP who has committed $10 million dollars to a $200 million fund will contribute 5% of the total amount of any capital call. Fig. 2 shows the average cumulative capital calls over a fund's life, for an LP with a $10 million commitment, broken down by strategy.[e] Calls are depicted as negative numbers because they are outflows from the LP's perspective. The figure shows that on average, committed capital is gradually called up during the first 5 years of the fund's life. For an individual fund, the pattern is less smooth than Fig. 2 suggests. The time it takes for a fund to be fully called up varies by fund strategy, deal flow, the length of the investment period, and other considerations. There is considerable heterogeneity in the rate of capital calls across vintage years and funds, as shown by the size of the shaded area in the figure, which captures the range between the top and the bottom 5% of the distribution.

After the investment period, the fund enters the "harvest period." GPs' workload drops significantly at this time, as they switch from deal sourcing to managing the fund's investments and realizing exits. If the fund still has "dry powder" (uncalled capital), follow-on investments in existing portfolio companies may still be made, such as participation in new fundraising rounds of previously backed startups in VC.

Exits take the form of acquisitions, usually by strategic acquirers but in some cases by other PE funds, or—in venture capital and buyout—an initial public offering (IPO) of the portfolio company. In some strategies, investments are self-liquidating, for example the maturing of loans in private credit. Not all investments are successful, however, and some may be written off completely. This is especially common in venture capital: Kerr, Nanda, and Rhodes-Kropf (2014) show that of all startup firms in the Venture Economics database that received their first round of early-stage financing between 1985 and 2009, about 55% resulted in a loss. Only 6% returned more than 5 times their investment, but this small subset of startups accounted for roughly half of the gross return that was realized over this sample period. This observation suggests a high level of skewness in VC returns, a topic I will return to in the next section.

Cash that returns to the fund is distributed to the LPs, after withholding of any fees due to the GPs. Like capital calls, distributions are pro-rata to LPs' commitments. In VC, distributions stem solely from portfolio company exits, since startups do not pay dividends, but in other strategies there may be additional distributions from intermediate cash flows that realize before exit. For example, in buyout, portfolio companies sometimes pay dividends (often through recapitalizations) and they

---

[e]Fig. 2 uses the sample of funds in Preqin for which cash flows are available. This is a subsample of the funds included in Table 1 (see section V of the Internet Appendix of Korteweg and Nagel, 2016, for a detailed comparison of the two samples). A second difference is that the sample for Fig. 2 does not use any post-2005 vintages, to allow for enough years of cash flow data to construct the figure, whereas Table 1 uses vintages all the way through 2019.

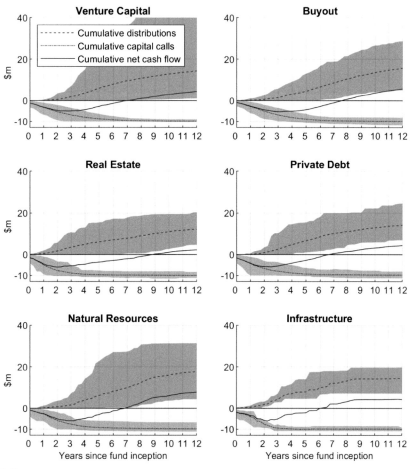

FIG. 2

Cash flow patterns for PE funds by strategy, for 1980–2005 vintages with a North American geographic focus for which cash flows are reported in Preqin. Funds of funds, secondary funds, co-investments, and venture debt funds are excluded. Cash flows are available until the end of 2019, they are normalized to a $10 million capital commitment to each fund, and are net fees to the General Partners. The dotted red line represents average cumulative capital calls since fund inception (in millions of U.S. dollars, shown as negative numbers) across funds that are active at a given number of years since fund inception (on the horizontal axis). The dashed blue line shows average cumulative distributions to LPs, and the solid black line is the average cumulative net cash flow (cumulative distributions minus capital calls). The shaded areas show the range between the 5th and 95th percentiles of the cross-fund distribution of cumulative capital calls and distributions. The distribution for net cash flows is omitted for readability.

Source: Preqin.

pay a variety of fees to the GPs, some of which are shared with the LPs. In real estate, property rental income generates a steady cash flow stream to the fund.

Fig. 2 shows the average after-fee cumulative distributions over a fund's life. Since it takes time for portfolio companies to mature and exit, distributions do not usually accelerate until the third year into the fund, and most tend to come in between years 4 and 9. The shaded area in the figure, indicating the range between the top and bottom 2.5% of the distribution, reveals a large degree of heterogeneity across funds and time.

The LPA sometimes allows GPs to reinvest proceeds from early exits. In such cases, after the money is distributed to the LPs, it gets "recalled" (or "recycled"). Global Investment Performance Standards (GIPS), a voluntary set of standards used by investment managers, requires that recalled distributions are both counted as an actual distribution and as additional paid-in capital. As such, a fund with recalled distributions may report cumulative capital calls in excess of its committed fund size. This can be seen in Fig. 2, where cumulative capital calls sometimes exceed the LP's $10 million commitment.

Fund cash flow data sometimes report negative capital calls. This usually represents a return of excess capital called, which can happen if the amount invested ended up being lower than the amount originally called, if a deal fell through at the last minute, or if the GP returns excess fees to the LPs. The returned amount can be called again later.

The solid line in Fig. 2 traces the typical pattern of cumulative net cash flows (defined as distributions minus capital calls) and reveals the well-known "J-curve" that also shows up in common performance metrics such as cash multiples and IRRs: cumulative net cash flows are negative in the first few years of the fund (the "valley of tears" as some call it), before turning positive later in the fund's life.

The holding time for an individual investment can vary, depending on the type of investment, macro-economic conditions, managerial skill, and luck, among others. For example, buyout investments often take 3–7 years from initial investment to IPO or acquisition, whereas early-stage VC investments can at times last 10 years or longer (and the average time to liquidity in VC has been growing longer in the past two decades). If the fund still has unrealized investments by the end of its legal lifetime, it can be extended beyond the initial 10-year period. In VC, for example, the LPA often gives the GP the right to trigger two 1-year extensions. Any further extensions must be approved by the LPs, which involves some negotiating over management fees. Fig. 2 shows that fund extensions are quite common across strategies, as a material amount of distributions come in after year 10 (the figure cuts off at 12 years, but it is not uncommon to see funds that are over 15 years old, especially in early-stage VC). If the fund terminates while there remain unexcited investments, these may be sold to another fund, or the securities may be distributed to the LPs.

2.3 Fees

A fund's GPs charge two types of fees to their LPs: a management fee and a profit share called "carried interest" or simply "carry" (also known as "promote" in real estate funds). It is also common for GPs to charge certain fees to portfolio companies, some of which may be shared with LPs.

The management fee is typically 2% per year, with some variation around this number. The percentage fee number is usually applied to committed capital during the investment period, and often switches to net invested capital (the aggregate invested amount of remaining unexcited investments) during the harvest period. The percentage fee number may also drop after the investment period. Metrick and Yasuda (2010a) report fund fee statistics for a sample of 238 VC and buyout funds. They compute total management fees over the median fund's lifetime of 17.75% and 12% of committed capital for VC and buyout, respectively. Robinson and Sensoy (2013) find 21.4% and 14.2%, in a larger sample of 837 funds. These fees are paid out of committed capital, so if total management fees add up to 15% of committed capital, a $100 million fund only invests $85 million (if there are no recycled distributions).

Carried interest is the share of profits that GPs earn if the fund returns more than its committed capital to LPs. For VC and buyout, carried interest equals 20% for most funds, whereas in real estate there are usually multiple tiers. In some strategies, such as buyout and real estate, there may be an additional "hurdle rate" (also known as "preferred return" or simply "pref," typically equal to 8% per year on net invested capital) that needs to be returned to LPs before the GPs start to earn carry. Funds with a hurdle often allow for a "catch-up" period where the GPs receive a larger proportion (often 100%) of distributions until they have received their carry share on the fund's profits to date. There is variation across funds in the timing of carried interest payments. European funds typically assess carry on a whole-fund basis, that is, the GP does not earn carried interest until the entire committed capital plus hurdle has been returned to LPs. In contrast, American funds typically compute carry on a deal-by-deal basis. The deal-by-deal structure allows the GPs to earn carry earlier, but if a fund had lackluster performance following early success, the LPs may claw back any excess carry paid, which carries some credit risk for the LPs.[f] For more details on the timing of carried interest, see Litvak (2009) and Hüther et al. (2020).

Apart from LP fees, some funds also charge fees to their portfolio companies. These fees are especially common in buyout and are described in the management service agreement contract between the GPs and the portfolio company. They include, but are not limited to, transaction fees for investment banking services provided by the GPs to the company at the time of the buyout (and possibly for any add-on acquisitions) and annual advisory fees (also known as monitoring fees). Metrick and Yasuda (2010a), from informal discussions with buyout practitioners, report that one-time transaction fees are typically 1–2% of deal value, and annual monitoring fees range from 1% to 5% of the portfolio company's EBITDA. Phalippou et al. (2018) collect detailed fee data for a sample of 454 large U.S. leveraged buyout deals and find that total fees add up to 1.75% of enterprise value for the average portfolio company. About 70% of fees are rebated to LPs on average, with an interquartile range of 25–80%. Since most portfolio companies in buyout

---

[f]To limit the risk of GP clawbacks not getting repaid, the LPA sometimes arranges for early carry to be paid into an escrow account.

are fully owned by the fund, these fees are effectively dividend payments (with a different LP-GP split than carried interest). Their characterization as fees may carry a tax advantage as fee payments are tax deductible for the portfolio company.

Some LPs obtain fee breaks as part of side letters they negotiate with their GPs. Lee (2015) describes the content of side letters anecdotally. In a survey of 249 LPs across 30 countries, Da Rin and Phalippou (2017) find that 63% of large LPs always get side letters, compared to only 17% of small LPs. Begenau and Siriwardane (2021) provide suggestive evidence that carried interest rates differ across LPs invested in the same fund; larger LPs and those that have a longer investment history with the GP earn higher net-of-fee returns.

At present, fund fee data is very difficult to collect. Fee payments cannot be identified in publicly available fund data sets, such as Burgiss, Preqin, and Thomson VentureXpert (formerly called Venture Economics), as they only report cash flows and returns net of fees. Thus, fund data can only inform about risk and return from the LPs' perspective. To say something about GP skill, we need gross-of-fee returns. Looking ahead, it may be possible to get gross-of-fee fund data for a reasonably large and representative set of funds, as pressure to increase transparency in fee payments has been growing in recent years. For example, California Government Code Section 7514.7 requires annual public disclosure of the fees, expenses, and carried interest paid by California public pension funds—which includes some very large LPs such as CalPERS and CalSTRS—to GPs after January 1, 2017. But as of this writing, the most comprehensive coverage of gross-of-fee returns comes from portfolio company data, which I discuss in Section 6.

2.4 Fund sequences

GPs raise a sequence of flagship funds, typically distinguished by Roman numerals (e.g., Sequoia I, Sequoia II, etc.), and may have more than one active fund at any given time. Since the GPs' workload is very high during the investment period, and to avoid agency problems from actively investing in new deals out of multiple funds at the same time, the LPA prohibits GPs from raising a new fund that directly competes with the current fund until a prespecified, substantial percentage of the fund is invested. Note, however, that this does not prevent GPs from raising funds in other geographies or strategies, from raising "opportunity" funds (also known as "select" or "growth" funds) in early-stage VC,[g] or alternative vehicles that are offered to select LPs. I discuss alternative vehicles, the number and size of which has grown dramatically in recent years, in more detail in Section 4.

Based on the number of PE firms and the number of funds reported in Table 1, the average PE firm has raised between 2 and 4 funds during the sample period,

---

[g]Opportunity funds are funds raised by early-stage VCs to make later-stage investments in successful portfolio companies. These types of funds, as well as continuation funds (which purchase portfolio company investments from GPs' prior funds), have become more popular in recent years as more startup firms stay private longer, increasing their capital needs and time to liquidity.

depending on the strategy (e.g., in buyout, 431 firms raised 1300 funds, for an average of 3.0 funds per firm). Empirically, most GPs raise a new fund every 2–4 years. Consequently, subsequent funds overlap in time for 6 or more years. Accounting for this overlap is important for the calculation of correct standard errors of performance metrics (as well as for inference regarding return persistence, but this is not a focal issue of this chapter; see Korteweg and Sørensen, 2017, for a model of overlap and persistence).

3 Fund data
3.1 Data structure and notation

Table 2 shows an example of the type of cash flow data that researchers would typically work with, for a fictitious fund i. Calendar dates are denoted by t, with t_0 and T being the date of the first and last observation for the fund, respectively. For notational simplicity I suppress the dependence of t_0 and T on i. Based on the initial cash flow date of February 1, 2022, researchers would generally consider this fund to be a 2022 vintage year fund, though the GPs likely started raising the fund in 2021. Date T for this fund is December 31, 2024. Note that the fund is not yet liquidated at this time. This may happen because we are at the end of the sample period, or the fund may have stopped reporting after this date.

Cash flows are reported from an LP's perspective and are normalized to a $10 million commitment. Capital calls, $I_{i,k}$, are indexed by k, from 1 to K. Unlike Fig. 2, capital calls from here on out are defined as positive numbers (except for recalled distributions, which as considered negative capital calls, as described in the previous section). Thus, from Table 2, $I_{i,1}$, the initial capital call that occurred on February 1, 2022, equals $200,000. Distributions, $D_{i,d}$, are numbered from $d=1$ to D. Our fund only has $D=2$ distributions: $D_{i,1}=\$500,000$, which occurred on April 10, 2024, and $D_{i,2}=\$1,000,000$ on December 20, 2024.

Some performance measures are based on net cash flows, $C_{i,j}$, defined from the LP's perspective as the distribution minus the capital call for each date on which there is a cash flow (either a capital call or a distribution, or both). For example, $C_{i,1}$ in Table 2 is the net cash flow on the date of the first capital call, and since there was no distribution on that date, it is equal to $-\$200,000$. Net cash flows are numbered from $j=1$ to J, where $J \leq D+K$, with strict inequality if a capital call and a distribution occur on the same day. This happens for the fund in Table 2, which has $K=7$ capital calls and $D=2$ distributions, but only $J=8$ net cash flows because on April 10, 2024 it had both a capital call and a distribution, which combine into one net cash flow ($C_{i,6}=D_{i,1}-I_{i,6}=\$500,000-\$200,000=\$300,000$). As with fund start and end dates, K, D, and J vary by fund, but I suppress their dependence on the fund index i.

Apart from cash flows, GPs report fund net asset values (NAVs) to their LPs at the end of each quarter, which provide a snapshot of the aggregate value of the fund's

Table 2 Fund data for a fictitious private equity fund.

		Cash flow data				Quarterly data		
Date	Years since t_0	Capital calls	Distributions	Net cash flow	Stock market return	Net asset value	Net cash flow	Fund return
t	τ	$I_{l,k}$	$D_{l,d}$	$C_{l,j}$	$R^M_{t_0,\tau}$	$NAV_{i,t}$	$C_{i,t}$	$R_{i,t}$
Feb 1, 2022	0	200	0	−200	1			
Mar 31, 2022	0.16	0	0	0	1.020	190	−200	N/A
Jun 16, 2022	0.37	100	0	−100	1.022			
Jun 30, 2022	0.41	0	0	0	1.017	250	−100	0.789
Jul 16, 2022	0.45	1900	0	−1900	1.026			
Sep 30, 2022	0.66	0	0	0	1.054	2200	−1900	1.200
Dec 31, 2022	0.91	0	0	0	1.098	2200	0	1.000
Mar 31, 2023	1.16	0	0	0	1.159	2750	0	1.250
Jun 20, 2023	1.38	1500	0	−1500	1.178			
Jun 30, 2023	1.41	0	0	0	1.023	3800	−1500	0.836
Sep 30, 2023	1.66	0	0	0	1.044	4100	0	1.079
Dec 31, 2023	1.91	0	0	0	1.106	4100	0	1.000
Feb 1, 2024	2.00	500	0	−500	1.110			
Mar 31, 2024	2.16	0	0	0	1.062	4600	−500	1.000
Apr 10, 2024	2.19	200	500	300	1.095			
Apr 20, 2024	2.21	50	0	−50	1.108			
Jun 30, 2024	2.41	0	0	0	1.167	4500	250	1.033
Sep 30, 2024	2.66	0	0	0	1.222	4300	0	0.956
Dec 20, 2024	2.88	0	1000	1000	1.244			
Dec 31, 2024	2.91	0	0	0	1.250	3300	1000	1.000
Total		**4450**	**1500**	**−2950**			**−2950**	

Fund data for a fictitious private equity fund, indexed by i. The first column shows the cash flow dates, t, where dates of the first and last observations, t_0, and T, are February 1, 2022, and December 31, 2024. Column two shows years elapsed since t_0. The third and fourth columns are capital calls, I (indexed by k from 1 to K), and distributions D (indexed by d from 1 to D), respectively. Column five shows the net cash flow from the Limited Partner's perspective, C = D − I, indexed by j from 1 to J. Column six is the public stock market return since t_0 ($R^M_{t_0,\tau}$, where a 5% return is shown as 1.050). The final three columns show quarterly fund data: the end-of-quarter reported Net Asset Value (NAV) and its quarterly net cash flow and fund return ($R_i^{}$), based on the net cash flow and the change in NAV over the quarter. All cash flows (capital calls, distributions, and net cash flows) and NAVs are in thousands of U.S. dollars, normalized to a $10 million commitment. Cash flows are net of fees paid to the fund's General Partners.

ownership position in its portfolio investments, net of any borrowing at the fund level.[h] In other words, the NAV represents the value that has not yet been distributed to LPs. For a liquidated fund, the final NAV is zero. The fund in Table 2 reports a large NAV of $3.3 million on December 31, 2024, since it is not yet liquidated at the end of the sample period (in fact, it is still in the investment period, having called only $4.45 million of a $10 million commitment).

For most performance metrics we need the time difference, τ, between fund inception (t_0) and the date of observed cash flows or NAVs. The second column of Table 2 shows τ for our example fund. The time-since-inception of net cash flow number j, capital call k and distribution d are denoted by $\tau(j)$, $\tau^I(k)$ and $\tau^D(d)$, respectively. Table 2 does not show these numbers explicitly, but they are easily identified: For example, $\tau^I(2)$ in Table 2—the since-inception time of the second capital call—is 0.37. Like the other timing variables, I suppress the dependence of the τ variables on the fund index, i, to keep notation tractable.

I use the conventional notation R_t for a return from time $t-1$ to t. That is, $R_t = 1.05$ represents a 5% return over the period. Lower-case letters denote log-returns, i.e., $r_t \equiv \ln(R_t)$. For returns over an interval from time t to $t+\tau$, I use the notation $R_{t,\tau}$. For example, column 6 in Table 2 shows the return on the public stock market portfolio from fund inception to the date of each reported cash flow or NAV (these are fictitious market returns for the sake of the example, not the actual returns in the data, which are unknown as of the time of this writing). Stock market and other factor returns data must be collected by the researcher. PE data providers, such as Preqin or Burgiss, usually only provide the capital calls, distributions, and NAVs (as well as some GP and fund characteristics).

3.2 Traditional private equity return metrics

3.2.1 Definitions

The two traditional metrics of return in private equity are cash multiples and internal rates of return (IRR). Gompers et al. (2016) survey 79 buyout GPs and find that in over 90% of investments, they use one or both of these measures to evaluate the deal. Moreover, virtually all of them report that either the cash multiple or the IRR is the most important metric to their LPs. Similarly, of 546 VCs surveyed by Gompers et al. (2020), 63% use cash multiples, and 42% use IRRs to evaluate investments. As many as 84% of these VCs think cash multiples are an important benchmark metric for their LPs, and 81% think IRRs are important.

---

[h]Many funds have lines of credit. The amounts borrowed are traditionally small relative to the size of the fund and are used for transaction cost reasons by allowing the GP to combine multiple small capital calls into one, or to cover for any capital calls that are slow to arrive so that a deal does not fall through. Recently, some GPs have started to use credit lines more aggressively, possibly distorting performance metrics (Schillinger et al., 2019; Albertus and Denes, 2020). See Section 3.7.2 for more discussion on the impact of leverage on performance measurement.

The standard cash multiple used in practice is Total Value to Paid-in Capital (TVPI), computed for fund i as[i]

$$TVPI_i = \frac{\sum_{d=1}^{D} D_{i,d} + NAV_{i,T}}{\sum_{k=1}^{K} I_{i,k}}. \qquad (1)$$

For example, as of December 31, 2024, the fund in Table 2 had total capital calls of $4.45 million, total distributions of $1.5 million, and its most recent reported NAV is $3.3 million. Its TVPI is therefore ($1.5m+$3.3 m)/$4.45m = 1.08.

The other customary return metric, IRR, is defined as the discount rate (expressed as an annual rate) such that the net present value (NPV) of the fund's net cash flows discounted back to t_0 (the date of the fund's first cash flow) is zero.

$$\sum_{j=1}^{J} \frac{C_{i,j}}{(1 + IRR_i)^{\tau(j)}} + \frac{NAV_{i,T}}{(1 + IRR_i)^{T-t_0}} = 0. \qquad (2)$$

Based on the 8 net cash flows and the NAV as of December 31, 2024, the fund in Table 2 has an IRR of 4.24%.

Both TVPI and IRR include the most recently reported NAV as a pseudo-distribution, to reflect any undistributed value remaining inside the fund. For fully liquidated funds (for which $NAV_{i,T}$ is zero), both TVPI and IRR are based entirely on cash flows.[j]

Note that the classification of certain cash flows as capital calls or distributions—for example, whether a recalled distribution is accounted for as a negative distribution or as a capital call, or whether a return of excess capital called is a negative capital call or a distribution—matters for TVPI (and more generally, for any performance metric based on ratios of distributions and contributions, such as the Kaplan-Schoar public market equivalent (PME) discussed below). Metrics that are based on net cash flows, such as the internal rate of return (IRR), are invariant to this classification issue.

3.2.2 Data

Table 1 reports descriptive statistics of TVPI and IRR using the data introduced in Section 2.1, separated into six PE fund strategies. The average fund TVPI over the 1980–2019 sample period ranged from 1.28 for infrastructure funds to 1.89 for VC funds. Infrastructure funds also had the lowest median TVPI at 1.22, whereas buyout had the highest median at 1.61. An important feature of private equity fund TVPIs

---

[i] At the deal level, the cash multiple is usually referred to as Multiple on Invested Capital (MOIC). For all intents and purposes, MOIC is the same as TVPI.
[j] For not-yet-liquidated funds, TVPI is sometimes split into Distributed-to-Paid-In Capital (DPI) and Residual-Value-to-Paid-In Capital (RVPI), where the former only uses distributions in the numerator, and the latter only uses the most recently reported NAV. TVPI is the sum of DPI and RVPI. For a fully liquidated fund, RVPI equals zero so that TVPI = DPI.

across strategies is their high level of volatility and (positive) skewness. Venture capital funds especially stand out with a standard deviation of TVPI of 2.43. The high variance is in part due to time variation in average performance, but the lion's share is due to cross-sectional variation (this is not shown here, but see Section 3.7.1 below for more details). Since TVPI is bounded below at zero, it is not surprising that VC exhibits large positive skewness and excess kurtosis (in comparison, the Normal distribution has zero skewness and zero excess kurtosis). To illustrate the degree of skew and kurtosis more clearly, the left column of plots in Fig. 3 shows the kernel-smoothed distribution of TVPI, with VC at the top left.[k] The second and higher moments of the other PE strategies are for the most part not quite as striking as in VC, but they are still very large compared to traditional publicly traded asset classes such as stocks and bonds.

Turning to IRR, the mean (median) ranges from 9.59% (8.78%) for infrastructure to 16.19% (14.00%) for buyout. The shape of the IRR distribution is broadly similar to TVPI, with each strategy exhibiting large variation (again, mostly cross-sectional) and positive skewness and excess kurtosis. Two notable differences are the higher volatility, skewness, and kurtosis of the IRRs of natural resources fund, which are much larger than for TVPI, and the slight negative skew in infrastructure IRRs. Both strategies are relatively small, so these results may simply be due to the small sample of funds. Moreover, infrastructure has only recently grown to become a more common PE strategy, with many funds still in the early stages of their life cycle (as underscored by the fact that only 13% of infrastructure funds have been fully liquidated by year-end 2019, as reported in Table 1). Performance results are likely to change as these funds mature and more exits realize. The recency of most infrastructure funds may also (partly) explain their lower average performance, as performance metrics tend to exhibit a J-curve over a fund's horizon, like the cash flow patterns discussed in Section 2.2.

Unfortunately, no currently available private equity fund data set is comprehensive. Kaplan and Lerner (2017) describe the pros and cons of the main PE data sets that are available for purchase to researchers. Harris et al. (2014) compare the leading commercially available fund data sets—Cambridge Associates, Preqin, and Thomson Venture Economics (now called VentureXpert)—with Burgiss, a data set that is accessible to academic researchers. They make a strong case for the Burgiss data being the highest quality data set, but they find that performance metrics in Preqin (used for Table 1 and Fig. 3) and Cambridge Associates data are qualitatively similar to Burgiss. Preqin does miss a few top performing VC funds that did not accept public money, as their data is primarily sourced from Freedom of Information Act (FOIA) requests. This likely affects the mean performance numbers but should have

---

[k]In the initial few years of a fund, performance measures can be extremely volatile and are often primarily driven by NAVs. To provide a more informative picture, the sample used to construct Fig. 3 excludes post-2014 vintages, such that each fund has at least 5 years of performance data (which is collected through the end of 2019). Other than the earlier vintage cutoff, the sample is identical to the sample used in Table 1.

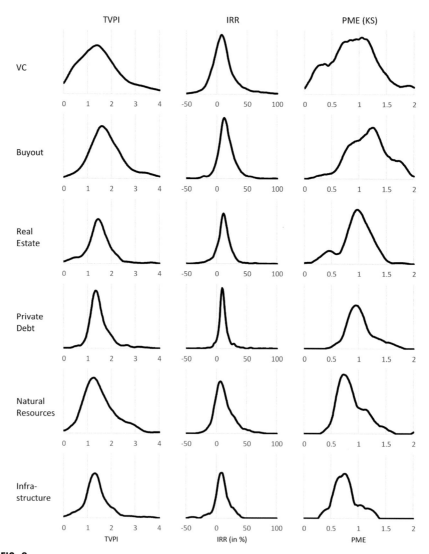

FIG. 3

This figure shows the Epanechnikov kernel smoothed distribution of three performance measures for private equity funds: total value to paid-in capital (*TVPI*), internal rate of return (*IRR*), and the Kaplan and Schoar (2005) public market equivalent (*PME (KS)*). The sample of funds is described in Table 1, except that vintages after 2014 are excluded to ensure that each fund has at least 5 years of data (performance is computed on cash flows and net asset values reported by the end of 2019). Each row represents a different private equity strategy. The distributions of the performance metrics for a given strategy include all funds and vintages for that strategy.

only a small (if not negligible) effect on medians. In contrast, the Thomson Venture Economics data has a strong downward performance bias compared to the other data sets, due to its failure to update cash flows and NAVs for about 40% of its funds after some point during funds' active lifetimes (Stucke, 2011).

3.2.3 Drawbacks
The traditional performance measures, while informative, suffer from several drawbacks. For example, TVPI ignores the time value of money: One dollar distributed in year 1 of the fund is considered just as valuable as a dollar distributed in year 10. IRR does account for the timing of cash flows, but it has several problems that are well described in any undergraduate-level corporate finance textbook worth its salt: First, an IRR may not exist in some (rare) cases. Second, there can be multiple IRRs. For example, while the IRR for the fictitious fund from Table 2 is unique, if there were an additional distribution of, say, $1.5 million on March 31, 2022, then there would be two IRRs, 42%, and 673%. Each number is a valid IRR, so it is not clear which is the "correct" number to report. Although such a large early distribution is admittedly rather unrealistic, multiple IRRs can happen in more realistic scenarios. A third drawback is that IRR implicitly assumes that distributions can be reinvested at the same rate. Phalippou (2013) constructs an example based on Yale's endowment track record that shows that early high returns can generate IRRs that do not vary much with subsequent, larger investments, even if those later investments have returns that vary substantially. Fourth, the IRR of a portfolio of investments is not the weighted average of the constituents' IRRs (Phalippou, 2008; Phalippou and Gottschalg, 2009). This means, for example, that the average IRR is not the IRR of the average fund. This is mainly an implementation issue but it is important to be aware that the portfolio IRR should be computed on the aggregated portfolio cash flows. Finally, IRRs can be manipulated to the extent that GPs can time cash flows, for example, by delaying a capital call. This latter concern is grounds for a more general call for research into the development of a manipulation-proof PE performance measure, possibly along the lines of Goetzmann et al. (2007).

The main critique of both the TVPI and IRR performance metrics, as far as this chapter is concerned, is that neither adjusts for risk. For example, consider the two fictitious funds in Fig. 4. Both funds have 5 years of cash flows, and both funds have a TVPI of 2.5 and an IRR of 50.2%. Yet, fund A looks considerably less risky than fund B (in fact, fund A looks very much like a fixed-coupon bond investment). A different benchmark return would seem appropriate for the two funds, yet the TVPI and IRR metrics do not provide any guidance in this respect. Moreover, while Gompers et al. (2020) report that of 546 institutional VCs, 64% say that they adjust their investments' target metrics for risk, it is not clear how those benchmarks are determined.

3.3 Risk and return: Factor models
At this point it is worthwhile to briefly review the standard asset pricing approach to assessing risk and return as it has been developed in the academic literature over the last 60 years. In this approach, one estimates risk and risk-adjusted returns by

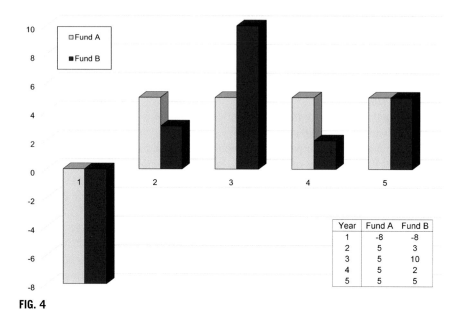

Year	Fund A	Fund B
1	-8	-8
2	5	3
3	5	10
4	5	2
5	5	5

FIG. 4

Example of cash flows for two fictitious private equity funds, called A and B, to illustrate differences in riskiness. Years are on the horizonal axis, and annual cash flows are on the vertical axis. The table in the bottom right corner shows the cash flow numbers. Both funds have a total value to paid-in capital multiple of 2.5, and an internal rate of return of 50.2%.

regressing a security i's excess return (its return minus the risk-free rate, R_t^F, over the period) on a set of G risk factors, whose returns are grouped in a vector $F_t = [F_{1t}, F_{2t}, ..., F_{Gt}]'$,

$$R_{i,t} - R_t^F = \alpha_i + \beta_i' F_t + \varepsilon_{i,t}. \qquad (3)$$

For example, the CAPM has only one risk factor, the excess return on the market portfolio, $F_t = R_t^M - R_t^F$.[1] The elements of the vector of factor loadings, β_i, represents the exposure of the security to each risk factor. These loadings represent systematic, undiversifiable risk exposures (as opposed to the residual, $\varepsilon_{i,t}$, component of returns, which represents diversifiable, or idiosyncratic risk). The security's benchmark portfolio is the portfolio that invests β_i in the factors, and therefore has the same (priced) risk exposures as security i. If the security is priced correctly, and if all factors are traded excess returns that capture all relevant sources of risk, then the intercept, α_i

[1]Formally, the CAPM does not have an intercept (α_i), and the model in Eq. (3) with the excess market return as the sole risk factor is known as the "market model". In empirical work in PE, researchers almost always include an intercept and use the CAPM and market model labels interchangeably. I will follow this practice, at the risk of upsetting theorists.

(sometimes referred to as risk-adjusted return), is equal to zero. A positive alpha means that an investor can achieve an excess return over the benchmark portfolio, on average.

It is tempting to take a similar regression approach in PE. However, there are few publicly traded funds for which returns can be measured on regular intervals, and the ones that are traded are a selected subset of the fund universe (see Section 5). An alternative for private funds could be to use fund IRRs (minus the risk-free rate over the fund's life) on the left-hand side of Eq. (3), and annualized returns to the factor portfolios over the same horizon as each fund on the right-hand side. While this is a cross-sectional regression across funds, the variation in vintage years allows for variation in the factor returns needed to estimate betas. For example, Kaplan and Schoar (2005) estimate CAPM betas by regressing fund IRRs on the average annual return to the S&P 500 stock index over the first 5 years of the fund. Assuming all funds have the same risk exposure, they estimate a beta of 1.23 for VC and 0.41 for buyout, meaning that VC is riskier than the public stock market (which has a CAPM beta of 1 by construction), and buyout is less risky. As Ilmanen et al. (2020) point out, it is problematic to compare IRRs, which are money-weighted returns in the sense that periods with higher cash flows get more weight, with factor returns, which are time-weighted such that each period has equal weight. Put differently, this procedure uses different definitions of returns on the left and right-hand sides of Eq. (3), and the estimated betas are therefore not true factor loadings. In simulations, Axelson et al. (2014) show that these types of regressions produce downward biased beta estimates. A better approach may be to regress fund IRRs on the IRRs of portfolios that mimic the capital calls and distributions of the PE fund but invest in the risk factors instead (see, for example, Ljungqvist and Richardson, 2003, for the construction of such matched investment portfolios). At present, the econometric properties of such regressions are unknown. However, in unreported work I find that this alternative approach still produces biased beta estimates, and that the bias is larger if expected returns vary over time or if cash flows are highly correlated with factor returns.

Another alternative that appears feasible, at least at first pass, is to use the quarterly fund NAVs together with the fund's cash flows to construct a quarterly return series. The next section explores this idea.

3.4 NAV-based returns

An intuitively appealing way to define a return on fund i for quarter t is to use the reported NAVs and the fund's capital calls and distributions over the quarter,

$$R_{i,t} \equiv \frac{NAV_{i,t} + C_{i,t}}{NAV_{i,t-1}}. \qquad (4)$$

Here, $C_{i,t}$, is the total net cash flow (distributions minus contributions) over quarter t. This definition is subtly different from $C_{i,j}$ in Section 3.1 above, where j

indicated the fund's cash flow number in the sequence of cash flows from 1 to J. Formally, the relation between the two cash flows can be expressed as

$$C_{i,t} = \sum_{j:t_0 + \tau(j) \in (t-1, t]} C_{i,j}. \qquad (5)$$

The final three columns in Table 2 shows the quarterly NAVs and net cash flows (based on a $10 million commitment), and the resulting return for the fictitious fund from Section 3.1. For example, in the quarter ending June 30, 2024, there was a $500,000 distribution and two capital calls of $200,000 and $50,000, for a net cash flow of $C_{i,t} = \$250,000$ (note that researchers have to construct these quarterly net cash flows themselves, data providers do not report $C_{i,t}$). With a NAV of $4.6 million at the start of the quarter, and an ending NAV of $4.5 million, the fund return for the quarter was $R_{i,t} = (\$4.5\text{m} + \$0.25\text{m})/\$4.6\text{m} = 1.033$, or 3.3%.

With the returns from Table 2 we can estimate a factor model, such as the CAPM: Assuming for simplicity that the risk-free rate is equal to zero (such that returns and excess returns are equal), the fund's beta is 1.22, and the intercept is -23% per quarter. However, as there are only 11 return observations, the standard errors of these coefficients are very large, at 0.66% and 67%, respectively, with beta barely significantly different from zero at the 10% level. To bring down the standard errors, one could estimate a common alpha and beta for a group of funds or even an entire strategy, such as VC. These pooled estimates are common across research methodologies (although a few papers estimate fund-level parameters, usually with the help of some additional identifying assumptions). When estimating a common beta across funds, it is important to correct the standard errors for cross-correlations, as residuals in the same calendar quarter are highly correlated.

To build intuition, it is worth highlighting a few characteristics of the quarterly fund returns as defined by Eq. (4). First, note that $R_{i,t}$ is not defined for the very first quarter of the fund's life, since the starting NAV is zero. Second, in any quarter in which there are no capital calls or distributions, the return is simply the percentage change in NAV. The first quarter of 2023 in Table 2 is an example: The fund's NAV grows by $550,000, from $2.2 million to $2.75 million, which is a 25% return. Third, distributions are analogous to dividends in public stocks: They represent a transfer of value out of the fund. For example, if a fund with a $100 NAV makes a $10 distribution, its NAV drops to $90. If there are no other cash flows, then its return is $(\$90 + \$10)/\$100 = 0\%$. Fourth, capital calls for investments work like equity issues by public firms, in the sense that they raise the fund's NAV, just like an equity issue raises the company's asset value. For instance, in the first quarter of 2024, the fund in Table 2 made a $500,000 capital call, which raised the fund's NAV by exactly the same amount. This could happen because new investments were still valued at cost at the end of the quarter, other investment marks remained unchanged, and the capital call was not used for management fees. If any part of the capital call is applied to management fee payments, then this lowers the return to the LP, as the money that is called up by the GP is not invested in any portfolio asset: a single $10 capital call in the quarter that is used for fees on a $100 beginning-of-quarter

NAV yields a -10% return to the LP (assuming the NAV did not change over the quarter, i.e., portfolio company valuations remained the same). However, capital calls for fees could result in anomalous returns, especially early in the fund's life when NAV is low. For example, suppose a fund started only recently and has made few investments, such that current NAV is $1 million. Let's also suppose that the GP makes a $2 million capital call for fees in the current quarter, and no other activity takes place. Leaving the portfolio company valuations unchanged, the fund return for the quarter is ($1 m–$2m)/$1m$=-1$, that is, a -200% return. This is a rather stark example, and it is not clear how often this actually happens in the data, but it is not inconceivable.

Two other complications with quarterly fund return series should be noted here. While most funds report NAVs at the end of the calendar quarter, not all of them do: Some GPs report at the end of January, April, July, and October, while other report in February and every 3 months thereafter. This complicates the comparison of returns across funds. A second complication is that, depending on the data source, some NAVs may be missing, such that returns cannot be computed. To the extent that these are random occurrences, it may not bias factor model estimates, but there is likely some selectivity as to which NAVs do not show up in the data.

Rather than computing returns at the fund level, one can define a return at the aggregate level, R_t, using the sum of NAVs and aggregate calls and distributions. This is equivalent to a NAV-weighted portfolio of all N_t existing funds,

$$R_t = \sum_{i=1}^{N_t} w_{i,t-1} R_{i,t} = \sum_{i=1}^{N_t} \frac{NAV_{i,t-1}}{\sum_{j=1}^{N_t} NAV_{j,t-1}} R_{i,t} = \frac{NAV_t + C_t}{NAV_{t-1}}, \qquad (6)$$

defining the aggregate $NAV_t \equiv \sum_{i=1}^{N_t} NAV_{i,t}$, and the aggregate net cash flow $C_t \equiv \sum_i^{N_t} C_{i,t}$. An advantage of aggregate returns, compared to fund-level returns, is that the first quarter of each fund can be used in the construction of the aggregate index, by setting the beginning-of-period NAV of newly raised funds equal to zero (such that $NAV_{t-1} \equiv \sum_{j=1}^{N_{t-1}} NAV_{j,t-1} = \sum_{j=1}^{N_t} NAV_{j,t-1}$). Another advantage is that anomalous fund returns due to capital calls for fees do not appear in the aggregate return series.

Examples of aggregate return series constructed in the spirit of Eq. (6) are the Cambridge Associates Private Investments Benchmarks, the Burgiss Global Private Capital Returns, and the State Street Private Equity Index.[m] To illustrate the properties of the time series of aggregate returns, Fig. 5 graphs the quarterly returns for the Cambridge Associates data for U.S. venture capital, U.S. buyout, and global real

---

[m]The Cambridge Associates, Burgiss, and State Street index returns are slightly more sophisticated than Eq. (6) suggests. CA and State Street compute an IRR for the quarter to account for the timing of cash flows within the quarter. Burgiss uses the Modified Dietz approach, which has the same goal. Differences in the timing of constituent fund NAV reports within the quarter could similarly be accounted for, although published index descriptions are not clear in whether this is in fact done.

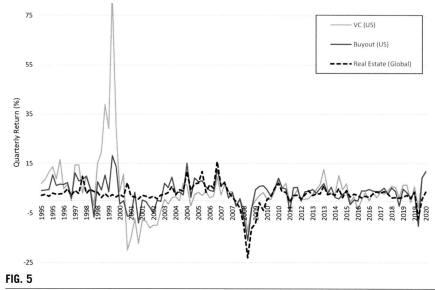

FIG. 5

This figure shows the times series of quarterly returns (in %) of the Cambridge Associates private equity indices from the first quarter of 1995 until the third quarter of 2020. See Table 3 for a detailed description of the data. The light gray line represents the VC fund index, the dark blue line is the buyout fund index, and the dashed black line is the private real estate fund index.

estate funds, which are freely available online for the period ending in the third quarter of 2020.[n] Table 3 reports descriptive statistics of the annualized returns. The average annualized returns are 17.06%, 14.17%, and 9.40% for venture capital, buyout, and real estate, respectively. These numbers are not so different from the IRR numbers in Table 1, even though this is not an apples-to-apples comparison as Tables 1 and 3 use different return definitions, as well as different time series and fund coverages. Pushing the IRR comparison further, despite these critiques, we see that the index returns have much lower volatility, skewness, and kurtosis than fund IRRs. The lower volatility is a result of diversification, and the "normalization" of index returns relative to individual fund returns is a natural consequence of the Central Limit Theorem. Still, there is considerable skewness and kurtosis left in VC returns even at the aggregate level. Buyout and real estate returns have, if anything, a slight negative skew in the aggregate, while kurtosis remains noticeable, especially for real estate.

For assets class returns with little or no skewness we can consider their Sharpe ratio—the ratio of the mean excess return to its standard deviation—ratios as a metric of the risk and return relationship. For a mean-variance investor, who does not care about higher moments such as skewness or kurtosis, a higher Sharpe ratio means a

---

[n]https://www.cambridgeassociates.com/private-investment-benchmarks/, accessed March 18 2021.

Table 3 Descriptive statistics for PE index returns.

	Venture capital	Buyout	Real estate	Public stocks
Returns (annualized, in %)				
Mean	17.06	14.17	9.40	11.46
St. Dev.	23.19	10.42	8.80	17.59
Skewness	1.75	−0.31	−1.07	−0.28
Exc. Kurtosis	5.67	0.53	3.09	0.15
Sharpe ratio (ann.)	0.65	1.15	0.83	0.52
Autocorrelation				
1 quarter	0.60	0.32	0.62	−0.06
2 quarters	0.48	0.24	0.56	0.04
3 quarters	0.32	0.12	0.32	0.02
4 quarters	0.04	0.06	0.31	−0.04
5 quarters	−0.04	0.00	0.08	0.12
6 quarters	−0.08	0.02	−0.03	0.03

This table reports descriptive statistics for Cambridge Associate quarterly private equity index returns data and the public stock market index from the first quarter of 1995 until the third quarter of 2020. The private equity indices in the first three columns are the U.S. Venture Capital, the U.S. Private Equity, and the Global Real Estate index, respectively. The public stock market index is the value-weighted return of all U.S. incorporated firms that are listed on the NYSE, AMEX, or NASDAQ (sourced from Kenneth French's data library). The mean, standard deviation, skewness, and excess kurtosis (relative to the Normal distribution) are reported as annualized numbers, in % (e.g., 5 represents a 5% annualized return). Sharpe ratios are annualized. Autocorrelations are reported for lags ranging from 1 to 6 quarters and are computed on quarterly returns.
Sources: https://www.cambridgeassociates.com/private-investment-benchmarks/ and https://mba.tuck.dartmouth.edu/pages/faculty/ken.french/data_library.html.

higher compensation for the level of risk taken. If there is no correlation among asset classes, then the Sharpe is closely related to optimal portfolio weights for a mean-variance investor (I do not explore the portfolio allocation question here, but see Korteweg and Westerfield, 2022, for an in-depth treatment). Table 3 shows that VC, buyout, and real estate had Sharpe ratios of 0.65, 1.15, and 0.83 respectively, over the 1995Q1-2020Q3 sample period. In comparison, the public stock market had a Sharpe ratio of 0.52 over the same period. As such, the private asset classes appear to be quite attractive investments. However, this is a premature conclusion, as there are several issues with the index returns that complicate matters.

While the PE index returns may serve as a benchmark to compare performance against (although representativeness, which may vary by data provider, is a concern), they are very difficult to realize in practice. There is currently no *investable* PE index, so investors must build their own portfolios of funds. Apart from the largest LPs, most institutional investors commit to only a couple of PE funds per year, given that GPs generally require a capital commitment of at least $5 to $10 million from a single LP (e.g., DeLuce, 2020). Since the cross-sectional variation in fund performance is extremely high, it is not feasible to achieve the level of diversification of the index with only a few funds. A second investability issue is that the index returns, when cumulated over time, presume that any cash distributions are reinvested. However, PE funds are closed-end, so one can only invest in new funds that are raising at the time, and these GPs may not be representative of the overall universe of active funds. Moreover, the commitments to new funds will be called up slowly over the next few years, and there is limited liquidity in the sense of being able to sell PE investments (or get out of future commitments some other way) if needed.

Apart from issues of investability, the PE returns constructed using NAV data inherit a number of drawbacks related to the use of NAVs. The next two sections delve into the concerns surrounding the use of NAVs and NAV-based returns.

3.5 Staleness in NAVs

Thus far I have worked under the assumption that a fund's NAV is equal to the market value of the PE portfolio. Current accounting standards (ASC Topic 820, formerly known as FAS 157, which has been effective since 2007) require that the NAV represents the fair valuation of portfolio companies. In funds that invest in publicly traded assets, such as most mutual and hedge funds, it is straightforward to compute the portfolio's market value because the constituents' current valuations can be easily looked up. But for PE portfolio investments (so-called Level 3 assets) there is currently no market to mark to. GPs, their consultants, and auditors, therefore have substantial leeway in determining the NAVs they report. GPs usually rely on recent deals and comparable assets to determine valuations, but this still leaves a fairly large degree of subjectivity and necessarily relies on historical data.[o] Before 2007 it was quite common practice to leave portfolio company valuations at cost. GPs tended to be conservative in marking up portfolio company valuations while being quicker to mark them down if they thought values had dropped (Anson, 2002, 2007). Since ASC 820/FAS 157, valuations have become more accurate (Jenkinson et al., 2020 Easton et al., 2021). Still, overall, Brown et al. (2019) find that NAVs remain on average conservative. Moreover, price staleness operates beyond the PE fund level: Agarwal et al. (2022) report that mutual fund family valuations of privately-held firms (mostly late-stage startups) are not updated in 46% of quarters, and it takes an average of 2.3 quarters for prices to update (the median is 2 quarters). Thus, prices tend to be stale, reflecting a mix of current and historical valuations.[p]

---

[o]See, for example, the "Valuation of Portfolio Company Investments of Venture Capital and Private Equity Funds and Other Investment Companies—Accounting and Valuation Guide" published by the American Institute of Certified Public Accountants (AICPA). To underscore that valuation is difficult even for relatively mature PE investments, Cederburg and Stoughton (2020), Agarwal et al. (2022), and Imbierowicz and Rauch (2021) show that there is large cross-sectional dispersion in valuations of PE investments by mutual funds, even within the same portfolio company and the same security.

[p]In index returns that use aggregated fund NAVs (e.g., Eq. 6), there is some additional staleness because not all funds report at end of a calendar quarter, as mentioned in Section 3.4. But, this particular source of staleness is relatively short-lived—operating on the span of one quarter—unlike the staleness due to conservative portfolio company valuations considered here.

Price staleness causes the observed time series of NAVs to behave like a moving average that smooths out the "true" underlying fund value. This causes autocorrelation in NAV-based returns, as well as downward biased estimates of the true fundamental return volatility, risk factor loadings, and correlations with other asset classes, and upward biased estimates of Sharpe ratios and alphas (see the literatures on return smoothing in real estate, e.g., Geltner, 1991, 1993; Fisher et al., 1994, and in hedge funds, e.g., Asness et al., 2001; Getmansky et al., 2004; Bollen and Pool, 2008; Cassar and Gerakos, 2011; Cao et al., 2017).

The empirical autocorrelation in NAV-based PE returns is indeed high. Table 3 shows that, for VC and real estate, the one-quarter autocorrelations in the Cambridge Associates returns are 0.60 and 0.62, respectively. It drops gradually over longer lags and reaches zero (effectively) by lags of four to five quarters. Buyout is less persistent, but the one-quarter autocorrelation is still as high as 0.32. It also takes about four quarter lags to drop close to zero. By comparison, the one-quarter autocorrelation in the public stock market over the same sample period is -0.06. Turning to factor loadings, Panel A of Table 4 shows that the market model beta estimated from Eq. (3) for VC, buyout, and real estate are 0.579, 0.465, and 0.166, respectively. These beta estimates appear surprisingly low, and much lower than the risk of the public market portfolio (which is one by construction). After all, venture capital invests in startups that in many cases do not yet have a marketable product or service, surely a risky proposition. As shown by Berk et al. (2004), even if this risk is often of a technical nature and idiosyncratic, the investment and financing decisions that must be made with respect to the startup result in a strong systematic risk exposure even at the earliest stages. Buyout is a highly levered equity investment, often in a publicly traded firm that is taken private by means of the buyout. Unless the bought-out companies have extremely low underlying asset risk, it is difficult to believe the PE fund's market risk loading would be as low as 0.5. Indeed, it turns out that estimated market betas are substantially higher when NAV staleness is corrected for. The next five subsections discuss various proposed ways to make this correction.

3.5.1 Longer-horizon returns
The previous section revealed that autocorrelations in NAV-based returns disappear at longer lags. Thus, a first proposed solution to the staleness problem is to use longer-horizon returns. Emery (2003) presents suggestive evidence that longer-horizon returns can indeed mitigate the staleness problem, by showing that the correlation between NAV-based PE index returns and public market returns is markedly higher when using annual returns instead of quarterly returns.

In implementing this solution, a choice must be made whether to use nonoverlapping annual returns (e.g., treating each full calendar year return as a separate observation) or a rolling window of overlapping returns (e.g., considering the return from the start of 1991 Q1 to the end of Q4 as one observation, the return from the start of 1991 Q2 to the end of 1992 Q1 as the next observation, etc.). The nonoverlapping return series has the advantage that it is easy to work with, because the residuals

Table 4 CAPM estimates for PE index returns.

	VC		Buyout		Real estate	
	Coeff.	s.e.	Coeff.	s.e.	Coeff.	s.e.
Panel A: Contemporaneous factor return only (S=0)						
$\beta_{i,0}$	0.579	0.153***	0.465	0.044***	0.166	0.089*
α_i	2.368	1.097**	1.909	0.320***	1.405	0.751*
Panel B: Dimson correction (S=6 quarters)						
$\beta_{i,s}$:						
s=0 (contemp.)	0.577	0.163***	0.476	0.034***	0.173	0.079**
s=−1	0.212	0.105**	0.143	0.032***	0.124	0.056**
s=−2	0.235	0.112**	0.090	0.029***	0.108	0.051**
s=−3	0.263	0.097***	0.084	0.024***	0.111	0.050**
s=−4	0.229	0.192	0.051	0.033	0.116	0.050**
s=−5	0.078	0.170	0.012	0.030	0.059	0.038
s=−6	0.064	0.091	−0.006	0.041	0.023	0.038
α_i	−0.052	1.186	1.140	0.328***	0.379	0.877
$\sum\limits_{s=-6}^{0} \beta_{i,s}$	1.658	0.327***	0.851	0.087***	0.713	0.236***

This table shows Capital Asset Pricing Model (CAPM) estimates for the quarterly Cambridge Associates venture capital, buyout, and real estate index returns from the first quarter of 1995 until the third quarter of 2020. The regression model is

$$R_{i,t} - R_t^F = \alpha_i + \sum_{s=-S}^{0} \beta_{i,s}\left[R_{t+s}^M - R_{t+s}^F\right] + \varepsilon_{it},$$

where i refers to the venture capital, buyout, or real estate index described in Table 3. The excess market return on the right-hand side is from Kenneth French's data library (see Table 3 for details). The intercept is in % per quarter (e.g., 5 means 5% per quarter). The columns labeled "Coeff." report regression coefficients, and the "s.e" columns show Newey-West standard errors that are robust to heteroskedasiticy and autocorrelation in the residuals. Panel A shows results for S = 0, i.e., regressions of index excess returns on contemporaneous market excess returns. Panel B uses S=6 quarters, i.e., the right-hand side contains the contemporaneous market excess return and its first 6 lags. The bottom row shows the Dimson beta estimates, which are the sum of the contemporaneous and lagged betas. ***, **, and * denote significance at the 1%, 5%, and 10% level, respectively.

should be uncorrelated as long as the return is calculated over a long enough horizon. In contrast, in the rolling window approach, standard errors must be corrected for overlap-induced autocorrelation, which generally requires additional assumptions about the nature of the residual autocorrelation. The Newey-West and Hansen-Hodrick estimators are classic examples.

The key disadvantage of using nonoverlapping returns is that few observations remain. Even VC and buyout, the strategies that have been around the longest, did not really become meaningfully large until the mid-1980s. Thus, by 2021, there are only around 35 nonoverlapping annual return observations. The low number of observations is especially troublesome for (co)variance estimates (including betas), which, unlike means, are more precisely estimated at higher frequencies (Merton, 1980).

A drawback to using longer-horizon returns, whether overlapping or not, is that the timing of cash flows within the period becomes more important as the chosen horizon grows longer. Eqs. (4) and (6) ignore such timing, which may be acceptable for quarterly returns, but more sophisticated return computations should be employed for longer horizons (for example, the above-mentioned methods used by Cambridge Associates, State Street, and Burgiss; see footnote m). Unfortunately, in many cases these techniques revert to IRR-type calculations, the very issue we tried to avoid in the first place.

Ultimately, the question of the optimal horizon remains unanswered. The trade-off is between mitigating the impact of staleness and having enough observations for meaningful inference (and keeping the intra-period cash flow timing issue in check). The answer likely varies by strategy and the level of disaggregation (for example, early-stage VC may have a different degree of staleness from VC overall). It may even vary at the individual fund-level, and may vary over time. For the aggregate VC, buyout, and real estate series in Table 3, annual returns appear to be a reasonable choice for the 1995–2020 sample period.

3.5.2 Unsmoothing
A rich literature in real estate, which shares many of the same concerns regarding staleness of valuations, and hedge funds, where return smoothing is common, revolves around methodologies to unsmooth a return series. Examples of unsmoothing algorithms are in Geltner (1991, 1993), Fisher et al. (1994), Getmansky et al. (2004), and Couts et al. (2020).

Unsmoothing algorithms rely on a specified relation between the observed, smoothed, returns and the unobserved returns based on nonstale fundamental valuations. For example, Geltner (1991) assumes that the observed return is a weighted average of the current and its p past fundamental returns,

$$R_t = \theta_0 R_t^* + \theta_1 R_{t-1}^* + \ldots + \theta_p R_{t-p}^*, \tag{7}$$

where R_t are the observed returns and R_t^* the fundamental returns. The θ's are all fractions, and they sum to one. Eq. (7) implies that R_t follows an infinite-order autoregressive (AR) process, but if $\theta_0 > \theta_p$ for all $p > 0$, then the higher-order terms quickly tend to zero, and the process can be approximated with a finite-order AR that includes the first k empirically meaningful lags of R_t,

$$R_t = \phi_1 R_{t-1} + \phi_2 R_{t-2} + \ldots + \phi_k R_{t-k} + e_t. \tag{8}$$

The residual $e_t = \theta_0 R_t^*$, so we can rewrite (8) to recover the fundamental return

$$R_t^* = \frac{R_t - \phi_1 R_{t-1} - \phi_2 R_{t-2} - \ldots - \phi_k R_{t-k}}{\theta_0}. \tag{9}$$

One additional assumption is needed to identify θ_0. One choice is to set $\theta_0 = 1 - \sum_{j=1}^{k} \phi_j$, which equates the true means of R_t and R_t^* (since the θ's sum to one, this equality of means must hold). An alternative strategy, proposed in Geltner et al. (2003), is to calibrate the volatility of R_t^* to a specific number, but this approach is rather ad-hoc, as there is little guidance what that number should be.

Korteweg and Westerfield (2022) apply the Geltner (1991) unsmoothing algorithm to the Cambridge Associates quarterly aggregate VC and buyout returns from 1998 to 2020, using k equal to 2. They show that unsmoothing dramatically changes many characteristics of the return series. Return volatility is magnified by a factor of approximately 2.5. Sharpe ratios drop by two thirds, from 0.48 to 0.16 in VC and from 0.93 to 0.31 in buyout. Higher moments (skewness, kurtosis) are closer to zero after unsmoothing, but the change is not very large. For VC, the correlation with public stock returns goes up by about 25% (from 0.42 to 0.51), whereas for buyout, the correlation increases only marginally. Finally, by design, the unsmoothed return series are not autocorrelated.[q] For other applications of unsmoothing methods in private equity, see Goetzmann et al. (2019), Aliaga-Díaz et al. (2020), and Brown et al. (2021b).

A drawback of many unsmoothing methods is that the specification of the observed returns process is typically based on a statistical model, rather than being microfounded with an economic model of price staleness. The resulting unsmoothed returns series can be sensitive to model specification. Moreover, parameter estimates tend to have large standard errors, and can be unstable over time. Imposing additional structure from an economic model has the potential to alleviate some of these issues.

A well-founded model of price staleness should also explain how fund-level staleness aggregates up. For example, if fund-level observed returns are a weighted average of past fundamental returns, as in Eq. (7), then aggregate-level returns follow the same process only if portfolio weights are fixed over time. Couts et al. (2020) present evidence that traditional unsmoothing techniques applied at a granular level can still leave substantial autocorrelation in aggregate returns.

A final, fundamental concern with many unsmoothing algorithms is that they aim to produce an uncorrelated return series. This is a reasonable assumption in efficient markets, where money can be moved around easily and costlessly, such that fundamental returns are likely (close to) independent over time. In PE, however, nonstale returns could still exhibit material autocorrelation, given the limited arbitrage opportunities due to the illiquid nature of PE investments. The model in Geltner (1993) is an example of an algorithm that does allow for autocorrelation in unsmoothed returns.

---

[q] Korteweg and Westerfield use the equal-means assumption for θ_0. They find that if they use the volatility-calibration method instead, estimates of means and variances change, but higher moments (skewness, kurtosis) remain unchanged, and Sharpe ratios are only marginally affected.

3.5.3 *Dimson correction*

As early as the 1960s, researchers in public equities recognized that nonsynchronous trading of securities could have a material effect on risk loading estimates. Nonsynchronous trading is like staleness in that a security's price does not reflect its current market value if there is no trade in the current period and its historical price is reported instead. Two key papers in this literature are Scholes and Williams (1977) and Dimson (1979). The latter is the focus of this section, by virtue of it having been applied to private equity in the literature.

Dimson develops an easily applicable method of correcting a security's beta estimates if observed expected returns are a weighted average of current and past realized fundamental returns. This specification is almost identical to Eq. (7), the key difference being that the left-hand side is an expectation. In its general form, if both the security and the risk factors are subject to staleness, the algorithm involves adding leads and lags of the factor returns to the model in Eq. (3). The corrected beta estimates are the sum of the loadings of all leads and lags, including the contemporaneous loading, for each factor. Since commonly used risk factors are not stale, it is not necessary to include leads, and the Dimson regression becomes

$$R_{i,t} - R_t^F = \alpha_i + \sum_{s=-S}^{0} \beta'_{i,s} F_{t+s} + \varepsilon_{i,t}. \tag{10}$$

Note that if the returns to security i do not suffer from staleness, and are serially uncorrelated, then the lagged factor loadings are all zero, and the model simplifies to the standard factor model of Eq. (3).

Table 4 Panel B shows an application of the Dimson method to the quarterly Cambridge Associates returns for the VC, buyout, and real estate strategies. The regressions use the CAPM and include 6 lags of the market factor, although only the first few lags (3 for VC and buyout and 4 for real estate) are statistically significant. The bottom row of Panel B shows the resulting Dimson beta estimate for each strategy, which is the sum of the contemporaneous and lagged betas. The VC beta estimate is 1.658, almost three times the size of the estimate of 0.579 that results from using only the contemporaneous factor return (see Panel A). For buyout and real estate, the Dimson beta estimates are 0.851 and 0.713, compared to 0.465 and 0.166 based on contemporaneous returns only. Given the higher beta estimates, it is not a surprise that alpha estimates are lower: Whereas alphas are positive and statistically significant for all strategies in the standard contemporaneous factor return model in Panel A, for both VC and real estate the null hypothesis of zero alpha can no longer be rejected in the Dimson method in Panel B. For buyout, the alpha drops from 1.9% to 1.1% per quarter but it remains statistically significant.

Table 5 summarizes the PE literature that has applied the Dimson method. Most papers use quarterly NAV-based aggregate returns. Exceptions are Woodward and Hall (2004), who use a monthly VC index constructed from portfolio company data (Metrick and Yasuda, 2010b, also report results for this same index, albeit over a different sample period, as well for the NAV-based Cambridge Associates index);

Table 5 Factor model estimates in private equity using the Dimson (1979) method.

Paper	Data source	Level	Sample period	Freq.	Lags	Model	Market factor	VC		Buyout	
								α(%)	β	α(%)	β
Woodward and Hall (2004)	SHE	Aggr.	1987–2002	Month	13	CAPM	Nasdaq	N.R.	0.9	N.R.	N.R.
Bilo et al. (2005)	D	Aggr.	1986–2003	Week	3	CAPM	MSCI World	N.R.	N.R.	−0.1[a,b]	1.1[b]
								N.R.	N.R.	10.4[a,c]	1.0[c]
Anson (2007)	VE	Fund	1985–2005	Quarter	3	CAPM	S&P 500	0.2	1.4	0.8	0.7
							Nasdaq	0.5	1.1	1.2	0.4
							Russell 1000	0.9	1.4	1.2	0.7
							Russell 2000	1.5	0.9	1.3	0.6
Woodward (2009)	CA	Aggr.	1996–2008	Quarter	5	CAPM	Wilshire 5000	0.5	2.2	1.4	1.0
Metrick and Yasuda (2010b)	CA	Aggr.	1981–2008	Quarter	8[d]	FF3 +PS	KF	0.1[a]	2.0/1.0/−1.5/0.2	N.R.	N.R.
Phalippou (2010)	SHE	Aggr.	1989–2008	Month	24[d]	CAPM	Local index	−2.1[a]	1.6/−0.1/−0.7/0.3	N.R.	N.R.
	D	Fund	1993–2008	Week	10	CAPM		N.R.	N.R.	6[a]	1.5
Ewens et al. (2013)	VE + P +LPS	Aggr.	1980–2007	Quarter	4	CAPM	CRSP-VW	−0.2	1.2	1.2	0.7
						FF3		0.5	1.1/−0.1/−0.9	0.9	0.8/0.1/0.2
Peters (2018)	CA	Aggr.	N.R.	Quarter	5	CAPM	CRSP-VW	0.6	1.4	N.R.	N.R.
Agarwal et al. (2022)	CRSP+SEC+R	Sec.	2010–2018	Quarter	2	CAPM	N.R.	0.5	1.3	N.R.	N.R.
						FF3		0.7	1.0/1.5/−1.0	N.R.	N.R.
Boyer et al. (2022a)	SMI	Aggr.	2006–2018	Quarter	1	CAPM	KF	N.R.	N.R.	−2[a]	1.8
	Burgiss				3					4[a]	0.8
	Preqin				3					4[a]	0.7
Stafford (2022)	CA	Aggr.	1996–2014	Quarter	3	CAPM	KF	N.R.	N.R.	5.0[a]	0.8
	Burgiss									4.5[a]	0.9
	Preqin									5.2[a]	0.7

This table summarizes the literature that estimates factor models in private equity using the Dimson (1979) method. The "Level" column shows whether data is observed at the aggregate/index level ("Aggr."), fund level ("Fund") or individual security level ("Sec."). "Lags" shows the number of lags in the Dimson regression. "Model" reports the factor model used, where CAPM is the Capital Asset Pricing Model, FF3 stands for Fama and French (1993), and FF3+PS is the Fama-French (1993) model augmented with the Pastor and Stambaugh (2003) liquidity factor. The return series used as the market factor is in "Market factor," where CRSP-VW is the CRSP value-weighted market index, and KF is the market factor from Kenneth French's data library. Alphas are in % and at the same frequency as the data (in "Freq."), except Bilo et al. (2005), Metrick and Yasuda (2010b), Phalippou (2010) and Stafford (2022), who report annualized alphas. For FF3 the "β" column shows loadings on the market/Small-minus-Big (SMB)/High-minus-Low (HML) factors, augmented with the liquidity factor loading as the final number for the FF3+PS model. If the same paper estimates multiple models, only the differences in specifications are shown in the additional rows (blank cells mean no change). Data source abbreviations: CA=Cambridge Associates; CRSP=Center for Research in Securities Prices; D=Datastream; LPS=LP Source; P=Preqin; R=Thomson Reuters; SEC=Securities and Exchange Commission; SHE=Sand Hill Econometrics; SMI=Secondary market intermediary (unnamed); VE=Venture Economics. N.R. stands for "Not Reported."
[a]Alpha is annualized.
[b]Based on equal-weighted buy-and-hold returns.
[c]Based on equal-weighted weekly rebalanced returns.
[d]Reported lags are for the market factor (the other factor loadings are estimated using half the number of lags used for the market factor).

Anson (2007), who uses fund-level returns; Bilo et al. (2005) and Phalippou (2010), both of whom uses publicly traded PE vehicles (see Section 5 for a description of these papers), Boyer et al. (2022a), who use a proprietary data set of secondary market transactions, and Agarwal et al. (2022), who use returns of individual startup company securities held by mutual fund families. The number of lags used in the Dimson regressions ranges from 1 to 8 quarters.

Estimated CAPM betas for VC range from 0.9 to 2.2, depending on the data set, sample period and factor used. For broad-based stock market indices such as the S&P 500, Wilshire 5000, or the CRSP value weighted index, the betas are centered around 1.2–1.4. Loadings tend to be closer to one in regressions of VC returns on the Nasdaq and Russell 2000. This result is to be expected, as these factors are closer proxies to startup firms, that is, small to medium-sized growth firms (based on the zero to positive loading on the small-minus-big (SMB) factor and the negative loading on the high-minus-low book-to-market (HML) factor in the Fama and French, 1993, model estimates in Metrick and Yasuda, 2010b; Ewens et al., 2013; Agarwal et al., 2022, among others; see Table 5). For buyout, CAPM betas for NAV-based PE returns are in the range of 0.7–1.0 when using a broad public stock index for the market portfolio. Loadings on the Nasdaq and Russell 2000 are lower, but these are less relevant benchmarks for buyout funds, which tend to invest in mid- to large-sized value firms (as indicated by the insignificant loading on SMB and the positive loading on HML in Ewens et al., 2013 (see also Stafford, 2022, for further evidence that, historically, buyout loads on value). Using the Russell 1000 index of large stocks as the factor, Anson (2007) finds a loading of 0.7. Finally, Phalippou (2010) reports a higher beta of 1.5 for publicly traded buyout funds, and Boyer et al. (2022a) estimate a buyout beta of 1.8 for an index constructed using secondary market prices (Sections 5 and 3.5.5 below dive deeper into publicly traded vehicles and secondary PE market data, respectively).

Estimated alphas for VC are generally close to zero, with estimates centered around roughly 0.5% per quarter, whereas buyout alpha estimates are higher, with most estimates around 1.2–1.4% per quarter. This pattern of low VC alphas and higher buyout alphas is one that is echoed in many other studies, across different methodologies.

Dimson uses a probabilistic model of trading to motivate his method, but this causes some tension with the specification of the return process that is the foundation for the beta correction. The trading model implies that expected observed prices are a weighted average of current and past (unobserved) fundamental prices. This weighted-averaging property carries over to expected observed capital gains, defined as the change in expected (log) observed prices. However, it does not apply to total returns that include cash flows, since capital calls and distributions are observed when they realize. Hence, more research is needed to work out the microfoundation of the empirical model.

Finally, the Dimson correction is subject to a similar concern as many of the unsmoothing methods in that it assumes that fundamental returns are serially uncorrelated. This is not necessarily a natural assumption in PE, as argued in the previous section.

3.5.4 Imputation and filtering

One of the earliest proposed solutions for the staleness issue in the PE literature was to simply impute any missing prices. Gompers and Lerner (1997) pioneered this approach. Using data on portfolio company holdings for a single large PE firm, E.M. Warburg, Pincus & Co., they mark each unobserved company valuation to market in each quarter by using the return to an equal-weighted index of publicly traded firms in the same three-digit Standard Industrial Classification (SIC) industry from the time of the last observed value. They then aggregate all valuations and cash flows, and compute the quarterly returns on Warburg, Pincus's portfolio for the period 1972–97 (this calculation is analogous to Eq. (6), using the portfolio's cash flows and valuations). They estimate a CAPM beta of 1.4 and an alpha of 2.0% per quarter. For the Fama and French (1993) model they find a loading of 1.3 on the market factor, 0.8 on SMB, and 0.1 on HML, and an alpha of 1.7% per quarter. The t-statistics on the alphas are 1.8 and statistically significant at the 10% level (for both models). Note that these factor loadings cannot be attributed to one single strategy, since Warburg, Pincus holds a diversified mix of VC, buyout, and other investments. This, and the fact that the loadings are estimated for a single firm, make it difficult to draw strong comparisons with other papers.

A drawback of the above imputation technique is that the mark-to-market value is only as good as the proxy that is used to update valuations. For example, in VC and buyout, there is an inherent tension in using public company returns as a proxy for private company returns, since being publicly traded is an endogenous decision, and these firms may be inherently different. A second drawback is that portfolio holdings information is needed to impute a fund's NAV (or the aggregate PE market). Portfolio company data is not part of standard fund data sets, and thus more difficult to obtain, especially if they need to be linked to specific funds.

Two papers develop methods to filter PE returns without the need for portfolio company data. Brown et al. (2021a) develop a state-space model to filter "true" valuations of individual funds. They assume that the evolution of (latent) true fund valuations follow a factor model, and that observed NAVs are noisy observations of the current and past true valuations (and thus, observed NAVs exhibit staleness). While their method imposes a high degree of structure on the problem, an interesting aspect is that they estimate fund-specific alpha and beta estimates. For a data set of funds raised between 1983 and 2008, they report an average (median) VC fund CAPM beta of 1.2 (1.1), with an annual alpha of 0.1% (-2.6%) per year. The average (median) buyout fund has a beta of 1.1 (1.0) and annual alpha of 1.5% (2.1%). They find a high degree of variation in these parameters across funds: for VC, the first and third quartile betas are 0.9 and 1.4, and alphas range from -11.4% to $+6.7\%$. For buyout the beta range is from 0.9 to 1.3, with alphas ranging from -5.5% to $+9.6\%$.

The second paper, by Ang et al. (2018), use Bayesian Markov chain Monte Carlo methods to filter a time series of realized aggregate PE returns from cash flows of funds raised between 1994 and 2008 (with cash flows until 2015). They then regress these returns on various sets of factors to estimate factor loadings and risk-adjusted returns. For VC (buyout) they report a CAPM beta of 1.8 (1.3), and Fama-French three-factor loadings of 1.7 (1.2), 0.8 (0.5) and −0.6 (0.6) for the market, SMB, and HML factors, respectively (the HML loading is statistically insignificant for VC, and the size loading is insignificant in buyout). For the CAPM and three-factor models the VC alpha is close to zero and insignificant, whereas it is positive and significant for buyout. For other models (discussed in Section 3.7.3) the VC alpha varies between −3% to −5% per year (−4% and +2% for buyout). The Ang et al. method does not use observed NAVs as an input to their model. As such, the paper is closer to the stochastic discount factor methods that are discussed in Section 3.7.

Finally, there is a small literature on imputing investment-level valuations in venture capital. Most of this literature revolves around constructing an aggregate VC index by adopting some form of repeat-sales regression (RSR), extended to account for the fact that failure is unobserved for many startups. Related work filters portfolio company valuations using a state-space model. I discuss these methodologies and the relevant literature in Sections 6.2 and 6.3, which deal specifically with investment-level data.[r]

3.5.5 Secondary market prices

A final option for dealing with NAV issues is to simply replace them with actual market prices of sales of fund stakes by LPs. This seems like a sensible solution, but there are some complications. The secondary market for LP stakes only started to become material after the turn of the millennium, so the observed time series is quite short. The market underwent massive growth in the wake of the global financial crisis of 2008, when many LPs needed to reduce their exposure to private equity (Hege and Nuti, 2011). Since then, the market has continued to mature, and it is in the process of transforming from pure liquidity provision to a widely accepted means for portfolio rebalancing. Despite the substantial growth, the market is still very illiquid, and transaction costs are high. Most sales are conducted in an auction format and can take up to 6 months to finalize.

Nadauld et al. (2019) collect data on fund transactions from a leading intermediary. They report that the average purchase price as a percentage of NAV in 2008 and 2009 was 78.1% and 54.4%, respectively, indicative of the high need for liquidity by sellers during this crisis period (but possibly also a sign of reluctance by GPs to mark down NAVs). Average purchase prices for the years 2010–14, the end of their sample period, fluctuated between 82.2% and 93.2% of NAV. There was substantial variation in prices paid within a given year, with a standard deviation of around 32%.

Boyer et al. (2022b) construct transactions-based PE indices for VC and buyout between 2006 and 2017, using a Heckman selection model to account for the fact that sellers choose which funds to sell. The resulting CAPM betas and volatilities are higher than NAV-based indices, and alphas are lower. They estimate a VC beta of 1.0, and a buyout beta of 2.3–2.4 (depending on whether they use price or size-weighting across funds). Alphas are negative but statistically insignificant for

---

[r]Another imputation technique is proposed by Woodward (2009), who shows how to invert the Dimson (1979) regression to impute valuations. Since this is a by-product of the Dimson approach, I do not separately discuss this method here.

both strategies. On the one hand, the transactions-based betas are considerably higher than NAV-based betas of 0.3 and 0.5, which they estimate on contemporaneous returns.[s] On the other hand, compared to Dimson-corrected betas in Table 5, the VC beta is on the lower end of the estimated range, whereas the buyout beta is considerably higher. However, the large buyout beta appears to be largely driven by the crisis: Eliminating the years 2008 and 2009 results in a transactions-based VC beta of 0.7 and a buyout beta of 0.9. The latter is more in line with Dimson buyout beta estimates. Whether or not it is legitimate to exclude the financial crisis is up for debate. On the one hand it is a dangerous practice to selectively exclude legitimate data. On the other hand, perhaps the large discounts that are the root cause of the high estimated betas (as transacted prices tumbled relative to reported NAVs), are due to the selected subset of LPs that were in a bind and willing to sell at almost any price (a subtly different selection problem than the fund selection problem mentioned above). But these prices, especially when realized in a thin market (Hege and Nuti, 2011, point out that the secondary market even temporarily froze in early 2009), may not be representative of the fundamental value of the transacted funds' portfolio companies for the vast majority of LPs that did not suffer a (large) liquidity shock and were not looking to get out of their commitments. Albuquerque et al. (2018) find evidence that liquidity provision in the secondary market is an important driver of the variation in discounts to NAV, so perhaps these types of illiquidity features are better captured by a separate aggregate liquidity factor; Section 3.7.3 discusses liquidity premia estimates from liquidity factors. A final complication with secondary market prices that should be mentioned, is that transactions often involve portfolios of funds, and it is at times difficult to assign prices to the individual funds that make up the portfolio.

With the continued growth in the secondary market, the transactions-based approach is a promising avenue for future research, not in the least because it can also circumvent some other concerns with NAVs besides staleness, as the next section explains.

3.6 Other concerns with NAVs

As is evident from the prior section, the issues surrounding staleness of NAVs occupies a fair amount of space in the PE literature, although there is some debate whether it's a bug or a feature.[t] However, besides staleness, there are other three

---

[s]Boyer et al. (2022a) update the results for buyout funds in Boyer et al. (2022b), extending the sample to 2018. They estimate a transactions-based buyout beta of 1.8. The updated results also include Dimson beta estimates of NAV-based returns from Burgiss and Preqin data, as shown in Table 5.
[t]Some long-horizon investors may in fact be attracted to the PE space exactly because of the lack of mark-to-market pricing. As Cochrane (2021, p. 8) puts it: "Why do so many institutions, like our endowments, prize assets like private equity, venture capital and real estate with no clear market values? Well, perhaps they like those assets precisely because the assets are hard to mark to market, easy to just pay out 5% of a made-up value, not to sell in a panic, and not fire the asset manager based on an irrelevant price [...]." Nevertheless, one still needs good estimates of alphas and betas to estimate the distribution of *long-term* payoffs, as the mark-to-market issue is a transitory one. Moreover, interim values undoubtedly matter for investors who suffer liquidity shocks and need to get out of their position.

other issues with using NAVs as proxies for fund market values: manipulation, fees, and, for VC specifically, the use of post-money valuations to compute NAVs.

Regarding manipulation, on the one hand there is evidence that some GPs may strategically manipulate reported NAVs, especially those who are underperforming and want to raise another fund (e.g., Phalippou and Gottschalg, 2009; Cumming and Walz, 2010; Jenkinson et al., 2013; Barber and Yasuda, 2017; Chakraborty and Ewens, 2018; Brown et al., 2019; Jenkinson et al., 2020; Smith et al., 2022). On the other hand, Hüther (2021) does not find evidence of inflated interim valuations at the deal-level, but instead, that valuation peaks before fundraising are the result of poorer investment opportunities that are also observed for non-fundraising firms with similarly-aged funds.

A second concern is that NAVs are usually reported as the value of the fund's investments, gross of fees. But fund cash flows are reported net of fees in commercial data sets. Therefore, performance measures that mix cash flows and NAVs in their calculation, such as the NAV-based returns above, are difficult to interpret and compare. One piece of suggestive evidence of the difference between gross and net of fee NAVs can be found in a sample of publicly traded funds of funds in Jegadeesh et al. (2015), who report an average discount of market prices to NAV of 11.8%, measured 1 year after IPO. However, Jegadeesh et al. show that there are other reasons why funds may trade at a discount. Moreover, public funds-of-funds are not representative of private primary funds that make up the bulk of the PE population (see Section 5 for details), so this number is best treated as an extremely speculative suggestion that the difference may be sizeable. Another dimension that is important for risk and return estimates, for which there is no existing evidence that I know of, is how strongly (if at all) the difference between gross and net of fee NAVs varies with factor returns.

For VC exclusively, a third issue is that portfolio company valuations are often marked to the post-money valuations of new financing rounds, when they occur. Post-money valuations are computed as the invested amount in a round divided by the percentage of equity that the investor owns upon conversion to common stock (the security sold is usually some form of convertible preferred equity). For example, a $2 million investment for 10% of the equity upon conversion would translate to a post-money valuation of $20 million. As pointed out in Metrick and Yasuda (2010b, p. 318), Gornall and Strebulaev (2020), and Ewens et al. (2022), post-money valuations are not equal to fundamental (market) valuations, as they erroneously assume that all investors own the same security (founders, for example, usually own common stock without any of the preferred terms that VCs typically receive, whereas Chernenko et al. (2021) show that mutual fund investors tend to negotiate for stronger downside protections). Post-money valuations usually overstate the fundamental valuation, and the difference can be large (Gornall and Strebulaev estimate an average of 48% for a sample of unicorns, and Ewens, Gorbenko, and Korteweg estimate a 20% difference for a representative first-round contract). How this affects risk and return estimates is more subtle, as it depends on the correlation between contract terms and risk factor realizations. As far as I am aware, there is no existing empirical evidence regarding the strength of these correlations.

Table 6 Issues with fund net asset values and proposed solutions.

	Staleness	Manipulation	Fees	VC post-money valuations
Longer-horizon returns	Y	N	N	N
Unsmoothing	Y	N	N	N
Dimson correction	Y	N	N	N
Imputation/filtering	Y	Y	Y	Y
Secondary market prices	Y	Y	Y	Y

This table shows whether techniques proposed in the PE literature may be able to resolve the main concerns with using reported net asset values for fund performance evaluation (with "Y" for yes, and "N" for no). The columns show the concerns, which are described in detail in the text (Sections 3.5 and 3.6). The rows list the various techniques (see Section 3.5.1 through 3.5.5 for details). Most techniques were developed specifically to deal with the staleness issue, but some show promise to resolve other problems as well.

Table 6 presents a crude overview of the potential of the various methods from Section 3.5 in dealing with the above problems, possibly with modification. To be clear, these are my unverified speculations. To my knowledge, no extant research validates the claims from the table (in fact, it is not even established how first-order some of these problems are).

As far as NAV manipulation is concerned, imputation/filtering methods may be able to correct for manipulation by using information from public markets, or, if manipulation is transitory, discipline imposed from the time-series of valuations. Methods that base filtered NAVs on discounted future fund cash flows (e.g., Ang et al., 2018; Brown et al., 2021a) may also work. Secondary market prices can help if buyers see through any manipulation (Brown et al., 2019, show results that suggest they might). I do not see a way how the other methods (long-horizon returns, unsmoothing, and Dimson correction) can get around the issue. On this note, it is worthwhile reiterating the earlier call for more research into the development of a manipulation-proof PE performance metric.

For the problems with fees and post-money valuations, a solution using filtering methods might be possible but is not obvious. One potential solution is to base filtered NAVs on discounted future fund cash flows, especially if they filter PE returns directly as in Ang et al. (2018). To the extent observed NAVs are used as observations in the filtering process, the observation equation should recognize that the deviation of NAV from true values might have a permanent component. More research is needed here to show whether such solutions can work. A more intuitive solution to both problems, at least in principle, is the use of secondary market prices. The market price paid for a fund in a secondary transaction should account for the expected carried interest and other fees that may need to be paid on profits from portfolio company exits (in fact, this may be one of the reasons why there is a discount to NAV in the first place). Similarly, the market price should reflect the fundamental value of a VC fund's portfolio companies, not the (biased) post-money valuation.

3.7 Stochastic discount factors

Given the myriad issues with NAVs, many performance metrics either avoid using them altogether, or they use them as little as possible. For example, IRR and TVPI, the two most common metrics used in practice, rely solely on cash flows when applied to liquidated funds. For a not-yet-liquidated fund, both measures only use the last observed NAV, ignoring all previous NAVs in the fund's history. However, as mentioned in Section 3.2.3, a key drawback to IRR and TVPI is that they ignore risk. A natural way to account for risk is to consider the discounted cash flows of a fund, where the discount reflects the riskiness of the cash flows. If a fund is fair investment, then the net present value (that is, the sum of the discounted future capital calls and distributions) should be zero in expectation.

A popular way to perform discounting is to use a stochastic discount factor (SDF). I do not cover SDFs in detail (Cochrane, 2005b, is a great read on this topic), but I briefly illustrate the underlying intuition and mechanics. Consider the following, stylized two-period model. An investor wants to maximize the expected utility of today's (time t) and next period's (time $t+1$) consumption. Given a time-separable, increasing and concave utility function $U(X)$ in consumption, X, and a time preference $\rho < 1$ that measures the degree to which an investor prefers receiving a certain payoff of \$1 today vs \$1 tomorrow, the choice problem is

$$\max_{X_t, X_{t+1}} U(X_t) + \rho E_t[U(X_{t+1})]. \tag{11}$$

The investor has no sources of income but has wealth, W_t, out of which she can consume. Anything not consumed today can be invested in a risky security that costs P_t per unit today and returns R_{t+1} next period. The return is a random variable as of time t. From the first-order condition of this optimization problem it follows that[u]

$$E_t[M_{t,1}R_{t+1}] = 1, \tag{12}$$

with the SDF

$$M_{t,1} = \rho \frac{U'(X_{t+1})}{U'(X_t)}. \tag{13}$$

Eq. (12) is the key pricing equation underlying much of modern asset pricing. The expression can also be written in prices by multiplying both sides by P_t:

$$P_t = E_t[M_{t,1}(P_{t+1} + C_{t+1})], \tag{14}$$

---

[u]Proof of Eqs. (12) and (13): Let ϕ be the number of units of the risky security bought. Since $X_t = W_t - \phi P_t$ and $X_{t+1} = \phi P_t R_{t+1}$, the choice problem (11) can be rewritten as $\max_{\phi} U(W_t - \phi P_t) + \rho E_t[U(\phi P_t R_{t+1})]$.
The first-order condition is $-U'(X_t)P_t + \rho E_t[U'(X_{t+1})P_t R_{t+1}] = 0$. Divide by $U'(X_t)P_t$ and reorganize to find the solution.

where C_{t+1} is next period's net cash flow. Note that in Eq. (14) I swapped the two sides of the equation from Eq. (12), to emphasize that today's price is the (conditional) expected payoff multiplied by the SDF. As such, Eq. (14) clarifies how the SDF takes care of discounting future payoffs.

Intuitively, the SDF can be thought of as a close cousin of state prices. State prices are prices of (fictitious) assets that pay exactly \$1 in one state of the world, at one specific future time (here: next period). Bad states of the world have high state prices (and a high realization of the SDF): A payoff (here: $P_{t+1}+C_{t+1}$) will be highly valued when consumption (here: X_{t+1}) is relatively low, such that marginal utility is high. Conversely, good states of the world have low state prices (and low realizations of the SDF).[v] Another way to illustrate this intuition is to rewrite the expectation on the right-hand side of Eq. (14) as

$$P_t = E_t[M_{t,1}]E_t[P_{t+1} + C_{t+1}] + Cov_t[M_{t,1}, P_{t+1} + C_{t+1}]$$
$$= \frac{E_t[P_{t+1} + C_{t+1}]}{R^F_{t+1}} + Cov_t[M_{t,1}, P_{t+1} + C_{t+1}]. \tag{15}$$

The second line uses the fact that the risk-free rate is known at time t, such that $E_t[M_t R^F_{t+1}] = E_t[M_t]R^F_{t+1} = 1$. The first term in Eq. (15) is thus the value of the payoff discounted at the risk-free rate, and the second term is a risk adjustment that is positive if the payoff is positively correlated with the SDF. In other words, assets whose payoffs are positively correlated with SDF realizations (that is, assets that pay out in bad times), are more desirable and therefore have higher prices.

SDF pricing also applies to longer-horizon payoffs. For example, the present value of a single cash flow that realizes two periods from today is

$$P_t = E_t[M_{t,1}P_{t+1}] = E_t[M_{t,1}E_{t+1}[M_{t+1,1}C_{t+2}]]$$
$$= E_t[E_{t+1}[M_{t,1}M_{t+1,1}C_{t+2}]] = E_t[M_{t,1}M_{t+1,1}C_{t+2}], \tag{16}$$

where the last step invokes the law of iterated expectations. Thus, the two-period SDF is $M_{t,2} = M_{t,1}M_{t+1,1}$, and more generally, for h periods, $M_{t,h} = \prod_{s=0}^{h-1} M_{t+s,1}$. Also note that $M_{t,0} = 1$, since cash flows that occur immediately require no discounting.

3.7.1 Public market equivalent

A PE metric that discounts cash flows, popular in academia and increasingly so in practice, is the public market equivalent (PME). Building on earlier work by Long and Nickels (1996), it is defined by Kaplan and Schoar (2005) as[w]

---

[v] See Sørensen and Jagannathan (2015) for a more in-depth description of this state-price analogy.
[w] Other PME-type definitions have been proposed, such as PME+ and modified PME (see, for example, Gredil et al., 2022, for a description and critique of these alternatives). The Kaplan and Schoar (2005) version is the most commonly used definition, especially in the literature, and the one that is most closely linked to theory (as explained below).

$$PME_i = \frac{\sum_{d=1}^{D} D_{i,d} / R_{t_0,\tau^D(d)}^{M} + NAV_{i,T} / R_{t_0,T-t_0}^{M}}{\sum_{k=1}^{K} I_{i,k} / R_{t_0,\tau^I(k)}^{M}}. \tag{17}$$

A comparison with Eq. (1) readily reveals PME to be a discounted TVPI, using the realized public stock market return as the discount rate.[x] To demonstrate the mechanics, consider the example fund in Table 2. The April 10, 2024, distribution of $500,000 is discounted at the 9.5% market return since fund inception to a value of $456,621. The December 20, 2024, distribution's discounted value is $1,000,000/1.244 = $803,859. Together with a discounted final NAV of $3300,000/1.250 = $2,640,000, the numerator of Eq. (17) is $3,900,480. The denominator is the discounted value of the seven capital calls, which add up to $4,101,269. The PME of this fund is therefore $3,900,480/$4,101,269 = 0.95.

One (common) interpretation is that a PME greater (smaller) than one means that the fund performed better (worse) than a hypothetical alternative strategy that invested the fund's capital calls in the public stock market. Put differently, the fund is benchmarked against the public stock market. In the example above, since the PME is less than one, an investor would have been better off investing the fund's capital calls in the public stock market.

Table 1 shows descriptive statistics of Kaplan-Schoar PME for various PE strategies, using the S&P 500 as the proxy for the public stock market. Over the sample period, VC and real estate had a PME centered just below one (at a mean of 0.96 for both strategies, a median of 0.98 for VC and 0.97 for real estate). Private debt looked very similar with a mean PME of 1.01 and a median of 0.98. Natural resources and infrastructure had PMEs centered well below one. In contrast, the mean and median PME for buyout were 1.11 and 1.10. Like IRR and TVPI, the variation in PME is very high (especially in VC) and there is a large positive skewness (except for infrastructure) and excess kurtosis. The final column in Fig. 3 shows the kernel-smoothed distribution of PME for the various strategies.

Many papers report PMEs, primarily for VC and buyout, using different data sources and time periods. Table 7 presents a representative (but not comprehensive) overview of these estimates. The table focuses on main PE vehicles (Sections 4 and 5 discuss alternative vehicles, co-investments, and publicly traded vehicles).

Table 7 shows that the mean VC PME from Burgiss data tends to be higher (on the order of 1.2–1.4) than the Preqin-based estimates from Table 1 (and other

---

[x]The PME is sometimes computed as a ratio of future (rather than discounted) values. These calculations are equivalent. This can be shown by substituting $R_{t_0,\tau}^{M} = R_{t_0,T-t_0}^{M} / R_{t_0+\tau,T-\tau}^{M}$ into

the PME formula of Eq. (16), yielding the ratio of future values $PME_i =$

$$\left[\sum_{d=1}^{D} D_{i,d} \cdot R_{t_0+\tau^D(d),T-\tau^D(d)}^{M} + NAV_{i,T} \right] / \left[\sum_{k=1}^{K} I_{i,k} \cdot R_{t_0+\tau^I(k),T-\tau^I(k)}^{M} \right].$$

Table 7 Public market equivalent estimates of private equity funds.

Paper	Data source	Vintage	Table	VC PME			Buyout PME			Other PME			Notes
				EW	VW	Median	EW	VW	Median	EW	VW	Median	
Kaplan and Schoar (2005)	VE	1980–1994	II	0.96	1.21	0.66	0.97	0.93	0.80				
McKenzie and Janeway (2008)	LP2	1980–2002	VI	1.98	N.R.	1.21							
Phalippou and Gottschalg (2009)	VE	1980–1993	2B	N.R.	0.88	N.R.	N.R.	0.96	N.R.				
Higson and Stucke (2012)	CA+CP	1980–2008	VI				1.22	1.23	1.13				CRSP-VW
Axelson et al. (2013)	P	1987–2010	VI				1.36	N.R.	1.35				
Harris et al. (2014)	B	1984–2008	III	1.36	1.45	1.02	1.22	1.27	1.16				CRSP-VW
Phalippou (2014)	P	1993–2010	I				1.03	1.19	0.99				
Robinson and Sensoy (2016)	LP1	1984–2005	2	1.06	N.R.	0.84	1.19	N.R.	1.09				CRSP-VW
Brown et al. (2019)	B+St	1971–2016	1	1.19	N.R.	1.11	1.21	N.R.	1.18				
Gredil et al. (2020b)	P	1983–2012	I	1.08	N.R.	0.82	1.14	N.R.	1.09				
Harris et al. (2022)	B	1984–2015	1	1.29	N.R.	N.R.	1.18	N.R.	N.R.				
Lerner et al. (2020)	SS	1985–2010	App. B	1.44	1.19	1.09	1.21	1.20	1.15				
Andonov et al. (2021)	P	2002–2018	3	0.99	1.02	0.95	1.05	1.06	1.01	0.93	0.93	0.95	Infrastructure funds
	B	2002–2018								0.89	N.R.	0.91	Infrastructure funds
Brown et al. (2021a)	B	1983–2008	1	1.2	N.R.	0.82	1.1	N.R.	1.02				CRSP-VW
Jeffers et al. (2021)	IFD+P	1999–2016	1	0.88	N.R.	0.82				0.78	N.R.	0.77	Impact funds; CRSP-VW

This table shows a representative (but non-comprehensive) overview of estimates of the Public Market Equivalent (PME) of Kaplan and Schoar (2005) from the private equity literature. Results for funds of funds, secondary funds, venture debt funds, co-investments, alternative vehicles, and publicly traded vehicles are excluded (to the extent they are excluded or separately reported in the original papers). The results shown are for active funds (not only liquidated funds, to the extent that these results are separately reported). All PME calculations use the return on the S&P 500 as the discount rate, unless noted in the "Notes" column (where CRSP-VW stands for the CRSP value-weighted market index). The "Vintage" column shows the fund vintage years covered by the sample in the paper. "Table" is the source table number in the cited paper that contains the PME numbers. "EW" and "VW" stand for equal-weighted and value-weighted mean, respectively. The "Other PME" column shows results for PE strategies other than venture capital (VC) or buyout (see the "Notes" column for the name of the strategy). Data source abbreviations: B = Burgiss; CA = Cambridge Associates; CP = California Public Employees' Retirement System; IFD = Impact Finance Database; LPn = sourced from n limited partners (LPs); P = Preqin; SS = State Street; St = StepStone SPI; VE = Venture Economics. N.R. stands for "Not Reported."

papers). The medians are comparable between the two data sets. This finding is consistent with Preqin data missing a few top-quartile VC firms, which affects the mean but not the median. Buyout results are similar between Burgiss and Preqin. The Venture Economics numbers for both buyout and VC funds tend to be lower, due to the performance bias discussed in Section 3.2.2.

There is some degree of time-variation in average PMEs. Many VC fund vintages from the 1990s performed very well as they benefited from the internet boom: Harris et al. (2014) report an average (median) PME of 1.99 (1.26) for the decade. The first decade of the 2000s has been poor, however, as average PMEs dopped to 0.91 (0.84). Performance appears to be improving with the 2010–15 vintages (Harris et al., 2022), although many of these funds are still far from finished at the time of this writing. Buyout fund performance has been more stable over time (see also figs. 1 and 2 in Harris et al. (2014) for a more detailed time-series of VC and buyout PMEs by vintage). Notwithstanding this time-series variation, and the fact that there is a cyclical component to cash flows (Robinson and Sensoy, 2016), most of the high PME variance is explained by the cross-section (that is, variation in PMEs across funds of the same vintage year). This dominant role of cross-sectional variation in PE fund returns stands in contrast to other managed funds that primarily invest in public securities, such as mutual funds.

To make a more convenient comparison with alpha estimates from factor models, Gredil et al. (2022) develop an annualized version of the PME, called direct alpha. Although Gredil et al. derive it somewhat differently, direct alpha can be computed as the (fixed, annualized) rate of return that needs to be added to the benchmark return to make the PME equal to one. While useful, one caveat to this measure is that it presumes that one can reinvest at the same alpha, similar to the reinvestment problem with IRR.[y]

If the PME is interpreted as a benchmarking metric, then the choice of benchmark is important, as it is supposed to capture similar risk as the investment it is compared against. Under this interpretation, using the public stock market is equivalent to assuming that the CAPM holds, and that the asset being evaluated has a beta of one. While this may be a sensible choice for buyout funds based on CAPM beta estimates that are indeed often close to one (see Fig. 1), it may not be an appropriate choice for other PE strategies. For example, VC beta estimates are typically far above one, and comparing private debt to a public equity investment is a stretch even for risky loans. In recognition of this, some authors choose different benchmark portfolios to compute the PME. Ljungqvist and Richardson (2003) show PME results with the Nasdaq as the discount rate for distributions, which could be a natural choice for VC (see Section 3.5.3) and using the risk-free rate to discount capital calls (they call their metric the Profitability Index, but the calculation is the same as the PME).

[y]Other ways of calculating an annualized excess return are the index comparison method by Long and Nickels (1996), PME+, and modified PME. See Gredil et al. (2022) for more details and a critical comparison with direct alpha.

Harris et al. (2014), Phalippou (2014), Robinson and Sensoy (2013, 2016), and Hüther et al. (2020) use a levered version of the PME, essentially (exogenously) choosing the market beta at which to compute the discount rate. Phalippou (2014) also uses a variety of size and value-sorted portfolios. Gredil (2022) uses publicly traded industry sub-index returns. Munday et al. (2018) study private credit fund PMEs using four different benchmark indices: a high-yield index, a levered loan index, a publicly traded BDC index, and the Cliffwater direct lending index. They find PMEs just below one, except for the levered-loan PME, which is 1.14. Finally, Driessen et al. (2012) take the choice of discounting rate one step further and estimate the factor model parameters needed to make the PME equal to one, and apply their approach to a sample of VC and buyout funds.[z]

A drawback of the benchmarking interpretation as described above is that in most cases the choice of benchmark is rather ad hoc, without any quantitative guidance on whether the appropriate risk-matching was achieved. An alternative interpretation of PME, specifically, as an application of SDF pricing with log-utility investors, avoids the benchmark choice issue altogether.[aa] Under this interpretation, PME is a valid measure of risk-adjusted performance without any assumption or restriction on beta(s). To see this, first note that an investor with log utility over wealth has an SDF that equals the reciprocal of the return on her wealth portfolio. Using the market portfolio as a proxy for the wealth portfolio,[ab]

$$M_{t,h} = \frac{1}{R_{t,h}^M}. \tag{18}$$

Now consider the expected value (as of fund inception) of the PME numerator in Eq. (17). If we include all future distributions until liquidation, then the final NAV is zero, and the expected numerators is $E_{t_0}\left[\sum_{d=1}^{D} D_{i,d}/R_{t_0,\tau^D(d)}^M\right]$. Switching the expectation and summation, and using Eq. (18) yields $\sum_{d=1}^{D} E_{t_0}\left[M_{t_0,\tau^D(d)}D_{i,d}\right]$, which is the sum of the present values of all future distributions. By the same logic, the expected value of the denominator is the sum of the present values of all capital calls. Thus, the ratio

---

[z]This description is a bit of a misrepresentation: Driessen et al. (2012) do not use the Kaplan and Schoar (2005) PME. Instead, they use an NPV formula similar to Eq. (19) below and estimate the market model parameters that make this NPV equal to zero. The intuition is the same, however. Another way to think of their approach is that it modifies the fund IRR calculation in Eq. (2) by substituting *IRR$_i$* with a factor model.
[aa]Log-utility has a long history in (financial) economics. See, among others, Hakansson (1971), Roll (1973), Fama and MacBeth (1974), Kraus and Litzenberger (1975), Rubinstein (1976), and Long (1990).
[ab]Using the public stock market as a proxy for the wealth portfolio is common in empirical applications but invites the well-known Roll (1977) critique typically applied to tests of the CAPM, which says that the model may be rejected not because log-utility is the wrong assumption but because the proxy is poor. It is especially noteworthy that the proxy portfolio does not include any private equity investments. In the benchmarking interpretation, on the other hand, using the public stock market return is perfectly fine if that is indeed the (risk-matched) benchmark portfolio that we want to compare PE investments against.

of the two is how much money we expect to receive, in present value terms, over the life of the fund, for a present value investment of one dollar (importantly, this is not quite the *expected* PME, due to Jensen's inequality). For not-yet-liquidated funds, the final reported NAV is included and discounted at the SDF. This is correct, and the interpretation does not change, if the NAV indeed represents the true net asset value of the fund as of its reported date, but it is of course subject to the same issues with NAV as discussed above.

Under the SDF-pricing interpretation, no assumption on the beta of PE is needed, as the SDF properly values each cash flow depending on the state of the world in which it realizes. This implies that beta may even vary from fund to fund without invalidating the PME metric. For the same reason, the fact that the timing of cash flows may be endogenously chosen by the GP is also not a problem per se. Moreover, the SDF pricing model leaves the distribution of payoffs unrestricted, which is important given the skewed and fat-tailed distributions common in PE. Of course, this does mean that we must assume that the log utility function is correctly specified, which implies that we are also making an assumption about which risk factors matter to investors, as well as their level of risk aversion (I will return to this below).

To summarize, we have two valid but different interpretations of PME: either as a benchmarking exercise that assumes the investment has a CAPM beta of one (without assuming a specific utility function other than what's needed for the CAPM to hold), or as a ratio of present values under the assumption of log-utility investors (but without any restriction on beta).

3.7.2 Generalized PME

Korteweg and Nagel (2016) introduce the generalized PME (GPME), which, as the name implies, is a generalization of PME to an arbitrary SDF:

$$GPME_i = \sum_{j=1}^{J} M_{t_0,\tau(j)} C_{i,j} + M_{t_0,T-t_0} NAV_{i,T} \tag{19}$$

Besides allowing for a generic SDF, the difference with PME is that the above definition is based on net cash flows (including any final NAV as a pseudo-cash flow), rather than a ratio of distributions to contributions. To allow for comparisons across funds, cash flows (as well as the final NAV) can be scaled by the fund's commitment size.[ac]

Defining the performance metric on net cash flows has several advantages over the ratio definition. First, the expected GPME is simply the expected NPV of a $1 commitment, earned over the lifetime of the fund. Thus, unlike the ratio definition, the average GPME in the data has a well-defined interpretation. Note that the key threshold number to compare the GPME against is zero (not one, which is the

---

[ac]Note the deceptive similarity between Eq. (19) and the IRR calculation in Eq. (2). The GPME would indeed be zero if M is equal to $1/(1+\text{IRR})$, but it is important to realize that this is not a proper SDF because it varies from fund to fund.

threshold number in the ratio definition). A second advantage is that the GPME of a portfolio of funds is simply the weighted average of the constituent GPMEs, with weights proportional to capital committed (this is not true for the ratio definition). Third, the net cash flow definition allows for the comparison of two GPMEs through their difference: an "excess" GPME is a GPME itself, namely the GPME of the difference in cash flow streams and final NAVs (see, for example, Lerner et al., 2020, for an application of excess PMEs). Finally, the classification of negative capital calls and distributions is not an issue for the net cash flow definition, unlike the ratio definition (for the same reasons as those discussed in Section 3.2.1).

In their empirical application, Korteweg and Nagel (2016) specify an SDF that is exponential-affine in the market return:

$$M_{t,1} = \exp\left(a - br_{t+1}^M\right), \tag{20}$$

with r_{t+1}^M the one-period log return on the market from time t to $t+1$. This is the SDF for a power utility investor with risk aversion equal to b. It rules out arbitrage opportunities as the SDF is positive in every state of the world, and it compounds nicely for longer horizons,

$$M_{t,h} = \prod_{s=0}^{h-1} M_{t+s,1} = \prod_{s=1}^{h} \exp\left(a - br_{t+s}^M\right) = \exp\left(ah - b\sum_{s=1}^{h} r_{t+s}^M\right)$$
$$= \exp\left(ah - br_{t,h}^M\right), \tag{21}$$

where $r_{t,h}$ is the h-period log-return from time t to $t+h$.

Korteweg and Nagel estimate the SDF parameters to price the public market and risk-free rate.[ad] Applying this SDF to a sample of 545 VC funds from Preqin, they estimate a GPME of -0.103, which is statistically significantly different from zero at the 5% level, taking into account the uncertainty about the estimated SDF parameters as well as the cross-sectional correlations between funds due to their overlap in time. This estimate indicates that per \$1 commitment, the average VC fund lost a present value of about 10 cents over its lifetime. This loss is driven by the post-1998 vintages in their sample, as the earlier vintages have a GPME that is statistically indistinguishable from zero.

Several recent papers estimate GPME for various investments. Hüther et al. (2021) report positive GPME estimates for buyout funds. Andonov et al. (2021) and Jeffers et al. (2021) estimate a negative GPME for infrastructure and impact funds, respectively. Giacoletti and Westrupp (2018) apply the GPME model to real estate investments. Cordell et al. (2021) estimate multi-factor GPMEs for

[ad]To be precise, Korteweg and Nagel estimate the SDF on portfolios of public equities and Treasuries that match investments made in the private equity funds in their sample. While this approach should be asymptotically equivalent to simply weighing each time period equally, in samples with short time series it helps to concentrate weight in periods where the exposure to PE is highest and it is therefore most important to price factor realizations correctly. Also, per the results in Shanken (1992), it is better to estimate the SDF over the same period as the PE investments, rather than over a longer historical sample period.

collateralized loan obligations with a few different SDFs, including the Fama and French (1993) three-factor model and an intermediary asset pricing model.

Note that the SDF implied by the PME is a special case of Eq. (20) with $a=0$ and $b=1$.[ae] The SDF parameter point estimates in Korteweg and Nagel are 0.09 and 2.65, and the log-utility model is statistically rejected. Still, it is worthwhile to dig deeper into the differences between PME and GPME. To fix ideas, suppose a fund makes a \$1 capital call today and invests it in a portfolio company that is liquidated next year at a return of $R^F + \alpha + \beta(R^M - R^F)$. In other words, the investment pays off according to the CAPM plus a risk-adjusted return α (I suppress time subscripts to avoid clutter). For simplicity, there is no idiosyncratic return (this could be easily added but does not change the intuition), these are the fund's only cash flows, there are no fees, and the fund is fully liquidated when the investment pays off. The expected PME of this fund is

$$E[PME] = E\left[\frac{R^F + \alpha + \beta(R^M - R^F)}{R^M}\Big/1\right]$$
$$= (R^F(1-\beta) + \alpha)\cdot E[1/R^M] + \beta \tag{22}$$

The first line uses the fact that there is only one capital call (of \$1) in the denominator, which is nonrandom as it occurs today, so that there is no Jensen inequality problem with taking expectations of ratios. If the β of the investment were equal to 1, then the expected PME simplifies to $\alpha\cdot E[1/R^M]+1$. If, in addition, α were zero, then PME equals one. This is not a surprise, because in this case the portfolio firm simply earns the market return.

Next, suppose we have an SDF that prices R^M and R^F, i.e., $E[MR^M]=E[MR^F]=1$. Then,

$$E[GPME] = -1 + E\left[M\cdot\left(R^F + \alpha + \beta(R^M - R^F)\right)\right]$$
$$= -1 + R^F(1-\beta)E[M] + \alpha E[M] + \beta E[MR^M] \tag{23}$$
$$= \frac{\alpha}{R^F}$$

where the last line uses the fact that the SDF prices the risk-free rate, such that $E[M]=1/R^F$. Gupta and van Nieuwerburgh (2021) point out that it is natural to discount alpha, which in this example realizes next year, at the risk-free rate. The important takeaway from Eq. (23) is that the value of beta does not matter for the expected GPME. Therefore, a levered investment in stocks (which increases beta) will be evaluated correctly by GPME.[af] A benchmarking interpretation to GPME

[ae] If the PME is implemented using net cash flows, as in Eq. (19), remember that in this Korteweg-Nagel type PME, zero is the counterpart to the PME=1 threshold in the Kaplan-Schoar PME.

[af] A more accurate modeling of a levered strategy shows that the alpha is in fact magnified by leverage: suppose the investor borrows x dollars (where x could be negative) on top of their own \$1 and invests the full \$$(1+x)$ in an asset that pays the market rate of return plus an additional alpha. Assuming that the investor can borrow at the risk-free rate, then $E[GPME] = -1 + E\left[M\cdot\left\{(1+x)(R^M + \alpha) - xR^F\right\}\right] = (1+x)\frac{\alpha}{R^F}$. Korteweg and Nagel (2016) show this "alpha magnification" in an exercise with artificially levered VC funds. They also show that PME does not properly account for leverage (see their table III).

is then that a GPME above zero means that there is a component of PE payoffs that cannot be replicated by a (possibly levered) investment in stocks and bonds (as the SDF prices these two assets in this example; more generally, the replication allows for investments in all of the factors priced by the SDF).

As one might intuitively expect, if investors have log utility, then PME and GPME are equivalent (such that PME equals one when GPME equals zero). This happens because under log preferences, $E[1/R^M] = 1/R^F$, so that $E[PME] = 1 + \alpha/R^F$ regardless of the value of beta. If, however, log utility does not hold, beta will enter the expected PME, and leverage will no longer be properly accounted for. With the recent increase in subscription lines of credit usage by PE firms (Albertus and Denes, 2020; Schillinger et al., 2019), this leverage issue becomes more problematic, as LPs often do not know how levered the fund is, so it becomes near impossible to determine what beta to use to construct a discount rate in a "levered PME" type exercise.

To illustrate the empirical importance of the log-utility restriction of PME, Table 2 in Korteweg (2019) shows its impact on effective discount rates used by PME, for each decade between the 1960s and the 2010s, and for various levels of beta. While PME works perfectly well when beta equals one, for an investment with a beta of 2 (which is in the range of estimates for VC) the PME-implied benchmark return can be off by as much as 10% per year or more. While the PME-implied benchmark rate is usually too low for investments with a beta above one, this is not necessarily true (for example, in the 1970s and the first decade of the 2000s the implied benchmark was too high). The reason for this result is that log-utility restricts both the risk-free rate (to $1/E[1/R^M]$) and the implied market risk premium (because it restricts the coefficient of risk aversion to one; see Korteweg and Nagel, 2016, for explicit expressions under lognormal returns). When beta equals one, the mismatch between the PME-implied and the actual risk-free rate and market premium happen to cancel out, but this is not generally true. In contrast, the GPME with the SDF of Eq. (20) and an additional assumption that returns are lognormal, implies a CAPM in logs:

$$\log E[R_{i,t+1}] = r^F + \beta\left(\log E[R^M_{t+1}] - r^F\right). \tag{24}$$

Thus, the GPME can properly benchmark any asset that conforms to this model (but note that the lognormal returns assumption is not necessary for GPME to hold, giving it an advantage over factor models, especially in PE). This duality generalizes to multiple factors, that is, $M_{t,1} = \exp(a - b'f_{t+1})$ corresponds to a multi-factor model in log returns.

Since SDF pricing works on expectations, per Eq. (12), the GPME method works well when taking averages over large samples (especially in the time series, to achieve more variation in the factor realizations). A downside is that the GPME for any individual fund can be very noisy. To address this, Korteweg and Nagel (2022) develop an extension to the GPME method that produces more accurate individual fund-level estimates of risk-adjusted performance.

A final important point is that Gredil (2022) shows evidence that VC and buyout GPs have skill in timing the public equity market, but any such type of factor timing skill is not recognized as outperformance by (G)PME, to the extent that the factors are priced by the SDF. While factor timing skill is valuable, it is better implemented through other, more liquid, securities with lower transaction costs, such as stocks and bonds, when possible. Rather, the (G)PME metric is geared toward identifying whether GPs possess skill that is specific to PE and cannot be realized elsewhere.

3.7.3 Other SDFs

With a machinery to use generic SDFs in place, we can turn our attention to exploring what risk factors besides the market may be in the SDF, or, in the dual representation, factor models. This is a recent but growing area of research in PE. Loadings on the Fama and French (1993) SMB and HML factors were described in Sections 3.5.3 and 3.5.4 above, so I will not revisit these results here. Ang et al. (2018) apply the Fama and French (2015) 5-factor model and find that VC funds do not have statistically significant loadings on the profitability or investment factors. Buyout funds have a significant positive loading on the profitability factor but do not load on investment.

Gredil et al. (2020a) estimate two consumption-based asset pricing models: the external habit and the long-run risks model. Results are mixed. They find small VC outperformance after the turn of the millennium, although this is not reliably statistically significant across specifications. For buyout they cannot reject the null hypothesis of zero outperformance for most specifications.

Illiquidity is a major feature of PE, but the size of the illiquidity premium is a priori unclear. On the one hand, most investors in PE have long horizons and should be well positioned to handle liquidity shocks. On the other hand, not only is there illiquidity in the realization of distributions, LPs are also exposed to funding liquidity shocks due to GPs having the discretion to call capital at any time (Lerner and Schoar, 2004), and penalties for defaulting on capital call are stiff (e.g., Litvak, 2004; Banal-Estañol et al., 2017). Franzoni et al. (2012), Ang et al. (2018), and Hüther et al. (2021) find that buyout funds load positively and significantly on the Pástor and Stambaugh (2003) illiquidity factor, with an illiquidity premium of about 3% per year. Buchner (2016) and Ang et al. (2018) find insignificant loadings for VC. Metrick and Yasuda (2010b) also estimate an insignificant loading when using the Cambridge Associates VC index returns, but a small positive loading for the Sand Hill Econometrics index (a VC index). Agarwal et al. (2022) also do not find any reliably positive loadings on the liquidity factor for mutual fund investments in private firms. However, the Pástor and Stambaugh factor may not be capturing the type of illiquidity that PE is exposed to, as it was developed to capture order-flow illiquidity in publicly traded stocks. A small literature considers the PE illiquidity premium from a portfolio allocation model perspective, but this falls outside the scope of this review. The interested reader can find a survey of these papers in Korteweg and Westerfield (2022).

Idiosyncratic risk may be important in PE. The potential benefits to diversification are large given the large cross-sectional variation in returns, but agents are under-diversified and risks are imperfectly shared (Opp, 2019): GPs hold a sizeable amount of wealth in their own funds, for incentive-provision reasons

(Ewens et al., 2013), and a typical LP commits to only three PE funds per year (Gredil et al., 2020b). Ewens et al. find supporting evidence that GPs in VC price their idiosyncratic risk exposure into the deals they negotiate with portfolio companies. In the cross-section of GPs, those with higher idiosyncratic risk earn higher expected returns. Peters (2018) takes a time-series perspective and shows that VC loads positively on aggregate idiosyncratic volatility shocks. This implies lower expected returns to VC, since investors prefer securities that pay off when idiosyncratic risk spikes unexpectedly (put differently, this risk carries a negative risk premium). Notably, the role of idiosyncratic risk for buyout returns has thus far been unexplored in the literature.

Gupta and van Nieuwerburgh (2021) introduce term structure factors, factors related to inflation, GDP growth, and price-dividend ratios and dividend growth rates of various public equity portfolios into the SDF. The introduction of term structure effects seems especially important for private equity funds, given their long investment horizon, and even more so for buyout given its reliance on leverage (see also Giommetti and Jørgensen, 2021). Overall, Gupta and Van Nieuwerburgh estimate negative average risk-adjusted profits for buyout, VC, real estate, and infrastructure funds. I discuss their empirical methodology, which is based on SDF pricing but implemented somewhat differently than GPME, in the next section.

Hüther et al. (2021) use a five-factor SDF with credit market factors, calibrated to price the loans and bonds of leveraged buyout deals. Using this SDF to price buyout PE fund cash flows using the GPME methodology (they call this the "Credit Market Equivalent"), the authors find positive but statistically insignificant risk-adjusted performance.[ag]

Korteweg et al. (2021) move away from a representative agent model in which there is one unique SDF, and instead use individual U.S. public pension funds' performance to evaluate the benefits of investing in PE. They find no reliable evidence that pension plans either over or under-allocated to PE, with the possible exception of buyout funds, which have historically looked attractive.

There are also a few potential risk factors that have not yet received much attention in the PE literature. First, while skewness in payoffs and returns is well-known, I am not aware of any work that quantifies (co-)skewness and its associated risk premium in PE (e.g., Harvey and Siddique, 2000). Is skewness mostly idiosyncratic or is there a large systematic component? Second, research in public equities suggests that many common risk factors, such as the value, profit, and investment factors, may be subsumed by a single cash flow duration factor (e.g., DeChow et al., 2004; Chen and Li, 2020; Gonçalves, 2021; Gormsen and Lazarus, 2021). Third, there is some suggestive evidence that there may be a PE-specific risk factor (Korteweg and Sørensen, 2010; Ang et al., 2018), but the nature and size of this potential factor has not yet been investigated.

[ag]A tangentially related paper by Fleckenstein and Longstaff (2020) uses secondary market data of securitized business credit card targeted to entrepreneurs. Calibrating a Merton-style model to this data they find an expected return on small entrepreneurial companies of 14% and a market beta of around 1.2.

Finally, generalizations such as time-varying SDF loadings (corresponding to time-varying risk premia) and using conditioning information in computing the expected GPME are as-of-yet left unexplored.

3.7.4 Critiques

I end this section on fund data with two critiques that future research can hopefully resolve. First, the use of SDFs and their close counterpart, factor models, is ubiquitous in asset pricing research, but little attention has been paid to how appropriate their application is in PE. Most importantly, a key underlying assumption to the derivation of both SDF pricing and factor models is that investors can make very small adjustments to their portfolios at very low transaction costs. While reasonable for public equities and other securities, this is clearly violated in PE. How does this affect implementations of the SDF/factor model approach in PE?

The second critique revolves around an empirical regularity documented by Martin (2012), which may impact the performance of the (G)PME method: for long horizons (i.e., large h), while the expectation of $M_{t,h}R_{t,h}$ equals one, most sample paths have realizations that are close to zero (mainly because M often ends up close to zero) and a few paths have very high outcomes (i.e., really bad times that coincide with high returns). A potential peso problem is that small samples may not include those high realizations, resulting in sample averages that can be significantly below one (or zero, in the case of GPME). Thus, while the (G)PME approach of using SDF realizations is consistent and unbiased, the distribution of realized (G)PME is skewed and may result in estimated performance that is below the mean in many cases. To be fair, the Martin result is for very long horizons, on the order of a century or longer. The effect for PE funds, which operate on the order of 10–20 years may be small, as suggested by simulations in Korteweg and Nagel (2022).

To the extent that the above peso problem does pose a problem, the approach by Gupta and van Nieuwerburgh (2021) is a potential solution, although it comes at the cost of assuming additional structure. Their two-step method first constructs replicating portfolios of each PE fund, using a series of zero-coupon bonds and dividend and capital gain "strips" that pay off at a single date. The second step is to specify and calibrate an asset pricing model that prices these strips. This model requires not only an SDF, but also a high-dimensional vector autoregression model for the state variables, with specific distributional assumptions. The benefit of this method is that it avoids SDF realizations and goes straight to expectations. The value of any nonreplicable PE fund cash flows, minus any difference in the cost of constructing the replicating portfolio and the PE capital committed, is then the risk-adjusted profit of the fund. Note that this risk-adjusted profit measure gives credit to the GP for market-timing capital calls, unlike (G)PME.

4 Alternative vehicles and funds of funds

The empirical results described in the previous section focus on flagship PE funds. Since the turn of the millennium, an increasing proportion of investments in PE are being made in vehicles outside of the main funds: In the 1980s, less than 10% of capital invested in PE went to alternative vehicles, compared to nearly 40% by 2017 (Lerner et al., 2020).

Alternative vehicles can be broadly classified as GP-directed and discretionary investments, depending on the degree of LP control. GP-directed vehicles (also called parallel or sidecar funds) leave the key decision powers with the GP. They generally make the same investments and dispositions as the main fund, their main purpose being to accommodate tax, regulatory, or other requirements of certain LPs. Sidecar funds with a lower fee structure than the main fund, and continuation funds (an increasingly popular way to keep exposure to portfolio companies when the original investing fund is at the end of its lifecycle) can also be included in this category.

In discretionary investments, the LP has a say in which investments are made. In some instances, select LPs are offered the opportunity to co-invest alongside the GP in a particular portfolio company, in other cases the GP sets up a separate fund. These funds may be in the form of a pledge fund where LPs decide on transactions on a deal-by-deal basis, or a co-investment or overage fund that is raised at the same time as the main fund. Finally, LPs sometimes engage in solo investments, in which they source and invest in a deal alone. These solo transactions are the playground of larger LPs that have the critical mass to support a dedicated PE team to generate deal flow and perform due diligence and post-transaction monitoring.

Lerner et al. (2020) report that the number of GP-directed and discretionary vehicles (including solo investments in previously PE-financed companies) are roughly equal, but the former represent about 25% more capital ($50 billion vs $38 billion).

Standard commercial data sets, as of this writing, either do not contain alternative funds and solo investments, or they are not well identified or classified. As such, the empirical literature on the performance of alternative vehicles is very small. The earlier key papers focused on co-investments and solo investments. Fang et al. (2015), in proprietary data from seven large LPs, find little evidence of net-of-fee outperformance. Solo transactions, while having PMEs above one, underperform fund benchmarks, especially in VC. For co-investments, PMEs are lower than the associated funds. This result is surprising, especially for solo deals (given that LPs pay no fees), and the authors say this is indicative of adverse selection. However, Braun et al. (2020) find no evidence of adverse selection in gross-of-fee PMEs from deal-level co-investments data in VC and buyout, sourced from CapitalIQ. While these contrasting results appear puzzling, the explanation could simply be that the two papers have very different data sets, representing distinct slices of the population. Lerner et al. (2020) use custodial data from State Street, which is more comprehensive than the data in prior studies. It also covers private debt in addition to VC and buyout. They find that performance in alternatives depends on the LPs' and GPs' qualities, and the match between LP and GP. While the average alternative vehicle has a lower PME than its corresponding main fund, the alternatives of top GPs tend to outperform. Top GPs offer preferential access to LPs that have high bargaining power (for example, due to their reputation as measured by past performance, or the size of their checkbook), and these LPs tend to earn higher PMEs in their alternative vehicle investments. The biggest difference in access is in discretionary vehicles, which on average tend to perform the best. Finally, alternatives have performed better in the years since the global financial crisis of 2008, a period that was not well covered by prior work.

Funds of funds are a potentially attractive investment for small investors. GPs typically require a minimum capital commitment, so that it is difficult to build a diversified portfolio of funds with a small PE budget. By pooling their money with other small investors in a fund of funds, LPs can achieve a higher level of diversification, and share the due diligence and monitoring expenses of running a PE portfolio. The ability to make larger commitments may also give the fund of funds opportunities to invest with high-quality GPs, which smaller investors may not be able to access. The main drawback is that they pay an additional layer of fees to the fund-of-funds manager. Since most fund performance studies are focused on direct fund investments, fund-of-funds are usually excluded from the data, so less is known about their performance. Harris et al. (2018) study the performance of fund-of-funds specifically. They main result is that VC funds of funds earn an average PME of 1.16, on par with the performance of direct VC fund investing, whereas the average PME of buyout funds of funds is 1.14, which is below the average PME of investing in direct funds.

Like funds of funds, secondary funds (which buy LP stakes in existing funds) are usually excluded from data sets that study fund PE fund performance. As described in Section 3.5.5, the secondary market in LP stakes has grown dramatically since the global financial crisis of 2008, and it is undergoing a transformation from pure liquidity provision to LPs to a more common portfolio rebalancing mechanism that encompasses a wider set of participants. Secondary funds performed extremely well in the aftermath of the financial crisis, when there were ample opportunities to buy fund stakes at deep discounts to NAV, but returns have come down since (Nadauld et al., 2019). It will be interesting to see how performance in this market develops as it matures.

5 Publicly traded vehicles

A small slice of the PE space is traded publicly, either over the counter or on stock exchanges. With regularly observed market prices, one can assess risk and return using traditional methods, thereby avoiding many of the issues that plague private funds.

There are two main types of publicly listed vehicles: management companies and funds. Listed management companies, such as Blackstone and KKR, provide investors the opportunity to share in the fees and carried interest income earned by GPs, and their risk-return profile should therefore be interpreted as approximating GPs' exposures in PE funds. Listed funds, on the other hand, can be thought of as traded net-of-fee LP stakes. These are dominated by broad, evergreen funds-of-funds portfolios, such as 3i Group, that are invested across the PE spectrum but also often include sizeable stakes in publicly traded securities. Additionally, in the U.S., many traded funds are business development corporations (BDCs), which invest primarily in debt securities such as high-yield loans to mid-cap sized firms, and Small Business Investment Companies (SBICs), a type of leveraged VC fund that is more heavily regulated than limited partnerships but receives favorable borrowing rates due to government guarantees (in fact, many BDCs have SBIC subsidiaries). Most publicly traded funds are listed in Europe and concentrate in the U.K. due to favorable tax rules for Investment Trusts and Venture Capital Trusts. Several indices of listed PE are widely available, such as the S&P Listed Private Equity Index, the Société Générale Privex index, the ALPS-RedRocks Global Listed Private Equity index, and the LPX Listed Private Equity Index Series. It is not uncommon for these indices to be used as PE investment benchmark returns, even though they usually include both the listed management companies and funds, despite their likely very different risk and return profiles.

Historically, the universe of publicly traded vehicles is extremely small. Martin and Petty (1983) identify 37 VC vehicles that traded publicly at some time during the 1970s, but only 17 had price data for their chosen sample period of 1974–79. Their sample is further reduced to 11 vehicles, eight SBICs and three VC firms, due to the fact that many are only sparsely traded. Similarly, Brophy and Guthner (1988) identify 12 publicly traded vehicles for 1981–85, all SBICs and BDCs, and all of which are traded over the counter (not on a centralized exchange).

In conjunction with the growth of PE as an asset class, the number of listed vehicles has expanded since the mid-1980s, and many institutions now have an allocation to listed PE. For example, Cumming et al. (2011) survey 171 European institutional investors, and report that 34% (primarily smaller and private institutions) have listed PE in their mandates. Bilo et al. (2005) identify 287 listed vehicles between 1986 and 2003, of which they analyze 114 that they find to be sufficiently liquid to plausibly estimate factor models. They estimate a CAPM beta of 1.2 for a value-weighted buy-and-hold strategy of listed PE, with an annualized alpha of −1.2%. An equal-weighted buy-and-hold strategy had a beta of 0.7 and an alpha of −0.1%, suggesting that the smaller vehicles performed better over the sample period. A fully rebalanced equal-weighted strategy performed remarkably well (with an alpha of 10.2% and a beta of 0.6). Applying the Dimson (1979) correction to account for staleness arising from thin trading raises the betas to around one but does not materially change the alphas (see Table 5 for the Dimson estimates, reported in the buyout column because this is likely the dominant strategy, although Bilo et al. do not provide information on the breakdown of strategies). But the apparent gains from the rebalancing strategy could well be wiped out by transaction costs, as accounting for bid-ask spreads alone reduces the annualized mean return by 8.3% (from 16.0% to 7.7%) over the sample period.

Phalippou (2010) identifies 19 publicly traded buyout funds and funds-of-funds in the CapitalIQ database as of 2008 that have at least 200 consecutive weeks of return data and for whom a zero weekly return is observed in Datastream for no more than once per 20 weeks. Using Dimson regressions with 10 weeks' lags, he reports an average beta across funds of 1.5 and an average annualized alpha of 6%.

Jegadeesh et al. (2015) provide a more detailed breakdown of risk and return across fund types and strategies. They analyze a sample of 129 traded funds and 24 traded funds-of-funds from 1994 to 2008. They separate the sample into VC and buyout vehicles, depending on their declared focus (for funds) or the strategy that has the greater asset allocation (for funds-of-funds). They find that VC and buyout funds have CAPM betas of 1.2 and 0.9 with respect to the MSCI World Index, and fund-of-fund betas are 1.0 and 0.7. In the Fama and French (1993) model augmented with a momentum factor (Carhart, 1997), all vehicles load positive on the small size factor and on the value factor (with insignificant loadings in VC), and all except buyout fund-of-funds load negatively on momentum. The fact that the loadings do not differ much across the types of listed vehicles highlights the mixed nature of their investments. Alpha estimates across factor models and vehicles range between -0.4% and $+0.2\%$ per month, with partnerships toward the upper end of this range and funds-of-funds at the lower end, but none are significantly different from zero.

McCourt (2018) studies 134 publicly listed PE funds, separated by strategy (VC, buyout, mezzanine, and fund-of-funds). His sample period spans 1995–2015, making this the only paper in the listed-vehicles literature that include post-financial crisis years. He estimates a market beta of around one for most strategies, except VC, which has a beta of 1.4. All strategies have a positive loading on SMB (close to 0.6 for most except VC, which has a higher loading of 1.1), and a negative loading on momentum of around -0.1. The loadings on HML are mixed: It is positive for buyout and mezzanine, negative for VC, and insignificant for fund-of-funds. This is consistent with the value and growth investing nature of buyout and VC, respectively, with funds-of-funds being a mixed bag. While alphas are statistically insignificant, the point estimates are positive for all strategies (around 0.3% per month for all but VC, which is 0.1%). Using tools from the mutual fund literature, such as cross-sectional bootstraps and false discovery rates, he finds evidence of that some managers in buyout and mezzanine funds are skilled, but not in VC, while the evidence for funds-of-funds is mixed.

While publicly traded vehicles are a useful alternative lens for assessing PE risk and return, the estimates should not be directly compared to those of private funds. First, the mixed investment strategies and highly diversified nature of listed vehicles makes it difficult to attribute risk loadings and risk-adjusted returns to any single strategy. The relative homogeneity in estimated risk loadings across types of listed PE vehicles and (inferred) strategies is consistent with the lines indeed being blurred here. Moreover, BDCs and SBICs, while also investing in startups, own very different securities with very different risk-return profiles than private VC funds, as described above. Second, public listing is an endogenous choice, and there is likely selection bias in the characteristics of PE vehicles that are traded. Selection on size is one obvious example, but there are bound to be many other variables that drive listing choice. Although both Jegadeesh et al. (2015) and McCourt (2018) argue that their samples are representative of the private fund space, future research should explore a formal model of the listing decision to analyze this question in more depth. Third, the pressures and incentives of having permanent public capital may change GPs' incentives and result in different risk and return profiles of the underlying investment portfolios compared to unlisted, private PE vehicles.

As a final point, many of the listed funds, though publicly traded, are still quite illiquid, raising the question how accurately market prices and returns reflect underlying valuations. Moreover, the permanence of public capital means that there is no forced final liquidation of the portfolio, so that misvaluation can persist for even longer periods of time than in the private limited partnerships. The fact that payout policies of the listed vehicles tend to be highly smoothed also does not help to alleviate this concern. Thus, market returns of listed funds may not capture all the underlying (co)variation of PE returns. Several papers in the traded vehicles literature use Dimson corrections to deal with this, but more work is needed to establish whether this is sufficient to obtain unbiased factor model estimates.

6 Investment level data

Analyzing returns at the investment level has two distinct advantages over fund-level data. First, investment-level data are reported before fees, allowing for direct assessment of GP skill. Second, one could estimate risk and return for specific industries, geographies, cohorts, and other characteristics, whereas funds are a mix of multiple investments across a broad set of attributes (this is true even for specialized funds such as early-stage U.S. VC funds). One could even assess performance for individual PE firm partners based on the portfolio companies they are associated with (see, for example, the VC partner fixed effect estimation in Ewens and Rhodes-Kropf, 2015).

Estimates of risk factor loadings and risk-adjusted returns differ between investment-level and fund-level data. Fig. 1 shows that for VC, the average (median) CAPM beta estimate across papers that use investment data is 1.8 (1.9), compared to 1.7 (1.4) from fund data. For buyout, the investment-level beta is 2.0 (2.2), vs 1.3 (1.1) for funds. Risk-adjusted returns are also materially higher in investment-level data. Fees are a natural explanation for the lower net-of-fee risk-adjusted returns, although the quantitative effect has not been analyzed directly.[ah] For betas, the effect

[ah]Metrick and Yasuda (2010a) and Stafford (2022) simulate the effect of fees on fund performance, but to my knowledge, no paper has analyzed the effect of a specific fund's (actual) fees on its performance and compared this with the gross and net-of-fee estimates in the literature. Robinson and Sensoy (2013) and Hüther et al. (2020) come closest. The former have fund-specific fee data and net-of-fee fund performance, but they do not have gross-of-fee data (without portfolio company level data, reverse-engineering the gross-of-fee fund returns is not possible in their data). The latter have both gross and net-of-fee data, but only for a small subset of funds, and their analysis focuses on the investment level, which is discussed in Section 6.

of fees is more subtle. Consider carried interest: the division of profits from investments implies that there is a degree of risk-sharing between GPs and LPs. As a result, the LPs' exposure is less sensitive to market (up)swings than the underlying portfolio of investments.[ai] On the other hand, management fees are paid according to a predetermined schedule, and so they might function somewhat akin to the way leverage raises a company's equity beta.[aj] Ultimately, the effect of fees on betas is still an open question.

While the differences in alpha and beta estimates could be consistent with the effect of fees, they can also stem from differences in data sources (which cover different parts of the population), sample periods, and methodologies. Hüther et al. (2020) is a unique paper in this respect, because the authors have data from one single (large) LP who collected both pre-fee and post-fee cash flows for 85 U. S. VC funds raised between 1992 and 2005 that invested in 3552 portfolio companies. This allows them to compute fund performance both before and after fees. The difference between the average (median) gross-of-fee and net-of-fee PME relative to the Nasdaq ranges from 0.23 to 0.41 (0.17 to 0.33), depending on vintage years. The difference is larger when PME is high, consistent with carried interest payments being higher when funds perform well. Unfortunately, the sample is rather small, and the paper does not consider the difference in gross and net betas (this is not its focal interest).

Besides sampling variation, beta estimates could differ because many fund beta estimates are based mostly or entirely on cash flows while investment-level estimates tend to rely on total returns that include both cash flows and valuations (for example, round-to-round returns in VC). In essence, the question is whether the difference is due to differences in cash flow and discount rate betas? Boyer et al. (2022a) report lower risk-adjusted fund returns after accounting for discount rate risk using secondary market transactions data, compared to using cash flows only. On the one hand, this suggests that discount rate risk indeed matters, and that "total" beta (including both cash flow and discount rate risk) of PE funds is higher than cash flow beta alone. On the other hand, their results further widen the gap between (lower) fund-level and (higher) investment-level risk-adjusted returns.

Finally, in VC, the heavy use of post-money valuations in investment-level data could distort results in a way that fund cash flows do not (apart from NAVs,

---

[ai]A more technical explanation is that carried interest can be thought of as a call option on the portfolio of investments that LPs have written to GPs. The factor loading of carried interest is the option's elasticity times the corresponding factor loading of the underlying portfolio of investments. Since the elasticity of a call option is above one, the beta of carried interest is higher than that of the underlying portfolio. As a result, the net-of-fee beta should be lower than the gross-of-fee beta. The strength of the impact of carried interest on betas may depend on the timing of carried interest payments (see Hüther et al., 2020). See also Metrick and Yasuda (2010a) and Ang et al. (2018) for a discussion of carried interest as an option.

[aj]Additionally, since there is some flexibility on the part of the GP regarding the timing of capital calls to pay management fees, this could lead to some degree of systematic risk in these fees. In practice, this risk is likely to be very low.

if used).[ak] With all these potential explanations floating around, future research should identify the relative importance of the various channels and reconcile the investment-level and fund-level estimates.

The remainder of this section considers an array of performance measures for investment-level data. A key issue in many of these data sets, especially in VC, is that data are nonrandomly missing, and a large part of this section is devoted to ways of dealing with this problem.

6.1 Cash flow-based performance measures

Investment-level performance can be computed based on each deal's cash flows, either for the portfolio company as a whole or as experienced from a single GP's perspective. Based on these cash flows one can compute the standard performance metrics, such as TVPI, IRR, and (G)PME, for each investment. In VC, the cash flows for a specific portfolio company are the investments made in each round of financing, and the ultimate payoff. The payoff can be measured as the value at exit (IPO or acquisition) or when the GP sells its stake in the startup (this may be post-IPO, as VCs often hold on to some of their stake in the company post-IPO, see Basnet et al., 2020, and Jenkinson et al., 2021). In buyout, there may be cash flows before exit, for example from portfolio company dividend payments and monitoring fees charged to the portfolio company by the GPs (as described in Section 2.3).

Most papers that report deal-level TVPIs, IRRs, or GPMEs consider buyout investments only. Overall, they find that gross-of-fee buyout performance has been consistently high over time.

For a sample of 25 public-to-private buyout deals from the early 1980s, Kaplan (1989) reports an average (median) total nominal return of the buyout capital, both the debt and equity claims, of 127.9% (111.3%), realized over an average period of 2.7 years. As this return is measured from the initial buyout date until exit, with no observed intermediate cash flows, this corresponds to a TVPI multiple of 2.28 (2.11). Adjusted for the contemporaneous market return, the average (median) return is 41.9% (28.0%). The returns to the equity investors (that is, the PE fund) are significantly higher.

Groh and Gottschalg (2011) collect data from private placement memoranda (PPMs) of buyout funds. A PPM contains the full history of deals for a GP, and include intermediate cash flows such as dividends, but there may be selection regarding the institutions that are willing to share their information. For a total of 133 U.S. buyout deals that took place between 1984 and 2004, the average (median) annual IRR is 50.1% (35.7%), earned by GPs over an average holding period of 3.8 years.

Franzoni et al. (2012) have data on 4403 completed buyouts that were closed between 1975 and 2006, sourced from CEPRES. The data, which are voluntarily disclosed by GPs, primarily cover buyouts in the U.S. and Europe. Like Groh and

---

[ak]I refer the reader back to Section 3.6 for a more detailed discussion of post-money vs fundamental valuations.

Gottschalg, the data also contain the exact cash flows, including any intermediate dividends, of each deal. They report a value-weighted mean TVPI of 2.52 and a modified IRR of 19%.[al]

Four papers report buyout PMEs. Guo et al. (2011) compute a market- and risk-adjusted return that is essentially a PME calculation but expressed as a percentage return. Their discount rate is a CAPM-based expected return estimate. For 90 public-to-private buyouts of U.S. firms between 1990 and 2006, they estimate that buyout investors earned an average (median) CAPM-benchmarked PME of 1.63 (1.41). However, these results are based on deals for which post-buyout data is available, raising success bias concerns. Acharya et al. (2013) compute PMEs using the sector return as the discount rate and report an average (median) of 1.88 (1.37) across 395 large buyout deals, based on proprietary deal-level data. Braun et al. (2017) report a median TVPI of 1.5 and PME of 1.3 for a large sample of 12,541 buyout investments between 1974 and 2013. Their data represent the near-complete deal history of GPs that raised capital from three large fund-of-fund managers. For the 7568 fully realized deals in their sample, the median TVPI and PME numbers are 1.9 and 1.4, respectively. Finally, Brown et al. (2020) have a large data set of portfolio companies collected by Burgiss. Across 15,095 buyout deals they report an average (median) TVPI of 2.14 (1.56) and an average (median) PME with respect to the S&P 500 of 1.45 (1.06).

Brown et al. (2020) have a large data set of 31,206 VC deals, showing an average (median) TVPI of 2.13 (1.00), and an average (median) PME of 1.35 (0.71). Not surprisingly, the outcomes of VC deals are significantly more volatile compared to buyout deals. In comparison, Hüther et al. (2020) report gross-of-fee VC fund PMEs (with respect to the Nasdaq) between 0.85 and 1.19 (0.85 and 1.06), across buckets of vintages. In line with the literature, pre-1998 vintages are at the high end of this range and post-1999 vintages are at the low end.

6.2 Index methods

An alternative to the pure cash flow-based approach is to incorporate additional valuation data. In particular, in VC, the post-money valuation of the startup (defined in Section 3.6) is observed when it raises a new financing round, providing intermediate indications of value over the investment horizon. I start by describing a two-step approach that first constructs an aggregate price index, and then estimates a factor model on the index returns.

6.2.1 Repeat-sales regression

Repeat-sales regressions are a standard approach to impute missing valuations, borrowed from the real estate literature (e.g., Bailey et al., 1963; Case and Shiller, 1987, 1989), where they are traditionally used to compute home price indices such as the

---

[al]The modified IRR allows for the specification of a reinvestment rate, making it less sensitive to the reinvestment assumption implied by the traditional IRR.

Table 8 Repeat-sales regression illustration.

Year	1	2	3	4
A	1	1.5	[1.875]	[2.5]
B		4	5	[6.67]
C	2	[3]	[3.75]	5
RSR return	N/A	50%	25%	33%

This highly stylized example illustrates the intuition behind repeat-sales regressions (RSR). The table shows the valuations for three fictitious startups (A, B, and C) at the time of their fundraising rounds. The numbers in square brackets are the imputed valuations that the RSR approach would assign to these startups in the periods where no valuations are observed. The final row shows the RSR index return. Note that there is no imputed valuation for startup B in year 1, as the company only raises its first round of funding in year 2.

S&P/Case-Shiller index. Its key intuition can be conveyed succinctly with a stylized example (see OECD, 2013, for a thorough yet accessible treatise). Suppose we have valuations for three startups (named A, B, and C) as shown in Table 8. Startup A raised money in year 1 at a valuation of $1 million and had another financing round in year 2 at $1.5 million. Company B raised its first round at a value of $4 million in year 2 and at $5 million in year 3, and C had funding rounds at $2 million and $5 million valuations in years 1 and 4. As is typical in VC, none of the companies paid dividends over the sample period.

RSR assumes that all startups have the same expected return over the same period. Since startup A had a 50% return from year 1 to year 2, we can impute company C's expected value to be $3 million in year 2 (shown in square brackets in Table 8 to indicate this is an imputed value). For year 3, we impute the value of A and C to have grown by 25% from year 2, which is the observed return on B over this period. The 1-year return from year 3 to year 4 can now be found from startup C, which grew from an imputed value of $3.75 million to an observed value of $5 million, or 33%.

Doing these imputations by hand is easy in this simple example, but quickly becomes intractable in large samples with many startups and time periods. Fortunately, it is possible to formulate the problem in regression form. Assume the following process for the natural logarithm of log-valuations of startup i,

$$v_{i,t}^{PRE} = v_{i,t-1}^{POST} + \phi_t + \varepsilon_{i,t}, \tag{25}$$

where $v_{i,t-1}^{POST}$ is the log of the post-money valuation (as explained in Section 3.6) at time $t\text{-}1$, and $v_{i,t}^{PRE}$ is the log of the pre-money valuation at time t. The pre-money valuation for a financing round is simply the post-money valuation (in the same round) minus the invested amount (if no capital infusion occurs, then pre- and post-money valuations in the same period are equal). The ϕ_t parameter is the one-period log-return on the repeat-sales index, which is common to all startups. The residual $\varepsilon_{i,t}$ is assumed to be mean zero.

The purpose of computing the log-value change from post-money to pre-money is to measure the actual return experienced by an investor. To see this, note that a capital infusion mechanically raises the (post-money) value of the company, but does not change the investor's wealth, just like a share issuance for cash in itself does not change a company's share price. For example, consider a startup with a $100 post-money valuation at t-1. Suppose that no value was created from *t-1* to *t*, and the company raises $50 in equity at time *t*. The post-money valuation at *t*, which is measured right after the cash infusion, is then $150, and the pre-money valuation is $100. Thus, the return measured as the post-money at *t*-1 to pre-money at *t* correctly reflects the investor's actual return over the period, which is zero.[am] Note that the resulting index represents an investor's buy-and-hold experience, not the aggregate value of all startups (to get the latter index, only post-money valuations should be used).

The log-return over a horizon τ, is then

$$v_{i,t+\tau}^{PRE} - v_{i,t}^{POST} = \sum_{s=1}^{\tau} v_{i,t+s}^{PRE} - v_{i,t+s-1}^{POST} = \sum_{s=1}^{\tau} \phi_{t+s} + \sum_{s=1}^{\tau} \varepsilon_{i,t+s}. \quad (26)$$

Eq. (26) suggests that we can estimate the ϕ parameters from a regression of observed log-returns (e.g., round-to-round returns or round-to-exit returns) on a set of indicator variables, one for each period except the very first one. The indicators for a given startup equal one if the period is in between sales, and zero otherwise (the period at which the investment is first made is also zero, but the period in which the next value is observed equals one). For example, the regression for the Table 8 example is (assuming that the first and second values for each firm are post-money and pre-money valuations, respectively, and there are no intermediate capital infusions)

$$\begin{bmatrix} \ln(1.5) - \ln(1) \\ \ln(5) - \ln(4) \\ \ln(5) - \ln(2) \end{bmatrix} = \begin{bmatrix} 1 & 0 & 0 \\ 0 & 1 & 0 \\ 1 & 1 & 1 \end{bmatrix} \cdot \begin{bmatrix} \phi_2 \\ \phi_3 \\ \phi_4 \end{bmatrix} + \begin{bmatrix} \eta_2 \\ \eta_3 \\ \eta_4 \end{bmatrix}. \quad (27)$$

The numbering of ϕ's and η's starting at 2 is a result of dropping the very first period of valuations. The η's are sums of ε's, per Eq. (26), and assumed to be mean zero and orthogonal to the indicator matrix, analogous to the standard ordinary least squares (OLS) identification assumption (we will revisit this assumption soon).

[am]Footnote 18 of Korteweg and Nagel (2016) describes a more elaborate example of the importance of computing post- to pre-money returns. Note also that Eq. (25) is consistent with a log-version of the fund NAV return calculation in Eq. (4) if NAVs are interpreted as post-money valuations (portfolio company values are usually equated to post-money valuations when financing rounds occur). With no dividends (i.e., no distributions), the return in Eq. (4) equals the pre-money valuation (post-money valuation minus invested amount, i.e., capital calls) at time *t* divided by the post-money valuation at *t-1*.

The OLS estimates of the ϕ's are 0.4055, 0.2231, and 0.2877. Exponentiating the estimates produces the 50%, 25%, and 33% returns that we found above.[an] Any additional financing rounds of the same startups can be added as separate return observations.

OLS estimation is efficient if the residuals in Eq. (27) have equal variance across observations. But the η's are sums of one-period residual log-returns $\varepsilon_{i,t}$ from Eq. (25). If the ε's have constant variance, σ^2, and if they are uncorrelated over time, then the η corresponding to a return over τ periods has variance $\tau\sigma^2$. In other words, the residuals in Eq. (27) are heteroskedastic. The weighted least squares (WLS) estimator is therefore more efficient than OLS, weighing each observation by the reciprocal of the time between sales. In the example, the weight matrix is a diagonal matrix in which the first two observations receive a weight of 1, but the third observation receives a weight of 1/3 (equivalently, one can multiply each observation by the square root of these weights and run OLS on the transformed variables). However, the real estate literature has found that residual variances do not scale linearly with τ, and do not approach zero as τ shrinks (e.g., Case and Shiller, 1987; Giacoletti, 2021; Sagi, 2021). This result is attributed to house-specific shocks that do not scale with time between sales, for example due to search frictions. Axelson et al. (2014) find a similar result for buyout investments, and I suspect a similar phenomenon applies to startups. Another critique of OLS and WLS estimation, and indeed much of the literature on investment-level returns, is that cross-correlations in the error terms are assumed to be zero. But, contemporaneous ε's are likely to be positively correlated, and to the extent that return horizons overlap, so are the η's. While the OLS and WLS estimators are still unbiased and consistent, reported standard errors that ignore these correlations are too low. Unfortunately, there is no easy clustering fix to allow for cross-correlations that is consistent with the underlying model. See Korteweg and Nagel (2016) for a standard error estimator that accounts for the return overlap.

The assumption that all startups have the same expected return (the same ϕ's) can be relaxed by allowing for covariates (e.g., Korteweg and Sørensen, 2016). For example, each industry can have its own price index, allowing for different expected returns in, say, biotech vs software. This approach is related to Gompers and Lerner (1997), who use publicly-traded industry returns to impute the unobserved valuations of portfolio companies (see the description in Section 3.5.4).

[an]There is more than one way to set up the RSR. The more traditional approach is to set the indicators to -1 in the period of the first observed valuation, and to $+1$ at the second observed valuation date, with zeros in between (and excluding the very first period, as above). The left-hand side is the same as in Eq. (27), and the regressor matrix is [1 0 0; -1 1 0; 0 0 1]. The estimated parameters are now the log price index (not the log-return on the price index), but the end result is identical. This formulation is slightly more efficient when there are many startups, due to the multiplication and inversion of sparser matrices, but it is one step removed from returns. For clarity of the exposition, which focuses on returns, I have chosen the alternative setup shown in the main text.

6.2.2 Selection bias

An important challenge that needs to be dealt with in commercial investment-level data sets is success bias. This is especially important in VC, as the final outcome for many startups remains unobserved. This can be seen in Fig. 6, which shows a pie chart of outcomes for 18,237 startups that were first funded between 1987 and 2005. By the end of the sample period, 10.4% has gone public, 23.4% were acquired, 15.9% had failed, and 50.4% had an unknown outcome. Some of these companies were still private at the end of the sample period, because not enough time had passed since first funding (a right-censoring problem). However, many firms had their last funding round years before the sample ended: in a different sample from the 2013 National Venture Capital Association Yearbook, as many as 35% of 11,686 startups that were first funded between 1991 and 2000, still had an unknown outcome by 2010. While these firms are likely out of business, this event was never recorded. As such, they are sometimes referred to as zombie firms, as they are dead but still appear to be alive.[ao] The reason for this success bias is that IPOs and large acquisitions are fairly easy to observe from filings and other disclosures, whereas failures and small acquisitions (many of which occur at a loss to the original investors) are not widely publicized. Thus, round-to-round or round-to-exit returns, which require at least two valuation observations for a given firm, are more likely to be observed for startups that are ultimately successful.

The consequence of the selection problem is that the RSR index returns are upward biased.[ap] Econometrically, selection shows up as a correlation between the error terms and the covariates in Eq. (27): firms that have a positive return shock (η) are more likely to be observed, that is, they are more likely to have ones in the indicator matrix. This correlation between residuals and explanatory variables violates the regression identification assumption and results in biased estimates of the RSR returns (ϕ).[aq]

Peng (2001) addresses the sample selection problem by estimating separate RSR indices for successes and failures with known outcomes. For the zombie firms (with unknown outcomes), he uses a nonparametric model to assign a probability of success to each firm in each period. He then distributes the value of the zombie companies

---

[ao]Other than zombie firms, the set of firms with unknown outcomes includes firms that have only recently started and haven't had enough time to reach an exit (a right-censoring issue), and "lifestyle" companies that are still in business but haven't had to raise funding in years. The latter are not likely to produce much value to the VC investors, even if they provide a means of income to the founders.

[ap]Success bias is also a potential concern for the cash flow-based measures discussed in Section 6.1, if failures are nonrandomly missing. Unlike commercial data sets, proprietary investment-level data often include the entire universe of deals that an LP or GP invested in, with final outcomes, and are therefore not subject to the same success bias. However, since these data are often sourced from one or a few LPs or GPs, selection bias can still be an issue if these investors are not representative of the population. Fund-level performance measures are also not usually subject to success bias at the fund level, since all investments (both successes and failures) will be accounted for by the time funds are liquidated. But, there may be selection bias in which funds are included in the data set.

[aq]The existence of sample selection bias in RSR was first suggested in real estate by Haurin and Hendershott (1991). Wallace and Meese (1997) show empirical evidence. A number of papers in real estate apply standard selection models to the problem (e.g., Jud and Seaks, 1994; Gatzlaff and Haurin, 1997, 1998; Munneke and Slade, 2000, 2001; Hwang and Quigley, 2004; Goetzmann and Peng, 2006).

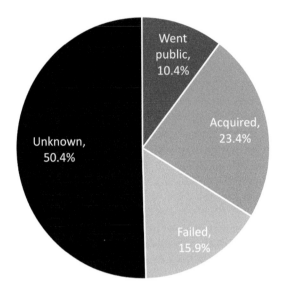

FIG. 6

Pie chart of the outcomes of a sample of 18,237 startup companies that were first funded between 1987 and 2005.

Source: Korteweg, A., Sørensen, M., 2010. Risk and return characteristics of venture capital–backed entrepreneurial companies. Rev. Financ. Stud. 23, 3738–3772.

across the success and failure indices, according to the estimated probabilities. Finally, he combines the two indices based on their relative NAVs. Peng then estimates factor loadings by regressing the monthly index returns on the excess return of the S&P 500. On a sample of 5634 startups that were first funded by VCs between 1987 and 1999, he estimates a market beta of 1.3 and a statistically insignificant alpha of −0.2% per month (and this is based on standard errors that too low since the second step ignores the estimation error in the index; more on this below). Using annual returns instead, he finds a beta of 2.4 and an alpha of −0.9% per year. This result is rather puzzling, since there is no obvious reason why the beta should change with measurement frequency, and why alpha does not scale with horizon.

Woodward and Hall (2004) use an RSR model and impute missing valuations after the last observed round for a company as a function of company characteristics and the amount of time that has passed since the last observed funding event. Unfortunately, the paper is not very detailed in how exactly this imputation is performed.[ar]

[ar]Hall and Woodward (2010) and Ouyang et al. (2021) appear to use a similar imputation method as in Woodward and Hall (2004), and provide more details on the algorithm: based on a subset of data without missing financing round data, they fit a regression on observed round data (primarily the round number, amount raised) and other covariates (e.g., Hall and Woodward include the increase in the Wilshire 2000 index in the preceding 2 years). They then use the fitted model to impute the missing round data in the full sample. Neither paper applies RSR: Hall and Woodward (2010) are interested in the returns to entrepreneurs, and Ouyang et al. compute GPME performance statistics.

A more fleshed out implementation of the same idea appears in Hwang et al. (2005), who follow Heckman (1979) and consider sample selection as an omitted-variables problem. They employ a two-step method. The first step is an ordered probit model that estimates the probability of observing a funding round of each firm in each period, as a function of observable characteristics. The second step uses the inverse Mills ratio of the first step to correct the RSR for selection bias. In an updated version of Peng's (2001) VC data, with companies funded between 1987 and 2003, they estimate an S&P 500 market beta of 0.6 and a statistically insignificant quarterly alpha of 0.9%. Relative to the Nasdaq, the alpha is 1.0%. Like most other papers in the literature, they find higher alphas in the pre-2000 period, of 3.5% per quarter.[as]

Some commercial indices also recognize the sample selection issue. For example, the Refinitiv Venture Capital Research Index (formerly the Thompson Reuters Venture Capital Research Index) estimates the value of each company over time, estimating missing values and interpolating values between financing rounds.[at] It uses a Heckman correction for missing rounds and assigns failures as having occurred 1 year after final observed round if the startup is currently listed as defunct.[au]

6.3 Round-to-round returns

The two-step approach of the previous section produces both an index (the first step) and factor model estimates (the second step). If we are only interested in the factor model estimates, we can skip the index and directly use the returns from one valuation observation to the next (e.g., from deal inception to exit, or, for VC, between financing rounds). This alternative yields proper standard errors, unlike applications of the index approach, which typically ignore estimation error in the index when estimating the factor model.

To estimate factor loadings directly from returns, replace the value process in Eq. (25) with

---

[as]Hwang et al. (2005) also explore a hybrid model that combines RSR with a hedonic model (hybrid models in real estate have been proposed, among others, by Case and Quigley, 1991). A hedonic price index can help to mitigate sample selection bias in real estate indices by allowing for the inclusion of single-sale homes, which may be systematically different from homes that have sold multiple times. In hedonic models, values are imputed using estimated shadow prices on a range of observed characteristics. A pure hedonic model is not particularly useful in PE, as very few portfolio company characteristics are usually observed, and most of their value is in difficult-to-observe and unique intellectual property and growth options.

[at]See https://www.refinitiv.com/content/dam/marketing/en_us/documents/methodology/venture-capital-research-index-methodology.pdf for a description of the index construction methodology.

[au]While not uncommon, setting values for deemed-liquidated companies to zero at some exogenously-chosen time after the last observed round is problematic, as the exact timing of exit can matter quite a bit for estimates of risk and return.

$$v_{i,t}^{PRE} = v_{i,t-1}^{POST} + r_t^F + \delta + \beta' f_t + \varepsilon_{i,t}. \tag{28}$$

Eq. (28) simply replaces the index return, ϕ_t, with a log-factor model, where f_t are (log) factors and β is a vector of loadings. The log risk free rate, r_t^F, accounts for the fact that factor models are specified on excess returns, so that δ is a risk-adjusted log-return. Note the similarity of this model and the log-factor model implied by the exponential-affine SDF model with lognormal returns from Korteweg and Nagel (2016) that was described in Section 3.7.2. The counterpart to the longer-horizon log return in Eq. (26) is

$$v_{i,t+\tau}^{PRE} - v_{i,t}^{POST} = \sum_{s=1}^{\tau} r_{t+s}^F + \tau\delta + \beta' \sum_{s=1}^{\tau} f_{t+s} + \sum_{s=1}^{\tau} \varepsilon_{i,t+s}. \tag{29}$$

The δ and β parameters can thus be estimated by regressing observed portfolio company returns (from round-to-round or round-to-exit) in excess of the log risk-free rate (over the same period) on the return horizon, τ (which varies by observation), and the log factor returns (also over the same period). Analogous to RSR, observations can be weighted to improve efficiency of the estimator in light of heteroskedastic residuals, and cross-correlations in the error term due to overlapping observations should be accounted for in computing standard errors. The δ and β estimates can be transformed from the log model to arithmetic alpha and factor loadings using the formulas in footnote 5 in Cochrane (2005a) for the market model and footnote 1 in Korteweg and Sørensen (2010) for the multifactor model (in the remainder of this section I will use alpha to refer to the arithmetic alpha).[av]

An application of the above methodology is in Axelson et al. (2014). They have data on all 2075 investments made by a single buyout fund of funds. Running a WLS regression on Eq. (29), they estimate a log-CAPM annual delta of -4.6% and beta of 2.4. The annual arithmetic return alpha implied by the model is 8.6%. Allowing for jumps in values (that may arise from the illiquid nature of buyouts), does not significantly impact the beta estimate, but increases the arithmetic alpha to 16.3% per year. Axelson et al. rationalize their beta, which is at the higher end of the estimated range (see Fig. 1), from a Modigliani-Miller calculation based on an unlevered asset beta of 0.66 and a leverage ratio that is typical for buyouts.

Axelson et al. (2014) argue that selection bias is less of a concern in buyout compared to VC, and they therefore do not make any adjustments for selection bias. Papers in VC do grapple with the issue. Ewens et al. (2016) adjust for selection by reweighing ultimate outcomes (IPO, acquisition, or known failure) in their observed-returns sample to match the exit rates in their full sample that includes companies with missing valuation data. Using returns from initial capital infusion to exit for 13,035 VC investments between 1990 and 2008, they estimate a log-CAPM beta of 2.3. Their estimated δ is -10.5% per year, which maps to an arithmetic annual risk-adjusted return of 45.6%. For the Fama and French 3-factor model, they estimate

---

[av]Since the RSR value process is also specified in logs, the index calculation also needs an adjustment to compute arithmetic returns (see Goetzmann, 1992).

a market factor loading of 2.2, an SMB loading of -0.4, and an insignificant HML loading. Korteweg and Nagel (2016) also follow the reweighting approach to estimate the average GPMEs for individual VC deals, and find estimates in the order of 0.52–0.61, depending on what they assume about the returns to known liquidations without liquidation valuations. Given an average time between round of about 1 year, this implies an approximately 52–61% annual return.

Two papers, Cochrane (2005a) and Korteweg and Sørensen (2010), take a more structural approach to the selection problem. Both papers use Eq. (29) and add a selection equation that models the probability of observing a financing round. Cochrane (2005a) considers the log-CAPM and models the selection as a function of the startup's underlying value only. Korteweg and Sørensen (2010) formulate the problem as a state-space model, allowing for multiple risk factors and for additional covariates in the selection equation. They also point out that the empirical problem is more complicated than the standard Heckman (1979) setup, which assumes that periods with unobserved valuations are uninformative about the valuation process. In reality, because valuations are dynamically linked over time through Eq. (29), these periods are still useful in estimating the parameters of the price process. Cochrane (2005a) estimates a selection-corrected log-CAPM beta of 1.9 with respect to the S&P 500, and an annual arithmetic alpha of 32% (39% if using the Nasdaq instead, with a beta of 1.4). In contrast, without selection correction the arithmetic annual alpha is a mind-boggling 462%. Korteweg and Sørensen (2010) estimate a log-CAPM beta of 2.8, and an alpha that's more or less equal to Cochrane's, at 3.3% per month. Splitting the time-series, they find that the positive alpha is primarily coming from the internet boom of 1994–2000, when the monthly alpha was 5.8%. From 2000 to 2005, the end of their sample period, the alpha was negative at -2.6%. For the Fama and French 3-factor model they estimate a market factor loading of 2.3, an SMB loading of 1.1, and an HML loading of -1.6, implying (consistent with the literature) that startup companies look like small-growth investments. In an extension of their model, they find that results are robust to allowing for startup-specific alphas and betas (see their appendix A.5).

Buchner (2020) deals with selection by explicitly modeling the cash flow process of each investment. He estimates a VC beta of 2.6 and an annual alpha of 8.9% using a sample of 6380 startups from 1980 to 2005. For a sample of 4418 buyout deals he reports a beta of 2.2 and an annual alpha of 7.0%. He finds a similar time-series pattern of VC alphas as Korteweg and Sørensen (2010). Consistent with the literature, risk-adjusted performance for buyouts has been consistently strong throughout the sample period.

Finally, estimates of idiosyncratic volatility for startups (that is, the standard deviation of $\varepsilon_{i,t}$ in Eq. 28) are of independent interest for a variety of applications, such as contingent claims valuation models that price the securities purchased by VCs (e.g., Metrick and Yasuda, 2010b; Gornall and Strebulaev, 2020). Reported volatility estimates range from just below 90% to over 140% per year: Cochrane (2005a) estimates 86% per year, Korteweg and Sørensen (2010), 142% (41% per month), and Fleckenstein and Longstaff (2020), using a very different sample and methodology, report 95%.

7 Conclusion

Over the last quarter century, significant progress has been made in our understanding of risk and return in PE. At the same time, much remains to be discovered and understood. A key challenge for the literature is to uncover the set of relevant risk factors and their loadings (betas), including gaining a better understanding of the impact of the various dimensions of illiquidity in PE and their impact on risk premia. A second unanswered question is whether PE payoffs can be spanned by public securities, or if there are components to payoffs that are unique to the PE space (and if so, whether these are priced factors or pure alpha)? Third, work is needed to further explore the time-variation in factor loadings and risk-adjusted returns, both in calendar time and over the life of a fund or portfolio company. Fourth, reconciling the pre- and post-fee risk and return estimates is important, especially given the apparent large differences in risk-adjusted returns. Finally, further research is needed into the extent of performance manipulation by GPs and the development of a manipulation-proof risk-adjusted return measure, if one such measure exists.

This chapter has largely been silent on the literature that documents the large heterogeneity in returns experienced by different types of LPs. Performance also appears to be persistently different across GPs. While there has been some recent work toward individual fund benchmarking, much is left to be done to better understand these differences, both methodologically and empirically. This in turn can help answer questions related to the source(s) of persistence in GP and LP performance, whether managers have styles, how contracts between GPs and LPs and between GPs and portfolio companies affect performance, and how PE fits into a portfolio of (public) stocks, bonds, and other securities.

To end on a positive note, the recent convergence in the literature toward the use of stochastic discount factor methods, and the continuing improvements in data quality and coverage, hold promise that significant progress can be made toward answering these questions.

References

Acharya, V.V., Gottschalg, O.F., Hahn, M., Kehoe, C., 2013. Corporate governance and value creation: Evidence from private equity. Rev. Financ. Stud. 26, 368–402.

Agarwal, V., Barber, B., Cheng, S., Hameed, A., Yasuda, A., 2022. Private Company Valuations by Mutual Funds. Rev. Financ. Stud. 26, 368–402.

Albertus, J.F., Denes, M., 2020. Private Equity Fund Debt: Capital Flows, Performance, and Agency Costs. Work. Pap. Carnegie Mellon Univ.

Albuquerque, R., Cassel, J., Phalippou, L., Schroth, E., 2018. Liquidity provision in the secondary market for private equity fund stakes. Work. Pap. Boston College, Univ. Oxford, and EDHEC.

Aliaga-Díaz, R., Renzi-Ricci, G., Ahluwalia, H., Grim, D.M., Tidmore, C., 2020. The Role of Private Equity in Strategic Portfolios. Vanguard Research.

Amornsiripanitch, N., Gompers, P.A., Xuan, Y., 2019. More than money: venture capitalists on boards. J. Law, Economics., and Organization 35, 513–543.

Andonov, A., Kräussl, R., Rauh, J.D., 2021. The subsidy to infrastructure as an asset class. Rev. Financ. Stud. 34, 3880–3994.

Ang, A., Chen, B., Goetzmann, W.N., Phalippou, L., 2018. Estimating private equity returns from limited partner cash flows. J. Finance 73, 1751–1783.

Anson, M.J.P., 2002. Managed pricing and the rule of conservatism in private equity portfolios. J. Priv. Equity 5, 18–30.

Anson, M.J.P., 2007. Performance measurement in private equity: another look. J. Priv. Equity 10, 7–21.

Asness, C.S., Krail, R.J., Liew, J.M., 2001. Do hedge funds hedge? J. Portfolio Manag. 28, 6–19.

Axelson, U., Jenkinson, T., Strömberg, P., Weisbach, M., 2013. Borrow cheap, buy high: the determinants of leverage and pricing in buyouts. J. Finance 68, 2223–2267.

Axelson, U., Sørensen, M., Strömberg, P., 2014. Alpha and beta of buyout deals: a jump CAPM for long-term illiquid investments. Work. Pap. London School of Economics, Dartmouth, and Stockholm School of Economics.

Bailey, M.J., Muth, R.F., Nourse, H.O., 1963. A regression method for real estate price index construction. J. Am. Stat. Assoc. 58, 933–942.

Baker, M., Gompers, P.A., 2003. The determinants of board structure at the initial public offering. J. Law. Econ. 46, 569–598.

Banal-Estañol, A., Ippolito, F., Vicente, S., 2017. Default Penalties in Private Equity Partnerships. Work. Pap. Univ. Pompeu Fabra and Univ. Carlos III Madrid.

Barber, B., Yasuda, A., 2017. Interim fund performance and fundraising in private equity. J. Financ. Econ. 124, 172–194.

Basnet, A., Pukthuanthong, K., Turtle, H., Walker, T., 2020. VC Ownership Post-IPO: When, Why, and How Do VCs Exit? Work Pap. Concordia Univ., Univ. Missouri, and Colo. State Univ.

Begenau, J., Siriwardane, E., 2021. How Do Private Equity Fees Vary across Public Pensions? Work. Pap. Stanford Graduate School of Business.

Berk, J.B., Green, R.C., Naik, V., 2004. Valuation and return dynamics of new ventures. Rev. Financ. Stud. 17, 1–35.

Bernstein, S., Sheen, A., 2016. Operational consequences of private equity buyouts: evidence from the restaurant industry. Rev. Financ. Stud. 29, 2387–2418.

Bernstein, S., Giroud, X., Townsend, R., 2016. The impact of venture capital monitoring. J. Finance 71, 1591–1622.

Bharath, S., Dittmar, A., Sivadasan, J., 2014. Do going-private transactions affect plant efficiency and investment? Rev. Financ. Stud. 27, 1929–1976.

Bilo, S., Christophers, H., Degosciu, M., Zimmermann, H., 2005. Risk, Returns, and Biases of Listed Private Equity Portfolios. Work. Pap. Univ. Basel.

Bisinger, M., Bircan, C., Ljungqvist, A., 2020. Value Creation in Private Equity. Swedish House of Finance Research Paper No. 20-10.

Bollen, N.P.B., Pool, V.K., 2008. Conditional return smoothing in the hedge fund industry. J. Financ. Quant. Anal. 43, 267–298.

Boucly, Q., Sraer, D., Thesmar, D., 2011. Growth LBOs. J. Financ. Econ. 102, 432–453.

Boyer, B.H., Nadauld, T.D., Vorkink, K., Weisbach, M.S., 2022a. Discount rate risk in private equity: evidence from secondary market transactions. J. Finance. forthcoming.

Boyer, B.H., Nadauld, T.D., Vorkink, K., Weisbach, M.S., 2022b. Private Equity Indices Based on Secondary Market Transactions. Work. Pap. Brigham Young Univ. and The Ohio State Univ.

Braun, R., Jenkinson, T., Stoff, I., 2017. How persistent is private equity performance? Evidence from deal-level data. J. Financ. Econ. 123, 273–291.

Braun, R., Jenkinson, T., Schemmerl, C., 2020. Adverse selection and the performance of private equity co-investments. J. Financ. Econ. 136, 44–62.

Brophy, D.J., Guthner, M.W., 1988. Publicly traded venture capital funds: implications for institutional "fund of funds" investors. J. Bus. Venturing 3, 187–206.

Brown, G.W., Gredil, O., Kaplan, S.N., 2019. Do private equity funds manipulate returns? J. Financ. Econ. 132, 267–297.

Brown, G.W., Harris, R.S., Hu, W., Jenkinson, T., Kaplan, S.N., Robinson, D., 2020. Private Equity Portfolios: A First Look at Burgiss Holdings Data. Work. Pap. Univ. North Carolina, Univ. Virginia, Burgiss, Univ. Oxford, Univ. Chicago, Duke Univ.

Brown, G.W., Ghysels, E., Gredil, O., 2021a. Nowcasting Net Asset Values: The Case of Private Equity. Work. Pap. Univ. North Carolina and Tulane Univ.

Brown, G.W., Hu, W., Kuhn, B.-K., 2021b. Private Investments in Diversified Portfolio. Work. Pap. Univ. North Carolina and Burgiss.

Buchner, A., 2016. Risk-adjusting the returns of private equity using the CAPM and multi-factor extensions. Finance Res. Lett. 16, 154–161.

Buchner, A., 2020. The Alpha and Beta of Private Equity Investments. Work. Pap. Univ. Passau.

Buchner, A., Stucke, R., 2014. The Systematic Risk of Private Equity. Work. Pap. Univ. Passau and Univ. Oxford.

Cao, C., Farnsworth, G., Liang, B., Lo, A., 2017. Return smoothing, liquidity costs, and investor flows: evidence from a separate account platform. Manag. Sci. 63, 2049–2395.

Carhart, M.M., 1997. On persistence in mutual fund performance. J. Finance 52, 57–82.

Case, B., Quigley, J., 1991. The dynamics of real estate prices. Rev. Econ. and Stat. 73, 50–58.

Case, K.E., Shiller, R.J., 1987. Prices of single-family homes since 1970: new indexes for four cities. N. Engl. Econ. Rev., 46–56.

Case, K.E., Shiller, R.J., 1989. The efficiency of the market for single-family homes. Am. Econ. Rev. 79, 125–137.

Cassar, G., Gerakos, J., 2011. Hedge funds: pricing controls and the smoothing of self-reported returns. Rev. Financ. Stud. 24, 1698–1734.

Cederburg, S., Stoughton, N., 2020. Discretionary NAVs. Work. Pap. Univ. Arizona and Vienna Univ.

Chakraborty, I., Ewens, M., 2018. Managing performance signals through delay: evidence from venture capital. Manag. Sci. 64, 2875–2900.

Chen, S., Li, T., 2020. A Unified Duration-Based Explanation of the Value, Profitability, and Investment Anomalies. Work. Pap. Southw. Univ. Financ. Econ. and City Univ. Hong Kong.

Chernenko, S., Lerner, J., Zeng, Y., 2021. Mutual funds as venture capitalists? Evidence from unicorns. Rev. Financ. Stud. 34, 2362–2410.

Cochrane, J.H., 2005a. The risk and return of venture capital. J. Financ. Econ. 75, 3–52.

Cochrane, J.H., 2005b. Asset Pricing, second ed. Princeton Univ. Press, New Jersey.

Cochrane, J.H., 2021. Portfolios for Long-Term Investors. Work. Pap. Stanford Univ.

Cohn, J.B., Hotchkiss, E., Towery, E., 2020. The Motives for Private Equity Buyouts of Private Firms: Evidence from U.S. Corporate Tax Returns. Work. Pap. Univ. Texas Austin, Boston College and Univ, Georgia.

Cordell, L., Roberts, M.R., Schwert, M., 2021. CLO Performance. Work. Pap. Fed. Reserve Bank of Philadelphia and Univ, Pennsylvania.

Couts, S., Gonçalves, A., Rossi, A., 2020. Unsmoothing Returns of Illiquid Funds. Work. Pap. Univ. Southern Calif., Univ. North Carolina, and Univ. Arizona.

Cumming, D., Walz, U., 2010. Private equity returns and disclosure around the world. J. Intern. Bus. Stud. 41, 727–754.

Cumming, D., Fleming, G., Johan, S.A., 2011. Institutional investment in listed private equity. European Fin. Manag. 17, 594–618.

Da Rin, M., Phalippou, L., 2017. The importance of size in private equity: evidence from a survey of limited partners. J. Finan. Intermed. 31, 64–76.

Davis, S.J., Haltiwanger, J., Handley, K., Jarmin, R., Lerner, J., Miranda, J., 2014. Private equity, jobs, and productivity. Amer. Econ. Rev. 104, 3956–3990.

DeChow, P.M., Sloan, R.G., Soliman, M., 2004. Implied equity duration: a new measure of equity risk. Rev. Acc. Stud. 9, 197–228.

DeLuce, A., 2020. Private Equity Fees and Terms Study. Callan Institute Research Study.

Dimson, E., 1979. Risk measurement when shares are subject to infrequent trading. J. Financ. Econ. 7, 197–226.

Driessen, J., Lin, T.-C., Phalippou, L., 2012. A new method to estimate risk and return of nontraded assets from cash flows: the case of private equity funds. J. Financ. Quant. Anal. 47, 511–535.

Easton, P.D., Larocque, S., Sustersic Stevens, J., 2021. Private equity valuation before and after ASC 820. J. Inv. Manag. 19, 105–135.

Edgerton, J., 2012. Agency problems in public firms: evidence from corporate jets in leveraged buyouts. J. Finance 67, 2187–2213.

Emery, K., 2003. Private equity risk and reward: assessing the stale pricing problem. J. Priv. Equity 6, 43–50.

Espen Eckbo, B., Lithell, M., 2021. Merger-Driven Listing Dynamics. Work. Pap. Dartmouth College and Norwegian Sch. Econ.

Ewens, M., 2009. A New Model of Venture Capital Risk and Return. Work. Pap. UC San Diego.

Ewens, M., Marx, M., 2018. Founder replacement and startup performance. Rev. Financ. Stud. 31, 1532–1565.

Ewens, M., Rhodes-Kropf, M., 2015. Is a VC partnership greater than the sum of its partners? J. Finance 70, 1081–1113.

Ewens, M., Jones, C.M., Rhodes-Kropf, M., 2013. The price of diversifiable risk in venture capital and private equity. Rev. Financ. Stud. 26, 1854–1889.

Ewens, M., Rhodes-Kropf, M., Strebulaev, I., 2016. Insider Financing and Venture Capital Returns. Work. Pap. Caltech, MIT, and Stanford Univ.

Ewens, M., Gorbenko, A., Korteweg, A., 2022. Venture capital contracts. J. Financ. Econ. 143, 131–158.

Fama, E.F., French, K.R., 1993. Common risk factors in the returns on stocks and bonds. J. Financ. Econ. 33, 3–56.

Fama, E.F., French, K.R., 2015. A five-factor asset pricing model. J. Financ. Econ. 75, 3–52.

Fama, E.F., MacBeth, J.D., 1974. Long-term growth in a short-term market. J. Finance 29, 857–885.

Fang, L., Ivashina, V., Lerner, J., 2015. The disintermediation of financial markets: direct investing in private equity. J. Financ. Econ. 116, 160–178.

Fisher, J.D., Geltner, D.M., Webb, R.B., 1994. Value indices of commercial real estate: a comparison of index construction methods. J. Real Estate Finance and Econ. 9, 137–164.

Fleckenstein, M., Longstaff, F.A., 2020. Private Equity Returns: Empirical Evidence From the Business Credit Card Securitization Market. Work. Pap. Univ. Delaware and UCLA.

Fracassi, C., Previtero, A., Sheen, A., 2022. Barbarians at the store? Private equity, products, and consumers. J. Finance 77, 1439–1488.

Franzoni, F., Nowak, E., Phalippou, L., 2012. Private equity performance and liquidity risk. J. Finance 67, 2341–2373.

Gatzlaff, D.H., Haurin, D.R., 1997. Sample selection bias and repeat-sales index estimates. J. Real Estate Finance Econ. 14, 33–50.

Gatzlaff, D.H., Haurin, D.R., 1998. Sample selection and biases in local house value indices. J. Urban Econ. 43, 199–222.

Geltner, D.M., 1991. Smoothing in appraisal-based returns. J. Real Estate Finance and Econ. 4, 327–345.

Geltner, D.M., 1993. Estimating market values from appraised values without assuming an efficient market. J. Real Estate Res. 8, 325–346.

Geltner, D.M., MacGregor, B.D., Schwann, G.M., 2003. Appraisal smoothing and price discovery in real estate markets. Urban Stud. 40, 1047–1064.

Getmansky, M., Lo, A.W., Makarov, I., 2004. An econometric model of serial correlation and illiquidity in hedge fund returns. J. Financ. Econ. 2004, 529–609.

Giacoletti, M., 2021. Idiosyncratic risk in housing markets. Rev. Financ. Stud. 34, 3695–3741.

Giacoletti, M., Westrupp, V., 2018. The Risk-Adjusted Performance of Asset Flippers. Work. Pap. Univ. Southern Calif. and AQR.

Giommetti, N., Jørgensen, R., 2021. Risk Adjustment of Private Equity Cash Flows. Work. Pap. Copenhagen Bus. Sch.

Goetzmann, W.N., 1992. The accuracy of real estate indices: repeat sale estimators. J. Real Estate Finance Econ. 5, 5–53.

Goetzmann, W.N., Peng, L., 2006. Estimating house price indexes in the presence of seller reservation prices. Rev. Econ. Stat. 88, 100–112.

Goetzmann, W.N., Ingersoll, J., Spiegel, M., Welch, I., 2007. Portfolio performance manipulation and manipulation-proof performance measures. Rev. Financ. Stud. 20, 1503–1546.

Goetzmann, W.N., Gourier, E., Phalippou, L., 2019. How Alternative Are Alternative Investments? The Case of Private Equity Funds. Work. Pap. Yale School of Management.

Gompers, P.A., Lerner, J., 1997. Risk and reward in private equity investments: the challenge of performance assessment. J. Priv. Equity 1, 5–12.

Gompers, P.A., Kaplan, S.N., Mukharlyamov, V., 2016. What do private equity firms say they do? J. Financ. Econ. 121, 449–476.

Gompers, P.A., Gornall, W., Kaplan, S.N., Strebulaev, I.A., 2020. How do venture capitalists make decisions? J. Financ. Econ. 135, 169–190.

Gonçalves, A.S., 2021. The short duration premium. J. Financ. Econ. 141, 919–945.

Gormsen, N.J., Lazarus, E., 2021. Duration-Driven Returns. Work. Pap. Univ. Chicago and MIT.

Gornall, W., Strebulaev, I.A., 2020. Squaring venture capital valuations with reality. J. Financ. Econ. 135, 120–143.

Gredil, O., 2022. Do private equity managers have superior information on public markets? J. Financ. Quant. Anal. 57, 321–358.

Gredil, O., Sørensen, M., Waller, W., 2020a. Evaluating Private Equity Performance Using Stochastic Discount Factors. Work. Pap. Tulane Univ. and Dartmouth College.

Gredil, O., Liu, Y., Sensoy, B., 2020b. Diversifying Private Equity. Work. Pap. Tulane Univ., Purdue Univ., and Vanderbilt Univ.

Gredil, O., Griffiths, B.E., Stucke, R., 2022. Benchmarking Private Equity: The Direct Alpha Method. Work. Pap. Tulane Univ., Ares Manag. Corp., and Warburg Pincus LLC.

Groh, A.P., Gottschalg, O., 2011. The effect of leverage on the cost of capital of US buyouts. J. Bank. Finance 35, 2099–2110.

Guo, S., Hotchkiss, E.S., Song, W., 2011. Do buyouts (still) create value? J. Finance 66, 479–517.

Gupta, A., van Nieuwerburgh, S., 2021. Valuing private equity investments strip by strip. J. Finance 76, 3255–3307.

Hakansson, N.H., 1971. Toward a general theory of portfolio choice. J. Finance 26, 857–884.

Hall, R.E., Woodward, S.E., 2010. The burden of nondiversifiable risk of entrepreneurship. Am. Econ. Rev. 100, 1163–1194.

Harris, R.S., Jenkinson, T., Kaplan, S.N., 2014. Private equity performance: what do we know? J. Finance 69, 1851–1882.

Harris, R.S., Jenkinson, T., Kaplan, S.N., Stucke, R., 2018. Financial intermediation in private equity: how well do funds of funds perform? J. Financ. Econ. 129, 287–305.

Harris, R.S., Jenkinson, T., Kaplan, S.N., Stucke, R., 2022. Has Persistence Persisted in Private Equity? Evidence from buyout and venture capital funds. Work. Pap. Univ. Virginia, Univ. Oxford, Univ. Chicago, and Warburg Pincus.

Harvey, C.R., Siddique, A., 2000. Conditional skewness in asset pricing tests. J. Finance 55, 1263–1295.

Haurin, D.R., Hendershott, P.H., 1991. House price indexes: issues and results. Real Estate Econ. 19, 259–269.

Heckman, J.J., 1979. Sample selection bias as a specification error. Econometrica 47, 153–161.

Hege, U., Nuti, A., 2011. The private equity secondaries market during the financial crisis and the "valuation gap.". J. Priv. Equity 14, 42–54.

Hellmann, T., Puri, M., 2002. Venture capital and the professionalization of start-up firms: empirical evidence. J. Finance 57, 169–197.

Higson, C., Stucke, R., 2012. The Performance of Private Equity. Work. Pap. London Bus. Sch. and Univ. Oxford.

Hüther, N., 2021. Do Private Equity Managers Raise Funds on (Sur)Real Returns? Evidence From Deal-Level Data. Work. Pap. Indiana Univ.

Hüther, N., Robinson, D.T., Sievers, S., Hartmann-Wendels, T., 2020. Paying for performance in private equity: evidence from venture capital partnerships. Manag. Sci. 66, 1756–1782.

Hüther, N., Schmid, L., Steri, R., 2021. Credit Market Equivalents and the Valuation of Private Firms. Work. Pap. Indiana Univ., Univ. Southern Calif. and Univ. Luxermbourg.

Hwang, M., Quigley, J.M., 2004. Selectivity, quality adjustment and mean reversion in the measurement of house values. J. Real Estate Finance Econ. 28, 161–178.

Hwang, M., Quigley, J.M., Woodward, S.E., 2005. An index for venture capital, 19872003. Contrib. Econ. Anal. Policy 4, 1–43.

Ilmanen, A., Chandra, S., McQuinn, N., 2020. Demistifying illiquid assets: expected returns for private equity. J. Altern. Investments 22, 1–15.

Imbierowicz, B., Rauch, C., 2021. The Pricing of Private Assets: Mutual Investments in 'unicorn' Companies. Work. Pap. Deutsche Bundesbank and Amer. Univ. Sharjah.

Ivashina, V., Lerner, J., 2018. Looking for Alternatives: Pension Investments Around the World, 2008 to 2017. Work. Pap. Harvard Univ.

Jeffers, J., Lyu, T., Posenau, K., 2021. The Risk and Return of Impact Investing Funds. Work. Pap. Univ. Chicago and Yale Univ.

Jegadeesh, N., Kräussl, R., Pollet, J.M., 2015. Risk and expected returns of private equity investments: evidence based on market prices. Rev. Financ. Stud. 28, 3269–3302.

Jenkinson, T., Sousa, M., Stucke, R., 2013. How Fair Are the Valuations of Private Equity Funds? Work. Pap. Univ., Oxford.

Jenkinson, T., Landsman, W.R., Rountree, B.R., Soonawalla, K., 2020. Private equity net asset values and future cash flows. The Accounting Rev. 95, 191–210.

Jenkinson, T., Jones, H., Rauch, C., 2021. Long Goodbyes: Why Do Private Equity Funds Hold Onto Public Equity? Work. Pap. Univ. Oxford and Amer. Univ. Sharjah.

Jud, G.D., Seaks, T.G., 1994. Sample selection bias in estimating housing sales prices. J. Real Estate Res. 9, 289–298.

Kaplan, S.N., 1989. The effects of management buyouts on operating performance and value. J. Financ. Econ. 24, 217–254.

Kaplan, S.N., Lerner, J., 2017. Venture capital data: opportunities and challenges. In: Haltiwanger, J., Hurst, E., Miranda, J., Schoar, A. (Eds.), Measuring Entrepreneurial Businesses: Current Knowledge and Challenges. Univ. Chicago Press, Chicago, pp. 413–431.

Kaplan, S.N., Schoar, A., 2005. Private equity performance: returns, persistence, and capital flows. J. Finance 60, 1791–1823.

Kerr, W.R., Nanda, R., Rhodes-Kropf, M., 2014. Entrepreneurship as experimentation. J. Econ. Perspect. 28, 25–48.

Korteweg, A., 2019. Risk adjustment in private equity returns. Ann. Rev. Financ. Econ. 11, 131–152.

Korteweg, A., Nagel, S., 2016. Risk-adjusting the returns to venture capital. J. Finance 71, 1437–1470.

Korteweg, A., Nagel, S., 2022. Risk-Adjusted Returns of Private Equity Funds: A New Approach. Work. Pap. Univ. Southern Calif. and Univ. Chicago.

Korteweg, A., Sensoy, B., 2023. How unique is VC's American history? J. Econ. Lit. 61, 274–294.

Korteweg, A., Sørensen, M., 2010. Risk and return characteristics of venture capital–backed entrepreneurial companies. Rev. Financ. Stud. 23, 3738–3772.

Korteweg, A., Sørensen, M., 2016. Estimating loan-to-value distributions. Real Estate Econ. 44, 41–86.

Korteweg, A., Sørensen, M., 2017. Skill and luck in private equity performance. J. Financ. Econ. 124, 535–562.

Korteweg, A., Westerfield, M., 2022. Asset allocation with private equity. Foundations and Trends in Finance 13, 95–204.

Korteweg, A., Panageas, S., Systla, A., 2021. Evaluating Private Equity From an Investor's Perspective. Work. Pap. Univ. Southern Calif., and UCLA.

Kraus, A., Litzenberger, R., 1975. Market equilibrium in a multiperiod state preference model with logarithmic utility. J. Finance 30, 1213–1227.

Lee, A., 2015. How LPs are driving private equity fundraising. Int. Financ. Law Rev. published July 8, 2015.

Lerner, J., 1995. Venture capitalists and the oversight of private firms. J. Finance 50, 301–318.

Lerner, J., Schoar, A., 2004. The illiquidity puzzle: theory and evidence from private equity. J. Financ. Econ. 72, 3–40.

Lerner, J., Sørensen, M., Strömberg, P., 2011. Private equity and long-run investment: the case of innovation. J. Finance 66, 445–477.

Lerner, J., Leamon, A., Hardymon, F., 2012. Venture Capital, Private Equity, and the Financing of Entrepreneurship, first ed. John Wiley & Sons, New Jersey.

Lerner, J., Mao, J., Schoar, A., Zhang, N.R., 2020. Investing outside the box: evidence from alternative vehicles in private equity. Work. Pap., Harvard Business School Finance Working Paper No. 19–012.

Litvak, K., 2004. Governance through exit: default penalties and walkaway options in venture capital partnership agreements. Willamette Law Rev. 40, 771–778.

Litvak, K., 2009. Venture capital limited partnership agreements: understanding compensation arrangements. Univ. of Chicago Law Rev. 76, 161–218.

Ljungqvist, A., Richardson, M., 2003. The Cash Flow, Return and Risk Characteristics of Private Equity. Work. Pap. New York Univ.

Long, J.B., 1990. The numeraire portfolio. J. Financ. Econ. 26, 29–69.

Long, A.M., Nickels, C.J., 1996. A Private Investment Benchmark. Work. Pap. Univ. Tex. Invest. Manag. Co.

Martin, I., 2012. On the valuation of long-dated assets. J. Pol. Econ. 120, 346–358.

Martin, J.D., Petty, J.W., 1983. An analysis of the performance of publicly traded venture capital companies. J. Financ. Quant. Anal. 18, 401–498.

McCourt, M., 2018. Estimating Skill in Private Equity Performance Using Market Data. Work. Pap. Univ. of Melbourne.

McKenzie, M., Janeway, W., 2008. Venture Capital Fund Performance and the IPO Market. Work. Pap. Univ. Cambridge.

Merton, R.C., 1980. On estimating the expected return on the market: an exploratory investigation. J. Financ. Econ. 8, 323–361.

Metrick, A., Yasuda, A., 2010a. The economics of private equity funds. Rev. Financ. Stud. 23, 2303–2341.

Metrick, A., Yasuda, A., 2010b. Venture Capital and the Finance of Innovation, second ed. John Wiley & Sons, New Jersey.

Munday, S., Hu, W., True, T., Zhang, J., 2018. Performance of private credit funds: a first look. J. Altern. Inv. 21, 31–51.

Munneke, H.J., Slade, B.A., 2000. An empirical study of sample-selection bias in indices of commercial real estate. J. Real Estate Finance Econ. 21, 45–64.

Munneke, H.J., Slade, B.A., 2001. A metropolitan transaction-based commercial price index: a time-varying parameter approach. Real Estate Econ. 29, 55–84.

Nadauld, T.D., Sensoy, B.A., Vorkink, K., Weisbach, M.S., 2019. The liquidity cost of private equity investments: evidence from secondary market transactions. J. Financ. Econ. 132, 158–181.

OECD, Eurostat, International Labour Organization, International Monetary Fund, The World Bank, United Nations Economic Commission for Europe, 2013. Repeat sales methods. In: Handbook on Residential Property Price Indices. Eurostat, Luxembourg, pp. 66–71.

Opp, C.C., 2019. Venture capital and the macroeconomy. Rev. Fin. Stud. 32, 4387–4446.

Ouyang, S., Yu, J., Jagannathan, R., 2021. Return to Venture Capital in the Aggregate. NBER Work. Pap. 27690.

Pástor, L., Stambaugh, R.F., 2003. Liquidity risk and expected stock returns. J. Pol. Econ. 111, 642–685.

Peng, L., 2001. Building a Venture Capital Index. Work. Pap. Univ. Colorado Boulder.

Peters, R.H., 2018. Volatility and Venture Capital. Work. Pap. Tulane Univ.

Phalippou, L., 2008. The hazards of using IRR to measure performance: the case of private equity. J. Performance Measurement 12, 55–66.

Phalippou, L., 2010. Risk and return of private equity: an overview of data, methods, and results. In: Cumming, D. (Ed.), Private Equity: Fund Types, Risks and Returns, and Regulation. John Wiley & Sons, New Jersey, pp. 257–282.

Phalippou, L., 2013. Yale's endowment returns: case study in GIPS interpretation difficulties. J. Altern. Investments 15, 97–103.

Phalippou, L., 2014. Performance of buyout funds revisited? Rev. Finance 18, 189–218.

Phalippou, L., Gottschalg, O., 2009. The performance of private equity funds. Rev. Financ. Stud. 22, 1747–1776.

Phalippou, L., Rauch, C., Umber, M., 2018. Private equity portfolio company fees. J. Financ. Econ. 129, 559–585.

Robinson, D.T., Sensoy, B.A., 2013. Do private equity fund managers earn their fees? Compensation, ownership, and cash flow performance. Rev. Financ. Stud. 26, 2760–2797.

Robinson, D.T., Sensoy, B.A., 2016. Cyclicality, performance measurement, and cash flow liquidity in private equity. J. Financ. Econ. 122, 521–543.

Roll, R., 1973. Evidence on the "growth-optimum" model. J. Finance 28, 551–566.

Roll, R., 1977. A critique of the asset pricing theory's tests part I: on past and potential testability of the theory. J. Financ. Econ. 4, 129–176.

Rubinstein, M., 1976. The strong case for the generalized logarithmic utility model as the premier model of financial markets. J. Finance, 551–571.

Sagi, J., 2021. Asset-level risk and return in real estate investments. Rev. Financ. Stud. 34, 3647–3694.

Schillinger, P., Braun, R., Cornel, J., 2019. Distortion or Cash Flow Management? Understanding Credit Facilities in Private Equity Funds. Work. Pap. Techn. Univ. München and Blackrock.

Schlingemann, F.P., Stulz, R.M., 2022. Have exchange-listed firms become less important for the economy? J. Financ. Econ. 143, 927–958.

Scholes, M., Williams, J., 1977. Estimating betas from nonsynchronous data. J. Financ. Econ. 5, 309–327.

Shanken, J., 1992. On the estimation of beta-pricing models. Rev. Financ. Stud. 5, 1–33.

Smith, E.E., Smith, J.K., Smith, R.L., 2022. Bias in the reporting of venture capital performance: the disciplinary role of FOIA. Rev. Corp. Fin. 2, 493–525.

Sørensen, M., Jagannathan, R., 2015. The public market equivalent and private equity performance. Financ. Analysts J. 71, 43–50.

Stafford, E., 2022. Replicating private equity with value investing, homemade leverage, and hold-to-maturity accounting. Rev. Financ. Stud. 35, 299–342.

Stucke, R., 2011. Updating History. Work. Pap. Univ. Oxford, Oxford, UK.

Wallace, N.E., Meese, R.A., 1997. The construction of residential housing price indices: a comparison of repeat-sales, hedonic-regression, and hybrid approaches. J. Real Estate Finance Econ. 14, 51–73.

Woodward, S.E., 2009. Measuring Risk for Venture Capital and Private Equity Portfolios. Work. Pap. Sand Hill Econ, Palo Alto, CA.

Woodward, S.E., Hall, R.E., 2004. Benchmarking the Returns to Venture. National Bureau of Economic Research Work. Pap. #10202.

Short chapter summaries

IV

Short overview of chapters

Part I: Early-stage financing
Chapter 1: The contracting and valuation of venture capital-backed companies

Will Gornall and Ilya Strebulaev

Fast-growing innovative companies—startups—operate unlike other businesses and raise money in similarly distinctive ways. Perhaps most importantly, while their investment needs are front-loaded, their cash flows are typically far in the future and uncertain, with success coming from a new product or service that has not yet been rolled out or created. These special circumstances raise numerous economic and business issues and necessitate special forms of financing and particular relationships with financiers. They make it difficult for these companies to access capital through traditional means, such as traditional bank and receivables financing or public equity markets. Eschewing traditional banks and equity markets, they turn to a startup financing ecosystem that includes corporate and institutional venture capital (VC) funds, crowdfunding, angel investors, growth equity, and private equity. Venture capital is a high-touch form of financing used primarily by high-growth, innovative, and risky companies. VC funds invest in these companies on behalf of limited partners, who are mostly large institutional investors.

Startups often write complicated financial contracts tailored to their specific needs. The complex nature of these contracts and the economic uncertainty the companies face leads players in this space to modify standard financial valuation methods. In this chapter, we analyze the economic foundations of the contractual relationships between innovative companies and their financiers as well as the valuation of such companies and the financial securities that they issue.

We aim to detail the economic nature of contracts used in practice in the United States and to relate the existing contractual relationships to the mainstream contract theory. While we concentrate on the recent US landscape, our analysis could also be applied to a broader international context, with some necessary modifications.

We start by discussing key relevant stylized facts and how they lead to contracting frictions. In particular, we show that modern economic theories of contracting are ideally suited to understanding both these challenges and how startups and investors respond to them. Principal–agent problems, contractual incompleteness, information asymmetry, insufficient collateral, the inalienability of human capital, and other core contracting frictions bind especially tightly for startups. The startup financing ecosystem has evolved to allocate capital to promising innovative ventures despite these many frictions. Startups operate within the nexus of complex sets of relationships between many interested parties. All these relationships are interlinked and operate both within the formal contractual relationships as well as informal arrangements based on trust and reputation. To illustrate young companies' evolution and the associated financing contracts, we classify startup lifecycle stages through the lenses of financing.

We then discuss several characteristics of VC-backed companies that are worth noting to understand the contractual arrangements, including the nature of their cash flows, the nature of the information about the startup outcomes, and moral hazard issues. This enables us to discuss the general economic features of VC contracting.

We proceed to discuss in detail the various investment contracts used by startups and their associated cash flow and control rights. These investment contracts include convertible preferred stock, convertible notes, venture debt, and Simple Agreement for Future Equity (SAFE) securities. Given that startups almost invariably raise multiple rounds of funding, we then discuss contracting issues associated with the evolution of cash flow and control rights. Overall, we provide an economic analysis of most contractual terms used by early-stage companies. We finally discuss approaches to valuing startups, their financial securities, and the impact of contractual terms on valuation.

Chapter 2: Venture capital and innovation

Josh Lerner and Ramana Nanda

Venture capital is associated with some of the most high-growth and influential firms in the world. In this chapter, we begin by tracing the growth of the institutional venture capital industry, from its origins in 1946, when Harvard Business School professor Georges Doriot formed the American Research and Development Corporation, through the rapid growth of the industry from the 1980s onward following a change in the so-called "prudent man rule," to the massive explosion of venture capital in last decade. Entirely new financial intermediaries such as accelerators, crowd funding platforms, and "super angels" have emerged at the early stage of new venture finance, competing with traditional early-stage funds. Meanwhile, mutual funds, hedge funds, and sovereign wealth funds have deployed large sums of capital into more mature, but still private, venture capital-backed firms. We discuss how technological and institutional changes in the past two decades have also narrowed the focus and concentrated the capital invested by VCs and review recent research examining the potential real effects that these changes can have.

Academics and practitioners have effectively articulated the strengths of the venture model. In Section 2, we review this literature, highlighting the intensive hands-on engagement of VCs with portfolio companies as well as contractual provisions such as staged financing that enable align incentives and exercise effective governance. We also discuss research noting the real effects of venture capital in terms of innovation, as well empirical approaches that aim to distinguish the impact of VC funding on startup innovation as distinct from their selection of the more innovative firms in the economy.

At the same time, venture capital financing has had real limitations in its ability to advance substantial technological change. As we noted in Lerner and Nanda (2020), we discuss three limitations that are particularly concerning to us: (1) the narrow band of technological innovations that are typically financed by institutional venture capital investors; (2) the relatively small number of venture capital investors who hold, and shape the direction of, a substantial fraction of capital that is deployed into financing radical technological change; and (3) the relaxation in recent years of the intense emphasis on corporate governance by venture capital firms. While academics and practitioners have effectively articulated the strengths of the venture model, we believe much less attention has been devoted to understanding the causes and consequences of these limitations. Yet, these features are likely to continue having important real effects on the rate and direction of innovation in the broader economy and are thus too important to ignore.

We conclude by summarizing some recent thoughts of ours about potential adaptations to the venture capital model might enable a broader base of ideas and technologies to receive risk capital. We call for greater research in this area, as we believe that understanding and addressing frictions in the ability of venture capital to have the greatest impact on innovation is an important challenge for both academics and practitioners alike.

Chapter 3: Small-firm financing: Sources, frictions, and policy implications

Ramana Nanda and Gordon Phillips

We review the growing literature on small-firm financing and potential financial constraints they may face. Small firms form the backbone of the economy. In the United States, they account for over 90% of all firms and over 40% of economic activity (SBA, 2019). Moreover, startups—the vast majority of which start small—have been shown to play a particularly important role in driving productivity growth and net job creation, making them an important set of firms to understand for academics and policymakers alike. Young and small firms also have particular features that make them more susceptible to financing constraints: They may depend more on external finance to support their growth, yet they often have less "hard" data available on which to make funding decisions. This can often lead them to be perceived by financiers as more "opaque" or subject to asymmetric information. In addition, small firms often have a single relationship with financial intermediaries such as banks, making them more subject to informational hold-up by financial intermediaries and hence face worse terms when raising external finance.

But how salient are these financial frictions and to what extent do they have a quantitatively important impact on real outcomes such as employment or productivity growth? We provide an overview of the large and growing literature on understanding financing constraints facing small businesses with a view to answering these questions. We begin by using representative data from the US Survey of Business Owners to describe the main sources of financing for US business owners, broken down by firm size. We also show using data from the Small Medium Enterprises Finance monitor for the United Kingdom that these patterns appear consistent with the financing patterns in the United Kingdom. These statistics provide an organizing framework for reviewing the literature on the sources of small-firm financing and associated frictions, and also shed light on financing sources that appear understudied relative to their use by small businesses. Among small firms that report using external financing, bank and credit card–based borrowing by the business and its owners accounts for the overwhelming share of external finance. Credit card financing, both to the owners and the business, stands out as a key area that received comparatively less attention relative to the intensity with which it appears to be used by small firms. Recent studies have begun to address this gap, including linking data from credit registers to census-level administrative data on firms and individuals.

After presenting these early statistics, the chapter discusses studies looking at the real effects of relaxing financing constraints. In many of these studies, identification concerns play a key role: Do small firms benefit from increased access to credit or do firms with better investment opportunities borrow more? These papers have addressed these identification concerns in multiple ways including expansion of branch banking in the United States, SBA lending cutoffs, and also the removal of consumer bankruptcy flags for borrowing on their own account by entrepreneurs. These studies show large measured effects on real outcomes when financing constraints are relaxed, although the magnitudes vary.

The overall conclusion that we make from reviewing these studies is that the relaxation of constraints that increase bank capital and personal financing availability has overall been shown to relax financial constraints and increase employment, investment, and efficiency for small firms that are likely to be financially constrained. However, this conclusion is nuanced. A key insight from this section is that there is growing evidence of heterogeneity in financing frictions facing small firms: A substantial share of firms may not even seek external finance or may not benefit from relaxed constraints because they do not wish to grow; on the other hand, relaxing constraints has large measured effects on investment and employment for certain subpopulations of small firms. This heterogeneity has important implications for how average effects are interpreted in academic studies, as well as for how policy is enacted.

The chapter concludes by discussing research on potential technological and policy interventions to reduce financing constraints for small firms. Several elements have contributed to making this an active area of work. First, there is growing availability of micro data on small-firm financing linked to credit registry data with the potential to tie this to longer-term firm outcomes. The data availability enables a much deeper understanding of the causes and consequences of financing constraints, as well as an understanding of heterogeneity among different subpopulations of small businesses. Second, there has been a massive rise of financial technology in recent years, both within traditional banks and with new "fintech" startups, several of whom are looking to exploit inefficiencies in small business lending. Studying their impact enhances our understanding of what frictions such fintech might address and what remain. Third, there have been several government interventions aimed at helping small businesses, particularly in the wake of the COVID-19 pandemic, which again enables a deeper understanding of the nature of financing frictions and the policies that might be most effective at alleviating them.

Part II: Later stage financing
Chapter 4: Private equity financing

Victoria Ivashina

As compared to other asset management institutions, private equity (PE) has a unique funding structure. At the core, this is tied to the illiquid assets they invest in and arrival of investment opportunities. The goal of this chapter is to understand the common practices for PE funds' structure and funding. The chapter covers three topics. First, it gives an overview of traditional PE financing; then, it discusses other investment vehicles like direct and coinvestments; and third, it introduces ongoing trends in the industry. It provides both core institutional features of the asset class and relevant real-world examples.

The chapter begins with the traditional PE fund structure, starting with the relationship between General Partners (GPs) and Limited Partners (LPs). It explains how PE funds typically raise capital from LPs through overlapping blind, closed-end funds. Then, it defines fundamental concepts like drawdown notices, defaults, management fees, and vintage years. After establishing the basics, the chapter discusses how the need for repeated fundraising acts as a disciplining mechanism in the industry and lists factors LPs might consider when reinvesting with a GP. It also allows the reader to contemplate the decisions PE managers face when timing their next fundraise and the tension in the industry around fixed percentage fees. The chapter introduced several essential PE concepts including the J-curve, which captures the distribution of LPs' cash flow throughout a fund's lifetime.

Then, the chapter moves to subscription lines, low-interest credit facilities used by PE funds to finance acquisitions. These credit facilities, typically backed by the LPs' commitments, allow GPs to delay capital calls. This can serve several purposes, such as liquidity management flexibility and quickly fulfilling capital requirements for a competitive deal. However, their widespread usage has attracted criticism in recent years due to their impact on internal rates of return (IRRs).

The last subsection on traditional PE financing shifts attention to the LPs. It lists dominant players in the industry, including pension funds, sovereign wealth funds, and endowments, and it provides a real-life example of a prominent PE firm's diverse investor base. Finally, it gives a brief overview on LP coordination and structures, like the Limited Partner Advisory Committee, that are often put in place after a fund has closed.

The second major topics covered in the chapter are direct investments and coinvestments. LPs typically use these vehicles to invest directly in a private company. Coinvestments allow LPs to invest in parallel to a fund, while direct investments are made on a solo basis. An attractive aspect of coinvestments for LPs is reduced fees, as these investments are often done on a low/no fee basis. The chapter then describes how GPs choose coinvestment deals and problems that may arise. After explaining the conceptual aspects of coinvesting, the chapter then analyzes studies that seek to understand coinvestment performance relative to corresponding fund investments.

The results appear mixed, with one study showing general underperformance by coinvestments on a net basis and another that found comparable performance on a gross basis. Yet, coinvestments have grown significantly in popularity, making this an important area to understand.

The final section of the chapter dives into three trends in PE financing. First, it discusses the increased fund flows into PE, with double-digit average growth rate between 2010 and 2019. This trend is partially driven by the near-zero interest rate environment since the Great Financial Crisis, pushing large investors toward alternative asset classes. Other factors include more retail investors, specifically defined contribution pension plans, and a rise in "nonflagship" funds. The second trend is the lengthening of fund horizons, or investors moving from a traditional 5-year investment holding period to perpetual capital vehicles that allow longer holding periods. In addition, the industry has seen a proliferation in cross-fund investments, secondary transactions, and GP-led secondary transactions, which can all stretch an investment's holding period. The chapter concludes with a brief reflection on the rise in environmental, social, and governance (ESG)-related strategies.

Chapter 5: Buyouts: A primer

Tim Jenkinson, Hyeik Kim, and Michael S. Weisbach

Private capital markets have entered the public consciousness. They are responsible for financing the most valuable companies in the world and restructuring many of the existing ones. With assets under management of about $2.5 trillion and $1 trillion in new assets being raised each year, private capital markets continue to grow and will undoubtedly play an increasingly important role in the economy. While economic growth in the 20th century was financed largely through public capital markets, in the 21st century, private capital is becoming the most important (and interesting) form of finance.

A new set of financial institutions has developed that has enabled private capital markets to thrive. In this chapter, we explain how these institutions function, present up-to-date evidence on them, and discuss the relevant academic literature. Our discussion focuses on the buyout component of private capital markets, which is sometimes referred to as the leveraged buyout (LBO) market because of the extensive use of debt in these transactions.

In a buyout fund, the LPs make capital commitments that can be drawn down at the discretion of the fund managers, known as the general partners. These "drawdowns" are used to acquire portfolio companies, which are managed and ultimately sold by the fund. The returns that the LPs receive come from the difference between the cost and the sale price, plus any dividends received.

To raise a fund, the GPs must offer potential LPs a sufficiently attractive return distribution to induce them to invest in the private market rather than in alternatives. Investments in buyout funds tend to be riskier, due to the extensive use of leverage, and less liquid than those in public markets. In addition, their fees and profit shares are substantially higher than vehicles that invest in public securities such as mutual funds. Private market returns, net of these high fees and profit shares, must deliver a premium over comparable public market returns to induce suppliers of capital to invest. Yet, despite this high hurdle, investors have chosen to make extremely large capital commitments to buyout funds because their expectations of returns are high enough to justify taking on the additional risk and illiquidity.

How do buyout funds manage to earn sufficiently high net returns to induce LPs to invest? Part of the answer is the real changes that the GP can make in its portfolio firms. Sometimes, the GP does as Jensen (1989) argues and creates value by reducing wasteful expenditures of free cash flow. But not always—often the value increases come from other sources such as strategic expansions or consolidations, professionalization of management combined with pecuniary incentives for them, providing the firm with capital at times when it does not have other sources of finance, or privatization of an inefficient government operation. In addition, GPs can produce returns for their investors by transferring value from other parties, in particular tax authorities, via the greater use of debt, which is normally tax deductible (within limits). Recent literature has documented that it is not just the government that is targeted for wealth transfers; it appears that there are, in some circumstances, systematic wealth transfers from customers, workers, and suppliers to buyout fund investors.

This chapter details some of the particular strategies that buyout firms adopt. These strategies vary from "bust up" LBOs designed to sell off assets and reduce cash flow, to expansions in which the fund provides capital for "bolt on" acquisitions to a firm, to transition-oriented deals where the fund provides an exit for some of the firm's owners while allowing others to remain in control. By being flexible in their investing strategy, buyout funds are able to come up with many ways in which they can earn returns for their investors.

We present a set of the most up-to-date facts about buyouts. Buyout markets tend to be correlated with the credit cycle. Purchase price multiples and debt contributions tend to go up (down) during economic booms (busts), but returns show a countercyclical pattern: Years when relatively little capital is raised tend, ultimately, to produce the best returns. While in the past, trade sales to corporate acquirers were the dominant way of exiting, secondary transactions whereby one buyout fund sells to another have become increasingly common. Fund fees have deviated surprisingly little from the 2 and 20 model—a 2% annual management fee and 20% profit share, or "carried interest"—even as buyout funds have increased dramatically in size.

Finally, we survey academic research on buyouts. This research has addressed a number of questions. Perhaps most importantly, it has devoted much attention to the buyout returns and the extent to which these returns are abnormally large, once one adjusts for the funds' risk and illiquidity. An important branch of the literature addresses the underlying sources of the gains that buyouts generate. A third section concerns the investors in the funds and the way they choose to allocate capital. Overall, the buyout literature has taught us much about these important institutions, but there is much more work yet to be done.

Chapter 6: Gender and race in entrepreneurial finance

Michael Ewens

This chapter reviews the intersection of race, gender, and entrepreneurial finance with the broad goals of providing the background and citations for those interested in contributing to the field.

A primary motivation for the chapter is picture that emerges from Table 1. That table shows the representation of women and minorities of all genders in the entrepreneurial finance market. The chapter begins with a normative statement that these numbers are too low. One need only compare the proportion of high-growth startups that are women-run (12%–28%) to their population representation or labor force participation (45%) to see why this is called the "entrepreneurship gender gap." Similar comparisons for Black entrepreneurs (1%–10%) reveal similar gaps. The sources of these disparities are many and not necessarily an indictment on investor's preferences or bias. In fact, that is the whole point of many academic articles on the topic: what explains the disparities? Is it a skills gap, wealth inequality, educational differences, culture, norms, or investor bias? Or perhaps some historical institution led to differences in human capital that persist today. That said, an unspoken motivation of the chapter equality of participation across all stages of the startup lifecycle. Why? Beyond how they correlate with characteristics like wealth, education and preentry economic characteristics, race, gender, ethnicity, and other innate characteristics should not predict participation or success in entrepreneurship ex ante.

Recent events and controversies in the venture capital and private equity industry show that this topic is likely to be top of mind for practitioners and policymakers for years. Several investors and limited partners have reacted to these developments with resignations and firings. Others have taken a proactive approach to address concerns about underrepresentation. Understanding if and how demographic characteristics matter from startup founding to exit is critical to assessing the industry's progress.

The setting is the financing of high-growth entrepreneurial firms in the United States. Many of the topics covered in the chapter apply to all small businesses, but several will be specific to venture capital, angel investors, and private equity. The unique setting of entrepreneurial finance includes firm insiders contributing a substantial amount of capital, who later tap the private equity markets as the firm develops. The high level of informational opacity distinguishes it from the public firm setting and plays an important part in understanding the financing lifecycle. This lifecycle involves multiple players—banks, angels, VCs, and private equity firms—and thus presents situations where bias, stereotypes, and discrimination could affect underrepresented founders. The informational opacity found at nearly every stage only exacerbates the frictions underlying most models of discrimination.

As will be clear as one proceeds through the chapter, it devotes more time to gender issues than to race. This focus is not a statement about relative importance. Instead, it is a by-product of several factors: the literature's own focus, low participation rates by minorities that lead to low statistical power, and data issues.

The chapter aims to achieve six objectives:

1. Presentation of a simple framework for understanding how gender and race matter for startups raising capital from banks, angel investors, venture capitalists, or private equity firms.
2. Extensive summary of the motivating "facts" about participation of women and minorities in startups.
3. A financial economist's summary of the economics of discrimination. It provides the citations, terminology, and models for researchers interested in testing the myriad alternative explanations when exploring differential treatment by race or gender.
4. Review of the contemporary literature in entrepreneurial finance—with an economics and finance bias—related to race and gender. The literature review attempts to connect the work and summarize its lessons for future work.
5. A list of unanswered questions for researchers interested in exploring topics in the area.
6. The Appendix provides references for data sources, methods for assignment of race and gender, and a review of methods used to detect discrimination.

The chapter is aimed at two audiences. First, it provides a literature review and "facts assessment" for practitioners and policymakers who do not have the will or time to review dozens of academic papers. The second audience—research faculty, PhD, and masters students—will find these sections only part of the story. Here, the chapter provides a resource for those who seek to conduct research at the intersection of private equity and discrimination broadly speaking.

Part III: Impact and performance
Chapter 7: Stakeholder impact of private equity investments

Morten Sorensen and Ayako Yasuda

We survey the academic literature about the impact of private equity investments on the broader economy. Private equity fund managers respond to high-powered incentives and seek to maximize shareholder value via a variety of channels. While research suggests that the private equity management model has a positive effect on shareholder value, its effects on the company's other stakeholders and society at large are less clear. This is natural because the logic and rationale of the private equity management model are traditionally shareholder-centric, and the effects on other related parties are side products of the pursuit of a single-objective maximization.

We start out by critiquing the traditional dichotomy where the impact of private equity ownership is presumed to be either predominantly positive, as proposed by Jensen (1989), or negative, as proposed by Shleifer and Summers (1988), with competing mechanisms underlying each of those views. In practice, both the positive and negative impacts can be present in a given transaction, and the two views are not mutually exclusive.

The empirical literature indicates that there are two distinct approaches to value creation by private equity funds with sharply divergent outcomes for stakeholders and the aggregate economy. The first approach, typically associated with public-to-private deals, exploits leverage and interest tax shields, cost reduction, and operating margin improvement. The second approach, typically associated with private-to-private deals, targets growth-oriented and capital-constrained companies and adds value by relaxing financing constraints, imparting operational and managerial expertise, increasing investment, and inducing top-line revenue growth.

Innovation tends to increase with the latter approach (private-to-private deals) while it either declines relatively or becomes more narrowly focused with the former approach (public-to-private deals).

For either workers at private-to-private targets or workers who perform IT-complementary tasks in their jobs, private equity ownership is associated with increased employment and improved long-run wage growth in general. In contrast, for either workers at public-to-private targets or workers who perform automatable or offshorable tasks, private equity ownership is associated with heightened risk and longer spells of unemployment, and slower long-run wage growth.

For consumers, private-to-private deals can lead to greater variety and broader geographic availability of products, whereas public-to-private deals may lead to higher prices and reduced availability.

In regulated industries, high-powered incentive of private equity owners is a double-edged sword and can either powerfully aid the implementation of the policy when the incentives are well aligned with the policymakers' intended goals (e.g., failed bank resolutions), or significantly exacerbate distortions when incentives are misaligned (e.g., federal aid capture, oligopolistic price bargaining between hospitals and insurers, capital regulation forbearance in insurance, and roll-backs of environmental regulation on federal land).

For governments and taxpayers, as a greater portion of the economy becomes owned by private equity firms, the permanently higher leverage of these companies significantly reduces corporate tax revenues. Beyond increased leverage, minimizing tax payments more generally (e.g., via cross-border tax arbitrage) is one of the value-creation strategies pursued by private equity owners, especially for companies with moderate growth prospects, and this also has a potential negative effect on government tax revenues.

Collectively, the emerging evidence suggests that welfare outcomes for the broader environment and society depend on the regulatory and competitive structures within which the private equity portfolio companies operate. Thus, regulators need to consider the impact of the high-powered incentives of private equity when assessing the market impact of a given regulatory policy or decision.

Finally, impact funds are posited as a mechanism for explicitly aligning the shareholder preferences with the broader public interest. Impact fund investors derive utility from holding impact funds that generate positive impact, and thus are rationally willing to invest in them even though their expected financial return alone may be lower than that from investing in nonimpact private equity funds. The result is consistent with the theory of sustainable investing in equilibrium with explicitly pro-ESG investors.

Beyond pro-ESG investors, traditional investors also increasingly demand that private equity funds incorporate material, or value-relevant, ESG-related informa- tion into their investment analysis (ESG-aware investors). The private equity fund structure allows limited partners and general partners to write contracts that fix the identities of the limited partners and aggregate their preferences at the time of the inception of the fund. The 10-year commitment requirement of private equity funds prevents limited partner turnover and temporal shift in aggregate investor preferences. Thus, the recent debate on the challenge of ESG incorporation raises a possibility that, with effective contracting, private equity-owned companies can make choices that are more consistent with ESG preferences of their ultimate owners than either public companies or nonprivate equity private companies.

Finally, we offer some suggestions for future research:

- What policy interventions can mitigate the misalignment of incentives between private equity and public interests?
- What is the aggregate impact of private equity's greater presence in the tech industry on innovation?
- How should impact funds govern and provide incentives for impact generation at portfolio companies?

Chapter 8: Risk and return in private equity

Arthur Korteweg

Estimates of expected returns and the risks that must be borne to earn them are important inputs for portfolio allocation decisions, the study of agency problems between investors and managers, and many other important questions in financial economics. The study of risk and return in private equity (PE) is an active field of research, not only because PE has grown dramatically as an asset class in recent years, but also because it poses unique and important challenges relative to the more mature literature on public equity.

Most PE investments are made by private funds that raise capital from institutions and wealthy individuals. Ownership stakes in such funds, as well as the individual companies or securities in a fund's portfolio, are highly infrequently traded. Although funds do report valuations on a quarterly basis, these tend to be stale and provide biased estimates of fundamental values at a given point in time. Unlike public equities, it is therefore not possible to construct a fund return series that is observed at regular intervals, and the standard methods developed for the public markets are not directly applicable to PE.

The PE field has adopted a set of standard performance metrics that are custom- arily reported. Cash multiples and internal rate of return are almost universally used.

Both provide a measure of the total return of a PE fund, but neither compensates for risk. Some of the first studies to estimate risk and risk-adjusted returns aimed to build a PE index from which regularly spaced returns could be computed so that standard techniques could then be applied. Many of these studies were inspired by (or replicated) approaches from the real estate literature, which has grappled with similar issues such as infrequent trading and appraisal bias of observed valuations.

Recent work has focused on fund-level data to employ stochastic discount factor (SDF) valuations of fund cash flows, premised on the idea that if funds are properly priced by the SDF, an investment in the fund should yield zero net present value in expectation. Examples of such metrics are the public market equivalent (PME) of Kaplan and Schoar (2005), which has become a widely used performance measure, and its generalization (GPME) by Korteweg and Nagel (2016), which is discussed in detail in the chapter. While these two papers consider stock market risk as the only risk factor, the SDF method is amenable to including additional risk factors, and several papers have started to explore multifactor SDF specifications.

The chapter takes a brief look at alternative vehicles and funds of funds. These have grown in importance relative to the traditional flagship funds, but they have not received as much attention in the literature. Their performance appears to depend quite heavily on the quality of managers and investors, and how they are matched. Another small literature concerns publicly traded funds, which represent a small subset of the PE fund space. While most studies find no significant under- or overperformance of publicly traded funds, the chapter stresses that the comparison with private vehicles is complicated by the fact that public listing is a choice, which may be related to their risk and return characteristics. The publicly traded funds also tend to be more diversified and many mix together various strategies, further complicating the interpretation of their estimates.

The final section of the chapter describes methods and results for data at the portfolio-company level. These data provide an alternate lens through which to consider risk and return, as they are measured gross of fees (as opposed to fund returns, which are observed net of fees to the fund managers), and with higher granularity than the funds that mix a number of these investments together. At the same time, using these data introduces new issues, most importantly the fact that many data sets (especially in VC) suffer from success bias: It is easier to observe success (initial public offerings or large acquisitions) than failures (bankruptcies and liquidations). The chapter describes techniques that have been proposed to deal with this issue, and how the empirical results between fund-level and investment-level data diverge.

The chapter describes a host of empirical results. To summarize a few of the key findings from the literature to date: The average VC fund earned positive risk-adjusted returns before the new millennium, relative to a market beta-matched investment in public stocks, but most studies find insignificant or even negative results since. In contrast, the average LBO fund outperformed a public stock investment strategy with similar beta throughout. Other risk factors beyond the public stock market risk, such as size, value, liquidity, and idiosyncratic risk, also appear to matter. The gross-of-fee risk-adjusted returns are higher than net-of-fee returns, and it is not clear if fees alone can explain the difference. While much has been learned, much more still needs to be uncovered. To that end, the chapter concludes with suggestions for future work.

Author index

Note: Page numbers followed by "*f*" indicate figures, "*t*" indicate tables, and "*np*" indicate footnotes.

A

Subject index

Note: Page numbers followed by "*f*" indicate figures, "*t*" indicate tables, "*b*" indicate boxes, and "*np*" indicate footnotes.